FRONTIERS OF KNOWLEDGE

A RESEARCH FRAMEWORK FOR HADRIAN'S WALL, PART OF THE FRONTIERS OF THE ROMAN EMPIRE WORLD HERITAGE SITE

VOLUME I
RESOURCE ASSESSMENT

Edited by:
Matthew F A Symonds & David J P Mason

With contributions by:-
Lindsay Allason-Jones, Paul Austen, Justine Bayley, Paul Bidwell, Andrew Birley, Robin Birley, Mike Bishop, David Breeze, Richard Brickstock, Ian Caruana, Mike Collins, Robert Collins, Jim Crow, Tim Gates, Elizabeth Greene, Kaye Hartley, Mark Hassall, Martin Henig, Peter Hill, Richard Hingley, Nick Hodgson, Jacqui Huntley, Rachael Newman, Tim Padley, John Pearce, David Petts, John Poulter, Jenny Price, Margaret Snape, Graeme Stobbs, John Shipley, Sue Stallibrass, Vivien Swan*, Jane Webster, Humphrey Welfare, Tony Wilmott, Steve Willis, David Woolliscroft, Robert Young and John Zant

Bust of Hadrian by M Buonarroti. Corbridge Museum, reproduced by kind permission of English Heritage

Contents

Volume 1: Resource Assessment

(N.B. More extensive accounts of PAS data along with full details of relevant material in the Cambridge University Collection of Air Photographs and a comprehensive list of Observations of the Wall remains can be found on the HWRF website *www.durham.ac.uk/archaeological.services/research.*)

List of Illustrations

Tables

The authors are extremely grateful to the institutions and individuals listed below who have given their permission for the reproduction of images in their ownership.

Archaeological Services Durham University: 22, 34, 128, 141, 146

Cumberland & Westmorland Archaeological & Architectural Society: 16, 18, 36, 50, 51, 52, 59, 60, 61, 73, 74, 76, 78, 79, 80, 105, 106, 109

Cumbria County Council: 113

English Heritage: 103, 121, 123, 126, 127, 129, 135, 136, 138, 147, 148, 149, 151, 153, 156, 157, 158, 160, 162, 163, 164, 166

Museum of Antiquities, Newcastle upon Tyne: 6, 11, 14, 19, 23, 25, 41, 81, 94, 96, 97, 150, 152, 155, 159

Oxford Archaeology (North): 32, 33

Society of Antiquaries of Newcastle upon Tyne: 1, 4, 7, 8, 12, 13, 20, 24, 56, 58, 62, 63, 64, 65, 66, 70, 77, 84, 87, 89, 90, 92, 93, 108, 110, 112, 115, 118, 134, 142, 144

Tyne & Wear Museums: 9, 27, 82, 83, 85, 88, 130, 131, 132, 133, 139

The Vindolanda Trust: 21, 28, 29, 140, 145

Alan Biggins: 104, 114, 122

Jim Crow: 95

Tim Gates: 38, 48, 72, 102, 120, 161

Matthew Symonds: 2, 3, 5, 10, 15, 17, 26, 30, 31, 35, 37, 39, 40, 42, 43, 44, 45, 46, 47, 49, 53, 54, 55, 57, 67, 68, 69, 71, 75, 91, 100, 107, 111, 116, 117, 119, 124, 125, 137, 143, 154, 167

David Woolliscroft: 86

Abbreviations

AHRC: Arts and Humanities Research Council

ALSF: Aggregates Levy Sustainability Fund

C14: Carbon 14

CSIR: *Corpus Signorum Imperii Romani*, Corpus of Sculpture of the Roman World. 1977- published by Oxford University Press for The British Academy.

EDXRF: Energy Dispersive X-ray Fluorescence

GIS: Geographical Information System

HE: Historic Environment

LiDAR: Light detection and ranging, an optical remote sensing technique

LPRIA: Late pre-Roman Iron Age

NERRF: The North East Regional Research Framework (Petts 2006)

NMP: The National Mapping Programme

NWRRF: The North West Regional Research Framework (Brennand 2006; Brennand and Chitty 2007)

RIB: Collingwood, R G & Wright R P 1965. The Roman Inscriptions of Britain:I. Inscriptions on Stone, Oxford. (reprinted with *addenda* and *corrigenda* in 1995 by R S O Tomlin).

PPG16: Planning Policy Guidance 16, covering the Secretary of State's policy on archaeological remains on land

TW: An abbreviation of Turf Wall, used to distinguish between milecastles built to the Turf Wall specifications and their Stone Wall replacements

WHS: The World Heritage Site of Hadrian's Wall

Acknowledgements

This project has relied upon voluntary contributions from a large number of archaeologists working on Hadrian's Wall issues and we are very grateful to all those who have given freely of their time and expertise in order to produce this research framework. As well as producing the summaries of current knowledge that make up the Assessment section of the framework, 49 individuals attended one or more of the three public seminar days devoted to devising the Research Agenda and Strategy. Representing a range of organisations and viewpoints, it is thanks to the engagement of the archaeological community and the support of bodies that allowed them to contribute that the creation of this document has been possible. The project was funded by English Heritage and facilitated by Durham County Council and Archaeological Services, Durham University. Peter Carne of the latter institution was co-manager for the project. This role subsequently passed to David Petts, originally the Project Officer for the Research Framework, on his return to Durham University following a brief sojourn at Chester University. Matthew Symonds took over from David Petts as Project Officer at the stage when the Assessment phase was nearing completion.

Particular thanks are due to the Steering group, chaired by David Breeze, for their help, guidance and advice. As well as agreeing the structure and methodology of the project, they provided valuable feedback on early drafts of the text. The members were Lindsay Allason-Jones, Paul Austen, Paul Bidwell, Andrew Birley, Colin Burgess, Mike Collins, Jim Crow, Jacqui Huntley, David Miles, Rachel Newman, Richard Newman, Tim Padley, Kathy Perrin, Sarah Rushton, Tony Wilmott, Pete Wilson and Rob Young.

The eight thematic groups were co-ordinated respectively by Matthew Symonds with Rob Young, Nick Hodgson, Paul Bidwell with Peter Hill, David Mason with Jim Crow, Jacqui Huntley with Sue Stallibrass, Richard Hingley with Lindsay Allason-Jones, Jenny Price with Daniel Robinson and later David Petts and Tony Wilmott with Colm O'Brien. As well as delivering the text for the Assessment, many of the coordinators led the discussion of their themes at the three seminar days. The project is also grateful to Rachel Newman, Margaret Snape and Humphrey Welfare for leading thematic discussion at the seminar days and David Breeze for chairing them. Thanks are also owed to those not mentioned hitherto who contributed to discussions at the seminars and/or submitted comments electronically: Alan Biggins, Patricia Birley, Yvonne Boutwood, Mark Brennand, James Bruhn, Alex Croom, Ian Haynes, Birgitta Hoffman, Fraser Hunter, Valerie Maxfield, Georgina Plowright, Daniel Robinson and David Shotter.

We are grateful to the Society of Antiquaries of Newcastle-upon-Tyne, The Cumberland and Westmorland Antiquarian and Archaeological Society, Tyne and Wear Museums Service, The Vindolanda Trust, The Museum of Antiquities, Cumbria County Council, English Heritage, Tim Gates, David Woolliscroft and David J. Breeze for permission to reproduce their illustrations within the text.

Finally we would like to thank all of the many individuals who downloaded the project documents from the website and gave us their observations.

David JP Mason

Summary

Hadrian's Wall is probably one of the two most famous archaeological sites in Britain and its importance is formalised by its World Heritage Site status and, since 2005, it has been part of the Frontiers of the Roman Empire World Heritage Site. The linear barrier and its immediate hinterland contain a wealth of individual sites and monuments of varying types set in spectacular landscape. An archaeological resource of unsurpassed importance to the professional researcher, Hadrian's Wall is also embedded in the popular imagination and is a much visited tourism destination.

The subject of antiquarian observation and collecting since the sixteenth century, Hadrian's Wall was first subjected to scientific excavation in the 1890s and this has continued to the present day. Gradually and painstakingly, information has been gathered and published, surveys conducted and elements of the monument conserved and placed on display. Interpretations and theories have been, and continue to be, advanced, discussed, modified and replaced. Today, there is a vast body of information on Hadrian's Wall available in academic and popular publications, in museums and in archives although it is not always easy to access.

The availability and application of new techniques in recent years have not only led to major advances in knowledge but have also shown just how much there is still to discover and understand. Geophysical survey that has revealed the extent of civil settlements outside forts is just one example. The advent of paleoenvironmental sampling that is yielding invaluable information about past climatic conditions, agriculture, diet and so forth is another. Similarly, wider ranging and innovative artefact studies are casting new light on social, ethnographic, cultural and economic aspects of life in the frontier zone. This new information is requiring previous perceptions and interpretations to be re-examined and adjusted.

Yet despite the vast corpus of information that now exists, there are still yawning gaps in our knowledge, a situation that is due in no small part to the uncoordinated way in which research has been conducted on the frontier in the past. Future research will not only improve understanding of the Wall itself but also has the potential to contribute to the study of the frontier systems of the Roman Empire in general. Changes to the garrisoning and organization of frontier areas over time and their effectiveness as well as the impact of Roman occupation on the local population and economy are areas of study pertinent to all frontier regions of the Empire. These are also questions that have resonances in the modern world. Excavation, the most visible form of research, not only affords the opportunity to train the next generation of archaeologists and refine techniques but also stimulates and maintains public interest. It does of course entail the destruction of archaeological deposits while the resources required for major projects of this type are always likely to be limited. For these reasons, it is highly desirable to have a universally agreed and prioritised set of research themes and topics to which those planning future excavation projects can refer.

The Hadrian's Wall Research Framework, a collaborative exercise involving a broad spectrum of specialists at the forefront of research in their own area of interest, has been prepared with two broad aims in mind. Firstly, it summarizes and assesses the existing knowledge base for our understanding including the surviving physical remains of the monument and its associated installations, the sum of evidence produced by investigations so far, and the collections of artefacts recovered. The scope of this exercise includes the remains of military installations in the area belonging to the period before the Wall was constructed as well as those along the Cumbrian coast. Secondly, it identifies and prioritises an agenda of key themes for future research and then sets out a strategy by which this initial set of objectives might be achieved. The Research Framework is designed to be a 'living' document with the Agenda and Strategy reviewed and, if necessary, revised at five yearly intervals.

Résumé

L'un des vestiges archéologiques les plus célèbres de Grande-Bretagne, le Mur d'Hadrien, est inscrit au patrimoine mondial de l'UNESCO et fait également partie depuis 2005 du patrimoine mondial des Frontières de l'Empire Romain. La fortification et son arrière-pays immédiat recèlent un grand nombre de sites et de monuments très variés, implantés dans un paysage spectaculaire. Source archéologique d'importance inégalable pour tout chercheur professionnel, le mur d'Hadrien est aussi ancré dans l'imagination populaire et est une destination touristique très prisée.

Objet d'observations scientifiques depuis le seizième siècle, le Mur d'Hadrien a attiré de nombreux antiquaires voulant enrichir leurs collections, jusqu'à ce que des fouilles archéologiques y soient menées à partir des années 1890. Les informations ainsi progressivement et minutieusement collectées, couplées aux sondages, ont amené dans un premier temps à leur publication, puis à la restauration et à la mise en valeur de certains sites appartenant au Mur. Des interprétations et des théories ont été, et continu d'être, avancées, discutées, modifiées et remplacées. Bien que parfois difficilement accessible, une masse d'informations sur le mur d'Hadrien est désormais disponible sous forme de publications académiques ou d'ouvrages de vulgarisation, dans les musées et les archives.

L'application de nouvelles techniques au cours des dernières années n'a pas seulement contribué à l'amélioration de nos connaissances, mais a également révélé l'ampleur de ce qui reste à découvrir et à comprendre sur ce monument. La prospection géophysique qui a montré l'étendue des implantations civiles à l'extérieur des forts est un exemple de ce manque à gagner. L'avancée de l'échantillonnage paléoenvironnemental qui a fourni des informations inestimables sur les conditions climatiques, l'agriculture, les régimes alimentaires, etc., en est un autre. De la même façon, des études novatrices menées sur les artefacts nous ont éclairé sur les aspects sociaux, ethnographiques, culturels et économiques de la vie dans une zone de frontière. Ces nouvelles informations ont rendu nécessaires une réévaluation des théories préalablement émises.

Cependant, malgré cette masse d'informations, nos connaissances restent lacunaires, une situation en partie liée au manque de coordination avec lequel les recherches sur la frontière ont été menées dans le passé. Les travaux scientifiques à venir n'amélioreront pas seulement notre compréhension du Mur lui-même, mais pourront également contribuer à l'étude des aménagements architecturaux frontaliers de l'Empire Romain en général. Les changements de garnison et d'organisation des zones de frontière au cours du temps et leur efficacité sont des domaines d'étude pertinents à toutes les régions de frontière de l'Empire. Il en est de même pour l'impact de l'occupation romaine sur la population et l'économie locales. Les fouilles archéologiques permettront non seulement de former la prochaine génération d'archéologues et d'affiner les techniques archéologiques, mais stimuleront et maintiendront également l'intérêt du public. Parce que ce type d'opération implique la destruction des dépôts archéologiques et se confronte à des budgets limités, il s'avère essentiel de poser une série prioritaire et universellement approuvée de thèmes et de sujets de recherche auxquels se réfèreront ces futurs projets de fouilles.

Le cadre de recherche sur le Mur d'Hadrien, impliquant la collaboration de nombreux spécialistes venus d'horizons différents, a donc été mis en ?uvre avec deux objectifs en tête. Dans un premier temps, il récapitule et évalue les connaissances acquises, qui constituent la base de notre compréhension. Sont pris en compte les vestiges matériels du monument et des installations qui lui sont associées, ainsi que l'ensemble des indices déjà obtenus et les collections des artefacts découverts. Le champ d'application de ce travail concerne les restes des aménagements militaires antérieurs à la construction du Mur même, ainsi que ceux construits le long de la côte cambrienne. Dans un second temps, ce projet de recherche identifie et établit les priorités d'un Agenda de thèmes-clés pour une future recherche et met en place une Stratégie pour réaliser ces objectifs. Le cadre de recherche est désigné pour être un document vivant avec l'Agenda et la Stratégie revisités et, si nécessaire, il pourra être révisé annuellement pendant cinq ans.

Zusammenfassung

Der Hadrianswall ist sicherlich eines der beiden berühmtesten archäologischen Denkmäler Grossbritanniens, dessen Bedeutung durch die Erhebung in den World Heritage-Status auch formal unterstrichen wurde. Seit 2005 ist der Hadrianswall ebenfalls Teil der Frontier of the Roman Empire World Heritage Site. Das lineare Befestigungswerk und sein unmittelbares Hinterland beinhalten eine Vielzahl von archäologischen Stätten und Denkmälern in einer spektakulären Landschaft. Der Hadrianswall ist eine unübertreffliche Quelle für den Wissenschaftler, die jedoch auch in der populären Vorstellung eine bedeutende Rolle spielt und darüber hinaus ein vielbesuchtes Touristenziel ist.

Der Hadrianswall war seit dem 16. Jahrhundert das Objekt antiquarischen Erkundens und Sammelns, mit ersten archäologischen Ausgrabungen in den 90er Jahren des 19. Jahrhunderts, die bis heute fortgesetzt werden. Nach und nach wurden sorgsam gesammelte Informationen veröffentlicht, Geländebegehungen unternommen und Teile des Bauwerks restauriert und für Besucher zugänglich gemacht. Interpretationen und Theorien wurden und werden weiter entwickelt, diskutiert, verändert und ersetzt. Heutzutage gibt es eine Fülle an Informationen zum Hadrianswall in akademischen und populärwissenschaftlichen Publikationen, Museen und Archiven, die jedoch nicht immer leicht zugänglich sind.

Die Entwicklung und Anwendung neuer Techniken in den letzten Jahren hat nicht nur unser Wissen bereichert, sondern auch demonstriert, wie viel es noch zu entdecken und zu verstehen gibt. Beispielsweise haben geophysikalische Untersuchungen den Umfang ziviler Siedlungen in unmittelbarer Nähe der Militärlager aufgezeigt. Die Entwicklung umweltarchäologischer Untersuchungen ergab u. a. wichtige Informationen zu Klima, Ackerbau und Ernährung in der Antike. Ebenso haben weitreichende und innovative Artefaktstudien neues Licht auf soziale, ethnographische, kulturelle und ökonomische Aspekte des Lebens in einer Grenzzone geworfen. Diese neuen Informationen machen eine erneute Überprüfung und Korrektur ursprünglicher Beobachtungen und Interpretationen notwendig.

Trotz dieser nun vorhandenen grossen Menge an Informationen gibt es immer noch gähnende Lücken in unserem Wissen. Dies ist letztlich auf die unkoordinierte Art und Weise zurückzuführen, wie die Erforschung dieser Grenzzone in der Vergangenheit betrieben wurde. Zukünftige Forschungen werden nicht nur das Verständnis des Hadrianswalls selbst verbessern, sondern auch generelle Beiträge zum Studium der Grenzen des Römischen Reiches liefern. Veränderungen in der Besatzung und Organisation der Grenze im Laufe der Zeit, ihre Effektivität und der Einfluss der römischen Besatzung auf die ansässige Bevölkerung und Wirtschaft sind Themenschwerpunkte, die allen Grenzstudien zu Eigen sind. Darüber hinaus finden einige dieser Fragen auch Anklang in der modernen Welt. Archäologische Ausgrabungen, die sichtbarste Form der Forschung, bieten nicht nur die Chance, die nächste Generation von Archäologen auszubilden und archäologische Techniken zu verfeinern, sondern erhalten und stimulieren auch das Interesse der Öffentlichkeit. Ausgrabungen beinhalten jedoch naturgemäss die Zerstörung archäologischer Befunde, zumal die Ressourcen für grössere Projekte in der Regel eher beschränkt sind. Aus diesen Gründen ist es höchst erstrebenswert, dass eine einheitlich vereinbarte und ihrer Priorität nach geordnete Anzahl an Forschungsthemen und -zielen vorhanden ist, auf die sich zukünftige Ausgrabungsprojekte beziehen können.

Das Hadrianswall Forschungsrahmen-Programm, ein Kooperationsprojekt unter Beteiligung einer Vielzahl von Spezialisten, die an der Spitze ihres Wissensgebietes stehen, wurde unter zwei Gesichtspunkten geplant. Erstens wird die existierende Wissensbasis erfasst und bewertet. Dazu gehören die bestehenden Denkmäler und die mit ihnen assoziierten Anlagen sowie die Aufarbeitung der Hinweise, die von bisherigen Untersuchungen erbracht wurden, und die Sammlungen der gefundenen Artefakte. Der Anwendungsbereich umfasst auch die Überreste militärischer Anlagen in der Region, die vor der Entstehung des Walles errichtet wurden sowie jene an der Küste Cumbrias. Zweitens soll eine Agenda für die Hauptthematik zukünftiger Forschungen identifiziert und nach ihrer Priorität geordnet werden, um eine Strategie zu entwickeln, mit der diese anfänglichen Zielsetzungen erreicht werden können. Das Forschungsrahmen-Programm ist als ‚lebendiges' Dokument konzipiert, dessen Absicht und Strategie im Fünfjahres-Zyklus überdacht und gegebenenfalls angepasst wird.

Preface

When the UK drew up its first list of potential World Heritage Sites, it naturally included Hadrian's Wall. Within Britain, Hadrian's Wall is probably one of the two most famous archaeological sites. It is certainly the largest archaeological monument in the country as well as being one of its most explored monuments. Further, its significance is enhanced by its spectacular landscape setting.

Hadrian's Wall was already famous in its own day. The visit of Hadrian to Britain in AD 122 was mentioned in ancient literature. The names of the regiments based on the Wall line were recorded in the *Notitia Dignitatum*, a list of all the senior officials of the Roman Empire created about AD 400. Enterprising tradesmen produced souvenirs of the monument, some of which listed the names of a number of its forts.

When the Romans abandoned Britain to its fate in 409 or thereabouts, information about the date of the building of the Wall was soon lost, but knowledge of its existence was not. It was written about from the sixth century onwards, though the gloss these writers placed on its date, history and function may have deviated from modern views. The Wall is marked on a number of medieval maps and knowledge of its existence was widespread, but the Renaissance brought a resurgence of interest. The new wonder of printing made ancient texts more readily available. People of an antiquarian frame of mind now offered their opinions, often based on personal experience. The publication of a new and extended edition of William Camden's *Britannia* in 1600 may be said to mark a particular watershed.

The eighteenth century witnessed great advances in recording and interpreting the military remains. The nineteenth century saw both the beginning of excavation and a new scholarly rigour with the Wall we now know as Hadrian's Wall finally acknowledged as being the work of that emperor.

The age of scientific excavation began in the 1890s and has continued to this day. From the beginning, excavations were carried out for different reasons: curiosity on the one hand, attempts to understand the monument better through sustained campaigns of research on the other. Gradually and painstakingly, information was gathered - and published - interpretations were advanced - and fought over. Today, there is a vast body of information on Hadrian's Wall available in academic and popular publications, in museums and archives. It is a formidable task to access these wide-ranging sources and decide whether you agree with the favoured interpretation of the day or if the time is ripe for an alternative assessment.

Such re-assessments are essential for, as every historian knows, there is no absolute truth about the past. Each generation interprets Hadrian's Wall in the light of its own experience. Moreover, new information continues to come to light. Excavations over the last decade have led to the discovery of totally new elements on the frontier, pits on the berm, the space between the Wall and the ditch. Geophysical survey has led to an enormous increase in knowledge about the extent of the civil settlements outside forts. Re-examination of the monument itself and its component parts has shed new light on its building history and function. Study of the artefacts from the Wall casts light on the ethnic background of the soldiers and their daily lives.

In short, there is no space for complacency about our knowledge of Britain's premier Roman monument: quite the reverse. Hadrian's Wall offers a vast archaeological database against which the ideas of theoretical archaeologists can be tested. Our understanding of the Wall casts light on how the Roman Empire functioned, how the army operated, whether frontier controls were successful, and how the local population responded to the Roman occupation - all very modern problems.

Yet, in spite of over four hundred years of collecting inscriptions, three centuries of surveying and mapping and one hundred years of archaeological investigation, there are still enormous gaps in our knowledge. This is largely because of the haphazard way in which research has been carried out on the frontier. This volume is the result of the deliberations of the many archaeologists who work on Hadrian's Wall. Here we seek to define the gaps in our knowledge. There are many ways in which they could be filled.

Although Hadrian's Wall is well protected through legislation, we all have to live in a real world in which, sometimes, parts of the monument have to be sacrificed to the greater good. Such occasions offer a chance for investigation of the archaeological remains. The visiting public wants - and needs - to understand the monument better and thus excavation to display its component features can be justified. Finally, archaeologists want to understand Hadrian's Wall better and will wish to undertake research excavations. Such information from all sources is published in archaeological journals, but it is further disseminated through more popular books on the Wall, museum displays and site interpretation panels.

This is emphatically not a book to sit on a shelf. It forms part of the strategy for managing and interpreting Hadrian's Wall. Its purpose is to aid decisions on what to survey, study and excavate, what to display, how to improve understanding of the whole monument. We hope that it will be used to promote and encourage research and understanding.

David J Breeze
Chairman,
Hadrian's Wall Research Framework Steering Group

Introduction

The Hadrian's Wall Research Framework has been prepared with two broad aims in mind. Firstly, it assesses the existing knowledge base for our understanding of the monument including the surviving physical remains of the monument and its associated installations, the totality of evidence produced by investigations so far, and the collections of artefacts recovered. Secondly, it identifies and prioritises key themes for future research and sets out a strategy and action plan by which the initial set of objectives might be achieved.

Purpose of Research Strategies
Research Strategies have been, or are in the process of being, prepared for all English regions. Funded by English Heritage, their purpose is to provide a research focus for the vastly increased volume of fieldwork that has resulted from the implementation of *Planning Policy Guidance Note 16: Archaeology and Planning* (PPG16) in 1990 that made archaeology and heritage conservation an integral component of the development control process. They also provide a guide for grant-giving institutions as to the priorities for research when deciding how to distribute their limited resources.

Although superficially different from previous exercises of this type - because it deals with a period-specific monument or group of monuments rather than the entire archaeology of a region - the Hadrian's Wall Research Framework does in fact share many aspects with equivalent exercises in other areas of the country.

Although perceived as a comprehensively protected and extensively investigated monument set in an exclusively rural environment and managed by a single entity, archaeological research of the Hadrian's Wall zone is beset by many of the complications and problems true of other regions of the country. At both ends of the continuous barrier the remains of the Wall lie in a modern urban environment with the usual problems of research objectives only latterly being incorporated into project designs. The changes wrought by the adoption of a preservation *in situ* policy and the switch from state to developer-funded fieldwork resulted in a move from the large-scale removal of archaeological deposits to restricted investigations located on the basis of where the foundations of new buildings were to be inserted rather than any consideration of archaeological priorities. This mechanical and narrow approach is being transformed by the incorporation into project designs of the priorities set out in Research Frameworks.

Hadrian's Wall is of course one of the best known ancient monuments in Britain and is recognised throughout the world as one of the most impressive frontier works of the Roman Empire. Its international importance received formal recognition in 1987 when it was inscribed as a World Heritage Site (WHS). This designation required the preparation of a Management Plan, and in the second version of this produced in 2002, it was recognised that further research was required to enhance understanding of the monument, stating that 'Developing further understanding of the WHS is intrinsically important in relation to the values for which it was inscribed. This understanding is also vital for interpretation, and thus to increasing the enjoyment and appreciation of visitors through communicating accurate information. It is also essential for the management of the resource: recent survey and investigation have demonstrated that in many cases important remains exist beyond the boundary of legally protected areas.

In recent years, English Heritage has facilitated the preparation of regional research frameworks for the Historic Environment which set down clear methods and approaches to the development and implementation of research policies for specific themes, topics and geographical areas. This builds on the publication of national policy documents such as *Exploring Our Past* in 1991 and a draft *English Heritage Archaeology Division Research Agenda* in 1997. The need for regional research frameworks was set out in *Frameworks for Our Past* (Olivier 1996, 5) and in the full MARS report (Darvill and Fulton 1998, 231) and led to a policy statement on Research Frameworks Implementation in 1999. The regional research frameworks for the North-West and the North-East regions were completed recently. Because of the importance of the Hadrian's Wall World Heritage Site, and its unique set of issues, it was felt that it required its own research framework, although obviously this should take account of, and articulate with, the relevant regional frameworks.

The proposal for a research framework that covers the whole of Hadrian's Wall, with its sites and monuments of varying type and location in both rural and urban environments, and which seeks to identify objectives within a national and international context, is timely in view of the imminent appearance of the revised Management Plan for the period 2008-12. However, to be of the highest value, it was considered essential that the process of writing the framework should be fully inclusive and involve the whole of the heritage sector in its widest sense. Future directions for research into the historic environment ought to be informed not only by archaeology but also by local history, architecture and the natural landscape, integrating all aspects of the built and historic environment (as described in the DCMS/DETR 2000 report *Power of Place*). Clearly, therefore, full participation in the preparation of the Research Framework by the archaeological community of the Frontier Zone was vital so that it could be a truly collaborative process resulting in an end product agreed and adopted by all parties.

The first part of the Research Framework (Volume I) is the Assessment. This is an analysis of the current state of the Hadrian's Wall resource, both in terms of the surviving physical remains in the ground and collections of artefacts and the accumulated knowledge existing in publications and archives. The second part (Volume II) consists of an analysis of the Resource Assessment and identifies the principal directions and themes for research suggested by the assessment including those prompted by gaps and areas of difficulty in the current knowledge base. The overall purpose is to identify subjects and themes for potential future research set out as a Research Agenda. The third and final element of the Research Framework (also in Volume II) is a Research Strategy that sets out ways in which the Agenda items might be addressed.

It is hoped that over the life of the existing document - it is planned to be revised on a five year cycle - the Research Framework will assist archaeological and related organisations to: consider the needs, objectives and opportunities for new research; identify appropriate partnerships; locate sources of funding; use resources to best effect; establish training opportunities and formulate strategies for succession planning (i.e. the next generation of Wall investigators and specialists in particular disciplines); as well as seeing their work in the broader social, economic and environmental context.

It is equally important to state what the Research Framework is not. It should not be seen as an absolute, proscriptive or exclusive document. New avenues and opportunities for research will undoubtedly occur in the future and circumstances will change. New work on the Wall will not only improve knowledge but will also itself give rise to the formulation of additional lines of investigation as will advances in scientific techniques.

Geographical Scope of the Study
The brief for the preparation of this Research Framework determined that the boundaries of the study area should be those of the World Heritage site. Thus it consists of: the Wall itself, along with its forts, milecastles, turrets, and the Vallum; the forts and other installations on the Cumberland Coast west of Bowness and as far south as Ravenglass; the forts and other sites associated with the line of the Stanegate; the coastal site of South Shields; the major centres associated with the Wall at Carlisle and Corbridge; and the outpost fort at Bewcastle.

The forts and military infrastructure to the rear of the Wall Zone, although integrated with the functioning of the Wall, are not included in this study as they have already been encompassed by the regional research frameworks for the North-East and North-West regions. However, cross-references are made to the relevant sections of those documents, and to the individual sites themselves and to other features, as and when appropriate.

Geology and Geography
Unsurprisingly, the geology and geography of the region had a great influence on the positioning of the frontier works. The general location of the linear frontier was determined by the existence of the Tyne/Solway isthmus while its precise route in individual locations was carefully chosen to meet the requirements of the builders. The terrain traversed by the Wall varies considerably. From South Shields to Chollerford, it crosses the lowlands of the North Sea coast and the lower stretch of the Tyne Valley.

As far as Heddon-on-the-Wall the geology consists of a succession of sandstones, shales, siltstones and numerous coal seams belonging to the Upper Carboniferous Coal Measures. Beyond this lie an earlier but similar group of Upper Carboniferous rocks and in both sectors the solid geology is overlain by deposits of boulder clay or till. It is in the next sector - between Chollerford and Brampton - that the solid geology has a more visual presence in the landscape. The land is typified by an east-west oriented scarp-and-dip topography where the Wall runs along the imposing north-facing escarpment of the Whin Sill. This last is a volcanic intrusion of magma which cooled to form dolorite, while the earthworks comprising the Vallum follow the lower ground to the south. In clear weather conditions this is a landscape of far-reaching views to both north and south of the frontier.

Beyond Brampton, the geology changes to sandstones, siltstones and mudstones of Permo-Triassic strata. Largely overlain by drift deposits of boulder clay or till this area is a softer landscape of gently undulating terrain. West of Burgh-by-Sands, the Wall crosses on to low-lying silts and clays bordering the Solway Estuary. Further south, the defences along the Cumbrian coast lie mainly on glacial deposits.

The Monument, its Study, and the Sources
Begun in AD 122 on the orders of the Emperor Hadrian, the construction of Hadrian's Wall set the parameters for events in and beyond the northern part of the province of Britannia for the next three centuries. It was the focus of military activity in the province and both it and the garrisons stationed along and close to it had a major influence on social, political and economic developments in the neighbouring regions.

The many and various installations of the frontier system contain a wealth of archaeological and related data which, in terms of scale, variety and integrity, is unsurpassed in Britain. Hadrian's Wall functioned as an integrated system and clearly it should be studied in the same way, the evidence from each constituent part contributing to the understanding of the monument as a whole.

Located in an island province Hadrian's Wall has a history and evolution peculiar to itself. However, it was part of an empire-wide frontier system and as such its study is inseparable from that of the other static limes systems. This important international aspect is reflected in the existence of the Congress of Roman Frontier Studies.

The existing data relating to Hadrian's Wall has accumulated as the result of more than 400 years of study, initially by antiquarians and historians and more recently by archaeologists. The corpus of information is considerable and much is readily accessible in either published works or public archives. Collected over such a long period, under varying circumstances, using various methodologies, and by individuals with differing priorities and preconceptions, the nature and quality of the evidence is inconsistent but all of it is of value.

An important element, however, does not exist in written form but rather as the combined knowledge and expertise of the archaeological community of Hadrian's Wall. The full engagement of this community in the Research

Framework construction process has been crucial to the success of the project.

Description of the World Heritage Site

At its greatest extent, in the second century AD, the imperial frontier stretched for over 5000 km, starting on the western coast of northern Britain, which it divided into two parts. The frontier in Europe then ran along the rivers Rhine and Danube, looping round the Carpathian Mountains to the Black Sea. The Eastern frontier, from the Black Sea to the Red Sea and running through mountains, great river valleys and the desert, faced Rome's greatest enemy, Parthia. To the south, Rome's protective cordon embraced Egypt and then ran along the northern edge of the Sahara Desert to the Atlantic shore in Morocco.

Hadrian's Wall was inscribed as a World Heritage Site (World Heritage Site) in 1987 as the most complex and best preserved of the frontiers of the Roman Empire. Since 2005 it has been part of the Frontiers of the Roman Empire World Heritage Site, along with the Roman Frontier in Germany, the Upper German-Raetian Limes ("Obergermanisch-Raetischer Limes").

The linear frontier works popularly known as Hadrian's Wall appear to have been constructed on the direct order of the Emperor Hadrian during his visit to Britain in AD 122. Hadrian's Wall underwent various modifications and alterations throughout its long history. Elements of it also continued to be used and adapted after the Roman period. The World Heritage Site is not restricted to the Wall itself. It also includes the chain of military installations that extended the system down the Cumbrian coast, other Roman sites and structures which pre-date the building of the Wall and which in some cases continued to develop after its construction, along with a few of the outpost forts to the north of the barrier. The term Hadrian's Wall should thus be understood to mean the Hadrian's Wall zone.

Our knowledge of the World Heritage Site is largely the result of antiquarian and archaeological interest and excavation. The same processes have collected together a huge assemblage of artefacts which illustrate the life of the Wall in the Roman period. The text of some of the building inscriptions and altars on stone identify the names of the units occupying the forts at certain dates and their country of origin. The finds from the frontier include a wide range of Roman objects including coins, metalwork, glass and ceramics. Excavations at Vindolanda have revealed an unparalleled collection of writing tablets, preserved in anaerobic conditions, ranging from official documents to personal correspondence, which is the largest such assemblage in Britain and contributes significantly to understanding of life on Hadrian's Wall.

Another valuable resource is the body of archive material that has been assembled relating to the World Heritage Site, particularly excavation records, some of which are often the only record of parts of the Site now available for research. Buried deposits of the World Heritage Site and its Buffer Zone contain not only artefactual evidence but also increasingly important scientific evidence in the form of preserved paleo-environmental material.

The Hadrian's Wall World Heritage Site falls within four of the character areas defined by Natural England. These are the joint products of the geology (described in Part 2, 2.4) and of human intervention in the development of the landscape.

Stakeholders in the World Heritage Site

The World Heritage Site and its Buffer Zone is part of a settled and heavily utilised landscape. The population living within 10 miles either side of Hadrian's Wall is just under a million inhabitants representing approximately 430,000 households. Local communities also include very many people who visit and enjoy the World Heritage Site as well as those who manage the sites accessible to the public or run tourism-related businesses. Education also provides links between local communities and the World Heritage Site.

There is therefore no one community or a single community of interest in relation to the World Heritage Site.

Given the extent and complexity of the Hadrian's Wall World Heritage Site it is hardly surprising that the individuals and bodies with an interest in it are large in number and varied in outlook. A number of bodies have statutory, official or other promotional and economic links with the Wall. There are institutions and individuals whose interest in it is as a great archaeological site and subject for study, wonder or visiting. Then there are those who own parts of the World Heritage Site or who live and/or work within its boundaries. These can be individuals or organisations, both public and private and operating at national, regional and local level.

There has long been international interest in Hadrian's Wall on a scholarly level. Now that it forms part the Frontiers of the Roman Empire World Heritage Site, that international interest has expanded to include the management of the site especially its potential contribution to defining best practice in the management of monuments of world importance.

The Summary Nomination Statement for the Frontiers of the Roman Empire World Heritage Site, to which UNESCO has agreed, states that "the responsibility for the management of individual parts of the World Heritage Site must rest with the individual State Parties and be carried out by each in accordance with their legislative and management systems. Equally, it is essential that individual parts within the World Heritage Site are managed within an overall framework of co-operation to achieve common standards of identification, recording, research, protection, conservation, management, presentation and understanding of the Roman frontier". This has led to agreement to form an international committee, comprising an administrator and an archaeologist representing the State Party, from each part of the frontier that has been inscribed as part of Frontiers of the Roman Empire World Heritage Site. ICOMOS, the International Council on Monuments and Sites, is a non-governmental organisation, set up in 1965, and is an official advisory body to UNESCO, and to the World Heritage Committee on the implementation of the World Heritage Convention on cultural sites.

The World Heritage Convention was ratified by the United Kingdom in 1984. The Convention provides for the identification, protection, conservation, presentation and transmitting of cultural and natural sites of outstanding universal value. Individual governments are responsible for the nomination of sites and ensuring protection of sites inscribed in the List. The Department for Culture Media and Sport is the government department responsible for World Heritage Sites.

Since the 1990s much of government involvement has been implemented through regional government offices or along the same regional boundaries. The Hadrian's Wall World Heritage Site is split fairly evenly between the North East and North West regions. The Government Offices for the North East and North West represent eleven central government departments across the entire region.

The United Kingdom National Commission for UNESCO was formally re-established in March 2004. An independent body working in partnership with Government and United Kingdom civil society it has the overarching objectives of developing United Kingdom input into UNESCO policy making, effecting reforms in UNESCO and encouraging support in the United Kingdom for UNESCO's ideals and work. ICOMOS-UK, founded along with the parent organisation in 1965, is one of 110 national ICOMOS committees and aims to be the lead voice in the United Kingdom for the world's cultural heritage, providing a forum for all those involved in the conservation of cultural heritage.

English Heritage is the only national body with a specific remit related to the World Heritage Site's inscription, including the protection and conservation of the World Heritage Site. Its responsibilities and functions mainly derive from the 1979 Ancient Monuments and Archaeological Areas Act, as amended by The Heritage Act of 1983. Sponsored by the Department for Culture Media and Sport, it is recognised by the government as the lead body for the historic environment.

Natural England was formed in March 2006, by bringing together English Nature (EN), the landscape, access and recreation elements of the Countryside Agency (CA) and the environmental land management functions of the Rural Development Service (RDS). Natural England works towards the delivery of four strategic outcomes, which together deliver on its purpose to conserve, enhance and manage the natural environment for the benefit of current and future generations.

Responsibility for museums within the World Heritage Site rests with the Museums Libraries and Archives Council, which works through its regional organisations for the North East and North West.

The Regional Development Agencies - ONENorthEast and the North West Development Agency - were established in 1999 and are responsible for economic and business development, including tourism, regeneration and improvement. The Regional Development Agencies will also become the Regional Planning Bodies and will take over responsibility from the current Regional Assemblies for preparing the regional spatial and economic strategies in their respective regions.

Tourism development and promotion in the North East is the responsibility of Area Tourism Partnerships and those covering Hadrian's Wall are Northumberland Tourism and Tyne and Wear Tourism; in the North West this responsibility lies with the Destination Management Organisation, Cumbria Tourism.

The Hadrian's Wall World Heritage Site as currently defined lies within 12 different local authorities many with overlapping jurisdictions and powers. Within Tyneside, parts of the Site lie within the three unitary authorities of Newcastle, North Tyneside and South Tyneside. The remainder comes under the jurisdiction of either Northumberland or Cumbria County Councils. In Cumbria, the frontier system passes through the district councils of Copeland, Allerdale and Carlisle. In Northumberland it runs through Tynedale and Castle Morpeth, although as from April 2009 these will be subsumed within a single unitary authority for the whole of the county. The powers of local authorities that potentially have the most impact on the World Heritage Site relate to planning, highways and transport and to economic development. The World Heritage Site also extends into two National Parks, the Lake District and Northumberland National Parks which have responsibility for planning within their areas.

A further level of local government outside Tyneside is provided by parish councils. The World Heritage Site itself falls within the areas of 42 parish councils with more parishes within its Buffer Zone.

The pattern of ownership and management within the World Heritage Site is very complex. A considerable number of bodies own and manage approximately ten per cent of the World Heritage Site specifically for conservation and access. In addition to the local authorities mentioned above other bodies are English Heritage, the National Trust, and the Vindolanda Trust. The remainder of the World Heritage Site, except for the areas controlled by highway authorities, is in private ownership as is most of the Buffer Zone of the World Heritage Site.

Four organisations mentioned above - ONENorthEast, the North West Development Agency, English Heritage and Natural England - jointly fund Hadrian's Wall Heritage Limited which has a key role in the overall management of the World Heritage Site. The company was established in May 2006, principally to co-ordinate and promote the growth of the economic contribution of the World Heritage Site to the regional economies through a programme of capital investment in the Site and its effective marketing.

As described below, academic interest in Hadrian's Wall has developed over four hundred years starting with the first antiquarians. Prominent among the current academic interests are the archaeology departments of universities, particularly those at Durham, Newcastle upon Tyne and Manchester, independent bodies such as the Vindolanda Trust, and local/regional societies such as the Society of Antiquaries of Newcastle and the Cumberland and

Westmorland Antiquarian and Archaeological Society along, of course, with a galaxy of individual scholars.

The World Heritage Site and its Buffer Zone are important economically for agriculture and tourism. The latter has increased as the former's viability has diminished and Hadrian's Wall is now a major feature of regional and local economic strategies. Hadrian's Wall is seen as an icon of the north of England. Agriculture and forestry cover most of the World Heritage Site and its Buffer Zone outside the urban areas. In the central sector, farming is primarily pastoral, as it is in parts of Cumbria where dairy farming is an important sector of the industry. Farming in the remainder of Cumbria and east Northumberland is primarily arable. There are approximately 700 farms that contain elements of the World Heritage Site, varying from large estates divided into tenanted farms to owner-occupied farms. The number of farms is greater if the Buffer Zone is included.

Heritage related tourism makes a very important contribution to the regional economy through admission fees and sales at displayed sites and of course through accommodation provision. A considerable number of jobs are dependent on the tourism economy and the importance of tourism has increased as other, more traditional, industries in the region have declined. Equally, however, both agriculture and tourism can, and in some cases do, have detrimental effects not just on the visual amenity of the World Heritage Site but also on the surviving above-ground fabric of the Wall itself as well as the remains of the other elements of the frontier works and associated sites. This is a consideration of fundamental importance to the integrity of the WHS and is an issue highlighted in the Research Agenda/Strategy section of the Research Framework.

The Roman Empire is of undoubted outstanding universal value. Spanning three continents, the Empire developed and transmitted over large parts of Europe a universal culture based on Greek and Roman civilisation. Its influence reached far beyond its actual boundaries in Europe and around the Mediterranean. Its culture framed and guided the cultures of Europe and beyond up to and including the present day.

The frontiers of the Roman Empire form the single largest monument to this civilisation. They helped define the very extent and nature of the Roman Empire. As a whole, they represent the definition of the Roman Empire as a world state. They also played a crucial role in defining the development of the successor states to the Roman Empire. The frontiers and their garrisons were also a crucial tool of Romanisation on both sides of the border line.

The frontiers also have high significance as illustrating the complexity and organisational abilities of the Roman Empire. With only the technology and communications of a pre-industrial society, the Empire was able to plan, create and protect a frontier of some 5,000 km and garrisons of tens of thousands of men. It was then able to manage and use this system, on the whole successfully, for periods of many centuries, both as a physical barrier, and also as the basis for diplomatic and military intervention far beyond the actual frontier line itself.

As a whole, the Frontiers of the Roman Empire World Heritage Site meets three criteria for inscription as a cultural World Heritage Site, which are those which Hadrian's Wall met in 1987 and still meets today. These are numbers (ii), (iii) and (iv):

(ii) exhibit an important interchange of human values, over a span of time or within a cultural area of the world, on developments in architecture or technology, monumental arts or town planning and landscape design

The Wall is the most intact and most elaborate frontier of the Roman Empire. As such, it demonstrates the advances made by the Romans in the development of fortifications during their occupation of Britain. At its outset, it was a complex and very large work, requiring a high degree of technological competence and great organisational skills. While no part of it demonstrates great technological innovation, the combination of its various elements and the scale of the whole work was a very significant achievement.

(iii) bear a unique or at least exceptional testimony to a cultural tradition or to a civilisation which is living or has disappeared

During the three centuries of the Roman occupation of northern Britain, the military presence developed an elaborate social structure and culture. This depended on the presence of the Roman army which in turn was a manifestation of the power of the first pan-European state. The combination of the army and its followers with the local population resulted in a very particular material culture based on the universal attributes of the Roman Empire tempered by local influences. The remains of the frontier system, and of the settlements contemporary with its use, are well preserved and, as such, are exceptional evidence of Roman culture and civilisation.

(iv) be an outstanding example of a type of building or architectural or technological ensemble or landscape which illustrates [a] significant stage [s] in human history

The Romans developed great skill in the building of fortifications reflecting their use of a standing army organised to a common pattern across the Empire. They were the evidence of the military might which underpinned and supported the Empire. Hadrian's Wall is the largest and best preserved of those works. As such, it is a major resource for the study and understanding of Roman military architecture

Brief History of Research

The origins of Hadrian's Wall were soon forgotten in post-Roman Britain. In the sixth century Gildas opined that it was built by a Roman army returning to Britain after its abandonment about 410 in order to protect the former provincials from attacks by the Picts and Scots. Bede, writing in the early part of the eighth century in the monastery at Jarrow/Monkwearmouth, was able to use the ancient historians, Gildas and his own local knowledge of the physical remains of the Wall. He assigned the Vallum (the great earthwork which accompanies the Wall to the south) to the Emperor Septimius Severus while retaining Gildas' date for the construction of the stone Wall, which he added still survived to a thickness of eight feet and a height of twelve feet. This continued to be the state of knowledge and understanding until the sixteenth century.

John Leland and others wrote about the Wall in the sixteenth century, but the first important account is by William Camden, the great Elizabethan antiquary, written in 1599 and printed in the fifth edition (1600) of his *Britannia*. Camden visited the Wall in person but some parts were inaccessible because of the activities of the robbers known as the Border reivers. He advanced a complete explanation of the Wall and its works which remained the orthodoxy for the next two hundred and fifty years.

The *Britannia*, written in Latin, was translated into English in 1610 by Philemon Holland, in consultation with Camden; Henry Holland, his son, produced a new edition in 1637. The Holland translations long remained standard works on the archaeology of Britain, and passed through many revisions. The later revisions by Bishop Gibson (1695, 1722, 1753, 1772) and Richard Gough (1789, 1806) incorporate the results of a fresh examination of the Wall in 1708-9 and, for the first time, an account of the whole line. Gough's edition is based upon the work of John Horsley, Presbyterian minister and schoolmaster at Morpeth, whose original thoughts about the Wall were presented in his *Britannia Romana*, published in 1732 shortly after his death.

William Stukeley's *Iter Boreale*, published in 1776, includes memoranda of a journey made along Hadrian's Wall in 1725 with Roger Gale. It contained a new theory of the relation between Wall and Vallum, and a number of useful drawings showing the contemporary state of preservation. The first notable observation in the 19th century occurred in 1807 when the Rev. Dr. John Lingard walked from Wallsend to Gilsland, making manuscript notes entitled *Mural Tourification*. A few years later, another member of the clergy, the Rev. John Hodgson, incumbent of Jarrow and Heworth, wrote *The Picture of Newcastle upon Tyne* (1812) with a comprehensive and useful account of the Wall. In 1840 he devoted a large part of the last volume of his *History of Northumberland* to the Walls of Hadrian and Antoninus. Using the evidence of inscriptions, Hodgson saw that Vallum and Wall must be contemporary whereas previously the former had been seen as Hadrianic and the latter as Severan.

Hodgson also excavated on the Wall, as did his contemporaries John Clayton and Anthony Hedley. Clayton inherited the Chesters estate in 1843 and during his long life purchased sections of the Wall along with several forts. He had his workmen replace fallen facing stones on the Wall and excavate many structures including MCs 37 (Housesteads), 39 (Castle Nick) and 42 (Cawfields), Chesters fort, and the bath-house and Coventina's Well at Carrawburgh.

The middle years of the century saw significant events in the history of Wall studies. In 1848 John Collingwood Bruce commenced his study of the monument. The following year he led the first Pilgrimage along Hadrian's Wall, followed two years later by publication of *The Roman Wall*. Two further editions were published in 1853 and 1867. The second of these contains a detailed description of the remains along with accounts of Roman sites near the Wall as well as inscriptions and other objects. In 1863 Bruce produced a summary version, *The Wallet-book*, later *Handbook, to the Roman Wall*. This offered the first, modern, statement of the function of Hadrian's Wall: "The Roman Wall...is a great fortification intended to act not only as a fence against a northern enemy, but to be used as the basis of military operations against a foe on either side of it".

The first accurate topographic survey of the Wall was prepared by Henry MacLauchlan in the years 1852-1854 for the Duke of Northumberland, and published in 1858 with an explanatory Memoir, which records his acute observations of the frontier works. MacLauchlan's survey was the basis of the map which appeared in all editions of the *Handbook* from the second to the tenth, eventually replaced by Ordnance Survey maps.

Systematic excavation on the Wall began in the 1890s. Francis Haverfield commenced his examination of the Vallum in 1894 on behalf of the Cumberland Excavation Committee and in 1898 R. C. Bosanquet excavated Housesteads. Arguably of even greater significance was the investigation of T 44b (Mucklebank) by J. P. Gibson in 1892 for this led on to a series of partnerships and the beginning of a long programme of research intended to establish the structural and chronological history of the Wall. F. G. Simpson joined Gibson in 1907. His association with the Wall was to endure for 40 years and it is the results of his work that provide much of our knowledge of the Wall. Gibson died in 1912 and I. A. Richmond joined Simpson in 1928. Another important member of this group was R. G. Collingwood. He it was who established the system of numbering the structures on the Wall and he also wrote a number of papers setting the Wall in its wider context. Eric Birley joined the team at Birdoswald in 1929, an excavation which led to the formation of a revised framework for the history of the Wall.

Noting damage at Housesteads in 1856, Bruce understandably assigned it to hostile action, in that case an invasion around 180. Nearly forty years later Gibson recognised three periods in T 44b (Mucklebank) and suggested that the need for repair was the result of repeated attacks on the Wall. The Gibson-Simpson investigation of MC 48 (Poltross Burn) in 1909 led to a chronology for the Wall being postulated. At the end of the first phase (IA), the pivots at milecastle gateways were damaged or removed, this being related to the abandonment of Hadrian's Wall in favour of the Antonine Wall about 142. The second phase of the first main period (IB) closed with the invasion of about 180 and in both milecastles and turrets this level of destruction was marked by considerable quantities of masonry debris. The end of the second period, which was also marked by masonry debris, occurred after the loss of a coin of Claudius II dating to 269. Coins indicated that the third and last occupation began before 300, with final abandonment occurring as early as 330. This third period continued in the forts until 364-69, when they were destroyed, to be subsequently re-built, surviving down to 383.

The results of an excavation at Birdoswald in 1929 caused this sequence to be refined. Four main periods were discerned. Period I commenced with the building of the Wall and, broken by the occupation of the Antonine Wall, continued until about 195 when the northern tribes took advantage of the absence of the army on the continent to invade the province. Period II commenced with the repair of that damage in 200/205 and lasted until about 295, when again the absence of the army defending the island from attack was an invitation to invasion from the north. Period III ran from 297/300 until 368, the year following the concerted barbarian attack on Britain known as the '*barbarica conspiratio*'. Period IV covered the final years of occupation down to about 383. This, together with the elucidation of the history of the Turf Wall over the decade 1925-1935, led to the premature assertion that all the problems of Hadrian's Wall had been solved.

It has become clear that not all sites on the Wall fit into this strict framework. Evidence recovered subsequently suggests the invasion of about 180 only affected the forts in the vicinity of Dere Street, namely Rudchester, Halton Chesters and Corbridge. The problem with the reasons advanced for the destruction of the Wall in the 190s and 290s is that no invasion is recorded at either time. Hadrian's Wall is not mentioned in the account of the invasion of Britain in 367, but archaeologists have tried to link the treachery of the *areani* (frontier scouts) at that time to a consequent destruction. Finally, re-analysis of the coin evidence has demonstrated that the Wall continued in occupation until at least the end of the fourth century.

The late 1920s and early 1930s were years of intense activity on Hadrian's Wall. The rejuvenated Cumberland Excavation Committee under F. G. Simpson and I. A. Richmond investigated the nature of the Turf Wall while the North of England Excavation Committee was founded by the Society of Antiquaries of Newcastle in 1924 to encourage "under proper supervision the excavation of sites in the North". Naturally, it tended to concentrate on the eastern end of the Wall. Also in the east, the improvement of the Military Road resulted in a series of rescue excavations. The importance of this work was recognised by Durham University, which appointed Simpson as its director of excavation in 1924, a post he relinquished in 1931 to allow Eric Birley to be appointed as a lecturer. Birley was to stay at Durham for 40 years, directing his students to research on a wide range of aspects of the Wall and the Roman army. Throughout these years, excavations took place at Corbridge. Wide-ranging exploration from 1906 to 1914 provided a basic plan of the town. In 1933, the core of the site was placed in state care and the following year a new campaign of excavation commenced, focused on the Roman fort under the town, which continued, with a break for the Second World War, until 1973.

Research on Hadrian's Wall through the nineteenth century and well into the twentieth was primarily undertaken by private individuals, local societies and, latterly, by Durham and Newcastle Universities. In 1928 the Government joined this group when it first took sections of the Wall into its care. Since 1945, the Ministry of Public Buildings and Works, the Department of the Environment, and latterly English Heritage have funded or sponsored much excavation on the Wall including clearing and consolidating many miles of the Wall and undertaking a major operation to examine and expose the buildings within the fort at Housesteads. Much has been discovered as a result of rescue excavations in advance of developments.

This work has been complemented by the activities of the National Trust in the central sector, which included investigation of MC 39 (Castle Nick) as well as the discovery of an additional tower at Peel Gap. Excavations in advance of developments have also taken place, for example at Wallsend, and in Carlisle, which have revolutionised our knowledge of the history of that city. Cumbria County Council has sponsored excavations at Birdoswald and Tyne and Wear Museums at South Shields and Wallsend. As well as providing valuable evidence relating to the later history of the Wall these also enabled the large-scale public display of remains thus enhancing the tourism offer of these locations. Also in the west, the second half of the twentieth century saw the real beginnings of research of sites along the Cumbrian Coast with the single-handed endeavours of Richard Bellhouse.

The long-running research excavations at Vindolanda have led to the display of additional buildings in the fort and extensive areas of the civil settlement. Of major international importance has been the discovery there of some 2000 writing tablets dating to the years around 100. The writing tablets not only shed a fascinating light on life on the northern frontier during the years immediately before the construction of the Wall - military intelligence, building, supply, and the *minutiae* of daily life - but, as so many of the documents are broadly similar to those found on the Roman Empire's eastern frontier, they allow these other documents to be used with confidence to illuminate life on the northern frontiers as well. Excavations, accompanied by academic research, have continued to extend and amplify our knowledge of Hadrian's Wall, challenging past assumptions and offering new interpretations.

David JP Mason

RESOURCE ASSESSMENT

"It is well known to all readers...that the investigation of Hadrian's Wall has advanced rapidly during the last few years: so quickly, indeed, that it has not been easy for those deeply immersed in the subject to keep pace with the inquiry. Not a few important points have been settled, and the correlation of new results with old has required considerable adjustment of ideas. Again, the removal of old difficulties has raised new questions. Thus, a statement of how knowledge of the subject now stands is desirable, so that all who read it may share in the thoughts and inquiries of those at work on the problem."

Ian A. Richmond 1939

1. The Historical Framework of Hadrian's Wall: An Assessment
by N H Hodgson

In the first half of the twentieth century the commonly held framework for understanding the history of Hadrian's Wall proposed a series of episodes of destruction followed by reconstruction. These episodes were not closely dated until 1929, when two re-used building inscriptions were found at Birdoswald: one of *c.* AD 205-8, the other of *c.* AD 297-305. As a result the 'Wall-periods' became standard, for all Wall structures, turrets and milecastles as well as forts.

Wall-period I ran from the building of the Wall under Hadrian to 196-7. It was supposed that in 196 the Wall garrison was withdrawn by Clodius Albinus, who proclaimed himself Augustus and left his British base to confront his rival for the purple, Septimius Severus, in Gaul. This, it was believed, gave the northern barbarians an opportunity to wreak destruction on the Wall and far to the south of it. Wall-period I was divided by the occupation of the Antonine Wall in Scotland into IA and IB.

Wall Period II was seen as starting with reconstruction under Severan governors and ending in 296-7. Once again the Wall garrison was withdrawn, this time by Allectus, to counter the invading forces of Constantius Chlorus, who succeeded in recapturing Britain, separated since 286 from the central empire. Again the Wall was overrun, and again reconstruction was necessary - referred to in the literature as 'Constantian'. This was the beginning of 'Wall-period III'.

Period III ended with the destruction wrought by the 'barbarian conspiracy' of 367. The subsequent reconstruction, the beginning of the final Wall-period, IV, was always referred to in Hadrian's Wall studies as 'Theodosian': nothing to do with the emperor Theodosius, but referring rather to his father, the *comes rei militaris* Theodosius, sent by Valentinian I to put things right in Britain. Wall-Period IV ended in the late-fourth or early-fifth century.

The whole framework was based primarily on history - or assumed history - as recorded in or implied by written sources, and phases observed on archaeological sites were dated by reference to the framework in a literal way that now seems inconceivable. From the 1930s the Wall-period framework went unchallenged until the 1960s, when there are the first signs of attempts to modify or break away from it. The Wall-periods were still in evidence in Charles Daniels' 13th edition of *The Handbook to the Roman Wall* (1978), but that this usage was no longer wholly representative of its time is shown by Breeze and Dobson's *Hadrian's Wall* (1976). This revolutionary book ignored the Wall Periods altogether, tearing up the framework and offering a new narrative - and social history of the Wall - based much more empirically on the actual evidence available. One problem with the Wall periods was the lack of direct literary evidence for the pivotal invasions actually having taken place. The irruptions of 197 and 296 were entirely hypothetical, whereas an invasion is actually recorded in the 180s. The barbarian conspiracy of 367 at least existed in the pages of Ammianus Marcellinus, but even here there was no actual mention of Hadrian's Wall being crossed or destroyed.

By the 1970s it was obvious that not every site displayed an identical sequence of structural change that could be equated with the events of 180/196, 296, or 367. This was the beginning of the age of the only really big, modern excavations on Wall sites, Wallsend, Housesteads, Vindolanda, eventually South Shields and Birdoswald. It was

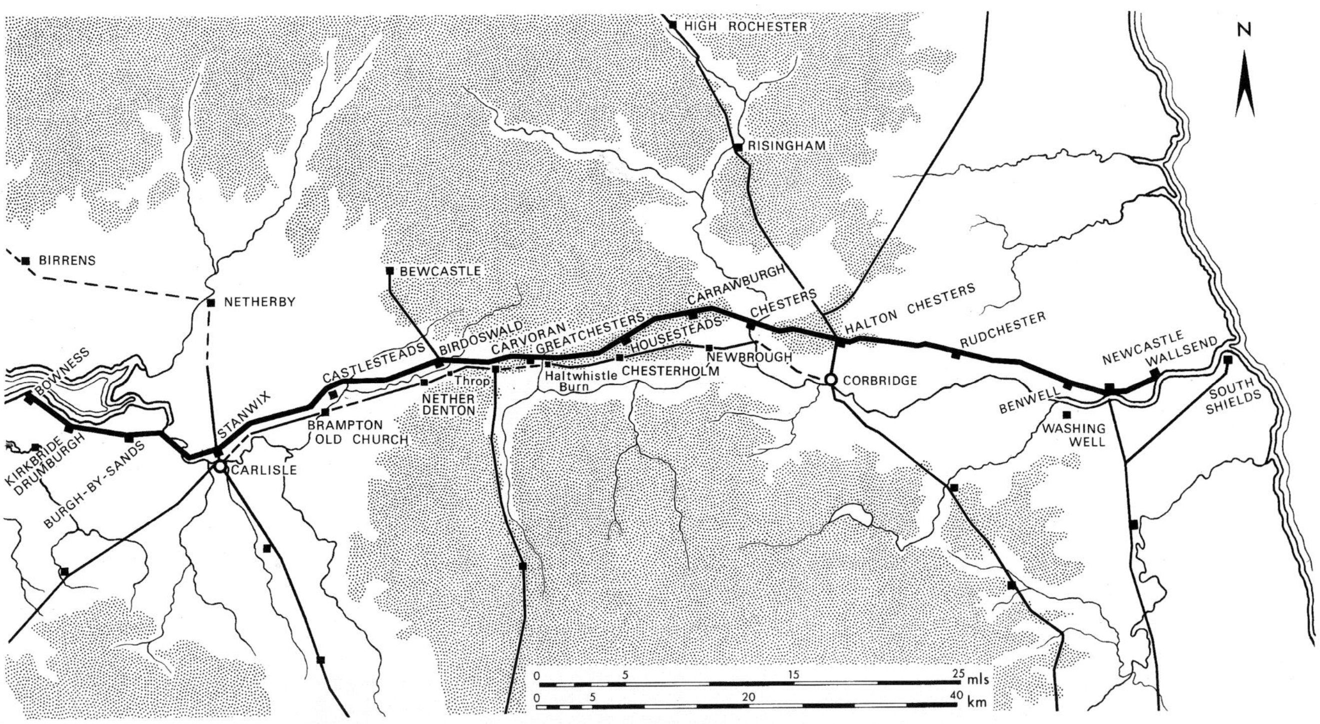

1. Hadrian's Wall and its installations as existing at the end of his reign

also the time when, with the problem of the chronology of the building the Wall seemingly solved, interest in researching the milecastles, turrets and Vallum dropped away (with the exception of the work in the 1980s on the National Trust Estate in the central sector). All of these big digs were to throw up a massive amount of information, but the results neither backed up the old historical scheme for the Wall or suggested an obvious new one. In fact results of excavations still tend be evaluated against the hypotheses advanced by Breeze and Dobson and others in the 1960s and 1970s as a cautious replacement of the Wall-periods. So for example, there is still an expectation that forts might have been run down or derelict in the later-third century (something predicted in the 1970s on the basis of small-scale excavations at Rudchester and Halton Chesters) although few of the big excavations listed above that subsequently took place provided any support for this. It is almost as if, despite the flood of information from excavations, and the development of mature and sophisticated study of previously neglected or unavailable categories of evidence (environmental material; numismatics; small finds, the palaeography of the Vindolanda and Carlisle tablets, high-resolution geophysical survey), historical thinking about the Wall stopped around 1980. General historical accounts of the Wall still tend to begin with the literary evidence, rather than starting with the archaeology.

Although they have yet to be generally agreed upon, fully tested, or even properly discussed, the following chronological and social-historical conclusions have

2. Bronze head of Hadrian found in the River Thames

emerged from archaeological studies over the generation since Breeze and Dobson's *Hadrian's Wall* was first written. Subsequent editions of Breeze and Dobson (1987, 2000) have made a conscientious effort to take account of these developments, though they do not always sit comfortably within the narrative as originally set out. They can be used to propose a framework of major historical developments on the Wall, into which historically recorded events somehow have to be fitted.

- Hadrian's Wall was at least partly decommissioned only 20 years after its inception with the move north into Scotland under Antoninus Pius. It remains particularly uncertain however to what extent the Hadrian's Wall forts were really abandoned, if at all. Most now agree that re-examination of the excavated evidence from Scotland shows that the Antonine Wall was finally abandoned by the 160s, after a single period of occupation. Hadrian's barrier was once again the fully functioning northern frontier wall from the 160s.

- There may have been a further reorganisation in the later-170s or early-180s (arguably when troops were returned to Britain after service in the Marcomannic Wars), and it is now certain that in some cases it is at this time that the Wall-forts received the garrisons that would occupy them throughout the third century and that would still be in place in the fourth century according to the *Notitia Dignitatum*.

- What we traditionally think of as the 'third-century situation' on Hadrian's Wall - actually beginning, if we accept the above, c.180 - is an epigraphically rich period which sees the peak of development of the military *vici*. The formerly unsuspected scale of these civilian settlements has been graphically revealed in recent years by the series of pioneering geophysical surveys published by Alan Biggins, David Taylor and others.

- Recent excavations of barracks have suggested that certain sociological changes within units occur during the course of the third century rather than in a reform by Diocletian around 300. These are marked by a diversity of building techniques in barracks. The barrack plans imply that reorganisation may have involved the reduction of century sizes in cohorts in northern Britain before the middle of the third century. There is no independent historical evidence for this, but that is no reason to ignore the suggestion of the archaeological evidence. The import of units recently raised in Germany could possibly have been intended to counter-balance the reduction in the 'regular' forces.

- A near-absence of historical sources for third-century Britain after the campaigns of Septimius Severus (208-11) has led to a perception of this period as a time of peace and stasis on the northern frontier. There is much epigraphic evidence for rebuilding and provision of facilities for the auxiliary units now permanently associated with their bases. There are, however, suggestions in the archaeological evidence that the third century was not the long period of peaceful and homogeneous character presented in many accounts.

3. The Wall crossing Walltown Crags

One sign of this is the growing evidence that the military *vici*, so characteristic of this period, were often enclosed by defences.

- The military *vici* both on the Wall and in its hinterland were abandoned or went into drastic decline somewhere in the period 270-330. This must betoken a major change in the sociological make-up and methods of supply of the Wall communities, but the apparent disappearance of these vibrant settlements has been little discussed or followed up. The third quarter of the third century is the time the long-standing traffic through the Rhineland and northern Gaul of products destined for the Wall-zone, such as samian ware and olive oil amphorae, expires. A link between these phenomena and historically-attested unrest on the German frontier demands consideration.

- Inscriptions speak against the argument that the decisive break with the military traditions of the principate, including epigraphy, was caused by the separation from the Mediterranean world under the separatist Gallic empire (260-73), which included Britain. A few inscriptions indicate that epigraphic practices continued after Aurelian's recapture of the Gallic empire, at least until the 280s. At Birdoswald an altar of *Cohors I Aelia Dacorum* dating to 276-82 is the latest certain epigraphic attestation of the long-standing Wall units, and after c. 300 with the exception of tombstones and milestones, epigraphy has ceased.

- Control of the area north of the Wall through the outpost forts had, it is now widely accepted, been relinquished by the early-fourth century, with High Rochester, Risingham, Bewcastle and Netherby abandoned. Henceforth Roman influence north of the Wall was achieved by other means.

- For much of the fourth century the Wall forts were manned by effective military units, not largely civilian communties or farmer-soldiers. There is no good reason to disbelieve the evidence of the *Notitia Dignitatum*, which has the same units in the Wall-forts in the fourth century as in the third. At least some commanding officers maintained their social status and Mediterranean origins, to judge by the excavated *praetoria* at South Shields and Vindolanda. Barracks, where they have been excavated, were still organised on the basis of the traditional *contubernium*. Where the civilians associated with the forts were living is a major problem.

- The urban centres at Corbridge and Carlisle flourished in the fourth century in contrast to the military *vici*: the vitality of these two towns, mirroring that of the 'small towns' of the lowland province, is a striking characteristic of this period.

- Despite the fact that we no longer call it 'Theodosian' rebuilding, there is a horizon of change somewhere after the middle of the fourth century, probably after 370. The plans of barracks and *praetoria* cease to conform to the archetypes of the principate. Surfaces of crude paving, often incorporating sculptures and inscriptions, are ubiquitous. There are obvious and well-documented changes of use in principal buildings such as the granaries at Birdoswald. Stone defences are not replaced and properly maintained but encased in earthen ramparts or bolstered with other running repairs. Pottery is now predominantly of northern British origin, though not from the immediate locality

- Even with the end of coin-using communities and a break from the Roman world, there is much emerging evidence for the existence of communities in the Wall forts in the fifth century.

4. The offering to Fortuna undertaken at Birdoswald in 1929. The slab under the altar and that adjacent to it would prove to be the influential RIB 1909 and 1912.

This of course can only be a selection. The developments indicated here give some very broad indications of how certain different periods on the Wall might be characterised. They do not even begin to touch on the question of the history of the minor installations of the Wall, and the curtain and Vallum, and how that might divide into periods: much more evidence on these neglected areas is required to do that. The great outstanding question for general historians of the Wall is whether the changes from period to period indicated here were rapidly precipitated, or took place through some seamless transition. The suddenness with which, for example, the art of epigraphy and the military *vici* faded out may suggest an acute and traumatic discontinuity, but much more research is required into the critical periods of transition in Wall society - including the break or transition that occurs at the beginning of the fifth century.

There are indications that there were actual policy decisions that affected the Wall. For example, building work is indicated by a peak of inscriptions under Septimius Severus (the traditional beginning of Wall-period II), who probably initiated much rebuilding of the Wall itself. Similarly there is little doubt that there was restoration work on and great interest in the Wall under the Tetrarchy, around 300, after Britain had been recaptured from Allectus (old Wall-period III). Inscriptions from Housesteads and Birdoswald suggest this, and South Shields was completely rebuilt to a new plan at this time. There may well have been actual building programmes that did coincide in some way with the great reconstructions proposed in the Wall-periods scheme, and surely there were others that did not.

5. The Wall on Winshields Crags

The period of over thirty years since Breeze and Dobson wrote *Hadrian's Wall* has therefore seen a vast amount of new information, much of it being studied by scholars in highly specialised compartments, and a reluctance to synthesise the material to create a new narrative, one significantly different from that which emerged from the ashes of the Wall-period theory when the torch was put to it around 1976. It should be clear from the current Research Framework that there are materials at hand to allow a return to the problem, and to construct a narrative of Wall life that promises to add unexpected and exciting dimensions to a subject that has developed a reputation for being stale and overworked. In order to do this, archaeologists of the Wall will have to move, Copernicus-style, beyond the position where the northern frontier, with its comfortable set of internal problems, is seen as the centre of their studies. While the work of refining chronology on the ground has really only just begun, it is also true that a convincing account of the Wall will only be written with reference to the archaeology of the frontiers and the provinces outside Britain.

2. The Pre-Roman Archaeology of the Tyne-Solway Isthmus

by M F A Symonds

Introduction

Within the Tyne - Solway corridor, the distinction between pre-Roman and pre-Hadrianic activity is not always clearly defined. The fields that were being tilled immediately prior to the construction of the Wall and Vallum at Wallsend and Denton are closely comparable to those being worked over two centuries earlier at South Shields. The roundhouse was also a common feature of the landscape for millennia and while these buildings were used in a variety of contexts, the chronology of many of them has yet to be established. A 'Romano-British' type of indigenous settlement is recognised, although there has been little confirmation of this dating through excavation in the Wall zone and the extent to which such settlements had Iron Age predecessors remains an open question.

It is fair to say that the focus of research in the region has been the Roman-period remains, but there have still been substantial advances in the last 25 years, building on Jobey's seminal survey and excavation work in the 1960s and 70s. Gates' sorties over Northumberland Park have revealed a number of previously undetected upstanding 'indigenous-style' settlements (see p107-10), while the identification of 'cord rig' and increased environmental sampling have revolutionised our understanding of the Iron Age landscape. For the purposes of this framework, the pre-Roman theme is primarily concerned with the immediate context for the Wall and so concentrates on Iron Age, and in particular Late Pre-Roman Iron Age, activity as well as the pre-Roman/Roman transition. This is not to detract from the importance of the preceding periods and a full treatment of the early development of the region is available in the NWRRF and NERRF (Brennand 2006; Petts 2006).

Settlement

Hillforts are often described as dominating Iron Age archaeology (Frodsham 2004, 36). A model for the development of these monuments, known as the "Hownam Sequence" and based on the excavation of a site in the Cheviots in the 1940s, charts the evolution of hillforts from their origins as timber palisades, in around 800 BC, to the construction of simple stone defences by c. 300 BC (Piggott 1948). More complex defences were then developed, before there was a transition, in at least some instances, to unenclosed settlement. This progression, though still acknowledged, has been superseded by more recent research. The final phase of this sequence was originally interpreted as a consequence of the arrival of the Roman army, but at Broxmouth in East Lothian the defences seem to have been abandoned during the second century BC (Hill 1982). The general applicability of the 'Hownam Sequence' to a site is difficult to test without excavation, although it is certain that its dogma is not appropriate in every instance and the framework has often proved overly simplistic (Welfare 2002, 72). In order to achieve a fuller understanding of hillforts in Northumberland, the National Park has undertaken the *Discovering our Hillfort Heritage* project (Oswald, Ainsworth and Pearson 2006).

6. The hillfort on Warden Hill

The function and development of hillforts is of less significance to the present study as the Wall corridor is largely devoid of these monuments. The medium-sized, mulitvallate hillforts at Warden Hill, overlooking the confluence of the North and South Tyne, and at Cargo, on the Eden, are notable exceptions. It has been suggested that a further example existed on the promontory currently occupied by Carlisle Castle (McCarthy 2002, 46). However, it is certain that there is nothing to match the density of sites in the Cheviots and Coquetdale. This can hardly be attributed to the absence of suitable terrain and so a cultural explanation has been sought. The most commonly accepted reading of the historical sources places the boundary between the territory of the Brigantes and the Votadini on the Tyne and Solway (Frodsham 2004, 43). As such, divergent approaches to developing settlement foci could be linked to the different preferences and possibly also hierarchy of these tribes. Van der Veen's interpretation of archaeobotanical data from the region supports this, as she attributes different crop husbandry regimes north and south of the Tyne to cultural rather than environmental parameters. To the north there was a preponderance of emmer wheat and small-scale, intensive, subsistence cultivation. In the Tees lowlands spelt was dominant, while larger scale cultivation was practised, with a comparatively high use of perennials (van der Veen 1992, 158).

As well as indications of a north-south divide, Cunliffe has observed of Iron Age Britain in general that 'if there is a divide to be made an east-west division is far more significant' (Cunliffe 1983, 85) and this is also apparent across the Wall corridor. In the central sector the Black Dyke provides a physical indication of division. This enigmatic linear earthwork runs between the North and South Tyne, crossing the line of the Wall near milecastle 36. There is a ditch on the west side and, while the dyke is believed to be pre-Roman, its date remains uncertain (Spain 1922; see also **Life and Environment** chapter. Cumbria also differs from the North East by being aceramic between the Early Bronze Age and the Roman conquest and it has been emphasised that our knowledge of later prehistoric activity in the region is limited (Hingley 2002, 46). Whether there were Iron Age settlement foci in Cumbria, and if so where they were sited, remains uncertain, although Carlisle has been proposed as a possible candidate (McCarthy 2002, 50). The alternative, that there was a 'relatively shallow settlement hierarchy' in the west, 'perhaps reflecting an egalitarian society' (Hodgson and Brennand 2006, 51) has also been mooted.

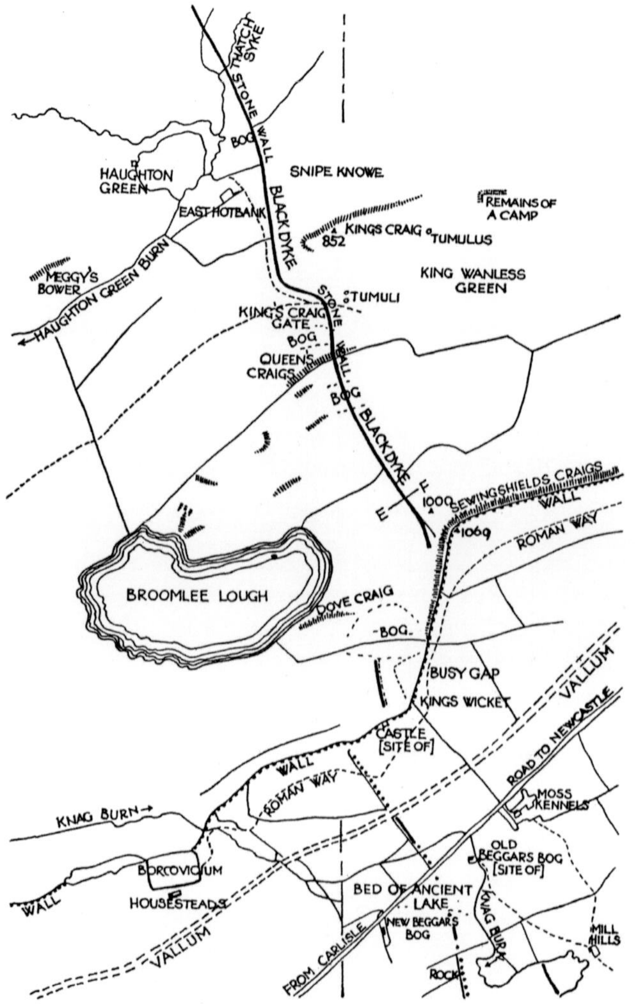

7. The course of the Black Dyke as it cuts the line of the Wall

More modest farmsteads are well attested in the Wall zone, although their chronologies remain almost entirely unknown (Gates 2004, 237). This inability to date the vast majority of the extant sites prevents any attempt to determine settlement density over time (Gates 2004, 240). Settlement in the region can be subdivided into two basic types: enclosed and unenclosed. 'Romano-British-type' farmsteads are prominent amongst the former, although as these have only rarely been independently dated their restriction to this period should not be considered certain. Such settlements are set within stone or turf enclosures, often rectilinear, occupying c. 1,500m^2. The entrance, normally east facing, would open onto a track that led past a range of open yards before reaching a cluster of roundhouses. These farmsteads are particularly prevalent in the central section, although Milking Gap, dug in the 1930s, remains the only Romano-British settlement in the immediate vicinity of the frontier to have been excavated in this sector (Kilbride-Jones 1938). As such, it is impossible to answer definitively the fundamental question of whether or not the Romano-British-type farmsteads in the Wall corridor had Iron Age predecessors. Without this basic information the extent to which the Roman conquest impacted on the indigenous settlement pattern in the Tyne-Solway corridor cannot be quantified and models of the socio-economic effects of occupation cannot be tested. While there were no indications of continuity with pre-Roman structures at Milking Gap, where pottery suggested a late-first- to early-second-century AD occupation, Jobey's work in nearby North Tynedale revealed that the visible stone settlements could have as many as three timber precursors, yielding radiocarbon dates of the first or second century BC (Gates 2004, 241-2). Some of the North Tynedale timber farmsteads were also found to have been rebuilt in stone as late as the mid-second century AD and it remains entirely plausible that a number of the upstanding stone farmsteads in the Wall corridor obscure timber pre-Roman and early Roman predecessors (Gates 2004, 242). Equally, stone-built roundhouses in the Cheviots have been radiocarbon dated to the second millennium BC and so the use of stone in domestic structures can in no way be considered diagnostically 'Roman' (Burgess 1984, 145). It is certain that a broader understanding of Romano-British-type farmsteads would be invaluable for our perceptions of both pre-Roman settlement and the impact of occupation on indigenous communities.

Enclosed settlements are also known in Cumbria, with circular, polygonal, rectangular, square and "D" shapes all attested. Although these are generally believed to be Roman in date, 'unequivocal Iron Age occupation is difficult to identify owing to the scarcity of identifiable material culture' (Hodgson and Brennand 2006, 52). Late Bronze Age or Iron Age dates are possible for two ovoid enclosures at Scotby Road, Carlisle and Burgh-by-Sands, although neither of these produced buildings (McCarthy 2002, 46). It has been proposed that such enclosures were a solution to the need to provide secure overnight stalling for cattle, although in some cases the ditches are considered too slight to hold livestock (McCarthy 2002, 47).

Unenclosed settlements consist of individual or clustered roundhouses. Such homesteads should not be dismissed as rudimentary; the roundhouses could be substantial, with diameters of up to 15m recorded. The standard design consisted of a thatched roof carried on a conical timber frame with an outer, wattle and daub, wall. Some may have had an upper floor, with livestock stabled beneath creating 'a primitive form of under-floor heating' (Frodsham 2004, 44-5). A lack of excavation once again hinders a broader understanding of unenclosed settlement, although Gates has proven that they were widespread in Northumberland (Gates 1983, 103). Identification is complicated by the number of other structures that can resemble roundhouses, including robbed cairns, sow kilns and bughts, while eighteenth-century highland huts were also noted by Dr. Johnson for their 'circularity' (Gates 1983, 107). Roundhouses are known to have been constructed from the Bronze Age until well into the Roman period in the Tyne - Solway corridor, and it has been suggested that in places they remained a staple of rural life into the post-Roman era (McCarthy 2002, 48).

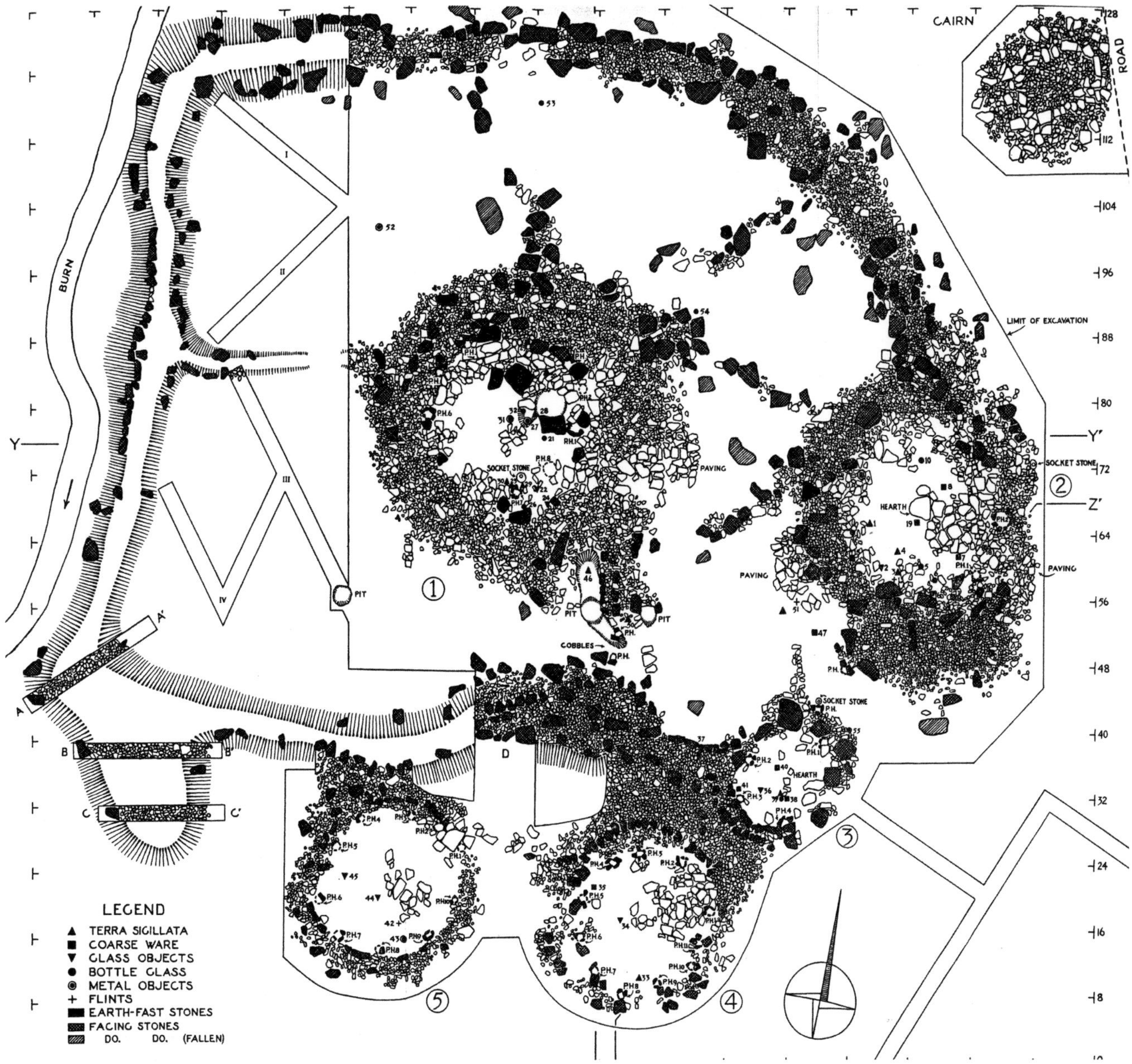

8. Plan of the excavated settlement at Milking Gap

An exceptionally well-preserved Iron Age unenclosed roundhouse was discovered beneath the Roman fort at South Shields. Although this middle Iron Age structure was abandoned at least two centuries before the arrival of the Roman army, it provides an excellent example of an Iron Age building in the Wall zone. The roundhouse, measuring 8.75m in diameter, underlay the south-east corner of the fort and was set 10m from a contemporary narrow-rig cultivation system. The wall-slot contained the impressions of round, upright posts, while a drainage gully lay 1.2m beyond it (Hodgson *et al* 2001, 96-98). Environmental sampling indicated an ordered division of space within the structure. Quantities of clean spelt grain near the entrance and scattered weeds, culm nodes and spikelets were suggestive of separation prior to food preparation. The northern part of the floor, as well as the area around the hearth, appear to have been kept cleaner, while heather and bracken from the rear, back-south quadrant may represent bedding (Hodgson *et al* 2001, 141). As phosphate analysis was not undertaken, it remains uncertain whether animals were also stalled within the roundhouse (Hodgson *et al* 2001, 151). Only two sherds of pottery were found in association with the structure and it has been suggested that there may have been only intermittent use of ceramics in the North East during the middle Iron Age (Willis 1999, 89).

Possible unenclosed settlements are known at The Lanes and the Cumberland Infirmary in Carlisle, and considered just as likely to be pre-Roman as early Roman (McCarthy 2002, 45). In general though, unenclosed homesteads are poorly represented at the western end of the Wall. Yet this may merely reflect our difficulty in recognising them. The extent to which enclosed or unenclosed housing was predominant in the Iron Age remains disputed. There is a growing feeling that the apparent prevalence of enclosed settlement in the first century BC is a consequence of its relative susceptibility to aerial photography. Certainly the few unenclosed settlements known in the North West are a consequence of accidental discovery (Hodgson and Brennand 2006, 52), while Hodgson (*et al* 2001, 155) has argued that 'open settlement occurred widely in the middle to later iron-age settlement pattern' in the Tyne-Tees lowlands. It has also been suggested that a shift from enclosed to unenclosed settlement was associated with the increased clearance and arable cultivation occurring in the first century BC (Haselgrove 1984). Excavation can reveal a more complex picture. In the North East, the enclosure ditch was filled during occupation at Thorpe Thewles, while West Brandon and Rock Castle were initially open settlements that were only later enclosed (Heslop 1987; Jobey 1962; Fitts *et al* 1994). Equally radiocarbon dates from this region provide no indication of a chronological distinction between enclosed and unenclosed settlement (Haselgrove 2002, 60).

Agriculture

Dixon discussed the apparently 'primitive system of cultivation' at Gallow Law in 1903 (Dixon 1903, 111), but it was not until the 1980s that the full significance of this agricultural technique became apparent. While the discovery of 'cord rig' has revolutionised our understanding of prehistoric agriculture in the region, much remains unknown about the chronology and specifics of its use. Cord rig is a form of ridge and furrow cultivation that varies from the medieval technique through the narrowness of its ridges, which range from 0.7 - 2m wide in the Wall area. The furrows served to drain the ground so that the crop can be grown at a higher temperature on the ridge, thus increasing the yield (Hodgson 2003, 30). Cord rig has been detected in proximity to enclosed and unenclosed settlements and was utilised in both small plots and more extensive field systems. Although this cultivation technique seems to have been practised for several centuries (Topping 1989a, 145; 149), its discovery sealed under a number of Roman structures makes a prehistoric usage certain, and a middle Iron Age context of no later than the second century BC has been proven at South Shields (Hodgson *et al* 2001, 153). Plough scores have been found to be stratigraphically earlier than Roman activity at sixteen locations on or near the Wall, leading Hodgson to state that 'their occurrence may be considered typical' (Hodgson 2003, 29).

9. The Middle Iron Age roundhouse under South Shields fort

The formation and usage of cord rig requires further clarification. The evidence for contemporary spelt and barley processing from South Shields in the middle Iron Age could imply that the technique was used predominately for cereals, but vegetable cultivation is also a possibility (Hodgson *et al* 2001, 154). It has been argued that the largest concentrations of cord rig can only have been created with the help of an ard (Topping 1989b, 166-7), although there is some evidence for hand-dug workmanship elsewhere. Much of the detailed evidence for field systems comes from features preserved under frontier elements and must therefore be thought of as pre-murus rather than pre-Roman. At Denton, where the remains were sealed by the Vallum mound, the excavators concluded that a plough was used initially to cut the furrows and the work was finished off with a spade (Bidwell and Watson 1996, 15). At South Shields the first two phases of cord rig were not associated with any underlying plough scores, while the later ard marks did not coincide with the overlying third phase of furrows (Hodgson *et al* 2001, 153). Excavations at Wallsend also found no certain connection between the ridge and furrow and plough lines (Hodgson 2003, 30) and it has been suggested in general that there is no need for an association between cord rig and ard marks (Fowler 1983, 154). This raises the question of the purpose of the plough marks. McCarthy has commented on the use of 'sod-busters' initially to break up ground in preparation for cultivation (McCarthy 2002, 45), but at Wallsend the quantity of plough marks running parallel and close together is seen as more indicative of 'year-in year-out re-ploughing of furrows'. This is interpreted as a consequence of switching between ploughs and hand tools (Hodgson 2003, 29-31).

Further details of farming practise emerged from Wallsend and Denton, where fields were being prepared for fresh cultivation when they were requisitioned for construction of the fort and Vallum. Deposits of black ash at these sites have been interpreted as a product of stubble burning, with the possibility that this formed a routine element of the agricultural cycle. The evidence suggests that the entire area of Wallsend fort was under cultivation and that it was subdivided into a series of fields or plots (Hodgson 2003, 32). While no continuity with the pre-Roman period could be proven at Wallsend, 'however likely that may seem', the 'pre-fort agriculture ... was entirely of the pre-Roman Iron Age tradition of the region' (Hodgson 2003, 34).

The demonstration that there was widespread arable cultivation has shifted our perception of Iron Age agriculture away from the extensive cattle ranching typified by Piggot's (1958, 25) view of 'footloose and unpredictable Celtic cow-boys' (Frodsham 2004, 45-6). However, the extent to which cattle were important remains ambiguous, largely due to the poor suitability of the local soil to preserve faunal assemblages. Evidence for cattle and a horse were forthcoming from the sparse bone assemblage associated with the South Shields roundhouse (Hodgson *et al* 2001, 146-7). Despite this, the consensus is that 'the Iron Age population practised a mixed agricultural regime' while 'the relative importance of stock rearing and cultivation probably varied from place to place and over time' (Frodsham 2004, 47). Where the cord rig survives best, in the central sector, its extent suggests crop growing on a limited scale (Gates 2004, 244 and see p. 109). This is consistent with local agriculture being predominantly 'small-scale, intensive, subsistence cultivation' (van der Veen 1992). Wild resources were also tapped, with hazelnuts, sloe, rosehip and blackberry all present at South Shields (Hodgson *et al* 2001, 111-2).

Environmental sampling has also begun to shed light on Iron Age exploitation of the region, although some details, in particular the Roman contribution to deforestation, remain contentious. This is discussed further in the **Landscape and**

Environment chapter. In general though, while some episodes of tree clearance can be attributed to the Roman period, others clearly indicate Iron Age deforestation (Huntley 1999, 52). At Fellend Moss, south of Walltown Crags, deforestation dates back to at least the first century BC, with traces of cereal pollen indicating that cultivation was also taking place. Such a motive is not implicit, as clearance would also be desirable for stock rearing (Gates 2004, 243). Taken together, the evidence provides 'clear indications that a settled farming landscape already existed when Hadrian's Wall was built' (Gates 2004, 244). Interestingly even at Birdoswald, where clearance appears to be associated with the construction of the Wall, a human influence in the form of coppicing has been tentatively advanced (Wiltshire 1997, 37).

10. The site of Coventina's Well

Sites where agricultural traces have been found under Roman contexts (Based on Topping 1989a, 156)

Haltwhistle Burn
Greenlee Lough
Carrawburgh
Carlisle, Annetwell Street
Carlisle, Blackfriars Street
Stanwix, Tarraby Lane
Halton Chesters
Stanley Plantation
Rudchester
Stott's House Tumulus
Denton
Wallhouses
Throckley
Newcastle
Wallsend
South Shields

Religion and Burial

Evidence for Iron Age funerary traditions within the region remains, in general, elusive. One probable exception comes from the inhumation burial cut by the construction trench for the Rise How tower on the Cumberland Coast (Tower 25a or 26a.), although radiocarbon dates of the seventh-eighth century AD preclude a definite Iron Age origin (Bellhouse 1991, 266). Elsewhere, the majority of bodies appear to have been disposed of in a manner which had little impact on the archaeological record, such as excarnation or unurned cremation (Petts 2006, 39). A group of crouched inhumations from Cumbria only proved to be Iron Age following absolute dating, highlighting the danger that in the absence of such evidence the notion that Iron Age burials are not archaeologically visible can become self-fulfilling (Brennand 2006, 55).

Direct evidence for Iron Age religion is equally obscure. Probable votive offerings are known from the Tyne, while deposits have been found in bogs and watery places in the North West. The most macabre of these is a body discovered in Scaleby Moss, c. 4km north of the Wall, which has been posited a late prehistoric context (Hodgson and Brennand 2006, 56). Although the remains have been lost, the body is recorded as being accompanied with sticks and covered by a deer skin. It is seen as an example of the "ritual" deaths found in peat bogs throughout Northern

11. The 'Celtic head' found near the estimated site of Milecastle 8

Europe (Turner 1988). Some Iron Age religious activity has also been inferred from Roman practice. Frodsham sees parallels from Coventina's Well with the 'Iron Age obsession with wet places' (Frodsham 2004, 48), yet the goddess herself is attested on altars from France and Spain, and may have been imported by an auxiliary unit (Allason-Jones and McKay 1985). Carved stone 'Celtic heads' have been found at a number of Roman sites, including the extramural settlement at Vindolanda, milecastle 35 and near the probable site of milecastle 8, although these too may be Roman imports. A number of the deities with overtly Celtic names found in Roman shrines and on inscriptions, such as Cocidius and Antenociticus, could be local gods, unless they were also imported by the auxiliary units. Cocidius in particular, whose *principal* shrine was presumably at Bewcastle *(Fanum Cocidi)*, had adherents working or stationed over a wide area with altars found as far apart as Risingham, milecastle 37 and milecastle 65 (Breeze 2002, 60). Ultimately though, how reliable a guide this activity is to pre-Roman religious practise remains uncertain and the Iron Age religious landscape is largely unknown.

3. The Pre-Hadrianic Frontier on the Tyne-Solway Isthmus, and The Stanegate

Co-ordinated by N H Hodgson

Overview

N H Hodgson

When Hadrian ordered the building of his Wall in AD 122, the Roman army had already been active on the Tyne-Solway isthmus for half a century. The archaeology of this period in the Wall zone thus represents no mere prelude to the Wall, but a substantial chapter in the history of the province of Britain. The key sites for the understanding of this period in our area include those where there has been most intensive archaeological investigation - Corbridge, Vindolanda and Carlisle. These lie not under the forts later built on the line of Hadrian's Wall, but immediately to its south, in the natural corridor of communication between the Tyne and Eden valleys. Corbridge, Carlisle and other sites on the isthmus in occupation in the Flavian and Trajanic periods were obviously for most of this time part of a network of military control and communication that extended far into Scotland. They were themselves strong-points in an area recently subjugated, but by no means on a northern frontier line, and at times functioned as rearward bases for operations conducted up to the Scottish Highlands. Extraordinary light has been cast on the everyday life of one of these bases in this period by the discovery and publication of the Vindolanda writing tablets (see p. 140-1; 153-4).

'The Stanegate' is the modern name for a Roman road that has been traced in places to the south of Hadrian's Wall, running at varying distances from the service road ('the Military Way') that closely accompanies the Wall itself. Physically, the Stanegate road has only been traced between Corbridge and Carlisle, and even there only in places. The Stanegate has lent its name to the modern concept of a preclusive frontier (a line of forts and smaller sites along the road) predating the Wall. Opinion has waxed and waned regarding the date and interpretation of the final, most closely spaced arrangement of forts and smaller posts - fortlets and occasional towers - between Corbridge and Carlisle. This has been seen variously as a Trajanic frontier cordon following withdrawal from all of Scotland around AD 105, as corresponding to the earliest (pre-fort decision) phase of Hadrian's Wall, and, in a period of more recent scepticism, as a disposition of sites along a road without particular significance. The various stages of the debate are traced in the following assessment. The date of construction of the Stanegate road itself remains quite uncertain. It is no longer assumed, as was once the case, that the road was built under Agricola, but by how long, if at all, the known engineered road precedes the building of Hadrian's Wall, is still an unresolved question.

Modern archaeological thought uses the term 'Stanegate' in a very wide sense, to include all sites along the route from Corbridge to Carlisle and even to consider putative arrangements of sites, and possible roads continuing west of Carlisle to the Solway Firth and east of Corbridge to the North Sea. Accordingly this section assesses what is known about the 'western Stanegate' (as it has sometimes been termed) and the equivalent problem east of Corbridge. This entails making reference to the evidence for pre-Hadrianic occupation of a site such as South Shields, even though there

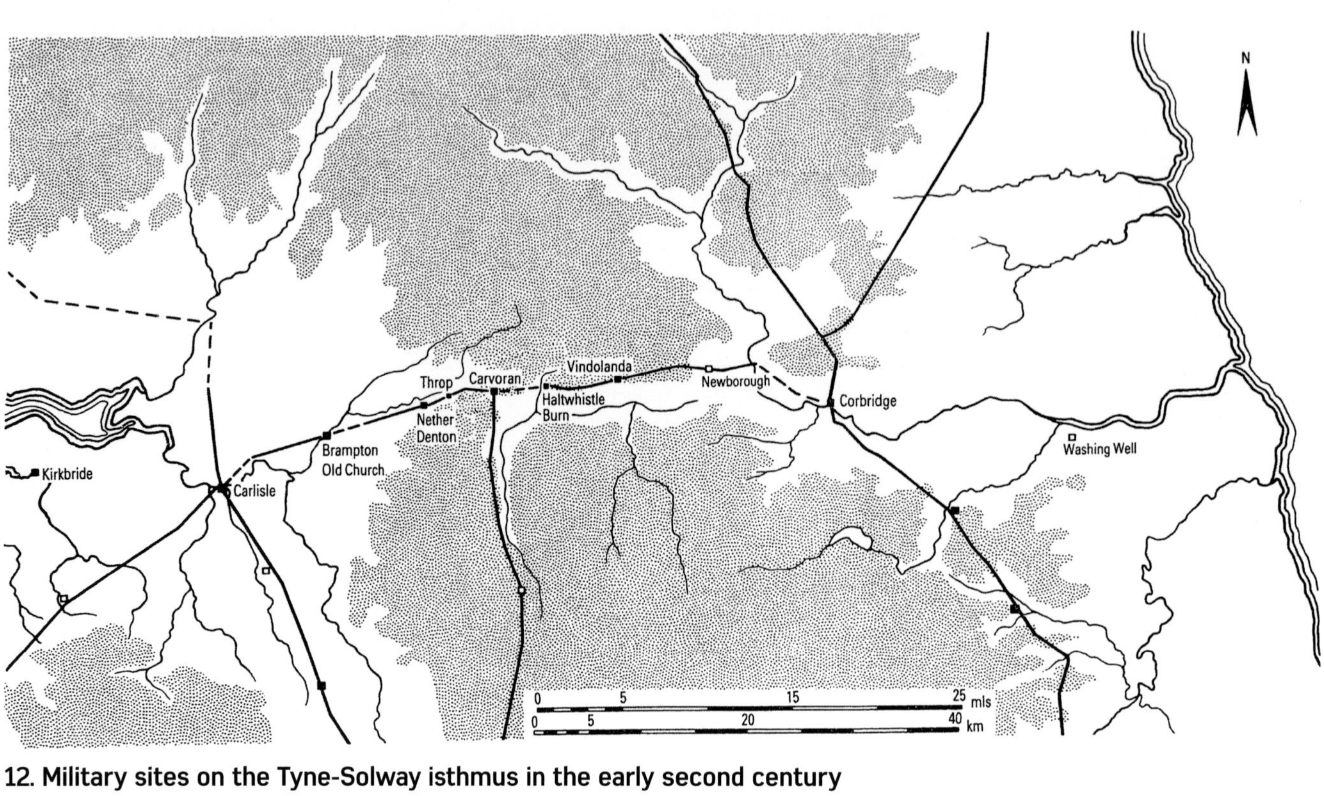

12. Military sites on the Tyne-Solway isthmus in the early second century

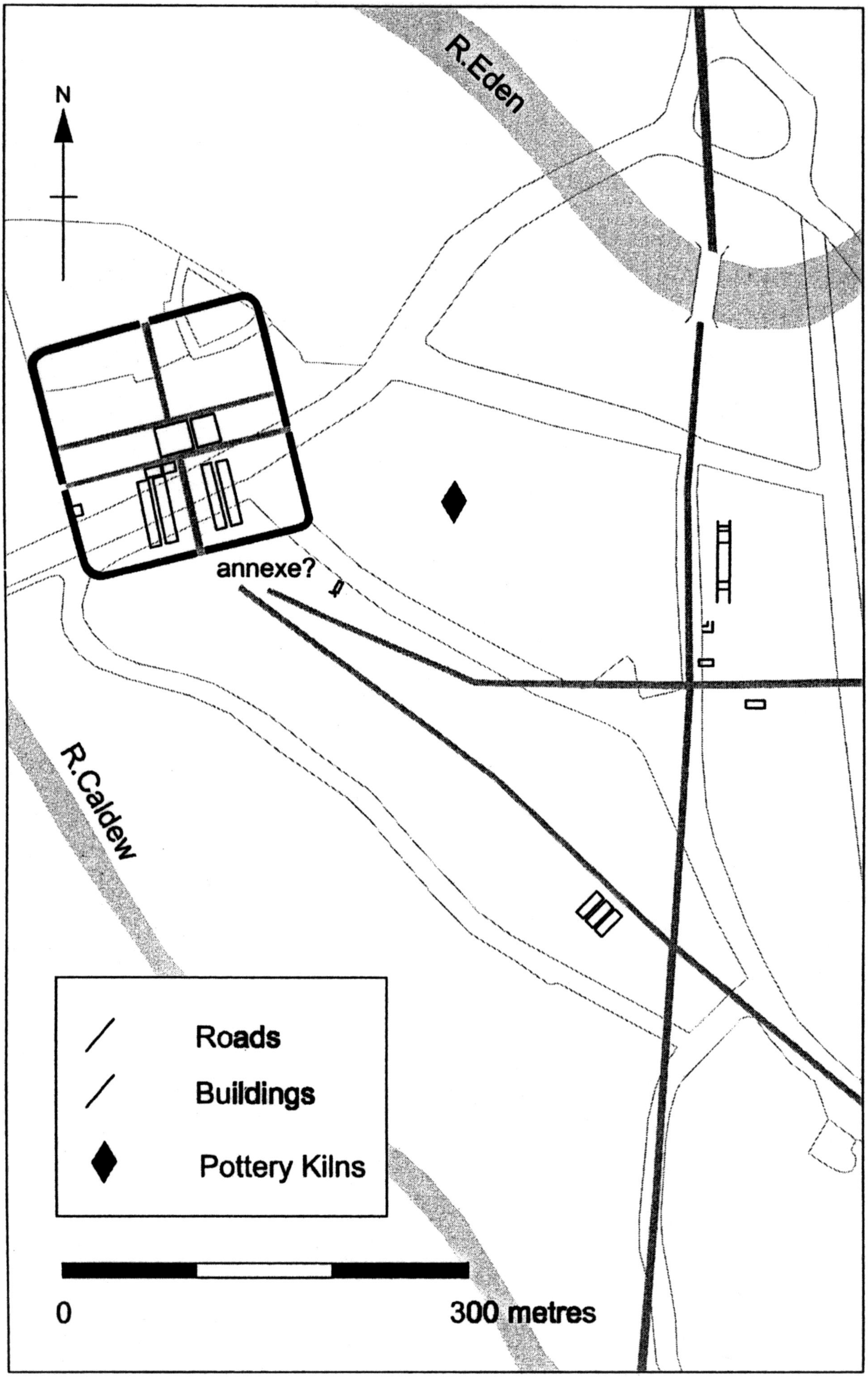

13. Carlisle in the late first century

is no evidence that the Stanegate road in the literal sense reached the North Sea or even extended east of Corbridge. Similarly, some assessment must be made of the claims by the late Prof. G.D.B. Jones to have discovered running barriers and other frontier works of pre-Hadrianic date south of the Solway between Carlisle and Bowness. Several claimed Roman military installations, including a site at Fingland Rigg, once interpreted in some detail as a fort, eventually turned out to be of native origin (and therefore of considerable interest in their own right). It will be apparent in the account that follows that several reported linear features running between Burgh-by-Sands and Kirkbride (ditches, fences), that have been thought to be Roman may actually have the character of Iron Age land divisions. Final judgement must be reserved until more extensive excavations are carried out and published. Jones' recognition of a predecessor ('Burgh I') to the Wall fort of Burgh-by-Sands, lying 1km south of the line of the Wall, remains a discovery of outstanding importance, although it is still uncertain whether Burgh I is a Trajanic predecessor to the Wall or in fact the earliest Hadrianic fort provision here.

Much of the archaeology of the Stanegate sites is pre-Hadrianic, yet the road itself and several of the sites either on the road or associated with 'the Stanegate' in the wider sense, continued to have an important function throughout the whole history of the Wall. Of the full-sized pre-Hadrianic forts along the line of the road only Nether Denton and Kirkbride did not continue in use as a permanent part of the military infrastructure of the Wall. Corbridge, Vindolanda, Carvoran and Carlisle all went on to have long histories as military sites associated with the Wall. The old notion of the Stanegate forts being emptied upon the 'fort decision' in order to provide garrisons for the Wall forts must be abandoned: the Wall represented an enhancement rather than a replacement of the pre-existing fort distribution.

Finally we may note that Carlisle and Corbridge went on to become the two greatest civil urban centres in the Wall zone, flourishing as such particularly in the third and fourth centuries, although both retained a military presence. In the case of Corbridge at least, milestones of the later Roman period along the Stanegate measured their distances from this town. In the west, Carlisle was almost certainly the capital of the *civitas Carvetiorum*, a civil polity that had been constituted by the early third century. These two urban centres offer the greatest potential for understanding the society and economy of the Wall zone in the fourth century and the relations between the communities of the Wall and the indigenous population in the northern frontier zone of a developed province of the Roman Empire. They would also appear to have flourished right down to the early-fifth century and beyond.

The Date of the Roman Conquest in this Region and the Withdrawal from Scotland

N Hodgson

The first fort at Carlisle is now known from dendrochronological evidence to have been founded in AD 72/3. This is the earliest known military establishment on the Isthmus. The discovery has confirmed longstanding doubts (Hanson 1987) about the traditional view that the governor Gnaeus Julius Agricola (77/8-83/4) was responsible for the conquest and garrisoning of the whole of northern England. Agricola's two predecessors, Petillius Cerialis (*c.* 71-3) and Julius Frontinus (*c.* 73-77/8) were obviously more active in this region than previously thought. It is possible that occupation on the eastern part of the Isthmus came some interval after the penetration to and establishment of Carlisle by Cerialis. At Corbridge the bath house associated with an early military base at Red House was seemingly in use from the late 70s or early 80s to judge from pottery published from its construction levels, but that does not necessarily date the establishment of the base. If we accept Tacitus' statement that Agricola penetrated as far as the river Tay in 79/80 (according to the generally agreed reading of the text), contacting in that area the first previously unknown peoples to be encountered in his governorship, then we are left with a period between 73 and 79 for the subjugation and garrisoning of that part of north-east England not taken in with the thrust to Carlisle, as well as the southern uplands of Scotland. A series of marching camps along the Devil's Causeway recently discovered from the air (Gates and Hewitt 2007) may date to this period, as must some of the examples along Dere Street.

14. The Red House baths, Corbridge

In this period there was no thought of a frontier on the Isthmus, which was just one more region to be subjugated, garrisoned and passed through on the way to Scotland. The abandonment of the Flavian conquest of Scotland lies outside the scope of this assessment, but the study of samian pottery by Brian Hartley (1972) has provided the datum by which we can trace the gradual fall back of the Roman army, first to the Tweed and south-west Scotland (after c. 86), and after c.105 to the Tyne-Solway Isthmus. The advance into Scotland and the progressive retreat from what had been conquered are marked in the closely excavated and documented episodes of rebuilding at Corbridge, Vindolanda and Carlisle. These culminate in a simultaneous rebuilding of all three sites around AD 105 (Bidwell 1999, 12-13), when the last holdings in Scotland were abandoned and the Tyne-Solway route consolidated as the northernmost set of military dispositions in Britain. Aspects of social, economic and military life in this period have been illuminated in extraordinary detail by the Vindolanda writing tablets (see p. 139-42; 154-5).

Pre-Hadrianic Military Installations and the Question of the 'Stanegate Frontier'

N Hodgson

That the Tyne-Solway isthmus (at least in part) saw a more intensive military occupation in the period after c. AD 105, with sites of more varied size and type than before, is not in dispute. What has been a constant matter of interest and debate is the extent to which these arrangements formed a system of frontier control or defence prefiguring the Wall of Hadrian. The idea of the Stanegate road as a pre-Hadrianic frontier originated with R.H. Forster, and was first attributed specifically to the Trajanic period by Collingwood (Collingwood and Myres 1937). The schedule of sites along it was formalised by Birley (1961a), who proposed a regular Stanegate system of forts at intervals of half-a-day's march, alternating with fortlets.

Forts at Carvoran and Old Church, Brampton are usually seen as additions of Trajanic or Hadrianic date to the earler series of Corbridge, Vindolanda, Nether Denton and Carlisle. Although there is a late-Roman fort at Newbrough, the early site predicted there by the Birley spacing has never been found.

The best established Stanegate fortlets are Throp and Haltwhistle Burn (0.31-0.36ha), although only the latter has yielded a plan, recovered in 1907-8, and this is not well understood in detail. Most significant is the extensive use of stone construction - something not seen in the reconstructions of c. 105 in the forts. Alongside work at Old Church, Brampton this apparently represents an innovation on the isthmus. Castle Hill, Boothby is vindicated as a fortlet by a convincing air photograph by J.K. St Joseph recently published by Jones and Woolliscroft (2001, 58). Other fortlets predicted by the scheme of regular spacing, as at Grindon and Wall, have never been found.

15. Turret 45a

Finally, a number of towers are thought to have pre-dated the Wall - Pike Hill, Mains Rigg, Birdoswald, Turret 45a, and Barcombe, and were fitted by Birley into his schedule, although no regular series of towers is known.

In the 1950s Birley followed Richmond and Gillam in abandoning the Trajanic date and Stanegate frontier interpretation of Haltwhistle Burn, concluding that the latest forts and the fortlets were Hadrianic, intended to function with the Wall in its first conception, before it was decided to place forts on the line itself. In fact the attribution has swung to and fro between Trajanic and early-Hadrianic periods, with the Trajanic view being reasserted by Hartley in 1966, with the additional suggestion that the pre-Hadrianic frontier will have extended from sea to sea, as far as South Shields in the east.

Doubts were voiced about the idea of a Trajanic frontier on the Stanegate shortly after its revival by Hartley (Daniels 1970). In 1986 Dobson subjected the whole notion of a 'Stanegate system' to a further critical review, emphasising the possibly disparate dates of the sites known and emphasising the lack of evidence for 'system'. Dobson concluded: 'There is no firm evidence that a frontier system was created on the Tyne-Solway isthmus between the abandonment of the Lowlands and the building of Hadrian's Wall' (Dobson 1986, 2).

In 2000 Hodgson returned to the question, this time from the perspective of exactly contemporary arrangements of military sites on the frontiers of Germania Superior and Raetia. Two main points were made. Arrangements of large and small forts, and fortlets, occurred along lines where there was no road or route, and where the formation of a screen or cordon controlling access to the province can have been their only *raison d'être*. Secondly, these combinations of sites do not form regularly spaced 'systems' like the milecastles and turrets of Hadrian's Wall. On the German frontiers sites were irregularly sized and spaced to suit local topographic circumstances. Thus, Hodgson argued, the failure of the regular system proposed by Birley to materialise does not give grounds for disposing of a frontier-control function for the installations on the pre-Hadrianic Tyne-Solway line. Meanwhile, in the light of the Continental parallels, fortlets such as Haltwhistle Burn or Throp are as likely to have exercised a frontier control function as to have guarded points where the Stanegate road crossed rivers.

There have in any case recently been doubts about the primacy of the observed Stanegate road within the sequence of development on the Tyne-Solway isthmus. A challenging contribution by Poulter (1998) argues, in essence, that the known course of the Stanegate road seems posterior to the fortlets (most convincingly at Throp, less so at Haltwhistle Burn). These fortlets are, on the available dating evidence, the latest sites to be provided in the sequence of development. The significance of this, if correct, is obvious: the safeguarding of the road can hardly have been the original function of fortlets which existed independently of and pre-dated the highway. In this model the road would be a consolidation of the late-Trajanic or early Hadrianic period. Poulter's suggestion is intriguing, but relies on a very small number of observed relationships between sites and the road.

In addition Hill (2002) has advanced the suggestion that that there is a greater concentration of Stanegate installations between Brampton and Haltwhistle Burn because of a particular threat of infiltration in that area, and has linked this to the occurrence of larger milecastles on Hadrian's Wall within the same sector.

There is, then, much mileage left in the debate about whether the Stanegate was a frontier before Hadrian.

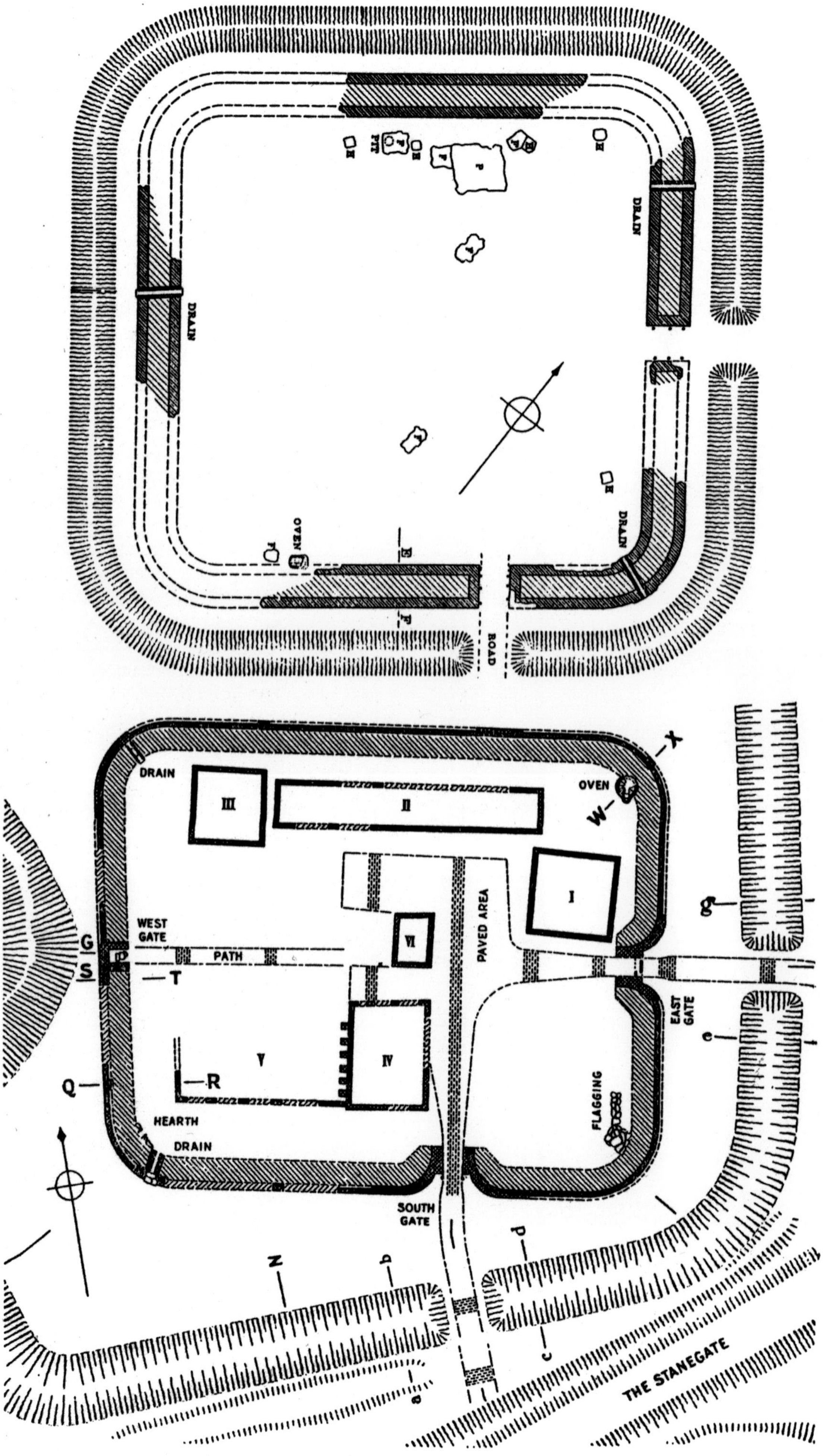

16. Excavation plans of Haltwhistle Burn and Throp fortlets

Hodgson's attempt to rehabilitate the Stanegate as a pre-Hadrianic frontier does rely on the acceptance of the view that sites like Haltwhistle Burn and Throp are Trajanic, and date to the period around 105 or shortly after. But this is not certain: the big outstanding question is whether the fortlets and towers really originated in the Trajanic period or whether they formed part of a first scheme for the Wall. All debate on this issue has been hamstrung by a lack of evidence from excavations carried out using modern techniques. Even with further excavation and the recovery of datable finds from the sites, such a fine distinction in date might be impossible to establish for certain. Grace Simpson (1974, 317-27) and Dobson (1986), pointing to the evident long period of use of Haltwhistle Burn reported by Gibson and Simpson (1909b) and its association with the Stanegate road rather than the Wall, rejected the idea that the Stanegate fortlets are Hadrianic and represent some short-lived early phase in the development of Hadrian's Wall. But of course a long period of use could be found in sites founded in the early-Hadrianic period and used for a time contemporary with the Wall: it is a simplistic assumption that these fortlets would be abandoned immediately the moment that the forts were built on Hadrian's Wall. Conversely, were it ever to be established, as has sometimes been suggested, that the forts were intended on Hadrian's Wall from the beginning, that would be a powerful indicator that the Stanegate fortlets belong to an earlier and distinct phase of frontier development. One final observation might strengthen the case for attribution to the period 105-22, and therefore to a 'Stanegate frontier': the situation of Castle Hill, Boothby south of the Irthing and therefore separated from the Wall and milecastle system.

The Date and Course of the Stanegate Road - Knowledge and Problems

N Hodgson

The course and character of the engineered road between Corbridge and Carlisle can be studied in detail by recourse to the original Ordnance Survey Map of Hadrian's Wall (1964) and Margary's Roman Roads in Britain, with reference, where appropriate, to MacLauchlan's detailed study in his Memoir and subsequent excavation reports on particular points.

The following points of interest, uncertainty or difficulty may be noted:

The date of the road in the sense of the visible engineered structure is now wholly open. There is absolutely no reason to follow the traditional Agricolan date. We have noted Poulter's argument that the road is posterior to Haltwhistle Burn and Throp and therefore likely to be late-Trajanic (110-7) at the earliest. The road is certainly not everywhere earliest in the structural sequence: two marching camps appear to pre-date it - Fell End and Markham Cottage 1 (Welfare and Swan 1995, 100-3; 113-15). On the other hand, a communication route must have connected such evidently pre-Hadrianic forts as Nether Denton, Vindolanda and Corbridge, and no doubt this could have been closely followed by the consolidated road of the Trajanic or Hadrianic period.

17. The stub of a milestone in situ next to the Stanegate, near Vindolanda

The pre-Hadrianic or Stanegate crossing of the North Tyne remains a particular problem (Sockett 1993, 7; Wright 1936; Wright 1939; Wright 1941; Wright 1958, 316). The Stanegate has been traced running westwards out of Corbridge, but is soon lost and its course is unknown until the next sighting, west of the North Tyne, where the road has been found running around the north side of Warden Hill. A crossing of the North Tyne near Warden is implied, but neither the course of the road nor the site of the crossing has ever been convincingly traced. This may be due to the short life of the route here: with the establishment of a road bridge at Chesters by AD 160, the main east-west route probably ran (via the known branch from the Stanegate to Chesters) to join the Military Way and cross the river there.

A road traced east of Carlisle at Linstock (NY 427 588), Buckjumping (NY 493 612) and High Crosby (NY 454 596), and east of Irthington, crossing the Irthing north of the fort of Old Church, Brampton is conventionally assumed to be the 'pre-Hadrianic' Stanegate, but there is a suggestion by Daniels (1978, 243) that this section of road dates to the period after the building of Hadrian's Wall and that the pre-Hadrianic road may have stayed wholly to the south of the Irthing, crossing the River Eden at Warwick Bridge. Bidwell and Holbrook (1989, 150-1) suggested the existence of a Hadrianic service road for the Wall predating the Military Way (not supplied until c.160). Such a road will have run south of the Vallum in those sectors where the Stanegate could not fulfil this function or where it was cut off from the Wall by rivers. The road from Linstock to Irthington could well have served this function.

The Problem of the 'Western Stanegate'

D J Woolliscroft

For many years, the 'Stanegate system' was assumed only to run from Corbridge to Carlisle, but the last decades of the twentieth century saw discoveries between Carlisle and the west coast which have led to suggestions (although not yet proof) that a frontier cordon of pre-Hadrianic date extended to the Irish Sea. Much of this work, including aerial surveys, was done by the late Prof G.D.B. Jones, who sadly died before his results could be fully published. His surviving papers, combined with a few published notes, do make it possible to reconstruct something of what was found, but the former, in particular, seem incomplete, making a detailed picture difficult to

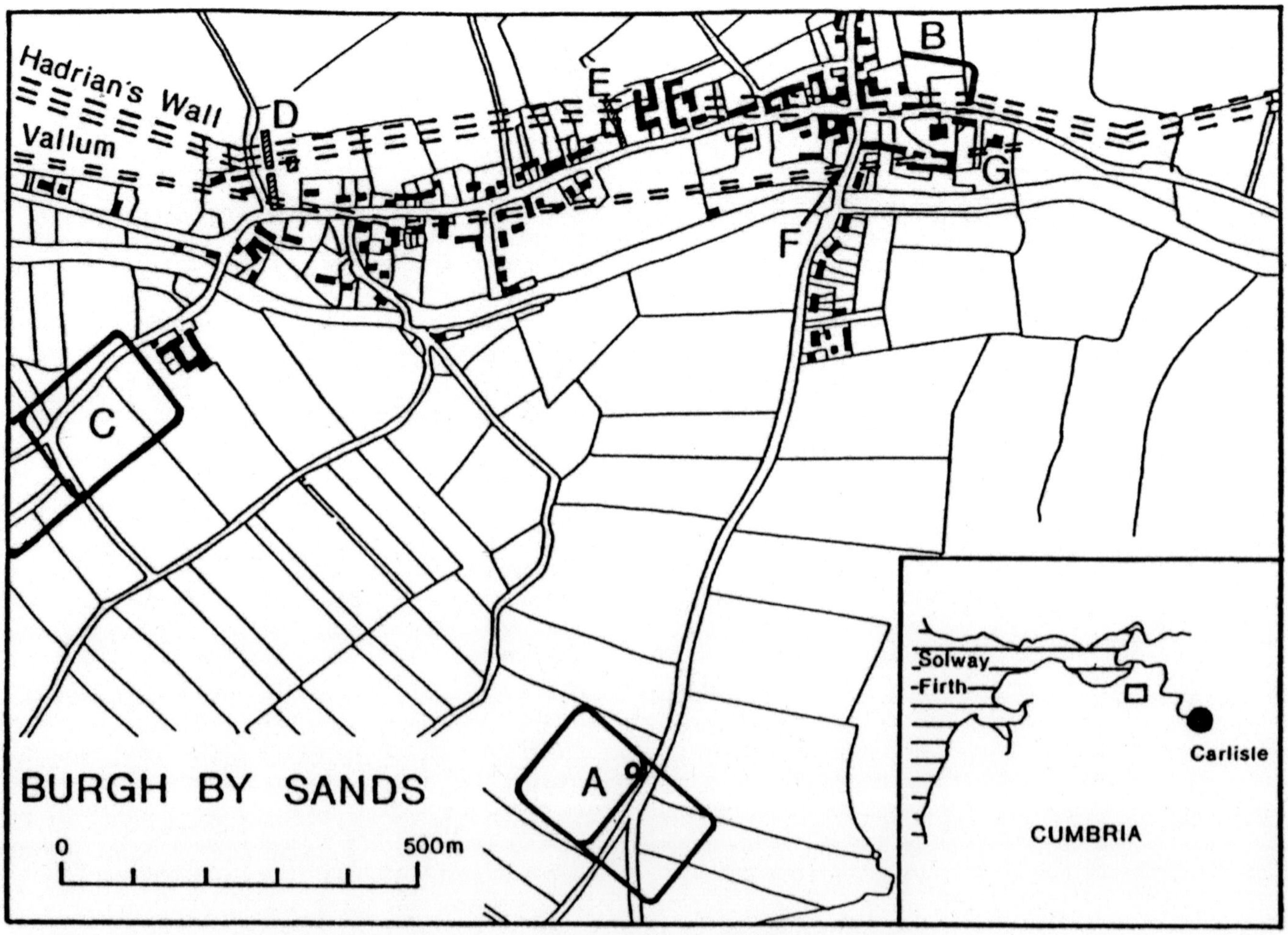

18. The complex of installations at Burgh by Sands. A: Burgh I; B: Burgh II; C: Burgh III.

obtain. This section will, however, attempt to summarise what has come to light and some of the research issues it raises.

Jones revealed what he believed to be a multi-layered system of defences based on two roads, and involving running barriers. The more northerly element involved a road from Carlisle to the fort of Kirkbride (on Moricambe), and Jones himself regarded this as a continuation of the Stanegate road. Only relatively short lengths of the road itself were discovered, of which the most significant were a c. 1.5km sector on Fingland Rigg (NY 261 572 - 276 576) and a shorter stretch leading east from Kirkbride. Woolliscroft (2004) excavated a section through the Fingland Rigg sector in the 1990s and found a gravel road or track. The road itself was badly plough damaged and only survived to 3m wide, but this was probably not its full original width. The aerial data show it running perfectly straight, but no dating evidence was recovered and it cannot yet be proven that it is Roman. The road appears to be associated with a V-shaped ditch, which runs some 18m to its north. This too is currently undated. The ditch is far more visible as a cropmark than the road and several additional sectors are known, notably on Farhill (NY 301 581 - 307 583) and Greenspot (NY 248 570 - 253 571). Jones sectioned the ditch in several places and, although the full records have not come to light, he claims to have found it to be fronted by a timber palisade or fence. No such timber barrier was found during Woolliscroft's work on Fingland Rigg however, where the ditch alone was revealed: 2.06m wide and 1.01m deep (Woolliscroft 2004). These linear features run along areas of higher, drier ground in what is a generally low-lying landscape, much of which would be moss land in its natural state. Jones interpreted this as showing what he called a *'clausura'* system, in other words, a system where discontinuous lengths of artificial barrier were used to seal off possible natural corridors for movement from the Solway into the interior.

A number of sites have been seen from the air and claimed as Roman watchtowers associated with the ditch and road. The Fingland Rigg sector has, since its discovery, proved to be an object lesson in the potential dangers of using air photographic data without subsequent follow up by fieldwork on the ground. Some of the earliest air photographs showed a rectilinear enclosure with rounded corners which was initially interpreted as a possible fort. It later proved to be of native origin, but soon afterwards a roughly circular feature came to light which was actually intersected by the running ditch and seemed likely to be the ditch of a Roman watchtower. The site was excavated on this expectation in 1973, but it too proved to be a native site, probably a small farmstead. Nevertheless, Jones seems to have been confident that genuine watchtowers would have existed in the area, and claimed sites at Farhill (NY 302 582) (intervisible with the Burgh I tower) and at Easton (NY 278 579). The latter has a rather unusual design, with its tower set into its defences, rather than in the centre of their interior, which has caused some questioning of its identity. Jones believed he had found towers at

Monkhill (NY 344 582), where a faint penannular cropmark is now largely destroyed by a modern building and at Kirkandrews-on-Eden (NY 350 585), but neither site can yet be classified with any confidence.

Jones associated a number of forts with this 'system'. Carlisle itself is treated in the key sites gazeteer, but other sites of pre-Hadrianic date are known at Kirkbride and possibly at Burgh-by-Sands. At Burgh a group of sites is known in and around the modern village, on the south side of the lowest Solway fords, the Sandwath (Durnock Wath) and the Peat Wath. These once made it a major crossing point. In the Roman period, a second- to fourth-century fort (Burgh II) lay where the eastern end of the village now stands. But two other sites have been revealed by aerial photography, each of which has been claimed as a fort.

BURGH I, occupies a hilltop on the line of the Burgh to Moorhouse road, 1km south of the village centre. A combination of both aerial photography and excavation here has led to the following sequence being proposed. Before the building of the fort, a watchtower was constructed close to the highest point of the hill, with a 20m diameter ring ditch. This has been taken to be contemporary with Easton and Far Hill and part of an integrated watch and signalling system. Doubts have been expressed about whether the timber tower within this ditch really stands independently of the fort. The present writer (Woolliscroft) sees no reason to support them.

The site of the watchtower was subsequently levelled and overlain by a timber fort with a stone central range (like Old Church, Brampton) of 1.58ha with a probable annexe to the south-east (often interpreted as the abandoned section of an earlier and larger fort). This fort possibly represents a Trajanic precursor of the Wall although the pottery from the site suggests that it was held into the Hadrianic period.

BURGH III - at the 'West End' of Burgh Village and 1km north-west of Burgh I lies a third site which, if a fort, would be difficult to fit into the sequence implied by the other two. A marching camp seems the most likely identification. The site was interpreted by Jones as a 3.4ha fort cut down to 2.1ha. It is said that excavations (not published) produced pottery dated to the first half of the second century and showed that it had been a permanent installation since, along with a 3.4m wide, V-shaped primary ditch, they also revealed timber structures and a road in the interior, and that air photographs have also shown faint traces of a *principia*. Unfortunately this evidence seems unavailable.

At **KIRKBRIDE** fort, excavations have confirmed the existence of a Trajanic fort where the River Wampool enters Moricambe, at the presumed coastal terminus for the emerging 'western Stanegate'. Air photographs show other associated installations and a harbour might be expected here. Bellhouse has also traced a Roman road running from Kirkbride to the Hadrian's Wall fort of Drumburgh.

Jones claimed as Roman frontier works a line of ditches traced in air photography between Old Carlisle fort and Beckfoot on the coast, running for c. 10km from Aldoth (NY 135 483) in the west to Aikhead, near Wigton, (NY 233 492). A section cut accidentally by a sand quarry at Hill House (NY 148 482) shows a ditch of similar size and form to that sectioned on Fingland Rigg. Again, most of the recorded ditch sectors are on high ground which would have been surrounded by mosses before the land was drained in relatively modern times.

Jones claimed a timber watchtower at Gamelsby (NY 269 523), about half way between Old Carlisle and Fingland Rigg, and an associated length of running ditch, stretching for at least 1,200m from NY 258 524 (just east of the River Wampool) to NY 270 522. This remains unexcavated but the cropmark suggests a feature of similar size to the ditch on Fingland Rigg and it again runs along a piece of higher ground, which is topped by the tower itself.

The Wigton to Aldoth line, if projected, would reach the coast somewhere in the vicinity of the fort of Beckfoot. The present writer (Woolliscroft) notes that aerial archaeology has long shown a possible precursor fort just southeast of the known Hadrianic site and, although this has never seen any excavation, it is tempting to wonder whether this may date to the Stanegate period. If so, he wonders whether it may have acted as a terminal fort for this southern ditch system, just as Kirkbride may have done for the more northerly line.

The Problem of the 'Eastern Stanegate'

N Hodgson

The very existence, let alone extent and nature of any pre-Hadrianic arrangement of forts and other installations between Carlisle and Kirkbride (at which two sites pre-Hadrianic forts can be accepted) remains uncertain, as the foregoing account must show. However, the problem is even greater east of Corbridge, where the Stanegate road is lost soon after leaving the eastern outskirts of the Roman site.

The failure to detect an extension of the road east of Corbridge has long taxed scholars. A fort which is often invoked in connection with the 'eastern Stanegate', Washingwells, is well known (Holbrook and Speak 1994), but at present it appears to stand in isolation, and apart from the obvious timber construction of its defences, and the fact that it shows at least two phases, nothing is known of its date.

On an early frontier line in Upper Germany or Raetia we would not expect a metalled road and a continuous cordon of installations in the earliest phase of frontier development, but rather individual sites placed and sized as local circumstances required, not necessarily connected by an engineered road. This may be the explanation for the failure to find a road to go with Washingwells. It is also possible that other military sites, forts, fortlets or towers, await discovery between Corbridge and the North Sea.

Washingwells lies south of the Tyne, so any connection between this fort and the road leading east out of Corbridge would have to have crossed the river somewhere in the vicinity of Bywell. Alternatively the pre-Hadrianic route may have continued east of Corbridge along the north side of the

Tyne. In 1990, Dobson (1990, 237), commented in a review on the suggestion by Bidwell and Holbrook (1989, 150-3) that there must have been a service road, south of the Vallum, and north of the Tyne, to allow communication to Hadrian's Wall east of Corbridge before the Military Way was provided. He wrote that: 'The notion of a road east of Corbridge north of the Tyne before the Military Way is a good one, but perhaps it is even earlier than the Wall: the Stanegate continuation east of Corbridge may well have run north of Tyne rather than south of it'.

19. Cropmarks of undated fort at Washingwells

More recently Bidwell has suggested how such a pre-Hadrianic road north of the Tyne might have tied into dispositions further east (Bidwell and Snape 2002, 256-9). Essentially he suggests that the crossing of the Tyne at Newcastle may have been pre-Hadrianic. Now that it is known from excavation that the fort on the Wall at Newcastle was not founded until the late-second or early-third century, a fort which will have guarded the river crossing has been theorised at Gateshead. Roman occupation which could have originated in connection with a fort is now firmly established at Bottle Bank in Gateshead, but the existence of an early fort is unproven. Such a crossing could have provided a secure link between the port at South Shields (where pre-Hadrianic occupation is possible but unproven) and Corbridge, via the Wrekendike, Gateshead, and the road north of the Tyne. Otherwise 'For a period of forty years...there was no secure established route from the mouth of the Tyne to Dere Street...and the rest of the northern frontier', and 'It is scarcely credible that supply by sea did not play an important part in the conquest and occupation of north-east England' (Bidwell and Snape 2002, 257).

Obviously this suggestion is speculative - 'nothing more than a possibility', in the words of its author. It seems as plausible as the loosely assumed route between Corbridge and South Shields via Washingwells - although it does not give a context for this last fort. However, the road leading east from Corbridge is not necessarily pre-Hadrianic: it could represent a Hadrianic road to service the Wall, as Bidwell and Holbrook had earlier suggested.

At South Shields, on the eastern seaboard, the earliest Roman occupation is very poorly understood, and there is no certain evidence for a pre-Hadrianic site, although a tentative case for this has been made on the basis of finds (Bidwell and Speak 1994, 14). It is now certain that one or more forts preceded the visible stone fort; but that stone fort, once so confidently dated to the Hadrianic period, is now known to be mid-Antonine. The Wrekendyke, from its junction with the road from Chester-le-Street to Newcastle at Wrekenton to the Roman fort at South Shields, has sometimes been postulated as being a continuation of the Stanegate 'system' to the east coast.

When Collingwood 'invented' the Trajanic frontier on the Stanegate in 1936, he actually suggested that east of Corbridge the frontier might have run along the Devil's Causeway to Berwick. This suggestion is also referred to by Daniels (1970). This takes us out of the immediate area of Hadrian's Wall, but it is a reminder that knowledge of sites along the Devil's Causeway (of which Low Learchild is the only permanent fort as yet known) may be essential to understanding the context of Trajanic period sites on the Tyne-Solway isthmus.

The Relationship between the Stanegate and Hadrian's Wall as First Planned and Actually Built.

N Hodgson

The commonly stated idea that the Stanegate forts were all simply given up and their units transferred to the new Wall forts when the 'fort decision' occurred can no longer be accepted. There is no evidence to support the old assumption that Corbridge was evacuated in the Hadrianic period. The evidence for Carlisle in the Hadrianic period is given in detail in the gazetteer of key sites. It suggests changes of function in the fort, including a possible growth in industrial activity, but the *principia* still functioned and there is no doubt that the site was still occupied. Some Trajanic forts in the area were given up, but as the chart shows, a number were retained in the Hadrianic period alongside the new Wall forts. This meant that significant pairings of sites occurred at Corbridge/Haltonchesters, Vindolanda/Housesteads and Carlisle/Stanwix, and this may be seen as a deliberate policy. Bidwell (1999, 20) has written that: 'The fort decision... can now be seen much more as an augmentation of the number of units in the Wall zone rather than a transfer of units from the Stanegate to new forts on the line of the Wall'. In fact, we can only identify for certain three full-size Stanegate forts that might have been abandoned to transfer units to the Wall, Kirkbride, Old Church and Nether Denton, and at the first and last of these there have been suggestions of occupation continuing into the Hadrianic period.

If, as is usually accepted, the decision to place forts on the line of the Wall was secondary, then the initial retention of the manpower required to support the frontier in the Stanegate forts means that these served as a fundamental element of the new border configuration. Woolliscroft (1989) has asserted that this is acknowledged in the provision of a signalling system. He found that on the stretch from Wall mile 30 to 57 only turret 56b was not intervisible with a conventional Stanegate site. In an emergency this would enable the small milecastle and

Trajanic or Early Hadrianic		Hadrianic	
Forts and Fortlets	**Towers**	**HW Fort Decision**	**Retained with HW**
South Shields			South Sheilds
		Wallsend	
?(Gateshead)			(? (Gateshead)
Washingwells, or site on N side of Tyne?		Benwell	
?		Rudchester	
Corbridge		Haltonchesters	Corbridge
? Newbrough		Chesters	
	Barcombe		
Vindolanda		Housesteads	Vindolanda
Haltwhistle Burn		Greatchesters	
Carvoran			Carvoran
Throp			
	Birdoswald	Birdoswald	
	Mains Rigg		
Nether Denton			
	Pike Hill		
Castle Hill Boothby			
Old Church Brampton		Castlesteads	
Carlisle		Stanwix	Carlisle
Burgh by Sands I			Burgh by Sands I
		Drumburgh	
Kirkbride		Bowness	Kirkbride

Table 1. Schedule showing continuation or abandonment of Stanegate sites in Hadrianic Period

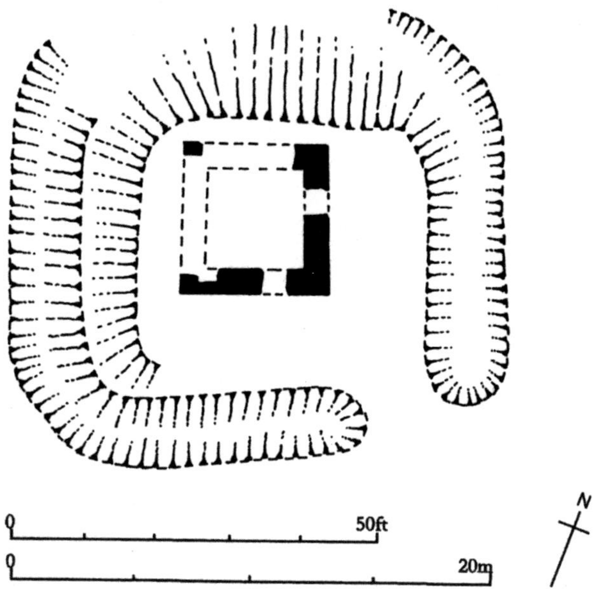

20. Plan of tower at Mains Rigg

turret detachments to signal for assistance from the much larger forces garrisoning the Stanegate forts. In those cases where a Stanegate fort or fortlet was not in direct visual contact, the towers at Barcombe Hill, overlooking Vindolanda, and Mains Rigg, between Throp and Nether Denton, could serve as relays. This need for intervisibility might also account for variations in distance between the milecastles, and the course of certain stretches of the Wall. However, as has been discussed, the continuation of the Stanegate forts beyond Carlisle and Corbridge remains to be proven, raising the crucial question of how the Wall forces were supported here, if such an arrangement was critical to the central sector. For the signal itself, Woolliscroft favours a simple beacon stance on top of the turrets or milecastle towers, initially to alert the Stanegate forces, used in conjunction with a messenger who would provide more detailed information.

The Stanegate and its Sites in the Later History of Hadrian's Wall

N Hodgson

Five sites along the Stanegate route were in occupation in the later-Roman period. These are: Corbridge, Newbrough, Vindolanda, Carvoran, and Carlisle. We might add South Shields, which, detached from the Wall system, had an enduring importance as fort and supply-base. Of the other five, Carvoran and Vindolanda were thought of as *forts per lineam valli* in the later period (as the *Notitia Dignitatum* shows). Although many research questions surrounding these sites can be considered in the section on the Wall forts, Vindolanda, at least, must have had a function connected with the Stanegate road on which it lies, for Housesteads was held simultaneously immediately north on the Wall. Perhaps the unit at Vindolanda represented a reserve of troops that could be moved more rapidly in an east or west direction than would be possible along the crags followed by the Wall itself. Carvoran lay at a point where the courses of the Stanegate and the Wall almost coincided. A small Roman fort yielding late-Roman pottery was detected at Newbrough in 1930, but very little is known about it. It does not seem safe to rule out the existence beneath or near this site of the earlier Roman fort that Birley's schedule of sites predicted. The known fort is the only site of its apparent type and date along the Stanegate, and the function of Newbrough in the later-Roman period is not understood: it could relate to the security of traffic along the road at a point out of sight of the Wall and its forts which lie 3km distant.

The two remaining sites, Corbridge and Carlisle, each retained a fort or military compound into the late-Roman period, but in each case a town grew up around the military centre. These two Stanegate sites are thus a key resource for the study of urbanism in the context of Hadrian's Wall in particular and the military zone of Roman Britain in general. At Corbridge the excavations of the 1940s to the 1960s concentrated on the earlier military levels, and our general knowledge of the later-Roman town derives largely from the pre-First World War excavation reports.

We know immeasurably more today about Roman Carlisle than could be guessed at in 1978, when Charlesworth summarised the then state of knowledge in an article that might have been deliberately intended to preface the flood of discoveries which the urban rescue archaeology of the 1980s was shortly to disclose. A fort at the strategic centre of the North West, guarding the bridge over the Eden leading into Scotland, was founded as early as AD 72/3. This fort, occupied by crack cavalry units, underwent many alterations and was not given up, as used to be believed, when Hadrian's Wall was built in the AD 120s. Instead it continued in use, the *ala Petriana* perhaps not moving to Stanwix until the 160s.

Outside the walls of the Carlisle fort and its annexe was a military *vicus*, already extensive by the 70s of the first century AD, augmented, by the early second century with official buildings, possibly associated with the *centurio regionarius* which the Vindolanda tablets attest at Carlisle. Even after the departure of the *ala* the fort was retained, and converted into stone by the early third century to house detachments of Legions II and XX. Outside the walls of their compound, a major urban centre had developed by the early third century. A possible forum, public baths, and aqueduct have been claimed in interim reports, but none of these is yet proven. More securely established by published reports are contrasting areas of strip-buildings and more open settlement of agricultural buildings and high-status housing, the latter being used to the end of the Roman period and beyond.

The town was almost certainly the capital of the *civitas Carvetiorum*, known to have been in existence by AD 222-235 (this date from the recently discovered Langwathby milestone) and probably constituted under Septimius Severus. Urban character was maintained into the late fourth or early fifth century. There is no firm evidence for a Roman walled circuit, although one has been assumed in the past. Possibly unfinished early third-century defences have been found at one point. The wall famously shown to St Cuthbert in AD 695 (*Vita Sancti Cuthberti*) was perhaps that of the military enclosure.

The pattern of rural settlement relating to the *civitas* capital is presently unknown: there is a notable contrast with the north-eastern region where some villa-style settlement is known in the hinterland of Hadrian's Wall. However, at Hawkhirst, just south of Old Church, Brampton, some 1.5km east of Carlisle, there is a site which has produced many Roman finds, including third- and fourth-century material, and what sounds like a hypocaust (Simpson and Richmond 1936, 197-82). Here there is the possibility of a civil site, maybe even a villa, belonging to the hinterland of late-Roman Carlisle.

There is abundant evidence that the Stanegate remained in use into the late-Roman period. At Crindledykes (1.5km east of Vindolanda; NY 786 669) five complete and two fragmentary milestones, dating from Severus Alexander (AD 223) to Constantine I (AD 307-337), were found in 1885 (*RIB* 2299, 2300, 2301, 2302, 2303, 2304 and 2305). The earliest (*RIB* 2299) records a distance of fourteen miles, showing that the distances were measured from Corbridge. Close to Fell End a milestone (*RIB* 2309) dating to Aurelian (AD 273-75) was found in 1932 (Birley 1932). There is good evidence for a major re-engineering of the road as it passes westwards from Corbridge as late as the Valentinianic period (364-75) (Wright 1941).

Finds from the Stanegate Forts

L Allason-Jones

The limited archaeological investigation of the Stanegate forts means that the finds assemblage is dominated by the forts of Corbridge, Vindolanda and Carlisle, where extensive excavations over the years have resulted in large and comprehensive assemblages. Some material from the Stanegate forts, such as the inscriptions and sculptured stone, is covered in general publications, eg *RIB* and *CSIR* I.1 and I.6, along with material from the Wall forts. Snape (1993) offers a synopsis of the brooches from the northern frontier with particular emphasis on the Stanegate forts (see case study).

Material from individual forts has been covered variously: The material from Corbridge is covered in the excavation reports by Forster and Knowles in *Archaeologia Aeliana* 3rd series. The excavations from 1947-1980 are published by Bishop and Dore 1988, where references to earlier excavations can be found. The Corbridge Hoard is discussed in Allason-Jones and Bishop 1988.

The material found at Vindolanda has been published in a series of fascicules, such as Birley, R E, 1996; 1999; Blake 1999; Birley and Green 2006 as well as Bidwell 1985. The Vindolanda writing tablets have been published by Bowman and Thomas 1983; 1994; 2003.

The series of forts at Carlisle is undergoing a programme of publication at the moment, although the finds from some sites are already in the public domain in McCarthy 1990; 1991, 2000; McCarthy, Padley and Henig 1982; Padley 1991; Padley and Winterbottom 1991; Taylor 1991 and Tomlin 1998. Finds reports currently in preparation include those for Annetwell Street, South Lanes, Fisher Street and the Millennium site.

The smaller forts have produced a limited amount of material, mostly samian and coarse pottery, although it is noticeable that there is a curious similarity in the discovery of glass armlets, melon beads and vessel glass on these sites. See Simpson 1913: Throp and Nether Denton; Simpson and Richmond 1936: Old Church, Brampton; Birley and Bellhouse 1963; 1975: Kirkbride; Gibson and Simpson 1909; Simpson 1976: Haltwhistle Burn. Excavations at Kirkbride produced several furnaces and the associated finds confirmed that these had been used for lead working (see also Wilson 1972). Throp was unusual in this series in producing a noticeable amount of mortaria, although Simpson (1913) makes a point of stressing the similarity between the other finds from Throp and those from Haltwhistle Burn.

A single piece of an undiagnostic greyware base was found by a man walking his dog at Washingwells. This has not been published but is in the Museum of Antiquities at Newcastle (accession number 1981.1); it remains the only Roman artefact to be found on the site.

The site just south of Old Church Brampton at Hawkhirst is known to have produced a sizeable amount of bronze work in the eighteenth century (MacLauchlan 1858, 64), including a statuette of a nude deity, possibly Mercury, an openwork Jovis balteus mount and a fourth-century crossbow brooch, and a hoard of third-century coins in the early nineteenth century (Hodgson 1840, 233-4).

On the whole the material found on the Stanegate forts covers the same range of material found in the assemblages from the Wall forts. There are however some apparent differences; whether these differences are valid would be worth exploring through future research:

- As might be expected, the Stanegate fort assemblages include more first-century AD material than the Wall forts. This is particularly important for the study of glass and pottery in the region. The proportion of fourth-century material appears to be similar to that from the Wall forts.
- The Stanegate forts, particularly Vindolanda and Carlisle, include more organic material. This is largely due to their position in the lower lying areas of the Tyne Solway gap, the Wall forts tending to be sited on the better draining Whin Sill.
- More field-army equipment, such as tenting, has been found on the Stanegate forts. This may reflect the more suitable conditions for organic preservation at Vindolanda and Carlisle but may also suggest an army that is less settled in its bases in the earlier years of the occupation.
- Whilst the material from the first- and early second century AD layers of Stanegate forts reflects an army on campaign, once Hadrian's Wall is built there is a noticeable change in the range of objects found, with more domestic material, including glass and luxury goods, from the Stanegate forts than the Wall forts. This may be largely due to the gradual development of some of these sites into towns as opposed to forts with military *vici*, but may also suggest that their position to the rear of the frontier line led to them being regarded as safer postings, suitable for administration and supply staff.

Case Study: Roman Brooches from Sites on the Stanegate

M Snape

Amongst the large number of Roman brooches from North Britain are examples of types thought to have gone out of use by the end of the first century; data collected in 1990 was used to study their distribution (Snape 1993, 97-100). This produced useful results for South Shields (Snape 1993, 100-1; Bidwell and Speak 1994, 182-4), and suggested that the same approach might in future be usefully applied to Stanegate sites.

Not surprisingly, Stanegate sites produced a higher percentage (5.6%) of first-century brooches than did sites on Hadrian's Wall (2.6%) (Snape 1993, Table 7). Unfortunately the total number of early brooches from the Stanegate was only 21, so it was not possible at the time to deduce anything meaningful from the relative proportions of Flavian and Trajanic brooches (eight belonged to types with an accepted date range of early/mid-first century, seven to the later first century, the remainder being not closely dateable within that century). However, as many more brooches will have been recovered in excavations since 1990, the same analysis might now produce more useful results.

Two caveats arose from the study:

- Some of these brooch types might have survived longer than previously thought. Several types thought to have gone out of use by the end of the first century were found at sites on Hadrian's Wall (Snape 1993, 99-100, Table 8).

• It is only the distribution pattern of types which is meaningful, as there are many reasons why an individual brooch might have been lost or discarded at any one site.

21. The recently discovered Quintus Sollonius Brooch from Vindolanda

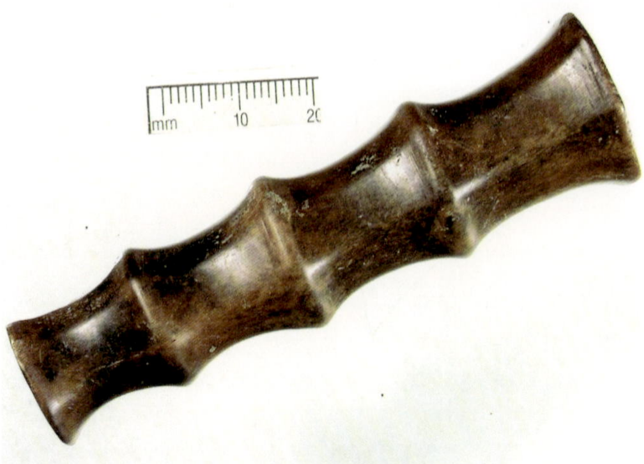

22. Roman Sword handle from Carlisle

The Brampton Kilns

P Bidwell

In 1963 six tile and two pottery kilns were found, along with a large quantity of pottery (mainly wasters), during an extension to the recreation ground of the former Irthing Valley School (now called William Howard School). A large quantity of pottery was recovered, mainly waster debris (Hogg 1965). A year later a large hoard of ironwork was discovered at the same place, from within a deep pit (Manning 1966). More recently, in 1997, possible buildings were noted during an evaluation (Esmonde Cleary 1998, 381).

23. A kiln at Brampton

Pottery vessels which can be identified as products of the Brampton kilns have been found in Period 3b levels at the Carlisle Millennium site which are dated between 83 and 92/3. They also occur at Vindolanda in IIb levels (92-7; no coarse pottery has been published from the earlier levels). Brampton products occur in later levels at both sites, but it is clear that the kilns were never their main suppliers of coarse pottery. It is likely that the Brampton tile kilns also supplied Carlisle and Vindolanda (as well as the intervening forts) but their products have no characteristics which would distinguish them from material from other kilns. Neither tiles nor mortaria were stamped. Pottery continued to be made at Brampton at least until the early Hadrianic period, as is shown by the presence of BB1 imitations at the kilns.

It is doubtful whether the pottery so far recovered from the site represents the full range and chronological span of the types made there. There is also a strong possibility that the kilns were part of a much more extensive industrial complex.

Key Investigated Sites

This section provides details of those Stanegate sites where major work has been undertaken. A brief synopsis of the remaining sites then follows in the schedule. South Shields, while of relevance to this theme, is traditionally regarded as a Wall fort and so the summary of its investigation history is given in the **Forts and Extramural Settlement** section.

Corbridge

M C Bishop

Location

The main Roman site at Corbridge lies on the second river terrace of the north bank of the Tyne at 45m above sea level, to the west of the modern village of Corbridge on a slight promontory to the east and south of the Cor Burn. It is strategically situated at the junction of the Dere Street (Margary 8) and the Stanegate (Margary 85) and is some 4km south of Hadrian's Wall. The predecessor to the main site, at Beaufront Red House, lies 1km to the west.

Current Condition

The central portion of the settlement (some 1.8ha) was

24. The urban centre of Corbridge

given to the nation in 1933 and is now in the care of English Heritage. The area to the south and south-east of that lies under permanent pasture, whilst most of the rest of the site is under the plough, with the exceptions of parts that lie beneath Corchester Towers (and the adjacent playing field) and the housing estate to the east and south-east of that.

History of Exploration

Nineteenth-century excavation by Coulson revealed the northern end of the Roman bridge over the Tyne, but all finds and documentation have disappeared. The first major campaign of work was undertaken between 1906 and 1914 in preparation for the volume on the parish of Corbridge for the Northumberland County History under the direction of Haverfield and supervised by Woolley. From 1908 onwards the excavations were run by Forster and Knowles and uncovered some 7ha of the settlement.

In 1933, the central part of the site was given to the nation and consolidation and clearance led to a new campaign of work by Birley, later joined by Richmond, which concentrated on the area in care until war brought it to a close in 1940.

In the post-war period, Corbridge was chosen as the location of the principal training excavation for the University of Durham (and subsequently that of Newcastle upon Tyne) and this ran from 1947 through to 1973. An important development came in 1974, when the construction of the new A69 Corbridge bypass led to rescue excavations at Beaufront Red House, Bishop Rigg, and on the cremation cemetery lining Dere Street. In 1976, the Ancient Monuments Laboratory undertook magnetometer and resistivity surveys in the grounds of Corchester Towers and the adjacent playing field.

25. Excavations underway at Corbridge, Site XI, 1970s

The final major excavation on the main site occurred in 1980, prior to the construction of the new museum. This and the post-Second World War training excavations were ultimately reported upon comprehensively in 1989, for which a new plan matching the excavated settlement to the evidence of aerial photographs was prepared by the RCHM(E).

The bridge was surveyed in 1906 and again in 1963-6. Excavations were undertaken by Coulson in 1861 and later by Forster and Knowles, before major work was undertaken by Tyne and Wear Museums in 2004 on the southern approach ramp and abutment.

Military bases

Garrison

Although long known as *Corstopitum*, following the (almost certainly corrupt) entry in the Antonine Itinerary, it is now widely held that references in the Vindolanda writing tablets to '*Coris*' may indicate a locative case of *Coria* (a form considered, but rejected, by Rivet and Smith 1981). Other suggestions, including *Corioritum* and *Corsobetum*, may be noted.

The *ala Petriana* is often associated with the early occupation of Corbridge, on the strength of the late-first-century tombstone of Flavinus from Hexham Abbey (*RIB* 1172). The Vindolanda *pridianum* indicates that a detachment of *cohors I Tungrorum* was outposted to *Coria* in the last decade of the first century AD. The discovery of the Corbridge hoard of armour and other artefacts could be seen as suggesting a legionary presence in the secondary fort (Allason-Jones and Bishop 1988, 110). The *cohors I Lingonum* is known from an undated inscription from the site , whilst *cohors I Fida Vardullorum* is recorded for the period AD 161-9.

The military compounds apparently held elements of two legions, and *II Augusta*, *VI Victrix*, and *XX Valeria Victrix* are all attested from the site in the second to third centuries AD (Richmond 1943, 134-136).

Plan

Only the central range of the primary fort is known with any certainty, including a granary and store-building(?) to the east of the south-facing *principia* and fragments of what may have been a *praetorium* to the west. An east-west aligned barrack-like building was identified to the north-west of the *principia* with another narrow structure to the east of it.

The secondary fort was, like its predecessor, aligned facing southwards, its *via principalis* comprising the Stanegate and its *via praetoria* being retained after the demolition of the secondary fort. The *retentura* of the secondary fort always contained six barrack blocks, but the central range seems to have alternated its granaries from east (II, IV) to west (III) of the *principia*. The east to west measurement of 121m within the ramparts has been established by excavation (Gillam 1959).

26. The marked subsidence of later structures at Corbridge

The military compounds each had their own *principia* facing each other across the former *via praetoria*.

Defences

A complex series of early ramparts and ditches indicate that the primary fort was larger than cohort-sized and is, as yet, imperfectly understood (Bishop and Dore 1988, 87-104). Ditches to the north and east of the main site seem to have been late Flavian, whilst a similarly early pair of east-west ditches beneath the later military compounds (probably associated with the reduction from Ia to Ib) are manifested by subsidence of later buildings into them. Part of a gateway was identified beneath the later *via praetoria*. The east and west turf ramparts of the secondary fort have been excavated within the area in care, together with timbers belonging to the gates, and appear to have served throughout the life of that establishment. The location of the northern and southern defences are not known with any precision, although if Site 17 represents an extramural bath-house and Site 14 a rampart-back structure and the scarp to the south is taken into consideration, the north-south distance within the ramparts would have been around 150m, so the secondary fort may have had a 5:4 proportion and enclosed an area of 1.8ha within its ramparts (which were between 6.7m and 7.3m broad).

The military compounds were undefended except for a wall around each and these seem to have been more symbolic than defensive in nature. Ultimately the two compounds were joined into one with a uniting wall across the former *via praetoria* (Birley and Richmond 1938, 249).

Structural History

The earliest military occupation was at Beaufront Red House (the excavated strip usually being identified as an Agricolan "supply base" (Hanson et al 1979)), but occupation shifted slightly eastwards by the middle of the AD 80s, when the primary turf and timber fort (Ia) was constructed on the main site. This was subsequently reduced in size (Ib) before being abandoned around AD 103. The secondary, cohort-sized, fort was built around AD 105 (II) and lasted until around AD 122, when a successor was constructed (III). This was in turn replaced around AD 139 (IVa) and for the first time stone was employed for at least some of the central-range buildings. The final phase (IVb) came around AD 158 and lasted until about AD 163 (Bishop and Dore 1988, 126-141).

The end of the cohort-sized fort was evidently not the end of military occupation, however, and some details of mid-second-century stone-built structures suggest army involvement in their construction before the east and west compounds were constructed in stone on either side of the former *via praetoria* at an unknown date (although they were believed by their excavators to be Severan in origin).

Changes of Plan

The defences of the secondary fort replaced those of the primary but appear to have been retained throughout the subsequent phases. It may be noted that all of the forts faced south.

Late Development

Since the conventional cohort-sized fort was abandoned during the second century, later development was confined to the military compounds, which were ultimately united.

Civil Settlement

Most of the civil settlement lies outwith the area in care and so was only examined during the pre-First World War campaigns.

Form

The form of the civil settlement was largely dictated by the road system, which comprised the Dere Street passing over the bridge to a junction with the Stanegate. Its northern continuation was to the east of the main site, but whether this was the original configuration is unknown. Strip buildings lined the Stanegate to either side of the central area and the Dere Street to the east, with east-west branch streets (an unexcavated one of which was located by the geophysical surveys at Corchester Towers). The civil settlement is often classified as a 'small town'.

Extent

The limits of the site are crudely defined to the west, north, and east by cemetery areas, but probably more accurately by the Cor Burn to the north and west and the Tyne to the south.

27. Reconstruction of one of the temples at Corbridge

Development History

The nature of the early excavations suggests that only the final form of the civil settlement has been recorded, so it is difficult to comment upon the development of the site other than that it resembles an enlarged military *vicus*, possibly a survival from that of the secondary fort.

Civil Settlement Boundary

Although long thought to have been a walled settlement, partly on the (possibly misleading) evidence of MacLauchlan's survey, no clear evidence of a wall around the civil settlement has ever been produced despite the early excavators seeking it exhaustively.

Official Buildings

Site 2, a corridor building to the south-west of the site in care, has been suggested as a *mansio*. Site 11, a near-square courtyard building located directly on top of the former *principia* and *praetorium* of the secondary fort, has variously been interpreted as a forum or legionary *principia* (Birley 1959). This structure was never completed. The two stone granaries of Phase IV of the secondary fort were retained after the rest of the base was decommissioned, whilst a fountain-head was constructed by *legio XX* between the east granary and Site 11, at the southern end of the aqueduct. Two further stone granaries, Sites 17W and 56, existed to the north of Site 11 and appear to post-date the secondary fort.

Shrines and Temples

Epigraphic and sculptural evidence makes it plain that a number of temples and shrines were located in (and possibly around) Corbridge. Inscriptions record deities of the conventional pantheon, those of eastern origin, and native and syncretised Roman gods and goddesses. Although architectural and sculptural fragments support the identification of temples and shrines in the vicinity, attempts to equate these with structures immediately north of the military compounds (Richmond 1943, 136-149) have been called into question recently.

Bath houses

The Red House baths (Daniels 1959) were recognised by Gillam as belonging to the military base at Beaufront Red House, whilst a small bath building to the north of the site in care has been suggested as that of the secondary fort on the main site. A further bath building is suggested by aerial photographic evidence to the east of the site in care and this may have belonged to the primary fort.

Cemeteries

A cremation cemetery was found in 1974 adjacent to Dere Street, under the south-western slip-road to the A69 (Casey and Hoffmann 1995). A square mausoleum was excavated to the west of the Cor Burn, next to the Stanegate, at Shorden Brae (Gillam and Daniels 1961).

Aqueduct

The course of the aqueduct south of Corchester Lane was revealed during the original campaign of excavations (Forster and Knowles 1910, 217-220) and unpublished Environment Agency LiDAR data suggest it continues northwards after a course change to the north-east, before crossing the line of the Dere Street where it was examined in 1974 (although dismissed in publication as a modern field drain). The entire course of the aqueduct to its source in the Cor Burn was allegedly traced by Gillam and Birley.

Bridge

The bridge carrying Dere Street over the Tyne has been suggested as one of a series of monumental stone bridges in the Wall zone and its stone piers were evidently still standing in the post-medieval period.

Vindolanda

R Birley

The majority of the site of the Roman site of Vindolanda has been owned since 1970 by the Vindolanda Trust, a registered Charity. Since then the Vindolanda Trust has pursued its long-term aim of total excavation of the Roman remains, and in 2006 estimated that it had completed some 12% of the total that lies within its land-holding. The research agenda is now determined by the Trust's Research Committee, formed by the Trustees with archaeological experience and the archaeological and curatorial staff. The Museum houses a number of important archives, including the bulk of Eric Birley's unpublished Roman Army research files, a large body of material from John Mann's files, the Charles Anderson photographic records of Wall conservation, and the full photographic records of the Vindolanda Writing Tablets.

Artefacts, sculptured and inscribed stones and coins found before 1929 are now in a number of Museums, including those holding the Clayton Collection at Chesters, the Museum of Antiquities in Newcastle, the British Museum and in the custody of the Dean and Chapter of Durham Cathedral. The bulk of the material from Eric Birley's work in the 1930's and all finds since 1967 are housed at Chesterholm Museum, with the exception of the writing tablets, which are held by the British Museum. The best of the reserve collection is displayed at the Roman Army Museum (at Carvoran).

Brief statement of the currently known occupation history

Primary occupation

The period I timber fort lay almost entirely under the later remains on the platform ultimately occupied by the 'visible' stone fort, known as Stone Fort 2. To date, only a part of its western rampart and ditches have been excavated, and it is so deeply buried that further investigation would require a very considerable excavation, involving the seven or eight occupation levels overlying it. Evidence of its date rests upon the deposit of La Graufesenque pottery dumped in its inner western ditch (suggesting the mid to late AD 80's) (Birley 1994, 19-35), and its garrison (the First Cohort of Tungrians) is assured by the recovery of two strength reports from the same ditch.

The periods II and III pre-Hadrianic forts

The evidence for their presence is based upon the work undertaken on their southern rampart and south gate, together with the examination of structures to the north of the gate (excavations of 1973-1994), with additional evidence gained during the excavations to the west in 2001-2005). A bonus was the discovery and excavation of the large bath house associated with these early forts (A Birley 2001), to which reference had been made in one of the writing tablets. The period III fort is the most closely dated of all Vindolanda occupations, with firm consular dates on writing tablets, dendrochronological dates and numerous coins, indicating occupation within the years AD 98-105. The garrison was undoubtedly the Ninth Cohort of Batavians, possibly with a detachment of the Third Cohort of Batavians. The period II fort appears to have been a short-lived temporary affair, soon converted into the period III fort. The garrison was also the Ninth Cohort of Batavians, but the only indicator of date was on a stylus tablet, of AD 97.

Further work on the remains of these forts would undoubtedly produce important evidence, especially if any areas with barrack buildings were examined, for in spite of the vast amount of information that has been recovered so far, most of it is related to higher status soldiers, and little is known of the conditions in which the soldiers lived.

The period IV pre-Hadrianic fort

This appears to have been constructed in late AD 105 (on the evidence of writing tablets and dendrochronology), and was certainly still occupied beyond AD 112 (writing tablet dated AD 111 and *Via Traiana dupondius* of 112-114), and there has been one early coin of Hadrian amongst a large assembly of Trajanic coins. It perhaps survived to c. AD 119.

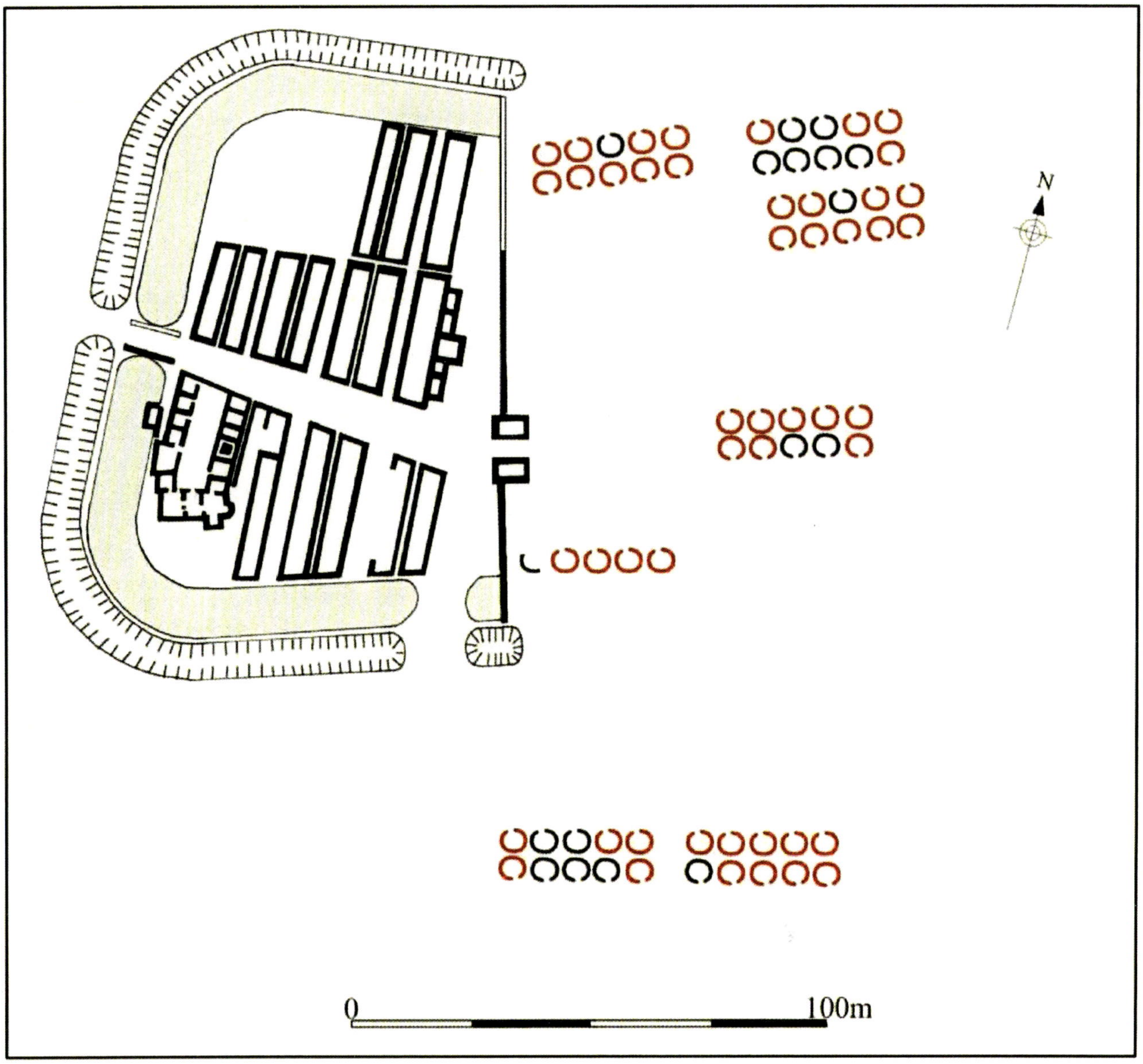

28. Vindolanda, Severan fort and circular hut compound

The garrison was then the First Cohort of Tungrians (graffiti and writing tablets), with, at times, detachments of legionaries and cavalry of the First Cohort of Vangiones (writing tablet evidence). The remains of this fort have been found in the same contexts as the remains of the period II and III forts, but also extending further to the west, where efforts are still being made to locate its western defences. This was clearly a very large fort, in excess of 8 acres - sufficient for the full *cohors I Tungrorum milliaria*, together with other detachments.

The period V wooden fort

The remains of this fort, almost certainly of Hadrianic date, have, on the evidence so far obtained, been severely mangled by the subsequent construction of stone buildings. It is likely that this fort was the same size as the period IV fort, but the date of its abandonment remains unknown (although likely to be associated with the departure of the Tungrians for the new Housesteads fort in the mid to late 120's). Some evidence implies that it may have been used as a major supply base for the Wall builders.

Period VI

Vindolanda's period VI is the most difficult to interpret, and needs much further attention. The notation 'period VI' was given to the military remains that succeeded the period V fort, and that was the fort usually referred to as Stone Fort 1, whose ornate, south-facing *principia* had been examined by Eric Birley and Ian Richmond (1936). Those excavators dated it to the early third century on somewhat lax reasoning, based on the fact that it was earlier than their preferred date for Stone Fort 2 (early fourth century) and therefore 'logically' of third century date, but Paul Bidwell argued that it was probably of Hadrianic date. Little of its remains other than the *principia* have been examined so far, although its southern wall was located in 2000, some 7m to the north of the corresponding wall of Stone Fort 2. Work by the Trust in the extramural area in recent years has examined two of that fort's western ditches, which were certainly back-filled around AD 180 at the latest, and in the course of 2006 a further examination of its western gate will take place (reported on in Birley and Richmond 1936, 233-235). The 2005 work below the clay rampart backing inside the western wall of Stone Fort 2 revealed a substantial and very well made turf rampart, which had been cut away at some subsequent date to facilitate the construction of a stone wall on its western side. It was clear, therefore, that 'Stone Fort 1' had started life with a

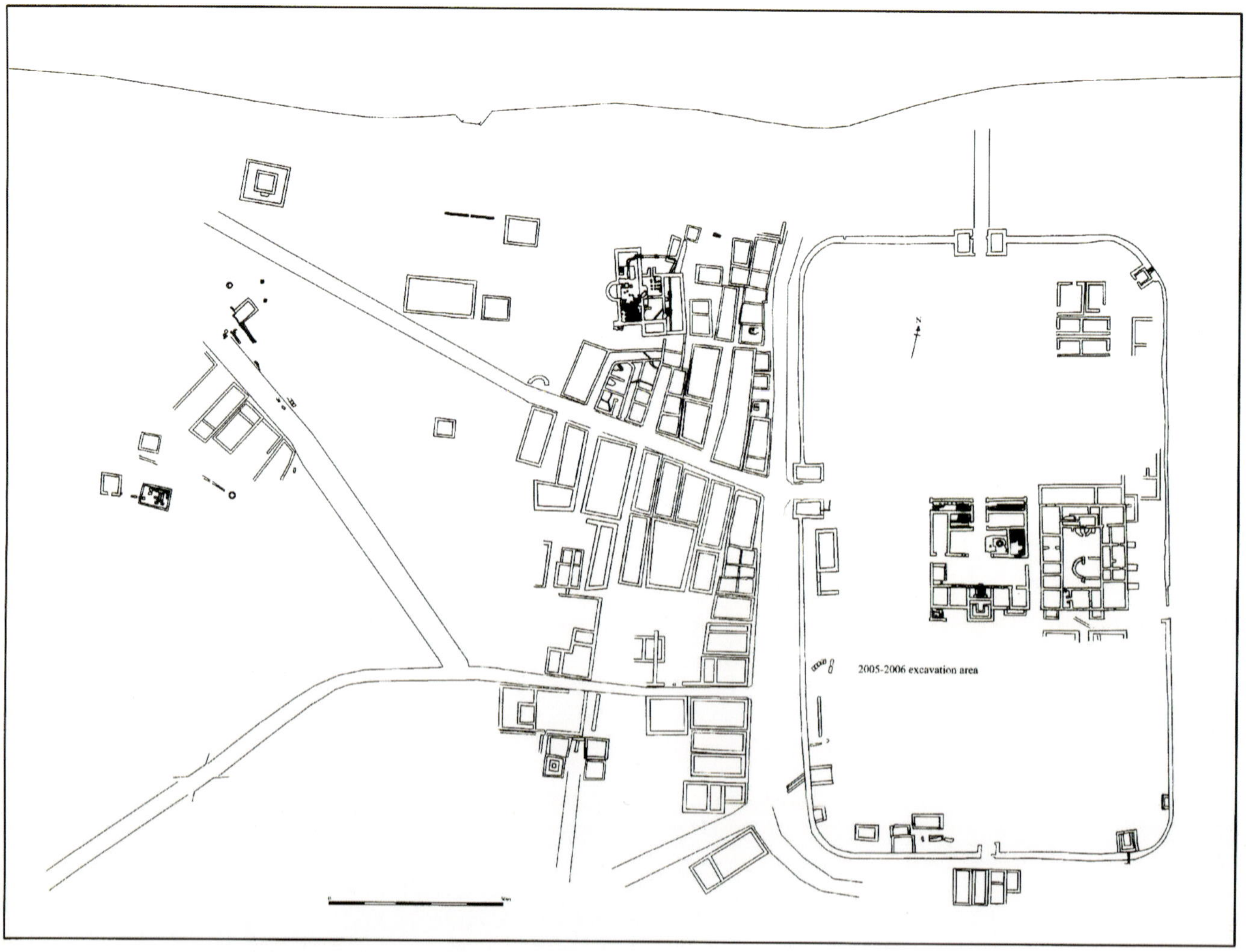

29. Vindolanda. Plan of fort and annexe in 3rd and 4th century

turf rampart alone (A Birley and Blake 2007). At that point the archaeologists recalled that at the very western limit of the 2000 excavation trench, which had revealed the southern wall of Stone Fort 1, a major oak timber had been seen standing in the turf of a rampart. At the time it was assumed that this post must have been a survivor from a pre-Hadrianic phase, but it is now realized that it was almost certainly a post of the original timber angle tower of Stone Fort 1. Subject to SMC being granted, there is therefore an outstanding chance of recovering a contemporary oak timber that could well provide a dendrochronological date - and thus put the start date of Stone Fort 1 beyond doubt.

30. The mysterious circular structures at Vindolanda

Period VIA

Work outside the western walls of the stone forts had revealed that the multiple ditches of Stone Fort 1 had been backfilled around AD 180, and that a regular series of large timber buildings had been erected, partially on top of the old ditches. As these lay below stone structures dating to the early third century, it is thought that they were probably a part of a military annex attached to Stone Fort 1, and they were therefore given the notation 'period VIA'. Little else is known of this period, and any further remains are likely to have been severely mauled by the subsequent stone period.

Period VIB

Early in the Trust's excavations, the stone remains above the period VI Stone Fort 1 had been assigned the title of period VII, or Stone Fort 2. Similarly, in the extramural area the stone remains of the civilian and quasi-military buildings appeared to be associated with Stone Fort 2, and were thus also assigned to period VII. But later excavations revealed another sequence of stone buildings below those extramural structures, and they proved conclusively (on considerable coin evidence) to date to the time of the Severan campaign (AD 208-212). As periods VI and VII were already assigned, they had to become another division of period VI, and were thus labelled period VIB. This Severan military establishment is of considerable interest, and needs further investigation, both under the civilian buildings (especially on the north side of the main road), and under the remains of Stone Fort 2. Apart from anything else, the strange circular buildings, first located by Eric Birley (Birley, Richmond and Stanfield 1936, 238-241) near the north gate of Stone Fort 2, and subsequently found north of the later *praetorium* and near the southern wall of that fort, also date to that same Severan period (Birley, Blake and Birley 1998, 13-18; Blake 2001). Clearly something very unusual was going on, and only excavation can supply the answers.

31. Third century baths at Vindolanda

Period VII Stone Fort 2

This relates to the 'visible' stone fort and its associated extramural settlement structures. The gateways, two latrines, two angle towers, the headquarters building and the commanding officer's residence have been excavated and consolidated for permanent display, and the bulk of the fort walls are similarly now exposed. Bidwell's 1980 excavation produced a wealth of information about the third- and fourth-century barracks in the north-east quadrant (Bidwell 1985). Further work on barracks, possibly stables, workshops and granaries is called for in due course, and only after that work is done can excavation continue to the levels below them. Outside the fort walls, perhaps half of the extramural buildings have been examined, and it remains a high priority to complete this work and then publish a full account of the civilian and military remains there.

It should be noted that Stone Fort 2 was largely rebuilt around AD 300, and this is regarded as **period VIII**, and that further substantial modifications were made after Count Theodosius 'restored' the frontier around AD 370, called **period IX**. Post Roman activity has been found on parts of the fort platform, and this is identified **as period X**.

Extent of occupation

There are qualifications to those last paragraphs. The current work has still not established the limit of occupation at the western end of the site, and magnetometer surveys have demonstrated that there has been a great deal of activity in the 6.5 ha field to the north. This is likely to include third- and fourth-century remains, and probably earlier material as well. The land is now owned by the Vindolanda Trust, and some sort of trial work should be undertaken there in the future.

The main sites of the cemeteries appear to lie outside Vindolanda Trust land, to the west and south west. In due course permission from the land-owners might be sought to investigate them.

Aerial photographs have indicated possible industrial sites on the western bank of the Chineley Burn, opposite Codley Gate farm (a likely place for a mill, for example). Again, permission to examine this area should not be difficult to obtain.

Finally, no trace of what must have been major rubbish dumps have been found, and possible sites outside the east gate of Stone fort 2, or to the south-east of the south-east corner of the fort could be investigated.

The Forts at Carlisle

J Zant

Evidence for pre-Roman activity was restricted to cultivation marks, the remains of a field system of possible Iron Age date. The arrival of the Roman army saw the construction of a turf-and-timber fort during the autumn/winter of AD 72-3, a date known from the dendrochronological dating of timbers recovered from the south rampart in the 1980s (Caruana in prep). The Millennium excavations (Zant in press) fixed the position of the west rampart and located the junction of two major roads, and in the southern part of the fort, the remains of barracks, workshops/stores, and external areas were investigated. A small part of the central range, including fragments of what may have been the *principia* and the *praetorium*, was also exposed.

An extensive internal reconstruction undertaken in the autumn/winter of AD 83-4 saw the replacement of almost all the original buildings with new structures. The barracks were rebuilt to a slightly larger specification, but otherwise the layout remained essentially unchanged; the fort defences do not appear to have been modified at this time. Following a minor episode of refurbishment c. AD 93-4, the fort was demolished around AD 103-5. The break in occupation appears to have been a short one, however, and rebuilding, again in timber, occurred c. AD 105. Barrack blocks in the southern part of the second fort were aligned north to south, as in the earlier fort, and part of the *principia* and an adjacent structure that might possibly have been a *fabrica*, or perhaps workshops attached to the *praetorium*, in the central range, were investigated.

A shift in the character of occupation during the Hadrianic period suggests that the fort may have evolved from a conventional base into something like a works depot, a change precipitated, perhaps, by the construction of Hadrian's Wall and the fort at Stanwix less than 1 km to the north. In the possible *fabrica* in the central range, an important cache of articulated armour fragments was deposited towards the end of this period. Exceptional preservation of waterlogged organic materials, including the remains of timber buildings, and outstanding artefactual and environmental assemblages, were a feature of the late first-century to mid-second-century levels over the greater part of the site.

The fort was again demolished in the mid-second century, perhaps as a consequence of the Antonine re-occupation of southern Scotland in the early AD 140s. The status of the site during the second half of the century remains obscure.

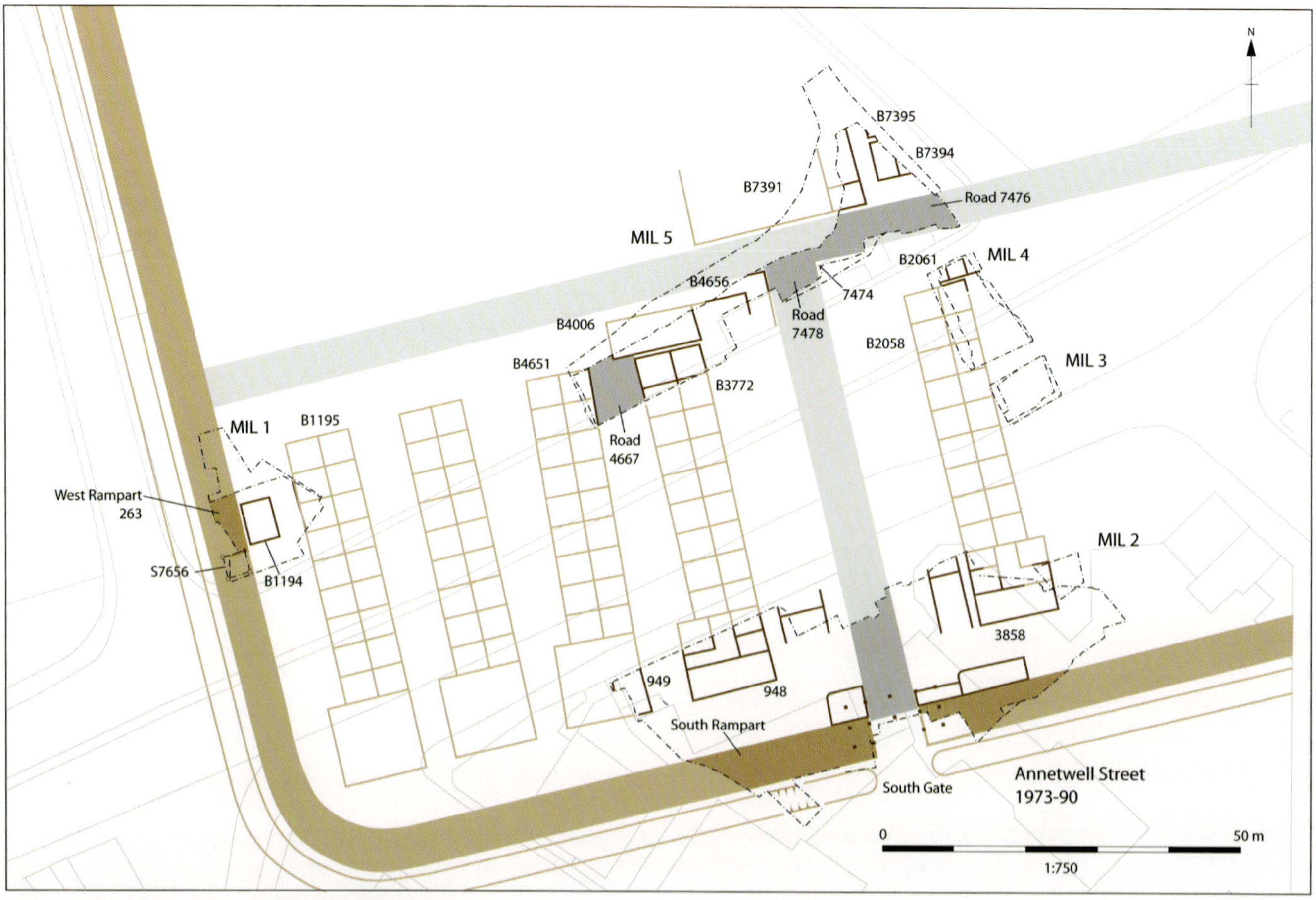

32. Carlisle. Remains of Period 3B fort

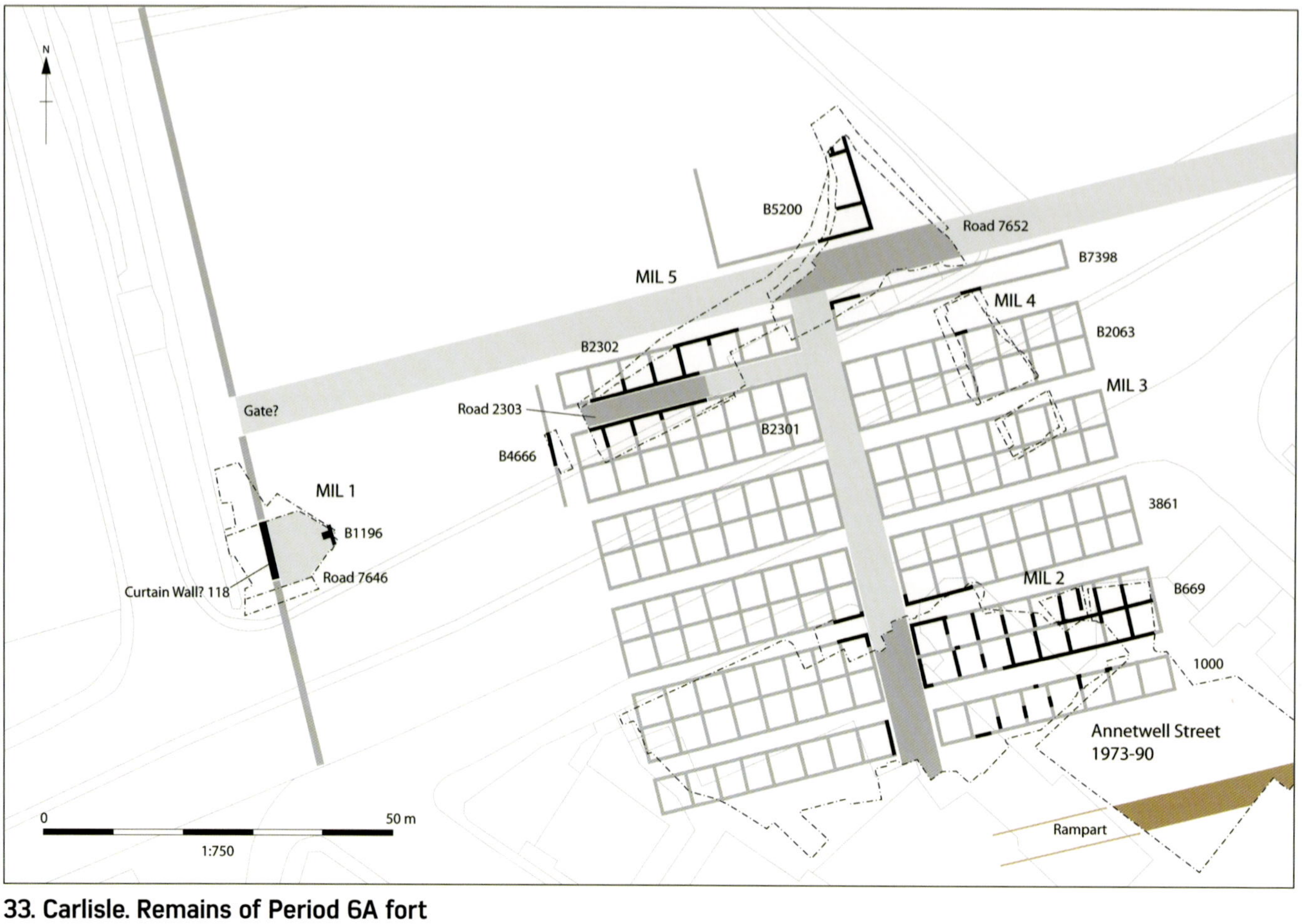

33. Carlisle. Remains of Period 6A fort

Intermittent occupation occurred, but the site does not seem to have been used as a conventional fort. The early third century saw extensive rebuilding in stone, but it is not clear whether the new installation was a conventional fort or something else, although for the most part the new layout followed that of the earlier forts. What was probably the west curtain wall lay inside the Flavian rampart, the *principia* was constructed on the site of the earlier headquarters buildings, the position of the major roads was maintained, and barracks were erected to the south. These were now aligned east-west, however, at right-angles to their predecessors. A building stone in the east wall of the principia suggests that the reconstruction was the work of *Legio VI Victrix*, although epigraphic evidence from elsewhere suggests that the fort was garrisoned by detachments from the other two British legions.

34. Articulated Roman armour from Carlisle

Thereafter the site was occupied to the end of the Roman period, with occupation certainly extending into the fifth century. Minor repairs were undertaken on most buildings, although rather more extensive refurbishment was evident in the *principia*, where a hypocaust was inserted into one room in the south range, and a latrine pit dug immediately outside the building. This continued in use to the very end of the occupation. In addition, the portico around the south front seems to have been enclosed. Heavy coin loss outside the *principia*, associated with large quantities of animal bone and an increase in items of personal ornament, suggest that the fort may have taken on a market function in the late fourth century. Eventually, the excavated buildings were levelled and their remains covered by 'dark earth', although parts of the *principia* probably remained upstanding for centuries.

The Stanegate: a General Schedule

G Stobbs and N Hodgson

Consult Birley, *Research on Hadrian's Wall*, for pre-1961 information on all sites.

The Installations:

South Shields see p. 71-5

Wrekenton (NZ 269 591) Suggested Roman site in the form of a distinct platform within the middle of Ravensworth Golf Course (Selkirk 1983, 43). Situated close to the junction of the Wrekendyke with the Chester-le-Street to Newcastle road.

Bottle Bank, Gateshead (NZ 2535 6355) Excavation on the site of the Gateshead Hilton has revealed a settlement lining the road leading down towards the Roman bridge across the Tyne. This may possibly be associated with an undiscovered bridgehead fort at Gateshead predating that at Newcastle, which was not founded until the late-second or early-third century (Burnham et al 1995, 344; 1998, 384).

Washingwells, Whickham (NZ 219 603) Apparently a turf and timber fort (2.38ha) of more than one period, known entirely from aerial photographs (McCord and Jobey 1971, 120; Holbrook and Speak 1994). The function of the site in relation to the Stanegate 'system' is unclear, as the outlook is predominately over the valley of the River Team to the east.

Corbridge - see key investigated sites

Newbrough (NY 868 680) A fortlet, roughly square and covering about 0.35ha, lies under the churchyard and has produced exclusively fourth-century material. No evidence has yet been found for the early-second century cohort fort predicted by the regular spacing of Birley's schedule of Stanegate sites. (Simpson 1929-1930)

Sitgate (NY 878 677) Crop mark of a skewed large rectangular enclosure with the character of a Roman camp, 5.1ha in area, within which lies a double-ditched probable Iron Age enclosure, on the east side of the village at Sitgate (Frere 1990, 316, 319; Maxwell and Wilson 1987, 14).

Barcombe Hill (NY 783 668 and NY 773 657) Two freestanding watch or signal towers. Barcombe A, consists of a small enclosure surrounded by a ditch, and lies within the northwest corner of a presumed Iron Age enclosure situated close to the summit of Barcombe Hill to the east of Vindolanda. Investigation in 1939 revealed a turf rampart 0.76m in height built upon a flagged foundation 3.06-4.26m wide. There was no trace of a structure within the interior. Later work, in 1950, re-examined the turf rampart, which was found to contain a stone oven. Pottery from this excavation was thought to be Flavian. Barcombe B was located on the westernmost spur of the hill in 1986. Limited excavation revealed stone footings of a wall, which formed a corner of a possible structure. Finds consisted of mortar, decomposed tile fragments and a piece of Roman glass (Jobey 1969; Woodfield 1966; Woolliscroft, Swain and Lockett 1992).

Vindolanda (Chesterholm) - see key investigated sites

Haltwhistle Burn (NY 715 662) This 0.31ha fortlet had a stone-fronted rampart, with three gates, facing south, east and west. The interior contained metalled roads and the remains of five stone buildings. The installation sits awkwardly within a single V-shaped ditch, 6.1 - 10.67m wide by 1.83 - 2.44m deep. Finds from the site included a single coin of Trajan and a quantity of pottery which was not closely dated, though it was suggested that this assemblage contained forms similar to those found in primary deposits on the Wall (Gibson and Simpson 1909b; Simpson 1974; Simpson 1976).

Turret 45a, Walltown East (NY 675 664) The origin of this turret remains disputed, with the traditional view that it was initially a freestanding tower challenged by an investigation of its foundations. This indicated that it could be a Narrow Wall structure (Crow 1991b).

Carvoran (NY 665 657) **(See Forts section)**. A precursor to the known Wall fort at the junction of the Stanegate road with the Maiden Way has been suggested on the basis of AP evidence showing a possible corner of an earlier, larger fort to the south-west of the Wall fort (Frere 1986, 381; Jones and Birley 1989). The presence of an early large fort (hence the name *Magna*?) has also been suggested as an explanation for the northward diversion of the Vallum at Carvoran. A complete bronze *modius* of Domitianic date was discovered on the site in 1915, while more recently military-style ditches revealed under Carvoran House produced pottery dating to the first and early second century.

Throp (NY 632 659) A 0.36ha fortlet enclosed by a turf rampart laid on a stone platform (MacLauchlan 1858; Simpson 1913). Finds from the site were sparse and the small amount of pottery was assigned a Hadrianic date, though the presence of later forms suggests a re-use of the site in the fourth century.

Birdoswald (NY 616 663) A freestanding stone watchtower 6.1m square, noted during excavations at Birdoswald in 1930 (Richmond 1931, 130).

Mains Rigg Tower (NY 613 652) A Freestanding stone watchtower 6.4m square, surrounded by a ditch, situated to the east of Nether Denton. No datable finds (Collingwood 1929, 141-142; Richmond 1929, 314-315; Hassall et al 1972, 308; Binns 1972).

Nether Denton (NY 596 646) A pre-Hadrianic fort with a complex structural history, not elucidated by any modern excavation. It was interpreted by Jones as a fort of 1.21ha enlarged to 3.2ha, with aerial evidence of a military *vicus* lying to the south-west. Late-first and early-second-century pottery came from the fort, while pottery from the second half of the second century was found in the vicinity of the military *vicus*. (Shipman 1874; Simpson 1913; Simpson and St Joseph 1934; Welfare 1974; Jones 1976, 28-9; Frere 1977, 373-374; Higham and Jones 1985, 62-63).

35. The truncated remains of the Pike HIll Tower

Pike Hill Tower (NY 577 648) A freestanding pre-Wall stone tower that was subsequently incorporated into the Hadrianic curtain. Its position provides a good view of both Nether Denton and Castle Hill, suggesting that its function pre-dates the Wall and that it is associated with forward observation and/or signalling on the Stanegate (Ferguson 1878, 214-215; Simpson 1928; Simpson and McIntyre 1932; Simpson and McIntyre 1933b).

Castle Hill, Boothby (NY 544 630) The site of a probable fortlet. A ditch 5.18m wide by 1.83m deep lay in front of the remains of a clay rampart. South Gaulish samian came from the ditch fill. Air photography shows the outline of one corner of the site, although much has possibly been destroyed by landslip (Simpson 1934; St Joseph 1951, 55).

Hawkhirst (NY 515 613 and NY 517 613) Two separate sites of uncertain form and function, situated upon a broad ridge to the south-east of Old Church, both of which have produced, over time, Roman material of predominately third- and fourth-century date (Simpson and Richmond 1936; St Joseph 1951).

Old Church, Brampton (NY 510 625) Fort of 1.5ha, roughly square in shape, with a stone central range and a turf rampart protected by a single ditch 4m wide by 1.5m deep (Simpson and Richmond 1936).

Watchclose (Watchcross or Steadfolds) (NY 4757 6019) Included by Birley in his schedule. A small camp of 0.6ha located to the south of the Stanegate road (now within the area of Carlisle airport). Trenching in 1935 established its size and temporary nature (Richmond and Hodgson 1936).

High Crosby (NY 4554 5977) A fortlet was postulated in the Birley schedule based upon the spacing and scant pottery finds made in 1934-5. Work in 1994-5 found a ditch containing fourth-century pottery. Further ditches and pits were located to the east of this and these contained flints and Iron Age pottery suggesting that the site is a native/Roman farmstead continuing in use into the fourth century (Frere 1986, 383-384).

Carlisle - see key investigated sites

Burgh-by-Sands I (NY 323 582) See p. 17

Burgh-by-Sands II - See p. 95-6

Burgh-by-Sands III ('West End') (NY 317 588) See p. 17

Kirkbride (NY 230 573) Fort of *c.* 2ha or somewhat over with timber internal buildings sited on a low ridge of boulder clay on the south side of the river Wampool. Pottery roughly dated to AD 80 - 110, suggests a Flavian-Trajanic occupation followed by abandonment in the Hadrianic period (Birley and Bellhouse 1963; Bellhouse and Richardson 1975; Bellhouse and Richardson 1982). The site has been suggested as the terminus of the "Western Stanegate" road running from Carlisle.

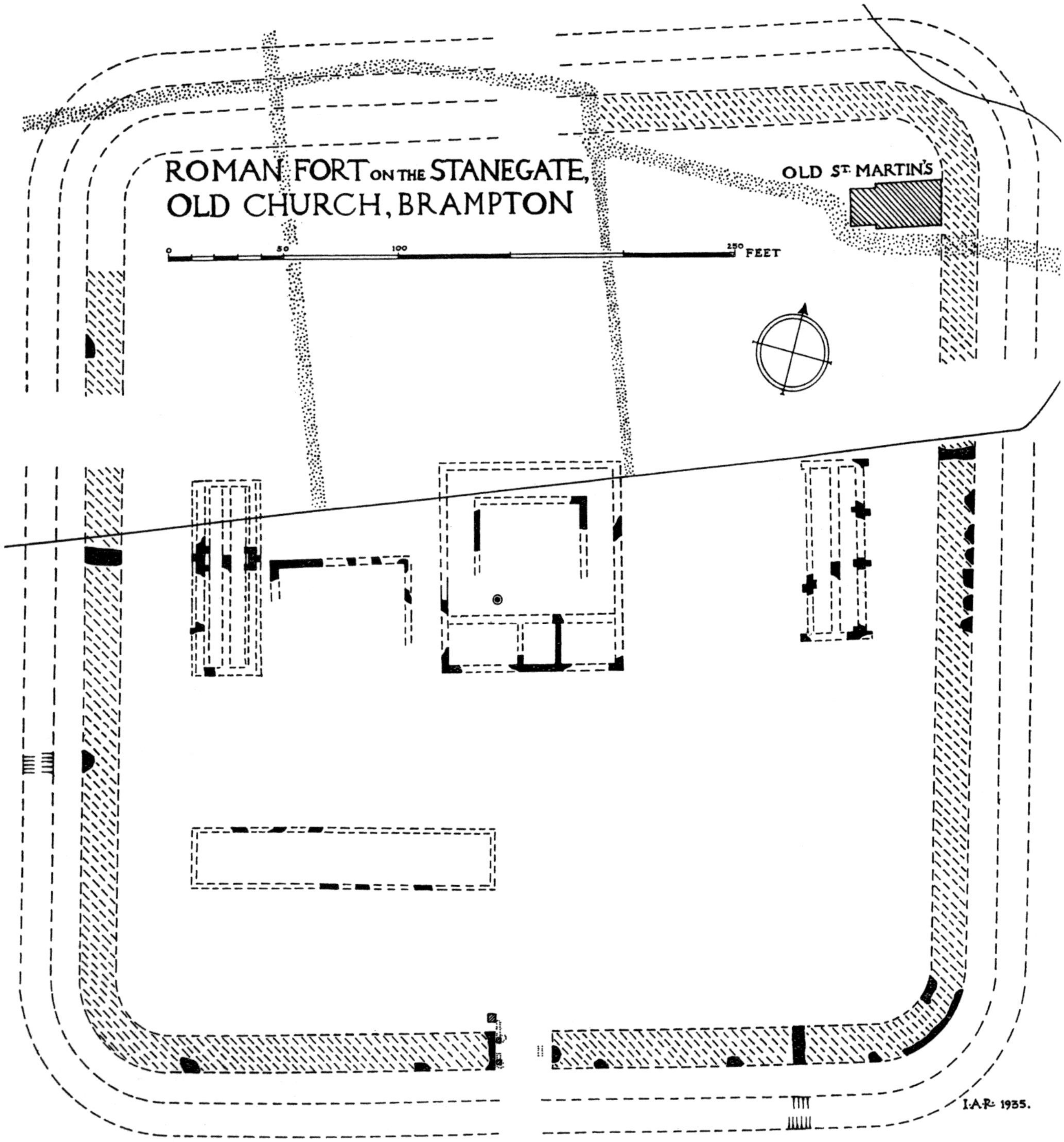

36. Excavation plan of Old Church, Brampton

4. The Wall
Co-ordinated by P T Bidwell

Overview
P T Bidwell

Hadrian's Wall represents the most elaborate of all Roman frontier works, combining elements drawn from the standard repertoire of military engineering, such as turrets and towers (watch-towers) and milecastles and milefortlets (fortlets), with at least one feature, the Vallum, which appears to be unique. The complexity of its structural history matches its elaborate design. Major additions were made to the original plan at an early stage in the building of the Wall, and its structures were altered, rebuilt or, in some instances, demolished at various junctures throughout the second and early third centuries. The later history of the Wall is poorly known, although some milecastles were still occupied in the later fourth century and repairs were made to the curtain in the third and early fourth century, if not later.

Building of the Wall probably began in AD 122 when Hadrian visited Britain. An earlier start is sometimes proposed but lacks any supporting evidence. The original design was for a Wall fronted by a ditch and obstacles, and with milecastles separated by pairs of turrets along its length. Construction was entirely in stone to the east of the Irthing, but to the west turf and timber was used, except for the turrets. The zone of control was extended down the Cumbrian coast by free-standing towers and milefortlets; there is no reason why they should not have been part of the original plan. The installations on the line of the Wall would only have held a very small force, and it is far from clear how it was intended to accommodate the main military strength needed to support the Wall. In the central sector and part of the western sector pre-existing forts of the Stanegate system could have held the necessary forces, although the siting of some of the forts, three to five kilometres south of the Wall or separated from it by a river, was hardly convenient. East of Corbridge no fort is certainly known which could have supported the Wall, and to the west of Carlisle there was only one fort near the line of the Wall, at Burgh-by-Sands, that was probably in occupation when the Wall was built. Ultimately, while construction was underway, it was decided to build a series of forts on the line of the Wall. At about the same time the width of the Wall was reduced and construction of the Vallum began.

The fort decision was taken in the governorship of A. Platorius Nepos who probably left Britain by the end of 126, if not earlier. For how long the main building programme continued is uncertain, although forts were added to the Wall at Great Chesters in or after 128 and at Carrawburgh in the early 130s. Rebuilding of the first five miles of the Turf Wall west of the Irthing was undertaken at the end of Hadrian's reign. The abandonment of Hadrian's Wall when the frontier was advanced northwards was marked by the removal of milecastle gates and slighting of the Vallum. The return from the Antonine Wall saw the restoration of the

37. The Wall in the central sector

38. Milecastle 48 and turret 48a at Gilsland

milecastle gates and the laying of new floors in the turrets. The Military Way was built behind the Wall, in places overlying the north mound of the Vallum, which however remained as a prominent earthwork, although it was never restored to its original form. Magnificent road-bridges were built at Chesters and Corbridge; rebuilding of the bridge at Willowford followed perhaps a little later. The rebuilding in stone of the remainder of the Turf Wall probably also took place after the return from the Antonine Wall. The final large-scale programme of work on the Wall was in the early third century when the Narrow Wall was replaced by the Extra-Narrow Wall in the central sector. At the same time all the turrets in this sector were demolished, and elsewhere one in every five or six turrets was removed. Demolition of the turrets was preceded by a period of disuse when their doors had been blocked. The Wall to the west of the Irthing was perhaps also rebuilt extensively in the Severan period. Subsequently, running repairs were made to the Wall and milecastles.

The structural sequence given in the preceding two paragraphs is generally clear enough and much of it had been worked out by the end of the 1930s. The chronology of the sequence, however, needs qualification to varying degrees at almost every point. In particular, the dating evidence for the various stages in the replacement of the Turf Wall in stone is unsatisfactory. The dating of the Extra-Narrow Wall depends on a *terminus post quem* supplied by a single group of unpublished pottery, and improvements in our understanding of pottery supply in the later second and early third century tend to suggest that the occupation of the demolished turrets continued for longer than was previously thought. The casual or running repairs to the Wall are very poorly dated, which deprives us of any real indications of when any attempts to maintain the continuous barrier were given up.

39. The southerly aspect of the Wall at Pike Hill

40. The view north from Limestone Corner

Inseparable from investigation of the structural sequence and chronology is the question of function. Bruce, Parker Brewis, and most notably Collingwood used the form of the Wall and the design of its installations to make deductions about the function of the Wall, although they reached different positions because they used different categories of evidence. Eric Birley and John Mann gave greater weight to general observations about Roman frontiers as a whole, and the latter, having stated that the Wall was a piece of imperial rhetoric, effectively denied that details of its design could be used to make any inferences about how it functioned as a barrier - it was there simply to impress and overawe. Breeze and Dobson combine these two approaches, studying the Wall in penetrating detail (and encouraging others to do likewise in specialised areas), while attempting to show how the use of the various installations on the Wall could fit into a generally consistent picture of frontier control around the empire, where the aim was to regulate the peaceful movement of people. Continuous barriers, whether natural or artificial, were not used as fortifications, and any attempt to force the frontier would be dealt with in the field. This is the view of Hadrian's Wall which is found in most general works on Roman frontiers, but it was always resisted by many involved in excavation and research on the Wall, from Gillam onwards. A particular problem, first raised by Collingwood, is the exceptional nature of Hadrian's Wall. If its function was the same as the *Pfahlgraben* (essentially a palisade replaced by a heaped-earth bank and ditch) or other artificial frontiers in Germany, why was it so much more elaborate and held in such greater strength? Frere has been the only modern writer in Britain to maintain Collingwood's argument that the differences corresponded to threats from beyond the frontier in Britain which were far graver than in Germany. The same explanation is favoured by those studying the limes at first hand in Germany.

Lively controversy encourages interest in a subject, but in this particular instance it has some dangerous implications. The opposing views necessarily carry with them contrary views about most political, social and economic aspects of society in the Roman and non-Roman north, and perhaps in Roman Britain as a whole. There is a risk that other areas of research, where clear results and a consensus might be easier to reach, will prove more attractive than a topic which is becoming increasingly complex and difficult. The need for more research in the field is self-evident, but that needs to be underpinned by some agreement about the principles and scope of archaeological argument. No better starting point could be found than in the philosophical works of Collingwood where he explained what he understood about historical method.

The Planning of Hadrian's Wall

J S Poulter

A recently devised test has enabled the directions of planning of Hadrian's Wall and the Vallum to be diagnosed (Poulter 2005; forthcoming a). Broadly, the Wall appears to have been planned inwards from the coast towards the crags. That is, the eastern sector seems to have been planned from east to west, from Newcastle to Sewingshields, whilst the western sector, running from Bowness-on-Solway to Carlisle and Carlisle to Walltown, was apparently set out from west to east. The Vallum, in contrast, generally appears to have been planned outwards from where each of the early Wall forts was sited or was due to be sited. The exception lies in the central sector, from Walltown to Sewingshields, where the Vallum runs at the foot of the crags and there it seems to have been set out uniformly from west to east.

The planning methods used by the Roman surveyors seem to have been similar to those used in setting out Roman roads. That is, the overall direction of travel would first be set out by means of long distance alignments, and then deviations from these alignments would be made in response to the local topography (Taylor 1982, 53-8; Lewis 2001, 218, 233-42; Poulter forthcoming b). Where the Wall and the Vallum differ from roads lies in their planning objectives. The objective for the Vallum appears to have been to set it out, as far as possible, in straight lines lying reasonably close to the rear of the Wall. As it happens, this results in alignments that are not unlike those typical of Roman roads, in their directness and disinterest in the local topography. The laying out of Hadrian's Wall, in contrast, shows a considerable concern with its positioning in the landscape, and, after much analysis, it appears that the primary objective for the Wall was to maintain a view to the south rather than the north.

This observation seems to complement the work of Woolliscroft, who has demonstrated that, at least in the central sector of the Wall, the positions of the turrets and milecastles along the Wall may have been adjusted to enable them to signal back to the Stanegate sites to the rear (Woolliscroft 2001, 58-67. The latest survey shows that the priority given to a rearward view now appears to extend all the way along Hadrian's Wall, even in the low-lying landscape to the east and west of Carlisle. The reasons for this south-facing aspect for the Wall are now being considered. The likeliest possibility is that the need to signal to the rear remained paramount all the way along Hadrian's Wall. The problem with this is that, as yet, no Roman military installations to the east of Corbridge are known to have been in commission at the time, and, apart from the fort at Carlisle, the contemporary picture to the west of the fort at Old Church, Brampton, also remains hazy (see p. 32). Hence other possible causes for a south-facing aspect for the Wall cannot yet be ruled out.

The Stone Curtain

P T Bidwell and P R Hill

The building programme

Construction of the Wall is traditionally believed to have begun at Newcastle with work proceeding westwards, the implication being that each part was completed before moving on to the next. This would not have been practical, and there will have been many gangs beginning on discrete sections all along the Wall, although perhaps with a predominance towards the east. Breeze and Hill (2001) have argued that work began at Portgate on Dere Street as the obvious primary access point. Symonds (2005) has put the case for the large milecastles 47 and 48 coming very early in the programme, a suggestion which would also explain the anomalous design of turrets 48a and 48b. The date of the start of work is not known, but the Roman army had been operating in the area for some 40 years, and preparation time could have been short enough to allow work to begin while Hadrian was still in the province.

41. The inscription from Milecastle 38 naming Hadrian and the governor Aulus Platorius Nepos

Inscriptions from four milecastles name Aulus Platorius Nepos as governor (*RIB* 1634, MC37; *RIB* 1637, *RIB* 1638, MC38; *RIB* 1666, MC42; *RIB* 1937, MC50 TW.) The dedication from milecastle 47 (*RIB* 1852) does not name the governor; this could be an indication that work began in an interregnum before Nepos arrived in the province in mid-122, but this is perhaps unlikely. There is clear evidence, at for example milecastle 37 and at turrets such as 26b, 33b, and 34a, that work on milecastles and turrets was still in progress when work was dislocated by major changes to the design of the Wall. At some point in the programme forts were added to the line of the Wall. *RIB* 1340 and 1427, from the portico of the granary at Benwell and the west gate at Halton Chesters respectively, show that at least some of this work was carried out under Nepos and that considerable progress had been made. Nepos probably left the province in 126. Another major change was the decision to reduce the gauge of the Wall from 10 Roman feet to 8 Roman feet (the standard Roman foot or *pes Monetalis* = 296mm). The point at which this took effect is not known, although the fact that the fort ditch at Chesters was backfilled to allow for, and that at Great Chesters respects, the line of the Broad Wall suggests that it came some time, although perhaps quite soon, after the fort decision was taken.

42. The Broad Wall at Denton

There is also no certainty about the time that elapsed between the start of work on the Wall and the implementation of the fort and Narrow Wall decisions. Milecastle 37 was certainly completed after the dislocation of work and still under Nepos, which may suggest that the fort decision was early in Nepos' governorship. The amount of Broad Wall surviving is actually very small. There are numerous points between T7b and the river North Tyne where small excavations in the 1930s revealed two or three courses of Broad Wall, and around T7b and T26b there are short lengths up to 2m high. But there are also many instances of Narrow Wall, at least some of which appear to be Hadrianic in date, such as between Planetrees and T26b. It is clear that work east of North Tyne was uncompleted while Broad Wall was begun between there and the river Irthing, although much less progress had been made.

The amount of surviving Broad Wall represents only a few weeks' work by a number of gangs spread out along the line. Of course, much may have been destroyed but it is important to remember that any wall is built in a series of horizontal courses, with a course being completed within the gang length before starting on the next course. Additionally there is a natural division into 'lifts' representing scaffolding levels. When the order to reduce the gauge was made, the builders would have narrowed the Wall in the same way as can be seen where the Narrow Wall overrides Broad wing walls, that is with a horizontal offset. It may be, although this is not susceptible of proof, that the surviving

Broad Wall is all that was ever built, and that it is Narrow Wall which has been lost. Either way the existence of a few Broad courses at the base of the Wall or a milecastle gives no indication of the gauge of the Wall at a higher level.

43. The north gate at Milecastle 37

Building seems to have begun to a reasonably high standard, with care being taken to achieve a decent, professional finish on those parts where large squared stones were needed; that is the milecastle gateways (see generally, Hill 2004). Evidence is very sparse, but the north gates of milecastles 10 and 37 show this. There was then some reduction in the degree of care taken, again visible at milecastle 37. Apparently very soon afterwards there was another change, this time with half-finished stones being fixed as though getting the work finished took priority over all else. There is very clear evidence for this at milecastle 37, probably at milecastle 10 (although the few stones there have been moved since excavation), and at the south gate of milecastle 42. The stone at milecastle 48 is so poor that no judgment can be made of the workmanship. The same changes are seen in the fort gateways. The north gate and east gates at Chesters started very well, with high quality work, but the latter was completed to a much lower standard, with one stone in the south-east pier very clearly unfinished. The same effect is seen at Birdoswald, with a good start to the west gate, some small deterioration, and a truly appalling third phase on the *spina*. This is mirrored at the *porta quintana dextra*. Given that Birdoswald was begun as a turf-and-timber fort, changed to stone before completion, with a hiatus in the building when part-completed, all these changes must have been followed very closely on one another, and to have begun very early in the building programme. It would also seem that work on milecastles and forts was proceeding in parallel. Much more excavation of gateways is needed before these theories can be attached to the Wall as a whole, or any definite conclusions can be reached.

Characteristics of the various stages in the construction of the curtain

The structural characteristics of the various phases in the building and renewal of the curtain of Hadrian's Wall can be summarised in tabular form (Table 2). The average dimensions are given and conceal wide variations (for which see Hill 2004, 19-23 and Appendix 1).

First in order of construction was the Broad Wall, which might have been largely completed to full height between Newcastle and Portgate (not accepted by Hill 2004, 139-49, but cf. Hill 2001, 13, and see above). Elsewhere the Broad Wall was only rarely built above the level of its footings and was completed to Narrow gauge. Between Portgate and the North Tyne the width of the Narrow Wall is consistently smaller than elsewhere and this seems to be a local variation which can be termed the Six-Foot Narrow Wall. It appears to be quite distinct from the Extra-Narrow (or Severan Wall) which replaced the Narrow Wall between milecastles 35 and 42. Replacement of the Turf Wall apparently began in the late Hadrianic period with the building of Narrow Wall (but without offsets) for four or five

Type	Width of footings		Foundations, type and width	Offsets
	Metric	Imp.		
Broad	2.9m	9ft 6in	Flagged, 0.35m (10ft) wide	A. Above 1st course B. Above 3rd or 4th course
Narrow	2.3m	7ft 6in	In trench, 2.45m (8ft) wide	Above 1st course
Narrow (6 feet)	1.8m	6ft	Uncertain	Above 1st course
Narrow, W of R. Irthing	2.3m	7ft 6in	Uncertain	No offset
Intermediate	2.45m	8ft	Flagged, 2.75m (9ft) wide	Uncertain
Extra-Narrow	1.8m or less	6ft or less	Uncertain	No offset?

Table2. Structural characteristics of the various stages in the construction and repair of Hadrian's Wall.

Wall miles to the west of the Irthing. Completion of the remainder, to Intermediate gauge, was undertaken after the return from the Antonine Wall or perhaps later. However, Hill (2004, 22-3, but cf. Hodgson and McKelvey 2006, 52) has shown that the supposed differences in dimensions between the Narrow Wall west of the Irthing and the Intermediate Wall are not clear-cut. The date of the replacement of the Turf Wall and its stages are still very much in question.

44. Surviving portion of Wall core at Hare Hill

The present state of knowledge is fragmentary. Table 2 shows that there are uncertainties about some of the most obvious structural characteristics of parts of the Wall such as the composition of the foundations or presence of offsets. It now seems certain that the Broad Wall generally had a clay and rubble core, with a poor brown mortar used for the facing stones in some places. The specifications for the Narrow Wall and its 6-Foot variation are less certain. The Extra-Narrow and Intermediate Walls had mortared cores and in some places herring-bone coursing is visible, but it is not known whether this typically later-Roman style of construction was universal in these two late stages in the building of the Wall.

The Wall nowhere survives to its full height and it is impossible to be certain whether it took the standard form of a Roman defensive wall, with a wall-walk protected by a parapet with merlons and embrasures. The alternatives which have been proposed are a wall with a simple parapet or one with a sloping top (Hill and Dobson 1992). The discovery of systems of obstacles on the berm supports the notion that the Wall was of the conventional defensive type (Bidwell 2005, 71-4).

Sources of materials

The Wall facing stones are almost exclusively of sandstone, which is readily obtainable between the rivers Tyne and Irthing. Just west of the Irthing the stone is covered by thick deposits of clay, and is visible only in deep valleys.

East of the Irthing there are numerous small quarries along the line many of which may well have a Roman origin, but in the absence of inscriptions or petrological assessments they cannot be certainly identified as such. The latter may only prove useful in a general way, as many sandstones vary little over long distances, but this will not be known until the exercise is undertaken. The quarry at Fallowfield Fell is proved by an inscription to be Roman (*RIB* 1442). It is very similar to that at Black Carts, a short distance to the north, which is where stone for Chesters Bridge is believed to have come. The side of the valley immediate west of Haltwhistle Burn fortlet carried a now destroyed inscription of Legion VI (*RIB* 1680), and thus presumably was used for Wall building.

Stone slates used for roofing the *praetorium* at Housesteads have been identified geologically as coming from a small quarry on the south side of the Military Road (Williams 1968). Further Roman quarries are identified by inscriptions, none of which are closely datable: the sandstone quarry at Queen's Crags, north of Housesteads, (Wright 1961, 194), Coombe Crag (*RIB* 1946-52), Lodge Crag (*RIB* 1953-4), and the group of quarries in Cumberland (*RIB* 998-1016). The proximity of the quarries to the Wall suggests that they were used for its building or rebuilding. The stone used for the gate piers and walling of milecastle 48 came from the adjacent valley of the Poltross Burn, despite the fact that it is not at all suitable for working large blocks.

Much of the Wall was probably built from small quarries opened all along the line, wherever reasonable stone could be found near enough to keep transport to a minimum. There is no evidence that the stone was carefully selected.

45. A reconstruction of the possible original appearance of the Wall at Wallsend

Repair and maintenance of the Wall

A distinction needs to be made between work that completed or renewed the Wall, such as the Narrow Wall or the replacement in stone of the Turf Wall, and running repairs needed to keep the curtain intact. The only apparent repair that was part of an overall programme seems to be the Extra-Narrow Wall (Crow 1991a and b). Large-scale rebuilding of the Stone Wall has also been suggested at turret 54a and near milecastle 79, but the evidence is capable of more than one interpretation. Vertical offsets visible at the rear of the Wall west of Housesteads probably represent repairs occasioned by the collapse of the original face. At Denton repairs of this type were of Severan or later date. Repairs of late third-century date are known just to the west of the fort at Wallsend. There seems to be epigraphic evidence for repairs to the Wall in 158 (see p. 152), but it cannot be connected with any structural remains.

46. A small quarry on Walltown Crags

A few observations in the eastern and central sectors suggest that the Wall was maintained in good order down to the end of the Roman period, but the sample is perhaps too small to be relied on (Bidwell 1999, 26).

State of preservation	Length in metres	% of total length of Hadrian's Wall
Fabric not visible	108,210m	91.49%
Destroyed in late nineteenth and twentieth centuries	1,440m	1.22%
Nineteenth-century restoration	2,416m	2.04%
Min. Pub. Build. Wks programme and continuation	6,055m	5.12%
Consolidated for display since 1985	159m	0.13%

Table 3. Estimate of the state of preservation of Hadrian's Wall.

Preservation and investigation

The table above showing the current state of preservation of the Wall is a broad estimate using a variety of OS maps, with some details confirmed by checking aerial photographs and a series of studies of specific stretches of Hadrian's Wall commissioned over the last ten years by English Heritage (unpublished). The figures must be regarded as indicative; a fuller survey, even if it relied only on documentary sources, would be a major undertaking. It is nevertheless considered that Table 3 below gives a tolerably accurate picture of how much of Hadrian's Wall is visible, and of how and when the visible stretches were uncovered, investigated and preserved.

47. The line of the Wall approaching Eppies Hill under the B6318

48. The line of the Stone Wall (top, under the modern road), Turf Wall and Vallum at High House

Commentary

A. Fabric not visible: this includes some stretches of the Wall which survive as earthworks, with no masonry visible. Much of the Wall in this category is buried under roads or, in the urban areas, is concealed under buildings.

B. Destroyed in twentieth century: lengths totalling approximately 700m were destroyed by quarrying at Walltown and Cawfields. Lengths totalling slightly more were obliterated where the A69 was built across the Wall in the 1970s and by the A1 by-pass at Denton in the late 1980s. Some stretches included in Category A above might also have been destroyed, although only a few cases are known where buildings or roads earlier than the later nineteenth century have entirely obliterated the Wall.

C. Nineteenth-century restoration: this represents the so-called Clayton Wall which is confined to the area west of Housesteads.

D. Ministry of Public Building and Works programme with its continuation: this was largely a post-war programme of clearance and consolidation that came to an end in the early 1980s. The programme was very largely confined to the Central Sector and the area immediately to the west of the River Irthing.

E. Consolidated for display (or in the process of consolidation) since 1985: these stretches were revealed as a result of comprehensive archaeological investigations in the Central Sector and at the eastern end of the Wall.

49. The Wall quarried away at Walltown quarry

Archaeological knowledge of the Wall is shown on Table 2. As might be expected, the largest gaps are in the Western Sector, but more surprisingly, there also many gaps in the Eastern Sector.

The Turf Wall

T Wilmott

The Turf Wall was the western counterpart of the Stone Wall, and formed the primary main curtain from the river Irthing at milecastle 49 to the western end of the Wall at Bowness-on-Solway. The reason for the contrasting construction materials of the curtain to east and west of the Irthing remains obscure, but may be at least in part due to the lack of limestone for mortar west of the Red Rock Fault, near turret 53b. It has been remarked at various times that the Turf Wall was more typical of Roman frontier works than the Stone Wall (Breeze 2006, 59).

Exploration

The existence of the Turf Wall was predicted by Cadwallader Bates (1895), and proved by Haverfield at Appletree in 1895 (Haverfield 1897, 187-191). By 1898 Haverfield had traced the course of the Turf Wall in the Birdoswald sector from milecastle 49 to milecastle 51 (Haverfield 1899, 347-51; Hodgson 1899). This section is the only place where the Turf Wall is known to follow a different course to its stone successor for any distance.

One of the objectives of Simpson's long-running campaign of excavation during the 1930s was the establishment of the length and character of the Turf Wall. Following the discovery of the Turf Wall in the Birdoswald-High House area, this question became important to the final unravelling of the history of the linear components of the frontier and their relationships one to another. The site of milecastle 50 TW was identified in 1933 and excavated in 1934 (Simpson, Richmond and St Joseph 1935a). This important excavation yielded a fragment of a wooden building inscription which, though heavily restored, suggests that the Turf Wall was constructed during the reign of Hadrian, and under the governorship of Platorius Nepos (AD 122-5/6) (Collingwood 1935b; *RIB* 1935).

50. A section through the Turf Wall

A series of exploratory excavations in the 1930s sought the sites of the characteristic Turf Wall milecastles and turrets (see p. 45-9). This operation moved steadily westwards from milecastle 50 until 1934, when the campaign had reached T57a near Castlesteads, and it was decided to make a jump to the far end of the Wall (Simpson et al 1935a, 213). The idea was to attempt to find the final turret on the line. If this was a free-standing, stone-built turret, without integral wing walls, it would be typical of the turrets of the Turf Wall, and would afford positive proof that the Turf Wall did indeed extend from the Irthing to Bowness-on-Solway; 'the [Cumberland Excavation] Committee's quest of forty years duration would be ended'. This approach was successful, turret 79b was found to be a Turf Wall turret, and the point was proven (Simpson, Richmond and McIntyre 1935, 217 8). This also meant, however, that the programme of methodical location of one site after another was suspended, and therefore this sector of the Wall, particularly in the stretch between Castlesteads and Burgh Marsh, has received little detailed archaeological attention.

Description

The Turf Wall was constructed on a flat base. At High House (Simpson, Richmond and St Joseph 1935a) this was constructed of three or four courses of laid turf blocks, but at and to the west of milecastle 72 at Burgh-by-Sands (Austen 1994, 38-40), and possibly at milecastle 53 (Simpson and McIntyre 1933a, 267-70) a basal layer of cobbles was built. The turf base of the Wall was normally some 6m wide. At High House, sufficient survived to suggest that the southern side of the Wall sloped at an angle of about 75%, while the north face was almost vertical towards the base, perhaps changing to a gentler slope higher up. The height of the Turf Wall has been

51. The reconstructed Hadrianic building inscription from Milecastle 50TW based on the surviving fragment

estimated at some 3.7m. The berm separating the Wall from the ditch, generally about 6m wide in the Stone Wall sector, is some 1.9 -2.4m for the Turf Wall, though wider berms have been recorded to the west.

The ideal picture of the Wall is that it was built of coursed turf blocks. Certainly where turf was available for building it was clearly stripped from the areas to the north and south of the Wall. This was graphically demonstrated at both Appletree and Crosby-on-Eden. At both sites the line of the Wall was marked out, and turf was then stripped from the areas north and south of the Wall line. The Wall was built by piling this material onto a band of turf which was left in situ to mark the desired line. This was most clear at Appletree, where the base of the counterscarp of the Wall ditch, the Vallum mounds, and a track to the south of the Wall were all placed upon natural boulder clay which had been denuded of turf and topsoil, and on which no regeneration had taken place (Wilmott forthcoming).

In actuality, the Wall appears to have been constructed using whatever materials were to hand, and Breeze (1982) has suggested that the term 'Earth Wall' would be more accurate. At Birdoswald the Wall was built following the clearance of dense woodland, where no convenient turfs were to hand, and it appears that the building material was brought from a few hundred metres north, having been stripped from the surface of the Midgeholme Moss (Wilmott 1997a, 50). The classic section at Appletree does not show turf block-work throughout, but turf facing-blocks going back into the core a certain distance, then a core of turf clods, unevenly deposited. This use of turf extended from Appletree (in Wall mile 51) as far west as milecastle 53 and resumed at turret 54b. At milecastle 54 and turret 54a however, clay was used. This area of clay construction apparently coincided with a belt of scrubland within which useful turf could not be found (Simpson and Richmond 1935b). At turret 54a, a turf-built rampart replaced the clay original, though even this included 'consolidated slime blocks' cut from a stream bed (Simpson, Richmond and McIntyre 1934a, 140) at the base. It is possible to speculate that the clearance of scrub had allowed the regeneration of turf for the construction of the replacement Wall. The Garthside area is the only place other than the Birdoswald sector where the Turf and Stone Walls are known to diverge.

A much-overlooked aspect of the Turf Wall relates to its course along the Solway coast. Excavations at milecastle 79 revealed that it had been built on a 'substantial sea-bank' (Richmond and Gillam 1952b), built of alternating layers of turf and gravel. This carried the curtain Wall along the edge of high-water mark and protected it from the encroaching sea. Only observed once, and never drawn in section, this would benefit from further research.

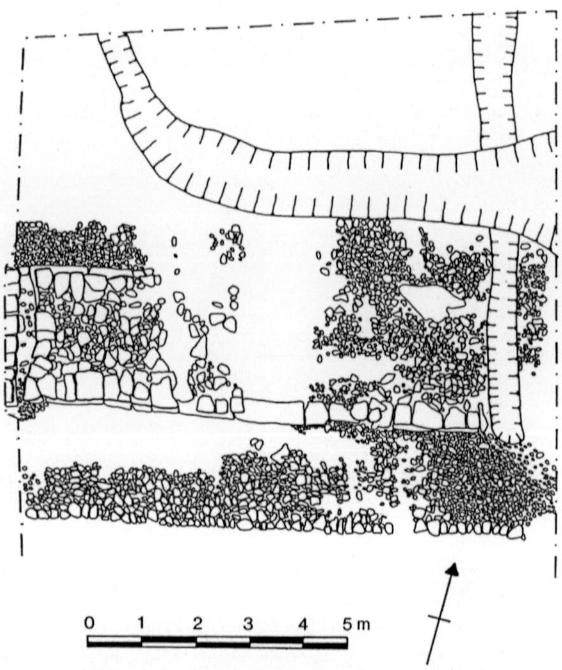

52. Plan of the Stone Wall built over the cobble base of the Turf Wall, west of Burgh-by-Sands

As with the Stone Wall, the treatment of the Wall-top is not known for certain. In a reconstruction drawn for Simpson (Simpson, Richmond and St Joseph 1935a) the Wall is reconstructed with a boardwalk on the top, and a breastwork of split timber. Evidence from pollen analysis at Appletree indicates a greater likelihood that if any breastwork was provided it might more likely have been of hurdling made from the birch and alder scrub woodland which grew in the area (Wilmott 2001a, 44; Wilmott forthcoming).

The destruction of the Turf Wall took place when the Stone Wall was constructed as its replacement. The lapse of time between the construction and destruction of the Turf Wall is demonstrated at Appletree by the fill pattern in the Turf Wall ditch. A peaty primary deposit formed, and the clay edges of the ditch slumped on top of it before the turfs of the Wall were dumped into the ditch from the north (Wilmott forthcoming). The deposition of the demolished Turf Wall into its ditch has also been noted at Birdoswald (Wilmott 1997, 47). On other sites, such as Crosby-on-Eden (Wilmott forthcoming), Stanwix (Smith 1978, 23-4) and Burgh-by-Sands (Austen 1994, 39) the Turf Wall material was not deposited into the ditch. This is probably because at Appletree and Birdoswald the construction of the Stone Wall on a new line, and the provision of a new ditch, made the primary Turf Wall ditch unnecessary. West of milecastle 51 the new Stone Wall was built on the line of the Turf Wall, and it was necessary to retain the primary ditch. At Crosby the occurrence of masonry chippings within the ditch defines the point at which the Stone Wall was constructed. As at Appletree, primary silt was followed by slumping, and the chippings appeared in the subsequent natural silting sequence. At Crosby spread material from the Turf Wall covered an area 20m wide to the south of the Wall. This was also partly sealed by masonry chippings from the building of the Stone Wall. By contrast on the berm between Wall and ditch there was no spread Turf Wall material, and the chippings lay on the ground surface. At Stanwix (Smith 1978, 23-4), Turf Wall material filled a hollow way to the south of the Wall. This evidence suggests a deliberate effort to ensure that the integrity of the ditch and berm to the north of the stone curtain was maintained from the Turf Wall phase in these areas.

Apart from the exceptions already noted at Appletree and Garthside, the stone replacement of the Turf Wall mostly followed the same line. The stone rebuilding of the Turf Wall seems to have occurred in two stages; the sector between the River Irthing and Wall mile 54 was built during the reign of Hadrian, with the remainder apparently replaced after the return from the Antonine Wall (Willis forthcoming).

It is characteristic of the Stone Wall in this sector that there is no foundation trench beneath the bottom course of stone, which consists of flat flags (cf. Simpson 1913, 301; 1932, 150). Often the facing stones of the flag foundation have a linear crack some 240mm from the face. This represents the pressure point where the face of the curtain wall stood on the flag foundation, which was offset to the north, and is a virtual signature feature of the Stone Wall in the former Turf Wall sector (Richmond and Gillam 1952, 19; Caruana and Fane-Gladwyn 1980, 21). The foundation width is generally some 2.75-2.89m. Often, the face of the Stone Wall was set back from that of its turf-built predecessor (Hodgson and McKelvey 2006, 50), and at Burgh-by-Sands the Stone Wall was built almost centrally on the cobble foundation of the Turf Wall.

Building Records from the Wall-curtain and Vallum

P T Bidwell

About 10% of the total number of inscriptions on stone from Britain consists of building records from Hadrian's Wall. The stones from the Wall-curtain and Vallum can be divided into eight categories, one of which includes 'anepigraphic' markings.

1. 'Centurial stones'. There are 211 stones (excluding those certainly or probably from the forts), which represent a total of 126 names of centurions (although in a very few cases they might be the names of ordinary soldiers). There are two main types: at least 94 stones give the cohort and century and at least 107 specify only the century (some are fragmentary and it is uncertain whether they named the cohort). The name of one centurion (Lousius Suavis) is given on six stones, and Cocceius Regulus certainly appears on four stones and probably on a fifth. Four centurions are represented by four stones each (Gellius Philippus, Caledonius Secundus, Julius Candidus and Valerius Verus), and many other names appear on two or three stones each.

53. Centurial stone of the century of Lousius Suavis found near Chesters

Forty-eight of the 211 stones are not in *RIB*, having been found after 1954, which is the cut-off date for inclusion in that volume. The later discoveries are published in *JRS* and from 1970 in *Britannia*, generally without photos or drawings. There have been very few finds since the 1960s, the most recent being stones of Gellius Philippus (at Willowford in 1986) and Hellenius (west of turret 22a, 1999). Both centurions are known from previous finds. An unknown but significant number of uninscribed stones with various types of borders either carried painted inscriptions or were prepared for carved inscriptions which were never executed (Whitworth 1994, 73).

54. Portion of building record carved on two sides of stone slab recording work done by the turma of Lucius A Fanus. Found near Turret 26b

2. 'PP' stones. Eight stones carry these letters and the centurial sign, for 'century of the *primus pilus*'.

3. (Supposed) cohort stones. Records of 10 or 11 stones (one might be a duplicate) show only the name of a cohort. Some look as if they are broken 'centurial stones' and the remainder do not seem to represent a regular series of building records.

4. Cohort and legion stones. There are two groups towards the eastern end of the Wall. Four such stones were reportedly found at Heddon in making the Military Road. One refers to rebuilding, and a fifth stone with the name of the Sixth Legion but not giving a cohort also carries a consular date of 158. In view of their scarcity elsewhere, it is likely that all these stones are of the same date and are associated with repairs to the Wall by the Sixth and Twentieth Legions. The second group is apparently from Denton and consists of three small stones of the Second Legion, all with elaborately decorated frames. They are perhaps also associated with repairs. The only other cohort and legion stones are two examples from towards the western end of the Wall.

5. Legionary stones. This is a very mixed category. There are only two stones of the size of the 'centurial stones' which give only the name of a legion, and three or four more elaborately-decorated legionary stones, one of which can be dated to the reign of Gordian. A group of Sixth Legion stones to the west of Birdoswald are all very similar in style, but they appear to be connected with the turrets and milecastles rather than the curtain (Mann 1990a). Two stones mention legionary vexillations.

6. 'Special' stones. The stones mentioning the *classis Britannica*, the *civitates* and the work done by Vindomoricus (if that is a personal name) have often been discussed and need only be noted here (see p. 152).

7. Numbers and other marks. These appear quite commonly. Numbers are recorded in *RIB* but there are some omissions and many subsequent finds. Other marks, for example crosses, saltires and phallic symbols, have not been systematically catalogued and published, although those noted in the recent English Heritage recording programme have been reported annually in Britannia (Whitworth 1994, 71-3).

8. Vallum stones. In 1936 five stones were found by the north and south mounds of the Vallum at Denton and a sixth stone was found to the west in 1953. One stone gave the name of an auxiliary unit, *cohors I Dacorum*, and the other five all seem to have named centurions. The stones, clearly building records for the Vallum, are thin, square slabs, and seven further examples, two with the names of different auxiliary units, have been recognised elsewhere on the Wall.

The total number of building records at present amounts to at least 275 and represents an epigraphic collection of outstanding potential. Brick-stamps apart, there is probably no other structure in the Roman world which has produced so much information which might indicate how its building was organised. C. E. Stevens made two detailed analyses of these records and their relationship with the fabric of the Wall. The first (1948) he (and others) regarded as not wholly satisfactory, and the second was written while the most informative series of stones was being found during the disinterment and restoration of the Wall to the east and west of the Irthing (Stevens 1966). The conclusions based on the second analysis were extremely complicated and tempered by many qualifications, partly because his arguments had to be adjusted as the new stones were found. Only the most general of his conclusions have been accepted by scholars subsequently (cf. Hooley and Breeze 1968), and it seems fair to say that the intricacies and back-trackings of the detailed arguments have persuaded many people that study of the building records in depth might well be a hopeless enterprise. A narrative of the building programme of the sort that Stevens was trying to write could well be impossible, but many other aspects of the stones might well prove very rewarding.

Systems of Obstacles on the Berm of Hadrian's Wall

P T Bidwell

Since 2000 systems of pits have been seen on the berm at ten sites in the easternmost 20km of Hadrian's Wall. All these observations have resulted from work undertaken in advance of development, often in very difficult conditions (Bidwell 2005a; Frain et al 2005; McKelvey and Bidwell 2005). As for the remainder of the Wall, there have been no opportunities to test for the pits by excavation, although a reassessment of old excavation records suggests that, at the very least, there was space for them along the entire length of the Wall except along the crags of the central sector. The pits were emplacements for timber uprights. They were filled to their tops around the bases of the uprights and were definitely not open pits containing sharpened stakes. The uprights were probably forked branches with sharpened, fire-hardened ends, described as *cippi* by Caesar or *cervi* or *cervoli* (in the sense of deer's antlers) by other writers such as Tibullus or Hyginus, their purpose being to form an impenetrable entanglement. This cannot be proved, so for the present they are best described simply as obstacles.

The systems of pits are usually arranged in three rows parallel to the Wall, although the pattern varies. A quite different type of obstacle has also been seen west of Wallsend - an irregular pattern of post-holes (i.e. the impressions of post bases driven directly into the ground) which is reminiscent of the *Flechtwerkzaun* (discontinuous lengths of fencing) on the Raetian limes. On three sites a small bank about 1.7m in width has been seen on the lip of the Wall-ditch, extending back to the outer line of pits. Its purpose seems to have been to block off the bases of the branches which formed the entanglement. At three sites it was clear that the pits were of more than one period. The original pits had either been re-dug, as at Byker, or were cut through by later pits, as at Throckley in Wall-mile 11 and at a site in Byker 420m to the west of the 2000-1 excavations (begun in 2006 and continuing).

The best indication of the date of the obstacles is the width of the berm, the exceptional width of which suggests that space was allowed for rows of obstacles in the original design, although their actual construction might possibly have been deferred to some later stage.

The Wall-ditch and Upcast

P T Bidwell

The ditch is perhaps the best-preserved feature of the entire Wall-complex. Except in the gaps, it was omitted along the crags of the central sector, and it was also dispensed with where the Wall ran long the left bank of the Eden and at some points on the Solway shore. Recent work by Welfare (2004) has shown that the profile of the ditch varies considerably and that there are additional points where it was not dug or where its dimensions are very slight. Material deposited on the north side of the ditch represents either a wide *glacis* or a much narrower counterscarp bank. In some places there was also a small bank on the south lip of the ditch, apparently blocking off the base of the entanglements of forked branches on the berm (Bidwell 2005). The ditch seems to have swung in towards at least some turrets, reducing the width of the berm from 6.1m to about 1.8m; at turret 11b the ditch seems to have been re-dug to form a berm of conventional width, and this may have been repeated at other turrets following their demolition. Finally, Wilmott (2006) has demonstrated that nowhere does the profile of the ditch correspond to the often-illustrated V-shape with a cleaning slot at its base.

55. Uncompleted ditch at Limestone Corner

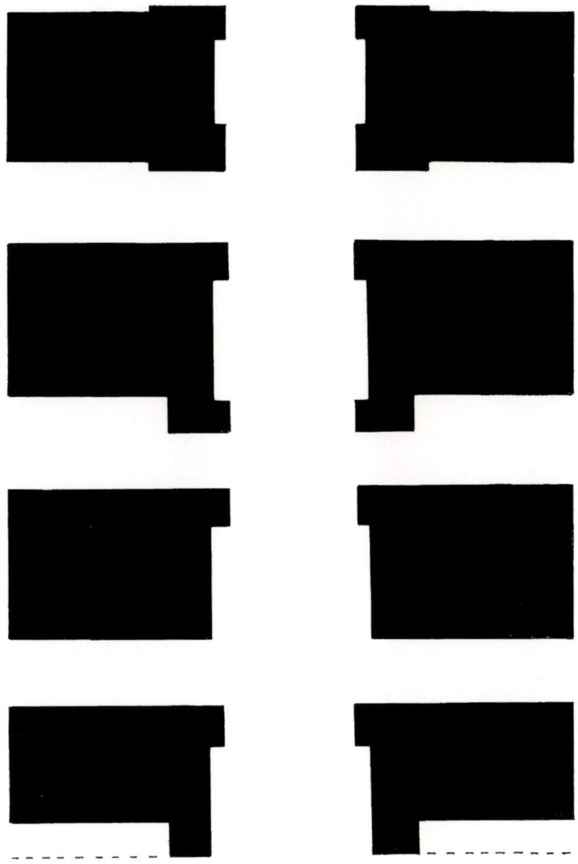

56. Milecastle gate types. From top, Type I, Type III, Type IV, Type II.

The Milecastles

M F A Symonds

The term 'milecastle' was introduced to the scholarly community in 1708 by Robert Smith, who noted that it was then current amongst the inhabitants of the Wall zone (Birley 1961a, 89). It is applied to an installation type that is recognisable as an adaptation of the fortlet class and was spaced at intervals of approximately 1 Roman mile (1,479m) along the course of the Wall. Physically anchored into the frontier curtain, which served as a north rampart, the milecastles normally contain two gates and permitted passage through the frontier. They were constructed of stone on the Stone Wall and of turf on the Turf Wall. Milecastles are small by the standards of freestanding fortlets, with an average internal area of 277m^2 on the Stone Wall. The largest attested example, the stone rebuild of milecastle 52, enclosed 644m^2. The original scheme would have seen the milecastles holding the bulk of the forces stationed on the Wall line. However, the 'fort decision' fundamentally altered this relationship and the full consequences of this for the milecastle sequence remain incompletely understood. Welfare has observed that 'much of the debate about the changing function of Hadrian's Wall centres around the role of the milecastle...' (Welfare 2000, 14), while Dobson dubbed them 'one of the great mysteries of the Wall' (Dobson 1986, 9).

The milecastles were numbered 1-80, from east to west, by Collingwood in 1930(a), and Hill (2001) has recently put the case for a milecastle 0. West of milecastle 9 their locations are, with the exception of the stretch between milecastles 65 and 71, reasonably certain. East of milecastle 9, under modern Newcastle and Wallsend, the picture is less clear. Much of our information is dependent on antiquarian observations, with Stukeley, Horsley, MacLauchlan and others all recording possible sites. However as Hill (2001, 3) observed, the locations they identify do not coincide. Furthermore, the Westgate Road milecastle does not correspond with the measured locations of milecastles 4 or 5, although it is currently considered most likely to be the former. The distance between MacLauchlan's milecastle 1 and the Westgate Road milecastle is 271m longer than 3 Roman miles, while the stretch west to milecastle 9 is 282m less than 5 Roman miles (Hill 2001, 11). The slight variations in intervening distance between the milecastles elsewhere on the curtain prevented them from occupying streams or split-levels. Woolliscroft (1989) has also demonstrated how they would complement a signalling system linking the milecastles and turrets with the Stanegate forts in the central sector. Despite this limited flexibility, the overall system is remarkably rigid and the awkward relationship that a number of milecastles enjoyed with the local topography has been well documented.

The provision of gates through the frontier barrier has earned the milecastles the epithet of 'fortified gateways' (Breeze and Dobson 2000, 33). Four different stone gateway types are recognisable in plan, although type II is a Narrow Wall adaptation of type IV. These were attributed to named legions, but as Hill (1991, 36; see p. 37-9) has pointed out, it is unlikely the legions commemorated on the building inscriptions are the same as those that commenced work there, due to a dislocation during the construction phase. The north and south gates in the stone installations are mirror images, yet what little is known of the turf milecastles indicates less uniformity. At milecastle 50 TW the north gate structure consisted of 10 posts, while the south had 6. It is generally assumed that both gates carried towers (Hill and Dobson 1992, 36), although the matter remains contentious (Crow 1988, 147; Breeze 2006, 67). The regular spacing of the milecastles has resulted in gates that are not always in the most apposite locations. Exceptionally, the 30m vertical drop to the north of milecastle 35 is acknowledged by the apparent absence of a north gateway. Indeed, there is no indication that a north tower was erected here either. The fundamental question of whether civilians were permitted to pass through the milecastle gates remains unresolved. Welfare (2000) has discussed the futility of having gateways through the Wall without an attendant provision to cross the ditch, and concluded from field survey that earth causeways were originally retained at these points.

57. Milecastle 35, directly south of a 30m drop on Sewingshields Crags

Two types of milecastle are discernible in plan and known as either long or short axis. The single known exception is the stone rebuild of milecastle 79, which was square. On the Stone Wall, all known short-axis milecastles, and the long-axis milecastle 18, have type I gates. All other long-axis installations have type IV / II or III gates. Hunneysett (1980) has discussed the implications of differences in the use of setting-out lines when constructing the milecastles.

Simpson believed that the Broad and Narrow gauges found on the curtain were replicated in the milecastle perimeter walls (Simpson 1931, 310). Milecastle wall widths range from 2.9-2.1m on the Stone Wall and 2.5-2m on the rebuilt Turf Wall. It is likely that those milecastles with Broad perimeter walls were begun during the lifespan of the Broad curtain and Symonds (2005) has suggested that at least some were completed to this gauge. The majority of milecastles on the Stone Wall with Narrow side and south perimeters have a Broad north wall. This has been attributed to either the completion of milecastles designated for modular construction after the reduction to Narrow gauge (Stevens 1966, 53) or a policy to provide narrower perimeter walls from the start (Hooley and Breeze 1968). Wilmott's confirmation that the short-axis milecastle 14 had Broad ramparts means that all three Stone Wall milecastle types are known to have been initially constructed to the Broad gauge. The building schedule may have been influenced by a desire to complete first those milecastles in areas where the topography facilitated unregulated north-south transit across the Wall line (Symonds 2005, 72).

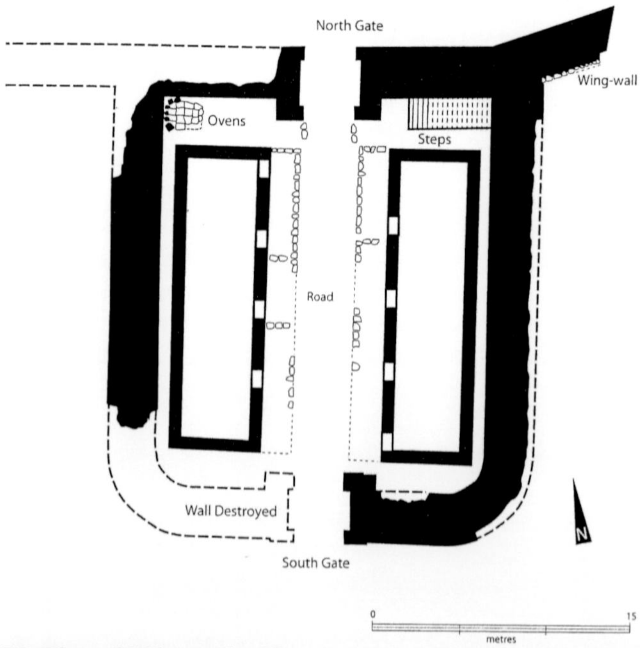

58. Plan of Milecastle 48

There is evidence for the primary internal arrangements of six of the milecastles: 9, 35, 37, 47, 48 and 50 TW, with some details also available for 39. With the exception of 50 TW, the known barrack blocks are of stone and it remains possible that they had timber predecessors. There are indications of wooden structures in some of the Stone Wall milecastles. A posthole was detected in the western half of milecastle 9 (Birley 1930, 156), while early timber buildings in milecastle 39 have been associated with construction work (Woodside and Crow 1999, 40). Nevertheless, the one certain example of a Hadrianic milecastle barrack block, from milecastle 50 TW, is sufficiently similar to the stone examples from milecastles 9, 35 and 37 to sustain the possibility that they accurately reflect the original internal layout. If so, then the discrepancy between the large double barrack blocks in milecastles 47 and 48, and those in milecastles 9, 35, 37 and 50 TW is marked. It has been suggested that this equates to a divergence in garrison size from 8 to 32 (Breeze and Dobson 1972, 188-9). The remains of a stone staircase providing access to the rampart were found in milecastle 48. Stone ovens are widespread. Milecastles 9, 23, 25, 29, 51 and 73 had perimeter ditches.

In addition to the famous building inscriptions (see p. 37) altars and tombstones have been found in or near thirteen milecastles. Religious dedications are most common, with Cocidius the named deity on eight inscriptions at six sites (Breeze 2002b, 60). The altar found outside milecastle 19 (*RIB* 1421) refers to an accompanying temple and it should be noted that the immediate vicinity of the milecastles has only rarely been investigated. Geophysical survey at milecastle 73 suggested the presence of undated extramural timber buildings and these deserve further attention (Biggins, Hall and Taylor 2004e). Finds from the milecastles include a range of pottery types, coins, tools, weapons, spindle whorls, millstones, lamps, gaming counters and boards. Particularly interesting are a plumb-bob casing from 79, harness pieces from 40 and 48, and a wooden writing tablet from 50 TW. Allason-Jones has commented on the similarities to material found in the turrets, while noting the absence of finger rings and intaglios from the latter. She also uses a concentration of finds with Wheel motifs to suggest that milecastle 35 was manned by a detachment from Housesteads (Allason-Jones 1988, 217-218).

59. Excavator's reconstruction of Milecastle 50TW

Post-Antonine milecastle use

The advance into Scotland was accompanied by the removal of the milecastle gates, an act which necessitated the destruction of their pivot holes. One of the first steps in reinstating Hadrian's Wall as a viable frontier line must have been to replace both elements. Welfare has argued that it is likely that 'in the later second century the role of each milecastle was evaluated individually, according to its geographical and tactical position' (Welfare 2000, 18). At around this time the large milecastle double gates were removed and replaced by narrow posterns or, at milecastle 22, fully blocked. Most of the milecastle ditch causeways may also have been eliminated during this period (Welfare 2000, 13). The Westgate Road milecastle and a number of milecastle gate towers elsewhere may have been demolished. Tower superstructure from milecastle 79 SW was found in a pit containing early-third-century pottery (Richmond and Gillam 1952b, 19-20), while voussoirs from the north gate at milecastle 48 lay between the secondary pivots and the reducing wall (Gibson and Simpson 1911, 411-413).

There is evidence for a third-century expansion of internal buildings in at least some milecastles. In milecastle 9 the existing stone barrack was enlarged and a further stone building erected in the western half (Birley 1930, 157-158). However, there are no indications of the nature of this occupation, and it cannot be dated with any precision. There is a comparable increase in internal buildings at milecastle 35, with pottery suggesting that they survived into the early fourth century (Haigh and Savage 1984, 39-44). No coins from between AD 180 to 259 are known from the milecastles. The most recent analysis of the pottery, from milecastle 35, suggests occupation continuing throughout the third century, but notes that this may over-represent actual occupation as the examples given as early third century could be late second (Haigh and Savage 1984, 111).

Milecastles 9, 35, 37, 38, 39, 48, 50, 51, 54 and 79 have yielded fourth-century material, but associated structures remain scarce. The south gates at milecastles 51 and 52 were rebuilt in the late third or early fourth century with monumental uprights. (Simpson and Richmond 1935c, 252-256). Fourth-century 'chalet-style' structures have been reported from milecastle 39 (Woodside and Crow 1999, 38), but the most detailed evidence for internal arrangement comes from milecastle 35. At around the start of the fourth century this site appears to have been cleared and levelled. The fourth-century buildings are judged 'cruder than their predecessors', while part of the interior was devoted to metal-working. By the last third of the fourth century, the excavators concluded that the structure 'may no longer have been recognisable as a milecastle' (Haigh and Savage 1984, 46-51).

The Turrets

M F A Symonds

Together with the milecastles, the turrets created a regular sequence of small installations physically anchored into the frontier curtain. The now-familiar pattern of two turrets between every milecastle was confirmed during the closing years of the nineteenth century (Birley 1961a, 103-105), while Collingwood (1930a) devised the convention of numbering the turrets after the adjacent milecastle to the east, with the annotation 'a' or 'b'. This structural sequence served to subdivide the Wall-miles into thirds, resulting in an average distance of 495m between the smaller Wall installations (Breeze 2006, 68). Where the Wall miles vary in length, the turrets were usually positioned at approximately the one-third and two-thirds point between consecutive milecastles, rather than strictly measured third-of-a-Roman-mile intervals. It has been suggested that some of these variations are attributable to the need for the turrets to be intervisible with Stanegate sites (Woolliscroft 1989). The turrets are exceptional in being constructed of stone on both the stone and turf stretches of curtain, although there are differences in plan between the resultant structures. Both types had entrances at ground level and these were positioned at either the eastern or western end of the south wall, a variation attributed to work by different legionary gangs. The decision to add a series of forts to the Wall precipitated demolition at a number of sites where turret construction had been advanced to an uncertain stage, including Chesters (27a), Housesteads (36b), Birdoswald (49a TW) and possibly Burgh-by-Sands (71b).

The presence of Broad wing-walls projecting from a majority of the known Stone Wall turrets indicates that work commenced prior to the construction of the linking stretches of curtain, although it remains disputed whether the turrets would have been completed to full height at this stage (see Hill and Dobson 1992, 39-40). The face of a Stone Wall turret that was flush with the curtain, the north in almost every instance, was wider than the others, though still narrower than the curtain, resulting in a recess at ground level. The remaining walls were normally of equal width, with variation in size between turrets usually attributed to building styles rather than intended height (Hill and Dobson 1992, 38). The internal area at ground level ranges from 3.4m - 4.1m north-south and 3.4 - 5.8m east-west, excepting the anomalous 44b which measured c. 3m square (Hill 1997, 44).

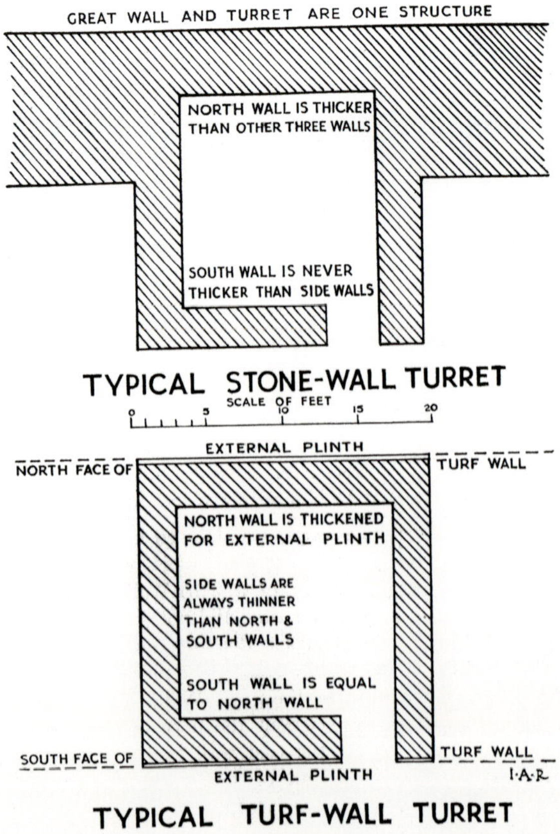

60. Plan of generic Stone Wall and Turf Wall turrets

The Turf Wall turrets were constructed to different specifications. These had narrower north walls, which were equal in width to the south wall, though wider than the east and west walls. The turrets measured c. 5.8m externally, and so were entirely enclosed by the 6m-wide base of the turf curtain. The north and south walls were gradually narrowed by external plinth courses, presumably in accordance with the tapering turf curtain. The narrower north wall resulted in a marginally more generous internal area of c. 4.2m north-south and c. 4.4m east-west. When the Turf Wall was rebuilt in stone, the north faces of the turrets were left projecting beyond the curtain, exceptionally by as much as 1.2m at 72b (Simpson, Hodgson and Richmond 1952, 15). Some have attributed this to the need to line up the rampart walk with pre-existing entrances into the towers. The re-routing of the Stone Wall around Birdoswald resulted in the obsolescence and demolition of turrets 49b-50b TW. Their replacements were constructed so as not to project beyond the curtain face, with walls of the Stone Wall specifications.

There is an important sequence at Garthside, where the original turret 54a collapsed (Simpson, Richmond and McIntyre 1934a). A new stretch of turf curtain and ditch was built to the north, while a replacement tower was constructed to the south. The pottery suggests that this was erected late in Hadrian's reign (Welsby 1985, 75-76). The provision of a freestanding tower has been used as an argument against the presence of a wall-walk (Breeze 2006, 327), although ultimately it was incorporated within a stone curtain of Intermediate width.

61. The collapsed north turret at Garthside, with its replacement to the south

Three turrets are exceptional to the overall sequence, being planned either before the frontier scheme, or after construction was considerably advanced. Both turret 45a and the Pike Hill tower in Wall mile 52 appear to pre-date the Wall proper, although this is disputed for the former (Crow 1991b, 62; Woodfield 1965, 166; Simpson and McIntyre 1933b, 272). These towers would originally have functioned in conjunction with the Stanegate forces. The workmanship of turret 45a is characterised as third rate, while Pike Hill surpassed the Wall turrets in terms of quality and stood on faced, mortared-rubble foundations (Hill 1997, 28-29). While 45a was incorporated into the Wall scheme, the retention of the Pike Hill tower did not prevent the construction of turret 52a less than 100m to the west. The Peel Gap turret was added to Wall-mile 39 at a point midway between turrets 39a and b where the curtain crosses a natural defile. The turret abuts the Narrow Wall (Crow 1991b, 53) and has walls of rough boulders and slabs with 'the appearance of having been built by a gang not well accustomed to the work' (Hill 1997, 29). Additional towers were also provided at the bridges (see p. 53-4).

62. Peel Gap Turret under excavation

There have been a number of attempts to reconstruct the superstructure of the turrets. A pyramidal roof similar to that portrayed on Trajan's Column is often considered most appropriate to the northern frontier (Hill and Dobson 1992,

41), although merlon capstones more consistent with a flat roof and crenellated parapet have been found (Crow 1991b, 61). Estimates of turret height vary according to the number of storeys preferred, with modern estimates ranging from 8 - 11.8m. A single voussoir from turret 44b suggests arched windows, and there is circumstantial evidence for the provision of at least one window on the ground floor of the Stone Wall turrets (Birley 1930, 150; Woodfield 1965, 120). Window glass has only been found at five sites (Breeze 2006, 71), so most windows were probably open or shuttered. Those turret doors that turned on pivots opened outwards (Brewis 1932, 199), and it has been observed that the corresponding upper pivot hole would best suit a flat lintel (Hill and Dobson 1992, 39). The arch at turret 44b would be appropriate for a door, although the absence of a formal threshold slab or pivot hole here suggests that the door was hinged (Hill 1997, 35). Stone platforms have been found inside a number of turrets, with that in turret 18a incorporating five steps and rising to a height of almost 1m (Brewis 1932, 202). An accompanying timber ladder (Brewis 1932, 202-203) or stair (Hill 1997, 37-39) would have provided access to the upper storeys. Platforms were normally positioned against the south wall, although they occur against the north wall in a number of Turf Wall turrets. There is considerable variation in quality and no consensus that all such structures had an identical purpose.

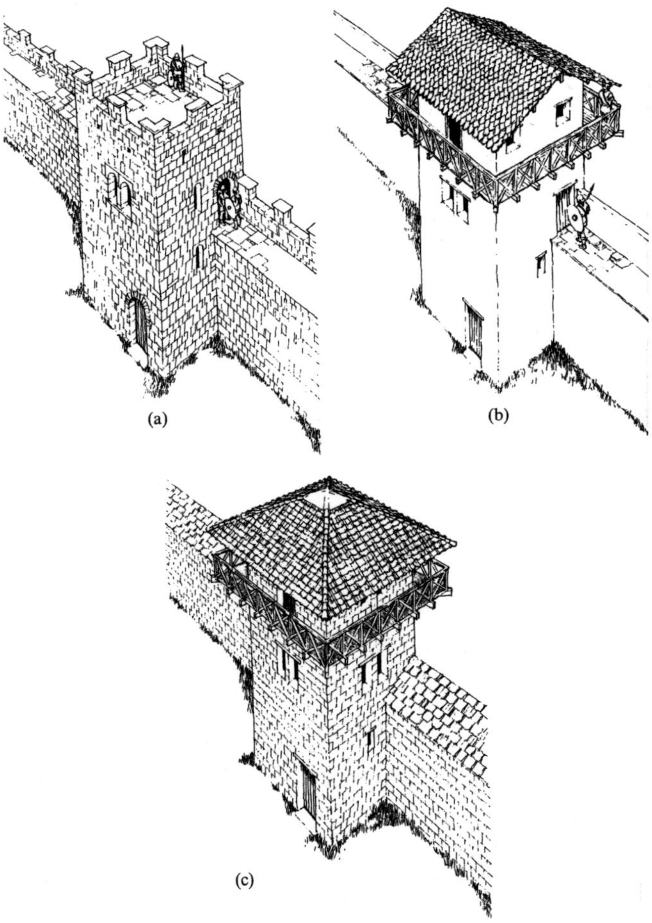

63. Three possible reconstructions of the Stone Wall turrets and Wall top

There is only evidence for the layout of the ground floor of the turrets. Hearths are common, although their locations vary, with some central and others positioned against the walls. Exceptionally, hearths in turrets 10a and 18b were placed on the entrance threshold and are incompatible with a functional door (Bennett 1983, 34; Woodfield 1965, 90). It has been suggested that the ground floors served as a mess area, containing food waste and broken equipment. Straw marks preserved on metal objects from 51b and a corroded coin with impressions of heather from 18b are consistent with organic carpeting (Woodfield 1965, 96; 173), while Allason-Jones has remarked that the loss of reusable items has implications for the conditions within the turrets (Allason-Jones 1988, 217).

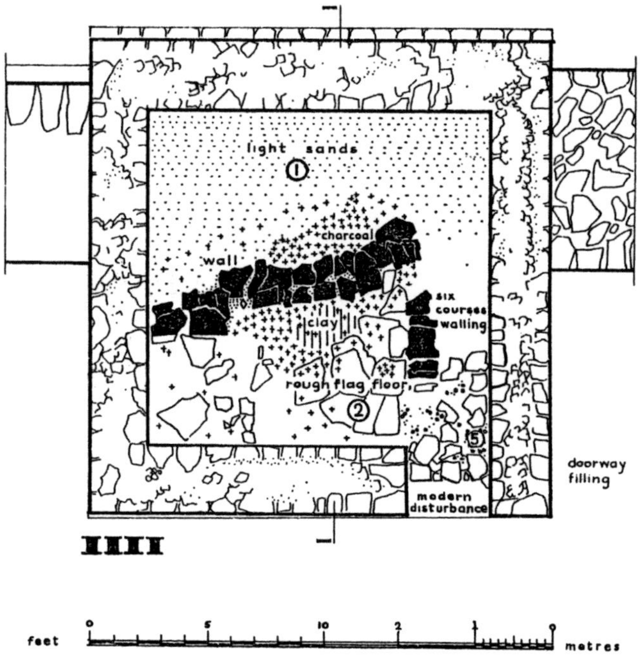

64. Plan of final phase of occupation at Turret 51b

The later history of the towers is not fully understood. They appear to have been reoccupied following the return from the Antonine Wall, although it is uncertain how intensive this was. Post-Hadrianic occupation at 33b has been described as 'very brief or spasmodic' (Miket and Maxfield 1972, 158), and a number of turrets were abandoned and then demolished in the late second or early third century. When demolition occurred, the recess into the curtain was blocked. The turrets on the central sector seem to have been judged most superfluous, with none between 33b and 41b known to have survived (Breeze and Dobson 2000, 136). Elsewhere the picture is more complex. Unstratified pottery from Pike Hill and 52a suggest they survived into the fourth century, even though they lie within 100m of each other. The latest feature preserved at 52a was a stretch of rough walling, in the correct position to act as a blocking wall, but without a rubble core (Simpson and Richmond 1934b). Turret 50a (SW) was abandoned in the second century and had its recess built up, while 51b went out of use, but does not appear to have been demolished. Its recess remained open and an undated rough hut was eventually built in the interior (Woodfield 1965). A comparable structure was detected in 7b, although the excavators assigned this to the eighteenth century (Birley 1930, 148-149).

Frontier Gates

M F A Symonds

While the overwhelming majority of the gateways through the frontier curtain lay at the milecastles or forts, a

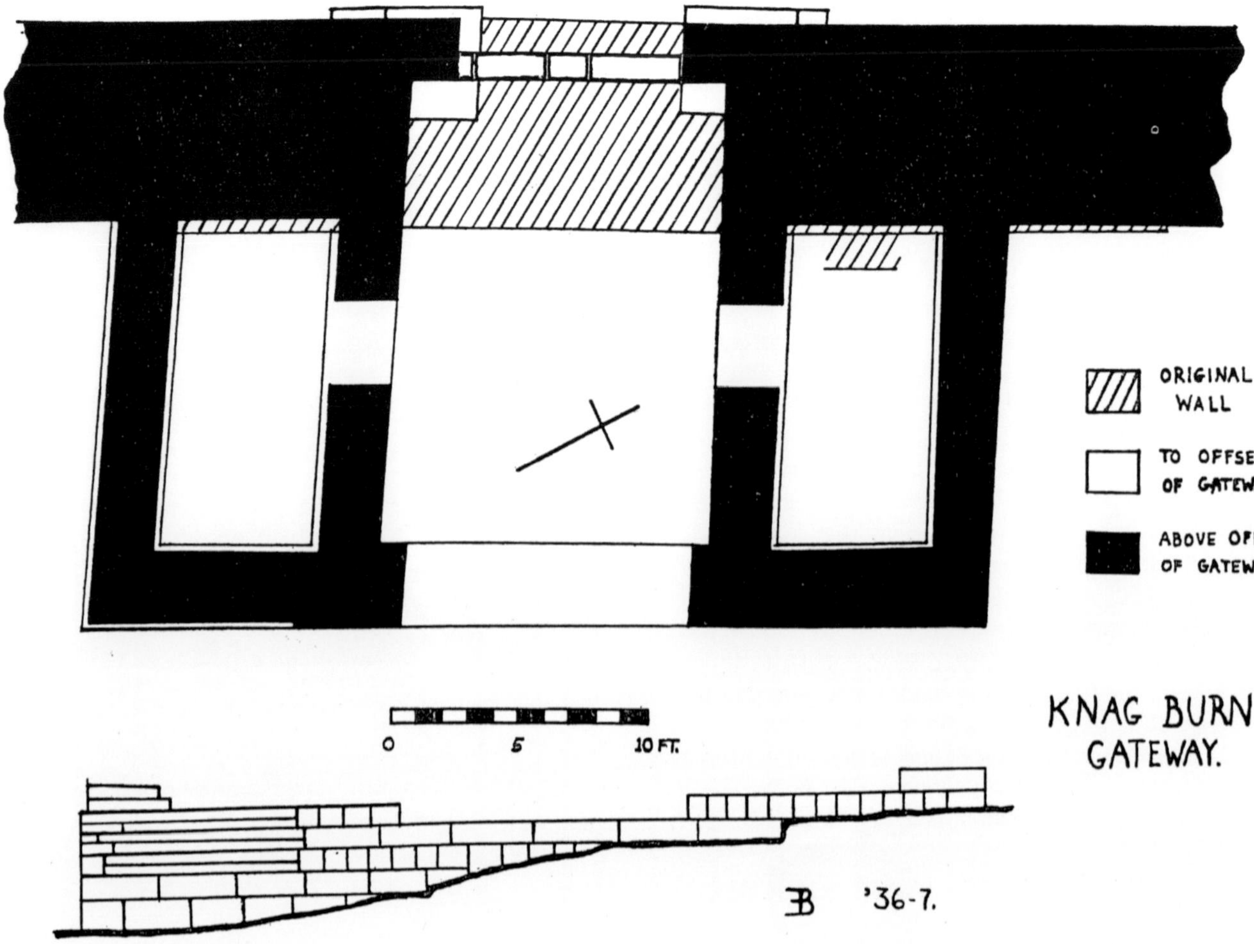

65. The Knag Burn Gate

small number of access points that were independent of these installations are known or suspected. The Portgate lies just west of milecastle 22, at the point where Dere Street crosses the line of the Wall. Horsley (1732, 121; 143) reported that this structure was comparable in size to a milecastle, about 17m square, but placed astride the Wall. The Wall ditch was diverted north to avoid it. Part of the north face of the Portgate was detected in 1966, projecting c. 3.5m beyond the curtain. The west side of the gate structure consisted of four large masonry blocks with a total length of 2.9m. Charlesworth (1967b, 208) noted that these dimensions are more consistent with a projecting gateway than the castellum described by Horsley. A similar provision is assumed to the west of Stanwix fort, where another major road crossed the frontier, but no trace of it has yet been found.

More structural details are available for the Knag Burn gateway, which lay in a valley only 100m north-east of Housesteads fort. It was discovered in 1855 and excavated by Clayton (1855-1857), before being re-examined by Birley (1937; see also Frere 1989, 273). The gateway is a secondary feature that required the demolition of a short stretch of Narrow Wall. The passage was flanked by two small guard chambers and accessed via a single, arched portal at the inner and outer ends. Clayton found fourth-century coins at the site, but there is no direct evidence for its construction date. Further gates have been proposed near Newcastle fort, in Wall mile 28, east of Great Chesters and near Carvoran, but these remain speculative (Birley 1961a, 111).

The Vallum

T Wilmott

Exploration

The Vallum is unique to Hadrian's Wall. It is a huge earthwork which runs from coast to coast south of the Wall. It was first mentioned by Bede (*Historia* I.12), who referred to a vallum, or earthern rampart, in distinction to the Wall or *murus*. We still use the term despite the fact that the essential element is a ditch, or *fossa*. It was for long thought that the Vallum pre-dated the Stone Wall, with the most elaborate phasing presented by Hutton (1802), who thought that the extant structure was a combination of Agricolan and Hadrianic phases. The first excavation was undertaken at Great Hill in 1893 (Holmes 1893), where it was observed that the Vallum ditch was cut through a seam of fire-clay which was deployed in both mounds, demonstrating that the main north and south mounds were both contemporary, and built using material won from the ditch.

Simpson and Shaw's (1922) paper on the Vallum has been superseded by more recent work, with the PhD thesis by Brenda Heywood and the 1965 article that derived from it providing the most recent thorough assessment.

The Vallum in the sequence of Hadrian's Wall structures

The sequence is now clearly understood. The fact that the Vallum was diverted to skirt the south side of many forts shows that it was conceived either contemporaneously with, or after, the fort decision, and this is confirmed by the

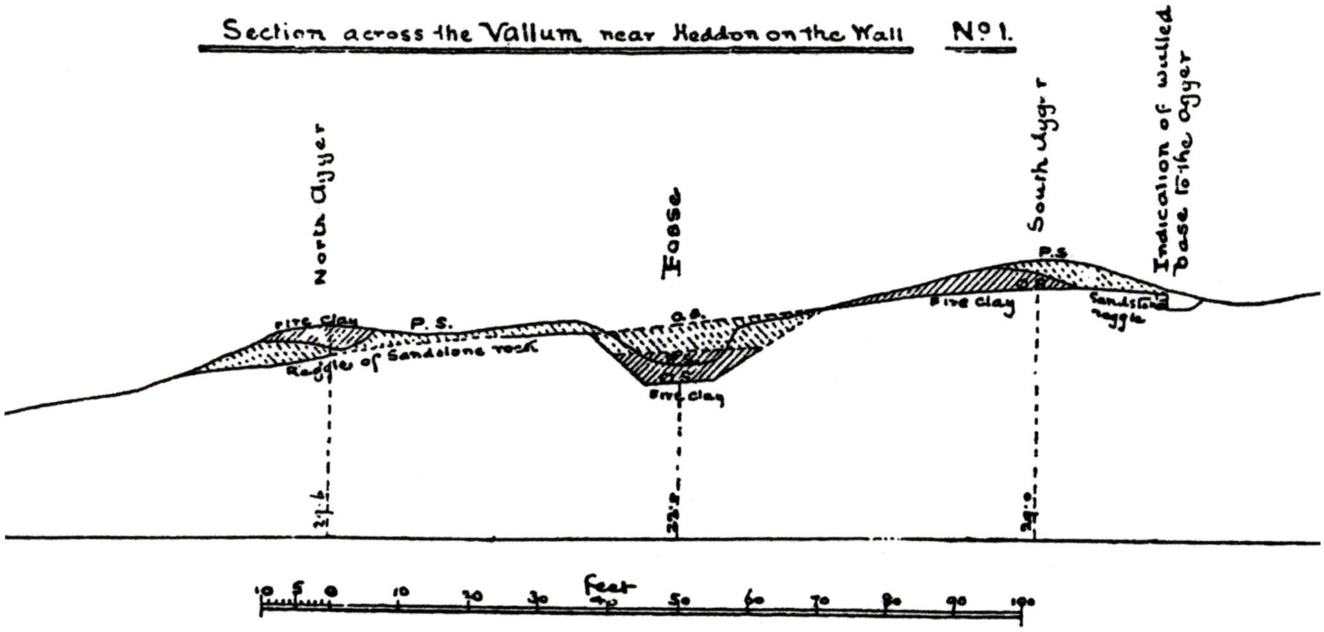

66. Section number 1 through the Vallum at Great Hill in 1893

retention of causeways of unexcavated material to the south of the forts. Great Chesters is epigraphically dated to c. AD 128 (*RIB* 1736), and a Vallum causeway was provided, indicating that the Vallum was later or contemporary with this date. The secondary fort at Carrawburgh (c. AD 130 - 133; *RIB* 1550) was built over the levelled and backfilled Vallum. At Birdoswald, pottery from the Vallum upper fill dates the backfilling of the Vallum to the late Hadrianic or early Antonine period (Wilmott, Cool and Evans, forthcoming).

Course and layout

The distance of the Vallum from the Wall varies. In general there was a preference for the earthwork to run close to the rear of the Wall where topography allowed. In the central sector the Vallum, laid out in long straight stretches, lies in the valley to the south of the Whin Sill. Similarly, from milecastle 68 to Bowness-on-Solway the Wall follows the line of high ground along the rivers Eden and Solway, while the Vallum, again in economical long, straight, alignments, follows the nearest practicable line. Between Kirkandrews-upon-Eden and Burgh-by-Sands this creates the broadest distance between Wall and Vallum on the entire line.

67. The Vallum ditch at Limestone Corner

Morphology and formation process

Classically, the Vallum comprises a steep-sided ditch, nominally 6m wide and 3m deep, with a flat bottom, flanked by two mounds, north and south, each set back some 9m from the ditch edges. For a great deal of its length a third mound, the so-called marginal mound occupies the south berm, right on the southern lip of the ditch. While excavation has shown that the depth and profile of the Vallum ditch can vary, the 6m width seems to be reasonably constant.

68. The Vallum at Cawfields

The design was adapted to meet local conditions, in particular the nature of the subsoil and geology. Variations such as the presence or absence of turf kerbs to the mounds, revetments to the ditch or differing ditch profiles are therefore largely matters of local detail rather than broader significance (Heywood 1965, 85-86). At White Moss in Wall Mile 60, marshland was crossed by a Vallum of four mounds. This effectively created a continuation of the ditch almost in embanked form (Haverfield 1895, 460-462; Hodgson 1897, 392). A determination to complete the Vallum ditch is also shown at Limestone Corner, where famously the Wall ditch is incomplete, while the Vallum ditch drives through the solid dolerite geology and is not intermitted. Indeed one of the main features of the Vallum in its primary form is the fact that the ditch is never interrupted, except at the primary crossing points provided at the forts. One other crossing has been claimed as original, that at milecastle 50 TW, where the excavation report (Simpson, Richmond and St Joseph 1936) interprets the Vallum crossing as part of the first conception of the works. A similar feature at the adjacent site of Wall Bowers is far less convincing, and even the milecastle 50 TW example is open to reinterpretation (Heywood 1965, 87).

69. The marginal mound (centre) and south Vallum mound (right), Cawfields

The idea that a service track or road was included in the Vallum system was suggested by Birley (1961a, 123). Metalling has been observed on the south berm at Black Carts (Wilmott, forthcoming) and Burgh-by-Sands (Austen 1994, 41). It has been detected on the north berm at Appletree (Daniels 1978, 217; Wilmott forthcoming), west of Limestone Corner, at Carvoran, High Shield (Wall mile 38), Mosskennels (Wall mile 35), near milecastle 34, and Down Hill (Wall mile 20) (Heywood 1965; Bidwell and Holbrook 1989, 152). These occasional patches of metalling do not add up to a system of communication - none was seen at Denton, for example, and they were probably installed for short-term local reasons.

Very few full ditch sections have been excavated under modern conditions, and the silting examined. The exceptions are:

1 A full section of the ditch at Denton (Bidwell and Watson 1996 35).
2 A full section of the Vallum at Appletree (Wilmott forthcoming)
3 A full section of the Vallum at Black Carts (Wilmott forthcoming)
4 A full Vallum section at Crosby-on-Eden (Bennet forthcoming),

What emerges from an examination of these, alongside the few other adequately recorded and full sections of ditch fill is that there is little or no evidence of human intervention in the ditch following its cutting.

Two further elements of the Vallum need to be considered, as they do show evidence of interference after the Vallum was constructed - these are the secondary crossings and the marginal mound. The marginal mound occupies part of the south berm. It has often been stated that the marginal mound comprises mixed material which has been cleared out from the ditch. This interpretation raises an immediate problem at Black Carts where there is a substantial marginal mound 4.2m wide and 0.8m in surviving height. It was built of clean material, clay and shale, like the south mound itself, and it directly overlies a subsoil scored with ard marks - in the same stratigraphic relationship as the main south mound. Stratigraphically, the two mounds should be contemporary. Given a clear sequence of slumping followed by silting in the ditch fill, the marginal mound does not derive from cleaning out the ditch, unless - and only unless - it was taken from the ditch after an early episode of slumping of the edges, and that this clearance was undertaken with archaeological scrupulousness.

Observations from Appletree and Cawfields also suggest that for some of its length the marginal mound may be primary, or at least near-primary. This idea is supplemented by the fact that often, as in the stretch from Denton westwards to Halton Chesters (Bidwell and Watson 1996), the south berm is wider than the north. The phenomenon has also been noted at Wallhouses (Bennett and Turner 1983, 67-8) and at Heddon-on-the-Wall (Tait 1962). It seems possible that in these areas provision was made for a marginal mound, which was never actually built.

The marginal mound is also relevant to the phenomenon of Vallum crossings. It seems probable that all Vallum causeways not at forts are secondary, and represent a slighting of the Vallum on the occasion of the Antonine advance into Scotland. The slighting of the Vallum was systematic, with causeways every 41m or thereabouts (Simpson and Shaw 1922). The causeways were presumably constructed by shovelling the material from the breach made in the mounds back into the ditch to create a crossing.

Based on observations between Wall Burn and Whittledean, Simpson and Shaw (1922, 414-16) concluded that the Vallum was reconditioned following the return from Antonine Scotland. This interpretation has enjoyed general acceptance (Breeze and Dobson 2000, 131). The evidence was that in this stretch there were gaps in the main mounds, no causeways, and a marginal mound. This led to the view that the marginal mound was the product of the removal of causeways and of the re-cutting of the ditch, especially as the marginal mound was not breached by the causeways. The latter consideration may not be crucial, as Simpson and Shaw (1922, 402) observed that the main mounds were not always breached to full depth to create the crossings, and in places the depth to which they are breached may be around the height of the marginal mound. The idea that the area between the south and marginal mounds might have been levelled with the spoil derived from the excavation of the breach has yet to be explored. At Wallend Common there is a ditch, no causeways, but breaches in the mounds, and no marginal mound. Are these unfinished causeways as Simpson and Shaw (1922, 401) proposed? If so why was the spoil not used to fill the ditch and create crossings, and simply spread around to north and south of the mounds, a procedure which would have been more difficult than backfilling the ditch (if this is the correct interpretation of the earthwork evidence here).

More importantly the whole idea is thrown into disarray at Black Carts, where there are many extant crossings, but excavation has revealed a substantial, apparently early, marginal mound built of clean material, and no evidence whatever for the re-cutting of the ditch.

The issue of the marginal mound and its relationship with the crossings remains ambiguous at best. It is important because if the mound is primary it is a second obstacle to the south, making the earthwork an even more formidable obstacle than currently acknowledged.

Function

Much has been written on the function of the Vallum and no firm conclusion reached. The curtain wall was adapted to keep to the highest available terrain, but this was not a consideration in the layout of the Vallum, which takes a totally undefensive course (Simpson and Shaw 1922, 360). This lack of even a remote defensive function is underlined by the fact that the course of the work happily ignores such useful natural defensive features as bogs, sometimes skirting the south, sometimes the north, sides of marshes.

Richmond's (1930) statement of the function of the Vallum remains valid.

'The Vallum takes its place as a prohibited zone delimiting the south side of the military area, an unmistakeable belt in which an obstacle is provided by the great ditch. Neither commerce nor interference with the soldiery could take place across it unchecked.'

The Vallum effectively reduces the number of crossings from 79 at the milecastles to 15 at the forts, but this could have been done simply by blocking milecastle gates. The gates were not blocked this early, which suggests that there was a need for greater control of access, with a double check for incomers taking place at milecastles and the Vallum gates at forts. As an unmistakable indication of forbidden territory the Vallum is comprehensible, but it is also a formidable obstacle.

Military Way and Other Minor Routes

P T Bidwell

The Military Way, which connected forts, milecastles and turrets, was not an original feature of Hadrian's Wall. Its relationship with the north Vallum mound, which in places it overlies, and the fact that it was connected by paths to turrets demolished in or by the early third century, makes it probable that the road was built when Hadrian's Wall was re-occupied following the withdrawal from Scotland. The earliest milestone from its course is dated to 213 (*RIB* 2298) and the latest to 305-6 (*RIB* 2311). There has not been much detailed investigation of its composition or route, although the former *RCHM*(E) has carried out some important surveys of its above-ground remains in Wall-miles 40/41 and 43/44 (Bowden 1999; Blood 1999). In sectors where the zone between the Vallum and Wall has been intensively cultivated, the Military Way seems often to have been ploughed out.

A metalled track was found immediately behind the Wall at Denton, but other recent investigations of the Wall on Tyneside have not uncovered anything comparable. The 'Lesser Military Way', not seen since the eighteenth century, ran between milecastles 28 and 34. It has been suggested that the Military Way was preceded by a Hadrianic service road.

Bridges and Culverts

P T Bidwell

Bridges are known at the points where Hadrian's Wall crossed the North Tyne, Irthing and Eden, and in addition the *Pons Aelius* (or *Aelii*) over the Tyne at Newcastle can be considered as part of Hadrian's Wall according to the traditional (and probably correct) view. Within the wider Wall-zone there were also Roman bridges at Corbridge and Risingham. Between Wallsend and Rudchester, and also to the west of the Irthing, there are many burns, some of considerable width, and it is possible that bridges of a single arch would have been needed to take them through the Wall, although none has yet been seen (although the abutment of a small bridge taking the Stanegate over the Cor Burn has been seen at Corbridge). For smaller burns culverts would have been sufficient; one was recorded at the Sugley Burn. (For a general account of bridges in the Wall zone, see Bidwell and Holbrook 1989).

The original bridges across the North Tyne at Chesters and the Irthing at Willowford were no wider than the Broad Wall and seem to have been designed to take the Wall-walk across the rivers (although this interpretation of their function has been disputed). The recess for a tower was found at Willowford and presumably there were originally pairs of towers at both bridges. Massive towers stood at either end of the later road bridge at Chesters and a tower of similar dimensions but slighter construction is known from a later phase at Willowford.

The plan of the Chesters road bridge is now almost completely known. It was a four-arched bridge of conventional design, with free-standing columns and parapets consisting of vertical stone slabs. Access to the carriageway was by means of road-ramps, their sides revetted by walls of massive blocks. The only unusual features were the towers at either end of the bridge, against which the Wall terminated. Construction of the bridge was of *opus quadratum* throughout; no use appears to have been made of concrete, which is remarkable for a bridge of this period. Pottery associated with the occupation of the western tower suggests that the bridge was built in the late 150s and early 160s, as part of a programme of improvements to lateral communications on the Wall which included the construction of the Military Way. The bridge at Corbridge has many of the same constructional features and is presumably of the same date. Recent work has uncovered the south road ramp which was a rebuilding of an earlier ramp. Less is known about the form and chronology of the bridge at Willowford. The Carlisle bridge, which is on the line of the Wall, is represented only by blocks dredged from the river and now displayed in Bitts Park. Nothing is known of the bridge at Newcastle and even its exact position is now in doubt. However, medieval and earlier deposits on both banks of the Tyne in the vicinity of the bridge are exceptionally well-

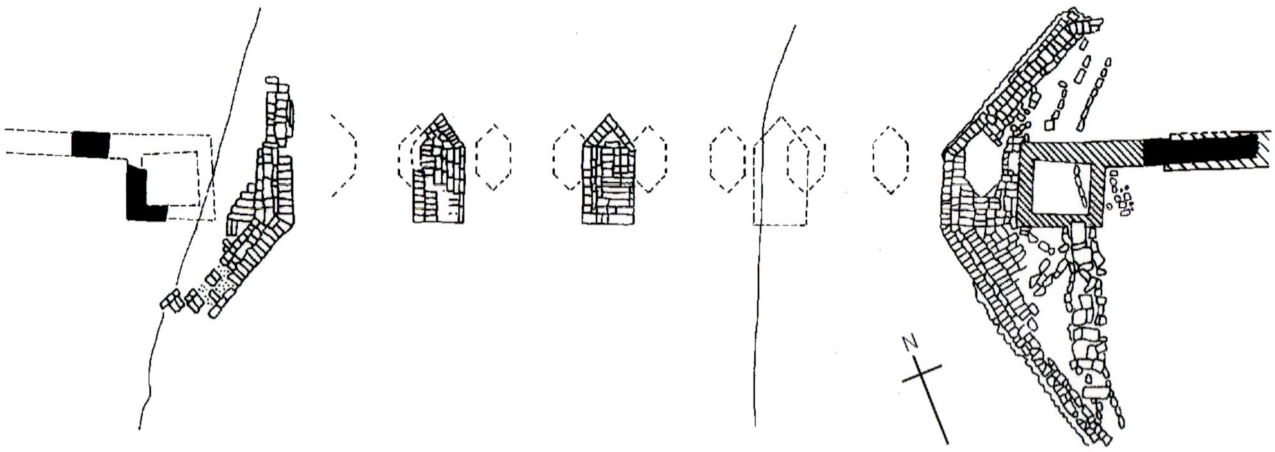

70. The bridge at Chesters

preserved and in places are waterlogged, and it is likely that there will be remains of the abutments and approach ramps.

71. The bridge abutment at Willowford

At Corbridge the Stanegate was realigned and a small bridge, noted above, built over the Cor Burn in the last quarter of the fourth century. A masonry causeway approaching the bridge over the Tyne from the southwest seems to be of similarly late date. Considerable efforts to keep the main lines of communication usable continued down to the end of the Roman period. Recent work on the crypt at Hexham suggests that the bridges at Corbridge and Chesters were demolished to build the later seventh-century church.

The Camps

H Welfare

The Hadrian's Wall corridor contains nearly 50 camps - the largest known concentration in Roman Britain. The evidence for them was assembled in Welfare and Swan (1995). The names adopted there are used here. The classification of a site as a camp is not straightforward; the criteria used in 1995 were a rectangular plan, rounded angles, and the diagnostic details of the gates; the topographical position could be a contributing factor, as well as the negative aspects that distinguish them from forts. For lack of certainty, a number of examples have not yet been accepted as camps (despite being published as such); these include Bishop Rigg, near Corbridge (Jobey 1979), and Newbrough, on the Stanegate (Frere 1990, 316, 319). Elsewhere, the evidence from excavation has been too slender to confirm a tentative suggestion: e.g. from below the fort at Carrawburgh (Breeze 1972, 86-9); at Etterby (Burnham et al 1997, 415); or at Stanwix (Burnham *et al* 2001, 335-6).

Within the Wall corridor the principal cluster of camps lies between the confluence of the North and South Tyne at Warden, and the Irthing at Willowford: here there are 35 camps in a stretch of 32km. Carlisle is a secondary focus. However, camps are - by definition - relatively insubstantial works, so the intensity of subsequent cultivation and of development will have affected this apparent distribution. 30 examples survive (whole or in part) as earthworks, in the portion of the corridor within Northumberland; in contrast, except for the site at Willowford, all those known in Cumbria (15) have been identified only as cropmarks on air photographs. In the rest of England the ratio of earthworks to cropmarks, as evidence for camps, is about 1 : 2.4; in the Wall corridor the ratio is reversed at 2 : 1. The rate of survival (and hence also our knowledge) should therefore be comparatively good.

The rate of new discovery is slow and sporadic. It may be that in the pastures of the central sector we are seeing something close to maximum survival; however, there is no inherent reason to think that the density of distribution should have been less intense elsewhere, so it is clear that our knowledge is, at best, partial. Even so, it is still surprising that more camps have not been identified in the arable land - long cultivated - to the east of the North Tyne.

72. Willowford camp, with Hadrian's Wall to the north

Our knowledge is further limited by a paucity of excavation. Only seven sites have been tested at all: Haltwhistle Burn 1 and 2 (in 1907-8), Limestone Corner (1912), Watchclose (1935), Sunny Rigg 1 (1981), Brackenrigg (1984), and Greenlee Lough (1984). In almost every case the investigations were restricted to very small sections of the perimeter.

These few excavations did, however, make it clear that a rampart was an essential element in the construction of a camp; a ditch was not. At Sunny Rigg and at Haltwhistle Burn 2 the amount of turf used in the rampart was too great to have been stripped from the area of the ditch alone; so more work had to be done in order to make the rampart complete. Moreover, ditches were often little more than shapeless quarries; the supposedly "diagnostic" qualities of "military" ditches have often been unduly emphasised.

As to proportions and size, a ratio of 2:3 in the lengths of the axes is common, although many of the smaller camps are square. Most are rectangular, but there are some parallelograms, and a few are markedly irregular (e.g. Milestone House, and Fell End). The reasons for the wide variations are unclear; some factors are likely to have been related to the needs and traditions of the original unit. There is, however, a little less variation in size. The camps discovered in the Wall corridor are markedly smaller than those known elsewhere in England. Almost all (14 out of 17) of the camps recorded in England as being less than 0.5ha have been identified along the Wall, along with half of those of an area between 0.5 and 1.0ha, and 8 out of 10 of those between 1.0 and 1.5ha. In the larger size-ranges, the Wall corridor is hardly represented, there being no more than nine camps between 1.7 and 16.8ha - a rather different picture from that in the rest of England.

Although there are still some puzzles around the orientations of some of the camps - such as those (differing greatly in form but sharing a common orientation) at Haltwhistle Burn - topographical convenience and tactical strength were no doubt the most decisive factors. The ground-plans suggest that a deliberate choice was often made on which way the camp should face - e.g. at Glenwhelt Leazes, Haltwhistle Burn 1, Seatsides 1 and 2, Burnhead, and Lees Hall. Intriguingly, the site at Burnhead appears to face away from Hadrian's Wall, which is immediately adjacent to its south angle. Was this camp constructed before the Wall?

Of the interiors of the camps we know almost nothing. Even when the perimeter is well preserved as an earthwork the interior will usually be featureless, and excavators have - wrongly - tended to ignore it. Even more surprisingly, none of the camps has been investigated with the type of extensive geophysical survey that has proved so worthwhile in the forts and military *vici*. Yet the questions to be answered about camps could be illuminated by a study of the interiors; after all, the troops lived within the defences, not on top of them. This ignorance of interior arrangements has also meant that some estimates of the size of the original detachment responsible for construction have been approached uncritically. For instance, the small stream within the perimeter at Lees Hall, and the steep slopes within the sites at Fell End and at Milestone House, all cast some doubt on the simple use of area as a direct indicator. Without better data the series of metrical assessments postulated by Richardson (2000; 2001; 2002) is difficult to evaluate.

The perimeters - and particularly the gates - have been more informative. The gates are the prime diagnostic feature for camps, although there has been little excavation of them in England. The variations in design may be due to unit tradition, or function - as well as the more commonly advanced distinction of date. There is a tendency to believe that the curving *clavicula* preceded the simple straight traverse but this remains uncertain. At Chapel Rigg and Glenwhelt Leazes - less than 1km apart, to the west of the Irthing, near Greenhead - *claviculae* and traverses are found in combination. At Seatsides 1 there are some grounds for thinking that the traverses may be secondary to the *claviculae* there. The probability is that the two principal designs overlapped to some extent in date.

The camps provided some protection for the troops. Beyond that, we know almost nothing about function: i.e. what those troops were engaged in, or in what circumstances the camp was constructed. A very few - such as Milestone House - appear to exhibit characteristics of a rapid pragmatic decision, and may be tentatively ascribed to a unit that was actually on the march. In contrast, the highly unusual site at Lees Hall, with its distinctive outer rampart, has every appearance of having been occupied for a significantly longer time - and yet it would still be classified as a camp rather than as a small fort.

Some of the other large camps in proximity to the major engineering works within the Wall corridor might be expected to relate to the construction phases of the Stanegate, the Wall, the ditch, the Military Way, or the Vallum, but without detailed excavation nothing is likely to distinguish a labour camp from one thrown up in any other functional circumstances. In addition, in the context of a long-standing garrison of occupation, extensive training will have been necessary: camps would have been constructed by detachments on manoeuvre (camps again indistinguishable from those constructed for any other purpose); these would have been every bit as much 'practice' camps as the tiny, un-utilisable enclosures to which this label has usually been ascribed. Although there are no examples along the Wall as suggestively non-utilitarian as those identified in Wales (Daniels and Jones 1969; Davies and Jones 2002), some of the camps in the central sector are so tiny that they may have originated in this way: e.g. Bean Burn 2, Coesike, Grindon Hill, Grindon School, Haltwhistle Burn 4, and Sunny Rigg 3.

Apart from their general ascription to the Roman period - here no better defined than being between c. AD 70 and the early fifth century - there is very little evidence for the dating of the camps. Although the beginning of the sequence is fixed by the first arrival of Roman troops in the area, we have no clear idea as to when the construction of camps ceased to be military practice, or of when the re-use of existing defences ceased to be thought necessary or desirable.

Excavation at Brakenrigg produced samian from the first half of the second century, and at Limestone Corner sherds of cooking-pot and mortarium have been dated to anywhere from the end of the second century to the fourth century. In terms of relative chronology, the camp at Red House was found to be later than the Agricolan vexillation fortress, but elsewhere the relationships are not instructive. For instance, the large camps at Fell End, Markham Cottage 1, and Seatsides are each crossed by the line of the Stanegate. What are the relationships here? If they were in use contemporaneously, the road would disrupt the internal organisation of the camp, but such an arrangement would provide stern policing of the route if that was thought necessary. Do these three camps precede the formal establishment of the road? Elsewhere, what is the relationship between the Wall itself and the camps that lie immediately north of it? There is no archaeological information at all.

The sites at Burnhead and at Cawfields - close together on either side of the Haltwhistle Burn, to the north of the Wall - share some features in common and may thus be broadly contemporary, or constructed by the same unit. The same may be true of Chapel Rigg and Glenwhelt Leazes, which are in close proximity to one another.

The most suitable sites were probably re-used time and again. At a significant number of camps there is evidence that the site was reoccupied or that the defences were modified for re-use: for instance, gates were blocked at Lees Hall and at Brown Dikes, and may have been refurbished at Fell End. Economy of effort is evident at Seatsides 1 and at Haltwhistle Burn 2 and 3, where the defences were re-used in an expansion or a contraction of the area enclosed. Where re-use is evident there is, however, no indication as to the length of time that separated the phases, and in many cases it is not clear which element came first. In the West, at Boomby Lane, and at Moss Side, the camps (one superimposed upon the other) are on different alignments - begging the questions as to how much was visible on the site when the second phase of construction began, and why a camp of a different size and orientation was necessary.

The Cumberland Coast

M F A Symonds

The scientific exploration of the western flank of Hadrian's Wall commenced in 1880 when the first coastal towers were excavated and Ferguson (1881, 130) confidently predicted the existence of more. Despite this promising start, the coast returned to obscurity until Collingwood (1929a) undertook a 'foray' in 1928. The rescue excavation of milefortlet 5 by Simpson and Hodgson (1947) followed in 1943-1944, and resulted in the recognition of a regular sequence of installations. In the second-half of the twentieth century a trailblazing campaign by Bellhouse located many new sites, while Jones has also worked extensively in the area. Most recently the Hadrian's Wall NMP project has conducted a survey of the western end of the Wall, including the Cardurnock peninsula (Boutwood 2005). Despite the wealth of data that this renewed activity has furnished, many details, including the nature or even existence of a running barrier, the terminus of the system and the evolution of the coastal towers, remain contentious.

Overview of the Cumberland system

As has been discussed (p. 15-7), the cordon of installations along the littoral may have been preceded by a build up of forces to the south, comparable to that seen on the Stanegate. Whether the coastal cordon itself was integral to the plan for Hadrian's Wall from the very start, or was contemporary with one of the many early adaptations to the original concept, remains uncertain. The closest indication of date derives from a near-mint coin of AD 119-121 in the foundation-layer at tower 13a (Bellhouse 1954, 49-50). The question of whether the extant coastal system was the product of a single plan or the result of a Wall-style 'fort decision' also remains unresolved (Breeze 2004, 79-80). The forts in question are considered in the forts chapter.

Milefortlet 1 is the first confirmed element of the Hadrianic coastal sequence and lies on a gentle rise dominating the Solway coastline, 1,676m west of Bowness fort. From milefortlet 1, with only one major interruption, a regular cordon of installations was constructed shadowing the Cumberland coastline. Small structures were placed at 490m intervals, mirroring the regular sequence of two turrets between every milecastle on the curtain. The resulting cordon can be divided into two sections: that directly continuing Hadrian's Wall around the Cardurnock peninsula as far as milefortlet 5, and that running south from milefortlet 9. This division is caused not by any structural difference in the installations (though see Breeze 2004, 80), but by the 2.5km wide mouth of the sea-inlet at Moricambe, containing the tidal estuaries of the Wampool and Waver rivers. The cordon was originally believed to encircle this inlet, and the designations 5a-8b were reserved for the anticipated sites. However, none of these have ever been located and they are now considered to be

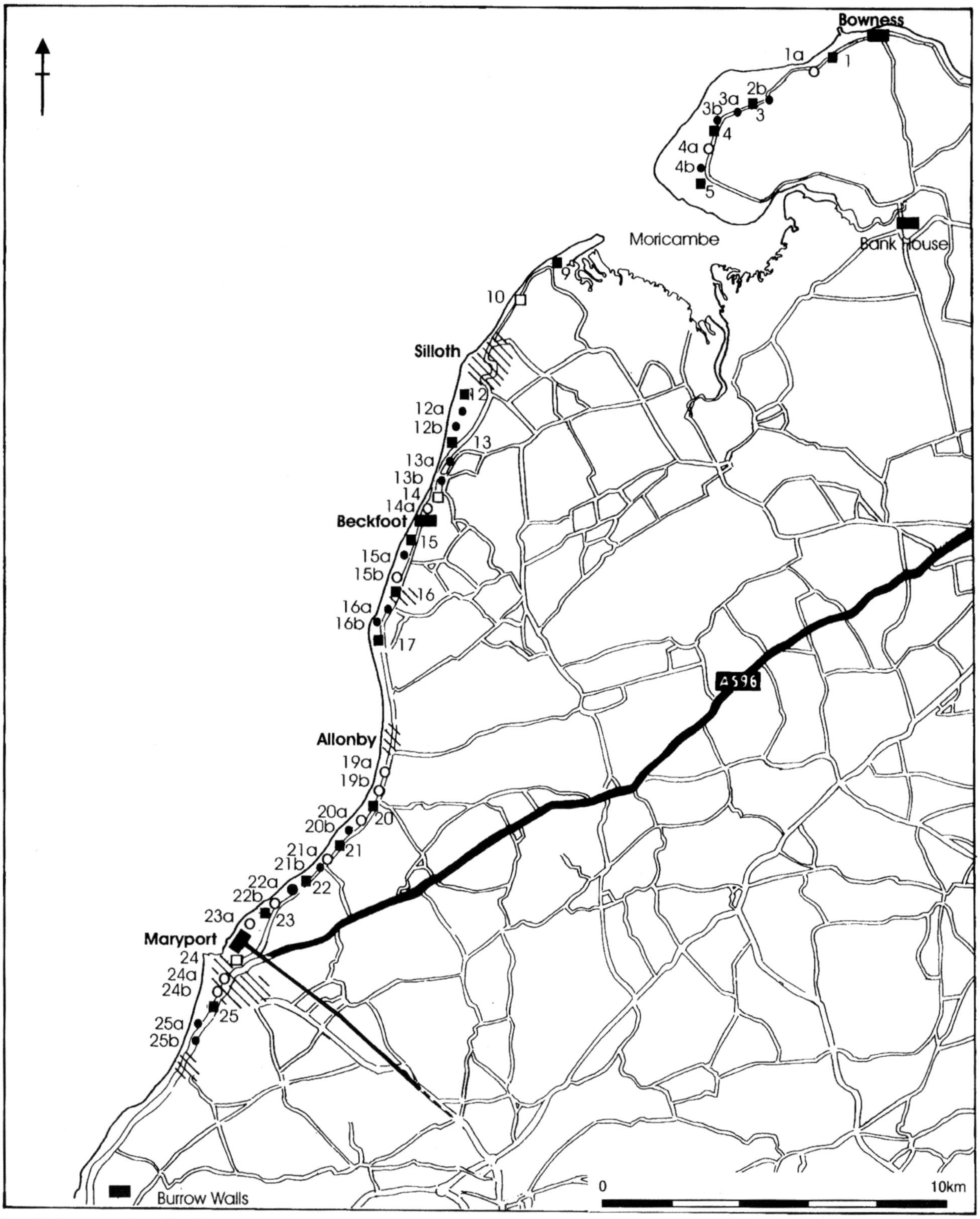

73. Cumbrian coast - all sites

illusory, hence the modern numbering leap from milefortlet 5 to 9 (Daniels 1990, 402). From milefortlet 9 the chain has been traced, at least in part, as far as Risehow tower, 2km south of the fort at Maryport. In the numbering scheme this represents either 25b or 26b, depending on which site schedule is preferred (Daniels 1990, 405-406; Bellhouse 1989a, 56). Although Bellhouse (1981b, 12) believes that this marks the end of the system, Jones (1982, 296) argued that a cropmark at Harrington indicates a further milefortlet, while Potter (1979a, 18) has proposed a continuation of c. 45km south to Ravenglass. This extension is based on the discovery of a possible fortlet under the late Hadrianic fort, but would seem to require an unfeasible number of missing sites. A further suggestion is that the Cumberland system may have 'just fizzled out and was not completed...' (Breeze 2004, 83), although ultimately 'we simply do not know where it ended' (Woolliscroft 1994, 57).

It has been asserted that the subtle variations in length between the milecastles and turrets were avoided on the Cumberland coast, resulting in installations at fixed 490m intervals (Bellhouse 1989a, 1; Woolliscroft 1994, 55). Although the milefortlets and towers along the Cumberland Coast were, in general, spaced more rigidly than their counterparts on the curtain, exceptions do occur. Milefortlet 21 was located 70m north of its measured

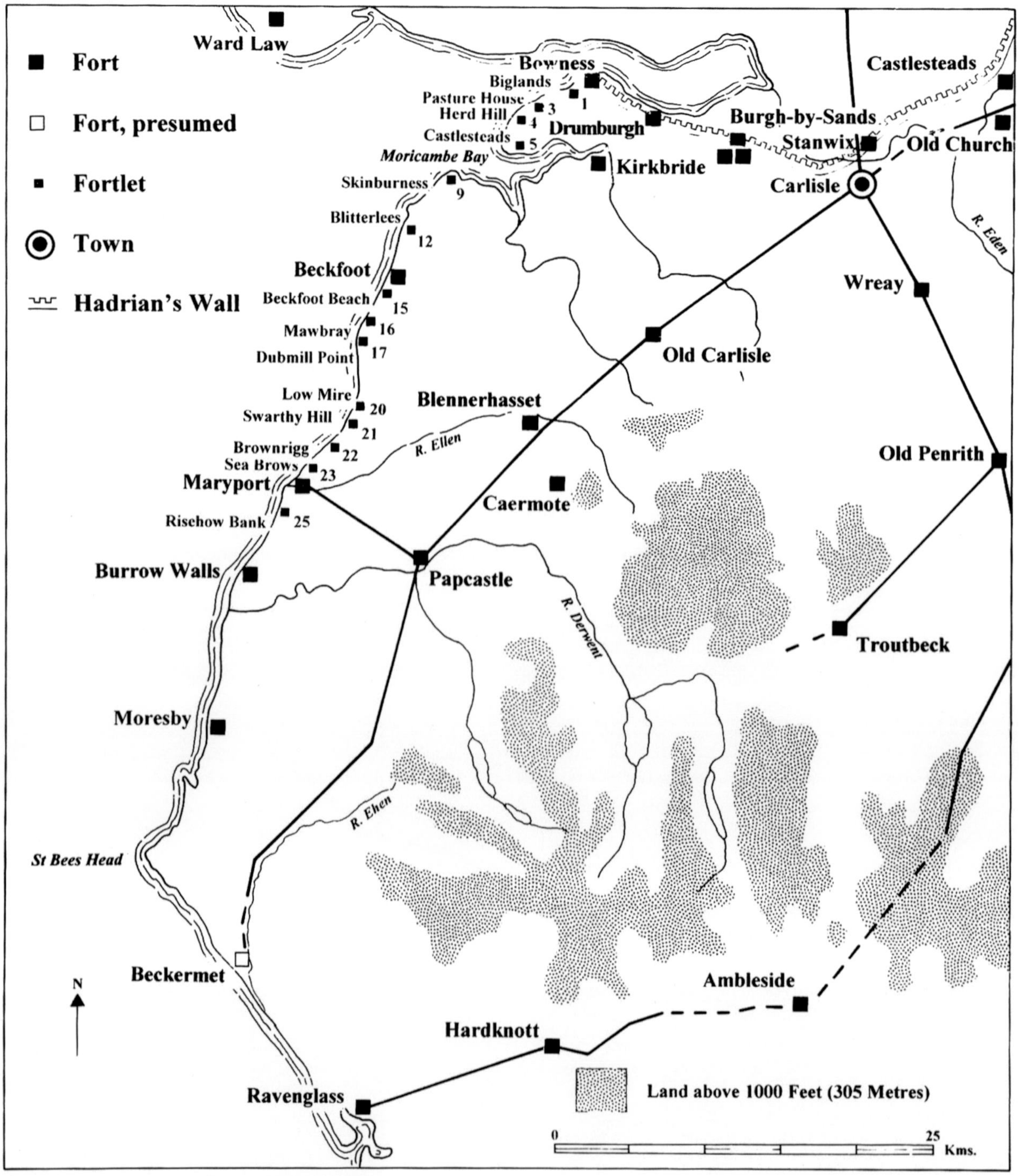

74. Cumbrian coast - principal military sites

position (Turnbull 1998, 63), while milefortlet 23 was 45m out, prompting the suggestion that there were long and short 'Wall miles' as on the curtain (Daniels 1990, 405).

The milefortlets

The bulk of the excavation data for the individual milefortlets come from limited test-pitting, intended either to confirm the presence of an installation or target specific research questions. These have proven misleading in two instances, when the sites of milefortlets 21 and 26 were subsequently found to be incorrectly attributed (Turnbull 1998, 77; Bellhouse 1984, 42). All of the known milefortlets were constructed of turf and, in contrast to their counterparts on the Turf Wall, there is no evidence that any of them were subsequently rebuilt in stone. Ditches were normally provided, although apparently not at milefortlets 15 and 16 (Breeze 2004, 76).

75. Allonby Bay viewed from Milefortlet 21

The limited evidence for the internal arrangement of the milefortlets is a serious gap in knowledge (Breeze 2004,

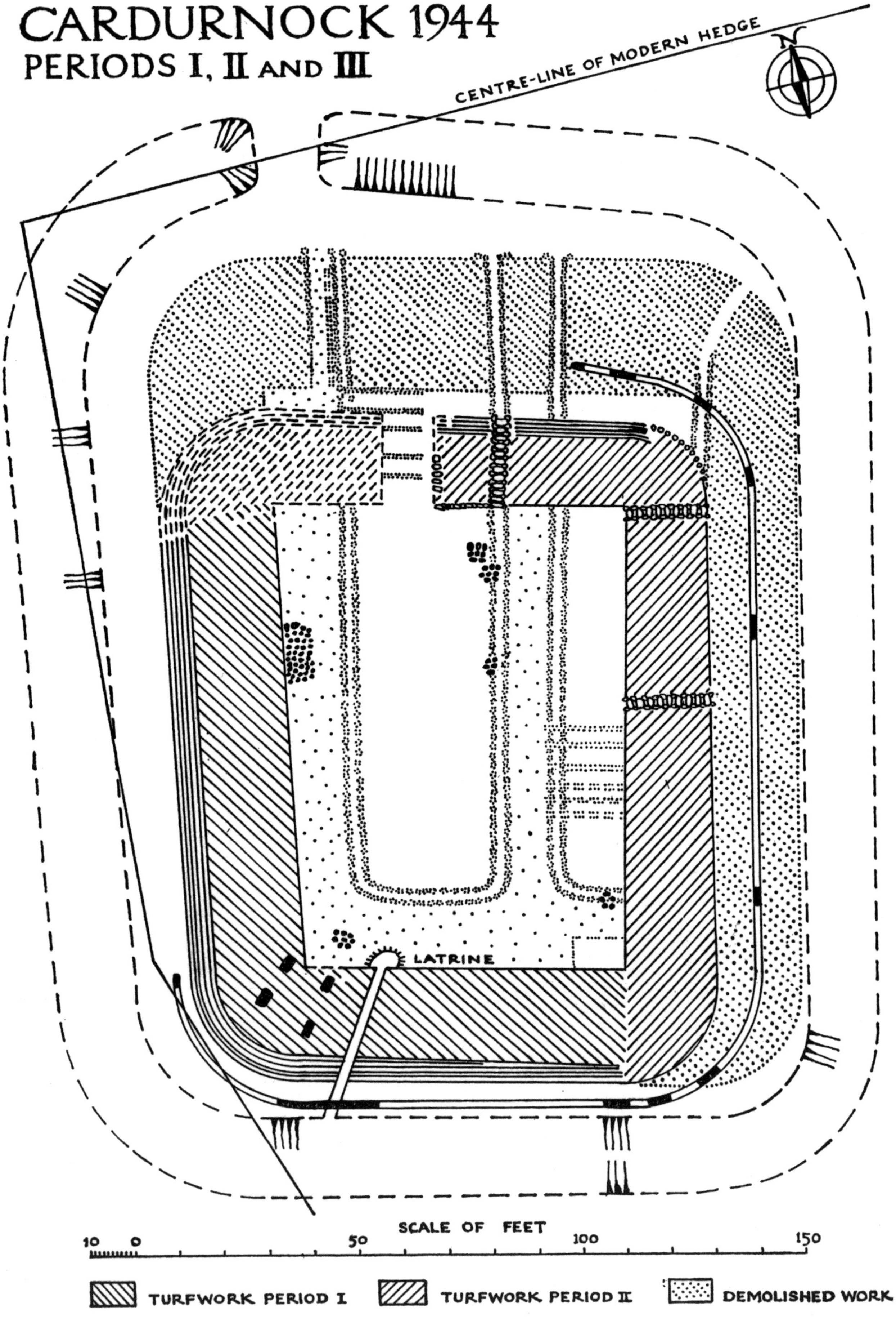

76. Plan of Milefortlet 5 as excavated

84). Only three have been subject to extensive exploration: 1, 5 and 21. Of these, milefortlet 5 is exceptional in terms of both its internal area, originally c. 40 by 29m, and its design. While its size has been attributed to the importance of its position on the northern lip of Moricambe, the single, off-centre, 1m-wide entrance contrasts with the double gates apparently standard for smaller milefortlets, including 20 and 21. Although milefortlet 5 did not have a gate-tower, a corner tower was detected in the south-west angle. A later reduction in size brought the installation closer to the estimated size of the neighbouring milefortlet 9 (Breeze 2006, 383). Milefortlet 5 yielded a conspicuously rich pottery assemblage, assignable to the second and fourth centuries AD (Simpson and Hodgson 1947, 124).

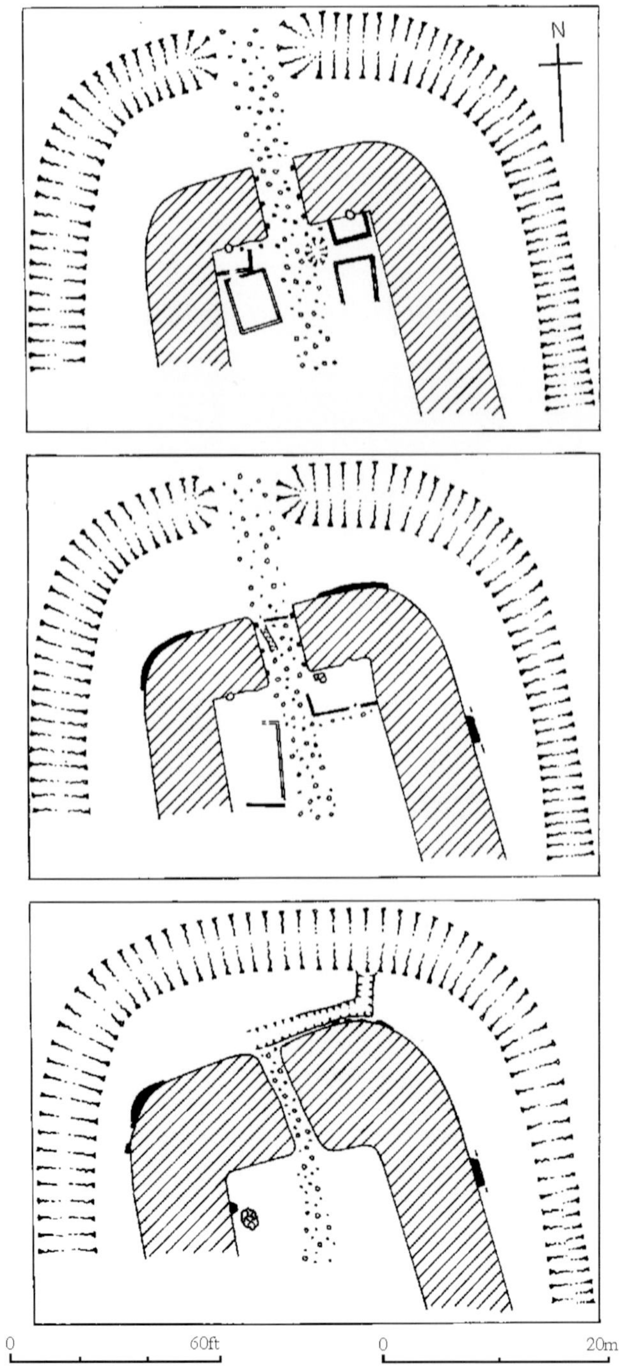

77. Plan of the three phases of Milefortlet 1

Milefortlet 1 has been characterised as 'a normal milefortlet ' and measured c. 14.5 by 20m internally (Potter 1977, 159; Potter 1979b, 198). Excavations revealed evidence for three phases, with occupation ceasing before the end of the second century. The internal buildings consisted of two timber buildings either side of the internal road, and two lean-to structures. The installation was reconditioned following demolition at the end of the primary phase, and while this could not be precisely dated, the excavator favoured a post-Antonine restoration (Potter 1977, 182).

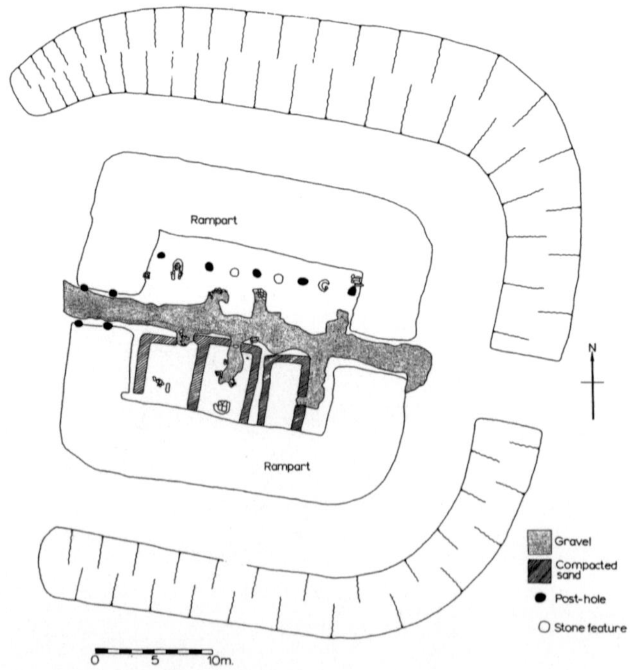

78. Plan of Milefortlet 21

Milefortlet 21 has produced the most complete internal building plan (Turnbull 1998). A 'flimsy' sand and turf rampart enclosed the vestigial traces of two buildings, one either side of the central road. The southern range comprised three rooms, while the northern building consisted of a line of postholes set back from the rampart. A garrison of six was proposed for the southern range (Turnbull 1998, 76), although its area, 59m^2, compares favourably with the smaller milecastle barracks. There is only evidence for a single phase of occupation at milefortlet 21, certainly not continuing beyond AD 140 (Turnbull 1998, 104-105).

Two of the milefortlets have been associated with burial grounds. While that in the vicinity of milefortlet 15 can be convincingly attributed to Beckfoot fort and military *vicus* (Caruana 2004a, 161), the burials c. 90m from the measured site of milefortlet 4 have no other obvious source. The cremations there were associated with Hadrianic pottery and are believed to have been carried out on site (Bellhouse 1954, 54-55), which may have some implications for our conception of the signalling system proposed by Woolliscroft (1994).

In most instances occupation seems to have been restricted to the Hadrianic period. Finds from the milefortlets include a range of pottery, knives, spearheads, keys, brooches, a quernstone and gaming boards and counters. A handful of sites have finds or structural evidence attributable to post-Antonine reoccupation, although Turnbull (1998, 104-105) has argued that this only occurred north of Moricambe. Either way, all of the installations seem to have been abandoned by the end of

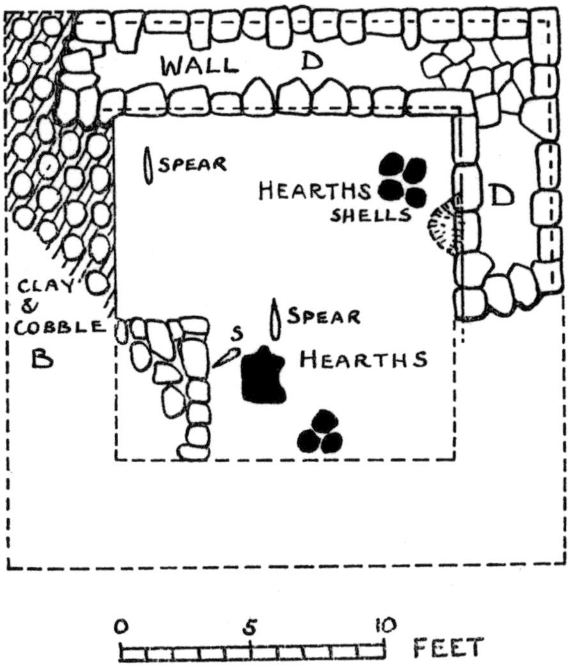

79. Plan of Tower 16b

the second century (Breeze 2004, 81). Fourth-century material has been found at milefortlets 5, 12 and 20.

A number of milefortlet sites remain undetected. The stretches of the coastal sequence which are reasonably securely traced can be broken down into three groups, running from milefortlets 1-9 to the west of Bowness fort, 12-17 either side of Beckfoot fort and 20-25b straddling Maryport fort. Previously it was thought that many of these missing stretches had been lost to erosion (Bellhouse 1989a, 38). However, recent work has questioned this (Clare 2000, 14-17) and it is conceivable that if the sequence was never completed to the south, gaps may also have occurred elsewhere. Even within the three groups the level of detail varies considerably and little to nothing is known of milefortlets 2, 4, 10-11, 13-15, 18-19, 24 and 25, excepting the presence of turfwork at 4, 13 and 15.

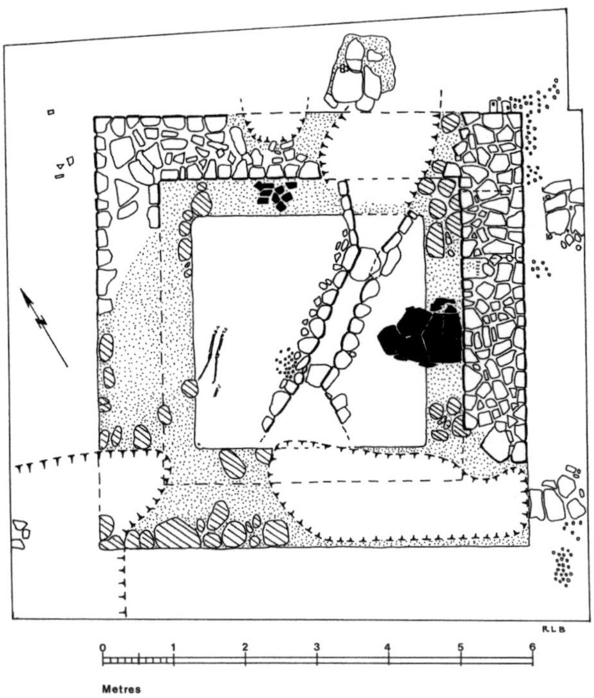

80. Plan of Rise How Tower

The towers

In general terms the towers along the Cumberland Coast are much better understood than the milefortlets, although Jones has queried their chronology. His excavations at towers 2b and 4b revealed possible timber predecessors to the stone installations (Jones 2004, 174). This has been described as creating 'more problems than solutions', and as these timber towers display unique features, it has been proposed that their existence should be discounted (Breeze 2004, 74). If so, then the general construction of the smaller structures mimics that on the original Turf Wall, with the milefortlets built of turf and the towers of stone throughout. The Cumberland towers had internal areas of c. 4 by 4m and unlike the Wall turrets the four outer walls were of approximately equal width, measuring c. 0.9m above the footings. The foundations consisted of layers of cobbles and clay (Breeze 2004, 72-74). Those under the south wall at 12a failed during the lifespan of the tower, triggering a collapse and necessitating the reconstruction of the wall c. 1.5m to the north (Bellhouse 1969, 55-59). The walls at tower 3b were also found to have fallen outwards, at an uncertain date, and could be traced for a distance of about 2.7m from the tower base (Ferguson 1881, 129). Estimates of original height range from 7.6-10m. The nature of the upper tower furniture remains uncertain, although two possible merlon caps from towers 16a and 16b have been taken to indicate flat roofs. No window glass has ever been recovered (Breeze 2004, 73).

Sand and, less commonly, gravel ground-floor surfaces are known. As in the Wall turrets, there are hints of organic carpeting, with the oxidised traces of rushes on the underside of an iron spearhead from tower 16b. Rough stone platforms were also found in 13b and 16b (Bellhouse 1954, 42-47). Hearths are common, with as many as five superimposed against the north wall at tower 12b (Breeze 2006, 384). Finds from turrets include pottery, quernstones, spears, knives, nails, coins, a whetstone and a gaming board. Towers 16b and 25a (or 26a) preserved particularly detailed evidence for the garrisons' diet and habits with oysters, mussels, whelks, winkles, cockles and pig and sheep bones littered around the hearths in the former (Bellhouse 1954, 45; Bellhouse 1984, 43).

The vast majority of the towers contain exclusively Hadrianic pottery, suggesting that they were not re-occupied following the return from the Antonine Wall (Breeze 2004, 80). Some appear to have been tidily demolished in a manner comparable to the decommissioned Wall turrets, although the walls of 3b were still standing to an appreciable height when they collapsed. A single sherd of third- or fourth-century pottery was found in tower 16a and two late-third-century coins were found unstratified at tower 2b. Towers 0a-2a, 9a-11b, 14a and b, 15b, 17a-19b, 21a and 22b-24b remain unaccounted for, while the recorded locations of 4a and 4b are contested.

The ditches and palisade

The strongest case for the milefortlets and turrets being linked and, to some extent, enclosed by a linear barrier was made by Jones (1982, 288) who argued that there is 'unequivocable evidence' for such an arrangement. During the droughts of 1974-5, he detected a pair of narrow, parallel cropmarks, 46m apart, approaching milefortlet 1's defensive ditch. The NMP has also charted similar ditches south of the Vallum between Bowness and Drumburgh (Boutwood 2005, 20). Further survey by Jones located additional stretches of linear cropmarks around the Cardurnock peninsula and he declared that 'the double ditches...connected originally into the outer ditches of the milefortlets' (Higham and Jones 1975, 22). The behaviour of the cropmarks is not uniform. Those immediately north-east of milefortlet 1 enclosed an area 46m wide, while the pair running east of milefortlet 5 are only 10m apart, with the northern one skirting the milefortlet ditch (Higham and Jones 1975, 20; Jones and Woolliscroft 2001, 125).

The Cardurnock cropmarks relate to ditches which vary in cross-section, ranging from c. 1-2m by 0.5m in size. Some may have been associated with a palisade fence, although further inferred instances of these, in the vicinity of Silloth, have subsequently proven to be field drains (Woolliscroft 2004, 189). The NMP survey concluded that this is also the origin of the features seen in the vicinity of towers 3a and b (Boutwood 2005, 17). Many of the ditches preserve evidence for recutting on two or three occasions. Jones judged the end result to be 'partly impractical' and suggested that it 'should be seen in part as a moral barrier' (Jones 1976, 237; 243). The rear ditch near milefortlet 1 yielded an early Hadrianic sherd, although this lay within the secondary fill (Jones 1976, 242), and the discovery that the rear ditch was cut by tower 2b (Jones 2004, 178) might also support an earlier date.

Bellhouse (1981a 139) argued that these trenches were intended as the first stage in the construction of a turf curtain. He attributes the failure to build this to the 'fort decision' (Bellhouse 1989a, 5) and highlights the presence of two gateways in some milefortlets (Bellhouse 1981b, 7-8), including 20 and 21. While two gateways are not typical for freestanding fortlets of this size, Bellhouse's corollary that the milefortlets were 'designed to allow traffic through a barrier' (Bellhouse 1989a, 5) is disputable. Daniels (1990) noted that small fortlets with double gates are known on the German frontier, but did not provide passage through the frontier barrier. Daniels' further statement that 'we do not yet fully understand the extent [of the running barriers], their date or their relationship to each other and to the milefortlets and towers' remains an accurate précis of current knowledge.

The road

Following Camden's observations, Ferguson (1881, 130) recorded that 'A paved causey can still be seen between Bowness and Campfield. There it is lost ... [it] re-appears between Skinburness and Silloth'. This road has proven elusive in more recent times. Bellhouse (1989a, 7) unsuccessfully sought the road between Bowness and Pasture House. Jones (1982, 288) reported 'unequivocable evidence of a patrol road', after sectioning a thinly-metalled, single-period feature between towers 4a and 4b. While this tallies with the description of the first-phase road entering milefortlet 1, Bellhouse (1989a, 7-8) was unconvinced and the precise course of any frontier road in this area cannot be considered certain.

There are strong indications that a road servicing the coastal installations did exist. A road running north-south through Beckfoot fort can be traced for over a kilometre on aerial photographs and there is evidence for a similar feature in Silloth playing fields (Breeze 2004, 80). The NMP recorded a road southwest of milefortlet 5 (Boutwood 2005, 19), although the reported width seems excessive. Wheel ruts were detected in the road surface at milefortlet 1 (Potter 1977, 157), indicating traffic there, while a 'gravel road' was identified on the cliff edge in front of milefortlet 22 (Bellhouse 1970, 15-16), though not at milefortlet 21 (Turnbull 1998, 71). Long stretches of the road may have been ploughed out, resulting in the slight and intermittent surviving traces (Breeze 2004, 80), but further clarification remains desirable.

The purpose of the Cumberland Coast

Bellhouse has stated that the 'purpose of this close watch and patrol was to deal with raiders from the other side of the Solway' (Bellhouse 1981a, 135). Woolliscroft concurs: 'one assumes that the Cumberland Coast was designed to prevent barbarian raiding parties outflanking the Wall and/or seeking booty in the hinterland'. He adds that 'this was a job that more isolated stations could not have carried out so effectively because it would still have been relatively easy for small raiding parties to slip past them at night or in misty weather' (Woolliscroft 1994, 60-61). In this context it is surprising that Moricambe was not encircled, as it created a 5km wide gap in the line, allowing the whole system to be outflanked only 7km from the Scottish shore. It is notable that the density of installations is well in excess of that seen on other coastal cordons, such as the North Devonshire coast, the western flank of the Antonine Wall and, in the fourth century, the Yorkshire coast. In many ways it is remarkable that the only acknowledgement of the shift from a land to a coastal frontier seems to have been the abandonment of a substantial running barrier.

5. Forts and their Extramural Settlements

Co-ordinated by J Crow and D J P Mason

Overview

DJP Mason

Forts constitute the major site-type within the study area. As bases for the units stationed both along the Wall itself and within the general frontier zone, and in most cases accompanied by significant civilian communities, they were the principal centres of population, economic activity and social interaction. Two, Carlisle and Corbridge, developed into sizeable towns in the later Roman period though in both cases with a continuing military presence. The evidence contained within the sites is the major source of information for many aspects of the frontier zone at both the macro and micro level: ranging from the evolution of the plan for the Wall itself and the deployment of military forces in the region over time through to the diet of the soldiers and the flora of the surrounding landscape.

Some of the forts within the study area were founded either during the conquest of the region in the early 70s of the first century (e.g. Carlisle, Red House Corbridge) or about a decade later in the mid-late 80s as part of the initial re-deployment of forces in the wake of the withdrawal of *legio II Adiutrix* from Britain and the beginning of the disengagement from much of Scotland (e.g. Corbridge, Vindolanda). A few were established in the early second century but were abandoned following the construction of the Wall (e.g. Brampton, Old Church). In one possible case - Castlesteads - a pre-existing fort lay sufficiently close to the line chosen for the Wall for it to be included in the space between the latter and the Vallum. The forts at Newcastle and South Shields were added c. 160 or a little later although there was probably a predecessor at the latter site. Some forts established before the Wall was built continued in occupation thereafter (e.g. Carlisle, Carvoran, Corbridge, Vindolanda). At some sites (e.g. Burgh-by-Sands and to an even greater extent at Vindolanda) there was a sequence of forts on neighbouring sites. In the original Wall scheme the auxiliary units were to remain in forts to the rear. Following the decision to move the units up to the Wall itself, this was done in stages. Where it has been possible to sequence them and according to current understanding Benwell, Haltonchesters and Rudchester were the first to be added, followed by Chesters and Housesteads, then Carrawburgh, Greatchesters and Wallsend. With the possible exception of Maryport, where there may have been a predecessor, the forts on the Cumberland coast were established in the Hadrianic period.

To some extent, the variation in the amount of investigation from one site to another has been dictated by their later settlement history. Thus while the majority lie in open country and are potentially available for research others, such as Carlisle and Newcastle, are overlain by modern settlement where investigation has been and is still largely dictated by re-development. Even in the case of those sites potentially available there has been a wide variation in the degree of investigation owing to factors such as the research priorities of individuals, location and ease of access, the attitude of landowners, restrictions imposed by legal status and, of course, resources. Thus whereas Housesteads fort (but not its *vicus*) has been extensively excavated many of the other 'open' sites have barely been touched. Conversely the forts in urban environments at South Shields and Wallsend have been - and at the former continue to be - the subject of large-scale excavation projects, both principally though not exclusively initiated as regeneration and heritage tourism economic development projects.

Of the twenty-seven forts (Carlisle and Corbridge included) with a military presence following the construction of the Wall at only three - Housesteads, South Shields and Wallsend - has excavation been sufficient to reveal anything like the entire fort plan. There are a few cases where even the overall size of the fort is unknown. At Newcastle this is because investigation is restricted by modern buildings. At Kirkbride however uncertainty about the size of the fort is due simply to a lack of investigation. The same is true at Drumburgh where the original size of the fort is in doubt. At Burrow Walls the situation is rather different as approximately one-third has been destroyed by coastal erosion and the precise dimensions will never be known. The north wall of the fort at Bowness has also been lost for the same reason and the effects of climate change are likely to accelerate destruction at coastal sites. Fort sites in open countryside have been affected to a varying degree by stone-robbing and in one case - Castlesteads - extensive levelling to form parkland, while at Moresby half of the fort interior is occupied by a cemetery. At Bewcastle, too, part of the fort interior is occupied by a cemetery and parts of the defences are overlain by a small medieval castle. Those in urban locations have obviously suffered considerable damage from later development though, as Carlisle in particular has demonstrated, their deeply buried remains can yield evidence of great importance.

Of the more extensively explored forts, Housesteads was excavated mainly in the late nineteenth century when investigation was confined to exposing the remains of the latest masonry buildings. The excavations at Wallsend in the 1970s and 1980s and those at South Shields begun in the 1970s and still continuing are the sole examples of modern investigations sufficiently extensive to provide a detailed picture of the plan and development of a fort over its entire history. Investigations at Housesteads and Birdoswald during the same period have also provided information of a similar quality but in both cases this was restricted to a small percentage of the interior. The long-running excavation campaign at Vindolanda has complemented contemporary work at other sites and produced results so far unparalleled elsewhere not least with regard to the number and varying size of its successive military installations (ten at the time of writing) and the collection of writing-tablets (in excess of 2,000).

At most forts only a fraction of the interior has been examined and in the overwhelming majority of cases the information derives from investigations carried out before the 1970s, and frequently before 1940. The information was recovered using what would now be regarded as primitive techniques. Exploration was usually confined to buildings of the latest phase thus providing no information about the earlier structural development of individual buildings or of changes in the fort plan over time. These early investigations are also unlikely to have recognised traces of timber buildings belonging to the late Roman or sub-Roman periods like those found in recent years at Ravenglass and Birdoswald respectively. At seven forts the interior remains completely unexplored (Beckfoot, Burrow Walls, Castlesteads, Carvoran, Drumburgh, Kirkbride and Moresby). At a further twelve sites investigations have encompassed less than 10% (Bewcastle, Birdoswald, Bowness, Burgh II, Carlisle, Carrawburgh, Greatchesters, Maryport, Newcastle, Ravenglass, Rudchester and Stanwix). At two sites (Housesteads and Wallsend) almost the entire plan has been recovered while at the remaining six the proportion ranges between 30 and 50% (Benwell, Chesters, Haltonchesters, South Shields, Vindolanda and both the early fort and later military compounds at Corbridge).

Aerial photography and, more recently, the extensive geophysical surveys carried out by Biggins and Taylor have provided a vast amount of additional detail about the layout of fort interiors. However, both techniques do not usually allow the structural remains of different periods/phases to be differentiated. The totality of available evidence suggests that in their internal planning the Wall forts conformed to the traditional layout employed by the Roman Army, the single deviation being the provision of secondary gates at either end of the *via quintana* at those forts which project north of the Wall.

Although the line of the defences has been established at most forts, and in many cases the gatehouses and towers explored (again mostly pre-1940), this has been done largely by means of narrow sections at widely spaced intervals. Large-scale examination of the defences (wall, rampart, rampart backing and ditch-systems) has rarely occurred. Understanding the often complex history of fort defences is best achieved by the investigation of large areas and this has occurred at very few forts (Housesteads, South Shields and Wallsend). Similarly, the potential of ditch fills in terms of environmental evidence remains largely untapped. Perhaps understandably, early investigators tended to target the principal and thus more substantial and display-worthy buildings such as the *principia*, the *praetorium* and granaries and at those forts where only a few buildings have been investigated these were usually the ones selected. The bulk of fort interiors were taken up with barrack blocks and the evidence these buildings can provide is key to understanding variations in the intensity of occupation over time as well as changes in garrison. Yet rarely have such buildings been investigated to any meaningful extent, Housesteads, South Shields and Wallsend being the exceptions with less extensive investigations having occurred (many decades ago) at Chesters, Greatchesters and Haltonchesters. A change in the strength of units in the third century is suggested by the introduction at South Shields, Wallsend and Housesteads of barracks with five or six, as opposed to eight or ten, *contubernia* and built as independent structures rather than conjoined in one long building as earlier. Recent analysis of the barracks at Wallsend has revealed the important discovery that where cavalry formed part or all of the garrison troopers and horses were accommodated in the same building.

Full-size structural reconstruction is something that has been attempted at three sites: South Shields, Vindolanda and Wallsend. At the second of these, representative sections of the Turf Wall and its masonry replacement have been erected along with reconstructions of a shrine and a shop. Wallsend features a reconstructed auxiliary bath-building based on that at Chesters while at South Shields a gatehouse, barracks and part of the fourth-century *praetorium* have been reconstructed on the original foundations.

In keeping with forts throughout the Empire, those along Hadrian's Wall were equipped with a number of military and/or official buildings and facilities which, either through choice or because of their size and/or function, were located outside the defences. These included the regimental bath-building, the parade-ground and, occasionally, a *mansio*. Bath-buildings have been excavated at Benwell, Carrawburgh, Chesters, Greatchesters and Ravenglass although even in the most recent case this occurred nearly a century ago.

The sites of regimental *balnea* are known at other forts either from antiquarian observations (Beckfoot, Bowness, Housesteads and Moresby) or geophysical survey (Birdoswald, Castlesteads, Haltonchesters and Maryport). At Burgh-by-Sands, a substantial building - possibly the bath-building - was destroyed by canal building in the nineteenth century. At Burrow Walls, Carvoran, Drumburgh, Newcastle, Rudchester, South Shields and Wallsend the location of the bath-house has yet to be determined.

Possible *mansiones* have been identified at Benwell (by excavation), Maryport (by geophysical survey), Chesters (aerial photography and geophysical survey) and Ravenglass (by structural debris).

Positively identified parade-grounds are few. One belonging to the predecessor of the known fort at South Shields has been tentatively identified while others, on the basis of large flat areas seemingly devoid of structural remains, have been proposed at both Housesteads and Maryport. The existence of such a facility at Benwell is attested epigraphically by an altar set up to the *Matres Campestres* (*RIB* 1334).

To complete the list of military extramural structures, aqueducts have been found at Corbridge, Greatchesters and Haltonchesters, tentatively identified at Carlisle and attested epigraphically at Chesters, while a circular feature 50m in diameter at Chesters has been proposed as a *gyrus* and a large circular depression north of the Wall at Housesteads as an amphitheatre.

That most forts were accompanied by civilian settlements had long been suspected from the evidence of antiquarian accounts, surface indications and chance discoveries as well as the partial uncovering of the *vicus* at Housesteads in the 1930s (Salway 1965; Mason 1984). This has been confirmed at many sites in recent years largely as a consequence of the geophysical surveys undertaken by Biggins and Taylor. Their surveys at Birdoswald, Carvoran, Castlesteads, Chesters, Haltonchesters, Housesteads and Maryport have in all cases demonstrated the existence of substantial civilian settlements of varying extent and complexity and including possible associated field-systems. The only substantial *vicus* excavation in modern times has been at Vindolanda where work is presently continuing with the exploration of buildings lying west of the third century fort. A recent programme of geophysical survey at many of the forts in Wales, in some cases accompanied by excavation, has confirmed the ubiquity of *vici* and demonstrated their appearance soon after the establishment of a fort (Hopewell, 2005; Sommer 2006). The placing of cemeteries at some distance from fort defences implies the growth of a *vicus* was anticipated. Indeed, as the evidence accumulates, *vici* appear increasingly as an inseparable and contemporaneous attribute of forts - or rather their garrisons - instead of the gradual and uncertain growth once envisaged.

In many of these settlements it is possible to discern the arrangement of roads and minor thoroughfares as well as the distribution and density of buildings, though the latter may be misleading given that it is impossible to determine if all were occupied contemporaneously. Precise regularity and detailed planning are not characteristics of these settlements even though the military set aside areas for them to occupy and probably dictated the position of the main thoroughfares. Rather they exhibit a more informal growth pattern based around the approach roads to the neighbouring fort and any by-pass routes. The new evidence reinforces the picture of the strip-building as the predominant form of building in these settlements although examples of larger and more sophisticated structures have been discerned in some of the larger *vici* such as that at Chesters. As usual with such buildings, these are generally placed end-on to the adjacent road, reflecting the essentially commercial nature of such settlements. In a few cases (Birdoswald, Chesters and Wallsend,), buildings - assumed to be civilian - are known beyond the Wall. The existence of wider than usual sections of road in some *vici*, such as that in the western *vicus* at Birdoswald, has been linked - on the evidence of Continental examples - with the provision of a market-place (Sommer 2006, 117-18).

The garrisons moved forward to the Wall-forts are likely to have been accompanied by civilian communities at their previous bases. Presumably moving with the military units these would have been prevented by the Vallum from establishing themselves immediately beside the Wall-forts. That they settled as close as possible to the new bases and immediately south of the Vallum is indicated by the discovery of a second-century *vicus* in just such a location at Housesteads (Birley 1961; 1962b). The civil settlement revealed by recent geophysical survey at Castlesteads may also have originated in this period and there is some evidence for a *vicus* of Hadrianic/early Antonine date at both Birdoswald and Rudchester. With the abolition of restrictions on the zone between the Vallum and the Wall, the *vici* were free to spread northwards close up to the fort defences.

At Castlesteads and Maryport geophysical survey has indicated the existence of what may have been a boundary ditch defining the limit of the *vicus*. As yet, actual defences around a *vicus*, or part of it at least, are known only at Wallsend within the study area. Although excavation within *vici* has generally been quite restricted, in the majority of cases the evidence suggests occupation terminated towards the end of the third century (e.g. Birdoswald, Wallsend and Vindolanda). The occurrence of Frisian style pottery in the *vici* - but not the fort - at Housesteads and Birdoswald is thought to have been made by the families of units of Frisii stationed here in the third century. Interestingly, its distribution at the latter site is restricted to one part of the *vicus*. What happened to the *vicani* in the fourth century is unknown.

Although religious structures are attested by epigraphy and/or sculpture at the majority of forts very few have been excavated. Those explored are the temple of Antenociticus at Benwell, *Mithraea* at Carrawburgh, Housesteads, Maryport and Rudchester, the temple of *Mars Thincsus* at Housesteads, Coventina's Well and the adjacent shrine to the Nymphs and *Genius Loci* at Carrawburgh, a temple to an unidentified deity at Vindolanda, along with another, circular, temple at Maryport. In addition, there are the five temple podia identified along the south side of the main east-west street at Corbridge. The demolition of these - and probably other religious structures nearby - in the fourth century resulted in the dispersal of their associated inscriptions, reliefs and statuary. This material records the worship of no less than twenty-five different deities, both classical and native, at Corbridge in the third century. Religious quarters of some considerable complexity are also attested by antiquarian observations and finds of inscriptions and sculptures at Carlisle and Housesteads. Others undoubtedly existed. The name of Bewcastle as recorded in the *Ravenna Cosmography* - *Fanum Cocidii* - implies this was the cult-centre of the god Cocidius but although several dedications are known the cult buildings have yet to be identified. With the exception of the example at Vindolanda, no religious structure has been investigated during the last forty-five years.

Cemeteries and religious quarters often existed in close proximity as demonstrated by discoveries at Benwell, Housesteads and Maryport. Chance finds of tombstones, sarcophagi or actual burials are known at the majority of sites suggesting, as one would expect, the presence of cemeteries along the approach roads. In some cases, these lie a considerable distance out from the fort (e.g. more than 1 km at Maryport) something which Salway - before the advent of geophysical survey - suggested long ago could suggest the intervening land was occupied by civilian buildings (1965, 166). Examples of mausolea have been excavated at Corbridge and Vindolanda. While small-scale investigations have occurred recently in cemeteries at both Beckfoot and South Shields there has been no large-scale research excavation to match that carried out for example at Brougham (Cool 2004).

Order of Forts and extramural settlement contributions (arranged east-west)

South Shields
Wallsend
Newcastle
Benwell
Rudchester
Halton Chesters
Chesters
Carrawburgh
Housesteads
Great Chesters
Carvoran
Birdoswald
Castlesteads
Stanwix
Burgh-by-Sands
Drumburgh
Bowness
Beckfoot
Maryport
Burrow Walls
Moresby
Ravenglass
Bewcastle

Schedule of Sites

South Shields (*Arbeia*)

N H Hodgson

The fort of *Arbeia* stood on the south side of the mouth of the River Tyne occupying the head of a promontory formed by a bend in the river. It was an easily defensible position having a steep slope to the south, the river to the north and west, and the sea to the east.

History of exploration

South Shields has the longest history of intensive excavation of all the forts in the Wall-zone. After High Rochester it was the second military site in the Roman empire to have part of its interior scientifically revealed and planned (1875). This was a rescue excavation, organised in response to the building of houses and schools that by the 1890s had covered the whole site except for the small area of 'The People's Roman Remains Park', where Richmond carried out the first modern excavations on the site in 1949-53.

The clearance of housing from the site began in the 1960s, leading to more excavation. Research and interpretation up to 1981 can be studied in detail in a series of publications. A new campaign of excavation initiated in 1983 has continued on an annual basis to the present time. This work has revealed a sequence of general major structural periods, reported on in 1994. Although since modified in detail, in broad terms this sequence is likely to be definitive as far as it refers to the known, and now extensively explored, stone fort. A policy of total excavation of selected areas has been pursued since 1983. This has allowed the recovery of complete archaeological sequences, from the prehistoric to the post-Roman levels. In addition the scale and totality of the work has allowed unprecedented insights into everyday life and social organisation in buildings such as barracks (of which no fewer than 15 have been excavated in their totality) and the *praetorium*. South Shields has the largest collection of finds from stratified contexts of any Wall site. As well as the collections, displayed remains and published reports, the results of research at South Shields are embodied in three full-size reconstructions of excavated Roman buildings *in situ*. These comprise the south-west gate of the first stone fort (opened 1988), a barrack-block of the period around AD 230 (2001), and most of the late-Roman commanding officer's house of the early-fourth century (2001). The design and decoration and fitting out of the superstructures of these buildings have in turn necessitated further programmes of research, much of it published.

81. South Shields fort re-emerges in the second half of the Twentieth Century

Layout and history

Despite gradual firming up of the chronological picture for the fort, there are still major gaps in our knowledge. The greatest problems involve the beginning of Roman occupation at South Shields, and correspondingly, its end or transformation into something else in the sub-Roman period. Spatially, understanding falls away immediately outside the walled area of the fort that is available for research. Even in the fort, 63% of the interior remains unexplored by modern excavation, with older trenches rarely penetrating below the latest Roman levels.

The total-excavation policy has resulted in the discovery of a multi-period prehistoric site beneath the east quadrant of the Roman fort. This included a mid-Iron Age roundhouse in an extraordinary state of preservation. The report on the prehistoric levels was published in 2001. The area in question was under cultivation at the beginning of the Roman period, so the whereabouts of the immediately pre-Roman settlement nucleus is unknown and we have no knowledge of how it was affected by the arrival of the army.

The date of the earliest Roman occupation remains unclear. Buildings, roads, and a possible parade ground found beneath the stone fort of c. 160 are not of a character likely to belong to a fort interior and are therefore interpreted as extra-mural activity associated with an as yet undiscovered early fort nearby. Finds from the site indicate the possibility of a Flavian presence but the earliest material that can be associated with Roman structural remains is Hadrianic. A road, timber buildings and an unfinished timber granary of

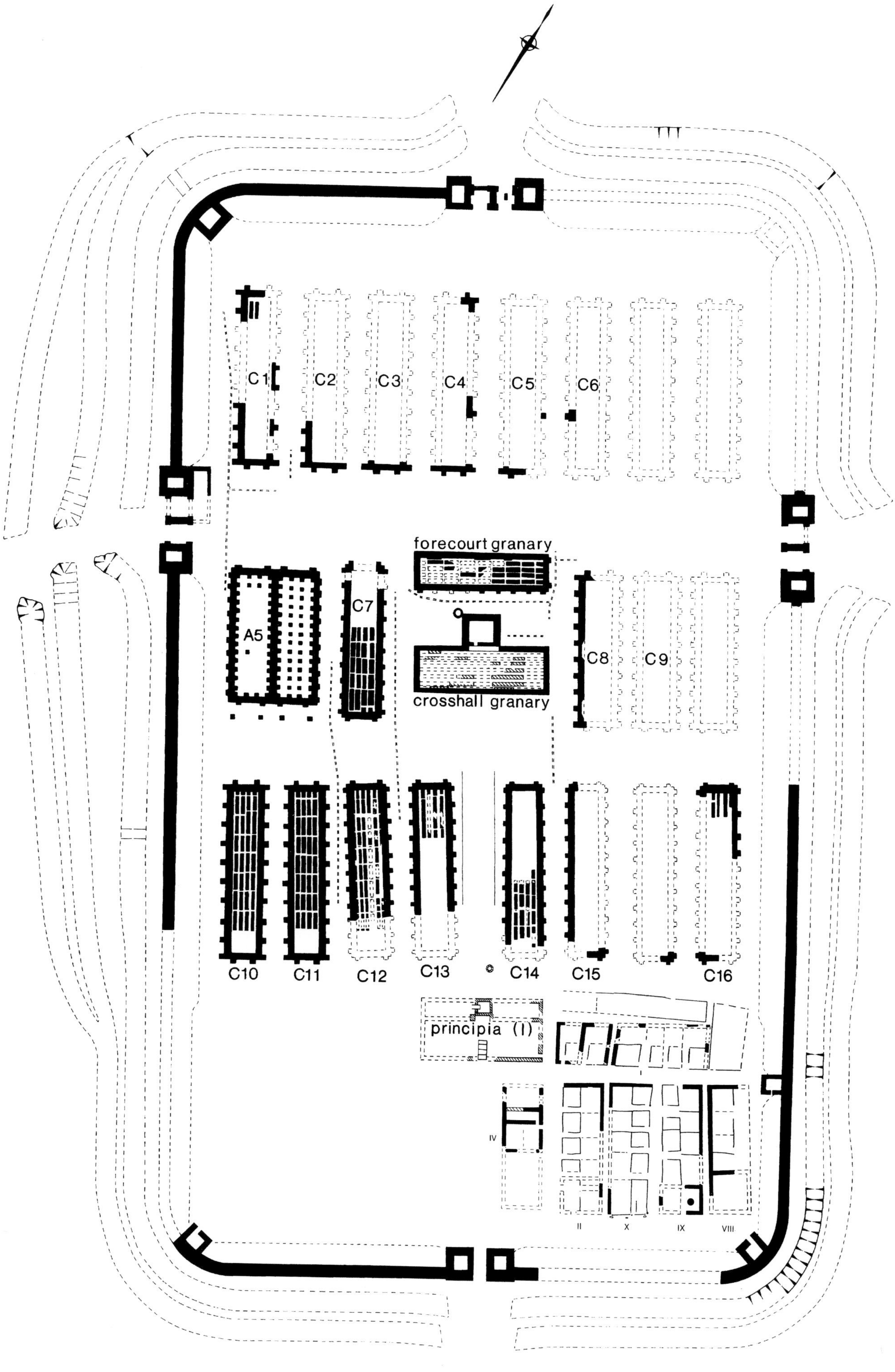

82. Plan of South Shields fort in the early third century

this date have been found beneath the later *vicus*, south-west of the known fort. The higher ground south-east of the known site is a possible location for an early fort.

The visible fort was built of stone from the outset in the mid-Antonine period (around 160) for a *cohors quingenaria equitata*. Its plan is similar to that of Wallsend, built around 35 years earlier. At South Shields two of the *retentura* barracks have been completely excavated and shown to be of the stable-barrack type first proven at Wallsend. As at Wallsend the barracks were timber to begin with and replaced in stone after an interval.

In 208-11 the fort was extended in area from 1.67ha to 2.1ha in order to form a supply-base for the Severan campaigns in Scotland. A remarkable and rare series of lead-sealings testifies to the movement of property of the Severan imperial family through the supply-base, and these seals have recently been found for the first time stratified in its construction levels. The supply-base, garrisoned by *Icohors V Gallorum*, outlived the Severan campaigns and remained in commission until at least the later-third century. The longevity of the supply-base is one of the outstanding historical discoveries of the recent excavations: the existence of a permanent coastal supply-base, evidently for the import of foodstuffs from a considerable distance for the Wall garrisons, casts doubt on the assumption that army supplies came predominantly from local farmers. Around 225-235 a permanent reorganisation of this unit is signalled by the rebuilding of its barracks to a new plan, in which each barrack possessed only five *contubernia*. This period was closed when a fire, probably the result of an enemy attack, destroyed parts of the fort.

The fire was followed by a general re-planning of the fort, or at least the southern half, the northern perhaps being retained as a reduced supply-base or used for some other special purpose. The new *principia*, ten barracks and a courtyard house formed a plan of recognisable late-Roman type (paralleled for example at Diocletian's place at Split) based on a cruciform arrangement of streets. The re-planning of the fort occurred in the period 286-c.318 and signifies the arrival of a new and larger unit (possibly the *numerus barcariorum Tigrisiensium* of the *Notitia Dignitatum*) to replace *cohors V Gallorum*.

As in the preceding period, the fourth century barracks contained five *contubernia*. As the complete complement of ten barracks is known, this allows the paper strength of the late-Roman unit to be estimated at around 400, divided into ten operational sub-units. The barracks were as formally arranged as their third-century predecessors, and even possessed officers' ends equipped with channelled hypocausts.

The courtyard house in the east quadrant, almost certainly the late-Roman commanding officer's residence, has been revealed as an architecturally ambitious peristyle house whose closest parallels occur in town houses in Mediterranean contexts as diverse as Ostia, North Africa and Syria. It functioned as an aristocratic residence until the period 350-80 and is of importance in demonstrating the high social status, and very probably the Mediterranean origins, of a fourth-century unit commander on Hadrian's Wall.

As it has emerged the plan of the fourth-century fort has confounded expectations and presented an alternative to the view of Hadrian's Wall manned in the fourth century by a peasant militia living in 'chalets'.

There was to be no further general re-planning of the fort, although many alterations were made to existing buildings in the second half of the fourth century. After c. 350-80 the commanding officer's house was no longer maintained to its former Mediterranean standards, but a nucleus of rooms was retained as a residential area which, on the evidence of coins running down to the Theodosian period, was occupied until at least the early fifth century.

There is evidence for a sudden dislocation in the life of the fort in the early-fifth century: this period saw the burial within the fort walls of victims of violent assault, whose remains have been radiocarbon dated. However, radiocarbon dating also shows that a community was present, working objects out of antler, in the mid- to late-fifth century, and a cemetery developed outside the south-west gate in this period. It is uncertain into what chronological context to fit the persuasive evidence that a church was constructed in the *principia* forecourt. A table altar belonging to the probable church was found *in situ* in the 1875 excavation. An Anglo-Saxon occupation of the site is signalled by the recent recognition of a number of seventh- to ninth-century objects from immediately above the latest Roman levels in the east corner of the fort, which can be linked with larger numbers in the collections deriving from the 1975 excavations. King Oswin was said in a tradition recorded by Leland to have been born in the fort at South Shields; if true this would have been in the early 600s, and it is plausible that the Roman fort was a royal site in this period. Very few structural remains have been recognised that may possibly be associated with this occupation. What there is includes a timber portal inserted into the south-west gate and a timber building over the ruins of a fourth-century barrack. Possibly some principal Roman buildings were retained and supplemented with humbler timber structures. A plausible model would be that with the shift of this Anglo-Saxon power centre to another site by the ninth century, the site was abandoned; Leland recorded another tradition that it was destroyed by the Danes. The excavators of 1875 recorded that the latest structures in the fort were covered with a 'sheet of ashes', of which all trace was removed at that time. In conclusion, although the post-Roman period is poorly understood, future excavation at South Shields has the potential to recover complete sequences from the late-Roman, through the fifth-century to the Anglo-Saxon period.

Extramural Area

Official buildings and structures

The discovery of a hypocaust in the area beyond the southern half of the eastern defences in 1798 hints at the location of the bath-house (Surtees 1820, 101-2).

The existence of a sea-port guarded by the fort at South Shields is certain given the existence of the supply-base. Despite a number of archaeological interventions in advance of development at various points between the Mill Dam and River Drive, on the river frontage west of the fort, its whereabouts remains unknown. However, the use of the mouth of the Tyne by troop transports in the Roman period is indicated by objects from the Herd Sand on the south side of the river entrance. Finds since 1830 from the sands or dredged from their northern edge include a shield-boss of the *Legio VIII Augusta*, a helmet cheek-piece, a *patera*, 67 coins, and other items. The finds are all remarkably close in date, falling in the second half of the second century, and the latest coin is of 176-80. It has been convincingly argued that the objects and coins, which still come to light from time to time, are being washed out of the wreck of a ship that came to grief entering the mouth of the Tyne in the later-second century. The presence of a legionary of *VIII Augusta* (based at Strasbourg) would suggest a troop ship bringing reinforcements into the northern frontier zone, perhaps in response to the invasion attested in the early 180s. It may one day prove possible to locate the remains of this shipwreck.

Civilian buildings
Nothing is known directly of the overall plan of the *vicus* belonging to the known fort. There is, however, an extensive record of finds and observations running back to the nineteenth century which indicates extra-mural activity on all four sides. Despite the problem of access caused by overlying housing dating to the 1970s, there is potential for further knowledge when opportunities arise. A rescue excavation 125m WSW of the fort in 2002 found well-preserved remains of second- to third-century timber *vicus* buildings at a depth of almost 2m, suggesting that the entire plan of the *vicus* may well survive intact beneath nineteenth- and twentieth-century housing. In common with other *vici* on the northern frontier, mainstream occupation seems to have finished before the end of the third century.

Religious structures
The building/restoration of a temple by Domitius Epictetus and his fellow soldiers is recorded on *RIB* 1056 but the location of the building is unknown.

Cemeteries
Important excavations were carried out in 1993 recovering both cremations and inhumations in a cemetery area 230m south of the fort. This was close to the find-spots of the tombstones of Victor and Regina, nineteenth-century discoveries which give a touching insight into the lives of members of the civilian population attendant on the fort in the mid-second century.

Wallsend (*Segedunum*)

N H Hodgson

The fort at *Segedunum* marked the eastern terminus of the Wall. Its remains were levelled by eighteenth-century agricultural improvement and suffered enormously when deep coal mining was pioneered at Wallsend from the 1780s. By 1900 the site was completely buried beneath the now-vanished streets of the ship-building town that Wallsend had become. As at South Shields, the setting of the fort in a decayed and regenerating industrial area has provided opportunities to reveal the site once again and to carry out extensive excavation.

History of exploration
The principal campaign was by Charles Daniels in 1975-84 (Daniels 1980; 1989. Still being worked up for final publication at the time of writing). This has been supplemented by further large-scale digging in 1997-8, published in 2003 (Hodgson 2003). Taken together this work offers a remarkable insight into aspects of the structural development of a Wall-fort.

83. Aerial view of Wallsend fort

Layout and history
This 1.64 acre fort was built directly over an Iron Age field system, still being actively cultivated on the eve of the selection of the fort site in the Hadrianic period. Wallsend contributes our only complete plan of a Wall-fort as first built in the 120s. Within the stone defences the barracks were entirely of timber, the principal central-range buildings of stone. The Hadrianic fort accommodated a *cohors quingenaria equitata*. Its four cavalry troops (*turmae*) were housed in the four barrack blocks of the *retentura*, without any separate stables. This way of accommodating men and horses under the same roof is now recognised as the standard form of barrack accommodation for cavalry in the principate.

During the second half of the second century the timber barracks were rebuilt in stone. The fort plan remained unchanged except for the addition of a courtyard building, almost certainly a hospital, and a forehall fronting the *principia*. The barracks were subsequently rebuilt and their plan rearranged to reflect a major reorganisation of the garrison, attested by inscriptions and the *Notitia Dignitatum* as being *Cohors IV Lingonum* in the third and fourth centuries. This rebuilding is not closely datable but had occurred before the mid-third century. The reorganised barracks are the buildings described by Daniels as 'chalets' and assumed to be of broadly fourth-century date. But it is now apparent that the fourth century levels were largely removed by agricultural and industrial activity before Daniels excavated the site.

The 1997-8 excavations confirmed that Daniels' work had left much of the surviving stratigraphy within the fort

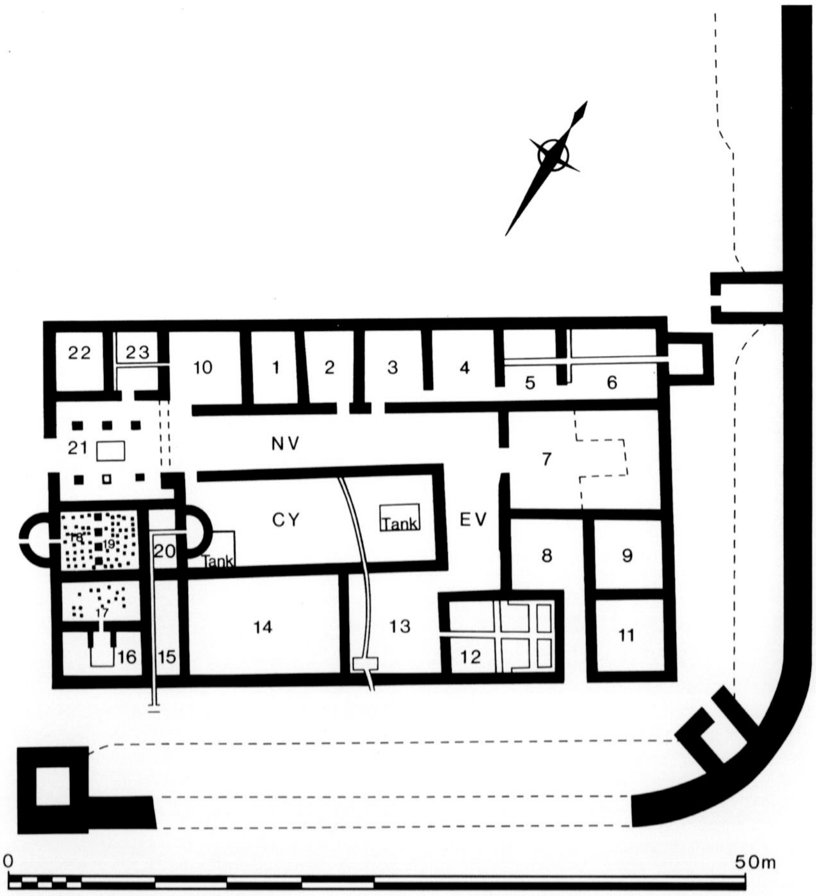

84. Plan of courtyard house at South Shields

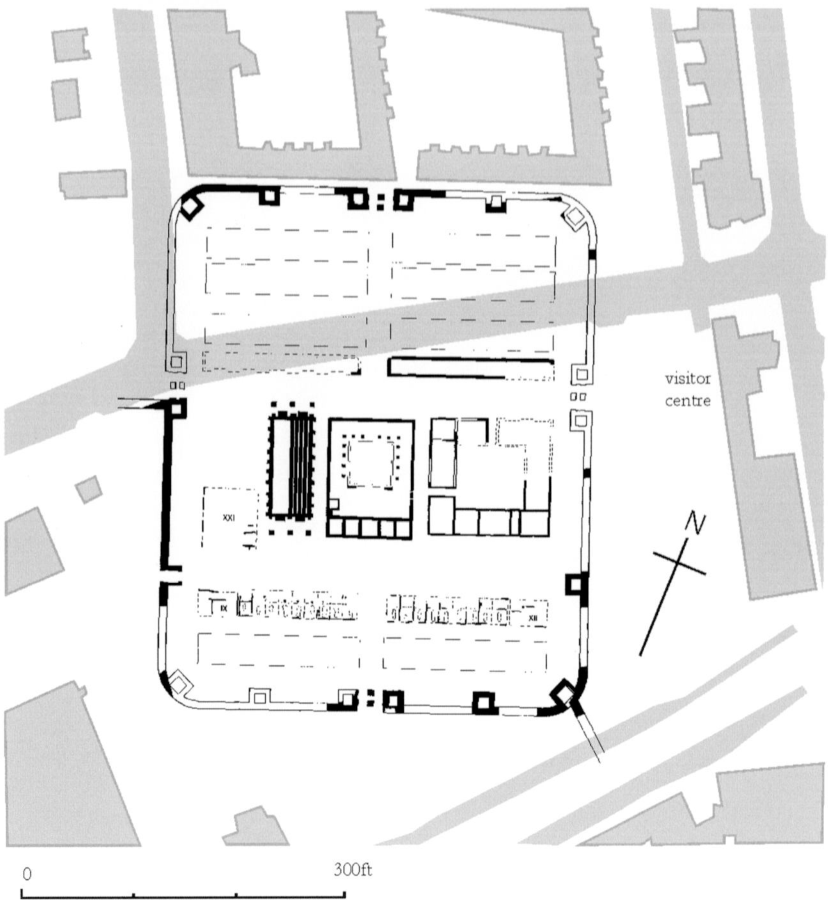

85. Wallsend fort, Hadrianic layout

intact, particularly the earlier levels. A swathe of the fort lies untouched by modern excavation beneath the highway of Buddle Street, which transects the site. Future excavation within the fort walls has the potential to clarify a number of outstanding problems. These include:

- The exact date of the third-century reorganisation of the fort and the details of the barrack plan that ensued. The new barracks included an additional insertion (re excavated in 1998) of irregular plan and timber construction. This has been interpreted as accommodation for cavalry irregulars of a type widely attested on the Wall in the early-third century. This hypothesis needs testing. Daniels' excavation plans suggest that there are other areas of the fort where such irregular barracks were inserted and where deposits relating to them will survive.

- The nature of the fourth century occupation. Much of the evidence for this has been lost, but the discovery of a zone of high coin-loss at the minor west gate, interpreted as a fourth-century marketing area, shows the potential. In general, fourth-century street surfaces survive even where the building plots have been truncated.

- Further finds and additions to the coin-list, already forming one of the larger collections of objects recovered from stratified contexts on a Hadrian's Wall site, would shed further light on the later history of the site and in particular the date when occupation ceased. At present the coin-list (numbering just over 400) does not indicate occupation beyond c. AD 380.

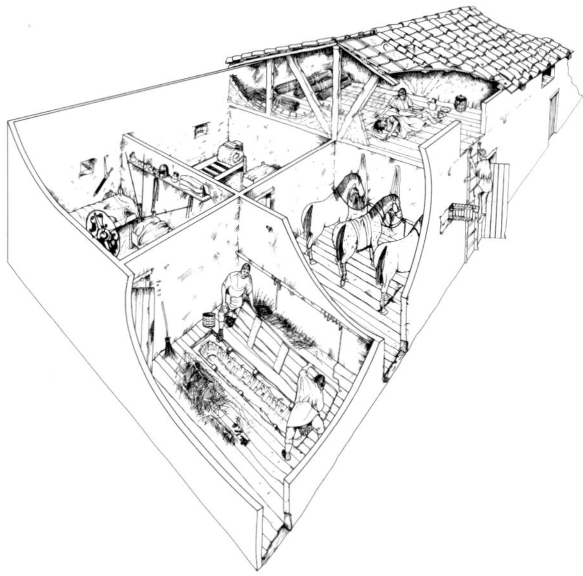

86. Reconstruction of front elevation of cavalry barrack

Extramural Area

Official buildings and structures
One can assume the existence of a riverside landing place or quay south of the fort. It would have been natural for the very end of Hadrian's Wall, which ran as a branch wall from the south-east angle of the fort for a considerable distance into the Tyne, to have been marked by a monument.

Civilian buildings
The *vicus* is fragmentarily known from excavations in 1993-8 and occupies the area south and west of the fort (Griffiths 1993; Snape & Bidwell 1994; Hodgson 2003). The settlement was enclosed in whole or part in the third century by a system of defensive ditches and banks, seen 65m west of the fort, running south from Hadrian's Wall, and presumed to turn to front the river Tyne 75m south, where a section of defences was found in the Swan Hunter yard in 2002. That there were outbuildings at a much greater distance from the fort than this is demonstrated by a series of religious dedications indicating an area of shrines some 400m to the west. These and other civilian buildings may be presumed to line the Military Way as it runs west from the minor west gate (*porta quintana*) of the fort. The extra-mural settlement and its annexe-like enclosure had passed out of use by the late-third century.

More recent work has demonstrated the potential of the extra-mural areas to yield information, a fact of particular note given the recent closure and forthcoming change of use of the Swan Hunter shipyard. This lies immediately south of the fort, and embraces much of the area of the outer defensive enclosure described above. A section recently excavated across the north-west ditches of the fort revealed a Roman stone building lying beyond the defences to the north of the Wall, a phenomenon already noted in the case of a timber building outside the East gate in 1998. As well as these buildings, fields or agricultural plots of Roman date are known to extend for at least 100m north of the fort and the Wall.

Religious structures
No evidence.

Cemeteries
No evidence.

Newcastle upon Tyne
P T Bidwell

The fort at Newcastle was situated on a bluff overlooking the Lort Burn to the east, and to the south the bridge over the River Tyne (from which the fort derived its name, *Pons Aelius* or possibly *Pons Aeli(i)*). The fort was detached from Hadrian's Wall which seems to have run down a small valley to its north, on the line of The Side.

History of exploration
Although fragments of Roman buildings had come to light from time to time during re-development the position and size of the fort were only determined beyond doubt in the late 1970s (*NCH* xiii; Snape and Bidwell 2002; Bidwell and Snape 2002).

Layout and history
The fort was built in the late second or early third century and had an estimated area of about 0.5ha (1.2 acres). Parts of the principia and two granaries have been excavated, as well as fragments of probable barracks. The principia has no forecourt and is of exceptionally small size, as are the granaries. Few new forts of this period are known anywhere in the empire, and the plan of Newcastle might

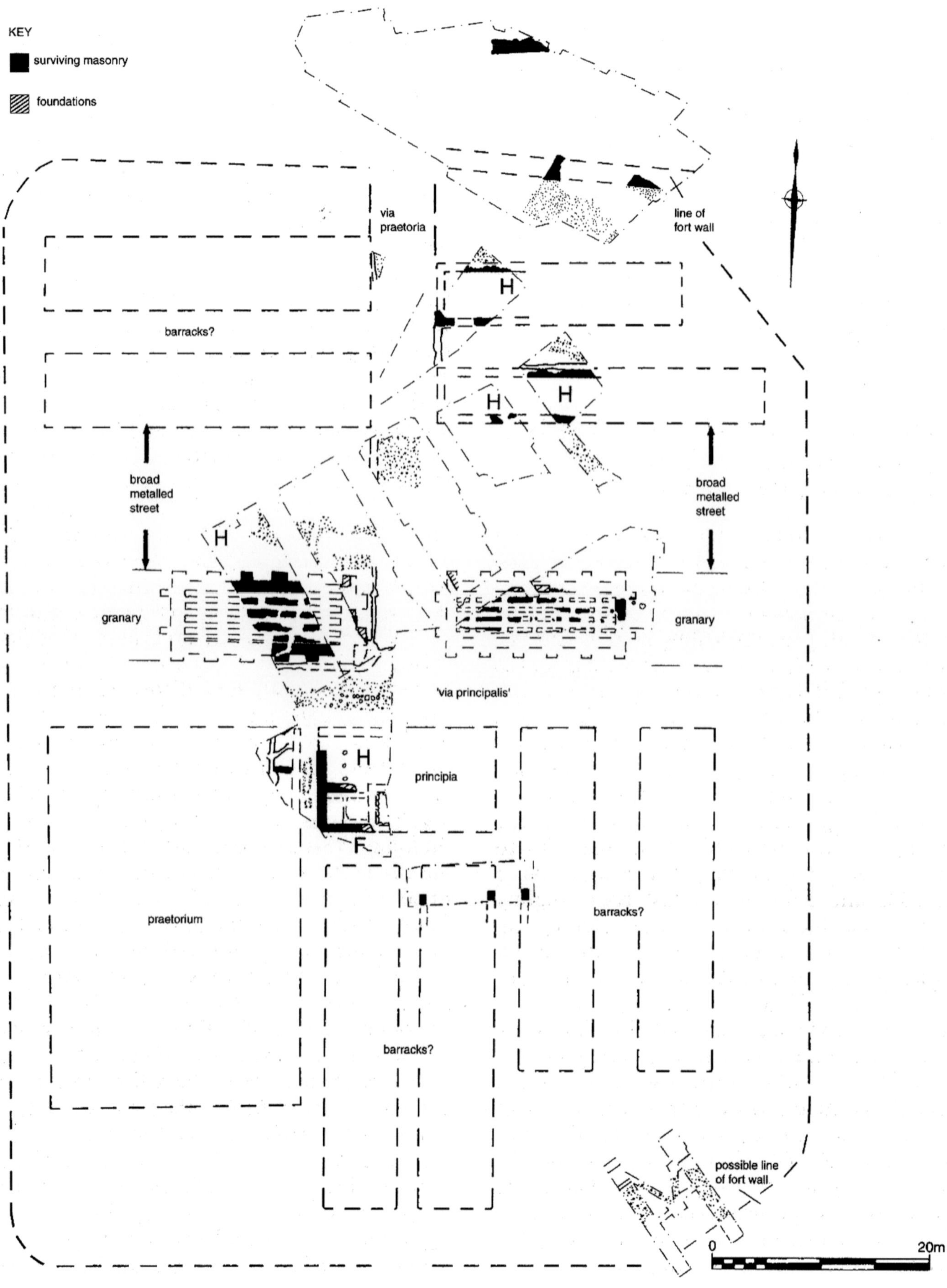

87. Reconstruction of the ground plan of the fort at Newcastle

reflect the reductions in unit size suggested by the plans of the third-century barracks at South Shields, Vindolanda and elsewhere. The plan of the fort, with the granaries placed in the *praetentura* opposite the *principia*, is also unusual and is perhaps an early occurrence of the cruciform plan typically of late-Roman date (cf. South Shields; Bidwell 1996). Newcastle is thus potentially of exceptional importance to our understanding of Roman castrametation in an age of transition. It is unfortunate that so many elements of its plan are uncertain.

The pattern and quantity of coin losses suggest that in the fourth century a market was established on the *via praetoria* (cf. subsequent discoveries at Carlisle). During its period of use (from the 330s to the 350s, or possibly through to the 360s or 370s), the fort can hardly have had a full garrison, although the *principia* might have been restored to use in the late fourth century. A cemetery (publication forthcoming) was established on the fort site in the late seventh or eighth century, following some poorly-understood building activity. The partial survival of post-Roman deposits and well-defined chronological horizons represented by later activities mean that Newcastle is one of the four key sites in the Wall-zone for understanding the transition of power between the Roman and Anglo-Saxon periods (the other three sites being Carlisle, Corbridge and South Shields).

Extramural Area

Although the area of the *vicus* and cemeteries is poorly known, discoveries include a stone sarcophagus and waterlogged features. A third-century cremation is known at the Gunner Tower, on the probable line of the Military Way almost a kilometre west of the fort.

Benwell (*Condercum*)

P T Bidwell

The entire fort and its environs are now built over, but small-scale rescue excavations and watching briefs (e.g. Holbrook 1991) have shown that the preservation of archaeological deposits is good.

Benwell (2.06ha, 5 acres) projects beyond Hadrian's Wall and appears to have been built to accommodate an *ala*; a cavalry regiment was certainly stationed at the fort by the 180s. Large areas of the *retentura* and the central range were investigated in the 1920s and 1930s, but the *praetentura*, covered by a Victorian reservoir, is a blank and elsewhere knowledge of building phases and the internal details of buildings are mostly lacking (Simpson & Richmond 1941).

Extramural Area

Official buildings and structures
The fort baths, revealed in the eighteenth century, stood 275m south-west of the fort.

A *mansio* lay just beyond the Vallum about 80m from the south gate of the fort and east of the road heading south. In its original form this was a simple rectangular structure measuring 23 by 17m (Petch 1928).

Civilian buildings
Excavations south of the fort in the 1930s revealed a group of civilian buildings overlying the filled-in Vallum to either side of the causeway. Of timber construction initially, these were later rebuilt in stone (see Salway 1965, 70-76). Other, presumably civilian buildings, lying near the *mansio* were partially examined in 1928 (Petch 1928, 74 n.8).

Religious structures
Excavations in 1862 explored a second century temple dedicated to Antenociticus lying 60m east-north-east of the fort's south-east angle. A second temple is attested by an inscription that records its restoration in 238 AD (*RIB* 1334).

Cemeteries
Little is known about the position and extent of the cemeteries apart from the discovery of a cremation burial at Benwell Lane, 400m south of the fort.

Post-Roman
Two late sixth- or early seventh-century Anglo-Saxon brooches have been found near the temple.

Rudchester (*Vindobala*)

D J P Mason

This fort guarded stood immediately east of the valley of the March Burn, an ancient route to the Tyne ford at Newburn. The land falls away to the March Burn on the west and to the Rudchester Burn on the south and east. The size of the fort is 1.80 ha (4.50 acres). *Cohors I Frisiavonum* constituted the garrison in both the third and the fourth centuries (*RIB* 1395; *ND* xl36).

History of exploration
The first major excavations were by Parker Brewis in 1924 which *inter alia* showed that the fort projected north of the Wall (1925). The next and also most recent investigations occurred in 1972 when part of the south-eastern quarter was investigated (Gillam et al 1973). An analytical field survey of the fort and its environs was carried out in 1990 (Blood & Bowden 1991).

Layout and history
Little of the fort plan is known apart from the headquarters building and a granary to its west revealed in the 1924 campaign and a barrack block found in the south-east quarter during the 1972 excavations. Destroyed by fire, this had been rebuilt to the same plan in the late second or early third century. By the last quarter of the third century this had fallen into disuse; its ruined walls covered by a layer of humus. This part of the fort was re-commissioned c. 370 AD when a series of timber-framed buildings set on stone sill-walls were erected.

Extramural Area

Official buildings and structures
None known as yet.

Civilian buildings
The land to the south and south-west of the fort is known to contain building remains, presumably those of *vicus*

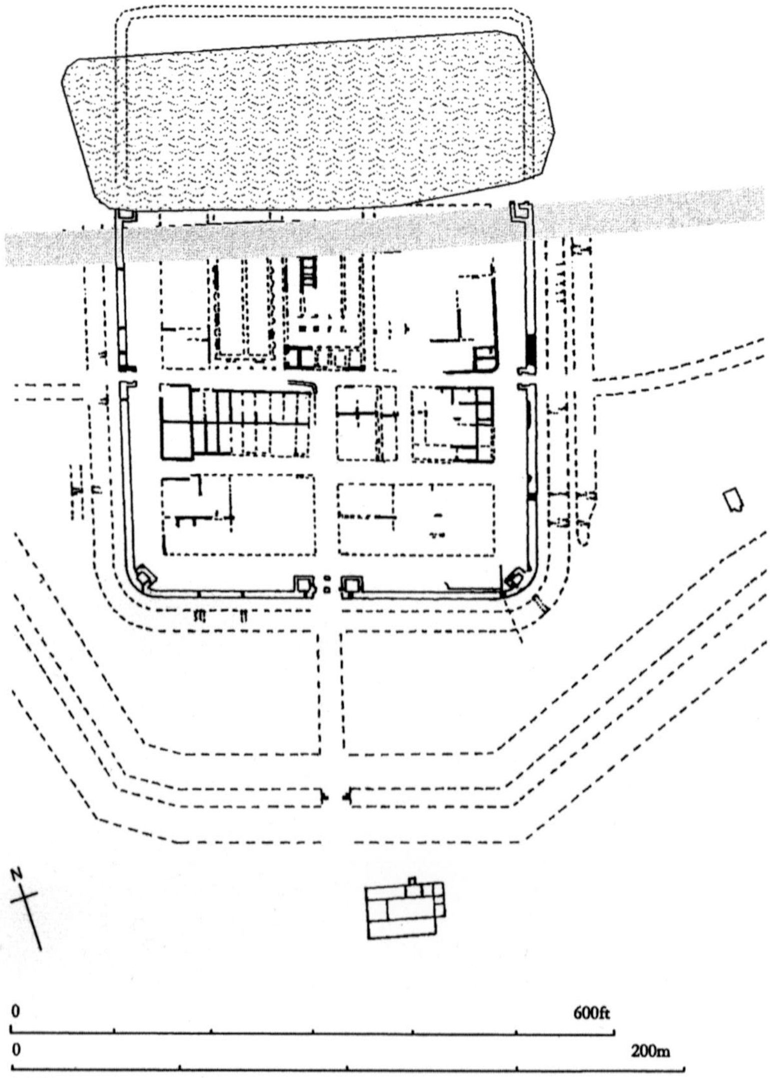

88. Plan of Benwell fort

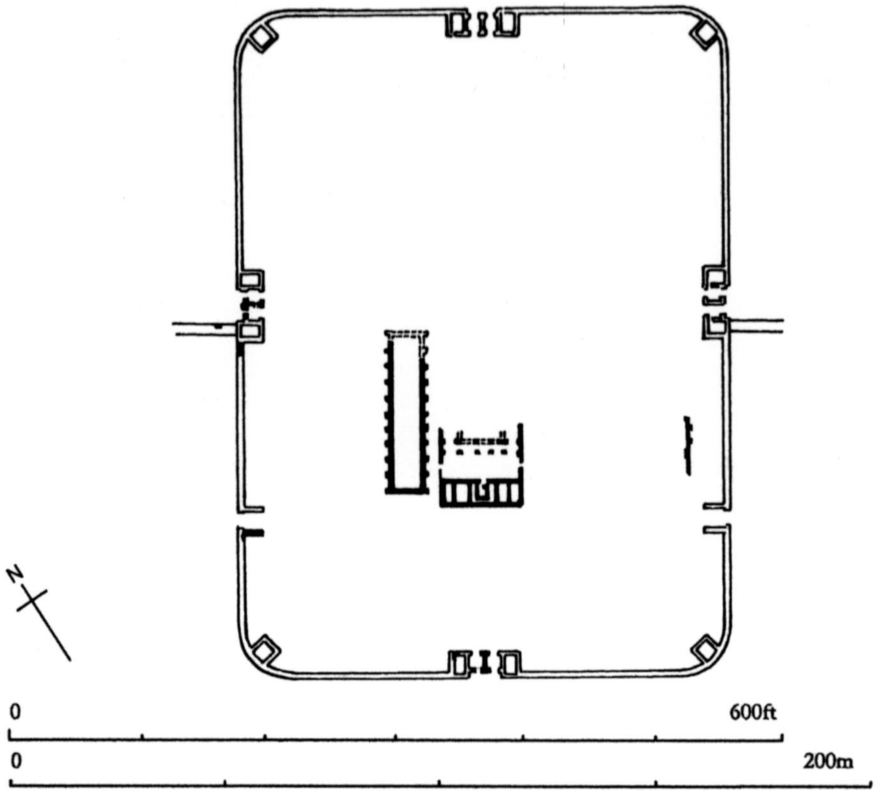

89. Plan of Rudchester fort

structures (Gillam et al 1954, 177). Excavation of a third century *Mithraeum* to the south-west of the fort in 1953 found traces of underlying and unrelated buildings associated with Antonine pottery (Gillam et al 1954, 183-6). Although the precise course of the Vallum here is unknown, these almost certainly lay to the south of it and thus would be most likely to belong to a second century *vicus*. Bruce refers to suburbs lying to the south-east of the fort.

Religious structures
A *Mithraeum* was excavated to the south-west of the fort in 1953 (above).

Cemeteries
As yet unlocated.

Halton Chesters - (*Onnum*)

D J P Mason

Located 8.5km east of Chesters, the fort at Halton Chesters occupied an area of high ground immediately east of the Fence Burn so as to command the ridge lying to the north. It appears to have been constructed to maintain a regular spacing of forts. The ground is reasonably level to the east and slopes down gently to the south. The fort platform is visible along with the denuded southern rampart and its accompanying ditch. The fort was 1.75 ha (4.37 acres) in size originally and was later extended to 1.95 ha (4.87 acres). It projected north of the Wall with the latter meeting the fort wall immediately south of the double-portalled gates as at Rudchester and, also like the latter, with minor gates south of the Wall. The garrison in the third and fourth centuries was the quingenary *Ala I Pannoniorum Sabiniana* (*RIB* 1433; *ND* xl 37). The Wall and ditch, dug to its full depth, crossed the site and were obliterated when the fort was erected. Whether the Wall was actually built is unknown as it lies beneath the road.

90. The bath-house at Chesters

History of exploration
A fourth century bath-house in the north-western quarter of the interior was excavated in 1823-7 (Hodgson 1840, 179-80, 316-20). Three excavation campaigns have been undertaken; by Simpson and Richmond in 1935-6 (1937, 151-70), and by Jarrett in 1956-8 and 1960-1 (1959, 177-90, 1960, 153-60; *JRS* 51 164, 52, 164). Further information about the fort and its *vicus* has been produced by geophysical survey in 1995 and 1999 (Berry & Taylor 1997; 1999).

Layout and history
The *principia* has been partly examined. It had a forehall attached to it - enclosing the *via principalis* - in the early third century. Geophysical survey has revealed the commandant's house to its east. To the west, excavation disclosed a granary and, beyond it, a hospital. Geophysical survey has revealed two double barrack blocks. In the north-east quarter a double-barrack, a stable and a store have been found. Two phases of buildings were found, the later with superstructures of wattle and daub. In the opposite half of the *praetentura* geophysical survey has revealed the bath-building seen in 1823 and another double barrack.

An extension was added to the fort on its western side south of the Wall in the early third century giving it an unusual L-shaped plan. The original fort wall was demolished. The extension contained another bath-house and other buildings of uncertain function.

For much of the third century the garrison was reduced considerably but occupation intensified towards the end of the century. Buildings of this period are characterised by timber superstructures resting on stone sill-blocks.

Extramural Area

Official buildings and structures
A large building outside the south gate revealed by geophysical survey may be the Hadrianic bath-house. The aqueduct for the fort is known. It entered via the north gate and its source was a spring 1.5 km to the north-west.

Civilian buildings
Antiquarian descriptions of buildings south of the fort (e.g. Horsley 1732, 142) have recently been confirmed by geophysical survey and a minor excavation. Civilian buildings can be seen lining both the Military Way, which enters the fort via the minor gates, and the road leading south beyond the Vallum. Some are typical strip-buildings while others appear set within their own enclosures. Metalworking is indicated by the discovery of a shale slab incised to form moulds for the casting of a variety of small objects. Jewellery was produced using both gold and local shale.

Religious structures
A relief of Mercury (*CSIR* I.1 206) and two reliefs and an altar associated with the Mother Goddesses (*CSIR* I.1 240 & 241; *RIB* 1424) hint at shrines outside the fort.

Cemeteries
South of the fort and immediately north of the hamlet of Halton at least one barrow can be seen.

Chesters (*Cilurnum*)

D J P Mason

This fort guarded the crossing of the Tyne, standing on its west bank. The land falls away gently to the south but more rapidly to the east down to the river while rising to the west. Projecting north of the Wall, the fort covered an area

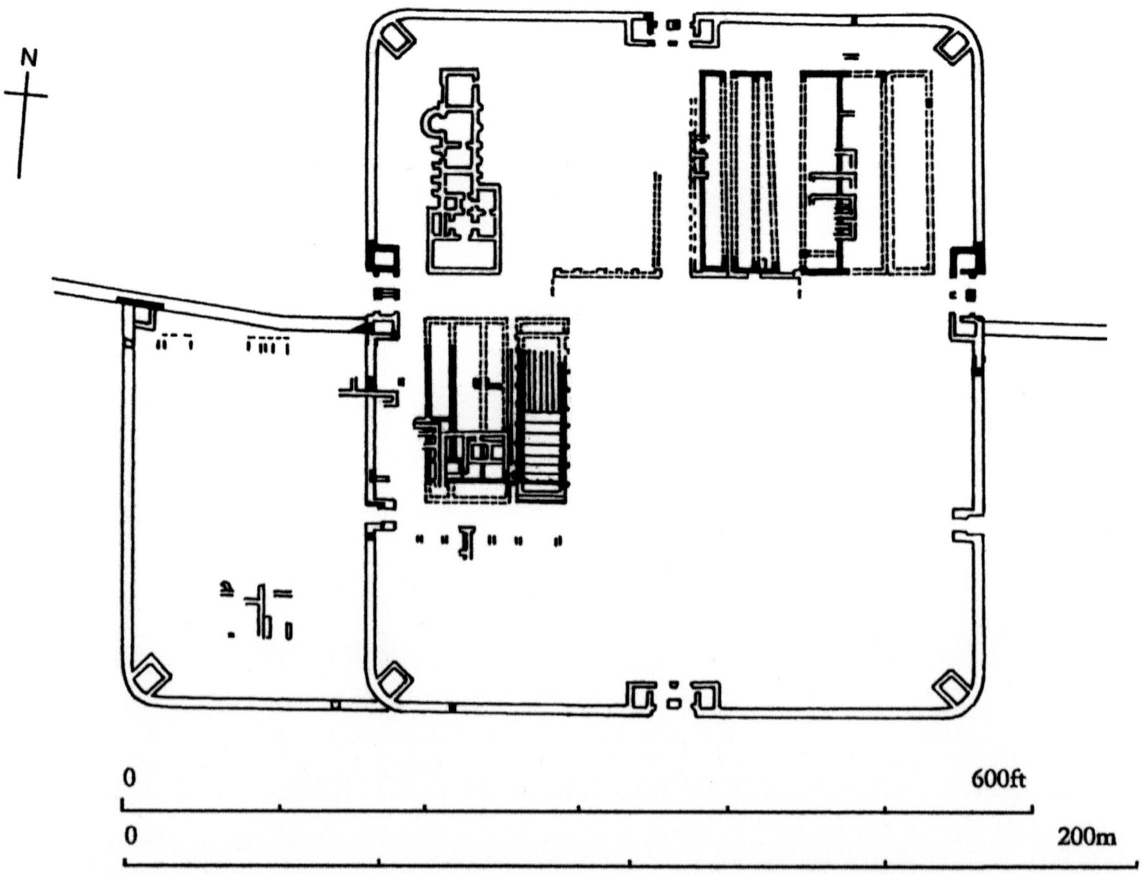

91. Plan of Halton Chesters fort

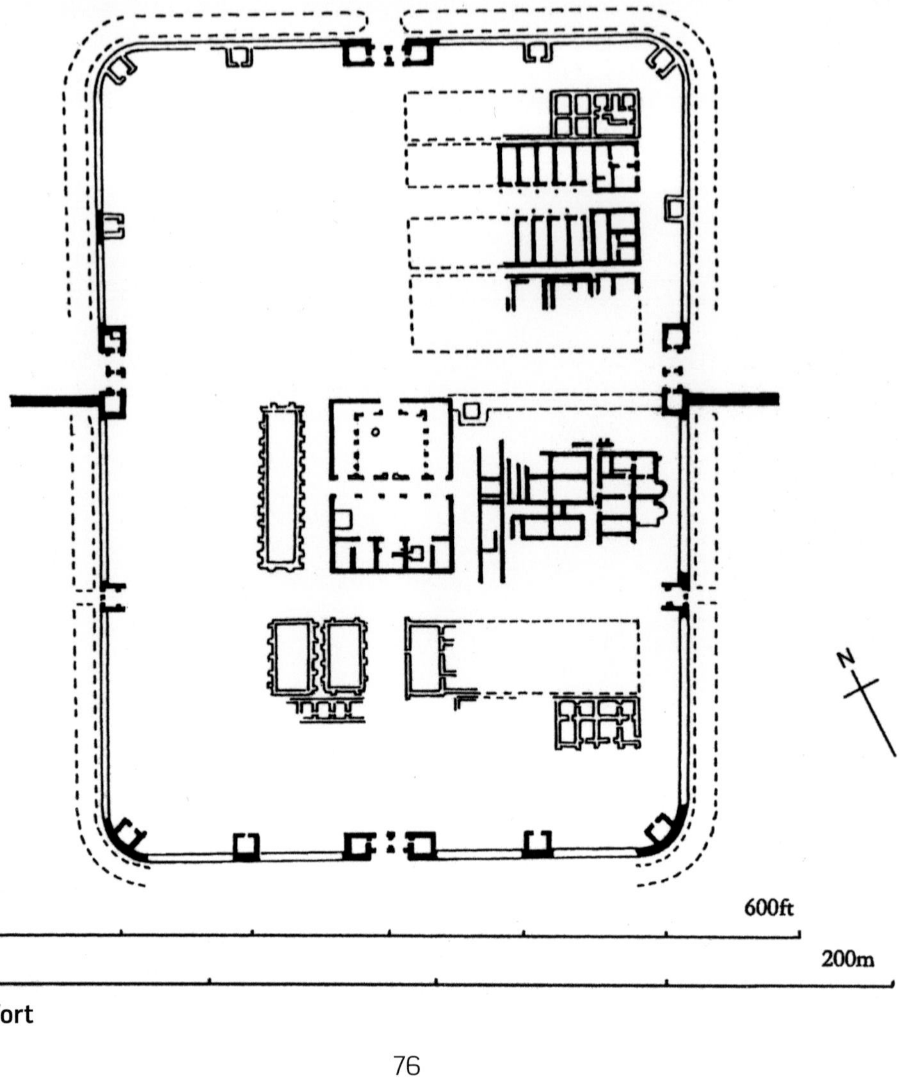

92. Plan of Chesters fort

of 2.32ha (5.75 acres). Successive units in residence were, Hadrianic, the *Ala Augusta* (Goodburn 1979, 346 No. 7), Antonine, *Cohors I Delmatarum equitata quingenaria* (Wright 1957, 229 No. 14), and, from the later Antonine period until the late 4th century, the *Ala II Asturum* (*RIB* 1462-6; *ND* xl38).

Owned for more than a century by the Clayton family, John Clayton began the exposure of the buildings visible today in 1843 (Clayton 1876; Bruce 1880; 1889a). Subsequently, Haverfield explored the relationship of the fort to the Wall and Vallum (*PSAN* 4 1907, 134ff), followed by Simpson (1923, 216). Simpson and Richmond investigated the relationship between the fort and the Broad Foundation of the Wall along with Turret 27a which it overlies (Anon 1946, 274).

Layout and history

Masonry of the fort wall is extant for considerable lengths as are the lower portions of the gateways. The lesser east and west gateways were single-portalled. The remains of the headquarters building are displayed as are those of the *praetorium* to the east of it and several barracks in the eastern part of the *praetentura*. Excavations in the nineteenth century revealed two small granaries in the *retentura* along with more barracks. Several phases of rebuilding were noted by the early excavators but these are undated while at some stage in the later Roman period the conventional barracks were replaced by individual 'chalet-type' structures (Daniels 1980).

Extramural Area

Official buildings and structures

The well-preserved remains of the regimental bath-building stand on the bank of the North Tyne 60m from the fort and immediately south of the road leading to the Roman bridge (Macdonald 1931; Breeze 2006, 204-9). A large building discernible on aerial photographs situated 70m south-east of the fort's south-east angle may be a *mansio* (Salway 1965, 55).

Civilian buildings

Remains hinting at the existence of an extensive civil settlement outside the fort and south of the Wall were noted by various antiquarians including Horsley (1732, 143-4) and Hutchinson (1776, 73). Buildings are also recorded north of the Wall. This was confirmed by aerial photography in 1949 carried out by St Joseph (1951, 55), the results of which were plotted by Salway (1965, 79-81 with Fig.8). A further plot of aerial photographs by RCHME in 1992-3 disclosed further details including the existence of buildings east of the fort extending right up to the rear of the Wall (Bidwell 1999, 117). The eroding walls of *vicus* buildings are visible in the river bank. Geophysical survey in 2003 revealed further details of the *vicus* including several possible courtyard plan buildings of considerable size and a circular feature over 50m in diameter, possibly a *gyrus* (Burnham et al. 2004, 273 and fig.8).

Religious structures

A number of religious dedications have been recovered but in no case has the location of a shrine or temple been confirmed.

Cemeteries

One cemetery is known to line the road which headed south-westwards from the fort and another lying on the east bank of the North Tyne (Horsley 1732, 143-4).

Carrawburgh (*Brocolitia*)

D J P Mason

This fort occupied a prominent platform east of the head of Newbrough Burn. The ground falls away gently to the south and west, is level to the north and rises steadily to the south. The fort was 1.52ha (3.80 acres) in size and lay entirely south of the Wall. Small sections of the defences and some of the internal buildings are visible. That it was one of the last forts to be added to the Wall is indicated both by the fact that the Vallum was levelled to make way for its construction and, probably, by a fragmentary building inscription of 130-33 AD (*RIB* 1550); this is supported by Hadrianic pottery from a primary context. The Hadrianic garrison was *cohors I Aquitanorum equitata quingenaria* (*RIB* 1550). The garrison in the third and fourth centuries was *cohors I Batavorum equitata quingenaria* (*RIB* 1534-6, 1544-5, 1553, 1559-60, 1562, *ND* xl 39).

History of exploration

Excavation occurred in 1876 (Clayton 1880), 1934 (Birley, 1935) and 1967-9 (Breeze 1972).

Layout and history

The 1960s explorations located the headquarters building on the south side of the *via principalis* and barrack blocks to the north. There was evidence of a major rebuilding in the early third century with occupation continuing into the late fourth century.

Extramural Area

Official buildings and structures

The regimental baths lay west of the fort immediately south of the Military Way and was excavated by Clayton in 1863.

Civilian buildings

There are antiquarian references to extensive suburbs on the west and south (Horsley 1732, 145-6; Hodgson 1840,183). Surface irregularities are still visible in the area east of the fort and aerial photography has shown development lining the Military Way and also extending around to the south of the fort (Salway 1965, Pl. IVb). Excavation for a new car-park in 1964 uncovered part of a possible *vicus* or funerary building outside the east gate and north of the Military Way

Religious structures

Carrawburgh has been described as 'exceptional - indeed unique - among the sites on Hadrian's Wall in being best known for remains of buildings of a religious rather than a military character' (Smith 1962, 59). Most famous is the Shrine of Coventina which lay on the south side of the Military way, 75m west of the fort. Excavated in 1876, this took the form of a 13m square precinct enclosing a natural spring encased in a stone-lined basin (Allason-Jones & McKay 1985). *RIB* 1522-1535 and 1543 came from the Well.

93. Plan of Carrawburgh fort

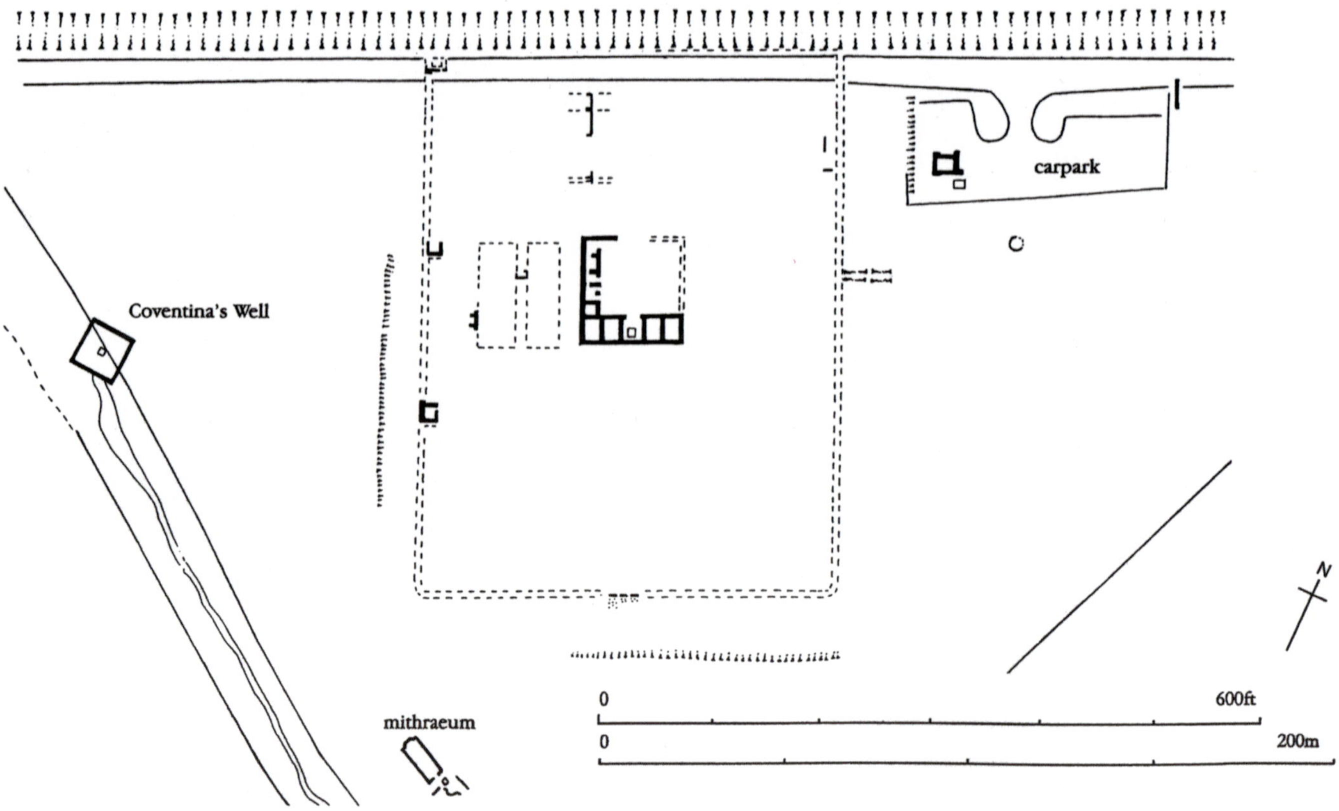

94. Excavations at Carrawburgh in the 1970s

A *Mithraeum* was discovered in the same valley in 1949. This was originally constructed in the early third century and measured 7.9 by 5.6m. It was later extended by 4.1m. A small narthex was screened off by a timber partition and wattle benches for worshippers lined the nave. Three altars at the northern end of the nave were dedicated by prefects from the First Cohort of Batavians (*RIB* 1544, 1545 and 1546). An altar dedicated to the Mother Goddess (*RIB* 1540) was reused in the nave and positioned so that its text was hidden by the eastern bench (Richmond & Gillam 1951, 33). A weathered statuette of a Mother Goddess was also installed in the narthex during the final phase. Pine cones, pork, lamb and chicken bones were found in the temple. The *Mithraeum* was abandoned by the early fourth century.

A small shrine to the Nymphs and *Genius Loci* lay directly south-east of the temple. This comprised a well, bench and an altar with an identical dedication on two faces. This latter named M. Hispanius Modestinus, prefect of the First Cohort of Batavians (Smith 1962, 61-66).

Cemeteries
Both Lingard (1807) and Hodgson (1840, 238) refer to the discovery of burials about 100m east of the fort in the vicinity of Milecastle 31. The structure under the car-park excavated by Charlesworth may relate to the cemetery.

Housesteads (*Vercovicium*)
J Crow

Housesteads is widely recognised as the most complete example of a Roman fort in Britain and amongst the best known throughout the Roman Empire. The visible remains of the fort include four imposing gates, a complete line of curtain walls and interval towers, and examples of all the main buildings found in an auxiliary fort: headquarters, commanding officer's house, barracks, granaries, hospital and latrines, plus part of the *vicus* outside the south gate. The remains of turret 36b represent an early stage in the construction of the mural barrier. The importance of the site is significantly enhanced by its archaeological and landscape setting on the line of the Whinsill crags. Since 1930 the fort and its environs have come into the public ownership and guardianship of The National Trust and English Heritage and the fort forms part of a well preserved and studied landscape 8km long and 1.1km wide (McGowan et al. 2002). Traces of the extra-mural settlement are known to extend to the east, south and west and since the 18th century the remains have been renowned as the most celebrated site on the Roman Wall, exemplified by William Stukeley's sketch 'A Cumulus of the Roman Antiquities at Housesteads' 1725, the earliest known illustration of a Wall fort. The site is particularly rich in stone inscriptions and sculptures collected and displayed in the small site museum, the Museum of Antiquities and the John Clayton Museum at Chesters.

The rich archaeological and epigraphic record from Housesteads ensures that the site remains central to continuing debates concerning the forts, garrisons and communities along Hadrian's Wall. The history of archaeological enquiry and conservation also provides a valuable resource to understand changing models of both archaeological interpretation and of preservation and display. Despite nearly two centuries of excavation there still remains great potential for further excavations within and outside the fort, although it is in the latter area where some of the major research questions lie. An outstanding concern must be the publication of the 1974-81 excavations and only then will the results be fully integrated in current and future Wall studies.

95. The 'chalet barracks' at Housesteads under excavation

History of exploration
Apart from 'diggings' reported by 18th-century antiquaries, the earliest excavations were carried out by Rev. John Hodgson, in 1822 and 1830-33, these included the excavation of the *Mithraeum*, south, east and west gates and part of building XV, with a clear description of the structures and early awareness of the stratigraphy. Records of these works survive in publications and in his notebooks, although his large scale plan of the site (one of the first, if not the first, to be made of a Roman fort) is lost. For almost the rest of the century, archaeological investigation was dominated by John Clayton, whose purchase of the site in 1838 was to form the core of his Roman Wall estate, one of the earliest archaeological estates in Britain and the basis for the contemporary conservation of the central sector of Hadrian's Wall. Clayton's legacy was the conservation of the Wall, although at the same time he undertook extensive excavations at Housesteads the results of which were reported in the various writings of John Collingwood Bruce. A more scholarly approach to the recording and investigation of the remains was undertaken in a single season by R. C. Bosanquet in 1898. This was the first academic description of the site, involving not just a systematic account of his excavations sponsored by the Society of Antiquaries of Newcastle upon Tyne, but an account of the earlier history and antiquarian enquiry. A significant photographic archive survives from this work. Further limited excavations including the north-west and north-east angles and a lime kiln (the latter being the only excavated example known from the line of the Wall) continued up to the First World War, carried out by F. G. Simpson, this work is characterised by careful draughtsmanship and description, although full publication had to wait until 1976.

After the war the attention of Wall-scholarship focused more on the problem-based agenda pioneered by R. G. Collingwood and no further work was undertaken until the fort came into the possession of The National Trust in 1930. However standards of recording appear to have sunk to the

96. Plan of Housesteads fort

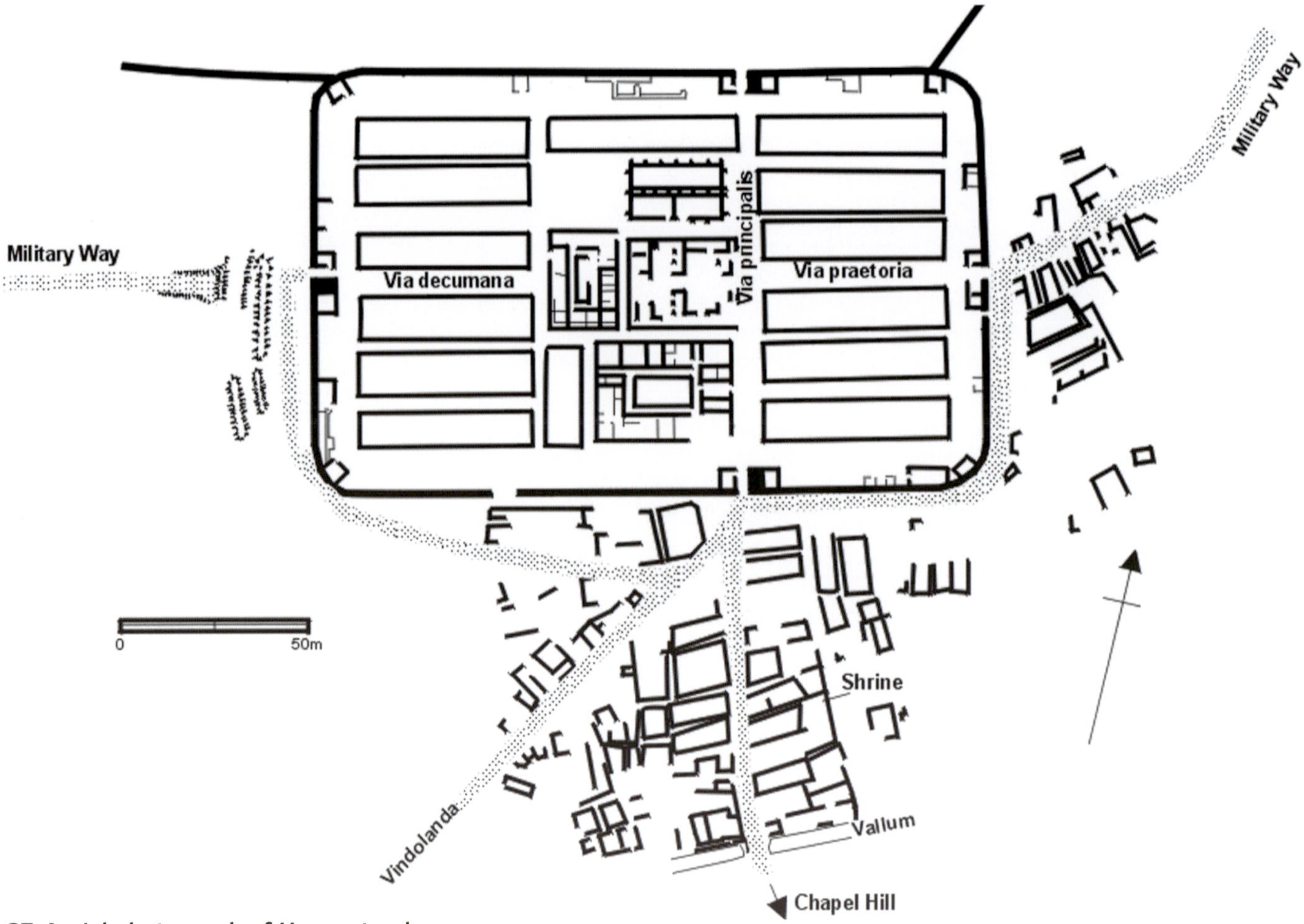

97. Aerial photograph of Housesteads

level of the days of John Clayton, when the granaries were cleared without record. Excavations directed by Eric Birley were concerned with the civil settlement outside the fort from 1931-34 and in 1936 the Knag Burn Gate was investigated. Of 27 known buildings only 6 were fully excavated and the remainder were only partially traced. These excavations were only published in interim form and many of the finds and pottery were either unpublished or lost. Much of a distinctive type of pottery known as 'Housesteads Ware' appears to derive from this area implying that part of the *vicus* was associated with units of Frisians known to have formed part of the garrison in the third century. No further excavations occurred until after the Second World War when the site came into guardianship, apart from the excavation of turret 36b, now displayed, but from which little excavation record is known. Over the next two decades excavations were carried out on the commanding officer's house, the 'hospital', and barrack XIV and building XV. The most intensive programme of excavations were carried out in the north-west corner of the fort from 1974-81 and for the first time the excavation was not limited to a particular building (barrack XIII) but included the roads and rampart areas. Publication of this work remains forthcoming. Since 1981 excavations have been limited to a section of the north rampart, area excavation of part of the terraces close to the museum and re-examination of the Knag Burn gate.

Layout and history

Little evidence is known for pre-Roman activity from the fort. The first Roman presence is demonstrated by the construction of the Broad Wall foundations along the north edge of the escarpment and the construction of turret 36b together with a cremation burial discovered in 1850 in the north-west corner the later fort. Construction began during Hadrian's reign of a large auxiliary fort (2.2 ha in area) intended to hold from the outset a milliary cohort of 800 men, probably the same *cohors I Tungrorum* known to have garrisoned the site in the third and fourth centuries. Although it is of conventional shape, because of its position on the crags the orientation known from most Wall forts was turned to the east through 90°. The fort's north curtain was set a little beyond the line of the earlier foundation. The early phases of a number of buildings are known: headquarters, commanding officer's house, 'hospital', together with angle towers, gates and sections of the curtain, which in places survives to ten courses in height. The height of the wall-walk can be estimated at 4.2 m. from stairs against the south curtain. The early layout of the barracks is best known from building XIII in the north-east corner.

The overall layout the buildings in the fort did not change significantly over the next two and half centuries. All the three major buildings of the central range underwent rebuilding and modification, but retained their original function into the late fourth century and only the granary was significantly reduced in size. In the *retentura* there were five barracks with another building IV containing evidence for use as workshops, a similar pattern is known for the *praetentura*, although building XV underwent a number of modifications before massive rebuilding c. AD 300. This was probably a store building close to the main east gate; a small bath house was later inserted in the east end. Detailed excavations of buildings XIII and XIV have revealed a complex structural history showing the transformation of contemporary barracks into distinctive rows of free-standing buildings, termed chalets. Significantly from the evidence of excavation over the past century there is no clear evidence for a reduction in the overall number of buildings during the course of the fourth century.

The gates and curtain underwent a number of changes. The north gate was reduced to a postern in the later second century and access north of the Wall was provided by the Knag Burn Gate. The west gate was reduced and subsequently blocked by the fourth century and access remained through the south and east gates. Initially there were only angle towers and single interval towers on the long north and south curtains. The curtain itself was backed by an earth rampart into which were constructed a regular sequence of cook-houses and ovens. In the third century much of this rampart was cleared and a number of rampart structures including workshops are known. In the fourth century however the rampart bank was reinstated and there is extensive evidence for major repairs to both the inner and outer faces of the curtain. In the final phase to the east of the north gate there is evidence to suggest the stone curtain had collapsed and was replaced in places by an earth bank and timber palisade.

Extramural Area

Official buildings and structures

The remains of a bath-house are known to lie east of the fort on the far side of the Knag Burn.

Civilian buildings

Outside the fort a civil settlement is attested from an inscription now displayed in the site museum. The visible remains are located on either side of the road leading from the south gate, but from field survey, air photography and most recently, geophysical survey, it is apparent that the settlement extended around the east and west sides of the fort. Roman structures extend down to the valley beyond the line of the Vallum, which is obscured by later field systems, but which was crossed by a causeway. Before recent geophysical surveys at Birdoswald and elsewhere, the remains at Housesteads represented the most extensive civil settlement known from the line of the Wall. In addition to ancient structures the hillsides around the fort preserve one of the most extensive relict field systems in northern England (fully surveyed by the RCHME in 1986). The terraces have now been shown to belong to the Roman period, probably after AD 200, although other linear field are late medieval or later in date.

Following the excavations in the 1930s it was argued that the *vicus* buildings south of the fort largely date to the third and fourth centuries, when settlement was allowed within the zone between the fort and the Vallum. In practice this historically determined model cannot be supported by the structural complexity known from many of the excavated buildings which indicate earlier timber phases. The earliest phase may have been more dispersed including occupation north of Chapel Hill and in the vicinity of the fort (Birley 1961; 1962b), this is likely to have expanded over the site of the Vallum at the same time as the extensive system of terraces was being laid out. Analysis of the coins from the *vicus* excavations suggests that most of the settlement was abandoned by the early fourth century.

Religious structures
Temples and/or shrines are known from antiquarian accounts and the discovery of many inscriptions and sculpture to have stood in the Chapel Hill area. A *Mithraeum* lying to the west of it has been excavated. A temple dedicated to *Mars Thincsus* and a shrine built around a spring were excavated in the 1960s.

Cemeteries
Three cemeteries are known at Housesteads: one flanking the Military way west of the fort; one west of the *Mithraeum*; and another in the Chapel Hill area, this last probably beginning in the third century after the demise of the early civil settlement.

Post-Roman
Immediate post-Roman activity is indicated by a cist-burial occupying a Roman water tank close to the north curtain, but no skeleton is recorded. This in turn may be associated with an apsidal structure nearby which is similar in size and form to a building identified as a church from Vindolanda. There are no documentary references to Housesteads during the middle ages, and the earliest use of the name appears later in the sixteenth century when Housesteads is reported as belonging to Nicholas Crane of Bradely Hall. By the end of the century the place was notorious as a lair of rustlers and thieves and famously, William Camden avoided the site for fear of the 'ranke robbers thereabouts'. The Armstrong family remained there until 1704 and soon afterwards it became the focus for antiquarian visitors to the Roman Wall, a pre-eminence it has retained until today. The main structural evidence for this era is the Bastle house, located at the south gate, one of several early modern buildings known from the fort and mostly removed by later excavators.

Great Chesters (*Aesica*)

J P Shipley

The Roman Fort of Great Chesters lies within the modern parish of Greenhead, (Tynedale district), in the county of Northumberland, approximately 65 km west of Newcastle upon Tyne, and 40 km east of Carlisle. Situated in the central sector, it occupies the site of milecastle 43, and lies on a relatively flat area of raised ground (approximately 210m above sea level) commanding fine views south across Haltwhistle Common which runs away towards the town of Haltwhistle, and the South Tyne Valley. To the east of the fort the land drops away towards the area of Cawfields Quarry and the numerous streams which feed the Haltwhistle Burn, with the whin sill escarpment visible as it cuts its way across the landscape towards the fort of Housesteads. Views to the west are dominated by the rolling landscape which continues to the settlements of Greenhead and Thirlwall, and the River Irthing which crosses the Wall near Gilsland. To the north, undulating moors roll away towards the old Forest of Lowes, with the immediate ground dipping towards the Tippalt Burn.

The forts name is recorded as *Aesica* on the *Notitia Dignitatum*, and as *Esica* on the Ravenna Cosmography and the Amiens Skillet. It is possible that the name can be identified in the post Roman period when it is reported, in the life of St Cuthbert, that the saint stopped mid way between Hexham and Carlisle at a *mansio* and people gathered at Ahse to hear him preach.

History of Exploration
The site of Great Chesters was investigated by a number of antiquarians during the nineteenth century however the fort never received the same intrusive study as other sites such as Housesteads and Chesters.

The earliest reference to an individual visiting the fort appears to be from 1691 when Thomas Machell mentions 'Chester by Woa-town', and although Raphaell Holinshed mentions 'Wall towne' and its position on the Wall earlier in 1577 he fails to mention Great Chesters by name. One can take Robert Smiths account (in the 1722 Gibson edition of *Britannia*) to be the earliest printed reference to the site when, in 1708, he notes 'at a place called the Chesters, two miles east of Caer-Vorran, are the ruins of another square city', while the fine preservation of the walls were noted by Alexander Gordon when he visited the fort with Sir John Clerk in 1724. This fine level of preservation was also noted by following antiquarians including William Stukeley and John Horsley who both make reference to structures standing within the fort, and the civilian settlement outside.

Intrusive investigation at Great Chesters seems to have commenced in the opening years of the nineteenth century, as when Lingard visited the Wall in 1807 he noted that the vaulted strong room in the *principia* had been exposed by the farmer (Daniels 1978, 182). It was not until the closing years of the century that the fort was host to its first planned excavations when, in 1894, the Northumberland Excavation Committee commenced its first season of work focusing on the south gate, west tower, south wall, and part of a barrack block in the south west corner. During this initial season a major hoard of jewellery from the latter part of the third century was discovered between floors of the west chamber of the south gate (Gibson 1903).

This work was followed up with a second season of work is 1895 when their attention turned to the *principia* (and a re-examination of the strong room), the south west angle, the south gate, and the east tower. In 1897 Northumberland Excavation Committee carried out a third and final season focusing on the west gate and bath house, however work on the bath house was never completed, and it was not until 1908 that the structure was fully excavated when Gibson and Simpson investigated the site (while working at nearby Cawfields Farm) discovering a hoard of late third century coins sealed by a destruction deposit (Gibson & Simpson 1909, 158-169).

In 1925 Simpson selected Great Chesters as the first site to be investigated by the newly formed Durham University Excavation Committee excavating sections of the north curtain wall and the northwest angle (Hull 1926, 197-203). This revealed a complete Broad Wall foundation to the

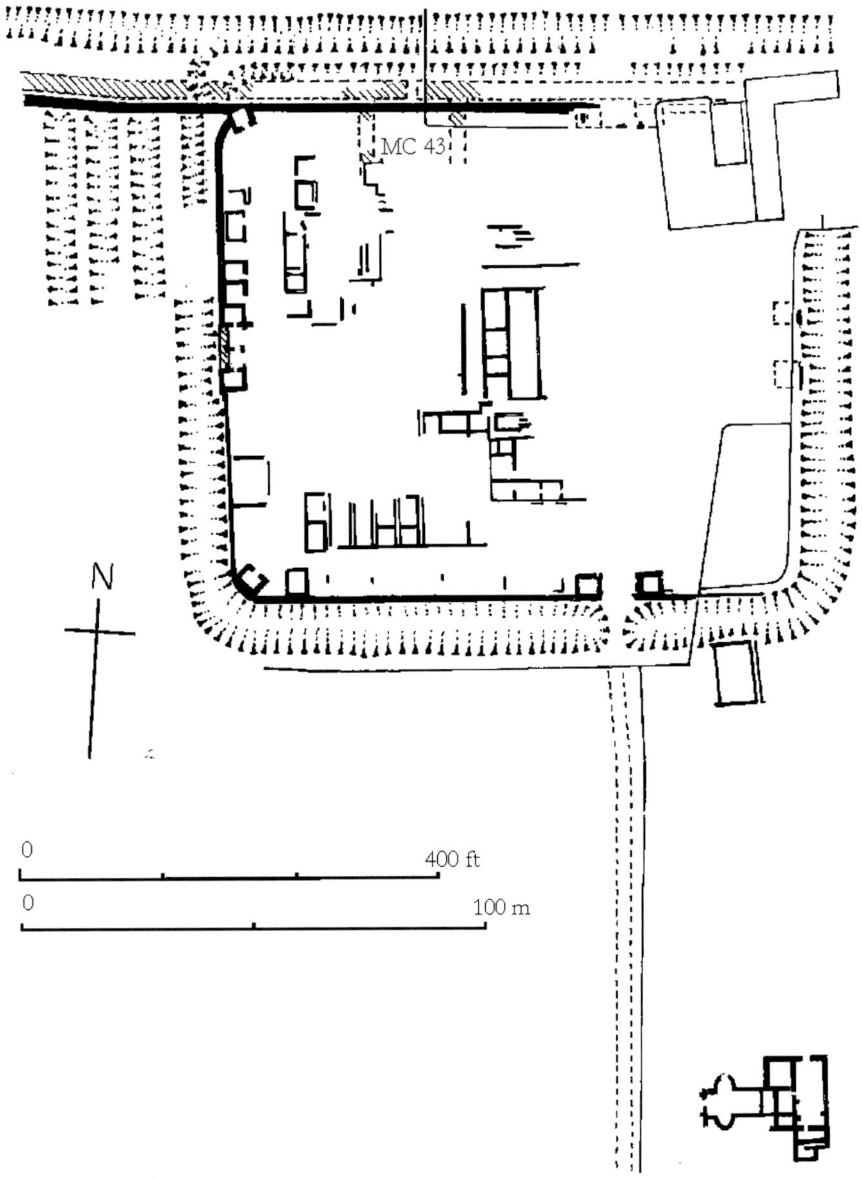

98. Plan of Great Chesters fort

north of the curtain, while it was also noted that the western ditches ran under the Narrow Wall (which also forms the north curtain) but did not continue north of this. This problem remained unsolved until the last major work to take place at the fort commenced in 1939 when Simpson returned with Richmond (Richmond 1939 162-165). During this season of work the remains of milecastle 43 were located attached to the Broad Wall, and were found to lie under the north curtain, thus for the first time it was suggested that the milecastle might relate to a different phase to the forts. This fact was proven in 1945 when a search was carried out at Chesters, Birdoswald, and Housesteads, and the same sequence was identified at all forts (Birley 1961, 191).

Work in the 1950's concentrated on the forts ditches and the Vallum causeway, however since these excavations work at Great Chesters has focused on consolidation and management issues. Problems regarding the condition of the site appear to have been noted during the mid 1970's, however it was not until the late 1980's that work started when a photographic survey was carried out detailing areas of significance. As a result of this survey the west gate (north and south chambers), the internal face of the west wall, and the east chamber of the south gate were the focus of consolidation work in 1988. This work involved the re-setting of loose masonry, pointing, and re-turfing some areas near the blocking of the west gate. At the same time the barrack block and bath house were filled in to reduce the remains to ground level, and therefore reduce damage caused by cattle.

Layout and History

Lying wholly south of Hadrian's Wall the fort of Great Chesters measures 128 by 108 metres enclosing just over 1.2 ha (3 acres), and faces east, with the Military Way entering by the *porta praetoria* and leaving by the *porta decumana*, while a road linking it to the Stanegate lies on the track of a modern farm road entering the fort through the south gate. West of the fort a series of at least four ditches can be observed, however these do not continue around the circuit of the fort with only two ditches apparent on the east, and a single ditch to the south. To the north an extra ditch was added between the Wall ditch and the north wall of the fort making Great Chesters the most heavily protected fort on the Wall (Breeze 2006, 273-274).

99. Aerial photograph of Great Chesters

100. The blocked west gate at Great Chesters

It is not clear when work commenced on the construction of Great Chesters, however a building inscription of Hadrian with the title *Pater Patriae*, a title he did not assume until AD128, suggests that the fort was not completed before this date. Further inscriptions indicate the granary was rebuilt by the Second Cohort of Asturians ('Severus Alexanders Own') in AD 225, while in the second century the fort appears to have been occupied by the Sixth Cohort of Nervians followed by the Sixth Cohort of Raetians (Daniels 1978, 179).

One of the most interesting features of the fort is the blocking of the western gate. Great Chesters is the only fort on the Wall to retain its blocking *in situ*, and although this is now obscured under a protective covering of turf, it was examined during the 1897 season of works. Study of this gate reveals a double Hadrianic gate extensively restored under Severus prior to the southern portal being blocked. The north portal was then blocked, with the final phase involving the construction of a new wall across both blocked portals (see Gibson 1903, Birley 1961, and Breeze 2006).

The bath-house was located to the south of the fort slightly to the east of the farm track that linked Great Chesters to the Stanegate. Excavated during the 1897 and 1908 the plan recovered a building containing (from east to west) a changing room with adjacent latrine, a cold room and a hot room (both with baths), a warm room, and large room, a second warm room, and a hot room (Breeze 2006, 274). During the excavations a hoard of 120 late third century coins were recovered from the hot room providing an approximate date of abandonment.

To the north of the fort the line of the aqueduct supplying the site can be traced for some 6 miles from its source at Saughty Rigg Washpool at the head of the Caw Burn (NY 7450 6879) to the point at which it approaches the northern limit of the fort (although it fails to actually enter the site). Limited excavations have observed an unlined channel (cut into clay) 0.56m wide and 0.28 deep with the upcast forming a retaining bank on the south side 0.30m high and 1.60m wide. At only one point (Benks Bridge) would the channel have had to cross a bridge, however no remains of this structure (that would probably have been constructed of timber) survive (Mackay 1990).

Extramural Area

Official buildings and structures
The remains of the bath-house lie south of the fort.

Civilian buildings
The civilian settlement associated with Great Chesters has received very little attention during the excavations carried out at the fort. Surviving as a series of earthworks to the south of the fort's defences, the *vicus* can be observed spreading out south of the gentle slope towards the Military Road. Detailed geophysical survey (such as those carried out at Birdoswald, Housesteads, and Maryport) would certainly further our knowledge and understanding of this important component of the Roman landscape of Great Chesters.

Religious structures
None known.

Cemeteries
Two clusters of tumuli have been identified a short distance to the south of the fort suggesting the location of the cemetery. The first is situated near the Stanegate, while the second lies by Markham Cottage on the Military Road, and although both clusters have yet to be excavated, a number of tombstones were recovered during excavations within the fort including one to a young child (Aurelia who lived 1 year and 4 months), and another to L. Novellius Lanuccus who, at the over end of the scale, died aged 70.

Carvoran (*Magna*)

A Birley

Carvoran lies at the junction of the Stanegate with the Maiden Way. The fort stood immediately east of the valley of the Tipalt Burn and the ground slopes gently down to the latter to the northwest, west and south-west of the defences. The ruins of the fort were very evident in Camden's time but these were levelled by agricultural operations between 1776 and 1837. The visible fort is 1.65 ha in size. The garrison throughout much of the second century was the First Cohort of Hamian Archers, originally raised in Syria (*RIB* 1778, 1792). The unit in residence in the third and fourth centuries was *cohors II Delmatarum*, a quingenary mixed infantry and cavalry unit (*RIB* 1705 and *NDXL*43), although a *numerus Magcensium* is also attested here (*RIB* 1825). The bulk of the site is owned by The Vindolanda Trust.

History of Exploration
Little of the fort interior has been explored. Investigation of the east, south and west walls of the fort together with the south gate in 2001-2 showed them to have been robbed extensively. The north gate was explored in 1973 when the west portal was found to contain secondary blocking. A geophysical survey of the fort and significant parts of the extramural area was carried out in 1999 (Robinson, Biggins & Taylor 1999).

Layout and history
The fort faced south. Aerial photographs showed what was thought to be evidence of an earlier fort but geophysical survey in 1999 failed to find any supporting evidence (Robinson, Biggins & Taylor 1999). The fragmentary tombstone of a soldier of the Twentieth Legion is thought on stylistic grounds to be Flavian (*RIB* 1826; Birley 1961, 194). Excavations under buildings attached to the Roman Army Museum found ditches containing early second century pottery. The 1999 geophysical survey revealed details of barracks in the forward and rearward sections of the interior but many details of the layout remain unclear.

Extramural Area

Official buildings and structures
The unit's bath-building and other official buildings have yet to be identified despite the extensive geophysical survey of 1999.

Civilian buildings
The geophysical survey in 1999 revealed numerous *vicus-*

type buildings lining the Stanegate to the south and south-east of the fort with further buildings lying beyond the fort defences on both the east and west (Robinson, Biggins & Taylor 1999).

Religious structures
The existence of a number of temples or shrines is indicated by the large number of religious dedications from the site, including more than a dozen altars to Vitiris (*RIB* 1793 - 1805). As yet, however, their location remains unknown.

Cemeteries
Burials have been found east of the fort (Bruce 1885, 240).

Birdoswald (*Banna*)

T Wilmott

Birdoswald is situated on a high spur contained to the south by a broad meander of the river Irthing. There is a road connection, the Maiden Way, to the outpost fort of Bewcastle. It is probable that the river cliffs below Birdoswald fort were used as quarries during the Roman period. An important element of the micro-topography of the spur is a dip of unknown extent, which occupies the centre of the site chosen for Birdoswald fort. The impermeable qualities of the boulder clay allowed a small peat bog to develop in this dip. This bog, the so-called 'morass,' was first identified during excavations in 1930 (Richmond 1931, 123).

The erosion of the eastern side of the spur is sufficiently distant to pose no current threat to the surviving archaeology on its summit. The western flank is a different matter, as here there is a steep slope down to the river, and this is being continuously undercut.

101. Birdoswald, the southern granary as found with *in situ* stone floor, from the south-west

History of Exploration
Birdoswald has a history of antiquarian and archaeological interest which goes back over four centuries. The following summary includes all of the main interventions and observations to have taken place over this time. The list is updated from that which appeared in Wilmott 1997a, 7-8.

The site was visited in 1599 by Reginald Bainbrigg, and the 'great ruynes thereof' described in an account sent to William Camden, who missed the site (Haverfield 1911, 365). The first reference to a Stonehouse at Birdoswald appeared in the 1603 Gilsland Survey for Lord William Howard of Naworth (Graham 1934). Horseley included an account of the surviving remains at Birdoswald, described by Birley as the best description of any Wall fort for over a century 1732; 1961, 197). Three altars were found inside the fort included the dedication to Silvanus by the *Venatores Bannienses* confirming the Roman name of the site (*RIB* 1905).

Excavations were undertaken in 1831/3 by the site proprietor, Thomas Crawhall, noted by Hodgson (1840, 207). These focused on the defences. Further work on the defences occurred in 1849, 1850 and 1851 following on from the visit by the First Pilgrimage in the former year (Potter 1855a, 1855b, 1855c). Minor excavations took place in 1859 (Norman 1860, 249; Bruce 1885, 203-4; Birley 1977, 161). It was not until 1896 that further work began when the Vallum was located south of the fort and the Turf Wall was found to underlie the stone fort (Haverfield 1897b; Hodgson 1897). The line of the Turf Wall east of the fort was established in 1898 and the existence of vicus structures was noted (Haverfield 1899; Hodgson 1899). F. G. Simpson decided to transfer his research work from Great Chesters to Birdoswald in 1927, thus beginning seven consecutive seasons of work, firstly by the Durham University Excavation Committee, and after 1930 by the revived Cumberland Excavation Committee. A notable discovery in 1928 was the finding of timber buildings to the south of the fort. The excavation of buildings north of the *via principalis* in the eastern *praetentura* was begun and the following year saw the identification of four Levels, which had considerable influence in the subsequent establishment of the idea of the four Wall Periods (Simpson 1930; Birley 1930c; Daniels 1989b, 10). In 1931 debris was found below Hadrianic levels, and the stone base for a turf rampart discovered below the stone fort defences (Simpson and Richmond 1932).

In the following year Simpson and Richmond (1933) continued excavation on the spur to the south of the fort. A polygonal ditched enclosure was cut by the Vallum. The excavation of the Vallum revealed the original Vallum-crossing, the first such feature to be identified. The south-east rampart was explored, including a range of ovens, the early rampart-base and a building butting the front of the south-east angle tower. The basis of a system of three Phases (as distinct from the four Periods of 1929) was established for the southern area. The three Phases of the previous season were broadly confirmed in 1933 (Simpson and Richmond 1934a). A rectangular enclosure stood within the polygonal ditches, and a 'native hearth' was found on the promontory. Work to the east of the *porta principalis dextra* established the relationship between the fort ditches and that of the Turf Wall.

Consolidation of the gates and curtain walls of the fort was carried out by the Ministry of Works in 1949/50 into whose care they had been placed by Lord Henley, the then proprietor (in 1939). Ploughing by J Baxter in 1959/60 led to the discovery of a cremation cemetery to the north west of the fort, in New Field. This was recorded by R Hogg (Wilmott 1993). In 1984 the Birdoswald estate was conveyed to Cumbria County Council and in 1987 a full earthwork survey of the Birdoswald area was undertaken by K Blood and D McKay of the Royal Commission on Historic Monuments (England).

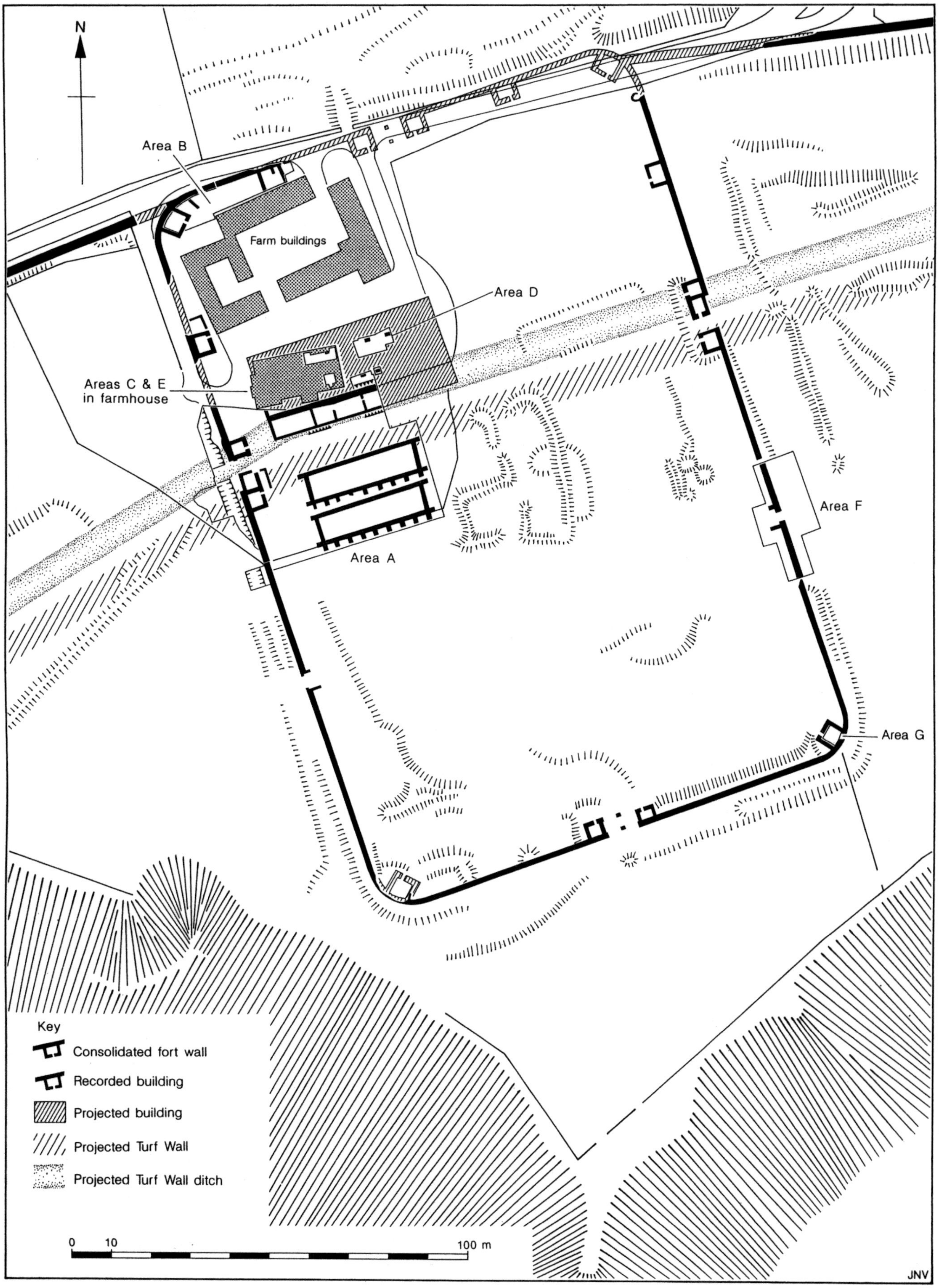

102. Plan of Birdoswald showing areas investigated 1987-92

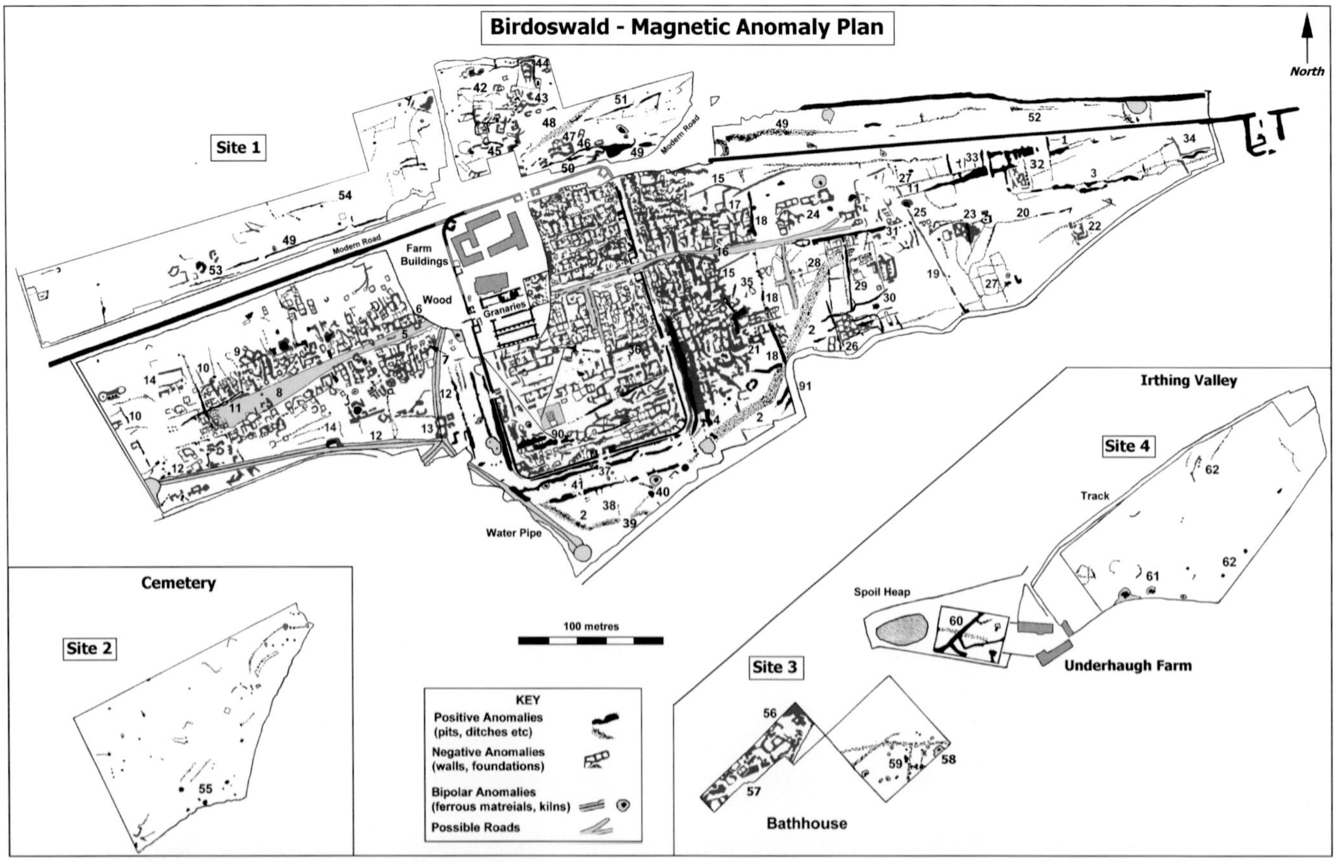

103. Results of geophysical survey, Birdoswald

In 1987 five seasons of excavation and consolidation work began under the direction of the writer for Cumbria County Council and English Heritage in the former gardens of the farmhouse, within the farmhouse, and in the north-west corner of the fort. An area over the two *horrea* and the *via principalis* were examined, demonstrating the presence of post-Roman timber buildings over the *horrea*. An area on the north wall of the fort, adjacent to the north west corner tower was opened up (Wilmott 1997a). A major discovery in 1989 was the existence of a basilican building and a workshop on the north side of the *via principalis*.

In 1996 three trenches were excavated on the promontory in order to examine the archaeology threatened by erosion to the south of the fort. These examined the Vallum, the ditch system, showing that the fort had three and not two ditches, and timber structures on the promontory (Wilmott, Cool and Evans, forthcoming).

Excavations were carried out in 1997-8 beneath the buildings and yards of Birdoswald farm, in the north-west *praetentura* of the fort. The plan of this entire sector of the fort was revealed, consisting of the basilican building previously identified, and a pair of barrack blocks. The history of the barracks was examined (Wilmott, Cool and Evans, forthcoming). Extensive geophysical surveys in 1999 on the fort and its surrounding area demonstrated the large size of the fort *vicus* for the first time (Biggins and Taylor 1999, 2004). Channel 4's Time Team undertook an evaluation of the western *vicus* and the known area of the fort cemetery. This demonstrated that the *vicus* had a complex history of stone buildings and industrial process, and that complete burials existed within the cemetery (Wilmott, Cool and Evans, forthcoming).

Summary of archaeological phasing as currently understood

Before the stone fort

The Birdoswald promontory before the arrival of the builders of the Wall was heavily wooded, and in the centre of the site lay a small basin mire (the Birdoswald morass).

The discovery of an apparent signal tower on the south east side of the fort (Richmond 1931, 130) may indicate that the first Roman structure of the promontory was associated with the Stanegate 'frontier'.

The construction of the turf Wall along the ridge between the Midgeholme Moss to the north and the Birdoswald morass required the clearance of the woodland on the site, an operation which took place so quickly that the pollen record beneath the Wall was undamaged.

On the south side of the morass a palisade trench, mirrored by a pair of parallel ditches on the northern (outer) side, described a polygonal course and cut off the spur end. In the bottom of these ditches a quantity of well-preserved Roman tent leather was found within the primary silt (MacIntyre and Richmond 1934). Though frequently regarded as prehistoric (Birley 1961, 143; Daniels 1978, 204), the tent fragments confirm their Roman date (Wilmott 1997a, 42), and the feature may have comprised a construction camp associated with the building of the Turf Wall. The stone-built turret 49b was at least begun (Soc Antiqs Newcastle upon Tyne 1946, 275).

The Turf Wall was demolished and its fabric deposited to fill the Wall ditch within the line of the walls of the later stone fort

104. Aerial photograph of Birdoswald

to allow the construction of a timber fort. Evidence for the fort has been found on the south rampart, where a stone base for an earth rampart was found (Richmond 1930a, 4; Simpson and Richmond 1933, 252-4), under the *horrea* (Wilmott 1997a, 42-4), and in the form of pits excavated to the north of the line of the turf Wall, which contained military metalwork etc (Wilmott *et al* forthcoming). It seems clear that like its stone successor this was a projecting fort.

The next feature to be constructed was the Vallum. Its line was originally traced together with the Turf Wall by Haverfield (1899, 347-51, pl 1), and in 1932 a primary Vallum crossing, the first of its type to be identified, was excavated to the south of the fort (Simpson and Richmond 1933, 246-52). At Birdoswald, for reasons which may be connected with the proximity of the Vallum to the Turf Wall, the north Vallum mound was omitted, and the upcast from the ditch disposed of in a double-size south mound. This state of affairs existed over the whole of wall-mile 50 between milecastles 49 and 50 TW (Simpson and Richmond 1937a, 171-3). At Birdoswald, the Vallum was diverted around the south side of the fort, but it passes extremely close to the south west angle of the stone fort. For this reason it has been suggested (Wilmott 1997a, 44-5) that the Vallum was built to work with the timber fort.

Building of the stone fort

The stone fort was also planned to project north of its timber predecessor. At the main west gate, the Turf Wall ditch was carefully backfilled with a deliberate layer of rubble and clay in order to make up the ground for the construction of the gate. A layer of black soil accumulated around the foundation, part of an extensive deposit covering much of the north-west quarter of the fort. It represents a complete cessation of work during the construction of the stone fort. There was continued human activity during the accumulation of these soils, and this was followed by a period of undisturbed plant growth and 'normal' soil development. Some scrub growth took place, which was subsequently cleared by burning, and the site was extensively used for animal housing or penning until just prior to the commencement of the completion of the stone fort (Wilmott 1997a 56-60).

Following this interruption, the west gate was completed in a noticeably less well-finished masonry style. The construction of the roads and principal buildings of the fort was contemporary with the completion of the gate, and levelling sealed the black horizon. Primary buildings were then constructed. In the north-western half of the *praetentura*, the *via principalis* frontage was occupied by a long, narrow building, behind which was a large basilican structure, interpreted as a *basilica exercitatoria* (Wilmott 1997b, 99). Behind this again was a broad alley while a pair of barracks, laid out facing each other, occupied the space between the alley and the intervallum. These were infantry barracks of eight *contubernia* each (Wilmott *et al* forthcoming). The 1929 excavations in the eastern *praetentura* (Richmond and Birley 1930) showed a long narrow building on the street front, behind which lay two pairs of confronted infantry barracks (Biggins and Taylor 1999). Construction of *horrea* ceased soon after the foundations were laid.

The buildings to the south and east of the excavated *horrea* were built in a deep, natural hollow from the base of which buildings were terraced upwards to north and south (Richmond 1931, 127; Wilmott 1997a, 27, fig 13). This means that the buried back wall of the *principia* survives to 15 courses. It seems likely that the northern part of the *retentura* is similarly deeply buried

It is possible that the Vallum was backfilled for the construction of the fort. The pottery from the Vallum is later Hadrianic in date, and was in deposits tipped from the west. This means that these were tipped from the outside of the fort, implying the existence of an early, Hadrianic, *vicus*. Finally the stone Wall was constructed to meet the north angles of the fort. As the fort was no longer projecting, the two minor gates on the east and west were blocked.

Evidence from the primary deposits of the stone wall turrets and milecastles west of Birdoswald, this replacement took place during the late Hadrianic period (Willis forthcoming)

Second major construction phase
There is little datable evidence for activity in the second century which could coincide with the return from Antonine Scotland, though it seems likely that the three primary fort ditches were cut at this time.

During the early third century a major reconstruction saw changes in the intervallum, and the wholesale remodelling of the barracks in the *praetentura*. Dating evidence provides a TPQ for the whole operation of AD 197 (Wilmott *et al* forthcoming).

The granaries were built as part of this activity, and an inscription (*RIB* 1909), records their construction between AD 205 and 208 by *cohors I Aelia Dacorum*. Renovation also took place on the eastern and western gates, and stones reused from Willowford Bridge were deployed in the eastern defences. It is likely that these works were the result of the arrival at the fort of a new garrison (Wilmott 2001a, 87-90; 2001f, 107). If so, this garrison was the *cohors I Aelia Dacorum*, which is attested on a great many inscriptions throughout the third century, and is the unit listed for Birdoswald in the *Notitia Dignitatum* (Wilmott 1997a, 14, 195-7; 2001b). In addition to the *horreum* inscription (*RIB* 1909), there is further epigraphic evidence to support the idea of a major building programme between c 198-219 (Wilmott 1997a, 197-8). An inscription (*RIB* 1914) found during the 1852 excavation of the *porta principalis dextra* (Potter 1855, 146-8) commemorates rebuilding at the gate under the governor Modius Julius (219). Two further inscriptions record building work during this period; *RIB* 1910 is a fragmentary dedication slab from a building constructed under Severus (198-209), while *RIB* 1911, an altar of the reign of Caracalla (212-217), also records building.

Third and fourth centuries
At some later stage the barracks were altered from the standard second-century form into the so-called chalet style with separate free-standing *contubernia* (Wilmott *et al* forthcoming).

It is clear that repairs which occasionally involved substantial works continued through the mid-third century, and a further dated inscription (*RIB* 1922) records a building 'built from ground level' in the consulship of Maximinus and Africanus, (AD 236). The mid-third century saw the blocking of the south portal of the west gate, the laying of new drains and resurfacing of the *via principalis*, together with the division of the long narrow building on the street frontage into two industrial buildings, one of which was used for metalworking, as was the blocked portal and the gate towers of the west gate.

There is evidence for change taking place in the latter part of the third century. The intensive iron working activity ceased abruptly, and layers of rubble and soil which lay between the end of industrial activity and rebuilding are redolent of collapse and a brief desertion. The TPQ for this collapse is c AD 280. The ditch, formerly re-cut and maintained was allowed to silt up. This evidence for possible desertion should be seen in connection with *RIB* 312, which records the rebuilding of a number of principal buildings in AD 297-305. There is evidence for refurbishment in the first half of the fourth century, when the ditch was re-cut for the penultimate time, and the buildings on the *via principalis* were rebuilt, though not for industrial uses (Wilmott 1997a).

In the middle of the fourth century, the northern granary collapsed and was not rebuilt. Its southern counterpart had its floor lifted, the sub-floor back-filled and the floor re-laid, clearly moving to other uses. This ushered in the post-Roman stratigraphic sequence to be discussed in the section on the post-Roman period on Hadrian's Wall

Extramural area

Official buildings and structures
No evidence.

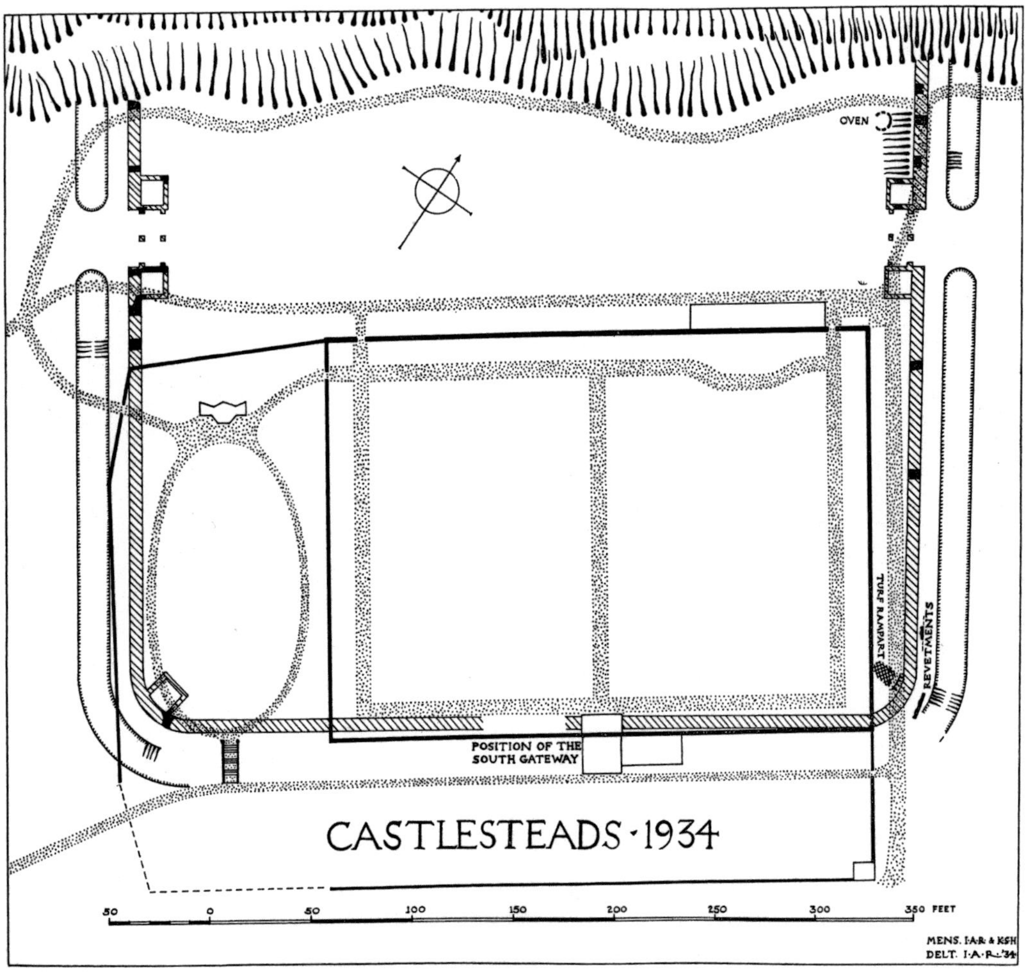

105. Plan of Castlesteads fort

Civilian buildings
Geophysical survey has proved the existence of an extensive *vicus* to east and west of the fort, and excavation has explored the area to the south of the fort (Biggins & Taylor 1999; 2004). This survey also revealed structures immediately north of the Wall.

The geophysical survey indicates that there are extensive areas of stone building to east and west. Evaluation (Wilmott et al forthcoming) has shown that the *vicus* to the west is stratigraphically complex and has a date range from the Hadrianic period to the late third century, when, in common with other *vici* on the Wall, it seems to have been deserted.

The area to the south of the fort has revealed a '*vicus*' of timber buildings, constructed in the mid-third century. And characterized by the Frisian pottery known as 'Housesteads ware' which is found in this area in quantity, while none has been found either within the fort, or in the area of the western *vicus*. This 'ceramic apartheid' requires explanation (Wilmott *et al* forthcoming).

Religious structures
Evidence restricted at present to inscriptions and sculptures.

Cemeteries
The fort cemetery is located to the west of the west *vicus* (Wilmott 1993). Excavation has shown that it was a cremation cemetery and has been damaged by medieval ploughing. A single excavated cremation burial shows rituals similar to those encountered in the cemetery at Brougham (Wilmott *et al* forthcoming).

Castlesteads (*Camboglanna*)

D J P Mason

Castlesteads fort sits on a high bluff overlooking the Cambeck valley. The site was levelled in 1791 when the gardens of Castlesteads House were laid out. Only the southern edge of the fort platform is now visible. The Cam Beck has eroded the north-west front of the fort to within 15 metres of the side gates. The fort is considered to have been a square originally with sides of 122 metres giving an area of 1.5 ha (3.75 acres). It is not impossible however that the fort faced south rather than north and thus could have been somewhat larger. Castlesteads is unique among the Wall forts in lying between Wall and Vallum but not being attached to the former.

Cohors IV Gallorum was the garrison for a time (*RIB* 1979-80), probably in the early second century, while the presence of *cohors II Tungrorum milliaria equitata* - or part of it in view the fort's size - is recorded in 241 (*RIB* 1981-3, 1999). Probably owing to an error, Castlesteads does not appear in the list of Wall units in the *Notitia*.

History of exploration
An extramural bath-house was excavated in 1741 (Hutchinson 1794, 115). The only modern excavations took place in the 1930s when the line of the defences on the east, west and south were located along with the double-

portalled east and west gates and the south-west angle-tower (Richmond & Hodgson 1934). Geophysical survey in recent years has taken place in the extramural area.

Layout and history
Nothing is known of the plan of the internal buildings. The 1930s excavations encountered the rampart and ditch of an earlier fort beneath the south-east angle apparently laid out on a different alignment. The existence of this fort may have influenced the decision not to attach its successor to the Wall.

Extramural Area

Official buildings and structures
Survey by the Royal Commission in the 1990s noted the remains of the regimental *balneum* beside the burn 200 m north of the fort (Bidwell ed 1999, 162). The recovery of two altars dedicated to Jupiter Optimus Maximus along with another set up to the emperor and god Vanauns from a spot 300 metres north of the fort may indicate the location of the parade-ground (*RIB* 1979, 1981, 1991).

Civilian buildings
Geophysical survey south of the fort between 1999 and 2001 disclosed the course of the Vallum, along with its causeway, and, beyond, the buildings, roads and property boundaries of a *vicus* (Burnham et al. 2001, 330-33). A system of field boundaries - apparently of two phases - lies to the east of the *vicus*.

Religious buildings and structures
The existence of a Mithraeum is attested by three altars (*RIB* 1992-4) while another inscription records the restoration of a temple to the Mother Goddesses of all the Nations, which had 'fallen in through age' (*RIB* 1988). Other deities represented include the Mother Goddesses beyond the Seas, Mars, Neptune and Belatucadrus (*RIB* 1989, 1986-7, 1990, 1976-7; latter rediscovered 1973 = Wilson et al. 1974, 463)

Stanwix (*Uxelodunum or Petriana*)
I Caruana

The fort lies on a plateau contained by the 30 metre contour on the north bank of the river Eden. The land rises gradually to the fort site from milecastle 65 (Tarraby) and falls again gently towards milecastle 66 (Stanwix Bank). The ground falls away more sharply from the north wall of the fort. The river flood-plain immediately south of the fort is marked by a steep bluff. The *ala Petriana* is the only known garrison unit (*RIB* 2427, 16; *Notitia Dignitatum* XL45). As a milliary cavalry unit, enlarged probably under Trajan (i.e. before 117 A.D.), it was the largest auxiliary regiment in the British province. The enlargement of the fort is likely to have been associated with its arrival c.160 AD. The unit probably remained in garrison until the end of the Roman period since it is the unit recorded in the *Notitia Dignitatum*.

The smaller Hadrianic fort may also have been garrisoned by a cavalry *ala* on the evidence of a cavalry tombstone (*RIB* 2028) of pre-Antonine style found when rebuilding Stanwix church. Alternatively, this could relate to a pre-Wall fort. Various items of cavalry equipment were found in King's Meadow, below the fort, in 1930 among a group of finds of Hadrianic or early Antonine date also point to the presence of cavalrymen in the primary garrison (Collingwood 1931).

The whole of the fort and most of its surrounds are built over to a greater or lesser extent. Survival of Roman levels beneath later structures appears to be good; in some cases as much as 2.50m of deposits as on the Miles MacInnes site (Caruana 2000, 57). Elsewhere, on the Stanwix School sites, Roman remains lie immediately below the modern surface. The line of the Roman Wall structures is left largely unencumbered in an L-shaped block of pasture land south of Tarraby Lane. South of Brampton Road, housing built from the 1930s onwards at Croft Road and adjacent streets, has obscured the cemetery site. Church Street and the east end of Kells Place may follow the lines of the *via decumana* and the *via praetoria* respectively and the west and east gates of the fort. Church Lane is close to the possible line of part of the via quintana and Well Lane may follow the line of the east ditch. The Brampton Road, one of the two arterial roads into Carlisle from the east, passes to the south of the fort.

History of exploration
The location of the fort at Stanwix had almost entirely disappeared by the time that early antiquarians began to study the Wall. Their speculations had proved entirely erroneous and can be seen in Birley's summary (1961, 205-8).

The first accurate results concerning the position of the fort were obtained by F.G. Simpson and I.A. Richmond during the 1930s. In 1930 a major hoard of military bronzes, coins, etc. was recovered during a watching brief on the Eden flood plain below the fort (Collingwood 1931). In the same volume of Transactions Eric Birley reviewed the evidence for the identification of *Petriana* (Birley 1931). At the same time as these two articles appeared, Eden Bridge was widened leading also to work on the approach road from the north. A triangular piece of land bounded by Church Street, Church Terrace and Scotland Road was cleared of housing (it remains as a car park). On then current thinking, this area should have been within the fort, but trenching failed to find any sign of the fort (Simpson 1932). It did, however, produce the important dated inscription of A.D.167 (*RIB* 2026; Birley 1932).

Trial-trenching in the grounds of Stanwix Primary School finally demonstrated the presence of fort buildings (Simpson 1933). Crucial evidence for the course of the Vallum was uncovered (Simpson 1933, 1934). It was not until a final campaign in 1939-40 that the limits of the fort were established (Simpson & Richmond 1941a; Simpson 1941).

The major findings from these excavations were published promptly but no full reports or finds reports ever appeared. Many of the finds appear to survive in Tullie House Museum and there are some additional records of the excavations: Simpson's annotated OS map recording his findings, a survey plan of November 1932 showing the remains in the schoolyard, a 1940 plan showing the SW angle of the fort. These are in the Dept. of Archaeology, Newcastle University

106. The site of the fort at Stanwix, on higher ground north of the River Eden

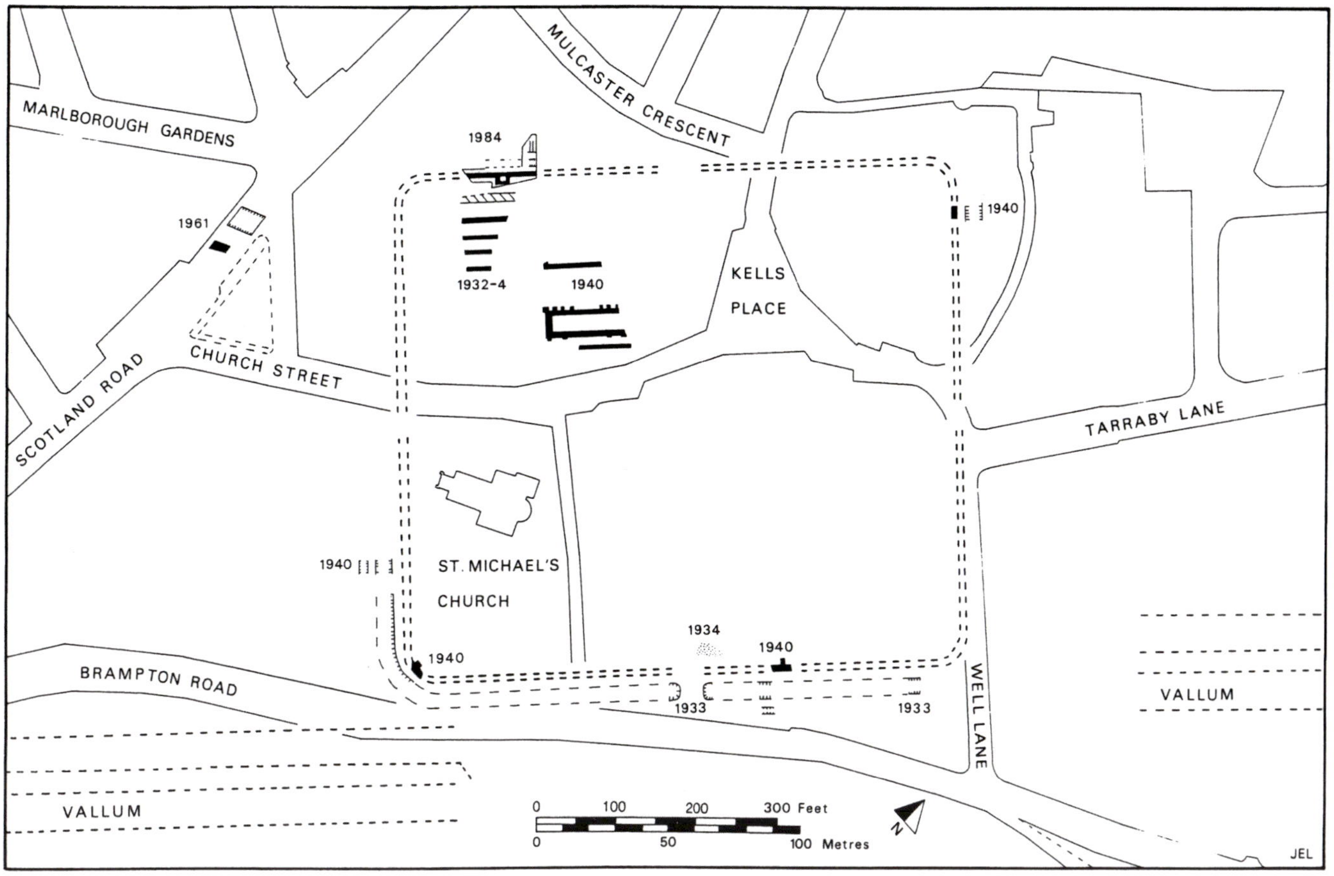

107. Plan of Stanwix fort

and Tullie House Museum. The Tullie House Accessions Register for 1934 has provenances for finds from that year's excavations.

Apart from minor chance discoveries no substantial excavation took place until the work on the northern defences in the car park of the Cumbria Park Hotel in 1984. To date, this is the only full excavation report for Stanwix to have appeared (Dacre 1985).

Subsequent to this, a series of evaluations, watching briefs, and excavations, mainly by the Carlisle Archaeological Unit (CAU) but also by Oxford Archaeology North (OAN) and The Archaeological Practice, Newcastle upon Tyne, (AP) working together.

Ditches of the large fort were found on the east and west sides in 1940 and on the south side in 1933. The north-west corner of the fort was identified in 1999 in further extensions to the Cumbria Park Hotel (*Britannia* 31 2001, 392).

Layout and history

The plan as currently understood shows that the fort was attached to the rear of the Wall with its long axis east-west, and facing east. The area is 9.79 acres (3.96 ha) slightly larger than the 9.32 acres calculated from the 1930s excavations (Dacre 1985, 68). The position of the south gate (but not the gate) was identified in 1933. A granary was identified in 1940, lying on the left side (north) of the *principia*. Further buildings in the central range were exposed in the grounds of Stanwix School in 1999 but remain unpublished (*Britannia* 31 2001, 392). Long buildings in the *retentura* were exposed in 1934.

Two pieces of evidence show that the plan of the 9.79 acre (3.96 ha) fort is not the Hadrianic fort. In 1933 F.G. Simpson recorded the Vallum appearing to deviate around a fort that was smaller than the 9.79 acre fort. The excavation in the Cumbria Park Hotel grounds demonstrated that the northern fort wall extended further north than the section of Hadrian's Wall found in 1934. Moreover, the original survey plan from the 1934 work (unpublished) shows a narrow barrack-type wall resting on the remains of Hadrian's Wall, a feature that was omitted in the published report of the excavation (Dacre 1985, 68). These buildings were reported as overlying an earlier gravel surface.

Two phases of occupation are reported to have been found in the grounds of Barn Close which would be in the praetentura of the fort (*Britannia* 25, 1994, 263).

It is entirely open whether the putative earlier small fort was built in stone or turf and timber, although turf, possibly from the fort rampart, is reported from the Stanwix School excavations in 1997 (McCarthy 1999, 163). Whether the Turf Wall arrangements were modified in conjunction with the conversion to stone, prior to the construction of the enlarged fort or whether the conversion to stone took place in conjunction with the enlargement of the fort is a problem that needs resolution.

The only significant structural sequence comes from the 1984 excavation in the car park of the Cumbria Park Hotel where the rampart and interval tower of the fort were found to overlie a ditch, presumed to be the Hadrian's Wall ditch. None of the earlier exposures of the defences did more than identify the location of defensive elements.

All the excavations where dating evidence has been reported show a significant peak in activity at the end of the second century and some show evidence of fourth-century finds. The coin lists from Stanwix, which show an almost complete absence of third-century radiates, are discussed by Shotter in the report on the Miles MacInnes site (Caruana 2000). The Cumbria Park Hotel site produced no third- and fourth-century pottery (Taylor in Dacre 1985, 66). It could be argued that the fort may not have been garrisoned in some or all of the intervening period. However, the *Notitia Dignitatum* does identify the *ala Petriana* as the final unit at the fort which suggests that any apparent falling off in occupation may reflect other factors such as artefact recovery. The chronology of the fort occupation is an issue which requires urgent attention.

Timber buildings are reported within the fort which must cannot be earlier than the fourth century but no further detail about the latest phases of occupation is available (McCarthy 1999, 166). It may be noted that the church of St Michael occupies part of the fort and there is evidence of pre-Conquest sculpture and coins from the site.

Annexes

None known.

Extramural Area

Official buildings and structures

There is no evidence for the location of the bath-house, *mansio*, aqueducts, or any other structures. A number of evaluations and excavations have identified a spread of stony clay east of the fort as a possible parade-ground (reconstructed plan in McCarthy 1999, 166-7 fig.55). However, the flimsiness of the surfacing and the lack of artefacts (hobnails, armour fragments) that might be expected from such a feature cast doubt on this. None of the interventions in the college grounds and to the east identified any remains of the Turf Wall and another possibility is that the clay layer was spread from the demolition of the Turf Wall (which was in places built of clay). Similar clay deposits were identified by George Smith in 1976 in the top of some of the gulleys close to Hadrian's Wall (1978, 26-9, fig.11) but these are not incorporated in the reconstructed plan.

Civilian buildings

Information about the *vicus* is scanty. Many archaeological interventions have taken place, mostly in the east *vicus*, between 1990 and 2000, but many of these were not reported even in summary form, even where client reports exist. A listing of this 'grey' literature is included in the bibliography but the list may not be complete There are hints of an extensive *vicus* both east and west of the fort. East of the fort structural features are largely confined to the area south of the Vallum. Buildings, probably in the form of ribbon development along the Military Way, were identified as far east as Dykes Terrace (Smith 1978). Closer to the fort occupation was identified at the Brampton Road entrance to the college (Phase 2b: LUAU 1999) and overlying the Vallum mound in Phase 3 (AP 2002). More significant was the absence of such features in trenches east, west (CAU 1998, LUAU 1999) and north (LUAU 2000) of the college buildings and in the walled garden of Homeacres, now the car park (Phase 5: LUAU Sept. 2000; OAN 2002). No information appears to be available from recent work in front of Stanwix House.

The main evidence for the western *vicus* comes from the watching brief on the Miles MacInnes site where roads and ovens were noted (Caruana 2000). Burnt clay was also noted during observations of utility trenches in 1993 (*Britannia* 25, 1994, 264). All these sites, unlike those in the eastern *vicus*, appear to be inside the Vallum. The other point to note is the presumed crossing of Hadrian's Wall, analogous to the Port Gate, by a road to the north leading from Eden Bridge. The road itself has been noted several times e.g. by Hogg in 1961, (Caruana 2000, *Britannia* 25, 1994, 264). Hogg recorded a break in Hadrian's Wall (Excavation notebook in Tullie House), although given the rather cramped nature of the trenches that he was observing the validity of this observation needs confirmation.

Religious structures

No religious buildings have been identified but two areas of less formal religious activity have been suggested. A small hoard of Flavian coins was found in the River Eden in 1962 (Robertson 1968). If they were not an unfortunate casual loss, they may have been a deliberate votive offering by a soldier of the army invading Scotland. More forceful is the suggestion that the King's Meadow deposit is a votive deposit in a stream, rather than a work-shop hoard as suggested by Collingwood (Manning 1972, 249, n148). Epigraphic and sculptural evidence from the site suggests devotions to Victory (*CSIR* I, 6 104), Mercury (*CSIR* I, 6, 83) and the Mother Goddesses (*RIB* 2025/ *CSIR* I, 6, 179)

Cemeteries

The only known burials come from the Croft Road/Whiteclosegate area where urns were uncovered in 1872 and 1936 (Hogg 1952, 154; Tullie House Acc. 30-1936 and 31-1937). No burials were found in any of the recent work in the Art College or Tarraby Lane area (Smith 1978) which might indicate that burials were confined to areas south of the Vallum and Military Road.

Burgh-by-Sands (*Aballava/Avalana/Aballaba*)

M F A Symonds

Three features interpreted as forts are currently known in the vicinity of the modern village of Burgh-by-Sands. None of these has been extensively excavated and all suffer from a shortage of detailed published reports documenting the work that has been undertaken. Although a precise chronology for the forts has yet to be resolved, the sites have been numbered I, II and III since the discovery of the two additional installations in 1976 and 1977. This complex of sites reflects Burgh's strategic importance as a base from which to ford the Eden. Details of Burgh I and III can be found in the western Stanegate section. Burgh II is the only one of the forts to have been placed on the line of the Wall. It occupies a low hill near the measured location of turret 71b and has been partially encumbered by the modern village. The name of one of the forts, presumably Burgh II, appears on the Rudge Cup and Amiens Skillet, but not the Staffordshire Pan. It is also noted in the *Notitia Dignitatum* and *Ravenna Cosmography*.

History of exploration

Although Burgh-by-Sand's association with Hadrian's Wall has been known since Leyland's visit in 1539, it was not until more recent times that the basic details of the fort were clarified. In the early eighteenth century Horsely believed that the Wall fort lay "a little to the east of the church...where there are manifest remains of its ramparts". However, this subsequently proved to be a castle and Maclauchlan concluded that the Wall-fort lay in the area of the village church. This was confirmed by Collingwood in 1922, who proved for the first time the existence of a fort. Since then there has been intermittent work within Burgh II. Jones excavated in the *vicus* to the east of the fort and in 1992 the Carlisle Archaeological Unit dug within it, revealing a stone building overlying what is believed to be the original Wall-ditch. Geophysical survey has confirmed Collingwood's interpretation of the course of the north and east defences. In 2002 Oxford Archaeology discovered buildings apparently associated with industrial activity to the east of the fort.

Layout and history

Burgh II has been described as 'one of the least explored and understood of all the forts on the Wall' (Breeze 2006, 351). Collingwood's excavations in 1922 revealed a 1.8-2.1m wide stone rampart, with facing stones 'so completely rotted that the spade cut through them without resistance' (Collingwood 1923, 8). He also noted indications of a turf backing. The heavily-robbed northern tower of the east gate was uncovered, along with a road of 'hard rammed gravel'; both of these preserved indications of a "long occupation" (Collingwood 1923, 9). Internally there were traces of stone buildings interpreted as barrack blocks. In 1993 excavation in the centre of the fort revealed a further stone building sealing an earlier, 6m wide and 2.2m deep, ditch. This latter is believed to be the original Wall-ditch bisecting the site. Geophysical survey revealed a linear feature adjoining the north-west angle of the fort, which would be consistent with a realigning of the Wall so that the fort lay entirely to the south of it, as at Birdoswald.

Austen has noted that Burgh II appears to postdate the Vallum and that Jones' excavations in the *vicus* did not reveal any second-century material, suggesting that it was a later addition to the Wall, possibly contemporary with the fort at Newcastle (Austen 1994, 53). In the third century the *cohors I Nervana Germanorum milliaria equitata* has been linked with the fort (*RIB* 2041) and an altar dating to AD 253-8 records Caelius Vibianus, tribune of an unnamed cohort and commander of a unit of Moors (*RIB* 2042). Traces of Frisian ware in the *vicus* raises the possibility that a unit of Frisians was also present in the third century (Breeze 2006, 353). References to a *cuneus Frisionum Aballavensium* occur on two altars from Papcastle (*RIB* 882, 883). The *Notitia Dignitatum* places the *numerus Maurorum Aurelianorum* in the fort. Little is known of the later occupation; Collingwood

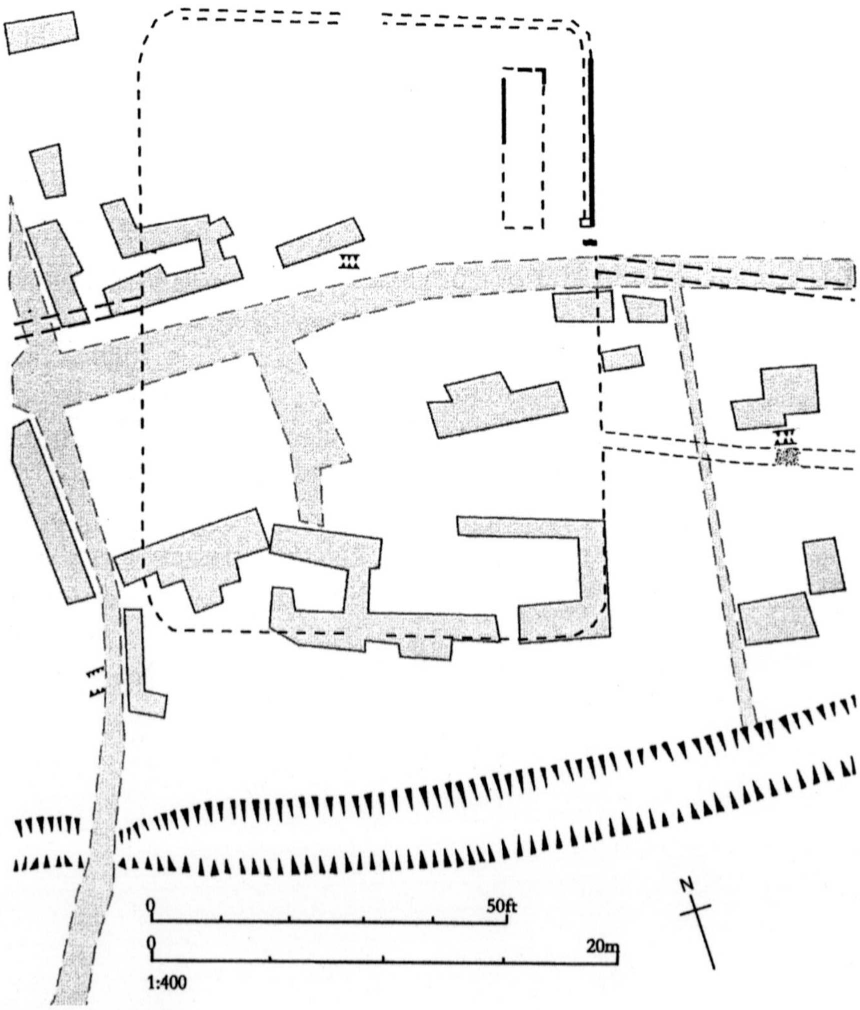

108. Plan of 'fort II' at Burgh by Sands

recorded a fourth-century minim, but noted that "the amount of pottery seeming to require a date at all late in the fourth century was not large" (Collingwood 1923, 10).

Extramural Area

Official buildings and structures
The bath-house stood south of the fort and was destroyed during the construction of the canal in 1821.

Civilian buildings
Excavations to the east of Burgh II in 1980 and 1982 revealed a sequence of timber and stone buildings opening onto a road and dating from the mid third - fourth centuries. Geophysical survey also revealed considerable evidence for extramural activity to the east of the fort (Burnham et al 1994, 263). Work in this area in 2002 is reported to have revealed a number of buildings with an industrial function. Timber buildings have also been excavated to the south of the canal cutting, some dating only to the second century and others extending into the fourth (Breeze 2006, 353).

Religious structures
Three altars dedicated to the god Belatucadrus found south-west of the fort hint at the existence of a shrine in this area (*RIB* 2038, 2039, 2044).

Cemeteries
Gravel quarrying south of the fort in the nineteenth century yielded bones and pottery perhaps suggesting a cemetery lay in this area.

Drumburgh (*Congavata/Coggabata*)

M F A Symonds

Drumburgh is an unusual installation, sited on a gentle hill with an expansive view in all directions over the surrounding lowland. The fort is positioned opposite a Solway ford and has been both partially overlain by modern housing and damaged by a substantial medieval ditch. Although its name is absent from the Rudge Cup and Amiens Skillet, the Staffordshire Pan records it as *Coggabata*, while it enters the *Notitia Dignitatum* as *Congavata*.

History of exploration
When Leyland visited the site, he recorded that the Wall had already been heavily robbed to provide for buildings in Drumburgh. Haverfield's excavations in 1899 revealed the Roman structure was not related to the visible ditch. He concluded that the fort 'was a milecastle or a fort very similar to a milecastle' (Haverfield 1900, 89). Simpson and Richmond judged the known stone fort details to be 'abnormal', and when their excavations revealed its turf predecessor, they found it 'hardly less so' (Simpson and Richmond 1952, 11).

Layout and history
The turf fort had a grey-clay rampart 5.8m wide, which

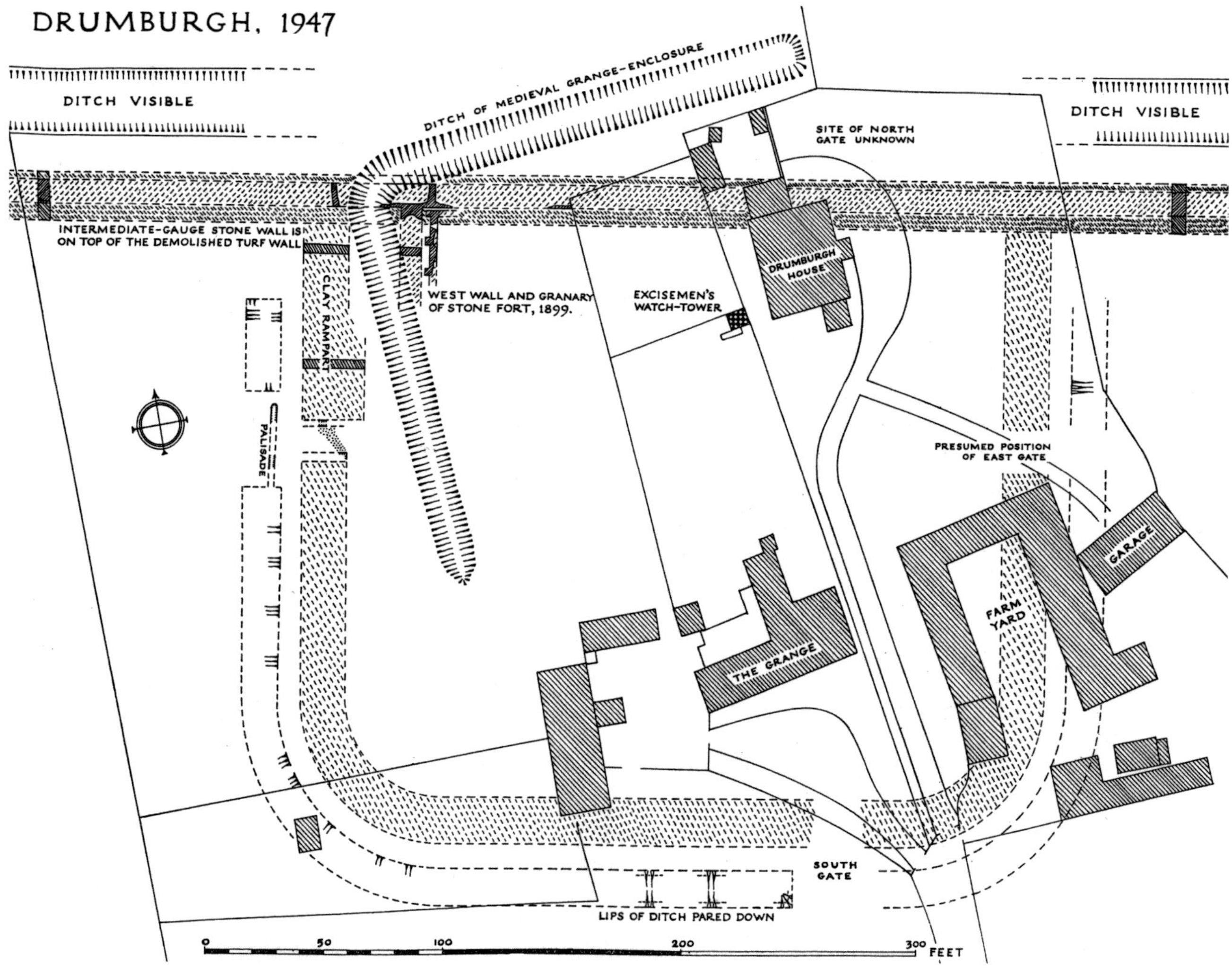

109. Plan of Drumburgh fort

thickened to 8.2m north of the west gate. This feature was interpreted as a stairway ramp. On the east side, the ditch varied from 3 - 4.6m in width and had been 'deliberately obliterated' by tightly packed rampart material, which was deposited after only a small quantity of silt had accumulated. The ditch was interrupted by a causeway, carrying a cobbled road, opposite the west gate. A butt-end in the ditch on the southern side of the fort indicated that the location of the south gate was abnormally close to the south-east angle, precluding an axial arrangement for the gates. The ramparts enclosed an area of 93.4 by 79.4m, making Drumburgh the smallest fort on the Wall. The Turf Wall was found to be built of turf rather than clay in the vicinity of the fort and given this divergence in material it was suggested that the two elements were not contemporary (Simpson and Richmond 1952).

The stone fort also remains poorly understood. Excavations in 1899 revealed footing courses 2.9m wide, from which a rampart width of 2.59m was calculated. At the junction of the Wall and the rampart, 'the foundations seemed to be bonded together' indicating contemporaneous construction. The west fort curtain joins the Wall at a right angle, in the manner of a milecastle, rather than displaying the curved corners usual in Wall forts. The remains of a buttressed building, probably a granary, were detected only 0.3m from the rampart junction. This unusual position left no space between the curtain and building for a turf backing, intervallum road or corner tower. The south and east ramparts were not detected (Haverfield 1900, 84-87). The *Notitia Dignitatum* places the *tribunus cohortis secundae Lingonum* at *Congavata*, although it has been noted that "the size of the fort as known precludes it being occupied by a complete unit" (Breeze 2006, 361). The presence of Huntcliff ware, as well as a coin of AD 350-360, suggests the continuation of the site into the late period.

Extramural Area

Official buildings and structures
The location of the bath-building has still to be determined. Squared blocks of red sandstone found in a foreshore creek could indicate the presence of a Roman harbour (Simpson and Richmond 1952, 14).

Civilian buildings
There are no indications of a military *vicus* in association with the installation. No bath building has been detected.

Religious structures
No evidence.

Cemeteries
Location unknown.

110. Bowness fort. View south over the Solway Firth

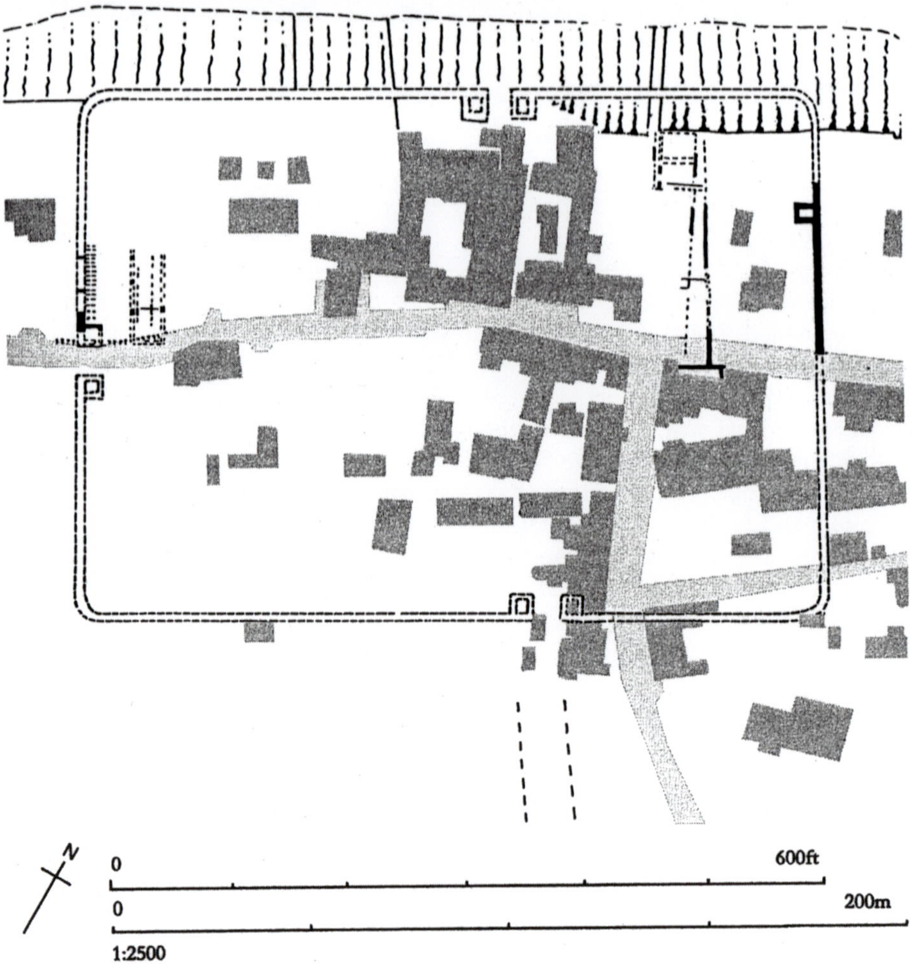

111. Plan of the fort at Bowness on Solway

Bowness-on-Solway (*Maia/Mais*)

D J P Mason

Bowness-on-Solway lies close to the western terminus of the Wall and commands a ford crossing the estuary. The fort occupies the presumed site of milecastle 80 on a clay promontory at the western end of the modern village. Housing was already encroaching on the eastern edge of the site in MacLaughlan's day and since the 1950s residential development has gradually covered the northern part of the west side of the fort. The modern road through the village respects the site of the east and west fort gates, although only the south-west corner of the fort is currently visible. The fort's name is recorded on the Rudge Cup, Amiens Skillet and Staffordshire Pan and occurs in the *Ravenna Cosmography*.

History of exploration

The position of the fort was recorded by antiquarians from Camden onwards, with references to the slight traces of the south defences close to the church of St Michael and of the position of the west defences common to all reports. MacLaughlan calculated "about 240 yards, by 110, giving an area of 5 1/2 acres" for the size of the fort. Subsequent research has proven these estimates to be flawed.

Most excavation hitherto, with the exception of Potter's work in 1976, has been concentrated at the western end of the fort and was conducted in advance of construction work. In 1930 Eric Birley carried out excavations on the west and south defences. He established the position of the north guard chamber of the west gate, and discovered that the south rampart lay a little to the south of MacLaughlan's line (Birley, 1931a). Birley also disproved the supposed course of the north defences. The west rampart continued north towards the Solway and disappeared at the top of the present scarp, indicating that the Solway had eroded the north side of the fort's defences. Using the west gate, Birley was able to calculate accurately the width of the fort as 128m.

In 1955 Daniels carried out trial trenching to the west of the fort, but found no evidence of an associated civil settlement or *vicus* on that side (Daniels 1960). Twelve years later J D Mohamed's excavations in Mill Field encountered the footings of the fort's west rampart, and two ditches, one of which was medieval in date. Potter's excavations in 1973 re-examined the north guard chamber of the west gate discovered by Birley, as well as the *intervallum* road and a succession of buildings bounded by it. These excavations established that the west gate was initially a timber structure and the primary fort defences consisted of a turf rampart. Potter returned in 1976 and dug within the northern *praetentura*, revealing a sequence of narrow buildings and evidence of quarrying for clay.

Excavations were conducted by Austen in the north-east of the site in 1988. As well as the eastern rampart and ditch, the excavations revealed that the Roman structures were built on top of an accumulated soil which covered pre-fort structures of unspecified date but also threw up two worked flints of late Neolithic or Bronze Age date. There has been no work since 1988.

Layout and history

The fort measured 128 by 188m and covered 2.3ha, making it the second largest on the Wall. The earliest construction was of turf and timber, with a 4m wide clay rampart. Four postholes at the western entrance have been interpreted as part of the original gate housing. When the fort was rebuilt in stone, the front of the clay rampart was cut back and a c. 1.4m wide wall with a clay and rubble core was inserted. This rested on clay and cobble foundations between 1.3 - 1.7m wide. There was a berm of 3-3.5m, which was also surfaced with cobbles. The inner ditch was between 4.6 - 6m wide and 1.5 - 2m deep and on both the eastern and western sides was found to contain fallen rampart masonry. The outer ditch was 2m wide and 1m deep on the western side and only extended as far as the northern interval tower. If an outer ditch also existed on the eastern side, it was obliterated by a medieval ditch 15.2m wide.

The survival, as an earthwork, of a short stretch of the *agger* of the road running south from the fort indicates the location of the south gate and reveals that the fort's central range faced east. Excavations in the north-east corner revealed traces of a north-south orientated multiphase timber building over 57m long, whose northern end had been lost to erosion.

Although of unusual design, the building is interpreted as a barrack block which was re-modelled three times during the second century. It was built on a red clay spread which sealed an earlier Roman rubbish pit. A new building was provided in the area during the fourth century. The northern part of the western gate-tower, and an interval tower on the eastern rampart, have also been excavated.

The garrison tribune, Sulpicius Secundianus, is named on two mid-third-century inscriptions, but the unit itself is not recorded (*RIB* 2057; 2058). An earlier, probably second-century inscription, records building work by the Sixth Legion (*RIB* 2061). Although the fort is not explicitly mentioned in the *Notitia Dignitatum*, this document has been used to suggest that the *cohors I Aelia Hispanorum equitata* was based here. Alternatively, the sparse late fourth-century material from the fort may imply that its omission from the list was deliberate.

Extramural Area

Official buildings and structures

Remains thought to be those of the fort baths lie east of the road exiting from the south gate. The remains of a possible quay wall are described by Hodgson (1840, II.iii, 227).

Civilian buildings

Earthworks are visible in a field to the south of the line of the southern defences of the fort. These have not been excavated, but the surface traces indicate a road, bordered by buildings on both sides, running from the probable position of the south gate of the fort. These buildings are believed to be Roman, although Bellhouse has argued for a medieval date.

Religious structures

The existence of a shrine, paid for by a trader, is attested by an inscription (*RIB* 2059).

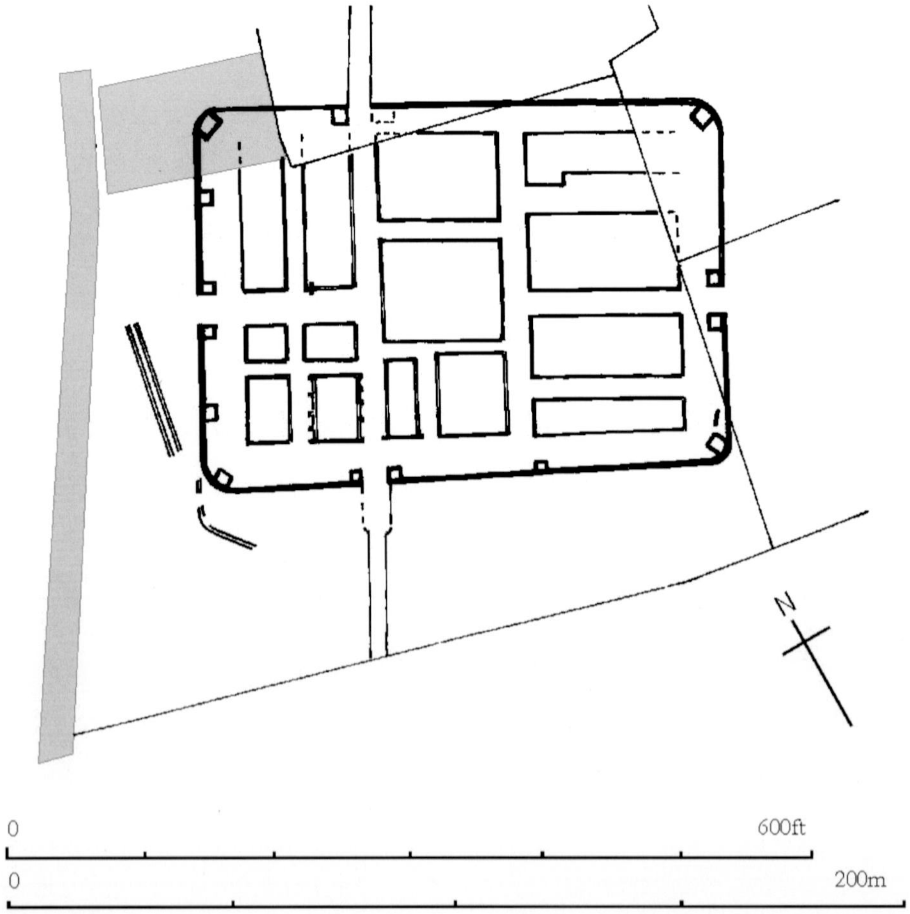

112. Plan of Beckfoot fort

Cemeteries
No evidence.

Beckfoot (*Bibra*)

D J P Mason

This fort occupies a slight rise a little to the south of the modern village of Beckfoot on the Cumbrian coast. A little over 1 ha in size is site is unencumbered by modern buildings. The only unit known to have been in garrison here is *cohors II Pannoniorum equitata quingenaria* (*RIB* 880).

History of exploration
Excavations in 1879 defined the fort outline and produced evidence for a long sequence of occupation extending from the Hadrianic period through to the 4th century (Robinson 1880).

Layout and history
Little of the interior has been explored although the general layout of the buildings has been revealed by aerial photography (St Joseph 1951, 56 Pl.IV.2).

Extramural Area

Official buildings and structures
A large building lying some 40 m north of the fort's north-east angle and partially explored by Robinson in 1879/80 is thought to have been the *balneum.*

Civilian buildings
Robinson's explorations encountered structural remains at various points outside the fort suggesting *vicus* buildings (1880, 142-6). Aerial photographs taken in 1949 revealed a series of strip-buildings lining the road south from the fort for a distance of at least 75 m (St Joseph 1951, 56 Pl. IV.2). Field-systems further out were seen during later aerial survey (Jones & Higham 1975, 28-30, fig.3).

Religious structures
Drainage works south of the fort in 1855 encountered five altars but only a fragment of one survives (*RIB* 852). There may have been a shrine at this spot.

Cemeteries
Cemeteries are known on the seaward side of the Roman coastal road both to the north and to the south of the fort. That to the south has produced interesting examples of second century cremations in the form of pyres with biers *in situ.* Later inhumations in stone-lined graves are also known. The southern cemetery is being affected by coastal erosion and is the scene of ongoing investigation. Discoveries relating to the cemetery are usefully summarised in a recently published article (Caruana *et al* 2004, 136-40).

Maryport (*Alauna*)

I Caruana

The fort is sited on a sandstone ridge 55 metres above sea level, at one of the highest points on the Solway coast. It lies 750 m north-east of the mouth of the river Ellen. The course of the Ellen loops north-east from its mouth past the south-east side of the ridge through an area of low lying marshy ground.

113. Results of geophysical survey at Maryport

114. Aerial photograph of Maryport

The Roman name for Maryport is now generally accepted to be *Alauna*, which is reflected in the name of the river Ellen. The first three units in garrison at the fort are known from epigraphic evidence to be *cohors I Hispanorum equitata* (Hadrianic, c.123-c.139), *cohors I Delmatarum* (Antonine, c139-c.165), and *cohors I Baetasiorum* (late Antonine, c.165-c.183). Nothing is known of the later garrisons. The *Notitia Dignitatum*, which for many sites identifies the third and fourth century unit name, appears to have a gap where *Alauna* should be (Holder 2004). The existence of such a *lacuna* makes better sense of the document and means that attempts to identify Maryport with *Alione* or *Axelodunum* in the *Notitia* may be discounted. There is, therefore, no reason to believe that either *cohors III Nervioroum or cohors I Hispanorum milliaria* were the third/fourth century garrison, as has sometimes been postulated in the past.

The fort and the northern *vicus* are free from modern buildings except for Camp Hill Farm on the north-east edge of the *vicus*. The fort field is under permanent pasture; the fields of the northern *vicus* are ploughed regularly. The fort is known to have been heavily robbed and the building lines visible on aerial photographs are actually robber trenches. Roman activity is known to the south-east of fort where large nineteenth century houses line the south-east side of Camp Road. Beyond this, geophysical work has proved activity beneath the playing field of Camp Hill School and the Roman road to Papcastle has been identified as far as the Ellen crossing in the grounds of Netherhall School. Immediately south-west of the fort is a recreation ground and playground surrounded by houses constructed since the 1920s. This area is known to have Roman remains and recent work has given indications that this might be the site of an earlier, pre-Hadrianic fort.

The Battery, now housing the Senhouse Museum, occupies the strip of land between the north-western fort ditches and the cliff edge. Observations when the tower was erected and results of the geophysical surveys suggest that Roman activity in this area may have been sparse. There are records of nineteenth century and later military activity on the fort site. Some of the earthworks in the area of the corner towers on the west face of the fort, which give the appearance of concealing external towers (Lax & Blood 1997, 55), may be the result of this or other post-Roman disturbance. A World War II anti-aircraft battery was sited in the fields of the northern *vicus*.

History of exploration

Investigation began seriously in the eighteenth century. These exposed the north-east ('north') gate (1787), the *principia* (c.1686 and 1766), the *praetorium* bath-house (1788) and unlocated work in 1779 and 1785 (summarised in Birley 1961, 216-22; Jarrett 1976, 1-8). The mound known as Pudding Pie Hill, south-west of the fort was investigated in 1742 and 1763 (Head 1773). Reports of this work appeared in eighteenth century volumes of *Archaeologia*. The chance discovery of Roman altars in 1870 led to the exposure of a series of pits and the recovery of 17 altars (Bruce 1874). In 1880 further excavation took place in the *vicus* (Robinson 1881). No further excavations were undertaken until 1966 when the C.W.A.A.S. celebrated their centenary by sponsoring an investigation of the fort interior. A detailed catalogue of the collection of artefacts from the site was produced in 1915 (Bailey 1915) with a supplement (Bailey 1926) and Bailey continued to record new finds and observations.

Since the publication of the 1966 excavations two major developments have been the creation of the Senhouse Museum Trust leading to the setting up of a museum for the Netherhall collection and the extensive geophysical surveys by TimeScape of the fort and *vicus* (Biggins & Taylor 2004a). A watching brief in the town discounted the traditional interpretation of the Roman harbour (Percival 1996, contradicting Bailey 1923). Excavations by the Maryport Archaeological Society south of the fort appear to have uncovered traces of a pre-Hadrianic fort (unpublished).

Layout and history

The fort is almost square with an internal area estimated from 1.87 ha (4.5 acres) (Lax & Blood 1997, 53) to 1.96 ha (Biggins & Taylor 2004a, 111) or 2.58 ha (6.5 acres) over the ramparts. The fort faces north-west. The *via principalis* lies only a short distance north-west of the central NE-SW axis. The *principia* can be identified in its conventional position on the RCHM plan (Lax & Blood 1997, Fig.3.1 nos 16 and 17) and in the geophysical surveys (Biggins & Taylor 2004a, 124). The *praetorium*, along with the bath-house excavated in 1788, lie north-east side of the *principia*. The 1966 excavation, in the *retentura*, uncovered a sequence of barracks in Periods I and II and long, narrow buildings of uncertain function (?stables, ?stores) in Period III.

The plan reconstructed from the geophysical surveys suggests that the *retentura* held only four buildings (barracks) and the *praetentura* may have held six barrack blocks and two other buildings (Biggins and Taylor 2004a, Fig.5.7). The unusually large size of the fort (6.5 acres) has tended to reinforce the idea that the fort was built for a milliary, equitate cohort. This explanation arose out of the use of the title *tribunus* for two of the unit's commanders, Maenius Agrippa and Caballius Priscus. According to this theory the unit was milliary in the 120s under its first two commanders, *tribuni*, with a title appropriate to such a sized unit, but later reduced in size to 500-strong, commanded by *praefecti*.

A milliary cohort would have needed ten infantry and four cavalry barracks plus stables. It is impossible to envisage how this accommodation can be reconciled with the likely plan established by the geophysics. The other part of the argument has also been challenged by Frere who, for various reasons, disputes the dating of Maenius Agrippa and his assignment as first commander at Maryport, preferring to see Agrippa arriving at Maryport in 128 or 129. He points out other examples of the use of the title *tribunus* in a quingenary cohort other than the size of the regiment (Frere 2000).

The 1966 excavations demonstrated that the clay rampart was fronted by a contemporary stone wall (Jarrett 1976, Plate IV). The excavations exposed three, and possibly four, ditches on the east face. The *porta principalis dextra*, excavated in 1787, was a single portal structure and the evidence for the other gates appears to be the same where no *spinae* are visible in the geophysical surveys (Biggins & Taylor 2004a, 112). There may also be later additions to the north-east and possibly the south-west gates (*ibid.*). Similar external masonry may also have been observed at the south-east gate (Jarrett 1976, 4 quoting Whellan 1860) Angle and interval towers are also identifiable on the survey plans.

A tentative structural history for the fort was established by excavation in 1966 excavation was to establish a dated structural sequence as follows:
Period I, Hadrianic
Period II, beginning after c.170 and possibly as late as 238-44
Period III, undated but possibly 238-44
Period IV, c.360+

The only evidence for changes in the arrangement of the fort again comes from the 1966 excavation which saw the pair of barracks of Periods I and/or II replaced by a long, narrow building in Period III and post-built structures of uncertain plan in Period IV

The 1966 excavations produced a final phase of timber post building which is characteristic of late occupation in a number of forts. The excavators assigned this phase a date of c. 360+ (Jarrett 1976, 40-41). Chance finds include late Roman military belt fittings believed to be indicative of military activity (Brown in Jarrett 1976, 76-82). One interpretation of this evidence is that there was an important line of late Roman garrisons running through Stainmore from South Shields to Maryport (Mann 1989). Several tombstones from Maryport show stylistic characteristics of late fourth or fifth century date (*RIB* 862-3). There is no evidence for destruction or the end of Roman occupation.

There is no evidence of any annexes which might be expected to have shown up in the geophysical surveys.

Extramural Area

Official buildings and structures
A large building (c.19 x 28 m) known from geophysical survey to lie outside the north angle of the fort has been tentatively identified as a *mansio*. Other large buildings have also been identified e.g. no.15, c.30 m by c.11 m, and no.16, c.26 m by c.11 m, with buttresses and no.17 on both sides of the main road in the north-east *vicus* (Biggins & Taylor 2004a, 114-5)

The existence of a third century parade-ground south-west of the fort has been postulated, based in part on an interpretation of the mound known as Pudding Pie Hill as an inspection platform. Recent investigations on the playing field (unpublished and unreported) seem to show evidence of a pre-Hadrianic fort but it is not clear whether there were also *vicus* remains overlying it. Limited geophysical work by TimeScape shows the presence of anomalies in this field but the report seems to conflate the excavation results with the geophysics (Biggins & Taylor 2004a, 122 & fig.5.6). The plan of the geophysics results shows nothing that can be interpreted easily.

The bath-house uncovered in 1788 is generally understood to be a suite attached to the commanding officer's house. A situation closer to the river Ellen on the south-east or south-west side of the fort may be possible locations for the regimental *balneum*.

Civilian buildings
Geophysical surveys have yielded a full picture of the north-east sector of the *vicus* and a partial picture of the south-east one. On the other hand since these investigations lack stratigraphical and chronological detail, we have only a generalised picture of the *vicus*. Moreover, any interpretation of the results shown on the geophysical maps is necessarily subjective.

The north-east sector of the *vicus* takes the form of ribbon development along the coast road heading northwards. The majority of the buildings are gable-end on to the road, most less than 7 metres wide but about a quarter with widths of 7 to 11 metres (Biggins & Taylor 2004, 115). Buildings also follow the line of the ditches up to and beyond the north and east corners. The road from the south-east gate of the fort, leading to Papcastle, has been traced as far as the crossing of the river Ellen (Dykes 1870, 169). Geophysics has identified features south-east of Camp Road school but they do not appear to have urban characteristics (unless they are cemetery enclosures). A watching brief in 2004 in the grounds south-east of Netherhall School found only a few pits and stake holes, all of which were undated, and may not even be Roman (HER 2/04/1259; CW3 v, 2005, 289). It is likely, therefore, the vicus was less extensive on the south-east side.

The overall extent of the *vicus* has been estimated as 70 ha. but this is a crude, and not very accurate, calculation based upon the 67 ha. extent of the geophysical survey (Biggins & Taylor 2004, 102). Any additional buildings present on the south-east and south-west may have been close to the fort in areas unavailable for survey because of housing and, therefore, not yet recorded. There has been no modern excavation within the *vicus* to provide details of its structural history and development.

There appears to be a ditch to the north and east which may mark the outer limit of the *vicus* around 600-700 metres from the fort (Biggins & Taylor 2004a, fig.5.10). Another indication of the *vicus* limit on the north-east side is a possible ditch (or series of linked ditches) which forms the rear of the properties fronting the road and running across the road in Field 4 (ibid. fig.5.9).

Civilian buildings seem to cluster mainly around the fort and along the roadside. However, at the rear of many buildings the apparent ditches, mentioned previously, may mark property boundaries at some distance back from the structures. Beyond these are traces of other ditches, suggesting field or enclosure boundaries, but whether they are pre-Roman, Roman or later is unknown.

Religious structures
Two of the buildings excavated in 1880 appear to have been temples. One circular structure with at least three external buttresses may have been a mausoleum (Robinson 1881, 246 and plan opp.256). The neighbouring structure, equipped with a rectangular nave and a shallow rectangular apse (ibid. 245; photograph in Wilson 1997, fig.1.8), is almost certainly a temple, possibly even a *Mithraeum*.

Cemeteries
Robinson's explorations uncovered a number of cremations on the edge of the *vicus*, in the fourth field from the fort, where the Serpent Stone appears to have been a burial marker and with numerous burial urns in its vicinity (1881, 242). These burials began immediately beyond the *vicus* edge but others in the area of the circular temple in the second field may have been built over by the expanding *vicus* (1881, 248-9). A gravestone was found in the 1920s close to Barney Gill (*RIB* 863) and another close to the Ellen crossing (*RIB* 862). Since these are likely places for the fort cemeteries they may have been at or close to their original location. A number of enclosures and smaller anomalies seen on the geophysical plots are also plausibly interpreted as enclosed cemeteries and cremations.

Epigraphy
J.B. Bailey calculated that there have been 213 inscribed and sculptured stones found at Maryport up to his time (Bailey 1926, 422). A few stones have been discovered since then. Of these about 40% are inscribed.

There is also an unusual stamped tile of the *cohors I Hispanorum* (*RIB* II 2474) which is a very early occurrence of tile stamping by an auxiliary unit.

The sculptured stones have been recorded for the *Corpus Signorum Imperii Romani* but await the appearance of the relevant volume. A discussion of the stones has appeared from the volume editor (Coulston 1997)

Burrow Walls (*Axelodunum*)

D J P Mason

The fort site is situated on the north-eastern outskirts of Workington but is free of modern buildings. The position is an old cliff top, slightly higher than the marshy area to the

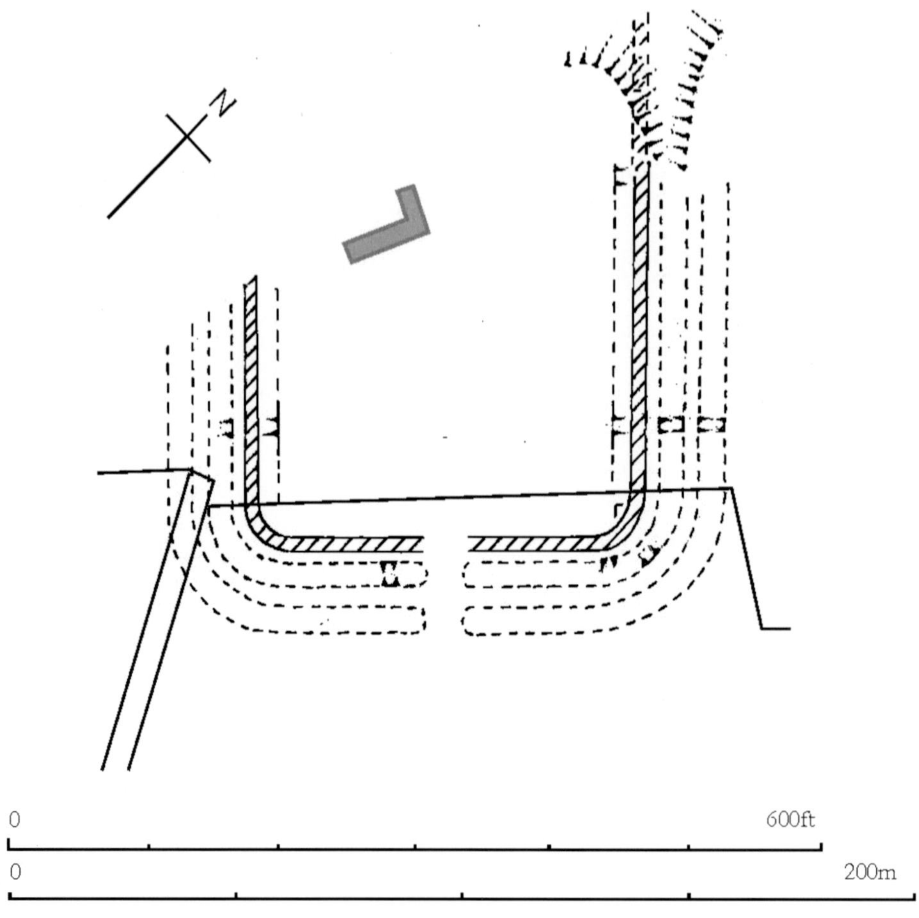

115. Plan of Burrow Walls fort

116. Site of the fort at Moresby

west and a little to the north of the mouth of the River Derwent. The north-western third - now occupied by a railway embankment - has been lost to coastal erosion. The original size of the fort is estimated as 1.2ha. The garrison is unknown except for the fourth century when the *numerus Pacensium* was in residence (*ND*xl29).

History of exploration
The only excavations to date occurred in 1955 (Bellhouse 1955).

Layout and history
The 1955 work was restricted to the defences. They produced plentiful evidence of occupation in the Hadrianic period and during the second half of the fourth century but activity in the intervening period was poorly represented.

Extramural Area

Official buildings and structures
Whellan refers to extensive building remains outside fort but there is now way of telling whether these were military or civilian (1859, 464).

Civilian buildings
See above. A fragmentary inscription on an altar refers to two boys - Aurelius and Secundus. They may have been *vicani* but could equally well have been the children of the commanding officer and lived in the *praetorium*.

Religious structures
Drainage works south of the fort in 1855 encountered five altars but only a fragment of one survives (*RIB* 852). There may have been a shrine at this spot.

Cemeteries
Burials have been found south and west of fort (Whellan 1859, 464).

Moresby (*Gabrosentum*)

D J P Mason

The site of the fort, 1.4ha in size, is partially covered by churchyard and faces the sea. A building inscription from the east gate records the construction of the fort in the latter part of Hadrian's reign (128-38, *RIB* 801). The garrison in this period was *cohors II Lingonum equitata quingenaria* (*RIB* 798, 800), succeeded in the third and fourth centuries by *cohors II Thracum equitata quingenaria* (*RIB* 797, 803-4; *ND* xl.50).

History of exploration
Excavations in 1859-60 located the north gate and determined the fort's overall size (Bruce 1867, 294-5). None of the interior has been examined.

Layout and history
Nothing known owing to lack of excavation.

Extramural Area

Official building and structures
Concrete floors and tiles seen during works south of the fort 1943 hint at location of the regimental bath building (Birley 1948, 71).

Civilian buildings
The foundations of what are assumed to have been *vicus* buildings were seen in the same general area in the nineteenth century (Jefferson 1842, 448; also Birley 1948, 71).

Religious structures
The bust of a Celtic horned god - probably Silvanus - was recovered from the area west of the fort in 1881 (Wright & Phillips 1975, No. 193). An altar dedicated to Silvanus has also been found here and the two objects may hint at the presence of a temple or shrine to this deity (*RIB* 798).

117. Walls Castle, the bath house at Ravenglass

Cemeteries
A cemetery was found east of the fort in the 1850s during alterations to Moresby Hall. (Whellan 1860, 420). An altar-shaped tombstone was recovered from a spot 550m east-south-east of the fort in 1962 (*JRS* 53 160 No. 5). This refers to two females who may have been resident in the *vicus*, Clanova and Fontia.

Other
A small natural harbour once existed at the foot of the cliff west of the fort and may have been used in the Roman period.

Ravenglass (*Itunocelum*)

D J P Mason

The fort site is free of modern building but was cut through by the construction of the railway line in 1850. Also, the western defences have been eroded by the sea. Until recently the site was afforested. The fort was 1.8ha in size and probably faced seawards.

The original garrison is unknown but in the third and fourth centuries it was *cohors I Aelia Classica* (lead sealing *RIB* 2411.94; also *diploma* of 158 (Holder 1997) (*ND*xl51)

History of exploration
Parts of the interior were examined in 1885-6 (Ferguson 1888). The evidence has been summarised on several occasions (Collingwood 1928; Birley 1958). Excavation in modern times consists of the 1976-78 campaign in the north-west quarter of the fort conducted by the late Tim Potter (1979). A survey of the site was undertaken in 1998 by the Royal Commission (Blood & Pearson).

Layout and history
The fort rampart was c. 7 m wide. A stone wall was added when the fort was rebuilt after a fire in the early third century. There were two subsequent fires and re-buildings, probably in the late third and mid-fourth centuries. The early fourth century barracks were built of timber and were reconstructed later in that century. Beneath the fort buildings were traces of an earlier fortlet 0.47ha in size belonging to the original Cumbrian coastal defence system of towers and fortlets.

Extramural Area

Official buildings and structures
The well-preserved remains of the regimental baths lie outside the north-east corner of the fort and were excavated in 1881 (Jackson 1883). Portions of the building's walls still stand to a height in excess of 2 metres above ground. The remains of another sophisticated building have been found north of the fort where coastal erosion has led to the discovery of box-tiles, bricks and *tesserae*. This may have been a *mansio*. (Fair 1948). There have been many other discoveries of material north of fort. A brick and pottery manufactory lay 5km to the north-east (Bellhouse 1960; 1961).

Civilian buildings
R.G. Collingwood stated that finds had been recovered from an area of 3-4 acres around the fort and as far as 460m out from defences though some of this material might derive from the as yet undiscovered cemetery (Collingwood 1929, 44; Fair 1948, 219).

Religious structures
No evidence

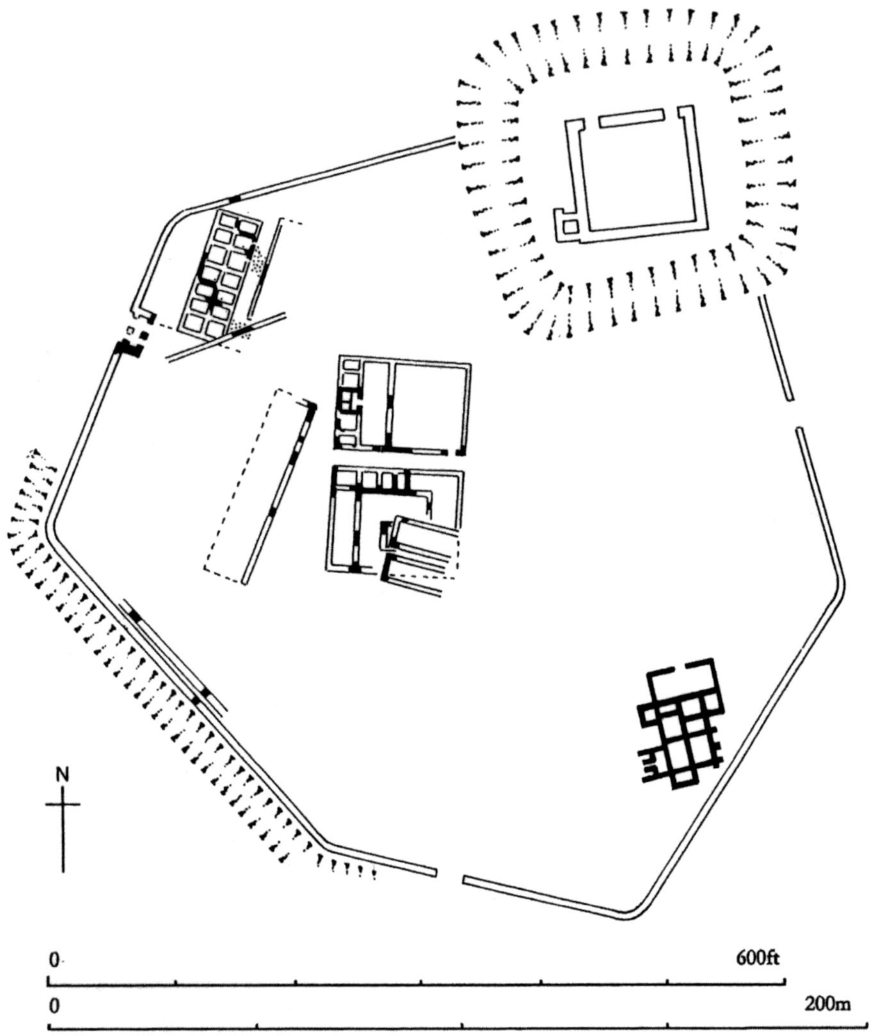

118. Plan of Bewcastle fort

Cemeteries
No evidence

Bewcastle (*Fanum Cocidii*)

D J P Mason

The fort site is partially overlain by farm buildings, the castle and a church. The fort was an irregular hexagon in plan, 2.40ha in size and faced north-west. The rampart and fort wall are visible and portions of the masonry of the NE, NW and SW gates survive

The Hadrianic garrison was *cohors I Dacorum milliaria peditata* (*RIB* 991). That in the early Antonine is unknown but in the third century it was *cohors I Nervorum milliaria equitata.*

History of exploration
Excavations occurred in1937, 1954-6 (Gillam, Jobey & Welsby 1993), 1977-7 (Austen 1991). An earthwork survey was carried out in the late 1980s (Sainsbury & Welfare 1990).

Layout and history
Excavated buildings consist of the *principia*, the *praetorium*, barracks and a possible store in the western half of the interior along with a bath-building in the south-eastern area. The rest of the interior is largely unexplored.

Excavations in 1977-8 by Austen (1991) revealed that the primary (Hadrianic) fort was equipped with turf defences and timber buildings but with stone gates and *principia*. The other internal buildings were rebuilt in stone in the mid-Antonine period or a little later. There was further rebuilding at the beginning of the third century with occupation continuing until the fort was abandoned in the early fourth century. Some of the latest buildings were on a different alignment to their predecessors and additional buildings were inserted into back of rampart. There was a possible realigning of the defences on the north-west side.

Extramural Area

Official buildings and structures
No evidence.
Civilian buildings
No Evidence.

Religious structures
A temple to Jupiter Doliche is attested epigraphically (*RIB* 992) as is one dedicated to the god after whom the fort was named - Cocidius (*RIB* 985-6, 988-9, 993).

Cemeteries
No evidence.

6. Landscape and Environment
Co-ordinated by J Huntley

Introductory Overview
J Huntley

Studies of the landscape and environmental background to the Wall have benefited greatly from the application of techniques typically used in other disciplines. Pollen analysis from naturally developing deposits (peat bogs, mires and water bodies), especially, has demonstrated the differing nature of woodland cover on either side of the Pennine watershed as well as indicating the effects, on a site-by-site basis, which the Roman military presence had on the local vegetation. In association with macrofossil analyses pollen has also shown us some aspects of grassland management, probably for fodder and hay, both important provisions for cavalry units. The use of pollen on archaeological material *per se* has yet to be explored in detail although the small amount of work done at Vindolanda shows that this could be rewarding so long as the questions are carefully targeted. Pollen has also shown us the highly cultivated nature of the landscape in the eastern lowlands with pasture and cereal cultivation both important. Pollen work on soils buried immediately under dated features on the Wall has provided several snapshots of vegetation although, unfortunately, pollen often does not survive in good conditions or adequate quantities. The presence of cord rig under many sites in the east further emphasizes the importance of cereal and, probably, other crop growing.

Other biological proxies, such as testate *amoebae* or diatoms (providing information about climatic parameters and water quality), have been used occasionally to good effect, but their potential remains to be explored in greater detail. Seeds and animal bones recovered from archaeological excavations provide data mostly about the economic aspects of the site, but also give indications of the conditions on the site itself. It is clear that many sites had areas of waste ground where weedy, ruderal *taxa* such as docks, thistles and nettles grew and this might be tied with periods at which the troops were deployed elsewhere - for example up at the Antonine Wall in the second century, or even as the Roman presence was 'winding down'. Small mammal bones offer the potential to look at pests and other commensals, but have rarely been studied due to a lack of sieving during past excavations at many sites. Animal *taxa* have provided some information about habitats, for example the red deer and black grouse bones recovered from Vindolanda suggest that extensive wooded areas were not that far away. Fishbones and marine shell have not been studied in any great detail but, even where large volumes of sediment have been sieved, the Roman military seems to have used these resources rather little.

Management of the landscape for production of timber and for water supply or disposal has been studied only occasionally, although these resources, and their control, are crucial to life on the frontier. Timber has also provided precise dating of structures, with Carlisle second only to London for its quality of Roman material. Water management is obvious on many forts with the complex systems of drains often surviving in good condition. How these relate to the wider landscape can probably be best studied through application of remote-sensing techniques and this certainly has high potential for the future.

Low-altitude aerial survey has determined just how much pre-Roman activity there was around the Wall, especially in the central sector. At least some of the features determined from such surveys may also reflect Roman and post-Roman occupation. The large number of boundary features of one sort demonstrated by these surveys leads us to the conclusion that much of the land was extensively managed and controlled. Chronological and economic understanding of these settlements and their landholdings remains, however, little studied. This is no doubt partially attributable to the poor resolution of radiocarbon as a dating technique during the late pre-Roman Iron Age and through the Roman period, due to calibration issues. Nevertheless, it also almost certainly reflects the historical interest in those structures associated with the Roman military and the rather lesser interest in the indigenous population.

Other remote-sensing techniques, again typically borrowed from other disciplines, are demonstrating their potential to address archaeological questions, although it is overwhelmingly clear that they need to be used as one of many techniques and not in isolation. Geophysical techniques have revolutionized our understanding of extramural settlements associated with the forts, demonstrating just how extensive these could be. Although many of these require highly specialized, and expensive, equipment, there is still a place for traditional techniques that can be undertaken at low cost. The main requirement is precise and accurate location of the work in order for all projects to be clearly linked, and displayed, together. Hence a Geographical Information System (GIS) for the Wall is an essential requirement.

Use of biological proxies and remote sensing is not restricted purely to interpretation of the landscape and environment. They have cross links with almost every aspect of study of the Wall and should be seen as part of that overall study. The assessment has shown that, to-date, rather too many studies, and not just landscape and environment ones, seem to keep within their own 'box'. It is more than time that a broader, more holistic approach is taken and the GIS would also help start to address this issue.

Landscape and Environment
J Huntley, T Gates and S Stallibrass

This section will assess the current state of knowledge regarding both the landscape (physical characteristics including sub-surface structures) and environment (especially climatic parameters) of Hadrian's Wall. Historic

119. Complex of landscape features around Housesteads

landscape and environment studies can encompass various broad categories of evidence - the physical remains still visible on the ground today, proxy evidence such as that derived from, for example, pollen surviving in ancient soils and other deposits, as well as old maps, documents and aerial photography, quite apart from place-name evidence.

As elsewhere in this framework, the chronology, although focused upon the Romans, essentially covers the period from the later pre-Roman Iron Age through to the fifth/sixth centuries AD.

Remotely sensing the landscape

Landscape survey - aerial photography

Studies of the physical historical landscape are probably best initiated from examination and transcription of aerial photographs for which there have been many flights over the last 60 or so years. In ideal conditions - low light, after periods of dry weather, under light snow cover - old field boundaries can often be discerned as well as the more frequent (and frequently targeted for subsequent analysis) settlements. One of the best documented areas is that covered by two flying and mapping projects carried out by one of the authors between 1998 and 2004 over the central section of the Wall, within the southern part of the Northumberland National Park (Gates 1999; 2004). For this purpose a territory of 160 km^2 was chosen and all of it was photographed except for 45 km^2 that was masked by forestry plantations. During these projects 1,280 new photographs were taken, including many stereo pairs. Data from these and 760 pre-existing photographs were transcribed onto 1:10,000 maps and over 600 'sites' of all types were described in an accompanying gazetteer. Of these, two thirds (407 sites) had not been documented in any other database. Indeed, the proportion of new material was much greater than these figures suggest as they take no account of the mass of post-medieval sod-cast dykes and enclosure boundaries which figure so prominently on the map overlays. The results therefore clearly demonstrate the extent of new information to be gained from such work.

120. Prehistoric and Romano-British site at Fingland

Boundaries

Boundaries of one sort or another make up the bulk of the detail portrayed on the map overlays produced from Gates' work. As noted above, these include a multitude of sod-cast dykes resulting from both piecemeal and Parliamentary enclosure during the historic period. However, there are a number, typically consisting of a bank accompanied by a ditch only on one side, which do not seem to fit in with the overall pattern of enclosure during the medieval or later periods. Fourteen linear earthworks of this type were identified during the course of this mapping project. These include sections of the so-called Black Dyke which has been recognised as a potentially early boundary since the early eighteenth century at least. In the great majority of cases, boundaries of this type run more or less north-south against the 'grain' of the landscape, cutting across the dry ridge tops which must have acted as the main east-west routes in these parts for millennia. The most likely purpose of these linear earthworks was probably to obstruct the movement of people and animals, and to act as territorial boundaries. In one or two instances there are indications that some linear boundaries of this type pre-date the construction of Hadrian's Wall and the Military Way, though others could be post-Roman in date. These important features are otherwise undated.

Unenclosed settlements - pre Roman Iron Age
Ten settlements of unenclosed roundhouses are now on record within Gates' survey area and most are accompanied by visible evidence of agricultural activity in the form of stone clearance, field boundaries or cord rig. Individual settlements are invariably small and none possesses more than four recognisable house stances. Although comparatively few unenclosed settlements have been excavated in the Tyne-Forth region, available radiocarbon dates indicate that they have a long chronological range, extending from at least the early second to the end of the first millennium BC. As a result it is not usually possible to assign even approximate dates to particular settlements on the basis of field survey alone.

Enclosed farmsteads - Romano-British
Enclosed farmsteads are a familiar sight in the Northumberland uplands and are usually attributed to the Roman period. However, the number of sites which have been excavated remains very small in relation to the total number on record, which now runs into several hundred examples, and there is still a lot we don't know about them. In the area covered by Gates' survey, there are roughly a dozen such farmsteads presently on record. Of these, eight were discovered by means of air photography carried out for this project. By contrast with the unenclosed settlements described above, the majority of these (presumably later) farmsteads are accompanied by developed field systems, sometimes incorporating walled trackways. Some fields also contain cord rig, as for example at Fold Hill.

Cord Rig
Cord rig comprises a series of narrow ridges generally less than a metre apart and formed as the result of cultivation. The recognition of extant cord rig at almost 100 locations within Gates' survey area supports the view, already attested by pollen analysis (see below), that cereal cultivation was practiced in this area during the first and second millennia BC, reaching altitudes as high as 270m. The technique was current in the middle Iron Age and still being practiced in the first half of the second century AD. How far it may have continued later into the Roman period is presently unknown.

The distribution of cord rig, at least in the form of visible earthworks, suggests a dispersed pattern of small scale cultivation with individual fields rarely exceeding 0.5ha in size. If this picture is a true reflection of the scale of cultivation in the central sector of the Wall during the later pre-Roman Iron Age then it is hard to see how much of a grain surplus could have been created locally, even on the unlikely assumption that all cord rig fields were under cultivation at the same time and that all were given over to arable crops. On balance the evidence points to small scale production for home consumption. Interestingly, the same conclusion has been reached by van der Veen (1992) following, her study of carbonised grain samples from excavated sites north of the Tyne. The story may not be the same to the south of the River Tyne, although more recent farming practices may well have obliterated any surviving cord rig and we become reliant upon charred grain assemblages for interpretation.

NMP
The Hadrian's Wall Project, which is part of the National Mapping Programme, represents a much broader survey than Gates' work. The project extends from Newcastle to Bowness and includes the Solway and Cumbrian coast defences. An interim report on the results of the survey from Carlisle to the Cardurnock peninsula has been prepared (Boutwood 2005). The project has recorded a range of sites from prehistory to twentieth-century military remains. Thus far it has enhanced 3,293 records of which 74% are new to the National Monuments Record database.

Landscape survey - LiDAR and satellite imagery
Satellite imagery is now available at a spatial resolution of less than 2m via, for example, the Corona, Gambit and Hexagon systems following declassification by the US military (Fowler 2004) although quality of image may not be that useful for our region where cloud cover is often high. Whilst it would not necessarily be that useful for picking up cultural features either, it would have the potential to help understand the topographic development of the river valleys and at least see the larger features, such as forts and military *vici*, in that topography.

Another remote-sensing technique that is being applied more frequently to archaeological issues is that of airborne LiDAR (Light detection and ranging). This also is used primarily to collect topographic data, although the different laser systems can produce chemical and velocity related data as well. The LiDAR instrument is fitted to an airplane and transmits light out to a target. This light interacts with and is changed by the target and some is reflected/scattered back to the instrument where it is analysed. The change in the properties of the light enables some property, in our case distance, of the target to be determined. The best spatial resolution from these surveys is currently about 15cm vertically and about 1m horizontally. The Environment Agency has flown airborne LiDAR surveys across most of the English coastline and major rivers as part of its flood risk management work and the high resolution makes it possible to distinguish cultural sites, as well as old filled-in stream channels that might well contain palaeoenvironmental records. It is not sufficiently sensitive to detect deeply buried ephemeral features such as post-holes or ring-ditches that might remain from non-military settlements of later Iron Age, Romano-British or post-Roman date in areas subject to alluviation.

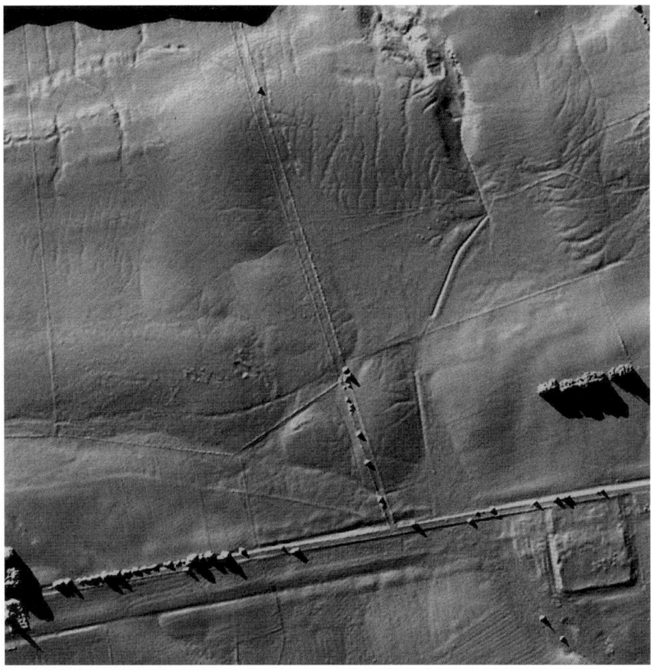

121. The results of the LiDAR survey at Carrawburgh

The technique has been used in several ALSF projects to good effect (see for example the Witham Valley project (Crutchley 2006)) and, no doubt, could add further to our knowledge of the landscape around Hadrian's Wall in critical areas. It is, however, expensive and the Witham project made it clear that LiDAR should not be used alone but 'ensuring that it is part of an examination of all readily available sources' (Crutchley 2006, 251) with the example of a feature initially thought to represent a Roman fort but, upon examination of old aerial photographs, determined to be, in fact, related to a Second World War airfield. Similarly, the Ribble Valley project combined desk-based archaeological survey, LiDAR survey and palaeoecological ground-truthing to develop a Digital Terrain Model that elucidated the development of the river terraces and their associated archaeology (Quartermaine *et al* 2006).

Generally, LiDAR does have significant potential to detect sites that do not show well on "traditional" aerial photographs in pastureland (by setting the instruments to detect leaf angle). This is a major advantage in rural areas under improved grazing or ley grassland but is less applicable to rough grazing, where the mosaic of vegetation need not reflect underlying soils or archaeological features.

Landscape survey - on the ground

On the ground survey work, using either modern hi-tech equipment and GPS (Global Positioning System) or the traditional plane-table surveys, can also define the "humps and bumps" of past landscapes at a very detailed, local scale. Work carried out by English Heritage's Survey Team on the hillforts in the Northumberland National Park (Pearson and Hunt 2004) demonstrates how much evidence of the past does survive at this level. In addition, for this site a nearby wetland produced detailed and dated pollen evidence for cultivation during the probable period of occupation of the site (Allen and Huntley 2004). The techniques are probably most applicable to our understanding of pre-Roman activity but could be applied to other single-phase or short-term sites, for example marching camps and practice camps.

Other non-invasive techniques are those that involve geophysical methods. Although highly effective at revealing detailed aspects of internal layout of specific sites e.g. Timescape's surveys at a number of sites including Maryport and Carvoran, they are not especially appropriate for landscape-scale work. Their place will probably remain in exploring specific archaeological sites, including the extramural settlements associated with forts on Hadrian's Wall, such as that associated with Birdoswald fort (Biggins and Taylor 2004d).

There is then the extremely old-fashioned, but reliable, tried-and-tested technique of walking around on the ground and simply observing and recording features - whether these are cultural in origin such like walls or boundaries, or natural such as river terraces and other geomorphological features. With modern high resolution GPS, again, spatial data can be produced and mapped onto standard Ordnance Survey maps. Associating such fieldwork with geoarchaeological investigations on the sediments, as in the Till-Tweed project (Passmore et al 2006), can lead to a better understanding of the development of the landscape thus leading to better focused research questions concerning how people managed and used that landscape in the past.

Desk-based work

We should not forget the value of desk-based work studying old maps and documents to provide data of past landscapes. Clearly these will relate to more recent times but can still be used to good effect - as for example the Second World War feature at Witham. For the Roman period, epigraphy and letters are relevant (see p. 151-4) with the Vindolanda writing tablets providing hints about some aspects of the landscape. For example, tablet 180 mentions supplying stores 'to the oxherds at the wood'. Lucco the swineherder is mentioned and, by implication, pigs also are rootling around in local woodlands.

The beauty of all of these remote techniques is that they create spatial data, albeit at very different scales, and, with modern computational power, these can be entered into the ubiquitous GIS for manipulation and analysis. The spatial covers can include descriptive data of whatever type needed and be linked to other databases, ranging from lists of animal bones, plant remains or finds from a specific site to structural details or visitors numbers. This should lead to integrated and innovative analysis of a wide range of information.

Environmental evidence

Proxy studies - pollen

Classic proxy data studies of landscape or, more strictly the environment, derive largely from traditional pollen studies for which the Wall, arguably, has more than its fair share. Palynologists over the decades have been fascinated with investigating the effects that the Romans did, or did not, have upon the contemporary vegetation. The individual papers are

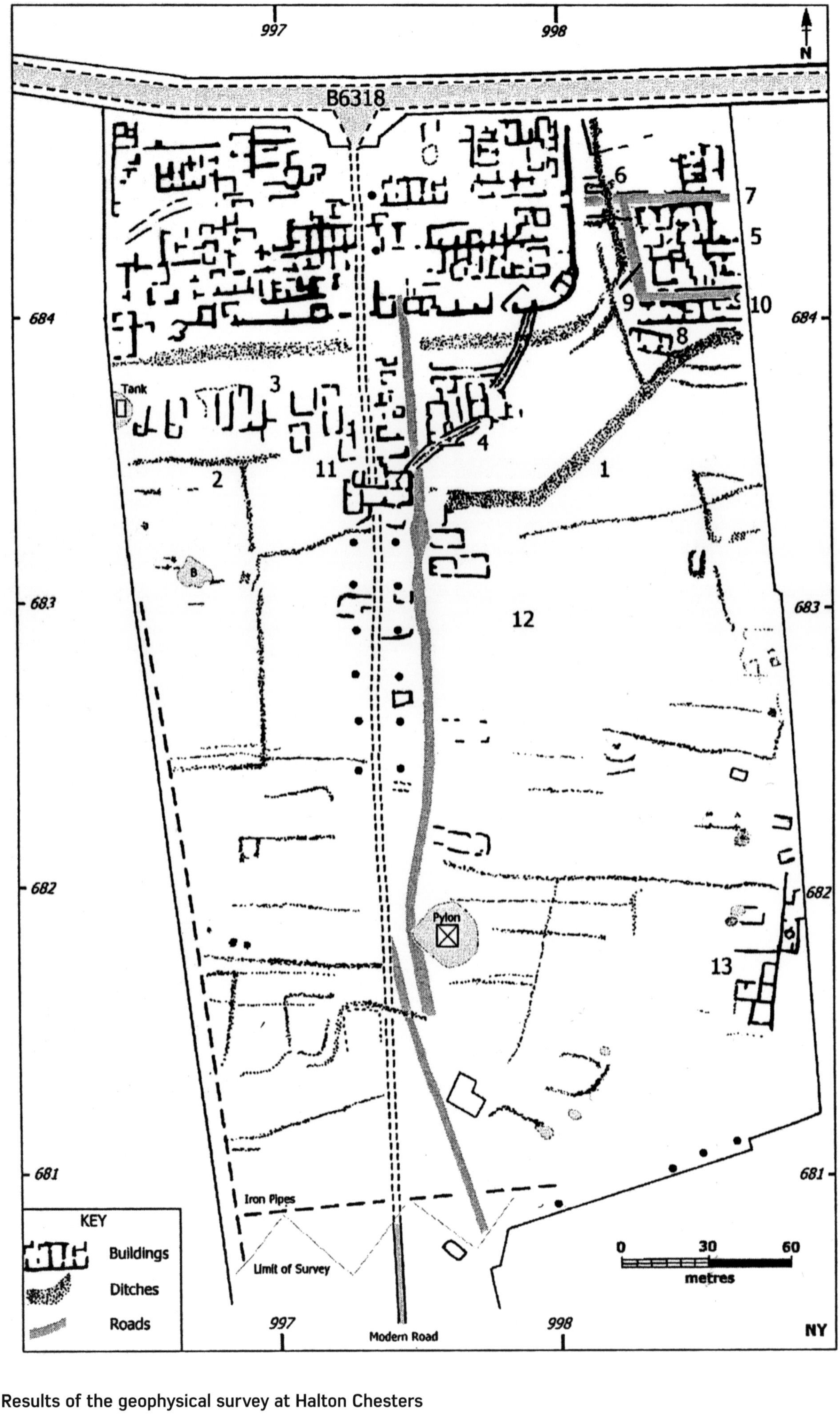

122. Results of the geophysical survey at Halton Chesters

too many to list but see Huntley (2000b) for a detailed review to that date. Very simplistically the picture that emerged was one of an essentially cleared landscape to the east of the Pennine watershed but with much more woodland to the west. See below for more details on the central sector. There are relatively few well-dated pollen diagrams from either the west or the east of the Wall region. To the east there are, obviously, the large conurbations on Tyneside and therefore suitable pollen sites are rare, though not absent. Pollen work has tended to concentrate in the Durham Lowlands for example see Bartley et al (1976), Hallowell Moss near Durham City (Donaldson and Turner 1977), Cranberry Bog, Beamish (Turner and Kershaw 1973) with a synthetic summary by Pratt (1996). In the western reaches, other than studies on the major Solway Mires very little has been done on pollen from the Cumbrian part of the Wall (Wells 2003). Most of the sites studied were purely in relation to questions of vegetation history and of only minor archaeological interest. This is probably a result of few archaeological sites being excavated in the area.

Although the major clearances of woodland were almost always discussed in these papers, and often radiocarbon dated, the main thrust is usually to describe the vegetation history over the Holocene as a whole. However, few papers considered the pollen catchment area and it may be that some of these 'wooded' sites had only very local woodland immediately in the vicinity of the pollen site - for example, Midgeholme Moss next to the fort at Birdoswald where alder pollen dominated (Wiltshire 1997). Alder is a wet-soil tolerant tree that certainly was growing on and around the moss, with alder stumps surviving in the peat, both swamping the surface with its pollen and filtering out much pollen from further afield. As noted by Huntley (2000b) a dense spatial network of small-catchment pollen sites would give a much better indication of vegetation cover around any specific site. Although suitable sites are plentiful along the Wall and within its hinterland, this type of work requires major resources of time and money.

In the immediate vicinity of the central sector of the Wall, pollen sequences obtained from Fellend Moss (Davies and Turner 1979) and Fozy Moss (Dumayne and Barber 1994) point to a landscape that was at least partly, if not mostly, cleared of trees before the construction of the Wall. However, estimating the extent of the impact of the Roman army on tree cover has proven controversial (Hanson 1996; Huntley 1999; Tipping 1997). Difficulties inherent in the precision of radiocarbon dates obtained from peat cores lie at the heart of this debate. In the case of Fozy Moss, air photography shows that there are no fewer than ten native farmsteads within a 4km radius of the sample site, any or all of which could belong to the late pre-Roman or Roman Iron Age (Gates 2004). As most of these are accompanied by organised field systems or cord rig, it would seem reasonable to attribute to native farmers at least some part in the process of wholesale deforestation which almost certainly began before the arrival of the Roman army in this area.

More recently, the emphasis has been focused on what happened after the Romans left the area, both from an archaeological and palynological point of view but, again, effort has tended to concentrate in the central section (Dark 2005). In very general terms the indications from most sites around the Wall are that woodland did regenerate to some degree during the period AD 400-800 but extent and duration varied greatly (Dark 2006). The problem reconciling these two lines of evidence is that the archaeology is highly specific to one site whilst the pollen evidence is not.

123. Coring expansive areas like this produces a regional scale picture of the ancient environment

Buried soils

One aspect of pollen which has been favoured recently is the material surviving in buried soils lying immediately under the Wall. Such deposits arguably provide a much more precise date for the deposit than the more usual radiocarbon, especially given its associated calibration issues for the Roman period (see Dumayne-Peaty and Barber 1997; McCarthy 1997)). Whilst the deposits under the Wall suggest that dating is more precise it is always possible that the former ground surface was truncated during construction. For example, at Black Carts, in Wall mile 29, pollen work suggested completely different assemblages on either side of the Wall (Huntley 1998c) NEED reference to David's full analysis report. Given the relative proximity of the two sites it is highly unlikely that the vegetation would be so different. Analysis of thin sections through the soil/sediment profiles did, in fact, demonstrate that a truncated podzol was present to the south of the Wall (Usai 1999) and that the pollen recorded from it was therefore not from immediately pre-Wall construction. Various other interventions have had buried soils sampled - see summary in Huntley (1999) - with pollen surviving to varying degrees. These data reinforce the evidence from the pollen diagrams from natural deposits that there was greater clearance to the east of the Pennine watershed before the Romans arrived than to the west. Recent work examined buried soils under a number of western milecastles, but the results proved disappointing with little pollen preserved (Tony Wilmott *pers. comm.*).

In some cases excavations have provided direct evidence of cultivation in the form of buried cord rig or plough marks, even though pollen has not survived. Sites that have yielded such evidence include Rudchester (Gillam *et al* 1973; Welfare 1985), and on lower lying land to the east, Denton (Bidwell and Watson 1996) and South Shields (Hodgson et al 2001). That from under the Westgate Road in Newcastle produced both ard marks and pollen suggesting some local alder woodland amongst essentially open grassland with some herbs, but no diagnostic evidence for cultivation (Huntley 1988).

The soils themselves from such deposits have been used to investigate the uses of land prior to the construction of forts. Work at Carlisle (Keeley 1989) and Stanwix (Hall et al 1994) has shown that both the fort at Annetwell Street and the parade ground at Stanwix were prone to waterlogging, suggesting that locations were chosen for strategic reasons despite unfavourable local ground conditions. The Stanwix investigation demonstrated the added value of combining a range of analyses, in this case plant, invertebrate and sediment analyses (see Usai 2002, 9 for a discussion).

Turf structures are most likely to have been constructed from materials close at hand, and so also give clues to the local vegetation. These have been investigated at Bowness-on-Solway and Appletreewick at least. At Lewthwaites Lane, Carlisle, early second-century turf derived from damp, possibly flooded grassland and all of the southern Lanes sites contained indicators of the use of moorland vegetation (Kenward et al 2000). Beetles and some woody plant remains that are indicative of such habitats can survive in deposits which contain the remains of turves, even when the turf blocks have lost their physical structure.

Although there are problems of differential and/or poor preservation from what is after all a dynamic and often aerobic material, i.e. soil, it nonetheless remains true to say that this is the sort of profile that does have potential to investigate quite local landscapes in the area and could be clearly related to specific archaeological sites.

Other proxies - climate change

Although the pollen tells us about vegetation in the landscape, other proxies can also be useful. Some, such as testate amoebae - present in many peats - give information about depth to water-table and wetness of the ground and thus, by implication, climate. Studies have been undertaken on some of the mires in the borders region and demonstrate a generally dry climate through the Roman period (Hendon et al 2001) which became significantly wetter from about AD 500. The very nature of the peats gives information about past climate and this has been well demonstrated by Hughes et al (2000) for both Walton and Bolton Fell Mosses where they investigated changes in species of Sphagnum (bog moss). These show an increased wetness during the late Iron Age, with the climate becoming drier through the Roman period. All of these sites are either to the west of the watershed or at higher altitudes in the Northumberland fells. It would be interesting to see the extent to which the 'rain-shadow' effect of the Pennines and generally lower river valley situations were visible to the east. If rainfall was considerably less to the east, this would have significant implications for crop husbandry.

The importance of determining the climate of the period is clear when we try to interpret patterns of husbandry for both domesticated plant and animal species. Climate, for example, has an effect on how well cereals grow, what the most effective method of storage is and, indeed, at what altitudes they will successfully ripen. It also influences whether animals can be over-wintered outside or not. If not then either large quantities of fodder would be required to over-winter them, or many would have to be slaughtered and the meat preserved in one way or another. Foddering has implications for vegetation management: small branches with green leaves, hay and other fodder need to be brought to the stalled animals and the semi-digested remains of consumed fodder will be deposited where the animals are kept. Rasmussen (1989) has demonstrated this very clearly in Neolithic deposits from Switzerland which revealed that cattle were fed a mixture of leafy fodder and cereal. Occasionally, deposits of discrete manure are found, as at Lancaster, where Wilson examined some very obvious horse manure (Wilson 1988). On the other hand, probably more evidence survives in the form of stable/byre waste, which consists of manure mixed with bedding material. There is certainly a classic 'suite' of stable manure taxa (Kenward and Hall 1997) that occurs in many of the organic deposits at forts along the Wall, suggesting that looking after housed animals was probably a mainstay of occupation for many of the troops.

124. Fellend Moss, directly south of Walltown Crags

Domestic animals and plants are not themselves indicators of local environmental conditions simply because they are domesticates and hence not the native local *taxa*. The possible origins of some of these domesticates are discussed further in the **Production and Procurement** section. The best environmental indicators, therefore, are commensals (where one species benefits from living with another, but not to its detriment, cf. parasites) that are likely to have grown and lived at the site and which are unlikely to have been imported from far away.

Native and commensals, and local environmental conditions

Elements of the native flora and fauna may have been living on the site or found their way onto a site where their remains were preserved. Likely contexts for their preservation would be wells, pits and ditches into which free-living organisms could fall and die, or in which faecal material and associated parasite eggs may have been deposited. Commensals include *taxa* brought accidentally to the site and may or may not be native to Britain - for example, grain pests imported along with grain. They all provide further evidence for living conditions and hygiene as well as the local environment. Many will only be recovered through the deployment of large sampling programmes and hence early investigations were unable to address relevant questions due to the lack of suitable recovery methods.

125. The Wall ditch with Fozy Moss beyond

Beetles and other invertebrates are especially good indicators of local environmental conditions, although unfortunately these have only rarely been studied on Wall sites. Carlisle is the exception and does have large and well-studied assemblages from first- and second-century contexts. The invertebrates recovered include one taxon, the nettle beetle, which today only breeds in Kent and further south. The presence of fragments from different ages of this species in Roman Carlisle and elsewhere in Northumberland strongly implies that the climate during the first century was somewhat warmer than at present (Kenward 2000). Returning to grain pests, parasites, dung beetles and so on, important work by Kenward *et al* (1991) demonstrates that grain pests were present in the earliest deposits at the Castle Street fort annexe in Carlisle (see overall review of Carlisle grain pests in Kenward, in press). This clearly shows that there were some problems with bulk storage of grain, and may also indicate that some, at least, of the grain was imported, as the grain beetles are not known from earlier sites. Once established in Carlisle, the grain pests could have spread to any stores of grain, whatever their origins. Sometimes the grain pests are associated with grain stores, but more frequently they appear to be associated with waste from animals: either bedding, spoilt feed or manure (frequently horse manure). Carlisle has also produced remains of many parasites (both internal gut parasites and external fleas, lice and keds) that afflicted a range of animals including humans, horses, cattle, sheep and pigs. Their distributions indicate different uses for different features, deposits and spatial locations, and also suggest that human excrement was disposed of separately to that from other animals.

Vertebrate bones, especially of wild species also provide some proxy environmental evidence. For example, black grouse (*Tetrao tetrix L.*) bones were equal in numbers to those from domestic fowl (chicken) from the *praetorium* at Vindolanda (Stallibrass 1998b) and were most likely hunted locally; indeed the species is ubiquitous on Wall sites, unlike in southern areas. They favour habitats that are transitional between open heathland or grassland and forest, although not closed canopy, thus providing roosting and displaying (lekking) areas. Catkins, fruits and other parts of birch and pine are favoured foods, although a variety of other fruits and seeds (bilberry and crowberry, sedges) are also taken (Cramp 1980). It is interesting to note that the two particularly favoured tree species are not that well represented in contemporary wood assemblages and identification of small wood from Vindolanda must be seen as high priority. Thus knowledge of modern habitats of black grouse contributes to the picture of what part of the local landscape must have been like in the first century AD. Likewise the presence of different species of sedge (*Carex spp.*) at Vindolanda strongly suggests the existence of different types of grassland (Huntley 2003). The presence of huge quantities of what was interpreted as horse dung/byre waste indicates quite intensive utilisation of different areas of land - either for grazing or hay production.

Small mammal bones - rats, mice, voles and so on - and invertebrate remains are more likely to reflect conditions specifically on a site. As noted earlier, invertebrate studies have been concentrated very much within Carlisle. Small mammals are also not well studied since they require processing and sorting from large volumes of bulk samples. The earlier work at South Shields is an exception and evidence for dormouse was forthcoming from a well (Younger 1994) and might indicate an import with grain. It remains disappointing that only a few sites have had extensive sampling and sieving procedures undertaken.

One of the most famous introductions to Britain's wildlife is the black rat (*Rattus rattus*) which may (or may not) have carried plague with it in the post-Roman and Medieval periods. The spatial and temporal distributions of this species are currently being researched by Reilly for a new volume on introductions and local extinctions of Britain's vertebrate fauna (Sykes and O'Connor, in prep.). Black rat was certainly found as far north as the Wall at South Shields (Younger 1994), but whether or not it spread from there is not yet known. Like other introductions, it may have arrived several times and it is not clear whether it was able to establish a permanent presence, or whether the population required constant 'top-ups' from new arrivals. The fate of the black rat is complicated by various factors: it is difficult to distinguish the bones of black and brown rat (*Rattus norwegicus*) and rat bones may be intrusive if they belong to the burrowing brown rat (black rats prefer warmer, drier conditions, and are good climbers but seldom dig burrows). It is quite possible that black rats were unable to survive as a viable population once their preferred habitat, urban settlements, declined in the late and post-Roman period. Direct dating of rat bones by AMS (a radiocarbon dating technique), and DNA testing for species could resolve several of the debatable finds.

Larger vertebrates (both wild and domestic) tend to be quite tolerant of a range of different environmental conditions, but there are some indigenous species of large wild vertebrates that might indicate the presence of habitats that were relatively undisturbed by people. These include some of Britain's largest carnivores and omnivores, all now extinct in the British Isles. No Roman wolf bones have been recovered from the Hadrian's Wall area and, perhaps surprisingly, bones of wild boar have similarly not been found, even though they were the 'mascot' of the Twentieth Legion and might, therefore, have been expected to have been targeted by troops for symbolic purposes. Further south in the Craven area of the Pennines, bones of lynx (Hetherington et al 2005) have been recovered from caves and one was directly dated by AMS to the post-Roman period, suggesting that they survived through the

Roman military occupation. Lynx, in particular, requires considerable cover from vegetation or rocks in order to hunt successfully (typically over 40% ground cover). The lack of suitable conditions for bone preservation and recovery may be the reason why similar remains have not yet been recovered further north in the Pennine uplands and valleys. On the other hand, the Craven area may have been sufficiently remote from human interference to allow the animals to survive.

Other wild animals were probably more common than they are today, although their remains tend to be restricted to the occasional bone from occasional samples. For example, a pine marten skull in a sieved sample from a stone surface in the late-first-century timber fort at Annetwell Street, Carlisle (Stallibrass 1991, 66) with skinning marks across its muzzle; and a beaver jaw from the 1907 excavations at Corbridge in a substantial house near the river (see Coles 2006). Other species that were present in much greater numbers than today include birds of prey and scavengers. Parker's (1998) review of Roman birds in Britain is out of date but even in 1988 he was able to demonstrate the almost ubiquitous presence of white-tailed sea eagle (*Haliaeetus albicilla*, which is by no means restricted to seaside habitats) and red kite (*Milvus milvus*) both of which were probably frequently seen scavenging at urban and military sites. Bones of sea eagles have been recovered from several sites along the Wall. Their post-Roman decline in numbers was mainly due to persecution and habitat loss in the nineteenth century. In rural areas of Hadrian's Wall, other birds of prey such as buzzards and harriers were probably much more common than they are today, although their bones have not yet been recovered from archaeological deposits. Common crane (*Grus grus*) was also much more common and widespread in Britain during the Roman period and remains have been found amongst food refuse at several sites on the Wall and in its hinterland. Its presence may reflect subsequent changes in habitat and/or in climate, as it survived in the relatively 'Continental' climate and wetlands of East Anglia after it ceased to breed further north and west.

Red deer provide a further, more substantiated, example of local fauna, the bones and antler of which are persistently present in small quantities. The natural habitat of red deer is woodland, where they attain much greater sizes than those compromised by poor nutrition on moorlands. The most frequently occurring red deer skeletal element at nearly all Roman sites in the Tyne-Solway corridor is antler, which can be collected as independent items after they have been shed, and then transported and curated for later use as a raw material for a wide range of artifacts. They may be traded over long distances and so their presence does not necessarily indicate the type of landscape close to the site at which they entered the archaeological record. However, it is noticeable that the red deer antlers are of a good size, indicating healthy animals that probably lived in woodland. The presence of bones does indicate the presence of carcases or joints of meat and it is assumed that these animals, at least, were caught locally. Vindolanda has rather more red deer bones than most other sites that have been analysed and this could reflect the presence of more woodland habitat around the fort as well as a high-status site. A size analysis of red deer bones from all of the Wall sites has not yet been undertaken, but would help to clarify whether or not the bones are likely to come from the same animals as the antlers. As yet, isotope analyses (such as strontium and oxygen) have not been assayed on material from Hadrian's Wall but might have potential to indicate transport of resources that grew in other localities.

Study of coastal and riverine resources is undermined by the pathetic quantities of fish bones that have been recovered from all sites. Recovery is nearly always hampered by a lack of sieving, so it is difficult to tell if this is genuine scarcity or just poor collection. However adequate and large volumes of sediment were processed from Lancaster, but still only produced about 100 fragments of fish bone (Stallibrass 1998a). Similarly, at Thornbrough Farm, Catterick, North Yorkshire on the banks of the River Swale, a total of 2,320 litres of stratified Roman deposits, sieved to 500μ, produced only 14 small fragments of fish bones, almost all of them from marine species that are not normally indigenous to the sea off the Yorkshire coast (Stallibrass 2002). *Vertebrae* and a few head bones from sea fish such as cod and saithe are large enough to be collected by hand, as evidenced from large Medieval assemblages in the region (Huntley and Stallibrass 1995) but are, nonetheless also almost completely absent from Roman assemblages. The few fish bones that have been recovered tend to be from species that are migratory (eels, salmonids) and which can be caught in estuaries where many of the migratory birds (geese in particular) can also be captured. Other fish represented include small flatfish that come right into shore. It does, therefore, seem that sea fish were probably genuinely hardly if ever exploited, but this needs checking by improved sampling and recovery procedures during future interventions. Riverine fish could have been important but poor recovery means the available data are totally inadequate for assessment.

Shellfish are also probably highly under-represented due to poor collection practices during excavation, particularly the tendency for them to be discarded without record from earlier excavations intent upon revealing structural elements. At present shellfish do not appear to have been heavily exploited by people living along the Wall, although the Solway and Tyne estuaries probably provided reliable sources. Excavations of the fort defences at South Shields produced shells of limpets, winkles and mussels (all of which require at least a modicum of rocky substrate) but there were only traces of oyster shells (Woodward 1983). Excavations at Carlisle have similarly produced comparatively few remains of marine molluscs. Elsewhere in Britain, particularly at small towns in the south and east of England, oyster shells are often extremely common, indicating an interest in the exploitation (if not the cultivation) of this species. Is the apparent lack on Wall sites a military versus civilian small-town issue rather than just recovery? In comparison to fish and shell-fish, bird bones are somewhat better recorded (as seen above) and 22% of those from the Carlisle Lanes-1 were from wild geese strongly suggesting exploitation of overwintering populations on the Solway marshes (Allison, 2000). This is interesting because it means that the marshes existed at that time and that the Solway, even if the river channel has moved to some degree, was in a similar hydrological state as today. The area has also remained an important site in long-distance migration of wildfowl for over two thousand years.

In summary then, the evidence suggests rather limited exploitation of estuarine/inshore habitats, for at least three types of resource: birds such as geese (in particular) and also possibly some waders, shellfish and small fish. Possibly most of these were a seasonal resource too. Vertebrate bones reinforce pollen and wood evidence for moderate woodland cover and underline the importance of using all possible forms of evidence for interpretation.

A slight diversion from classical environmental studies leads us to look at the environment in terms of living spaces and the contribution of biological remains to perceptions of that. Physical remains of barrack blocks at Wallsend have been interpreted as housing horses and men on the basis of a combination of evidence including phosphate analysis and the physical remains of drains through the centres of the floors. Reconsideration of barrack blocks plans from other forts has suggested further examples, even though in some instances the environmental evidence was never investigated (Hodgson 2003). Horses were very important as officers' mounts, pack animals and possibly also traction animals (alongside cattle). Accordingly, as briefly discussed above, fodder provisioning and management of manure were likely to have been important tasks for the military. As well as horses there has been a long-running debate about the presence of mules. At present the most northerly record of these is from Castleford, West Yorkshire (Cluny Johnstone *pers. comm.*) although recently bones identified as mule have been recorded from Vindolanda (Deb Bennett *pers. comm.*). With Johnstone's metrical definitions (Johnstone 2005) there is clearly great scope for further investigation and reinvestigation of sites already analysed along Hadrian's Wall: Mules, of course, are an unsustainable commodity since they are the infertile progeny of mares mated with male donkeys. Either donkeys had to be breeding in Britain alongside the horses, or they had to be obtained from other parts of the empire where male donkeys were available to breed with mares. The latter might be more likely in view of the absence of donkey bones.

Water supplies

Water was a crucial commodity, as it is today, for drinking, cooking, industrial processes and power. It is therefore perhaps surprising that rather little attention has been paid to its procurement, management and disposal at many Wall sites. Water mills have been described at Chesters, Haltwhistle Burn Head and possibly Vindolanda (A Wilson 2002). Pipes and drains abound on almost all sites excavated, with those at Vindolanda still running with water in places. Those at the Carlisle Millennium site were extremely well preserved and work was undertaken to determine whether they were bringing water to the industrial areas or carrying it away. There must be evidence for cisterns and water storage as well as leats and other channels used to manage supply. All of these should be surveyed and leveled into a GIS. As well as functionality during life these negative features were often convenient places to dump rubbish, thus making further environmental evidence available although it has to be said that the latrine drains at Vindolanda have, so far, proven extremely clean.

126. Coring a small basin produces a picture of vegetation in the immediate vicinity of the site

A further aspect clearly related to water is transport. At all appropriate sites quaysides might survive, although it must be remembered that some changes in sea level have occurred and this must be factored in to any investigations.

Timber supplies

The demand for timber for building as well as for fuel has had a long history of discussion, see for example Hanson and Macinnes (1980), but there have been few opportunities to study such material as it rarely survives in sufficiently large quantities for reasonable interpretations to be offered. Carlisle remains the best studied in the Wall area, with suggestions that woodland, although not necessarily formally managed in medieval terms, was nonetheless exploited heavily and re-grown woodland was used (Huntley 1987, 1989). The most frequent use of timber is for precise dating using dendrochronology (tree ring growth patterns), but it, too, can also contribute to our understanding of forest/woodland dynamics. In this respect Carlisle (first and second century) is one of only two places in Britain to have a master curve from Roman timber - the other being London. For example, at least 60% of the timber from the early phases at Carlisle: Lanes-1 reflects large trees that were more than 100 years old with very slow growth rates. This implied that the woodland from which they were drawn was probably quite dense, thus limiting their growth (Groves 2000). Groves commented upon the generally poor quality matching within the Roman timbers, suggesting exploitation of a large area of woodland. This was in accord with Huntley's interpretation of the smaller non-structural wood, from the later phases at least, where a wider variety of *taxa* was present than at first (Huntley 1989). It must be noted, however, that Huntley's material was from within the fort at Annetwell Street, as the comparable material from Lanes-1 was limited in extent and predominantly off-cuts from wood working. Groves (2000) also noted that intra-site cross-matching for the post-Roman period could suggest that these timbers were being obtained from a variety of sources. More recently, massive timbers dating to the late first to early second century at Vindolanda illustrate that some huge trees were still available to the Romans (Andrew Birley and Ian Tyers *pers. comm.*). What does not seem to have been done is to use the tree ring data to investigate climate signals within them and this could be an avenue for further research.

127. Charcoal can be used for reasons other than radiocarbon dating. Here, an ash stem shows an abrupt decrease in growth after seven years of fast growth. This may indicate pollarding or shredding to stimulate leafy/twig growth suitable as fodder for overwintering stock

Food production/cereal pollen

Food production has implications for landscape use but is not easy to demonstrate categorically. Livestock require grazing and/or fodder and this has been touched upon above. Plant species characteristic of hay, such as yellow rattle (*Rhinanthus minor*) are common at some sites, especially around Carlisle, although this probably reflects the larger number of samples and better preservation of material than necessarily more of the habitat. Vindolanda is beginning to produce similarly good evidence for hay meadows and pasturing. Cereal production per se will only be determined by the presence of cereal-type pollen and this is neither produced in abundance nor dispersed greatly. Taken with the fact that most pollen sites are mires, probably remote from fields, this means that cereal pollen is rarely recorded. However, cereal-type pollen is occasionally present at many sites, probably indicating quite extensive cereal cultivation and this ties in with the extensive survival of cord rig. Of especial interest are a few sites where more effort at investigating cereal pollen has recently been invested. (see page 145-6)

Summary

There is a wealth of data allowing us to interpret the landscape and environment around Hadrian's Wall throughout the Roman period, but it is neither uniform nor consistent. There are good sequences of aerial survey and photogrammetric transcription, especially in the central sector to-date, which allow us to say that the pre-Roman occupation was extensive although not necessarily intensive. Cultivation was also extensive, but again probably not that intensive. We remain less clear about Iron Age occupation in the urbanised east or the essentially pastoral west. As far as climate goes, invertebrates and other biological indicators suggest a slightly warmer and possibly wetter climate in very general terms, than today. This might well have implications for crop husbandry and whether livestock needed to be kept indoors through the winter or not.

Tree rings and pollen data allow us to say that the woodland in the west of the area was still extensive at the time the Roman military arrived, but that they rapidly gathered this material from a wide area to complete their construction work. Wells' (2003) review however, suggests that clearance had started in the later Iron Age and probably continued after the Romans arrived, although on a relatively small-scale and perhaps largely for pasture rather than arable cultivation. The data for east of the Pennines differ in so far as there was already well-established farming here, and as a result it is unclear where timber was obtained for the eastern forts and military *vici*. On the other hand, cereals probably were available in the east and it was the military in the west that might have had more difficulties in supply.

128. Wooden barrel top from Carlisle

In theory, from a consideration of the archaeology of Hadrian's Wall much indeed has been done. In practice, however, rather less has been achieved for the landscape and environment aspects. Some no doubt has benefited from recent developments in technology, allowing investigations previously impossible to conceive. Others, in particular the sampling of archaeological deposits, have suffered from a historical focus on structures rather than function and hence we have lost several major opportunities. This must not happen in the future. In addition, we are now more aware of techniques being used in other disciplines that can be borrowed and adapted to our cause. With non-invasive and remote techniques of investigation we should be able to provide detailed pictures of a continuing dynamic landscape through time and into which the structures so beloved of Wall Romanists can comfortably sit! By understanding that landscape, we should also be able to adapt management practices for optimal survival of the cultural heritage for future generations to enjoy. Some sites inevitably will be destroyed through natural agencies and we should seek to recognise, record and interpret the most vulnerable ones as soon as possible.

7. Production and Procurement
Co-ordinated by J Price and D A Petts

Overview
DA Petts

The establishment of the Northern Frontier with its substantial military garrisons and the associated civilian population directly or indirectly connected to the army led to a fundamental dislocation of the economic infrastructure in the North of England. The existing native British economy was unable to cope with the scale and range of logistic demands required by the step change in the population from the First century AD. Although the frontier zone was already integrated into regional, national and even international exchange networks before the arrival of the Roman army, these existing systems of procurement were fundamentally transformed. Equally, the system of local agricultural production of crops and animal resources underwent profound structural changes following the advent of Roman control.

Traditionally, approaches to modelling the patterns of production and procurement for the army have focused on exploring only individual classes of evidence (e.g. pottery, coinage, environmental evidence). This short overview attempts to integrate a wide range of sources to develop a better idea of the broad contours of exchange in the first to fourth centuries AD. Before exploring the data it is essential to be aware of some of the conceptual and methodological challenges facing any attempt to synthesis such disparate sources of data.

First, it is important to be aware of the basic biases in the recovery of archaeological data reflecting both patterns of fieldwork and post-depositional factors. In general, archaeological excavation has focused on excavating the intra-mural areas of forts, with less work having been carried out on *vici* and other civilian settlements. There is a particular lack of work on rural settlement, though recent unpublished work at sites such as Quarry Farm, Sedgefield East Park, Faverdale and Newcastle Great Park may well help to fill in this major gap in our knowledge.

This uneven coverage of sites has obvious implications for modelling supply networks. It is unlikely that civilian and military procurement strategies operated entirely independently, and there may have been extensive formal and informal trade between the army and civilians with the provisions of materiel and services flowing in both directions. There is also little known about such basic issues as refuse disposal strategies at Roman forts. Was rubbish placed in middens or dumps outside the forts or solely within pits within the fort? If dumped outside the fort, is it possible to distinguish between army and civilian deposits? It is clear that a better understanding of such basic issues is essential for developing a more nuanced appreciation of patterns of exchange, production and consumption on the Wall. It is clear that *vici*/civilian settlements were supplied in different ways from the forts. Steve Willis has noted that in assemblages of Samian at *vici* there is a greater proportion of decorated to plain forms. Sue Stallibrass highlights the contrast in the age at death of cattle from civilian and military areas at Carlisle. Animals from the fort were either young and meaty or old, indicating deliberate slaughter of cattle for meat, supplemented by opportunistic use of older animals when they were no longer usable for dairy or work purposes. In the civilian settlement the bones were mainly from older animals suggesting there was little consumption of animals deliberately bred for meat. Whilst it is important to recognise such differences it is also important to explore the socio-economic factors behind such variation.

It is apparent that such basic issues as variations in burial environment across the study area can also skew the archaeological resource. The wetter climate of the west and central areas of the Wall means that plant macrofossils survive better in these areas than in the eastern zone. It is important to be cautious when extrapolating resourcing strategies from evidence that is regionally biased. Indeed the wet climate that leads to such good preservation in the west of the Wall also has the implication that agricultural regimes and crop capacity is likely to vary along the frontier. Models of crop procurement and local production based on environmental evidence from the west are unlikely to reflect systems used in the east.

Production

Pottery production appears to have been mainly located in the western and central sectors (Carlisle, Brampton, Scalesceugh, Corbridge), though there was probably a production centre on the Lower Tyne. By the third century, this production appears to have contracted to the western sector.

Environmental evidence, such as spelt from the granaries at South Shields suggests that there was some local production of grain, though of course, it is not possible to be clear how locally such grain was acquired. It may have been produced in the immediate environs of the fort or elsewhere in Northern England and brought up by boat. The role of South Shields as a supply base also implies that such grain was being redistributed along the Wall and presumably north to the outpost forts and potentially bases along the Antonine Wall. Some forts may also have grown some or all of their own crops (though this may have been less likely in the central sector). South of the Wall the recent recognition of substantial Roman field systems around Binchester suggest that some installations could have been effectively self-sufficient for grain. There was also doubtless small-scale horticultural activity at all forts, though this is difficult to recognise in the archaeological record.

The bone evidence suggests that sheep were being raised primarily for meat consumption rather than wool, as were most cattle. However, it is not clear whether they were being raised in the immediate locality or were being brought in either on the hoof or as carcasses from elsewhere. The long-term regional traditions of transhumance and droving in the north of England remind us to look at meat supply mechanisms that may have operated across a wide geographical area.

There is some evidence for ferrous and non-ferrous metalworking on forts, though clearly not on large scale. Nothing has been found that suggests the presence of *fabricae*. Instead much of the evidence implies blacksmithing, or small-scale, perhaps relatively *ad hoc* production of minor pieces of military equipment, such as buckles.

Some local production may have re-worked materials. The production of glass bangles and bead is likely to have utilised glass circulating in the northern frontier region, whilst jet and shale objects appear in some cases to have been worked locally using raw material brought in from outside the region. Other small-scale industries recognisable through the archaeological record include shoe manufacture.

It is important to remember that the Northern frontier zone is rich in mineral deposits and forts such as Whitley Castle may well have been placed to exert control over lead, and potentially, silver, production in the North Pennines.

The wooden tablets from Vindolanda and Carlisle also provide some evidence for individuals at garrisons being involved in local production; they mention pig- and cowmen, as well as hunters, brewers and butchers. It is however not easy to assess the relative importance of such individuals to overall procurement strategies.

Trade

In addition to this clear evidence of local (-ish) production it is clear that much of the Wall was provisioned from further afield. Like the rest of the province the Hadrian's Wall Frontier was clearly plugged in to inter-provincial supply systems and was susceptible to the wider ebbs and flows in trade that is found elsewhere in the Western Empire, though there are clear differences in the pattern of military supply between the Northern Frontier and the south and west of Britain.

In the first and second centuries most pottery fine wares came from Gaul or Germany. Once the Wall was constructed assemblages of coarse wares are dominated by BB1, though forts in the eastern sector also drew their supplies from a range of other sources, such as London (Highgate Wood), Verulamium, north Kent, Colchester and East Anglia, whilst those on the western sector also utilised ceramics from Wilderspool and the Severn Valley. Supply patterns of coarseware appear to have followed the same broad pattern following the hiatus caused by the move forward to the Antonine Wall. BB1 continued to dominate at both ends of the Wall, although there were some changes in the source of other British wares, and perhaps an increased reliance on local production in the western sector.

In the third century Rhenish wares and Central Gaulish wares remain important and by the end of the third century and into the fourth century there is an increase in North African imports and imports from the west of France such as *céramique à l'éponge*. Glass, mainly from Gaul and the Rhineland, also seems to be most common in this period. These changes in the flow of international trade need to be seen in the context of a clear move towards regional supply. There was a change in the supply of coarse wares from the Severan period with BB1 being replaced by BB2 along much of the central and eastern sector of the Wall and Nene Valley ware also becoming common from this period. By the fourth century coarse wares were sourced mainly from Yorkshire, particularly in the form of Crambeck and Calcite Gritted wares. The wider move from inter-provincial to regional sourcing of ceramics noticeably appears to parallel with the spread of coinage across the region, with late third and fourth century coins making up the majority of site finds.

In addition to the trade in pottery as a commodity in itself, ceramics as containers, particularly in the form of amphorae (supplemented by the extensive evidence for wooden barrels from Vindolanda and Carlisle) provide plentiful information about the long-distance supply of other commodities, such as wine and olive oil. This suggests that wine was being supplied to the frontier from Gaul (barrels mainly from the Rhône valley) and Italy in the pre-Hadrianic period, with olive oil being sourced from southern Spain. There is a relative lack of wine amphora from South Shields after the mid-second century, and it may be that wine was being imported in barrels, probably from the Rhineland, which was also the source of other ceramics arriving at this period. Wine continued to be imported from Italy into the third century, and North African and East Mediterranean amphora seemingly attest to the continuation of wine importation, even if only on a small scale into the fourth, and even fifth, centuries.

Little is known about many other aspects of Roman trade. It is thought that tents were imported, probably fully fabricated, possibly from Gaul or Spain; the Vindolanda tablets refer to the import of hides from at least as far as Catterick (*Tab. Vindol.* 343). However, little is known about the procurement of weapons, armour or military ornaments, beyond the evidence for the small-scale production of buckles and similar items.

Procurement strategies

Finally, it is crucial to be alive to the likely complexities of networks of production and exchange in the Frontier zone. The army is likely to be using a range of procurement strategies ranging from local sources (but articulated how? Payment? Taxation? Commandeering?), as well as regional, provincial and inter- provincial exchange. At these wider scales, it is still often unclear precisely how goods were obtained, were producers directly under contract to the army with an element of directed trade or were goods bought on the open market? It is clear from the Vindolanda tablets that the ways in which goods could circulate once they had entered the military supply system could also vary widely. The tablets also serve to highlight the importance of other types of exchange, such as gift giving. Once the spatial and chronological issues are factored into any exploration of patterns of production and exchange on the frontier, it is clear that we must be cautious of overly simplistic models.
In addition to military procurement strategies it is likely that the civilian population operated their own exchange

mechanisms, although it is highly likely that the military and civilian networks were interlinked. It is probable that some military supplies found themselves, officially or unofficially, in civilian hands, whilst much of the population of the *vici* are likely to have been supplying services to the military market, again either in an official or unofficial capacity.

A more detailed understanding of the mechanics of exchange and production is difficult. Some evidence from the Vindolanda tablets suggests that civilians acting as *de facto* negotiators were integral to the military supply system (e.g. *Tab. Vindol.* II. 180, 343, 344). It is clear from these that external suppliers were entering into substantial contracts to provide the army with a range of supplies, including hides and grain. These men may not just have been drawn from the local population. The merchant who writes one tablet protesting at his ill-treatment calls himself a *hominem trasmarinum* (*Tab Vindol.* II, 344).

Several documents, including inscriptions and writing tablets record the presence and activity on the frontier of the *beneficiarii consulares*, soldiers seconded from their unit to the governor, who seem to have played a significant role in the organisation of military supply (e.g. *Tab. Vindol* II, 344) Epigraphic evidence for a number of such officers comes from forts within the frontier zone (e.g. Binchester *RIB* 1030, 1031; Greta Bridge *RIB* 745; Catterick *RIB* 725, 726).

Roman Pottery with a Brief Reference to Barrels

P T Bidwell

Kilns

Production sites have been investigated at Carlisle (Fisher Street and English Damside), Brampton and Scalesceugh. The largest and most important centre of production was at Corbridge, but its exact location has yet to be established. There would have been smaller potteries supplying forts up until the end of the Hadrianic period, and at least one on the Lower Tyne which distributed its products throughout the North-East. There was probably no pottery production in the eastern and central sectors after the early third century, although it is possible that in the western sector there was limited production throughout the third century.

Sites

From most forts on the Wall there are only small quantities of pottery, and from some there is virtually none. The only forts with stratified groups large enough to yield reliable information about the chronology and supply systems throughout the duration of their occupation are Wallsend, Newcastle, Housesteads and Birdoswald. The largest quantities of pottery are from forts which formed part of the Wall system but which were not on its line: South Shields, Corbridge, Vindolanda and Carlisle. The pottery from milecastles and turrets is more evenly distributed as far west as turret 54a, beyond which there is little.

Collections

The following museums hold significant collections of pottery: Senhouse Museum; Tullie House Museum, Carlisle; Vindolanda Roman Site and Museum; Chesters Museum; Corbridge Roman Site Museum; Museum of Antiquities, Newcastle upon Tyne; Segedunum Museum; Arbeia Roman Fort Museum.

Research and publication until the 1970s

Detailed pottery reports and catalogues began to appear in the early years of the last century (see Birley 1977). Almost as much pottery from the Wall zone was published in the first two decades of the century as in the following two decades. In the 1930s it was work on sites elsewhere that provided the most useful contribution to pottery studies of the frontier. Much work was carried out on the pottery from the Yorkshire industries, particularly the kilns at Crambeck, the main supplier of pottery to Hadrian's Wall throughout much of the fourth century, while Hull published the late Roman pottery assemblages from the Yorkshire signal stations. During the 1920s and 30s a more systematic approach was developed in the study of samian, identifying makers and refining the dating.

From the late 1940s onwards increasing amounts of pottery were published from the Wall. In 1948 Birley and Gillam published their study of the stamped mortaria from Corbridge, looking at their source of manufacture, date and distribution. During the 1950s the classification of vessels by type and source was developed in greater detail. In 1957 Gillam published his Types of Roman Coarse Pottery Vessels in Northern Britain (revised 1968, 1970), a dated typology of the more common forms of pottery to be found in the northern frontier zone. Also in this period Kay Hartley began her study of mortaria, which has continued to the present day, revealing the wide range of sources for the vessel type as well as their dating. In 1965 Callender published his study of Roman amphorae, with a discussion of types, dates and use, and an index of dated stamps.

Research and publication from the 1970s to the present

The mid-1970s can be regarded as the beginning of a short-lived era of large-scale research excavation on the Wall which continued for little more than two decades. Work had already been in progress at Vindolanda since the later 1960s, but new projects began at Housesteads (1974), Wallsend (1975), Newcastle (1976) and South Shields (1977). At the same time the scope of Roman pottery studies was much increased by the application of scientific methods, particularly in the field of petrology, and by the gradual introduction of agreed standards and techniques of quantification. Now there were the means of answering a much wider range of questions than just simple chronology. The publication of large assemblages from stratified sequences started with Vindolanda (Hird 1977), which still represents the largest series of pre-Hadrianic groups from northern Britain. Other large pottery reports were published from South Shields (Dore and Gillam 1979) and the Agricolan site at Red House, Corbridge (Hanson et al.1979). The first report which included quantification by weight was on the pottery from the 1980 excavations in the fort at Vindolanda (Bidwell 1985). Many subsequent reports have employed quantification more methodically than in the first attempt at Vindolanda, but its use is still not universal.

Trade and exchange

Amphorae (and barrels)

Studies of barrel remains and amphorae at Vindolanda, largely from the pre-Hadrianic levels, have produced information on the supply of wine, olive oil and other imported consumables which is unmatched elsewhere in Britain in its quantity and in its depth and detail (Marlière 2003). Most of the barrels were of fir or larch and probably came from the Rhône valley. Three types have been recognised, and they were all probably used for transporting wine. Wine also reached Vindolanda in Gaulish and Italian amphorae, although the majority of amphorae were olive-oil containers from southern Spain. On the barrels there are inscriptions of various kinds, and on the amphorae there are stamps, *dipinti* and *graffiti*.

The environmental conditions at Vindolanda are only matched at Carlisle, which has produced evidence of similar quality. For trends in the supply of wine and olive oil after the early second century, research depends almost entirely on amphorae. The study of amphora stamps shows that the origins of southern Spanish amphorae in northern Britain differ from those in Wales and southern England, and that of the three conventus in Baetica that exported to Britain, Astigi is much more strongly represented in the north than elsewhere (Funari 1996, 76-2). South Shields has produced a wider picture of amphora supply at the eastern end of the Wall from the mid-second century onwards. Of particular interest is the scarcity of wine amphorae, suggesting an increasing reliance on wine imported in barrels (probably from the Rhineland which was an increasingly important source of mortaria and fine wares). In the mid-third century Campanian wine amphorae begin to occur in large quantities at the eastern forts on the Wall (Bidwell and Speak 1994, 214-220). Eastern Mediterranean and North African amphorae are also being recognised in increasing (though still small) numbers. They are probably of third- and fourth-century date, although importation of North African amphorae seems to have continued into the fifth century, on the evidence of a rim sherd from Piercebridge which represents the latest type so far recorded from Britain.

Other imported fine wares

In addition to samian wares, other fine table wares were imported from Gaul and Germany. Much of the pattern of Claudio-Neronian importation continued into the Flavian period: *terra nigra* and Lyon ware occur on sites founded as late as the mid- to late-80s. A new pattern was established towards the end of the Flavian period with rough-cast beakers from Northern Gaul occurring from c. 90 and colour-coated beakers from Cologne with rough-cast or barbotine decoration appearing from some date in the early second century yet to be determined more closely. Beakers from the Argonne (Exeter Fabric 1) appear in the reign of Hadrian and seem to have been imported to the Wall along western coastal routes. The dating and origin of other types of rough-cast beaker found in second-century levels are uncertain.

The final main phase of importation consisted of 'rhenish ware' (or *Moselkeramik*) and Central Gaulish (Lezoux) ware. Vessels from these sources are common in third-century levels, but they are absent from well-dated Severan deposits at South Shields and, with the exception of a single unpublished sherd, from the Severan site at Carpow (although they are present at Cramond where there are significant quantities of post-Severan pottery). The date at which their importation stopped is uncertain, although there are late third-century 'rhenish-ware' motto-beakers from York. There were a number of minor imports, such as North Gaulish white ware which is present in Severan levels, *céramique à l'éponge* from Aquitania which dates to after c. 270 (the latter known at forts on Tyneside and at Vindolanda) and African red-slipped ware (at South Shields). The importation of fine wares (and other types of pottery) from outside Britain to the northern frontier area came to an end, with very rare exceptions, in the first half of the fourth century, and probably closer to the beginning rather than the middle of that century.

Coarse pottery

During the half century preceding the building of Hadrian's Wall coarse pottery was supplied to the army by local kilns, operated either by soldiers or civilian contractors. At Brampton the kilns supplied Carlisle to the west and Vindolanda to the east, and presumably the intervening forts. It is uncertain whether other kilns, such as those which probably existed at Corbridge, supplied only their nearest fort or distributed their products more widely. The pottery was related to the forms introduced from the Continent, especially the Lower and Upper Rhine, by the army from the conquest onwards. Little coarse pottery was imported from production centres further south in Britain, apart from Verulamium white wares. Small quantities of grey wares came from northern Gaul, probably via London, and their importation continued until at least the Severan period.

129. Black-burnished ware (fabric 2) dish, Arbeia

The building of the Wall was accompanied by a radical change in the pottery supply. Importation from the South began on a more substantial scale. BB1 from south-east Dorset seems to have reached every fort on the Wall. It was probably shipped up the west coast, but might also have reached the forts at the eastern end of the Wall via transhipments from London. West Coast imports also included Severn Valley ware and pottery from Wilderspool. Forts, milecastles and turrets in the central and eastern sector of the Wall drew on a much wider range of sources, including London (Highgate Wood), Verulamium (as earlier), north Kent, Colchester, East Anglia and the area on the south side of the Humber. Local production continued, although perhaps on a reduced scale, and included a new centre thought to have been located somewhere on the lower Tyne making oxidised wares with white and brown painted decoration and which exported its products as far south as Piercebridge. These local types were increasingly influenced by BB1, although there were other strands of production derived directly from continental antecedents.

130. BB2 cooking pot, Arbeia

During the occupation of the Antonine Wall most of the forts on Hadrian's Wall were presumably abandoned, with a clear exception at Corbridge and other possible exceptions (for example, South Shields and Carlisle). The move north was marked by another radical change in the supply of pottery. The bulk of the supply at the eastern end of the Antonine Wall consisted of BB2, from Colchester or north Kent, the latter perhaps being the main supplier. The origins and early development of this industry are poorly understood; it seems to have started in the early second century. It is possible, but unproven, that BB2 reached the sites on Hadrian's Wall which were occupied in the early Antonine period.

The abandonment of the Antonine Wall seems to have brought about another change in pottery supply. It used to be thought that the BB2 industries, having established themselves as suppliers to the army in the eastern sector of the Antonine Wall, then supplied the eastern part of Hadrian's Wall. It now seems that at the eastern end of the Wall, and presumably in the central sector, BB2 is scarce until the Severan period, and that as much BB1, if not more, was used in the second half of the second century. Importation from the areas in eastern Britain that supplied the Wall in the Hadrianic period continued or resumed, with the exception of London and Verulamium. Colchester was a new but minor source, supplying rough-cast beakers and perhaps other wares such as flagons. Local production of grey wares and oxidised flagons continued, the latter probably associated with the production of mortaria at Corbridge and elsewhere. However, locally-produced pottery became increasingly scarce, and it is likely that by the end of the second century its production had ceased in the eastern and central sectors of the Wall. Specialised production of mortaria and presumably of flagons may have continued longer but not beyond the early third century.

Large quantities of BB1 were used at forts along the western part of the Antonine Wall, and when full occupation of Hadrian's Wall resumed the BB1 potteries continued as the major supplier at forts on the Wall from Birdoswald westwards and in the rest of Cumbria. Severn Valley ware was also imported in significant quantities. However, there was much more reliance on local and regional production than in the central and eastern sectors. A kiln making grey wares is known at English Damside in Carlisle, and there were probably other small production centres at forts in the Eden Valley. The types produced were predominantly BB1 copies, although a few were more distinctive, as for example narrow-mouthed jars with frilled cordons in reduced or oxidised wares.

The Severan period saw an upsurge in the supply of BB2 which was so vigorous that BB1 no longer reached the eastern sector of the Wall and became scarce in the central sector. It is probable that all of the BB2 from this period onwards came from kilns on the Essex shore of the Thames estuary, such as those at Mucking and Grays. The kilns at those sites, and probably many others, produced a wide range of other types of jars and bowls, mostly derived from the indigenous pottery traditions of the area. Almost all these other types (usually referred to as Thameside or BB2-related) occur on Hadrian's Wall, especially after the Severan period when they are almost as common as BB2. The Essex pottery appears to have a very limited local distribution, and not much occurs in London which is only 20 miles upstream from the kilns. Its production seems to have been largely directed towards the military zone of northern Britain and specifically to Hadrian's Wall where it achieved an almost complete dominance of the market in the eastern and central sectors. The wares are less common at sites to the south along Dere Street and at York, and in the third century the existence of several different systems of supply are very evident at military sites throughout the north.

Nene Valley colour-coated wares were ubiquitous in the third century but are not known from definitely pre-Severan contexts. Grey wares from the same source are now known, especially at South Shields, although they are generally very scarce. Despite the dominance of the BB2 potteries, small quantities of pottery from many other sources are found at the forts on the lower Tyne and to a lesser extent in the central sector. Large storage-jars from Horningsea (near Cambridge) are of great interest. The use of storage-jars was well-established in parts of southern and western Britain but was not practised by the army in Britain in the second and third centuries. The Horningsea jars were presumably imported as containers, perhaps of grain or salt. It is likely that pottery from many other minor kilns in East Anglia, such as those at Brampton (Norfolk), Wattisfield, Pakenham and West Stow reached the Wall. There is a general correspondence in the types and fabrics with vessels from Hadrian's Wall, but the only specific source so far recognised is the Nar valley. East and South Yorkshire industries began to supply the Wall; products of the Norton (opposite the fort at Malton) and Cantley

(Doncaster) kilns have been recognised. A source of pottery of particular importance from the later third century onwards was an unlocated industry making jars in heavily-gritted wares, including Dales-type jars. Their distribution suggests a production site on Dere Street, possibly at Catterick or Piercebridge. Small quantities of *Eifelkeramik* are known from Severan levels and there are other possible North Gaulish or Rhineland coarse wares.

131. Nene Valley ware beaker decorated with hunting scene. Corbridge

The western sector of Hadrian's Wall and Cumbria saw little change in its systems of supply, although Nene Valley colour-coated ware seems to have reached the western sector at the same time and in the same quantities as along the remainder of Hadrian's Wall. Importation of BB1 seems to have remained at much the same level throughout the third century, although supplies of Severn Valley ware probably came to an end early in the second half of the third century. Local and regional production continued until at least the last quarter of the third century and possibly well into the fourth century. Only small amounts of the pottery from eastern England that flooded the eastern and central sectors of the Wall reached the western sector and the Cumbrian coast.

In the second half of the third century products from kilns in East Yorkshire (including those at Hasholme and Holme-on-Spalding Moor, but only at first) began to appear on the Wall. This was the beginning of a process which about a century later resulted in the Wall and its hinterland as far south as the Humber and Mersey being almost entirely dependent on the Crambeck kilns and sources of calcite-gritted wares nearby for their supply of pottery. There seem to have been four stages in the process:

A. 260/270-310/320: during this early stage Crambeck grey ware is many times more common than calcite-gritted ware, although the overall quantities of both wares are very small compared to BB2 and Thameside fabrics in the eastern and central sector (which continued until the beginning of the fourth century) and BB1 in the west.

B. 310/320-360/370: before the second quarter of the fourth century, calcite-gritted ware had become far more common although Crambeck grey ware is still up to twice as common. Overall, the wares are more common than in Phase A and by the end of this phase they were probably major components of the pottery supply. In the eastern and central sectors, BB2 and Thameside wares had been superseded by BB1 and heavily-gritted wares. Dales ware and other shell-gritted wares played only a very small part in the pottery supply.

C. 360/370-390/410: there now seems no reason to doubt the long-established dating of Huntcliff-type jars from c. 360 and Crambeck parchment ware from c. 370. In groups of this period there are roughly equal amounts of Crambeck grey ware and calcite-gritted ware. These East Yorkshire products were predominant but by no means the only sources of pottery for the Wall. Heavily-gritted wares continue occurring and it is by no means certain that supplies of BB1 had come to an end by c. 370, as has previously been thought. During this phase some jars, dishes and bowls were supplied in Nene Valley colour-coated ware. It is likely that the rare examples of Oxford, Hadham (?) and Swanpool (?) colour-coated wares date to this phase.

D. Early post-Roman: deposits where calcite-gritted ware is much more common than Crambeck grey ware seem to be of very late date. The contexts are either associated with the decay of buildings or post-date their disuse or are stratigaphically later than deposits containing Valentinianic or Theodosian coinage. In such deposits there is two to three times as much calcite-gritted ware as Crambeck grey ware.

The scheme set out above is based on quantifications of pottery of sites throughout northern England, most of which have been published recently or are still awaiting publication. There are two serious problems. First, many of these deposits contain a great deal of pottery which is residual from previous periods of occupation. Secondly, there is a lack of well-dated groups from the first three-quarters of the fourth century. Absolute dates are used because coins supply the primary dating evidence. Although the scheme must be regarded as provisional, it suggests very strongly that the rise of the east Yorkshire industry was not necessarily a gradual process but was subject to the sudden changes which are characteristic of pottery supply to the Wall in earlier periods. There was certainly a progressive increase in the use of cooking-pots rather than bowls and dishes, but other factors were also important. In addition, marked changes in the ratios of Crambeck grey ware to calcite-gritted ware continue beyond what can be reasonably regarded as the end of organised military occupation on the Wall sites. It seems possible that the manufacture and export of pottery from the East Yorkshire kilns continued after the end of the military economy.

Native (local traditional) ware

Only recently has it been realised that small but significant amounts of 'native' pottery occur at Roman forts in the central and eastern sectors of the Wall. The pottery is better described as local traditional ware (LTW) to avoid confusion with other types of pottery produced by indigenous communities in an Iron Age tradition which were imported from well outside the Wall zone (e.g. calcite-gritted Knapton ware from East Yorkshire). It is of importance as an index of trade and exchange between military and civilian sites, other evidence being largely lacking, and because the pottery is sometimes from well-dated contexts, which are lacking on indigenous sites. Preliminary research suggests that the petrology of these wares should allow their sources to be established.

Samian (*terra sigillata*) and the Stanegate-Hadrian's Wall Corridor: An Assessment

S Willis

The importance of samian to the study of the Stanegate-Hadrian's Wall corridor, and vice versa

Samian and its occurrence along the frontier zone in northern England represents a unique and key relationship in Roman studies. This has arisen from the exceptional sequence that this frontier presents and the extraordinary chronological value of samian ware (cf. Hartley 1969). The study of the samian from the area of the Wall is closely related to knowledge of the supply and consumption of samian on the northern frontier in general (cf. Birley 1958; Hartley 1972). Samian has provided vital dating evidence for horizons and events, particularly of course through the late first and second centuries and into the third. It has long been at the forefront of dating and discussion of events and sequences in this context (eg. Bushe-Fox 1913; Simpson 1913; Newbold 1913; Birley 1952; cf. Stanfield and Simpson 1958, xlii; cf. Willis in press C). Equally, the elements of the Wall that can be related to historical dates provide a means by which the dating of samian types, decorative styles and stamps etc. was verified. That there was a circular aspect to this framework is apparent, though since other checks and indices have made neither overly reliant on the other. Given that samian was so widely distributed across the central and western provinces of the Roman Empire the significance of dating derived from or supported by the stratification of Hadrian's Wall, etc., has been profound. The date-range of particular vessel forms, fabrics, decoration and finishes is now well understood and established.

This special relationship has been offset though by the increasing value of dating based on coarse wares. Since samian forms only modest proportions of groups (and the closely datable fraction of samian sherds may be a low percentage) this has been a significant development. Dating related to coarse wares along the Wall has become indispensable as by increment knowledge of these types has become robust. Yet the international context of samian means that its incidence on Hadrian's Wall is of exceptional interest and has much to contribute. The study of aspects of its occurrence, beyond chronology, has opened new opportunities for understanding economic and cultural practice in the Wall zone.

Samian and the Stanegate-Hadrian's Wall corridor: a brief history

Samian was a cornerstone tool of the pioneers of Wall studies, and was well published in the numerous reports on excavations between the late 19th century and c. 1950. Such evidence was worthy of illustration and documentation for the information it brought to studies of both Hadrian's Wall and the understanding of samian styles and dates (eg. Birley 1930; Detsicas 1962). This is most readily seen in the research of Prof. Eric Birley whose work formed a platform of data informing studies for the Wall through the mid-twentieth century (e.g. Stanfield and Simpson 1958; cf. Stanfield and Simpson 1990). One sees the vital use of records of the products of samian potters and their distribution and incidence on Wall and associated sites, with Birley emphasizing this in his introduction to that volume (Birley 1958). Particular studies have used the evidence of occurrence on Hadrian's Wall of particular types to establish the nuances and trends of the output of specific samian workshops/potters.

132. Decorated Dr 29 samian bowl, later 1st century. South Gaulish. Corbridge

133. Base of samian bowl shown in 132

It is surprising that no single project examining the samian from the Wall has ever been undertaken (cf. Davies Pryce and Birley 1935; Hartley 1972). Progress was made by piecemeal means. The studies by Birley and Simpson were of great significance and fed into publications. Subsequently from the mid 1950s Brian Hartley and his assistants took rubbings of stamps as the Leeds Corpus of Samian Stamps developed. The fine dating that the study of potter's stamps can provide is one of the great assets of samian, and recording these stamps in stratified contexts on the Wall sites has been an integral strand of the Leeds Corpus, providing a chronological anchor and point of reference for like stamps found at sites across the empire.

This was supported too in the reports that Hartley wrote, latterly with Brenda Dickinson, or solely authored by her (eg. Dickinson 1994; Dickinson and Hartley 2000).

The momentum of excavation, research and publication on the Northern Frontier was not maintained after the war. The excavations at Corbridge did not result in the systematic publication of the important samian collections, that were otherwise used as a key point of reference in, most notably, the work for the Central Gaulish Potters volume (Stanfield and Simpson 1958; cf. Bishop and Dore 1988; Dickinson and Hartley 1988). Work and publication by Charlesworth and Daniels resulted in significant contributions wherein samian featured (eg. Daniels 1959; Charlesworth 1967; 1975). In recent decades important excavations at Carlisle, Corbridge Red House, South Shields and Vindolanda have lead to key publications with samian prominent (Dickinson 1990; 1991; 1992; Hartley 1959; Hanson et al. 1979; Dore and Gillam 1979; Bidwell and Speak 1994; Bidwell 1985; Birley 1994; Hartley 1994). Indeed, the excavations at Carlisle, South Shields and Vindolanda have been ongoing. Newcastle has also been subject to significant investigation in recent years (Snape and Bidwell 2003), while the Wallsend millennium project will represent a notable contribution to samian study.

Samian from the Hadrian's Wall zone and its chronological horizons

The changing sources of samian are helpful in providing an index of dating. Attention to samian fabric is a recent development. The sources of supply to Britain are well-known. Nonetheless it is appropriate to briefly document this here, given its relevance.

The main source in the first century AD was La Graufesenque in Southern Gaul, normally associated with deposits dating up to c. AD 110 (eg. Hartley 1959). This is the main type found on late first century sites in the frontier zone. However, examples can occur in early to mid second century deposits, not necessarily as residual sherds but as items in use up to that date (Willis 2005a). Hence there is a 'tail' of this material in use through the second century, especially decorated bowls. It also occurs occasionally in layers associated with Hadrian's Wall (eg. Willis in press A; in press B).

From c. AD 100 the workshops at Les Martres-de-Veyre supplied Britain, and are mainly associated with deposits of c. AD 100-120/130. It can be a guide to Trajanic occupation or a Trajanic-early Hadrianic site, and thus is mainly seen on Stanegate sites and other pre-Hadrian's Wall sites and rarely in Hadrianic deposits associated with the Wall (eg. Dickinson 1990; Willis in press b; in press c; in press d). It should always be borne in mind that Les Martres ware is relatively uncommon in Britain and comparatively low amounts of it are not necessarily an indicator of minimal occupation.

The construction of the Wall coincided with the arrival of the first wave of main exports of Lezoux samian from c. AD 120. The Wall's manifestation provides a tpq. of c. AD 122 for samian in levels associated with its sites; the presence of normal second century Lezoux ware indicates a date later than c. AD 120. Lezoux provides the great bulk of samian from Hadrian's Wall deposits. Material from the Wall zone has provided evidence for the end of the supply of Lezoux samian ware to Britain, at the close of the second century. It is clear is that Lezoux samian was in use into the third century. East Gaulish samian is well attested on the Wall providing useful dating evidence into the third century (eg. Dickinson 1997).

Given that many sites on Hadrian's Wall were subject to alteration it is not surprising that there is a high residual element amongst its samian assemblages. This does not mean this material cannot be used as a dating indicator, simply that such material cannot be used to date specific layers/deposits. Site remodelling and rebuilding did, though, seal certain deposits and horizons.

Samian and the Hadrian's Wall zone: assessment of the present state of knowledge

Methodology: Tradition and potential in reporting samian
The established approach to reporting samian from Hadrian's Wall is to concentrate upon the decorated sherds and stamps as these were intrinsically the most closely dateable. The attraction of publishing the decorative style, associated with a potter and workshop, and of identifying the maker via the reading of a stamp was axiomatic and provided the excavator with the dating evidence they required. However, this tradition of publication is limited in scope.

Forts yield large quantities of samian, so traditional approaches meant that assemblages were dealt with via a selective concentration upon stamps and decorated pieces (eg. Dickinson and Hartley 1988). However, stamps are infrequent finds amongst assemblages; perhaps only 2-3% of an assemblage. These might not be usefully stratified, only indicative of the dates of consumption of samian at sites. Further, decorated samian vessels were rarely stamped. Detailed examination of such pieces may only provide a slightly more refined date than other typological indicators. There is then an argument for studying and dating all the stratified samian, as the identification and dating of plain wares is comparatively quick. Such an approach provides a much fuller indication of dates and trends. Hence the publication of full site lists is valid (cf. Pengelly 1975; 1985; Dickinson and Hartley 1979; Willis in press a; in press b). It is to be hoped that the days of selective publication of decorated and stamped sherds are gone, and that full listings are published not assigned to archives (cf. Mills 1997).

The supply of samian
The organization of the supply of samian is still poorly understood. Sites like Carlisle and South Shields, from where large assemblages (?consignments) of samian have been excavated, some usefully stratified, offer interesting possibilities for investigating such questions, as does the zone in general.

An interesting case in point is the distribution of Montans samian in northern Britain. Montans samian from South Gaul was supplied to Britain from the mid first century to the mid second, with a second *floruit* from the end of the

Trajanic period to c. AD 145/150. The ware was also supplied to sites in the north-west of England and to the Antonine frontier sites in Scotland, but, not to the Hadrian's Wall sites where few sherds occur, particular east of Birdoswald (Willis 2005a, 6.6; cf. Hartley 1972, 42-5; Hartley and Dickinson 1994, 206; Dickinson 2000, 62). This patterning of distribution seems to highlight areas which had specific supply patterns. Jeremy Evans discusses such matters for this region (Evans in preparation), but remind one of earlier discussions of supply arrangements prominent in the 1970s, but which tended not to incorporate samian supply (cf. Willis 2005a, 6.3). Differing trends in material culture and supply are variously noted between the east and the west sides of the frontier zone and East Gaulish samian is often mentioned in this connection. Yet how this geo-economic dimension relates to samian supply in detail is only slowly emerging.

Hadrianic samian from Hadrian's Wall

There is little Hadrianic samian from Hadrian's Wall (Willis 1997b; 1998; 2005a). The Hadrianic era was a period of construction; sites may have been occupied for only c. 10 years before the end of the era. During this time sites may have been kept clean of rubbish, minimizing deposition. Hadrianic samian on Wall sites, therefore, is of particular interest. Groups of Hadrianic samian (c. AD 120-140) are uncommon in Britain and important implications for the dating of the first half of the second century in the province may arise from this infrequency (cf. Willis 1998; 2005a).

Samian and the indigenous population/native settlements

Samian was in the vanguard of Roman imports to arrive on native sites, especially east of the Pennines where there was an established tradition of pottery use, in the Neronian and Flavian era (Willis 1994; 1997a). The ware was actively traded to or otherwise acquired by the people of such sites, perhaps as a diplomatic gift or as an exotic curiosity or status indicator. The quantities involved were small but decorated vessels were well represented. Elsewhere the question of indigenous attitudes to Roman material culture and its consumption is a firm matter for investigation. This is also true for the Wall corridor, but is hindered by the infrequency of such sites in this zone. The few sites that are known and which have been subject to examination such as Milking Gap (Kilbride-Jones 1938), Apperley Dene (Greene 1978), Thornborough Scar (unpublished excavations by Peter Clack in the 1980s) and Newcastle Great Park (Willis forthcoming) have yielded little or no samian. Thus it is possible to say little about samian acquisition and use at such sites. It may be that consumption at such sites was consistent with the pattern that emerges through the late first and second centuries at indigenous sites in the North; small-scale consumption, with a comparatively high proportion of plain vessel types, long curation and a character that confirms the supply/consumption was not a straight sub-set of consumption on nearby military sites.

Samian from vici/extra-mural areas: differing consumption from that within forts

A striking pattern to emerge from recent studies has been the realization that the assemblages recovered from vici and extra-mural areas are markedly different from those recovered from the adjacent forts. This is perhaps surprising given their proximity and their shared final point of destination in a long chain of supply, though this makes perfect sense since forts and their *vici* were markedly different social contexts.

Difference in assemblage composition is apparent at Birdoswald where recent excavations have lead to systematic quantification and comparison of samian assemblages between areas (Willis in press a; in press b; in press d), and at Carlisle. The proportion of decorated bowls present amongst samian assemblages as opposed to plain forms is much higher from the *vici* and extramural areas. These decorated forms are drinking vessels or for food consumption and of significantly greater value than plain forms. Similarly, the proportion of pottery assemblages formed by samian is higher from *vici* than within forts (as, for instance, at Birdoswald). The pattern is not unique to the Wall for this is seen too at Melandra and Caerleon (cf. Willis 2005a). *Vici* are likely to have housed places of entertainment, eating and drinking establishments, shops, places of accommodation for travellers and perhaps often the elite, and may have included residences for the families of officers; hence the use of better quality pottery table ware in these contexts.

An imbalance in knowledge of samian from the Stanegate-Hadrian's Wall corridor

The lack of samian assemblages from 'native' sites apart, there are inevitable imbalances in the knowledge we have of samian from this zone. Some sites were intensively explored decades ago and there are samian assemblages associated with such archives, albeit with little contextual information (eg. from Housesteads, Chesters and Corbridge, and the earlier work at Wallsend). Due to modern development or successful research projects several sites have seen considerable exploration in recent years with well-examined samian or samian collections (eg. Carlisle, Birdoswald, Vindolanda, Red House, Newcastle, Wallsend and South Shields). Other sites have been little examined or for other reasons there is little samian evidence available (eg. Nether Denton, Carvoran, Rudchester). *Vici* are a general category of site in this zone for which we have only a limited picture of samian consumption (eg. from Carlisle, Birdoswald and South Shields). Few cemeteries or burials have been examined in the zone, and elsewhere such contexts are known to have regularly included samian vessels.

Hadrian's Wall and Environs: Coin Research, a Summary

R J Brickstock

Introduction

The state of coin research in the vicinity of Hadrian's Wall is regrettably uneven, being well advanced in some areas but almost non-existent in others. This is partly a reflection of the pattern of excavation. Extensive numismatic research has been undertaken in recent decades, in particular by David Shotter, John Casey and the author; the former concentrating on the western sites and the latter two on the eastern sector. This has resulted in the recording, cataloguing and publication of many sites. Despite this,

134. *Sestertius* of reign of Hadrian bearing image of a warship. Found in River Tyne at Newcastle

there are sites still awaiting modern analysis and/or publication. In addition, there is as yet no complete numismatic overview of the region.

Several general points may be made of sites in the Wall zone:

- No major site has been fully excavated, so we have a no full numismatic pictures from any location.
- Some sites have been extensively excavated and have yielded large assemblages, which have been fully catalogued, discussed and published to modern standards.
- Other sites have been similarly extensively excavated and yet their coin assemblages have not yet been analysed or published to modern standards.
- Still other sites have undergone little or no excavation and have therefore yielded little or no numismatic material, beyond chance or surface finds.
- Much more is known about the numismatic assemblages of forts and major settlements than about the vici adjacent to forts, the minor structures of the Wall or the curtain wall itself.

Summary of current research at individual sites:

Hadrian's Wall: forts, some with *vici*

Wallsend:

- Partially excavated, and excavation on-going;
- Finds fully catalogued;
- Computer database exists;
- Coin reports published, including overview.

Newcastle:

- Partially excavated;
- Finds fully catalogued;
- Computer database exists;
- Coin report published.

Benwell:

- Excavation limited;
- Coin finds very limited;
- Catalogue published.

Rudchester:

- Excavation limited;
- Coin finds limited;
- Catalogue published.

Halton Chesters:

- Partially excavated;
- Extant finds fully catalogued, but numbers limited;
- Large numbers of surface finds unrecorded and lost;
- Computer database exists;
- Coin report awaiting publication.

Chesters:

- Partially excavated;
- Extant finds relatively limited;
- Extant finds partially catalogued;
- Computer database incomplete;

- Publication incomplete.

Carrawburgh:

- Virtually unexplored;
- Coin finds almost non-existent.

Housesteads:
- Extensively excavated, including parts of *vicus*;
- Coin finds catalogued, and recently recatalogued to modern standards;
- Computer database exists;
- Finds of sufficient quantity to allow comparison between fort and *vicus*;
- Reports and overview complete, but EH monograph as yet unpublished.

Great Chesters:

- Limited modern excavation;
- Coin finds very limited.

Birdoswald:

- Extensively excavated;
- Finds fully catalogued;
- Computer database incomplete;
- Coin reports published

Finds from the western sector forts are well covered by David Shotter's periodic publication of coin finds from Cumbria:

Castlesteads:
Stanwix:
Burgh by Sands
Drumburgh
Bowness on Solway
Beckfoot:
Maryport:
Burrow Walls:
Moresby:
Ravenglass:

Milecastles:

- A percentage quite extensively excavated;
- Coin finds sporadic;
- Finds catalogued but sometimes incompletely (and some finds now lost);
- Computer database as complete as foregoing allows;
- Summary report produced by the author but unpublished.

Turrets:

- A percentage quite extensively excavated;
- Coin finds sporadic and very limited;
- Finds catalogued but sometimes incompletely (and some finds now lost);
- Computer database as complete as foregoing allows;
- Summary report produced by the author but unpublished.

Curtain Wall, Ditch, Vallum, etc:

- Excavation very limited
- Finds extremely limited;
- Finds catalogued and computerised;
- Summary report produced by the author but unpublished.

On the Stanegate:

Corbridge:

- Fort and town both extensively excavated;
- Extremely extensive coin assemblage (8000 + hoards);
- Finds of sufficient quantity to allow comparison between various areas of site, including comparison between military, civil and religious.
- Coins fully catalogued;
- Computer database exists with the author and Corbridge Museum;
- Coin reports published, but modern reassessment required.

Newbrough:

- Excavation limited;
- Coin finds very limited.

Vindolanda:

- Extensively excavated, including parts of *vicus*, and excavation on-going;
- Coin finds fully catalogued;
- Computer database exists and available as CD Rom;
- Finds of sufficient quantity to allow comparison between fort and *vicus*;
- Older reports and annual interims published; modern overview required.

Carvoran:

- Limited excavation;
- Coin finds limited;
- Catalogues incomplete.

Nether Denton:

- Limited excavation;
- Finds limited;
- Finds catalogued.

Brampton Old Church:

- Limited excavation;
- Finds limited;
- Finds catalogued.

Carlisle:
- Extensively excavated, and excavation on-going;
- Finds fully catalogued;
- Finds computerised;
- Some reports published; others in prep.

Outpost Forts:

High Rochester:

• Partially excavated;
• Finds catalogued but not to modern standards;
• Computer catalogue lacking;
• Reassessment of finds desirable.

Birrens:

• Partially excavated;
• Finds fully catalogued;
• Computer catalogued to be compiled from above;
• Report published.

Netherby:

• Partially excavated;
• Finds catalogued though not to modern standards;
• Computer catalogue to be compiled;
• Reassessment of finds desirable.

Bewcastle:

• Partially excavated;
• Finds catalogued to modern standards;
• Finds published.

Risingham:

• Partially excavated;
• Coin finds limited.

Other forts:

South Shields:

• Extensively excavated, and excavation on-going;
• Finds fully catalogued;
• Computer catalogue exists;
• Reports published (though a modern overview required).

Hoards and other collections;

• Several dozen hoards are known from the region, including a dozen from Corbridge (some published; others merely catalogued); the Rudchester hoard (full publication in prep.); several hoards from Wallsend; a small unpublished hoard from Gilsland; the Coventina's
• Well assemblage (c.13,000 coins, poorly published and now dissipated); etc.
• Some are fully catalogued; others poorly or not at all;
• Some are extant, in known locations; others are lost or dissipated;
• Some are reported upon; some require a modern reassessment; some require full publication.

Major Museum Collections:

Much of the excavated material from minor sites is held either in the Museum of Antiquities, Newcastle upon Tyne or at Tullie House in Carlisle. Various major sites with museums attached retain their own numismatic material. These include South Shields, Wallsend, Corbridge and Vindolanda. By far the largest assemblage is that of Corbridge Museum.

135. ***Antoninianus*** **of Claudius II, minted 268-70. Corbridge**

Chronological Summary:

• Coin finds from the Late Pre-Roman period are extremely limited
• The earliest finds are normally late Claudian and Vespasianic issues, types still extant when the invasion forces came to the region in the AD 70s. The stable nature of the early imperial currency makes it difficult to attribute foundation dates to sites by analysis of numismatic data alone. This problem is exacerbated by the relative lack of excavations of the earliest levels of sites.
• The same problem of residuality has prevented concrete numismatic conclusion of a number of pressing problems, such as the degree to which Hadrian's Wall sites were downgraded or even abandoned during the Antonine Wall period.
• The numismatic crisis of the third century complicates the interpretation of Severan and later levels; the dating of Severan counterfeits is still not established beyond doubt.
• The relatively small quantities of coinage in circulation in the early third century compared with the later third- and fourth-century bronzes, present a grave interpretational problem. The absence of coin types of the period c.220 260 may be statistically insignificant in a small coin sample, making it hard to date sites or levels within that time period.
• Late-third and fourth-century bronze make up the majority of site finds. The quantity of finds and the often short-lived nature of coin types allow detailed interpretation of the later Roman levels of many sites.
• Roman coin ceased to reach Britain after the end of the fourth century. Coinage found in fifth-century levels is therefore necessarily residual, and numismatic

contribution to the fifth-century debate is therefore unavoidably limited.

Conclusions and Recommendations:

Conservation and Access:

In some instances coin collections are well cared for, being well-conserved, stored in a controlled environment and readily-available for further study. This is not always the case; some early assemblages (e.g. the Coventina's Well finds) have been dissipated or lost; while others are held in private collections which are sometimes difficult for scholars to access. In addition, other assemblages are held in Museums outside the region (e.g. various Corbridge hoards held in the British Museum), making comparative studies that much more difficult.

The majority of Museums have recently up-graded their record-keeping, storage facilities and access provisions - and others are in the process of so doing. Examples of good-practice in these areas may be observed at The Hadrian's Wall Museums, the Vindolanda Trust; Tyne and Wear Museums; Tullie House in Carlisle, and elsewhere. These moves, and in particular the growing trend towards providing digital images of collections, are a tremendous aid to the collation and dissemination of numismatic material. There is, however, the need to ensure a degree of standardisation as the developments progress.

Research: current status and future needs:

Significant numbers of coins have been recovered from more than thirty sites in the region, totalling several tens of thousands of coins. Thus, while there are many gaps in our potential database there is already a very considerable body of coinage that should be available for study. However, while some sites have been published, in whole or in part, some of the most important coin collections remain difficult of access and unavailable for general study.

The most urgent need, therefore, is to bring this data into the public domain in a useful and usable format. There is a pressing need for a concerted numismatic overview of Hadrian's Wall and the surrounding region, as well as comparative studies between the northern military zone and the coinage of Roman Britain as a whole.

A start has been made: the author has built up an extensive database of finds from the eastern sector of the Wall (east of the Irthing), Dere Street and the North East in general; and Cumbria and the western sector of the Wall have been well served by Dr. David Shotter's commendably rapid publication of recent finds (e.g. Shotter 2001; 2002; 2004; 2004a). The author is in the process of making his database available for general study by setting up a website on which both coin catalogues and discussion articles will be posted. A standardised format for publication is already available, whereby all interested scholars will be able to access sufficiently-detailed data for their various needs, including statistical analysis (see the author's The Production, Analysis and Standardisation of Romano-British Coin Lists, EH Guidance Note, 2004). In the absence of dedicated funding, however, work on this website is necessarily a slow "spare-time" activity. There is therefore a need for a co-ordinated, and funded, approach.

Additional recommendations:

- A reassessment of the numismatic material from the Outpost forts;
- Production of full, modern catalogue of all known Hoard finds from Hadrian's Wall and environs;
- An in-depth analysis of the Corbridge site assemblage, with particular emphasis on comparative studies between areas of known different usage;
- In-depth study and publication of material that allows direct comparison between the numismatic patterning of fort and *vicus* (i.e. in particular the assemblages of Vindolanda and Housesteads).
- Extension of on-going work on the EDXRF analysis of Severan counterfeit *denarii* to include those from Corbridge, Housesteads, Chesters, Blackgate, South Shields, etc.. This would greatly expand the current database of such analyses (which includes material from Catterick, York and Chesters (Bridge Abutment). The aim is to work out a more definitive method of identifying such counterfeits as well as to establish a more precise chronology for their production and circulation. The latter might well lead to a significant step forward in our understanding of the chronology of events in the north in the early third century.

Metals and Metalworking in the Hadrian's Wall Area

J Bayley

Sites

The number of sites producing finds of metalworking debris from Hadrian's Wall is considerable but none of these sites have produced very large quantities of material. Given the number of archaeological investigations in the Hadrian's Wall area, the number of sites with evidence for metalworking is not unexpected (cf Bayley 2001, Fig 2).

The selection and use of different metals and alloys has been investigated for certain classes of copper alloy artefacts found in the Hadrian's Wall area (Bayley 1985a; Bayley 1985b; Dungworth 1995; Allason-Jones and Dungworth 1997, 319-20; Bayley and Butcher 2004) and some patterns have been identified.

Bayley (1992) and Allason-Jones and Dungworth (1997) record finds from turrets, milecastles, forts and their *vici*. There are also finds from settlements close to the Wall such as Carlisle (see gazetteer below).

Collections

The older finds are lodged in a variety of museums (eg, at South Shields, Newcastle, Carlisle, Corbridge and Housesteads). More recent finds may still be with their excavators or the specialists studying them. Finds reported under the PAS will generally be with their finders or may have been sold to other collectors or museums.

Almost all the material referred to in this document is published either fully or in grey literature such as the AML Report Series.

Local trade and exchange

Small-scale metalworking was widespread in the Hadrian's Wall area with finds from the whole range of military and civilian settlements. Most of the metalworking evidence does not indicate the types of objects being made so it is almost impossible to link it to the production of artefacts whose distributions may suggest manufacture in the Hadrian's Wall area. Where specific object types can be identified from moulds, a small range of mainly military buckles and mounts are known to have been made. It would therefore appear that much of the local production was aimed at the military market, though the craftsmen themselves could be civilians.

As yet there is no good evidence for large-scale metalwork production in *fabricae*, though buildings in some forts have been identified as such. However, the lack of large assemblages of metalworking debris does not necessarily mean that there was no larger-scale manufacturing only that the diagnostic evidence has not survived in the areas where limited and partial excavations have been carried out. Future investigations may hit on the 'right' spots.

Gaps in current knowledge

Most of the publications consulted in drafting this resource assessment focus specifically, or mainly, on copper alloy working. There are no finds that relate specifically to the working of precious metals, except the mercury from Carlisle which is most likely associated with mercury gilding, and only a few that suggest lead or pewter working. Unless large new assemblages are found, there is only limited potential for increasing the understanding of the technical processes being undertaken.

Iron working must have been at least as important but as yet no syntheses of the evidence from the Hadrian's Wall area have been published. It is not an area renowned for its iron ores so no major iron smelting sites are to be expected. Despite this, small-scale smelting would not be unexpected in a civilian context, and iron smithing would have been practiced in most settlements of any size, whether military or civil. Until relatively recently iron slags from excavations were not routinely retained, so it is only more recent fieldwork that is likely to have the potential to contribute to this study.

The ways in which metalworking (of all types) fitted into, and contributed to, the local economy is not generally well-studied. Who the craftsmen were, whether they were military or civilian, and whether they came from the locality or from further afield, are all questions we cannot answer at present.

Gazetteer of sites with evidence for metalworking

(Based on Bayley 1992 and Allason-Jones and Dungworth 1997. Note this is unlikely to be a complete list of all published evidence, but should include all major groups unless they are from more recent excavations.)

Carlisle
Roman
A complete crucible with brimful volume of 540ml (tidemark at 430ml) and a thick extra outer layer of less refractory clay was found.
Refs: Wilthew 1985

Carlisle: Castle Street
Roman: c.100 AD
Annex to fort. Finds include many copper alloy offcuts '... clearly the residue of a recycling process ...'. In Per 9 (late 2nd to mid 3rd century), after the fort went out of use, a lead 'ingot' 56 x 53 x 29mm with cut (?chisel) marks on the upper face was found.
Refs: Padley 1992

Carlisle: Fisher Street
Roman
Finds include three crucible fragments, hearth lining, copper alloy waste and lead scrap, mercury, a haematite pebble worn flat on one side and two fragments of galena.
Refs: unpublished

Carlisle: Keays Lane
Roman
Finds include fragments of 2 crucibles used to melt copper alloys and bronze blobs and dribbles.
Refs: ?unpublished

Carrawburgh: Coventina's Well
Roman
Two flawed castings found.
Refs: Allason-Jones and McKay 1985
Corbridge
Roman
Finds include a pewter 'ingot' of oblate spheroid form weighing c.450g (94.78% Sn, 5.37% Pb) and an irregular lump (43.94% Sn, 56.30% Pb).
Refs: Hughes 1980; Smythe 1937/38

Corbridge: Red House site
Roman
Excavations in building 10, the *fabrica*, found three hearths and associated with one was a crucible used to melt copper alloys. Nearby was an area with other hearths and pits, two of which contained fragments of lead droppings.
Refs: Hanson et al 1979

Dunston:Tyne and Wear
Roman
Stone mould for ?brooches or studs.
Refs: Allason-Jones and Dungworth 1997

Halton Chesters
Roman
Found in the ditch of the Vallum near this fort was a shale slab 100 x 80 x 20mm cut in intaglio with many designs on one face and one end. The lack of runners shows it cannot have been used for casting; gold foil may have been pressed into the matrices.
Refs: Smith 1922

High Brunton (Turret 26A)
Roman: 160-190 AD
'Bronze working area' identified. Finds include crucible fragment, clay mould fragments for (?)mounts, scrap metal and a bone tool.
Refs: Woodfield 1965

Housesteads
Roman: mid second-late third
Finds include slag, fragments of c.50 crucibles (of a range of forms), clay piece moulds and copper alloy scrap and waste, mostly from a dump in the rampart area to the NE of the fort. Of the total weight of c.15kg of debris, c.13kg was iron smithing slag, half of which was from post-Roman contexts and so may be redeposited. The copper alloys were mainly bronzes and a few gunmetals, the scrap being essentially unleaded and the casting waste containing an average of 10% lead. Three of the moulds were for casting buckles of a common military type (cf Austen 1991, Fig 93), one of which was from a multiple mould. Excavations in the vicus found smith's tongs and a coin mould.
Refs: Birley and Keeney 1935, 241; Goodburn 1980, 359; Dungworth 2001

Murton High Crags
Roman: probably late first century onwards
Finds include part of a sandstone bar ingot mould with a single U-shaped groove 20 mm x 15mm x 100mm (to the break).
Refs: Jobey and Jobey 1987

Newcastle upon Tyne
Roman: later third century
Several hearths, scrap metal and 14 clay mould fragments for making openwork trumpet-motif mounts found.
Refs: Allason-Jones and Dungworth 1997

Sewingshields
Roman: fourth century
Small-scale copper alloy working. Hearths were found in association with a hand-made crucible, a possible tuyere and some clay mould fragments. Some slight evidence for iron smithing.
Refs: Bayley 1982b; Bayley 1984

South Shields
Roman: c.160 and fourth century
Clay piece mould, possibly for a harness mount, as well as crucibles. Mould for belt tag and stone ?mould for a domed stud found in early excavations.
Refs: Allason-Jones 1983, 134-5; Allason-Jones and Miket 1984; Allason-Jones and Dungworth 1997

Stanwix
Roman: second quarter of second century
Unfinished and flawed castings, scrap metal and part manufactures (bar, wire etc) found. They were apparently redeposited and not *in situ*. (In the smudgy illustrations some of the supposedly unfinished objects appear quite normal).
Refs: Collingwood 1931a and 1931b

Vindolanda
Roman: 270-350 AD
Vicus II. Evidence of iron and 'bronze' working includes three crucibles, one with a bar of clay across the pouring lip, five or six ingot moulds, a casting sprue and a flawed casting of a second or third century military buckle. XRF analysis failed to detect any metals on the ingot moulds which may be post-Roman in date.
Stone Fort I: Large scale iron working in buildings of E Rampart of in period 1B.
Refs: Birley 1977a, 41; Birley 1977b; Bayley 1982a; Bidwell 1985, 117

Wallhouses West (Turret 18B)
Roman: 120-150 AD
Ironworking debris found in pit in floor of turret.
Refs: Woodfield 1965

Glass in the Hadrian's Wall Region

J Price

Introduction

The glass finds from the region of Hadrian's Wall have not received as much attention as some other categories of material evidence. The comparatively late development of a research tradition in archaeological glass and the often very fragmentary state of glass finds from settlement sites which makes their identification difficult led to most early excavators ignoring it. In the majority of excavation reports published in the first half of the twentieth century, the glass found was mentioned only generally and not studied in depth or illustrated unless the pieces were substantially complete, decorated or in some way particularly unusual. In the past five decades, however, much more attention has been given to the subject. Detailed studies of numerous glass assemblages have led to a chronology being established for Romano-British glass vessels and glass objects such as beads, greater understanding of local and regional production traditions and recognition of differences in patterns of glass use by different communities in different parts of the province and at different periods.

Some glass from the Hadrian's Wall region was recorded in the nineteenth and early twentieth centuries (eg. Ferguson 1864, Wallis Budge 1907, Toynbee and Richmond 1954), but the regular recording of glass finds began with the work of Dorothy Charlesworth. From the late 1950s until her death in 1981, she studied most of the glass in the region and wrote reports on finds from excavations at Red House Corbridge, Chesters, Carrawburgh, Housesteads, South Shields and elsewhere (eg. Charlesworth 1959c, 1961, 1962, 1971, 1979a 1979b) as well as an account of Roman glass in northern Britain which included material from Carrawburgh, Chesters, Housesteads, Castlesteads, Nether Denton, Corbridge, Carlisle and South Shields (Charlesworth 1959a) and a note on glass in Tullie House Museum, Carlisle (Charlesworth 1959b). At around this time, the glass in the museum at Corbridge was also examined by other researchers (eg. Bulmer 1955, Halliday 1971).

Since 1980, the study of the glass in the region of Hadrian's Wall has become more detailed, as in most cases the total assemblages of material have been examined and assessed, but it has also become more fragmented, as various researchers have prepared glass reports, including Denise Allen, Hilary Cool, Sally Cottam, Birgitta Hoffmann, Christine Howard-Davis, Dominic Ingemark, Jennifer Price and Sally Worrell. This material has been studied for the excavators of individual sites, and no broader research projects or synthetic reviews have been undertaken. Many of the reports remain unpublished.

The glass

A wide variety of glass vessels and objects is known from sites in the Hadrian's Wall region. The vessels include tablewares, particularly vessels for serving and consuming liquids, household wares and containers. These tend to complement their ceramic equivalents, though they are found in much smaller quantities. The glass objects include personal items such as armlets, beads, finger rings and hairpins and accounting and leisure items such as counters and gaming pieces. Window glass is also commonly found, particularly in bath-houses and other public buildings and in high status residences. The glass finds range in date from the second half of the first to the late fourth century and occur in varying quantities, depending on factors such as the date and nature of the deposits, the status of the area excavated, the date and extent of the excavation, and the arrangements in place for collecting and recycling the glass, both at the time of breakage and at later periods. Some sites, particularly Carlisle, Corbridge, South Shields and Vindolanda have produced large numbers of glass fragments from different periods, which little is known about the finds from some of the others (see the List of Sites below for information available to me).

Early Flavian glass has been recorded at some sites, such as Carlisle and Red House Corbridge, and glass of the last decades of the first and early years of the second century is also known at Vindolanda, Corbridge and elsewhere. Overall, the majority of the glass finds in the region belong to the second and early third century. Glass is found in all the forts and civil settlements of this period, with smaller amounts from the milecastles and turrets and occasional pieces from native sites such as Milking Gap (Kilbride-Jones 1938, 346). After the middle of the third century there is a marked diminution in the quantity of glass surviving in the archaeological record, although there are some interesting groups at South Shields and Wallsend, and some fourth century vessel glass and objects have also been noted, particularly at South Shields and also at Carlisle, Chesters, Corbridge, and Vindolanda. In general, the surviving material suggests that glass was used less in the later periods, but this impression may well be biased by the organisation of recycling in the region.

Origins

With the exception of a very few exotic items, the glass vessels in the Hadrian's Wall region are closely comparable in form and decoration with finds of similar date found elsewhere in Britain and the north west provinces, although it is noticeable from the second century onwards that only a part of the range of contemporary vessels seems to have been present in the frontier region. The nature of glass production and the recyclability of broken glass make it difficult to establish precise centres for production of the vessels, and it is as yet unclear whether most of them arrived as finished vessels from glasshouses in the Rhineland and northern France or were produced within Britain by glassworkers with a common tradition of craftsmanship using raw glass and recycled glass (cullet) to blow vessels for local markets. A little evidence for glass working has been noted in Carlisle where a fragment from a ceramic crucible with bluish green glass and some pincered trails came from the Northern Lanes (Price and Worrell unpublished) and a tubular moil from Fisher Street (Ingemark unpublished), but no information about the date of these activities or the vessel forms being produced has survived. No other evidence for glass-working has yet been noted in the region, although there is some at Camelon (unpublished).

The majority of the objects, such as armlets and beads, are likely to have been formed in Britain, and some may have been made by personnel attached to the military units. No production waste has been identified in the Hadrian's Wall region, but some evidence for bead production survives at Camelon (unpublished). Some bead types, such as the colourless segmented beads with gold foil found at sites including Birdoswald, Carrawburgh, Chesters, Great Chesters, Housesteads and South Shields (mostly listed in Allason-Jones and Miket (1984, 278) have parallels in central Europe. These may have been brought to the region in the course of trade or by incoming military units. Beads of this kind have been discussed recently in connection with finds in the cemetery at the fort at Brougham in Cumbria (Cool 2004, 386-7). It is also assumed that panes of window glass were generally made close to the place where they were to be used, probably using recycled glass, although it could have been made elsewhere, as window glass has sometimes been found as part of the cargo in ships wrecked in the western Mediterranean.

Collections

Glass finds from early and some more recent excavations are held in the collections of the museums in the region, and it is noteworthy that little seems to have found its way into public collections elsewhere in Britain. Two of the museums, the Tullie House Museum in Carlisle and the Museum of Antiquities in Newcastle hold finds from sites at the western and eastern ends of the region, while the others, such as the Clayton Museum at Chesters, the Corbridge and Housesteads Museums, the Senhouse Museum in Maryport, the Arbeia Roman Fort and Museum at South Shields, the Vindolanda Museum and the Wallsend Museum principally house the material from their own sites, although the Clayton Museum also has early finds from Carrawburgh, Great Chesters and Nether Denton. Much of the more recently excavated material is, however, currently stored by the organisations directing the excavations or with the researchers writing the reports.

Trade and exchange

The tableware forms indicate close affinities with contemporary vessels in the lower Rhine and northern Gaul, and virtually all of them come from exactly similar traditions of production and decoration, but it is not always certain whether they were supplied from the continent or produced more locally by itinerant glassworkers, or arrived as personal possessions. There is no physical evidence for installations undertaking large-scale production of glass vessels anywhere in the north west provinces, while the large number of small furnaces now known points to small-scale production in many places. Overall, the forms in use at a particular time in different parts of the Hadrian's Wall region are broadly similar, though it is observable that some vessels frequently found in the eastern part of the region are much less common at western sites, which suggests differing patterns of supply. This is particularly noticeable among the later second and third century drinking vessels with linear and facet cut decoration which are present in some numbers at South Shields and also known at Benwell and in forts in the central Wall area but are virtually absent in Carlisle.

The large bluish green cylindrical and prismatic bottles present on every site in the late first, second and early third century contribute more direct information about trade and exchange, because they have reached the region as containers of liquid or semi-liquid materials, probably foodstuffs, supplied to the military units and perhaps also to the civil population. Vessels of this kind were used to supply military sites in many parts of the Roman world. Virtually all prismatic bottles were made with raised patterns on the bases, and while most of these were combinations of concentric rings a sizable group has more distinctive designs, which allows the distribution of similar pieces to be recognised. There are, however, some difficulties in interpreting these results because, unlike ceramic and wooden containers, glass bottles are easy to clean and could be re-used many times, so the findspot is not necessarily the place to which the vessel and its contents were originally supplied.

Charlesworth examined bottle base designs from Corbridge and elsewhere in the region as well as in other parts of Britain and produced some interesting results though much of her work remains unpublished, and recent publications of bottle base designs from other provinces in the western empire has shown that certain designs occur exclusively or principally in Britain. It is also apparent that some designs are concentrated in the northern frontier region and that certain bottle shapes, production details and basal designs are characteristic of different periods, so that it is often possible to distinguish between Flavian, Hadrianic and late Antonine bottles.

Gaps in knowledge

As no comprehensive overview of glass finds in the region has been produced, and the material has not been the subject of a doctoral thesis or postdoctoral project there are inevitably very large gaps in current knowledge. The study of single sites in the recent past has shown that large quantities of glass vessels and objects were in use, but much of this work remains unpublished. The information now available is variable; a great deal is either known or knowable about the large groups of late first to late fourth century glass found at Carlisle, Corbridge, South Shields or Vindolanda whereas little or nothing is known about many of the other sites. It is thus difficult for one individual to present a balanced and informed view of the material, although there is clearly much potential for future research.

Acknowledgements; I am very grateful for the assistance of Denise Allen, Hilary Cool and Christine Howard-Davis who have been most generous with their time in answering questions and providing information about their unpublished work (listed in the summary and in the bibliography below), as well as to John Shepherd who confirmed that he had never worked on any glass in the Hadrian's Wall region.

Glass found in the Hadrian's Wall region

Stanegate

Corbridge:
A lot of glass has been found at Corbridge, and some is published - eg.
Red House (Charlesworth 1959b; Charlesworth 1979a),
Fort and town (Allen 1988).
Glass from Corbridge is mentioned in Bulmer 1955, Halliday 1971, Allen 1983.

Newbrough:
No information

Vindolanda:
A lot of glass has been found at Vindolanda, and some is published.
Bidwell - (Price 1985)
Birley - (Hoffmann unpublished)

Carvoran:
No information
Nether Denton:
Vessels and objects listed in Wallace Budge 1907, 406

Brampton Old Church:
No information

Carlisle (see HW)

Hadrian's Wall

Wallsend
Charles Daniels - (Allen unpublished, written 1986, amended 1997)
Tyne and Wear - (Price, Cottam, Worrell unpublished, written in 1990s)

Newcastle
Barbara Harbottle - (Price unpublished)

Benwell
Petch (excavations in 1920s) - 20+ fragments, second-third century tablewares and bottles
Late second century vessel in burial in lead coffin (Honeyman 1935/6)

Rudchester
No information

Halton Chesters:
Charles Daniels - 187 fragments, second-third century tablewares and bottles (Price)
Tyne and Wear 2001 - 10 fragments, bottles (Price)

Chesters:
Vessel fragments, beads and counters from John Clayton's excavations listed in Wallace Budge (1907, 370-1, 374-5, 385)

Carrawburgh:
Coventina's Well - Wallace budge 1907, 389; Allason-Jones and Mackay 1985
Fort - Wallace Budge 1907, 395

Housesteads:
Glass from drain in Commandant's House (Charlesworth 1971 - dating to be amended) .
References to glass in Allen 1983
Glass from site H 20 (Allen unpublished b, written in 1987)

Great Chesters:
Vessels and objects listed in Wallace Budge 1907, 396

Birdoswald:
Wilmott 1987-92 - (Price and Cottam 1997)
Wilmott sites 585, 590, BRD99 (Cool unpublished b - written in 2001)

Castlesteads:
No information

Carlisle:
There is a lot of glass from Carlisle
Finds in Tullie House Museum - Charlesworth 1959b
Blackfriars St - 1108 fragments - Price 1990
Castle St - 469 fragments - Cool and Price 1991
Annetwell Street 1973-84 - 970 fragments (Cool and Price unpublished)
Annetwell Street 1990 - 753 fragments (Cool unpublished a)
Extension to Tullie House Museum - 168 fragments - Cool 1992
Southern Lanes - 816 fragments - summarised in Price and S Cottam 2000 (report unpublished
Northern Lanes - 1684 fragments - (catalogued by Price and Worrell, unpublished)
Millennium site - 634 fragments (Howard-Davis forthcoming)
Plus Fisher Street (Ingemark unpublished), Botchergate and other sites

Stanwix:
Oxford North - (Howard-Davis unpublished)

Burgh by Sands:
Jones and Mattingly - (Price unpublished)

Drumburgh:
No information

Bowness on Solway:
No information

Cumberland Coast

Beckfoot:
No information

Maryport:
Birley and Jarrett - Price 1976.

Burrow Walls:
No information

Moresby:
No information

Ravenglass:
Potter - (Charlesworth 1979c)

Outpost forts

High Rochester
No information

Birrens:
Robertson 1975

Netherby:
No information

Bewcastle:
Bath-house - a few fragments (Allason-Jones in Gillam et al 1993)

Risingham:
No information

Milecastles

Milecastle 35 (Savage) - some glass

Milecastle 39 (Crow) - (Allen unpublished c, written in 1985-6)

Turrets

No information

Other forts:

South Shields:
There is a lot of glass at South Shields; some is published eg. Charlesworth 1979b
Glass objects in Allason Jones and Miket 1984

Leather Artefacts in the Hadrian's Wall Region

E M Greene

Introduction

The largest concentration of Roman leather in Britain can be found on the northern frontier, provided primarily by the ever-growing assemblage from the fort and vicus at Vindolanda, but also by contributions from Carlisle, Birdoswald, and the outlying fort of Newstead (see Curle

1911). Leather artefacts known from the Hadrian's Wall area include shoes, tent panels, horse equipment, cobbler offcuts, and a variety of small artefacts such as patches, thumb guards, and laces. Shoes and much of the horse gear known are usually made from thick cowhide leather, while the thinner goat's skin is reserved for tent panels, some horse gear, clothing (there are no large examples of full garments, though fragments of leather may represent pieces of clothing), and other more delicate leather objects.

Footwear

Footwear is the most robust of leather artefacts and therefore preserved where conditions are suitable for preservation of organic material. Often only the thick cowhide sole layers remain with or without the iron hobnails, but commonly the upper portions that often reveal delicate cut patterning and stitching is also preserved. Shoe types and styles can vary greatly, with military boots naturally making up a large part of assemblages on Hadrian's Wall. There are also many examples of shoes clearly worn for everyday use and meant for less robust activity, evidenced by smaller hobnails often in a decorative pattern that covers less of the underside of the leather sole. The carbatina is also commonly found, and is used for light wear, perhaps in indoor spaces only. Its single layer of thick cowhide with a smooth sole free of any hard material such as hobnails or wood, certainly would not withstand constant outdoor walking. They are constructed from one piece of cowhide and often have cutouts on the top of the foot that took laces to hold the shoe together. Less frequent finds of wood and leather clogs were probably used in the bathhouse or a similar environment, but are not nearly as common as other shoe types.

Horse gear

The most impressive leather horse gear to be found on Hadrian's Wall are the chamfrons found at Vindolanda, that are similar to others known from Newstead (Driel-Murray 1989). The chamfron was often highly decorated with metal attachments and lines tooled into the leather. A second thinner goatskin layer was placed on the interior of the chamfron. Partial finds from Carlisle have been suggested to be from chamfrons, based on their similarity to the Vindolanda examples.

Leather saddle covers, better understood as the casing for the saddle, are known only in fragments from Hadrian's Wall, but which can be compared to an almost complete example from Valkenburg (Germany) (see generally Connolly and Driel-Murray 1991). Vindolanda and Carlisle have both produced leather finds that have been accepted as fragmentary saddle covers (Driel-Murray 1989 and Winterbottom 1989). Harnesses and other horse trappings are generally not found in these large leather assemblages, but must certainly have existed as part of the cavalry horse equipment.

Tent panels and other artefacts

Tent panels have been a focus of leather research since the early discovery at Birdoswald of a number of large panels (McIntyre and Richmond 1934). Many examples are known, whole or fragmentary, but Vindolanda has for the first time produced panels that can be linked together by the stitching patterns, and has provided the model for actual reconstruction of a Roman tent (rather than hypothetical, Driel-Murray 1993). Tents are made from thinner goatskin and often show signs of repair and patching throughout their period of use. Tentage from Hadrian's Wall can also be compared to finds from Ribchester further south.

Leather preservation and find contexts

The most common environment for the survival of leather is in the fort ditches, which eventually became rubbish deposits for the various people living in the forts and extra-mural settlements. At Vindolanda, the large Severan period ditches have revealed hundreds of shoes belonging to men, women and children, as well as concentrated deposits of cobbler's offcuts with leatherworking needles found nearby. Moreover, the pre-Hadrianic levels with anaerobic soil conditions have preserved leather artefacts within specific building contexts, and can provide a very good view of leather artefacts in their original context. In addition to the fort ditches located on almost all fort sites, the watery environment of wells also provide a suitable environment for the preservation of leather (compare Saalburg on the German Limes where all leather artefacts on site were found in the fort and *vicus* wells).

Sites with leather assemblages

Most sites along the wall should have the potential to produce leather artefacts in some quantity, but currently only three major assemblages stand out. In addition to the large assemblage at Vindolanda, finds are published from Carlisle and Birdoswald, with the outlying fort at Newstead also contributing but in need of updated research and publication.

Vindolanda carries by far the largest assemblage of leather artefacts in Britain, the number of catalogued finds through the 1992 season reaching 3897 (Driel-Murray 1993); since then that number has risen by at least half. Shoes are found from all occupation periods on the site from AD 85 through the third century. The largest contexts which preserve organic materials are the fort ditches of period VI, VIB and VII, dating mostly to the mid-second to mid third century, but also from the period I fort ditch dating to AD 85-90. The most intriguing leather artefacts from a contextual standpoint are those shoes found within fort buildings of the pre-Hadrianic timber phases (ca. AD 90-120). Shoes such as the 'Lepidina slipper', one of the highlights of the Vindolanda assemblage, have been tentatively tied to individuals living in the praetorium (Driel-Murray 1993). The vast majority of the assemblage is shoes of all types, sizes and purpose, but also large quantities of tentage, horse gear, cobbler's offcuts, and other small artefacts comprise this vast assemblage.

Carlisle adds to our understanding of leather artefacts through the discovery of footwear, tentage, horse gear and other small artefacts and scraps. The horse gear has been greatly helpful in understanding the use of saddles in the Roman period (Winterbottom 1989), as well as chamfrons and other cavalry equipment. Potential pieces of clothing are also suggested to be present at Carlisle (Padley and Winterbottom 1991).

Birdoswald produced leather finds quite early in its excavation history (see McIntyre and Richmond 1934), however, it is the recent excavations that have produced 692 examples of leather artefacts that highlight it as a major contributor to the leather assemblages on Hadrian's Wall (Mould 1997). Almost all examples come from the fort ditches of second-fourth century contexts, and comprise mostly shoes and waste leather, some tentage and basic scraps. The large amount of scrap leather together with the cut-outs discarded by cobblers suggests there was at least small scale production of shoes on site (Mould 1997: 327).

Current and potential research of the leather from the Hadrian's Wall area

There is certainly potential for much broader research of the leather assemblages in the area. Currently the Vindolanda footwear assemblage is being fully researched with a focus on demographic information provided by the footwear for each period of occupation on the site. The publication of this extensive assemblage will provide excellent comparison for individual finds from other sites. Stylistically, footwear might provide information about ethnic preferences, while shape and form could reveal deformations or disabilities present in the population. The potential for answering highly interesting research questions and for new lines of inquiry could certainly be provided by a closer look at leather assemblages.

The project website contains a list of select sources for further reading about the leather finds from the Hadrian's Wall area directly. These sources will provide detailed information about finds and contexts, as well as provide more general bibliography about leather in the ancient world and infantry and cavalry equipment. They can also be accessed for further reading on comparative assemblages of leather finds from elsewhere in the Roman Empire.

Wooden Objects from Hadrian's Wall and how they Relate to Trade.

T Padley

The amount of evidence and where it survives is variable. The survival of wooden evidence relies on waterlogged deposits. The largest amounts have been recovered from Carlisle and Vindolanda. There are some single objects, such as a turned box from Corbridge and fragmentary bowls from Birdoswald, but these are not common.

The Carlisle material is destined for Tullie House and the Vindolanda material is housed in the Vindolanda museum. However, much of this is unpublished as yet. The publication of the Millennium report in November 2007 will improve the Carlisle position. An examination of the current Vindolanda publications doesn't seem to have one that deals with the wooden artefacts. I have put a very basic bibliography at the bottom of this.

The range of material, where it survives is large. It covers personal items like combs, needle-cases, medicine boxes, through household items and writing materials to industrial items like wheels and barrels. Many of these could be seen to be evidence for craft and industry as well as trade and exchange. The latter can be looked at from the artefacts themselves, such as large wine barrels (found in Carlisle as linings for wells) and the type of wood used to make them. The barrels in Carlisle were made of Silver Fir (*Abies alba*) which is only found in the hills of Continental Europe. Box (*Buxus sp.*) was used for many small items such as combs and medicine containers, and this is only found as a native plant in Britain in the south of the country. Field maple is only found in South Cumbria and not further north and was used for things like some writing tablets and wheel spokes. The pattern of species used is rather like pottery sources in some ways, but there is also the problem of re-use. Writing tablets, particularly stylus ones are made of Silver Fir, but they could be a secondary use of barrels that had been imported rather than coming from overseas themselves.

The main gaps in our knowledge come from the lack of publication of major sites such as Carlisle and Vindolanda, which would put much information into the public domain where it could be examined and further questions posed.

Jet and Shale

L Allason-Jones

Traditionally, archaeologists have identified Roman artefacts with a black and shiny surface as being made from jet, with a geological source at Whitby in Yorkshire (RCHME 1962), whilst those objects with a grey/brown and matte surface were expected to be products of the Kimmeridge shale beds in Dorset and probably of Iron Age date (Calkin 1955; Davies 1936). Any artefacts of either material found elsewhere in the Roman Empire were presumed to be Romano-British exports or items which had been transferred by travellers returning to their homeland or soldiers arriving at a new posting. Even the large quantity of black Roman jewellery found in the area of Cologne and Bonn was presumed to be made up of Whitby exports, even though there were some stylistic disparities.

Recent analytical work has revealed that all that was black and shiny was not necessarily carved from jet (see Allason-Jones and Jones 2001 for a bibliography of the various analytical methods which have been explored). This analysis has tended to concentrate on identifying the geological materials which were utilised for jewellery and small domestic items; these are now known to include jet, shales, torbanite, cannel coal, and detrital coals with a range of different sources for each type. This has shed interesting light on the jewellery trade in the Roman period, particularly as some of the material found on the frontier, such as torbanite, was brought in from areas north of Hadrian's Wall. The local Coal Measures were also used, with the favoured sources being in South Northumberland near Alston and up the North Tyne Valley, beyond Hadrian's Wall, but the bulk of the products found in the Military Zone were made from sources in Yorkshire, Derbyshire and Midlothian. Two armlets found at Halton Chesters proved to be made from shale with a source less than two miles north of the fort.

Most of the objects of black material found in the area of Hadrian's Wall come from post 180 AD contexts, i.e. after the abandonment of the Antonine Wall, so the use of materials from North Northumberland and Scotland suggests that Hadrian's Wall was not hindering the movement of luxury source materials (Allason-Jones and Jones 1994). Identification of half worked objects or raw blocks at South Shields, which proved on analysis to be of Whitby/Robin's Hood Bay jet, suggests that material from the Yorkshire coast was not necessarily being worked at York but was sent out to other centres for working or completion. This evidence, plus the large number of black objects from South Shields, indicates that South Shields was a centre for jet/shale working in the Roman period and probably the main supplier for the other sites in the region (Allason-Jones and Jones 1994).

Analysis has also shown that the objects found on the Rhineland were not being imported from the north of Britain but were made from locally acquired material. Sources in Hungary, France and Spain were also being used, with two objects found at York proving to be made from Spanish jet; it is presumed that these were brought to the country as the property of individuals rather than evidence of a perverse trade route (Allason-Jones and Jones 2001).

The study of jet in Roman Britain has revealed that the bulk of the finds come from female graves or could be interpreted as being for female use. It is, of course, very difficult to label a particular item as being exclusively for use by either gender but in the case of jet there is an Empire-wide bias towards jewellery and artefacts which are traditionally associated with female activities (see Allason-Jones 2002). The inclusion of jet in predominantly female graves may suggest that the material had some religious or magical significance for women so the high proportion of jet artefacts from the Military Zone, an area often presumed to be dominated by men, is curious and worthy of future study.

The Documentary Evidence

J Pearce

Introduction

The documentary evidence for trade and exchange on Hadrian's Wall may be divided into three categories, documents written or found on this frontier, those created elsewhere in Britain or in other provinces which relate to the Wall, and those relating to trade and exchange on other Roman frontiers which shed light by analogy. This discussion deals primarily with the first category, covering the pre-Hadrianic frontier as well as the Wall itself.

The major pre-occupation in the study of trade and exchange on Hadrian's Wall has been the economic impact of the garrison, its dependence on long-distance supply from continental Europe, its use of the agricultural and other resources of northern Britain and the military's own production of food and other commodities. Breeze's 1984 study emphasised the complexity of supply, combining provision of supplies from local, regional and more distant sources, through levy or purchase, and supplies produced or procured by individual units or men (Breeze 1984: 282). This characterisation depends on documents found outside Britain; evidence from Hadrian's Wall has played a limited role in the broader study of trade and exchange on Roman frontiers. Whittaker (1994) and Elton (1996), for example, make little use of British evidence, though it features more strongly in the other work (e.g. Erdkamp 2002). The military presence is also argued to have an impact on the structure of the Romano-British economy as a whole (Fulford 2004). Roth (1998) focuses on the army on campaign. The frontier economy also receives little attention in the most recent edition of Breeze and Dobson's Hadrian's Wall (2002). There have been significant studies of individual categories of data or themes (see below), but no recent synthetic study of Britain's frontier economy.

The following discussion reviews the range of documents related to the topic of trade and exchange and notes where they are published. Whilst they are certainly a key resource for studying the impact of the frontier army, they also allow a detailed study of the movement of commodities within and between garrisons and the mechanisms by which they move, re-distribution, sale and gift. In this connection exchange cannot be divorced from the study of frontier society; social relationships within and beyond the army are structured around the exchange of goods and hospitality. The focus of discussion lies on the Vindolanda tablets, but the other categories of document are also considered.

Forms of Documentary evidence

Literary sources shed occasional light on the army's economic impact during the conquest period in Britain (e.g. Tacitus *Agr.* 19), but the limited evidence for the northern frontier (Mann n.d.; Breeze and Dobson 2000) does not provide insights of the type sometimes available for other frontiers (e.g. Tacitus, *Hist.* 4.64; *Germania* 41). The abundance of the Hadrian's Wall zone in stone inscriptions is well known, though these are at best indirectly relevant to this topic. More important is the corpus of texts placed on everyday objects during their production, circulation and use. The frontier is rich in these, especially where excavation of anaerobic contexts has yielded a wealth of wood and leather artefacts bearing texts of this type.

Exceptional, if not quite unique, in a British and broader Roman context are the hundreds of wooden ink tablets from Vindolanda and Carlisle, which on first discovery in 1973 were a hitherto unknown document type from the Roman world. The Vindolanda evidence shows that ink tablets were widely used among the garrisons: many more must await discovery on other sites. The difficulties of interpretation of many individual texts, due to their fragmentary survival or abraded condition, as well as the difficulties of transcription and understanding, even where well preserved, should not be underestimated.

The corpus of legible stylus tablets from this frontier is smaller and here Carlisle, with a higher proportion of surviving legible texts, is the most significant findspot. Most of the hundreds of tablets from Vindolanda remain unread (Birley et al. 1993; Bowman and Tomlin 2005). One late

136. Lower quernstone, probably from a mechanical mill. Corbridge

Flavian example, which anticipated that the addressee might be found at Carlisle or at Newstead (*RIB* II.2443.3) reminds us that these documents too circulated widely, as does their occasional discovery in excavations at other sites (Pearce 2004) and the wide distribution of writing equipment, in particular styli and seal boxes.

We should not however be misled by this abundance into thinking that a representative sample of documents is yet at our disposal. The tablets from Vindolanda date primarily to the half-century before the construction of the Wall. Documents related to property ownership and transmission are also mentioned in the Vindolanda texts (Bowman 2006), but have not yet come to light. Comparison of the Vindolanda tablets with documents from Carlisle and from Roman military sites in the Mediterranean suggest what might be absent (cf. Bowman 2006; RMR). For example there is no document at Vindolanda recording the disbursements of food for units, noted at Carlisle (*Tab. Luguval.* 1) and Bu Njem (Marichal 1992: 103). Elsewhere, evidence has been obtained in more significant quantities of soldiers and others obtaining their supply through purchase or gift (Bingen 1992; 1997; Davies 1971: 134-5). This is perhaps due to the Vindolanda tablets deriving primarily from the commander's household(s) rather than the garrison(s) as a whole. Some media for portable documents are scarcely represented. Papyrus survives as only the scraps with the Corbridge hoard. Texts on amphora (and other ceramic) sherds are not yet documented, in contrast to other frontiers. The textual evidence is also restricted by time and place. Few fourth century documents have been recorded and none so far on the farms of the indigenous population, although this possibility should not be dismissed (cf. Derks and Roymans 2002).

Britain is well served in terms of the publication of documents. Monumental inscriptions discovered up to 1955 were published in *RIB* I in 1965 (and the subsequent 1995 edition). Later discoveries have been reported in *JRS* and *Britannia*. *RIB* III, currently in preparation, will gather and revise all of these subsequent discoveries up to 1999. Instrumentum domesticum and portable documents, including writing tablets, have, with significant exceptions, been published in *RIB* II. Introductions to the fascicules put the inscriptions in their context and discuss their significance. For monumental inscriptions the annual report of inscriptions in *Britannia* is the first point of reference. The majority of documents discussed here are housed in site and city museums in northern England.

The major exceptions are:

(i) Ink writing tablets from Vindolanda and Carlisle
The tablets from Vindolanda and Carlisle are undoubtedly the most important documents for study of this topic. The Vindolanda examples excavated up to 1994 have been published (Bowman and Thomas 1983; 1994; 2003).

Volume III publishes tablets excavated in the 1990s and some revised readings of previously published texts. Many tablets are discussed by Anthony Birley (2002; see also Birley 2003; Birley and Blake 2005). The corpus of tablets from Carlisle has been published by Roger Tomlin (1998).

(ii) Stamps on pottery: samian and coarsewares
The key resource is the Leeds index compiled by Brian Hartley and Brenda Dickinson (Brock and Fulford 2005). For the study of the Romano-British coarsewares which bear stamps (Tyers 1996).

(iii) Amphora stamps
Amphora stamps are not published in *RIB* II. Callender's (1965) survey of amphora stamps in Britain has been updated (Funari 1996; Funari and Carreras Monfort 1998; see also Marlière and Torres Costa 2005 for Vindolanda).

(iv) Other writing tablets with no traces or only illegible traces of writing
Tablets on which no traces of writing survive are not published in these corpora. The most significance group of these are stylus tablets from Vindolanda (Birley et al. 1993). There are also small numbers of stylus tablets from other sites (see Pearce 2004 for references). Digital imaging analysis may provide significant breakthroughs in reading stylus texts on which little can currently be read (Bowman and Tomlin 2005; Terras 2006).

Research on trade and exchange

Commodities and supply routes
Textual evidence gives a view of the commodities arriving in the frontier area. The evidence of the Vindolanda (and to a lesser extent Carlisle) tablets is crucial, since many documents are concerned with the movement of commodities, sometimes with quantitative information. Most frequently mentioned are foodstuffs, clothing, footwear and vehicle parts (Bowman 2004; Whittaker 2002), but other items include vessels, lanterns, horse and hunting gear and medicines (?) (*Tab. Vindol.* II. 194; III 590; 591; 593; 596; 641). It is not always possible to identify the precise character of an item or commodities recorded (Pearce 2002; van Driel-Murray 2001). *Dipinti* (painted inscriptions) and *graffiti* on amphorae record the presence of wine (?) (RIB II.8.2503.4), fish sauce (*Britannia* 33 (2002), No. 7, 361), olives (*Britannia* 34 (2003), No. 36, 377), fruit (Tomlin 1992, *Britannia* 22 (1991), no. 28, 301) and, perhaps, coriander (*RIB* II.8.2503.1).

The Vindolanda tablets occasionally indicate the origin of goods (e.g. *Tab. Vindol.* III 588). However the stamps on amphorae and pottery provide a much larger body of evidence for the sources of commodities as well as the means by which these have come to the frontier. For example Carreras Monfort and Funari (1998) have demonstrated the differences in the producers / production areas in Baetica from which olive oil was supplied to Hadrian's Wall, Wales and southern England and the similarities in sources for the Hadrian's Wall and Rhineland garrisons. The distribution of stamps on coarse pottery from various production centres illuminates the orientation of some distribution patterns on the frontiers (for a recent summary see Tyers 1996: 116-35). Samian stamps are a key tool for the history of the frontier garrisons (Hartley 1972), but the emphasis in their study continues to be chronological (e.g. Dickinson, in Wilmott 1997: 256-257). The more limited evidence from other artefacts also has potential for shedding further light on supply networks.

Textual evidence is important for understanding military production of food and commodities. The Vindolanda and Carlisle tablets reveal individuals at the garrisons involved in food production, for example pig- and cowmen (*Tab. Vindol.* II 180), hunters (*Tab. Vindol.* III 615; RIB 1905), brewers (*Tab. Vindol.* II 182.14) and butchers (?) (*Tab. Vindol.* III 590). Braciarii (*Tab. Vindol.* III 646; *Britannia* 19 (1988), 496-498, no. 32), might be maltsters or grain dealers. The writing tablets also reveal the other building and artisan skills (e.g. *Tab. Vindol.* II 155, 160) and the abundant references to 'spare parts', for example for shoe-making.

Traders and transport
Textual evidence gives insights into military supply, although few individuals are explicitly labelled as the traders and contractors who might be anticipated as being involved with army supply (see Whittaker 2002). Rare exceptions aside (e.g. *RIB* 1065; 2059), we can only guess at such an identification, for example where a non-British origin can be detected from a stated *origo* or, less securely, by a name and lack of military rank. At Vindolanda in some cases circumstantial evidence suggests that individuals acts as *negotiatores* (e.g. *Tab. Vindol.* II. 180, 343, 344). Some tablets appear to indicate the involvement of members of the imperial household in military supply (*Tab. Vindol.* III.645; Bowman 2006: 83-84). A re-reading of *Tab. Vindol.* II.255 suggests that the writer may be an *annonarius*, rendered by Tomlin (1996b) as 'commissariat officer'.

Several documents record the presence and activity on the frontier of the *beneficiarii consulares* who seem to have played a significant role in the organisation of military supply. Their attestations in Britain, both on the frontier and elsewhere are discussed by Nelis-Clément (2000). At York (e.g. Lucius Viducius Placidus, *Britannia* 8 (1977), no. 18, 430-1), London (*Britannia* 34 (2003), no. 5, 364-5) and in continental estuaries and ports the individuals who designate themselves as *negotiatores* and other types of merchant may have a connection to trade with the frontier (Hassall 1978).

The Vindolanda tablets provide evidence for transport of men and material to the frontier and the agents responsible (see Breeze 2000). There are references to road vehicles of different names (e.g. *Tab. Vindol.* III 597, 598, 600), and to the variable condition of the roads (*Tab. Vindol.* II 343). One document suggests the use of requisitioned transport from the native population (*Tab. Vindol.* III 649) and also refers to fees for the carriage of goods.

The nature of exchange
The documentary evidence has potential for shedding light on the processes of commodity exchange. Individuals and posts referred to in the Vindolanda tablets and elsewhere suggest the existence of tax officials (Bowman 2006: 78-

79), including possible reference to local recruitment for the army (*Tab. Vindol.* III 594) and to corvée labour (*Tab. Vindol.* III 649). There is also evidence for the large-scale purchase of supplies, seemingly through the agency of middlemen (*Tab. Vindol.* II 343). A single document from Carlisle (*Tab. Luguval.* 1) records what seems to be the regular disbursements of cereals for a unit, in this case a *turma* of a cavalry cohort. Most commonly attested in the tablets are small-scale distributions to individuals of varying rank over several days or months (e.g. *Tab. Vindol.* II 180, 183, 186). There are also individual purchases by or between soldiers (*Tab. Vindol.* II. 181, 184, 310, 346) and slaves (*Tab. Vindol.* II 301). Many of these transactions involve money, shedding significant light on the monetization of the military economy. The many sums mentioned in the Vindolanda tablets comprise the only price data from Roman Britain (see Bowman 2006: table 1, for the most recent list).

Gift-giving appears to be a major exchange mechanism. *Tab. Vindol.* II 233, a request for hunting nets, appears to solicit a gift, *Tab. Vindol.* II 299 suggests receipt of a present of oysters. Gift-giving can also be seen in texts on artefacts, for example the dedication to Aemilia, the recipient of a gold ring found at Corbridge (*RIB* II.3.2422.1). The hospitality that high-ranking officers offer to their peers and seniors (e.g. *Tab. Vindol.* II 291; III. 581) should also be considered in the context of gift exchange, and sometimes too the sending and receipt of correspondence.

The use of documents
Although they have yet to be identified among the surviving documents, it is clear from other references that documents could serve as legal instruments in certain transactions, for example the *chirographum*, if used in its sense of 'bond' (e.g. *Tab. Vindol.* III. 647). The use of documents in commercial transactions in the Vindolanda tablets is discussed by Bowman (2006: 82-83) and the wider evidence for the operation of Roman law by Peachin (1999).

Some of the documents discussed above relate to the production of commodities at some distance (e.g. stamps on samian pottery or amphorae). The production, transport, disbursement, consumption and monitoring of resources seems to have involved the creation of documents at every stage. This is attested in the variety of documents surviving on the frontier. The production of artefacts is illustrated by the graffiti and brands surviving on barrels (e.g. Birley et al. 2003; Marlière and Torres Costa 2005), or by stamps of auxiliary units on bricks and tiles. Lead seals attached to goods in transport are illustrated by examples bearing unit names from South Shields (*RIB* II.1.2411.1-15), and Papcastle (*Britannia* 35 (2005), nos. 22-27, 487-489). Lead tags or labels (*RIB* II.1.2410, *Britannia* 20 (1989), no. 14, 334) also indicate the names of unit, as well as price and quantity. The movement of goods in northern Britain and beyond was accompanied and managed by the sending of letters along the same routes (e.g. *Tab. Vindol.* II 310; 343).

The evidence suggests that the military commodity consumption was closely monitored. In many cases the purpose of a list is not always certain. In some it is to list items disbursed, in others to record those consumed, for example poultry eaten over two years in the *praetorium* at Vindolanda (*Tab. Vindol.* III. 581) or to document missing items (*Tab. Luguval.* 16; Tomlin 1999). The marking of weights and volumes on jars presumably relates either to disbursement or inventorization of their contents. Property was sometimes marked with the name of an individual or unit. Dr 20 olive oil amphorae have been found at Vindolanda with graffiti referring to individuals and units who are also mentioned in the writing tablets (*Britannia* 34 (2003), no. 37, 377; *Britannia* 36 (2005), nos. 68 and 70, 495). Occasionally inscriptions of this type assumed a more monumental character. The best example is perhaps the 'Carvoran *modius*', bearing the (erased) name of the emperor Domitian (*RIB* II.2.2415.56).

Fauna
S Stallibrass

Faunal aspects can be divided into primary and secondary resources and into indigenous and exotic fauna. It is important to note the almost complete lack of animal bones from any rural sites in the entire Wall zone. The discussion below has to concentrate on military sites (particularly forts) and their associated urban settlements and *vici*. Most of the animals exploited in the area during the Romano-British period were domestic mammals: cattle, sheep, pigs and a few goats, chickens, horses and dogs. All of these had been basic livestock in the later Iron Age throughout the region. The arrival and establishment of the military required organised production and procurement of large quantities of animal resources, both primary and secondary, and it is still debated to what extent these were produced in the Wall zone and to what extent they were moved into the 'consumption' zone. Nearly all excavations of sites in the area have failed to use mass sieving procedures and so the faunal collections are all heavily biased towards the recovery of larger animals, and cattle bones, typically form 60-70% or more of the total numbers of identified fragments of cattle, sheep and pigs.

Meat production

Butchery marks and fragmentation patterns indicate that these three domestic species of livestock were butchered for food. Even if cattle were not the most common species deposited at the sites, their large carcase size still means that more than 50% of the meat represented by the bones of cattle, sheep and pigs came from cattle. The lack of butchery marks on all but a very few bones of horse or dog throughout the region together with their frequent recovery as partial or complete burials indicates that the flesh of horses and dogs was very seldom eaten. The ages at death, however, indicate that many of the animals that were butchered and eaten were not raised primarily for food. Typically, the age at death of the sheep does indicate that sheep were raised for consumption by the army, since most of them were killed in their second year. We do not have any complementary evidence for what remained at the rural production sites, but it can be predicted that more animals must have been kept to a mature age, in order for the flocks to remain viable. In addition, clips of fleece can be obtained from live sheep year after year, and the young sheep slaughtered to feed the army would only have produced one clip before they died. If sheep were being kept for wool production, or for milk production then most of these sheep presumably stayed at the production sites even after death.

Unlike cattle and sheep, pigs have few uses as live animals other than breeding, and their prolific breeding rate permits a high cull of young animals for meat. The pig remains at military and military-related sites are mostly from immature animals. Although this type of culling is sustainable, it can still be predicted that mature sows (and a few mature boars) will have remained at the production sites. There is a possibility that some pigs were raised in more urban settlements such as *vici*. They can be kept in backyards or on small plots of land and, being omnivorous, can be fed scraps from industrial and domestic processes. Domestic fowl may have been kept for eggs as well as for their meat and often played a role in sacrifices and special meals. We have no idea whether or not the military raised their own hens, or whether they acquired them from urban or rural settlements. They were killed at various ages indicating that at least some of them were slaughtered whilst relatively young and tender. The ages at death of the cattle tell a complex story. At Carlisle, the ages at death of the cattle from the fort (Annetwell Street) tended to group into two categories: a young, meaty age and an older group probably used for many other purposes before they finally died and were eaten. In Carlisle's civilian settlement in The Lanes, the bones nearly all came from the older group, with few meaty animals represented. Congenital traits and metrical analyses strongly suggest that the animals came from the same genetic stock, presumably raised locally in the environs of the site since it seems unlikely that people living in a civilian area of smallholdings would be able to import their cattle from elsewhere. Interestingly, the much smaller collection analysed at Birdoswald indicated that even the inhabitants of the fort were consuming aged local cattle carcases (i.e. the soldiers did not have access to prime meaty animals) (Stallibrass, 2000a).

The geographical area where the livestock were produced is not yet known, but PhD research is proposed at Liverpool to investigate the possibility of long distance transport of cattle through Carlisle using isotope analyses. Livestock such as cattle and sheep are quite easy to drove (i.e. 'transport' themselves whilst alive), and this is logistically much easier than transporting perishable carcases long distances. Tom Lord (*pers. comm.*) has suggested that the Craven area of North Yorkshire may have had large-scale livestock production linked to the military network, similar to the large land holdings of various abbey estates in the area during the medieval period. Several people have suggested that livestock and agricultural products may have been 'exchanged' between rural sites and the military as tax in lieu of monetary payments.

Transport

Horses played a major role for the military in terms of fighting method (cavalry, officers and communications) as well as transport of humans and goods. They do not appear to have been utilised as plough animals. Horses may have been brought in by troops or bred locally and crossbreeds of imported and indigenous horses should be looked for. Johnstone's research into equids indicates that some mules may have been utilised in Roman Britain (Johnstone, forthcoming). Many existing collections of animal bones from military sites in the Hadrian's Wall zone should be re-examined to look for mules and donkeys now that her metrical analyses have been developed to distinguish between asses, horses and crossbreeds. Mules, being sterile, have to be created 'afresh' for each individual. Donkeys do not thrive in cool damp climates although the slighter warmer climate in the Roman period may have permitted the husbandry of slightly more donkeys in northern England than are found there today. If large numbers of mule bones are found in the Hadrian's Wall area, then it may be an indication of repeated importation of livestock from more southerly parts of Britain or the Continent.

There is quite a lot of evidence from pathological alterations to cattle bones at several sites along Hadrian's Wall that these animals were utilised for heavy traction (e.g. carts and ploughs) (see Stallibrass 1991 for photographs of examples from Annetwell Street fort, Carlisle).

Exotic imports

There is some evidence that cattle of a different type (i.e. size and shape) were introduced to Britain during the Roman period. Generally, larger animals appeared in the vicinity of Rome first, spreading out to join the indigenous types within the empire, reaching the furthermost areas (such as northern Britain) latest and in the smallest numbers. Hadrian's Wall is a good example of this, with only a few bones of these larger cattle being found, generally quite late and only in small quantities. The numbers are smallest and the dating is at its latest in the western half of the Wall zone. It seems clear that these larger cattle were not a 'must have' in north-western Britain and their eventual uptake seems to coincide with a time when pottery from Yorkshire became more common import in the region (Stallibrass 2000a, using pottery data from Evans 2000). The purpose of these animals is not known. Being larger they may have been useful as draught animals. Alternatively, they may have had status as 'Roman' types for ceremonies or for personal or administrative kudos and visual impact.

A few bones have been found of animal species that were probably introduced, some of which may have been able to establish small breeding populations from time to time. Current knowledge is very restricted and requires an overview, although a useful synthesis is currently in prep for a range of British species that have been introduced or extirpated (Sykes and O'Connor, in prep). Riley is collating evidence for black rat (*Rattus rattus*) which has been recovered from South Shields, a site that also produced bones of edible dormouse (*Glis glis*). Both species prefer warmer climates to twenty-first century Britain; it is not clear whether their bones may derive from individuals who died without breeding, or whether local indigenous viable populations were established. The dormouse was considered an edible delicacy and was almost certainly imported deliberately, whilst the black rat was probably an inadvertent introduction. Other 'stowaways' that must have entered Britain via boats across a sea include grain beetles and other pests. All of these exotic species are small, and their remains are usually only found when suitable recovery and sampling techniques are employed: hence the recovery from a well at South Shields. Their actual distribution is not known. Other potential imports of animals include macaques, bones of which have been found at a handful of sites in Roman Britain, though not yet from any along Hadrian's Wall. Similarly, it is not at all clear whether bears were still alive in sufficient quantities to be hunted successfully in Britain during the Roman period, or if their bones derive from animals imported from other parts of the empire for entertainment and sport (or as skins for ceremonial clothing etc).

Other animal resources include fish and processed fish sauces, but evidence for these from sites along Hadrian's Wall is restricted by the poor history of fish bone recovery and the paucity of residue analyses of potential commodities containers. Similarly, although marine shellfish may have been food resources at some sites, their remains have seldom been recovered or analysed in any systematic manner. It is quite possible that these resources were recovered locally from the Solway or the Tyne estuaries, but equally they may have been imported from estuaries further south in Britain or elsewhere. They are easy to recover from excavations and would repay serious study. Marine, coastal and estuarine resources need consideration with regard to source areas, potential transport systems and markets. For instance, the common occurrence within the Hadrian's Wall zone of Black Burnished Ware manufactured in Dorset begs the question of whether it was the pottery itself that was the main commodity or its contents. Since the pottery production area was also a coastal salt producing area, perhaps the main item for sale or exchange was potted shrimps.

Exports

Despite the oft-quoted exports of hunting dogs from Britain prior to the successful military invasion, we do not have any information regarding the possibility that animals or their products were exported from Britain during the military occupation. Hadrian's Wall was a frontier zone for much of its existence, and may have served as an exchange centre for resources from both inside and beyond the controlled zone. A pine marten (Martes martes) skull with skinning marks around its muzzle from Carlisle may indicate that some indigenous fauna were exploited for home consumption or exchange.

Processed products

Dead animals provided a wide range of processed products including preserved meat. Deposits of processed cattle scapula at Carlisle indicate that mass production of filleted meat was undertaken at least upon occasion in some of the forts on Hadrian's Wall. Meat can be preserved by smoking, drying, pickling and salting. There is plenty of evidence for the extraction and processing of salt on an industrial scale at several sites in Cheshire (e.g. Nantwich and Middlewich) and artefactual evidence links these production sites with the military system (see Nevell and Fielding 2005). What is less clear is where the salt was used (i.e. at the production site or after shipment elsewhere). One of the salt production sites (Kingsley Fields, Nantwich) had large tanks that may have been used for tanning hides. Much more work is required to investigate processing and manufacturing sites, particularly those in the industrial hinterland that probably served the Wall (Cheshire, Lancashire and Yorkshire and, at times, south-west Scotland). Whilst the nature of the products of some of these industrial sites is clear, many other sites simply have evidence for processes utilising heat and water (e.g. Walton le Dale). These sites were probably processing organic resources such as animals and plants. Similar traces of industrial activities have been found at various military sites, particularly fort annexes such as Castle Street in Carlisle. Cattle hides and leather items were important materials for the Roman army as well (presumably) as for the indigenous population. Again, there needs to be more synthetic treatment of evidence for production (e.g. skinning marks on cattle footbones) and processing sites (e.g. waterproof tanks with botanical and chemical residues of tanning materials or parasites likely to have lived in animal hides) (see Halland Kenward 2003, Serjeantson 1989 and Stallibrass (2000b).

Carol van Driel Murray (1990) has investigated the use of hides for military tents and demonstrated that these preferentially used goat hides, which are much lighter than the thicker hides of cattle. Her estimates that approximately 70 goat hides were required to make each eight-man tent indicates the scale of hide processing that was required to equip the military. Like donkeys, goats prefer a warmer, drier climate to that enjoyed in Britain, and examination of animal bones from Romano-British sites shows that goats were kept in very small numbers, nowhere near the quantities required to provide the military. This suggests that soldiers' tents were imported, probably fully fabricated, from warmer parts of the empire, such as southern Gaul or Spain. Repairs may have been made with any pieces of leather to hand, although damaged tents may have been curated to provide suitable patching material. Leather pieces were found in the ditch at Ribchester, associated with large quantities of other materials that had been curated prior to the slighting of the fort, presumably when the garrison was moved on (Buxton and Howard-Davis, 2000)

Other textiles made from animal fibres included wool. Wild (2002) points out that the statutory requirements for each soldier to be issued with new clothing and bedding each year, even if only implemented every two years, would require about 202,000 - 270,000 fleeces for a garrison of 22,500 men and take about 400,000 person weeks of time to weave. Even allowing for considerable error in these approximate estimates, the scale of production is clearly industrial, and makes no allowance for the fleeces and weaving time required for non-military personnel's clothing and blankets. We need to create a methodology to investigate where and on what scale this production took place, both in the hinterland of Hadrian's Wall and throughout the empire. Similar investigations are required for textiles made from plant fibres such as flax (linen), and for coverings and containers made from straw, basket fibres etc as well as the more obvious basketry made from larger plant resources such as reeds and withies.

Impact on local societies

Scale of production, processing and manufacture of natural resources were clearly huge and more guesstimates are needed to try to get a handle on the quantities required both in terms of raw materials, hectares of land and time to process and transport. Similarly, more is required to investigate the possibility of shipments of bulk quantities by water, whether across seas, along coasts, or up rivers (cf. Allen and Fulford 1999) particularly for the western side of Britain, along the coasts of Cumbria and south-west Scotland to Carlisle.

Trade and Import - The Evidence from Plant Remains

J Huntley

The presence of exotic plant taxa on a site can be assumed to represent imports although with the proviso that some of the herbs, especially, could have been grown as pot herbs on windowsills. This could certainly include coriander and dill, both of which are commonly recorded from military sites along the Wall as well as the single seed of kalange (*Nigella sativa*) found at Annetwell St. Carlisle (Huntley, 1989b). These could have been imported as dried seed. The large numbers of seeds from the opium poppy are considered to represent an import and might well reflect their use as a condiment. Most of the exotics recovered, however, are Mediterranean fruits such as grapes, olives and figs and it is assumed that these were brought in as dried fruit, perhaps even in the barrels of silver fir whose remains are also common. The barrels can be re-used as linings of latrines, as at Carlisle, and possibly as writing tablets given that a barrel stave is approximately the same size as a typical tablet and would easily be split longitudinally into two or more such tablets.

In most cases these remains are preserved through water-logging. The distribution of these taxa along the Wall deserves further attention in the future. They are abundant in most sites studied at Carlisle, for example Busby (1988), Huntley (1989a; 1989b; 1991; 1992a; 1992b). Birdoswald, on the other hand, only produced one fig pip in one of the several waterlogged ditches (Huntley, 1997). Further east, Vindolanda, Steel Gap and Housesteads are like Birdoswald despite, in the case of Vindolanda, superb preservation and large numbers of samples being studied (Huntley, 1998a; 2003). To the east of the Pennine watershed the few forts studied have only produced charred plant remains - notably Newcastle (Huntley & Daniell, 2000) and Wallsend (Huntley, 1998b) although few were recovered from the latter.

It is therefore clear that we have a surprisingly restricted knowledge of food imports from forts along the Wall and, in fact, no evidence from the associated civilian settlements. Vindolanda is especially intriguing given the small find and bone evidence for high status and it has to be assumed, for the moment, that food debris and faecal material were disposed of somewhere not yet excavated. One research aim here for the future is to investigate the latrines on the north side of the fort where it is hoped they will not be as clean as those in the *praetorium* (Huntley, 1998a). Any opportunity to study waterlogged remains should not be missed and work on the *vici*/ civilian settlements is essential.

Another question that could be addressed is the one of the source of silver fir used extensively in barrels. This is a species of central Europe concentrated around the Alps and eastwards (Jalas & Suominen, 1972). Recent work on tree ring patterns of fir in Germany suggests a different response of trees from north and west of the Alps and there is, therefore the potential to look at ring patterns from barrel staves here on the Wall to see if they can be matched to one of the German chronologies. There seems to have been two routes for the timber to reach at least The Netherlands - one from the Jura, France and one from southern Germany along the Rhine (Sibylle Bauer, *pers com.*) - either of which could have continued through to Britain.

Linking to timber supply and craft is the use of various species in objects recovered from excavations. For example, the sycamore (*Acer pseudoplatanus*) identified by Blackburn from Vindolanda (Blackburn, 1970), if correct, has to mean an import since the species was not introduced for growing in Britain until the seventeenth century. The box (*Buxus sempervirens*) used in several small wooden objects is also likely to have been brought north from at least southern Britain and, more likely, from southern Europe especially Iberia or France where growth of this tall shrub produces much better quality wood (Meusel, 1978). Other species used in crafts include yew (*Taxus baccata*) but this was probably from locally sourced material (Huntley, 2000).

A broad definition of trade could include the acquisition of cereals and other large-scale food commodities from elsewhere within the region. Whether cereals were specifically traded, implying mutual satisfaction, or commandeered is not possible to determine from the plant remains, if at all.

The Roman army had a large demand for cereals given the often quoted requirement of 3 pounds (ca 1.5kg) of grain per man per day (Davies, 1971). Although the major supply granaries at South Shields were no doubt storing grain for distribution to other forts along and behind the Wall it is quite possible that some of this was local produce. Spelt wheat is frequently encountered in later prehistoric to Romano-British sites throughout the east of the Wall region (van der Veen, 1992) and is abundant in the few granaries studied in this region. Bread wheat (*Triticum aestivum*) is also abundant at South Shields, although absent elsewhere, and was perhaps brought in from further afield (van der Veen, 1988) as it is only ever found in very low numbers on native sites and thus interpreted as a weed amongst other crops. As an aside, it is interesting to see that all spelt recovered from granaries is in the form of grain and not spikelets which need further processing, allegedly on a daily basis by the soldiers, to extract the usable grain. If spelt was being stored in spikelets this would be obvious from the remains surviving a fire in the granaries. Thus, if soldiers are processing their own supplies it could imply that this was locally produced and acquired on a smaller-scale basis rather than them relying upon logistics and supply from granaries.

Using yields from modern spelt grown under subsistence-type conditions the author calculated that only about 300 hectares of cereal field would be required to feed a garrison of 500 each year. Thus the grain demand for a garrison of that size at Carlisle, or elsewhere in the lowlands, could be satisfied locally from an area of only about 20km radius of the fort assuming 25% of that land was cultivated. It may not be as feasible in the upland stretches as cereal yields may have been considerably lower, although it must be remembered that evidence from invertebrates (Kenward, 2000) suggests that the climate of the Wall during Roman times was more like that of Kent today. The presence of cereal-type pollen from various natural deposits along the Wall also shows that local cultivation was being undertaken, for discussion of this see Huntley (1999). Pollen work to address the effect that the Romans had upon the landscape has long been a favourite subject and is discussed further in the Landscape and Environment section of this framework. The question of whether cereals, especially spelt, were being cultivated locally has also been investigated through trace element analyses - minute amounts of specific chemical elements in the grains that might be associated with specific soil types, geology and hence region (Langston, 1994). Unfortunately this study produced no clear-cut conclusions. The presence of exotic weed seeds likewise could suggest cultivation further afield but a) their absence confirms nothing and b) most of the crops represented on fort sites at least are fully processed grain - after all why transport straw and weed "rubbish" further than necessary? Therefore the question of supply of cereals especially remains unanswered although it is clear that at least some were produced locally.

Legumes are referred to frequently in the classical literature, see for example Varro and Cato (Hooper, 1935) but rarely occur in the archaeological record. Under waterlogged conditions they rapidly rot and it is only when charred that they tend to survive. Whilst the typical peas (*Pisum sativum*) and Celtic bean (*Vicia faba*) may well have been a local produce the rare occurrence of lentils (*Lens culinaris*) from Carlisle presents another example of an exotic trade.

The writing tablets mentioned above in terms of silver fir are, clearly, an excellent source of information about trade. Pepper is recorded from Vindolanda (tablet 184) but has yet to be recovered archaeologically - perhaps imports were already ground or perhaps simply too valuable to dispose of/lose and, in any case, would have been fragmented after use and excretion. Other 'shopping lists' from the tablets refer to '*bracis*' which is generally translated as emmer, a species rarely recorded from any Roman site within Britain and it has to be considered whether *bracis* is in fact, spelt - another glume wheat after all.

We have not discussed trade of structural timber, good supplies of which were essential for building forts (Hanson & Macinnes, 1980). There is the presumption of local supply again but whether adequate supplies of suitably sized timber remained available throughout the 3-4 centuries of construction across the whole of the Wall is unknown. Large timbers survive and are regularly used in attempts at dating buildings but there is little other use of the ring widths - for example in climate reconstruction or whether statistics of cross-matching with master chronologies from different regions might suggest different supply areas. Especially where dating fails there might be other explanations. The smaller roundwood used in wattling, hurdles and construction of more ephemeral walls probably was locally obtained although even here, at Carlisle there are suggestions of different areas being exploited at different times - presumably as a result of sources being used up and the need to move elsewhere (Huntley, 1987, 1989c).

In summary then, plant foodstuffs and supplies were, no doubt being imported and traded across the Wall frontier, certainly within the forts and probably in the civilian settlements lying outside the forts although no archaeobotanical evidence has been sought from these as yet. Many of the imported foods are from the Mediterranean and probably reflect the origins of the garrisons, especially at Carlisle, at that time. Their recovery is predominantly from well preserved, anoxic, organic deposits and thus inevitably patchy across the Wall. Ironically we know less of the foodstuffs on the eastern side of the country through lack of waterlogged preservation although we know a reasonable amount about native crop husbandry from charred assemblages here. To the west this is in reverse, we have minimal evidence for charred assemblages but abundant waterlogged. Any opportunity to address this inconsistency should be taken. Where there is good survival of faecal material every effort should be made for thorough investigation - this is material that very obviously relates to what was eaten. It can also preserve epidermal fragments - the skins and leaves of plants - and this would help to determine an aspect of diet frequently under-recorded although probably mostly relates to locally produced greenstuffs.

8. Life and Society
Co-ordinated by R Hingley and L Allason-Jones

Overview
L Allason-Jones

The other sections of this publication assess the current level of knowledge of the physical remains of Hadrian's Wall, both its buildings and its surviving material culture. A considerable body of evidence, however, has recently been amassed, mostly through the re-assessment of museum collections, which is beginning to shed light on the lives of the people who inhabited the Military Zone.

It is through epigraphy that we are able, for the first time in Britain's history, to name individual people, and Hadrian's Wall is particularly rich in named inscriptions. As a result, scholars have become increasingly aware that the population of the frontier region was not just made up of serving military personnel. There is evidence for the families of serving soldiers, enough evidence in fact to indicate that the law banning soldiers from marrying, repealed by Septimius Severus in AD 197, had not been strictly adhered to on the frontier (Roxan 1989; Allason-Jones 1999; Allason-Jones 2003). Exactly where the ordinary soldiers' wives, such as Pusinna (*RIB* 1667) and Aurelia Aia (*RIB* 1828), lived, both before and after 197, is still not clear, since the suggestion that the 'chalets', which replaced the more conventional barrack blocks in several forts on the Wall in the third century, provided married quarters was dismissed, following the evidence from Housesteads (Allason-Jones 2006, 52-54). The accommodation of commanding officers' wives has never been in doubt, but the theory that the centurion's wives lived with their husbands in the centurion's quarters at the end of each barrack block needs more confirmatory evidence (Allason-Jones 1999, 44).

Wives were not the only dependants accompanying soldiers to the frontier. Lurio, a German serving at Chesters, had his wife, sister and son with him (*RIB* 1483) and there is no evidence that they were all squeezed into his *contuberum* with him and his colleagues, despite the analogy offered by Dutch Indonesia in the nineteenth century (van Driel-Murray 1995). It is currently presumed that such families, as well as the mothers and sisters of soldiers who are known to have been in the area, such as Aurelia Lupula at Risingham (*RIB* 1250) and Vacia at Great Chesters (*RIB* 1742), lived in the military *vici* but how they spent their time and how they earned their keep requires much more research. Auxiliaries, in particular, were paid a reasonable salary for one man to live on but hardly enough for him to support a family, so dependents would have had to earn a living. The numbers of dependents now attested alters the popular image of a frontier dominated by adult men with only a few 'camp followers' to provide female interest and only the children of the commanding officers to lower the age ratio.

Some work has been done elsewhere in the empire regarding the legal status of the wives and children of serving soldiers, mostly based on the law codes and Egyptian papyri (Gardner 1986, 34; Riccobono, 1940-3, 3.5; 3.19); however, the practice of conscripting the sons of veterans, not to mention the law that stated that a marriage was considered dissolved if the husband later joined the army, which will have affected the families of the *numerus Hnaudifridi* at Housesteads and those of the Tigris bargemen at South Shields, will have created a very confused legal situation in the Military Zone.

137. Cut-down remains of the tombstone of Dagvalda, soldier in the First Cohort of Pannonians. Set up by his wife Pusinna and found reused in Milecastle 42.

There is evidence that many soldiers settled in the military *vici* of the last fort they served in when they retired, returned to a favourite posting or moved to a nearby town; few seem to have returned to their country of origin. It is known from epigraphic evidence from other frontiers that many veterans set themselves up in business but there is little evidence from Hadrian's Wall to clarify whether veterans in the area survived on their savings or retirement bonuses or if they became businessmen. The evidence of manufacturing and retail outlets outside many forts indicates the frontier zone to have been a hive of industry but it is not always clear what was being made and sold, nor who was involved in the production and trade. The quantity of imported artefacts and foodstuffs must imply a complicated system of supply and demand; some of the Vindolanda tablets reveal that the army was acquiring a wide range of commodities but the role of civilian middlemen still remains obscure.

From inscriptions we can deduce that the ordinary soldiers had a range of ranks and military duties, such as *cornicularius* (*RIB* 1742), *medicus ordinarius* (*RIB* 1618), *librarius* (*RIB* 1134), and their time was not solely taken up with 'slaughtering a band of Corionototae' (*RIB* 1142). Considerable time appears to have been dedicated to building work; firstly the Stanegate forts had to be built, then the Wall forts, then the latter may have been decommissioned and then brought back into service before much of the Wall curtain was dismantled and re-erected under Septimius Severus, as was shown by Crow's excavations in the Central Sector. In between these major building programmes, individual sites and buildings were repaired or completely rebuilt (see, for example, *RIB* 1151, 1234, 1912). The Vindolanda writing tablets have also revealed that much military time was spent in bureaucracy, organizing and paying for supplies, ensuring discipline was maintained and that individual soldiers had their leave entitlement, and that their pay was accurately assessed. Despite all this evidence, as well as the evidence from literature and *comparanda* from other provinces, there is still much to learn about how an individual soldier on Hadrian's Wall would spend his day.

The daily lives of the civilian population also remain a mystery. Only two record their work, both of a religious nature: Diodorus, the priestess of Heracles of Tyre at Corbridge (*RIB* 1129) and Julius Maximus the priest at Wallsend (*RIB* 1314), but it may be assumed that there were many other professional clergy in the area. Excavations at Corbridge and Vindolanda have uncovered butchers', mortaria and glass shops but not the names of the owners of these emporia nor any indication whether they and their staff were retired from military life, related to military personnel or purely civilian. It is not even clear whether the potteries and tileries in the area which supplied the forts were manned by the military or by civilian contractors.

The lives of the local farming community still have much to reveal. The geographical limits of the Iron Age tribes in the region remain unclear nor is it known if these tribal boundaries with their associated loyalties and traditions continued into, or even beyond, the Roman period. That there were people who acted as a group - such as the Textoverdi (*RIB* 1695) - is beyond dispute but exactly who these people were and what their status was, is still uncertain. Even the relationship between the Roman occupiers and the Brigantes needs further study if we are to fully understand frontier life and society.

There is a presumption that the local communities were entirely self sufficient and their survival relied on farming; this may not necessarily be true and there is even some debate as to whether the 'native settlements' in Northumberland existed before the Romans arrived in the area. Through the excavations and surveys of Jobey, and the aerial photography of McCord and Gates, the layout of the settlements and their surrounding fields is well known, but how life was lived in these settlements still owes more to ethnographic parallels than to known facts. There is limited evidence for the crops such communities grew and the animals they raised (see **Landscape and Environment**); there is even less information about the relationship between these farmers and their local forts. A study of the small objects of Roman manufacture found on 'native settlement sites' and those of native manufacture found on fort sites in Northumberland suggested that the locals were not particularly interested in Roman material culture but were willing to exploit the marketing opportunities offered by the presence of a large military force (Allason-Jones 1989). The discovery of the Long Horsley coin hoard appears to support this argument (Abdy 2003), but a wider comparison of Roman and native material culture is required before we can be sure of the accuracy of this picture. The Carvoran *modius* may be taken to infer that the locals were expected to pay the corn tax (*annona*) in grain; this can be debated, but the apparent lack of coins on native settlement sites makes an alternative method of payment difficult to identify.

138. The Carvoran *modius*. Chesters Museum

Compared to the large body of information regarding the forts, almost nothing is known about the religious life of the local population. There has been a presumption that if a deity attested to on an altar has a 'Celtic' name then it must be of indigenous origin. However, evidence is beginning to build which suggests that many of these deities were native to other Celtic areas of the Empire, such as the Germanies or Gaul, and were alien to the north Britons. Even the 'Celtic heads' are now believed to be a Roman import; none have been found in a native settlement but their distribution clings to the line of Hadrian's Wall, one being carved into the walls of milecastle 35 (Allason-Jones 1994).

It is particularly interesting to use the epigraphic evidence from the area, coupled with evidence from excavations, to build up a picture of the lives of slaves and freedmen on the frontier. The tombstones indicate that some owners had a good relationship with their slaves; for example, Regina married her owner Barates (*RIB* 1065), but the need for slaves to join burial clubs may suggest that few slaves trusted their owners to accord them the traditional rites on death (*RIB* 1620). The tombstone of Victor, the Moroccan freedman of Numerianus, a trooper of *ala I Asturum* at South Shields, draws our attention to the fact that it was not just the officers who had slaves but ordinary cavalrymen owned servants, who presumably acted as grooms (*RIB* 1064; Spiedel 1989, 239ff). It is not known if these military slaves lived in the attics of the barrack blocks, in special blocks of their own or in the military *vici*.

Victor's tombstone, with its lavish appearance, may also hint that homosexuality was not unknown in the region.

139. Tombstone of Victor, the Moroccan freedman of Numerianus

Victor's birthplace in Morocco also reminds us that there were people from all over the Roman Empire present on the frontier and that they would have brought with them their native religions, traditions, cooking methods and social mores: life on the frontier would have been both cosmopolitan and diverse. Military units are known from Dacia, Gaul, Spain, Africa, Syria and elsewhere, although it is to be questioned whether every soldier serving in an auxiliary unit was born within the boundaries of that unit's original homeland. With the clear evidence of intermarriage between soldiers or veterans with Britons or other ethnic groups, it is unlikely that all the units retained an unbroken link with their homeland. However, the reference to the Sarmatians at Ribchester requiring a liaison officer several generations after they were first deployed in Lancashire may suggest that some units kept themselves to themselves and relied on recruitment from home to maintain numbers. In the third and fourth centuries the introduction of *numeri* may also have altered the pattern of recruitment as well as introducing different ways of life (Southern 1990).

Artefactual evidence confirms that both soldiers and civilians expected to spend some of their time in leisure pursuits. Excavations in the Housesteads military *vicus* in the 1930s uncovered an inn immediately outside the south gate. The discovery of the bodies of a man and a woman concealed in the floor structure of this building shows that life on the frontier could be sordid and dangerous for soldier and civilian alike. Throughout the empire the association of brothel and tavern or brothel and bath house became a tradition but the limited amount of military *vicus* excavation in the area has denied us any picture of this expected side of military life. Fragments of decorated pottery and glass imply that cock-fighting, boxing, horse racing, chariot racing, gladiatorial combat and so on were familiar to frontier dwellers but no sites have been discovered where any of these might have taken place. The large number of gaming boards and gaming counters, on the other hand, assures us that the population was keen on all types of board games, as well as playing dice, knuckle bones, etc.

140. Glass vessel decorated with depictions of gladiatorial combat from Vindolanda

It is very easy to presume that life on the northern frontier of Britain was much like life on the other frontiers of the Roman Empire; however, each frontier was different due to the terrain it ran through, the attitude of its local population, and the reality of the threat from the enemies beyond that frontier. The length of time each frontier was occupied and how many changes it went through during its history will also have affected the daily lives of its inhabitants. Despite the evidence of epigraphy, site excavation, and material culture we have still much to learn about the life of the people of Hadrian's Wall.

The Indigenous Population

R Hingley

We should not imagine that the Roman military forces that occupied the Wall zone formed a homogeneous and coherent whole and it is also inevitable that the indigenous people who lived within these landscapes were highly variable in character; the variable nature of occupying forces and local communities will have affected the ways that areas were incorporated and developed during the period of Roman control (see Mattingly 2004 and 2006 for the context). This brief paper explores the potential social structure and degree of assimilation of indigenous peoples in the Hadrian's Wall zone. It does not address details of the environment or agricultural practices, or the details of available settlement evidence.

Limitations

The main difficulty with addressing the indigenous people relates to the relatively limited work that has been undertaken across southern Scotland and northern England. Along the line of the German *limes*, innovative programmes of excavation have transformed our understanding of the character of society at this time (see

141. Plot of geophysical survey of the rural settlement at East Park, Sedgefield

Bloemers 1989; Haffner and von Schnurbein 1996; Creighton and Wilson eds. 1999; Derks and Roymans 2002; Roymans et al 2007). This work emphasises that the Roman conquest and incorporation of these areas transformed indigenous societies; as a result, research must address both the indigenous peoples and also the incomers. The local societies that developed as a result of the creation of frontier society can now be seen to have varied in character in space and time. Indigenous settlement patterns have often been viewed in a negative light, the backdrop to what is considered the far more important evidence left by Roman military activity (Willis 1999; Frodsham 2000). Despite proposals that we need to address the character of indigenous society in the frontier zone of Britain (Keppie 1989, Hanson and Breeze 1991; Breeze 1996; Hanson 1997; Hingley 2004), relatively little relevant work has been undertaken.

Zones of central Britain?

In a recently article on Roman-period settlement in northern Roman Britain (southern Scotland/Northern England), Hingley (2004) tentatively defined three settlement zones. In north-eastern England (north Yorkshire and south Durham), a pattern of settlement comparable to certain areas of southern Roman Britain is being recognised, with evidence for villas and 'small towns' (the evidence for villas is addressed in Hingley 2004; for the possibility of 'small towns' lacking association with military activity, see the results of the recent Durham County Council/Durham University project at East Park, Sedgefield (*Archaeology County Durham* 4, 34). To the north of this zone of central Britain are the brochs, duns and souterrains of southern Scotland (Hingley 2004, figure 18.1). It is possible that the substantial roundhouses typified by the brochs and duns form an indigenous mode of status display. Across the whole of central Britain a variety of enclosed and open settlements with roundhouses typify the settlement tradition, and artefacts, whether 'Iron Age' or 'Roman', are rare in domestic contexts. In the Hadrian's Wall area such 'native settlements' appear to predominate, while villas and substantial roundhouses are unknown. As a result, the Wall area has sometimes been viewed as characterised by an absence of significant evidence. One view is that the presence of the Roman army in this region prevented the development of an indigenous elite (Higham 1989, 168; Breeze 2002). Hingley has suggested, by contrast, that the Wall could have been placed here because an indigenous elite that could be effectively incorporated into the empire was absent (Hingley 2004, 339, drawing on Groenmann-van Watteringe 1980).

Evidence of absence?

Whether we should see the apparent poverty of settlement in the Hadrian's Wall corridor as a result of opposition, or failure to accommodate, to Rome is unclear. One reason for supposing such opposition is the scarcity of 'Roman' objects (wheel-made pottery, Roman coins, metalwork, etc) on indigenous settlements that have been excavated; another idea is that the characteristic settlements of this area do not become 'Romanized', hence the absence of villas. A dramatic contrast to the British evidence appears to be indicated by the excellent work of archaeologists in the Netherlands, which has indicated the widespread adoption of new forms of pottery, metalwork and even Latin literacy by one local society, the Batavi, just across the Channel (Derks and Roymans 2002; van Driel-Murray 2002). It is notable that such changes are accompanied by only fairly subtle transformations to the forms of rural settlements; indeed a 100 km zone to the rear of the limes has been identified as a non-villa zone. In this area, house forms and settlement types only change gradually, but recent excavations suggest that a comparable general continuity in settlement forms masks considerable changes in the details of the structure of houses through time and the layout of settlement (see the recent work at Tiel-Passewaaij, reviewed in Roymans et al 2007). Members of the Batavi were recruited in large numbers into the Roman auxiliary forces; excavation at Tiel-Passewaaij and elsewhere are now indicating that local communities modified their economies to help to feed the growing military and urban demand for food along the frontier. This evidence can be taken to represent a particular way of 'becoming Roman' for the Batavi (Derks and Roymans 2002), but Hingley has proposed (Hingley 2005, 97-9; forthcoming) that these people were actually exploiting aspects of a broadly-defined Roman culture to assist them to operate in their own terms in an imposed imperial system.

A sustained campaign of excavation on indigenous settlements in central Britain might well produce comparable evidence for the reaction of local people to imperial incorporation. Here there was no strong pre-Roman tradition of the use of pottery (although see Hunter 2007, 287 for some qualifications), so the relative scarcity of 'Roman' pottery on indigenous settlement sites may merely reflect a continuation of the pre-Roman traditions of storing and eating food. The evidence for relatively subtle changes in settlement forms amongst the Batavi may well be paralleled across northern Britain but without further excavation in the Wall zone such a proposal is impossible to assess. In contrast, in North Yorkshire and County Durham rescue excavations are producing evidence for the apparent assimilation of at least some members of the indigenous peoples into provincial society.

Evidence for assimilation?

Although available evidence for an accommodation comparable to that amongst the Batavi is scarce across much of central Britain, the evidence derived from prestige metalwork indicates one promising area for future research. The important research of Fraser Hunter (2007), which builds upon the earlier work of MacGregor (1976), proposes that a common fashion of 'Celtic' metalwork developed across central Britain and that items in this tradition occur on both military and indigenous sites. These items, although they often appear to draw upon pre-Roman 'art' styles only occur across central Britain from the late first century AD and appear to form a reaction or response to Roman control and influence (Hunter 2007, 289). It is possible that the items discussed by Hunter, which mostly appear to indicate high-status display objects (jewellery, weapons, feasting equipment, horse and chariot gear), may have united disparate communities into a relatively common and unified mode of display. This so-called Celtic metalwork might then have operated in a complex way to represent aspects of the identity of people, whether indigenous or incomers, and their relationships to one another across this extensive area. Hunter demonstrates that these items occur on 'Iron Age' (e.g. indigenous) settlements, although they are more common on 'Roman' (i.e. military) sites and in hoards (which might have been military or indigenous; see Hunter 2007, fig. 5). That there was no strong pre-existing tradition of metalwork deposition on settlements across central Britain could indicate that such items were once rather more common in indigenous contexts than the current evidence serves to indicate.

Conclusion

At present, the idea that the indigenous peoples of central Britain may have been at least partially assimilated into the economy and political structure of the empire is relatively difficult to support, but this is probably the result of our traditions of research, which have resulted in a scarcity of recent excavation of non-military sites. Indeed, the increasing discovery of villas in north-eastern England suggests a high degree of assimilation in certain areas. Past research traditions in Britain and on the Continent have tended to emphasise indigenous peoples and Romans as oppositional concepts and such approaches have helped to create a situation in which accounts of assimilation are difficult to support. Recent work in Germany and the Netherlands provides some idea of what we should expect to find in the frontier zone of Roman Britain. Future work should aim to explore the ways in which indigenous communities within the frontier zone were incorporated and marginalized, together with the relationship between the situation across the Hadrian's Wall area and societies in other parts of Britain and across the empire.

Inscriptions and Hadrian's Wall

M W C Hassall

The object of this survey is to present the different ways in which inscriptions on stone, wood, pottery and metal have contributed and continue to contribute to our understanding of Hadrian's Wall. Something shall also be said about the ways in which future discoveries may be expected some day to extend our knowledge. Where appropriate the lines that future work might take have been indicated. It is worth noting that literary documents provide an outline history of Hadrian's Wall, supplemented by coins which provide dates for archaeological contexts. The Vindolanda writing tablets shed considerable light on life on the northern frontier, but nearly all date to the period before the construction of the Wall.

Evidence for the building of Hadrian's Wall

Inscriptions from the milecastle gateways show unequivocally that the structure that we know today as Hadrian's Wall was built during the reign of that emperor and under the direction of the governor Aulus Platorius Nepos (AD 122-125/6), whose arrival in Britain shortly before 17 July 122 is demonstrated by a *diploma*, a certificate of privileges issued to a veteran. Further, the so-called 'centurial stones' found built into the fabric of the Wall demonstrate that the building of the frontier was divided amongst the legions *II Augusta*, *VI Victrix* and *XX Valeria Victrix* and their constituent cohorts and centuries. As a by-product of the discovery of these stones, we have partial rolls of the centurions serving in the three legions during the reign of Hadrian.

Only one fragmentary timber inscription survives from the turf stretch of the Wall (*RIB* 1935), and it will be a matter of extreme chance if any more are discovered.

Two inscriptions found at Benwell and Halton Chesters (*RIB* 1340; 1427) indicate that a major change in plan, the 'fort decision' took place during the governorship of Aulus Platorius Nepos, and others that work continued on the frontier almost until the end of Hadrian's reign in 138.

Finally, inscriptions found on the Vallum indicate that this was created by auxiliary soldiers rather than the legionaries who built the Wall and its forts.

Evidence for the later history of Hadrian's Wall

Epigraphic evidence for the building of the Antonine Wall comes from that frontier rather than the Wall of Hadrian, though inscriptions from the latter may indicate continuing occupation of some forts. A lost inscription (*RIB* 1389) records building work undertaken on the curtain in AD 158 thereby indicating an intention to return to Hadrian's Wall. A second inscription records building work at Birrens, an outpost fort, in the same year (*RIB* 2110). Many inscriptions indicate building work continuing through the second century and well into the third. Some of the later inscriptions are more informative and provide details of the buildings then being erected. They also provide information on the rebuilding of the turf section of Hadrian's Wall in stone.

142. Lost inscription RIB 1389 recording rebuilding of the Wall curtain in AD 158

Two newly discovered diplomas (*RMD* III 184, *RMD* IV, 293) cast light on the British war of 180. They show that the governor Ulpius Marcellus who led the campaign was already in Britain in 178. This solves a local problem as it can now be seen that the altar inscription from Benwell, which mentions Ulpius by name, is dated to the joint reign of Marcus Aurelius and Commodus (plural emperors are mentioned), i.e. before the death of Marcus on 17th March 180, at the very latest (*RIB* 1329).

143. A possible 4th century building inscription from Cawfields recording work done by the Civitas Durotrigum

Fourth-century inscriptions are rare on Hadrian's Wall. It has been suggested that the building inscriptions set up by corvées drafted from the southern *civitates*, eg the *Civitas Catuvellaunorum* (*RIB* 1962), the *Civitas Dumnoniorum* (*RIB* 1843, 1844), the *Civitas Durotrigum Lendiniensis* (*RIB* 1672, 1673) found along the line of the Wall, date to this time.

The Units on the Wall

The present state of knowledge of the units attested at the forts on the Wall and the Cumbrian coast from Wallsend to

Ravenglass is conveniently summarized by Breeze and Dobson (2000, Appendix 2). There are some 23 forts concerned and of these the garrisons of only five are known for certain in the Hadrianic period, though the identity of some others can be postulated. The presence of the *ala Augusta ob virtutem appellate* at Chesters during this period was established following the discovery of an altar there in 1978 (*Britannia* **10** 1979, 346) and it seems reasonable to suppose that future discoveries will provide the names of some of the units in the remaining forts. For the later second century after the abandonment of the Antonine Wall in the 160s when Hadrian's Wall once more became the frontier, seven of the 23 units in garrison are known, while for the third century the figure is 18. This figure can be increased by three if one extrapolates back from the evidence of the *Notitia* which lists the fourth-century units. This seems reasonable since all the *Notitia* units are identical to the third-century units where these are known, with only one exception. To sum up, there are considerable gaps in our knowledge of the army dispositions in the forts of Hadrian's Wall and the Cumbrian coast, especially during the earlier periods, but it is probable that some at least of these will be slowly filled by new discoveries, in particular chance finds, though no dramatic increase in our knowledge is likely.

Lead sealings can be stamped with the names of units, but as they sealed items in transit, they are not as informative about specific units' bases as might be hoped.

Inscriptions also provide information on the officers and soldiers of the Roman army, their ages, origins and careers, their social arrangements and their religious beliefs. Of particular importance is the collection of altars to Jupiter from Maryport dating to the reign of Hadrian. The annual dedications indicate that the average length of service of a commanding officer was three years.

Place Names

Our knowledge of the place-names of the forts along the line of Hadrian's Wall and the Cumbrian coast up to the time of its publication has been conveniently summarized by Breeze and Dobson (2000, Appendix 4). It is based on four types of evidence:

The Rudge Cup, the Amiens Skillet and the newly discovered Ilam Pan, are all vessels inscribed with the names of forts along the line of approximately the western third of the Wall;

The *Notitia Dignitatum* which lists by name units in garrison in the forts, and the names of the forts themselves, from east to west along the line of the Wall and then southwards down the Cumbrian Coast;

The *Ravenna Cosmography* which lists over 300 place names in Britain including some 20 in the area under consideration. The names are listed in geographical 'clusters' which do not always make identification easy;

Inscriptions found at various fort sites. These sometimes provide the name of a unit listed in the *Notitia* and thus enable a name to be assigned to a fort. Alternatively, they may provide direct evidence of a site name. The derivation of the place names of *Arbeia* (South Shields) and *Cilurnum* (Chesters) has recently been debated (Breeze 2001; 2004; Hodgson 2002).

144. The recently discovered Ilam Pan bearing the names of four wall forts

The recent discovery of the Ilam Pan (*Britannia* 35 (2004), No 2) which confirms the name *Congavata* (or similar) for the fort at Drumburgh, and a fragment of a military *diploma* from Ravenglass issued to a veteran in *Cohors I Aelia Classica* (*Britannia* 26 (1995), 389-90) demonstrates the possibility of more such valuable discoveries.

Civilians on the Wall

This is a subject covered by Salway (1965), who made full use of the epigraphic evidence such as tombstones, building inscriptions and religious dedications, sometimes set up corporately such as the dedication to Vulcan made by the villagers at Vindolanda (*vicani Vindolandesses*) (*RIB* 1700) cited above. This and other inscriptions demonstrate that people living in the civil settlements outside forts had self-governing rights.

145. A dedication to the goddess Gallia by Gallic citizens and 'like-minded Britons' from Vindolanda

Salway's study appeared in the same year that *RIB* 1 was published, and a review of the evidence that has accrued in the last forty years, perhaps covering both Hadrian's Wall and the Antonine frontier and including the evidence from the Vindolanda tablets, could appropriately be undertaken after the publication of *RIB* 3, which will cover new epigraphic material discovered during the past forty years.

Cults on the Wall

Inscriptions provide a large body of evidence for deities and religious practices on Hadrian's Wall. There were dedications to the official gods of the Roman pantheon, other Roman and Greek gods, foreign gods and apparently local deities (p. 157-9). Dividing the material in this way is natural, but an inscription recently found at Vindolanda (CA 205, September/October 2006, 4-5), cannot be so neatly categorised. It is a dedication to the Goddess Gallia, by the Gallic citizens (*cives Galli*) - presumably serving in the known third-century garrison, *cohors IV Gallorum*, along with 'like minded Britons' (*concordesque Britanni*), British recruits in their unit. Altars are the main continuing sources of new inscriptions. A general survey of religion in the frontier area of Roman Britain was carried out relatively recently but there is scope for further study (Birley 1986).

Conclusions

From the brief survey given above, it is clear that inscriptions provide unique insights into the way in which Hadrian's Wall was initially constructed and manned, and into its subsequent history, the careers of the officers and soldiers who were based on it, and their religious beliefs. Some of the gaps in our knowledge have also been indicated and these are likely to be filled both by chance finds and by discoveries made as a result of systematic excavation. It is hard to see how a specific programme of excavation or field work could be designed to produce more inscriptions, in the way that planned work at Vindolanda, say, could be designed to recover more writing tablets. The single most important requirement is the publication of the third volume of the Roman Inscriptions of Britain (*RIB* 3), since with this the discoveries made during the last 40 years would be made readily accessible in a standard work of reference. This would facilitate surveys on such topics as military dispositions, religion or the evidence for civilians in the frontier region to be readily updated.

Writing-Tablets

D J P Mason

The Vindolanda writing-tablets - now numbering in excess of 2,000 individual examples - constitute a unique source of information about the Roman Army in the North during the decades immediately preceding the construction of the Wall (Bowman and Thomas 1993; 1994; 1996; A Birley 2002; *http://vindolanda.csad.ox.ac.uk*). Approximately 250 of the tablets are of the wax-filled hollow type (*tabella cerata*) of imported spruce or larch, and largely indecipherable. The majority, however, are of the much rarer 'leaf' type (*sectiles* or *laminae*), mostly of alder or birch, practically unknown before the discoveries at Vindolanda. The largest diptychs are 9 x 20 cm in size and 0.25-3mm in thickness, they were normally scored down the centre to facilitate folding and pierced by tie-holds and v-notches so that they could be tied with thread and sealed. Several leaves could be tied together to form a 'concertina-like' document or small notebook. The writing surface was smoothed and treated with some material to prevent the ink from running.

The tablets include many official documents identifying the unit in residence and, in some cases, those based in other forts. Many are concerned with supplies or inventories of goods. A wide variety of foodstuffs are mentioned including wheat, barley, bread, pork, ham and bacon through to oysters, fish-sauce, eggs, spices and honey. Reference is also made to those other military staples, beer and wine. Raw materials also appear and include *inter alia* timber, lime, clay and lead. Perhaps understandably, items of clothing are prominent and include vests, tunics, boots, sandals, socks and underpants. Blankets and bedspreads are listed along with many utensils such as plates, dishes, bowls, bread-baskets, eggcups and lamps. The transport of supplies is also referred to, with the state of the roads to Catterick being a particular cause for concern. Soldiers' dealings with civilian suppliers are recorded along with the sums from the regimental coffers with which they were entrusted to make purchases. (see 139-42)

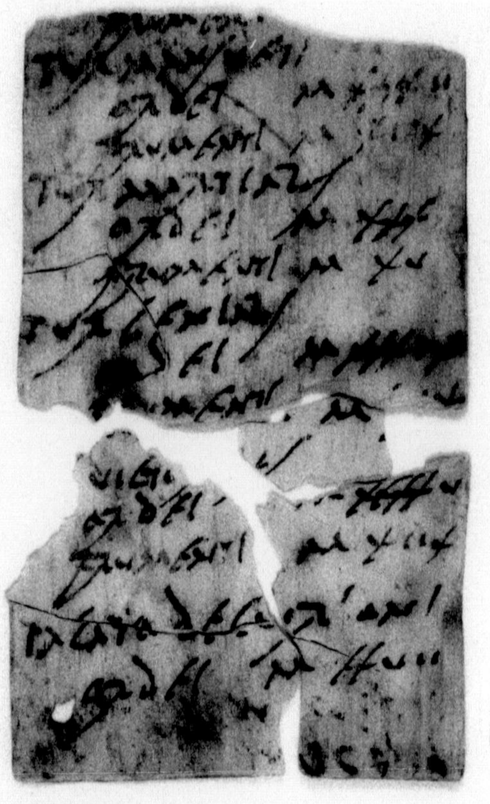

146. Writing tablet from Carlisle

Other military tablets include unit strength reports and give a fascinating insight into the number of soldiers actually present and fit for duty, compared with the theoretical maximum. On the 18th May, of the 752 soldiers in the first cohort of Tungrians only 265 were present at Vindolanda and fit for duty. A further 31 soldiers were unwell, including six wounded. Of the 456 absent, 337 were at *Coria,* while one centurion was as far afield as London. Others were absent engaged in the purchase of supplies.

The tablets have revealed previously unrecorded personal names and shown that the Batavians and Tungrians had a mix of Celtic, Latin and even Greek names. Some record purchases by individual soldiers and others correspondence with friends and relatives. One memorandum detailing the activities of the 'wretched Britons' might give an insight into either the shortcomings of British conscripts or the nature of the armed resistance that the Roman units faced.

Further tablets relate to the commanding officer and his *praetorium* and include correspondence between two commanding officers' wives, Claudia Severa and Sulpicia

147. Statue of Juno Regina from Chesters. Chesters Museum

148. Statue of Victory from Housesteads. Chesters Museum

Lepidina. Most famous is a letter from Severa inviting Lepidina to her birthday celebrations on the 11th September, and hoping that she will 'make the day more enjoyable for me by your arrival'. Other surviving letters from the archive of Flavius Cerialis, Lepidina's husband, include one written in October in which he promises to 'provide some goods...by means of which we may endure the storms even if they are troublesome'. Further concerns include lists of foodstuffs and expenses associated with entertaining the prefect's guests.

Carlisle has also produced examples of late-first-century wooden-leaf tablets albeit in far smaller quantities (Tomlin 1998; 1999). Probably all written by members of the *ala Gallorum Sebosiana*, the decipherable examples include references to missing lances, cloaks, an account of the routine issue of wheat and barley, and a soldier seconded to the mounted guard of the governor.

Both Carlisle and Vindolanda obviously have the potential to produce additional writing-tablets and there may well be waterlogged anaerobic deposits at other Wall-forts where similar material might survive.

Roman Sculpture from the Hadrian's Wall Region

M Henig

The northern frontier has provided us with the largest concentration of Roman sculpture from Britain. Together with associated inscriptions these stones provide some of the best evidence for the lives of Roman soldiers and their dependants in the Roman Empire, and consequently they have an international importance. This brief survey will be largely concerned with Hadrian's Wall and its outpost forts, but will also include Maryport, Carlisle, Corbridge and South Shields, all south of the Wall.

Publication

With the exception of a few recent finds such as the sculptures found on the 'millennium site' at Carlisle, we are fortunate that all the sculpture is already published to a high standard, mostly in the relevant fascicules of the *Corpus Signorum Imperii Romani* [Corpus of Sculpture of the Roman World] Great Britain, Vol.1 (British Academy). These are Fascicule 1 (Phillips 1977) and Fascicule 6 (Coulston and Phillips 1988). The Maryport material is accessible in Wilson (1997).

Collections: Many sculptured stones are to be found in the splendid English Heritage site museums at Corbridge, Housesteads and Chesters while other site museums with important sculpture include Vindolanda, South Shields, and Maryport. There are also sculptures in Hexham Abbey. There are major collections at Tullie House Museum, Carlisle, while those displayed in the Museum of Antiquities are currently being rehoused in the new Great North Museum, Newcastle-upon-Tyne. These collections include sculptures from their own localities as well as further afield.

Material: All the stone sculpture from the frontier region is carved from the local sandstone which is buff coloured in the east, but red in Cumbria. It may be noted that sandstone was also employed in Chester and Wroxeter in Shropshire (Henig 2004a) Indeed it is only when one reaches Yorkshire and proceeds down the Jurassic Ridge that limestone becomes the normal medium for sculpture, as was the case over most of Europe north of the areas where marble is readily available. Thus, despite the sculptures of the Wall region being an eloquent testimony to Romanitas, the limitations of the stone from which they were made means that they often appear somewhat rough to those familiar with Roman sculptures from elsewhere, even judged by the variable standards of the north-western provinces.

Style and workshops: There remains only a modest quantity of what might be described as official sculpture in the classical tradition, originally embellishing gateways and administrative buildings. Pride of place must be given to two images of Victory from Housesteads, one standing on a globe (now in Newcastle) and the other holding a palm (in Chesters Museum). A relief depicting Mars, likewise from Housesteads, may be from the *principia*.

With regard to other sculpture, there are several accomplished workshop groups. Most remarkable perhaps are two tombstones from South Shields whose distinctive style shows them to have been the work of a Syrian sculptor. One commemorates a Catuvellaunian woman called Regina, and was set up by her Palmyrene husband Barates, as the inscriptions upon it, both in Latin and Aramaic record. The other is the memorial of a Moor called Victor, a freedman and probably the boyfriend of Numerianus, a cavalryman from *ala I Asturum*. The characteristic closely detailed and linear cutting is very similar to work from Palmyra itself. Whether by the same sculptor or not, but on a more ambitious scale, is the quite splendid statue of Juno Regina from Chesters, as well as a fragment from a matching image of Jupiter Dolichenus.

Another remarkable workshop group appears to have been centred on Carlisle. The Carlisle school was, and is, remarkable mainly for its tombstones of women. Apart from the monument to Regina, the best-known representations of a woman from the region are the memorials of a lady with the fan in Tullie House Museum, and of Aurelia Aureliana in Newcastle. A statue of Fortuna from Birdoswald (now in Carlisle) can be assigned to the same tradition by virtue of the similar patterning of its drapery. Perhaps also related to the Carlisle workshop are some reliefs from Housesteads. A fine study of two women was unfortunately destroyed when the hut in which it was displayed was burnt down, but there are two tombstones of men wearing long-sleeved tunics in Newcastle of similar style and quality.

149. Relief of Mars from Housesteads. Chesters Museum

Religion: The Wall sculptures are of major importance for understanding life in the frontier zone, although our interpretation of them needs to be considered alongside related inscriptions and other epigraphic records such as the wooden tablets from Vindolanda and Carlisle.

Religion is especially important in this respect. Although in reality the division between 'official' Greco-Roman religion, native cults and the Oriental religions, at least in the minds of worshippers, may not have been a rigid one, it is convenient to examine them under these three headings.

Classical deities - There are few images of Jupiter, with the most convincing being torso fragments and a head from Corbridge. Figures of Mars are only to be expected in a military context and there are several reliefs from

Housesteads and the torso of a statue from Corbridge portraying the god. The latter site has also yielded two splendid reliefs of the Dioscuri, which have traditionally been assigned to a temple of Jupiter Dolichenus, but in fact the Dioscuri were widely venerated in military circles and it is best to see these as coming from a temple of Castor and Pollux. A statue of a river god leaning on a mask, most probably representing Oceanus, comes from Chesters while from Housesteads, a relief of Neptune with accompanying nymphs probably ornamented a fountain. The images of Mercury from the region are mainly votive reliefs which may be of little artistic worth but are a useful reminder of his ubiquity in the Wall region as elsewhere; two altars from Carlisle bearing representations of Mercury are of higher quality. Figures of Genii are widespread, including statues from Burgh-by-Sands and Carlisle which are of very reasonable competence, the latter including a figure identified as a *Genius Centuriae*. Hercules, who was regarded both as a god and as a hero, is represented by a number of sculptures, one of them a striking head from Housesteads and another a well-known relief from Corbridge upon which, aided by Minerva, he battles against the Hydra. This is a vigorous work, though decidedly provincial in style. The Labours of Hercules were evidently well known and an altar at Housesteads shows the Hydra episode, as well as Hercules and the Nemean lion, and the apple tree of the Hesperides.

150. Head of Antenociticus statue from the temple at Benwell

Goddesses include a representation of Diana from near Vindolanda, attesting the importance of hunting. Minerva is depicted not only with Hercules at Corbridge, but at Carrawburgh assisting Aesculapius in his work of healing. Venus appears at Maryport and especially at High Rochester, with two nymphs. There is an attractive pedimented relief of Fortuna, perhaps with Ceres, from Corbridge, which has also yielded a pediment from a shrine, probably of Roma, since it depicts Romulus and Remus being suckled by the Roman she-wolf. In a class of its own is the Fortuna statue from Birdoswald, as already mentioned a product of the Carlisle school.

Native deities - More interesting, perhaps, are the images of deities which are traditionally interpreted as local (although cf. p. 148 for an alternative perspective). Amongst them is Antenociticus represented by a head, an arm and a leg from his temple at Benwell. The head shows he was a youthful god - possibly, as his long hair indicates, a deity like Apollo. His tubular patterned hair is reminiscent of Carlisle work, but the almond shaped eyes and enigmatic 'archaic' mouth show that this piece is not altogether in the sophisticated tradition of most of the products of that workshop. Likewise belonging very much to a native tradition is the famous image of the *Genii Cucullati* from Housesteads and others from Netherby.

151. Coventina represented on a stele from Coventina's Well. Chesters Museum

Equally characteristic is a representation of a triad of nymphs together with a stele of a single nymph from Coventina's Well, Carrawburgh. A goddess stirring a tub on a relief from Corbridge, recalls the goddess with a tub or cauldron who sometimes accompanies Mercury on Cotswold sculptures.

Other native deities may reflect connections with the Rhineland including the Matres, which sometimes appear in triads as at Housesteads and Vindolanda. Even so, the style of some, like a relief from Bewcastle which is almost two-dimensional in its linearity, definitely displays local Romano-British workmanship. This also appears to be the case with the arch from Housesteads showing the Germanic Mars Thincsus with his goose, flanked by what look like wingless victories but are, in fact, the Alaisiagae.

Eastern deities - The *mithraea* at Carrawburgh and Housesteads have yielded highly important Mithraic sculptures. From Housesteads there are fragments from a large tauroctony and two figures of Cautes, but the most unusual piece is a relief depicting Mithras holding spear and sword being born from the cosmic egg. The figure is contained within an egg-shaped frame bearing the signs of the zodiac. Inscriptions indicate that Mithras was especially venerated here as *saecularis*, 'Lord of Ages'. Found *in situ* in the *mithraeum*, an altar from Carrawburgh shows Mithras conflated with *Sol Invictus*, the Sun god, wearing a radiate crown three of whose rays are pierced so that lamps mounted in a niche behind could illuminate the figure. This is a distinctively patterned relief. Sol appears in his own right on a vigorously carved relief from Corbridge which has sometimes been associated, though with little reason, with Jupiter Dolichenus. Other eastern deities attested from the region include the superb statue of Juno Caelestis, the work of a Syrian artist, from Chesters and a Cybele from Carvoran, though the upper part of the goddess's body and all except the front paws of the lion are lost.

152. Relief of Mithras emerging from the cosmic egg found in Mithraeum at Housesteads

Tombstones: In addition to the (mainly) civilian tombstones of the Carlisle school, there are one or two important military *stele*. Pride of place belongs to the tombstone of a cavalryman of the *Ala Petriana* called Flavinus, now in Hexham Abbey but probably originally from Corbridge. Another cavalry tombstone, presumably associated with the same regiment, was found at its home base at Stanwix. From Housesteads comes a tombstone of an archer as well as other probable examples of the Carlisle school. Also doubtless a funerary monument is the Corbridge lion, perhaps the finest and certainly the best known example of the ravening lion type, which seems to have been adapted later to serve as a fountain. Other stele, even those of a standard bearer from Carrawburgh and an *immunis* (military clerk) with his tablet case from Castlesteads are of such indifferent quality that they raise the question of the ready availability of competent sculptors, since soldiers were certainly amongst the best paid men in provincial society and cost should not have been an issue. There are also some splendidly naïve *stele* depicting women, for example from Vindolanda.

Cultural significance: A brief conspectus like this cannot hope to do full justice to the sculptures from Hadrian's Wall and its hinterland. They certainly rank in importance as indicators of frontier life and thought with the sculptures from the Rhine and Danube frontiers, even if the general technical standard is generally nowhere near so high. Although remote from the centre of the Roman Empire, they still reflect classical culture and a passable knowledge of Graeco-Roman myth. These are powerful reasons why they deserve to be conserved and displayed in a sympathetic manner.

They may, however, have an importance wider than their own period. After the end of the empire many sculptures will still have been visible to later generations, lying around the ruins of Roman forts and settlements. Both the late George Henderson and Henig have pointed out that it is possible that Roman tombstones of the Carlisle school had an influence on the carving of the eighth-century Bewcastle Cross, and perhaps on Northumbrian art of the middle-Saxon period in general.

Religion

J Webster

Hadrian's Wall yields key resources for the study of belief and practice in Roman Britain, and the extent of the epigraphic and iconographic record make this a unique resource for the analysis of the spiritual life of the cosmopolitan communities living at the edge of Rome's empire.

Altars and other epigraphic attestations

The epigraphic habit was stronger on Hadrian's Wall than in many other parts of Roman Britain. Many soldiers and officials, and some civilians, commissioned inscribed monuments honouring their favoured gods. As we might expect in a military zone, Jupiter is very well attested (particularly at Birdoswald, and on the well-known series of altars from Maryport) as are the imperial *numina*, and Mars, but Oriental and Celtic deity names are also common. With reference to the latter, the Wall is undoubtedly our best source of information on localized Celtic deities worshipped during the Roman period. Well-attested cults include those of Belatucadrus, Coventina, the Veteres and Cocidius. Belatucadrus is named on 19 inscriptions, mainly from the Cumbrian section of the Wall. Coventina is attested 14 times, with all examples coming from her shrine at Carrawburgh (*RIB* 1522-1535). The 61 altars honouring the Veteres come mainly from the eastern end of the wall, with notable concentrations at Carvoran and Vindolanda. The local god Cocidius gave his name to the fort at Bewcastle (*Fanum Cocidii*).

There are a few references to religious activities in the Vindolanda tablets, including a sacrifice on the day of the Kalends, the purchase of supplies for Saturnalia, a list of expenditure incurred by items for a festival and a request relating to a festival that a priest be sent to the prefect. A letter from Fatalis includes the caveat 'if the gods are propitious'.

RIB adopts a tripartite scheme for categorizing the gods of Roman Britain: Graeco-Roman, Eastern and Celtic. This scheme has the virtue of simplicity, but does not foreground two categories of deity especially common to Hadrian's Wall: syncretistic gods given both Roman and Celtic names (for example Mars Cocidius (Bewcastle, *RIB* 993), and deities with Germanic rather than Celtic names. Syncretistic deities like these are an especially important source of information on the process of *Interpretatio Romana* (Tacitus *Germania* 43 - the Roman interpretation of foreign gods) and - to a far lesser extent - its indigenous counterpart. In this context, it is also important to note that many of the Wall deities with Celtic and indeed Germanic names did not, or did not always, appear in syncretistic couplings (this is especially true of Coventina, the enigmatic *Veteres* and Belatucadrus), indicating that *interpretatio* was favoured by certain sectors of the Wall community, but not all.

153. Altar to Cocidius found north of Milecastle 37. Chesters Museum

Iconography (sculpture)

As the preceding section discussed, the Wall zone boasts the largest concentration of Roman sculpture in Northern Britain, and many of these sculptures depict deities. Unsurprisingly, Mars and Hercules (both favoured by soldiers) are well-represented on fort sites, including Birdoswald, Vindolanda and Housesteads. Deities imported from other provinces are also well represented. Amongst these are various *Genii* and the *Matres*.

There are obvious and sometimes surprising discrepancies in the iconographic and epigraphic treatment of individual deities. For example, Jupiter is very well attested epigraphically (especially on the important series of altars from Maryport), but images of the god are far less common. Similarly, the most frequently named Celtic deities (such as Belatucadrus and the *Veteres*) are not sculpted at all. The relative costs of epigraphy and sculpture may be a factor here, but it is also interesting to note, in this context, that whilst syncretistic epigraphy is relatively common in the wall zone, syncretistic iconography is not and only a handful of surviving images depict pairings of 'Roman' and 'Celtic' (or otherwise foreign) deities. The factors informing these iconographic/epigraphic disjunctures are not clear, but merit further investigation

The sculptures from Hadrian's Wall, like those of Roman Britain as a whole, have traditionally been studied from an art historical perspective. It has commonly been assumed that the artists who made these images were attempting to copy classical exemplars, and scholars have routinely made value judgements as to the status of these artefacts as 'good' or 'bad' art. Most have been found wanting. Attitudes to provincial art have changed radically in the last decade, and it is to be hoped that the religious imagery of Hadrian's Wall will be a beneficiary of the new willingness to regard provincial 'artworks' as localised manifestations of complex cultural negotiation. In this context the Wall museums curate numerous examples of small and supposedly 'poorly executed' carved heads and full body images which appear to represent deities. Perhaps these poorly studied images speak less of technical incompetence than of a different way of conceptualising deity under Rome. Again, this group of images would merit sustained study.

Non-figurative symbols

For the same reasons, far more attention should be paid to the non-figurative religious symbols (wheels, swastikas and the like) from the Wall zone. These can occur independently (wheel-shaped brooches have been found at Corbridge and Housesteads, for example), but are also found on altars, images and tombstones. These symbols have received some attention from scholars with an interest in 'Celtic' art and religion (notably Green), but have excited less interest among Romanists.

Temples and other ritual foci

The epigraphic and iconographic data point to Hadrian's Wall as a vibrant focus for spiritual activity. The paucity of evidence for temples and other cult foci is therefore particularly surprising. Excavated examples of cult sites are few, but include the temple of Antenociticus (a Celtic deity) at Benwell, the temple of Mars Thincsus (a syncretised Germanic Mars) at Housesteads, and the shrine of Coventina at Carrawburgh. Temples to the following gods are also attested or hinted at epigraphically: Cocidius at Benwell (*RIB* 985-6, 988-9. 993); Jupiter Doliche at Bewcastle (*RIB* 992), and the *Matres* at Castlesteads (*RIB* 1988). Evidence for the Christian religion is particularly limited. The recent discovery of an apsidal building at Vindolanda, interpreted as a church dating to c. AD 400, is therefore particularly exciting (see also p. 169).

The most visible category of cult site on Hadrian's Wall

154. The Carrawburgh Mithraeum

is the *Mithraeum*. Three have been excavated (at Carrawburgh, Housesteads and Rudchester), and another is attested epigraphically at Castlesteads (*RIB* 1992-4). The *Mithraea* at Carrawburgh and Housesteads have produced important sculptures, including taurochtony. In terms of the study of religion, at least, Housesteads and Carrawburgh remain perhaps the two most important sites on the Wall.

Burial on Hadrian's Wall

D A Petts

Introduction

Despite the extensive archaeological research carried out on the Wall, relatively little is known about Roman burials and cemeteries. While the location of a number of fort cemeteries are known, mainly through discovery of tombstones, there have been few significant excavations of cemeteries, and those that have taken place have tended to be relatively small-scale. There is nothing to compare with the cemetery excavations at Brougham (Cumbria) (Cool et al 2004) or York (Wenham 1968; Hunter Mann 2005) Due to the lack of such excavation, knowledge of the skeletal material is poor. This is exacerbated both by poor bone preservation in the region due to the predominantly acidic soils, and the apparent widespread continuity of the cremation rite in the third and even fourth centuries AD. Despite the lack of excavated evidence, the Wall zone has produced a significant quantity of funerary epigraphy. Over 100 tombstones are recorded in *RIB* and a further 15 have been recorded in subsequent issues of *JRS* and *Britannia*. This important corpus of epigraphic material has been relatively understudied.

Location

The location of the cemeteries associated with many of the Wall forts is suspected. They are either identified by the recovery of tombstones or by the survival of field monuments of a probably funerary nature. As would be expected from parallels elsewhere, most cemeteries are located along the main access roads leading to the forts and their associated military *vici* as at Great Chesters, Vindolanda and Housesteads.

However, burials are also known from non-fort sites: a cist excavated at milecastle 35 (Crow and Jackson 1997); a cist and a cremation burial from near the curtain wall to the east of Birdoswald (Wilmott 2001, pl.60); burials found in and around Turret 39a (Simpson 1976, 100, 102-3, fig.22); a cremation burial found below the fort at Housesteads (Crow 1995, 22); and a burial from milecastle 9 (Birley 1930, 154). Other probable evidence for burial along the course of the Wall includes the discovery of several tombstones re-used in the restoration of the Wall (e.g. *RIB* 1641, 1642, 1667; *JRS* 53, 161).

In addition to the placement of burials within milecastles and turrets, there are other cases of burials being placed within structures. Excavation of the temple of Antenociticus revealed three burials within the apse. These are likely to post-date the abandonment of the building in the late second or third century. On a more substantial scale 33 skeletons were found in the bath house at Chesters (Bruce 1885, 101; Birley 1960, 30); although often assumed to be of post-Roman date, there is no hard evidence for this. However, the burials found in the headquarters building in the interior of *Arbeia* are more likely to be of an early post-Roman date. These remains were disturbed and the precise number of interments is difficult to establish, though it is clear that at least one had suffered a major blade injury to the head (Bidwell and Speak 1994, 105, 143-4; Croom and Caffell 2005).

155. Statue of Cautes from the Carrawburgh Mithraeum.

156. Relief of woman stirring tub with long-handled patera, thought to be Rosmerta, consort of Mercury. Corbridge

157. Relief showing radiate head of the sun-god Sol, re-used in floor of the east granary, Corbridge

158. The 'Corbridge Lion'. Lion and stag tombstone, later converted into a fountain. Corbridge

159. The Shorden Brae mausoleum

Burial Monuments

Earthen barrows are known from several sites. The best recorded are those at Petty Knowes, High Rochester (Charlton and Mitcheson 1984). The Petty Knowes barrow burials comprised a central cemetery of around seventy-five barrows, with a number of clusters of outliers. Most barrows consisted of an earth mound surrounded by a shallow ditch and bank and were between 3m and 5m in diameter. Other barrows had no ditch or bank and were correspondingly smaller in size. A number of burials within the cemetery were located in the *interstices* between these barrows, and had no recorded above ground element.

Other probable Roman barrow cemeteries have been identified. Two groups are known at Great Chesters (Horsley 1732, 150; Jones 1976, 21) and others have been recognised at Chesters (Charlton and Mitcheson 1984, 19-20) and Bewcastle (Sainsbury and Welfare 1990, 144). An earth mound was recorded over one of the cremation burials excavated at Morton Walk, South Shields and ring ditches have been recorded surrounding cremations at Beckfoot (Mike Collins *pers. comm.*).

In addition to barrows and mounds, a number of more substantial masonry tombs are known. Again, the best recorded are from High Rochester. A row of four tombs, three square and one circular, lay along the course of Dere Street opposite Lamb Crag (Bruce 1867, 330). These were investigated in 1850 by William Coulson, revealing little in the square barrows, but an 'urn with bones, a fragment of glass unguent bottle and a coin of Severus Alexander' in the circular structure (Richmond 1940, 105). This latter tomb had an enclosing ditch and banks; it appears to be a more substantial version of the earthen mounds standing nearby at Petty Knowes (Wilson 2004).

A far more substantial masonry tomb is that sited at Shorden Brae, close to Corbridge (Gillam and Daniels 1961). Lying to the west of the town, this tomb consisted of a substantial central structure containing a burial shaft surrounded by a larger precinct wall. This massive structure was clearly decorated with stone sculpture, elements of which were recovered during excavation. This complex probably dated to the mid-second century on ceramic evidence. Outside the main enclosure the remains of a far smaller structure consisting of a central grave and a small outer wall was also recovered. This post-dated the larger structure and was dated, on coin evidence, to the early-mid fourth century.

In addition to masonry monuments and earth mounds it is clear that graves could be marked in other ways. Obviously many were provided with tombstones, though few have been found *in situ* above the grave, with the possible exception of some from Carlisle (Charlesworth 1978). Several of the burials at Petty Knowes contained a post-hole which may have supported a wooden marker post (Charlton and Mitcheson 1984, 6), while early-nineteenth-century records note the presence of strong oak stakes marking groups of cremation urns at Vindolanda (Hodgson 1840, 197)

Burial Rites

As elsewhere in Roman Britain, both cremations and inhumations are known from burials in the Wall zone. Excavations at Morton Walk, South Shields revealed a total of five late-third-/fourth-century inhumations. The earlier burials were aligned north-south; one grave (Grave 1) contained a significant group of grave-goods, including a jet spindlewhorl and possible distaff, at least eight bracelets (bone, copper and iron), rings, an iron knife and chain and a string of 100 glass beads. There is a range of evidence for coffins and grave linings. Grave 4 from Morton Walk, South Shields contained indications of a wooden coffin (wood stains and iron fittings) (Snape 1994; 1995). Two stone coffins, one containing a beaker of late-second-/third-century date were found at Clavering Place, Newcastle, and were presumably related to the fort which lay 160m to the north-east. Another stone coffin, containing two gold rings, was found in a mound to the east of the fort at Carvoran in the nineteenth century. Stone and lead coffins have also been found in the London Road cemetery in Carlisle (Charlesworth 1978). Stone linings and cist graves are also known; a burial from Morton Walk was lined with sandstone slabs (Snape 1994; 1995). A probable stone burial cist was found within a water tank at Houseteads (Crow 1995), a cist has been excavated at Sewingshields (Crow and Jackson 1997) and the remains of a cist burial next to the wall to the east of Birdoswald fort have been recorded (*ibid.*, 64-5). The three burials in the apse of the temple at Antenociticus were also placed in stone cists (Simpson and Richmond 1941).

Cremation is also common along the Wall; examples have been recorded at South Shields (Snape 1994, 1995), Vindolanda (Birley 1961, 187-8), Housesteads (Crow 1995, 22), Stanwix (Hogg 1952 154), Birdoswald (Wilmott 1993), Carlisle (Charlesworth 1978), High Rochester (Charlton and Mitcheson 1984), Herd Hill (Bellhouse 1954, 54-55), Beckfoot (Hogg 1949; Bellhouse 1954, 51-3; Mike Collins *pers. comm*) and Corbridge. These burials were often accompanied by grave-goods, such as the two flagons and hobnails from one cremation at Morton Walk, South Shields (Snape 1994, 1995). One of the cremations uncovered during excavations on the course of the Corbridge Bypass in 1974 was accompanied by a fine enamelled copper alloy vessel (Casey and Hoffman 1995, 24).

The cremation rite along the Wall, however, shows differences from that practiced elsewhere in Roman Britain. First, the practice clearly continues to be widespread into the late Roman period, and is never significantly supplanted by inhumation. For example, it appears that at least one cremation at Birdoswald was accompanied by a calcite gritted cooking pot, indicating a fourth-century date; whilst the vessels from the cremations excavated at Petty Knowes, High Rochester, ranged in date from early second century to early fourth century (Gillam, Jobey and Ramsay 1984). Material recovered from Beckfoot also indicates that cremation continued to be practiced into the fourth century (Mike Collins *pers. comm.*).

A second distinctive aspect of the cremation rite in the Wall zone is the recovery of *busta* (*in-situ* burial of the cremation on the pyre site). Examples are known from Herd Hill (Bellhouse 1954, 54-55) Beckfoot (Bellhouse 1954, 51-53; Hogg 1949; Mike Collins *pers. comm.*) and High Rochester, where at least eight of the excavated graves showed evidence for *in situ* cremation and records of one of the officer's tombs suggests it was also a *busta* burial. It is also likely that some of the cremations from Birdoswald were *busta* burials. Other probable examples of this rite from northern Roman Britain include the 'fire pits' at Camelon (Breeze and Rich-Gray 1978-1980). However, not all cremations in the Wall zone took place on *busta*, there is no evidence for *in situ* burning at Morton Walk, South Shields, and a probable *ustrinum* has been identified at Corbridge (Casey and Hoffmann 1995, 17-18). Little is known about bier furniture and fittings. Richard Bellhouse traced the remains of a possible bier at Beckfoot (Bellhouse 1954), and fragments of decorated bone veneer from a cremation at Birdoswald shows strong parallels with similar veneers found at Brougham, which have been convincingly interpreted as derived from funeral furniture (Greep 2004). It is likely that any attempt to divide the cremation rites into two categories (those in which the pyre is buried *in situ* and those in which the ashes are removed from the pyre and buried) is overly simplistic. It is clear from sites such as Beckfoot and Brougham (just outside the Wall zone) that the cremation rite could be extremely complex, with the ashes being given a range of different treatments (Cool 2004). The use of fire in complex mortuary rites is also seen at Shorden Brae, where, although an inhumation, the shaft above the probable site of the burial was filled with an inch-thick layer of 'soot' containing the burnt remains of a Roman pot. (Gillam and Daniels 1961, 43).

160. Excavation of the cemetery at Beckfoot

Human remains

Few human remains have been recovered from burials in the Wall zone. There may be several reasons for this: the acid soils in the region, the continuity of cremation into the late Roman period and the general lack of excavation within cemetery sites in the area. Although cremated remains have often been passed over for osteological analysis, the work of McKinley on the material from Brougham has clearly demonstrated the potential of close examination of burnt bone (McKinley 2004). One of the few considerations of the surviving human remains, from both inhumations and cremations is the overview of assemblages from South Shields (Croom and Caffell 2005).

Case study: Beckfoot Roman Cemetery

M Collins

The current state of knowledge about the archaeology of the cemetery at Beckfoot has recently been summarised by Caruana (2004a), to whom a debt is owed for much of the current knowledge of the cemetery.

Finds from the cemetery started to be reported in the early part of the twentieth century to Tullie House Museum at Carlisle. However, more systematic observation, and limited rescue excavation, by Bellhouse and latterly by Caruana and

James, from the late 1940's onwards has started to provide a fuller picture of the cemetery. This picture has also been added to by recent geophysical survey by English Heritage and evaluation excavations carried out by Healey of Oxford Archaeology (North), for which an unpublished report has been produced (Healey 2007).

- The cemetery lies some 370m from the fort at Beckfoot. Although part of the cemetery may have been associated with milefortlet 15, this location is comparable with cemeteries from other fort sites in the Roman north.
- Cremation appears to be the main burial rite found at Beckfoot, and although the possible presence of inhumations has not entirely been ruled out, the recent excavations covered a significant percentage of the site and noted a high density of cremation remains but no inhumations.
- The cremation ritual appears to be highly varied, with pit burials, burials within ditches, burial within ring ditches and pyre dumps all found to be present. The ditches mentioned above are thought likely to represent divisions within the cemetery or mark its edge, although these were not always respected as the cemetery appears to have expanded. The ring ditches are of particular interest, suggesting that these burials were made in particular plots, and there is also evidence that these plots were not respected by later burials. This, together with evidence for partial collection of material for final burial suggests the burial rites at Beckfoot were far from simple.
- Material recovered from Beckfoot indicates that the use of cremation continued into the fourth century, and while stone cists have been recorded here, none were located in the recent excavations.
- With reference to grave goods, Caruana draws attention to a number of interesting features of the Beckfoot assemblage known before the recent excavations: one particular burial contained a sword, shield and spear, a very unusual type of burial in Roman Britain. Other finds include hobnails from shoes or boots, although the nature of these finds cannot in itself indicate a military nature to the cemetery. In contrast to this, finds from the recent excavations have been few in number, and limited to nails and hobnails.
- A final feature of tantalising interest is the recovery in the recent excavations of a number of millstone grit boulders, and it is tentatively suggested that as well as ditches, the cemetery may also have used these as either grave markers or for division of space

Anecdotal reports also mention the erosion of large animal bones from the cemetery site. Although confirmation on the date and origin of this material (which has been suggested as being more likely to be recent animal burials than Roman in origin) it may be significant that no such material was recovered by the recent fieldwork.

As mentioned, the site of milefortlet 15 was thought to lie within the cemetery site. However, an absence of any traces of this structure looks to have confirmed earlier understanding (Breeze 2004) that it has been removed entirely by erosion into the Solway.

Osteology and Ethnicity

S Stallibrass

Analyses of stable isotopes (particularly those of oxygen and strontium) in unburnt human bone can investigate the geographical locations of people's childhood years. This has the potential to demonstrate the origins of military personnel serving (and dying) on the frontier, investigate potential settlements of veterans in the Wall's hinterland, and indicate the degree of 'local' involvement with the army. Its use in the Wall zone would provide an important opportunity to test the multicultural implications of the epigraphic evidence.

Ethnicity does not simply refer to people's geographical and biological affinities, but also to their perceptions, beliefs and cultural traditions. Within north-western England, many of the military and military-related sites demonstrate a cultural practice of preparing cattle metapodials (foot bones) by scorching them midshaft and then breaking them open to pour out the marrow from the central cavity. This has been observed at several sites on the western half of the military zone, but does not seem to be prevalent on the eastern side (Stallibrass 2000). Similar east-west differences have been noted with regard to the uptake of pottery manufactured in Yorkshire (Evans 2000) and with the uptake of new types of cattle emanating from the centre of the empire. In both cases, sites on the western side of the Pennines appear to be reluctant to take up the new resources on offer. Due to an extreme paucity of Iron Age material, it is not yet possible to suggest whether these east-west differences originated with the indigenous populations, or whether they were Romano-British developments.

Another aspect of ethnicity and cultural practices relating to the preparation and consumption of food concerns the different uses of flavourings and condiments at military sites in the Hadrian's Wall zone (Swan 1992). The uses of opium poppy seeds, coriander seeds, grapes and figs probably reflect soldiers' tastes developed in their home countries, and Huntley has drawn attention elsewhere to the variability shown by different forts, that might relate to the tastes of soldiers drawn from different parts of the empire.

Transport and Communications

D J P Mason

It is assumed that the main arterial roads in the North were constructed immediately following its conquest in the early/mid 70s of the first century. East of the Pennines, Dere Street (Margary 8) was the principal strategic road. Originating from the legionary fortress at York, this proceeded northwards to Corbridge linking a chain of forts at Aldborough, Catterick, Binchester and Ebchester. With the conquest of Scotland, Dere Street was extended to Newstead, Elginhaugh, Inchtuthil and perhaps finally Stracathro. A road now known as the Devil's Causeway (Margary 87) branched off from Dere Street just north of Corbridge leading first to the fort at Learchild and then on to the coast in the vicinity of Berwick where an early fort site surely awaits discovery.

West of the Pennines the main road north, leading back ultimately to the legionary fortress at Chester, headed for

161. Aerial photograph of the Maiden Way

Carlisle. The latter (Margary 7) is known to have been constructed from dendrochronological dating in the winter of 72/3 and the road would have been constructed around the same time. Its subsequent extension farther north linked the forts at Birrens, Tassieholm and Crawford. It then continued on to Elginhaugh and was crossed along the way by another road heading north-westwards from Newstead to Bothwellhaugh and eventually on to Old Kilpatrick on the Clyde (Margary 79 and 78).

East-west communication from the Solway to the Tyne was provided by the Stanegate (Margary 85 and 86). The precise date of its construction is unknown, but it has long been assumed that it was in existence by 86 when forts were constructed at Corbridge and Vindolanda as part of the initial redeployment consequent upon the first stage of the withdrawal from much of Scotland. Poulter (1998) has challenged this interpretation and the matter remains unresolved. The course of any continuation of the Stanegate east of Corbridge remains unknown, but see p. 15-18 for a discussion of possible routes.

East-west communication further south was afforded by a trans-Pennine road linking the forts at Brougham and Bowes and utilising the Stainmore Pass (Margary 82). At Bowes the road divided into two, one branch joining Dere Street south of Binchester (Margary 820) and the other connecting with it at Scotch Corner. Towards the western end of the trans-Pennine road another known as the Maiden Way ran northwards from the fort at Kirby Thore to that at Whitley Castle where it split into two; one branch proceeding to Carvoran, the other to Corbridge (Margary 84).

Some of the Cumberland coast sites (such as Maryport) are likely to have originated in the early Flavian period but the date of the road system is unknown. The principal road was that which headed south-westwards from Carlisle to Papcastle and beyond (Margary 75). A road linked the latter with Maryport and there may have been similar 'spur' roads to the other coastal forts (Margary 751). A road running along the coast linking the forts is certain if unproven (Margary 750).

A later addition to the road system in the north-east was that known as Cade's Road (Margary 80). This originated at Brough-on-Humber and proceeded northwards running roughly parallel with Dere Street and some 15 km on average to its east. After Chester-le-Street it continued to Newcastle from where there may have been a link to the Devil's Causeway, connecting with the latter somewhere near the crossing of the River Coquet. On present evidence, this road was established in the Hadrianic period. There may have been a road running roughly parallel with the coast beginning at the fort at Lease Rigg and merging with Cade's Road in the vicinity of the recently discovered settlement at East Park, Sedgefield.

The transportation of supplies, and on occasion reinforcements, by sea obviously played an important role in the logistical support of the Wall and its garrisons. The existence of a sea-port guarded by the fort at South Shields is certain given the presence of the supply-base. However, despite a number of archaeological interventions at various points between the Mill Dam and River Drive, on the river frontage west of the fort, its whereabouts remains unknown. The use of the mouth of the Tyne by troop transports in the Roman period is indicated by objects from the Herd Sand on the south side of the river entrance. The finds, which include a shield-boss of *legio VIII Augusta*, are all remarkably close in date, belonging to the second-half of the second century. It has been convincingly argued that the objects are being washed out of the wreck of a ship that came to grief entering the mouth of the Tyne in the later-second century (Bidwell 2001). The presence of a legionary of *VIII Augusta* (based at Strasbourg) would suggest a troop-ship bringing reinforcements into the northern frontier zone, perhaps in response to the invasion attested in the early 180s.

Substantial riverside quays capable of accommodating seagoing vessels are probable at Wallsend with perhaps minor facilities suitable for use by barges at sites such as Chesters and Corbridge further up the Tyne.

Most of the Cumberland coast forts possessed anchorages, while Maryport has often been suspected of having a more substantial harbour though evidence is lacking at present. Ravenglass, too, may have possessed significant facilities given that its garrison - *cohors I Aelia Classica* - had a naval background and may even have operated a small flotilla of warships. Kirkbride, overlooking the large and sheltered Moricambe Bay, would seem a logical location for an important early harbour. In later periods the focus for shipping would presumably have been closer to, or at, Carlisle.

9. The Post-Roman Archaeology of Hadrian's Wall AD 400-1000
T Wilmott

For the purposes of the Research Framework it was agreed that the Post-Roman section should concentrate upon the immediate post-Roman period, with the wider issues of Early Medieval archaeology within the region covered by reference to the NERRF and NWRRF, which together encapsulate the area of the former Roman frontier zone. These two documents (Newman 2006; Petts and Gerard 2006) now incorporate useful Resource Assessments on the Early Medieval period for the whole area.

162. Debris from mid 4th century collapse of roof at west end of north granary, Birdoswald

Until the last two decades, the fate of the Wall and its installations at the end of the fourth century was a subject which was little explored, and in which archaeologists of the Wall had little interest. Recent excavations, particularly at Vindolanda (Bidwell 1985), South Shields (Bidwell and Speak 1994), and Birdoswald (Wilmott 1997a) have revolutionised knowledge of this phase of the history of the monument. A first attempt to remedy the lack of synthetic work on this period, look at what was known and create a possible future agenda was made at the 1999 Roman Archaeology Conference in Durham (Wilmott and Wilson 2000). More recently the subject has been picked up more theoretically by Collins (forthcoming), who has demonstrated a series of traits whereby the organisation of fort interiors changed in the second half of the fourth century, and has effectively shown that these alterations became more pronounced in the fifth.

Environmental evidence for landscape change in the Wall zone is limited to a small number of regional palynological samples, principally Fozy Moss, where there is evidence for the regeneration of woodland in the fifth century (Dumayne and Barber 1994). At Glasson Moss increased clearance has been noted at cal AD 780-1020 (Cox et al 2000). Study of this important source of evidence has effectively only just begun, as emphasis has tended to be placed upon the palynological evidence for the Iron Age to Roman transition rather than the post Roman. Clearance of woodland in the seventh and eighth centuries can be confirmed by dendrochronological dates from Carlisle for trees felled in AD 633 (a post at Blackfriars Street; McCarthy 1990, 72) and AD 770-803 (a post at Castle Street; McCarthy 1991, 49).

In terms of settlement activity, evidence for the Early Medieval period derives almost entirely from the Wall forts. This is simply because the emphasis of modern excavation has been predominantly on fort sites.

There are two principal stratigraphic sequences which illustrate the development of sites during this period, from Birdoswald and from South Shields. That from Birdoswald is quoted in both the NWRRF and NERRF as a type site for the early post-Roman development of a Roman fort. The Birdoswald sequence centres on the two granaries (north and south) to the south of the *via principalis* and adjacent to the west gate of the fort (Wilmott 1997). Period 5 represented the late-Roman transition between the Roman occupation of Period 4, and Period 6 which may be described as 'non-Roman' in character. During this period, the ventilated sub-floor of the south granary was backfilled and the flagstone floor relaid. The latest coin from this fill was dated to AD 348 giving a *terminus post quem* for this work. Silty layers were succeeded by a relaid patchy stone floor, incorporating two hearths at one end of the building, around which were found high-status items such as a gold earring, a glass finger ring and a worn, silver, Theodosian coin (388-95). At the same time, the north granary roof collapsed (*terminus post quem* 350-53) and the building was robbed of its walling stone and floor flags, the former sub-floor being used as a dumping area. The coinage from these dumps ran on from 348-378, and the finds also included a small penannular brooch of a characteristic sub-Roman type (Snape 1992, 158).

163. Principal sub Roman building over site of north granary, Birdoswald

The 'non-Roman' Period 6 was characterised by the erection of timber structures over the remains of the north granary and over the roads of the fort. The first major building was post built with most of the posts placed in shallow post-holes located in the tops of the robbed granary walls. A new floor of re-used flagstones over facing stones was laid over the roof-tile spread from the building's collapse. This building was larger than the granary. A small service building was constructed as a post-built lean-to against the inner side of the fort wall, south of the west gate.

The second phase of timber buildings saw the erection of a free-standing, framed, building founded on post pads. The

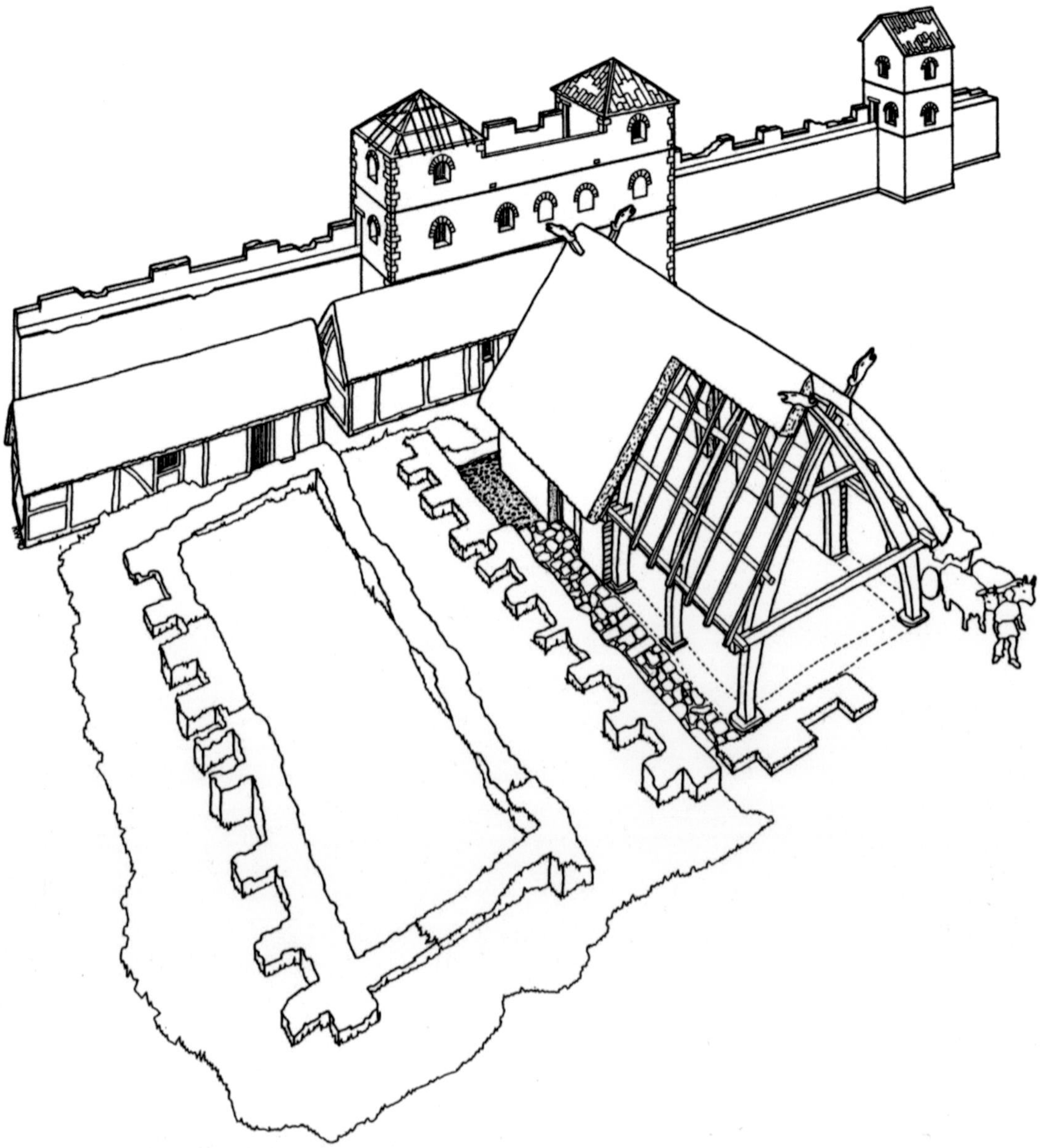

164. Reconstruction drawing of the period 6 building at Birdoswald

south wall was on the site of the former granary. However, the north wall lay on the former *via principalis* and was aligned with the *spina* of the west gate, thus covering the road inside the blocked south gate portal. This building was surface built, as were two small structures founded on surface-laid sleeper beams on the *intervallum* road. Apparently at the same time, the west gate was provided with a new, timber-built outer portal, possibly allowing gates to be hung to open outwards, and thus to be more defensible.

Dating for Period 6 is problematic. The south granary was clearly reused, possibly as a hall building, with the hearths at the western end provided for the leading figures in the fort community. If the timber structures were the functional successors of this building, as seems likely, the *terminus post quem* for the first is c. 388-95. As the Theodosian coin was worn, however, this could be assumed to be later, perhaps c. 420. An estimated life of 50 years for each building would bring the close of occupation to c. 520.

The South Shields sequence is located in and around the south-west gate of the fort. Here there is evidence for an extended sequence of activity. The *terminus post quem* for the start of the sequence was a coin of 388-402 which was found in the top layer of road metalling on a revetted causeway through the outer fort ditch. A subsequent ditch was cut through this causeway, isolating the gate. After a period of natural silting, this ditch was partly filled with rubble from the gate, including architectural fragments (Bidwell and Speak 1994, 45). After this the gate was reinforced by post-holes in the same position as those flanking the gate at Birdoswald. Subsequently an inhumation cemetery was located outside the gate. South Shields has yielded other important evidence for the period. A granary was provided with a solid floor in the mid-fourth century and was subsequently demolished and robbed. After this the fort road gravels were quarried in the vicinity of the granary (Bidwell and Speak, 1994, 45). Presumably these materials were taken in order to maintain some other, more active area in the fort. In the courtyard house in the south-east corner of the fort, two male skeletons exhibiting injuries were found, and radiocarbon dates suggest burial in the first half of the fifth century (Bidwell and Speak 1994, 45-6, 265).

Though Birdoswald and South Shields are the only detailed sequences on the Wall line itself, there is another similar sequence in the Wall hinterland at Binchester (Ferris and

Jones 1996, 58). These sequences clearly demonstrate continuity of occupation within at least some Wall forts beyond the conventionally understood end of the Roman period in Britain, and into the fifth century. Further, the character of this occupation clearly changes during the fifth century.

165. The possible church in the *praetorium* at Vindolanda

More fragmentary stratigraphic evidence exists at other forts. It is possible that surface-built timber structures like those at Birdoswald existed at Stanwix in the latest period, for instance. Most of this later activity is stratigraphically defined in fort defences. This is true at Vindolanda, where a repair of defences during the late fourth or early fifth century involved the deliberate piling of soil to a height of 3m against the wall to prevent collapse (Bidwell 1985, 45), and the collapsed north curtain wall at Housesteads was also replaced by an earth bank with a timber angle tower (Crow 2004a). Evidence for a similar late embanked fortification was found on the south wall at Birdoswald during the 1930s (Simpson and Richmond 1933, 260-61). At Carlisle the recent millennium excavations have revealed potential for the existence of early post-Roman structures (Zant, forthcoming). Late survival in the town is shown by the discovery in Scotch Street of a Valentinianic *solidus* buried early in a continuing sequence of mortar floors (Keevil et al 1989), and the well known seventh-century reference to a functioning fountain in the town (*Vita Sancti Cuthberti,* v). Also in Carlisle, a building sequence at Blackfriars Street (McCarthy 1990) must have continued into the fifth century.

It is important to stress that these sequences all reflect continuity of occupation from the Roman period into a different fifth century *milieu.* There is, for instance, no stratigraphic evidence for a hiatus in occupation at Birdoswald during the period between the backfilling of the south granary floor and the occupation of the final timber building phase. Two such occupational breaks have been recognized on that site, one at the end of the third century and one following the final timber building phase, so there is no doubt that a hiatus would have been recognized in excavation.

The interpretation of those sites where continuity of occupation has been recognized is problematic, but something of a consensus has emerged around basic ideas. The idea of this resulting from a re-occupation of the Wall, as suggested by Dark (1992), following a phase of desertion is unlikely, as no evidence for desertion has been found. At Birdoswald, a period of change, possibly to localized supply is shown by the disuse and changes of use in the granaries. The continuation of local supply to the fort in the early post-Roman period may have supported a community descended from the Roman garrison, but adopting more local ways, and it has been argued that the communities of soldiers on the Wall may have become small independent units, reliant for subsistence on a local *territorium*, which supplied the fort in a part-coercive but at any rate symbiotic relationship (for discussion cf. Casey 1993, Wilmott 1997, Collins 2007). A clear problem with this model is the failure as yet to identify a network of rural settlements which could have provided this supporting role, although little work has been done on known rural settlements which could be pre-Roman, Roman period or post-Roman in date, and in the North West such sites have returned Early Medieval radiocarbon dates (Newman 2006, 114). It seems clear that the forts which did continue in occupation became part of a network of different fortified settlements in the post-Roman north, which emerged from differing cultural traditions, whether Roman military, Roman provincial, or extra-provincial.

Recently there has been some evidence for the late presence and possibly continuity of Christianity in and around forts. In three forts, Housesteads, Birdoswald and Vindolanda, very late buildings with apses (admittedly all west facing) have been found. At Housesteads an apsed structure was built on a street in the north-west corner (Crow 2005, 95-96), at Birdoswald in the north-west corner (Wilmott 2001, 87; forthcoming), within a former centurion's quarters of a barrack, and at Vindolanda, within the courtyard of the *praetorium* (Birley et al 1998, 20-21). At South Shields there is some evidence that the *principia* forecourt was transformed into an east-facing church in the late fourth century (Bidwell and Speak 1994, 102-03). Also at Vindolanda the early Christian tombstone of Brigomaglos dating to c. 500 (*RIB* 1722) indicates a late Roman / early post-Roman Christian presence (Jackson 1982, 62), as does other recently discovered artefactual evidence. Additional inscribed stones attributable to this period have been tentatively identified at Castlesteads and Maryport (Dark and Dark 1996, 60-63). Long-cist graves (all empty) have been claimed adjacent to the church at Housesteads, at Sewingshields (Crow and Jackson 1997, 66-7) and east of Birdoswald (Wilmott 2000b, fig 16). It is possible that some of the forts persisted as Christian centres.

One of the main difficulties in the interpretation of stratigraphic evidence is that the associated deposits contain merely late Roman material, so that only stratigraphic depth and complexity following the deposition of the very latest Roman material can be confidently proposed as 'sub Roman' in date. Artefactual dating evidence is thus rare, and any attempt at identifying an early post-Roman material culture assemblage typical of the early post-Roman period on the Wall or in the Roman military north generally is not yet possible, despite the pioneering paper by Cool (2000). She has shown a development in material culture which might see specialized use of materials of different colours, particularly red and black. The only example of an artefact which can with confidence be dated to the period remains a variant of a Fowler D7 pennanular brooch found in contexts of this date at South Shields and Birdoswald (Snape 1992).

Other evidence comes from unstratified artifacts. Briefly, there is sixth-century Anglian material from Wallsend (Hodgson and Griffiths 1999), Corbridge (Knowles and Forster 1909, 406-8) and Benwell (Brewis 1936), and brooches of the same period come from Chesters (Miket 1978), Vindolanda (R E Birley 1970, 136) and possibly Birdoswald (Wilmott 1997, 216). Other objects of 'Germanic' origin, such as spearheads (Dark 1992) and the Frisian pottery known as Housesteads Ware (I Jobey 1979) are now seen as associated with ethnic Germanic auxiliary units of the third century.

166. Late or sub Roman penannular brooches from post-dismantlement deposit over site of north granary, Birdoswald

Immediate post-Roman settlement is as yet unrecognized outside the forts, and there is a similar paucity of Anglian settlement evidence. Most of the finds mentioned above fit with casual loss. The material from Corbridge, comprising two late-fifth-century brooches, beads, and fragments of an urn, and from Benwell, where two brooches, one cruciform and one square headed, together with a glass vessel were found to the east of the fort (Jobey and Maxwell 1957) both suggest the equipment of Anglian burials.

Settlement within the walls of former Roman forts does occasionally occur, as at Birdoswald (Wilmott 1997) where renewed settlement begins in the twelfth century, and also at Housesteads (Crow 2004). Prior to 1000 AD, however, this principally takes the form of churches within fort enclosures (Nether Denton, Old Church, Brampton), adjacent to Roman settlements (Corbridge), and churches re-using material from the forts but built at a distance from the source of robbed material (Hexham Abbey). Interestingly none of these are on the Wall forts, but lie on the Stanegate, whose very medieval name shows its utility into this period. These churches may have been built to partake of Roman legitimacy (Newman 2006, 104), but equally their situation in relation to the road must have been significant. The same conclusion may be reached for Bewcastle, where the remarkable eighth-century stone cross shaft (Bailey and Cramp 1988) probably denotes the presence of a monastic settlement within the former Roman fort enclosure, which lies at the head of a Roman road, the Maiden Way.

167. The eighth century Bewcastle Cross

Appendix 1

Hadrian's Wall Archive Project

Update 2006

The original Hadrian's Wall Archive project (HWAP) was carried out in the early 1990s by Eleanor Scott on behalf of the RCHM. The project archive is held by EH.

For the HWRF the original list of archives compiled by the HWAP was revisited. Where possible the archives listed were contacted to check whether they still held the relevant material, whether there were any additions and whether there were any changes to the either conditions or related cataloguing/search aids. Also, where additional archives were identified they have been listed. Where there are no notes next to an archive this indicates that either there is no change or it has not been possible to contact the archive.

DP July 2006

Table 4. List of archives, HW Archives Project

Listed Archive (as used in pilot study report)	**Notes**
Adam Welfare	
Alnwick Castle	Location confirmed
The Ashmolean Museum	Now in Sackler Library, Oxford.
Eric Birley	
Prof G.D.B Jones	Professor Jones died in 1999. His archive material is now in the NMR, Swindon
Frank Batchelor	
Richard Bellhouse	Archive material now in Senhouse Museum
British Library	British Library now has digital cataloguing of much of its holdings.
Black Gate Library	Electronic cataloguing underway
British Museum	
The Bodleian Library	The Bodleian Library now has digital cataloguing of much of its holdings
CUCAP	Extensive collection of aerial photographs. Digitally searchable via the CUCAP website
Carlisle Archaeological Unit	Trust disbanded in 2001. CAU archives now held by Tullie House Museum, Carlisle
CEU EH: Carlisle Castle	Archives relating to published sites have been deposited either in Tullie House for Cumbria or Newcastle for Northumberland. Archives relating to unpublished sites are in Portsmouth. No archives remain at the Castle.
CEU EH: Portsmouth	Now contains archives relating to unpublished sites transferred from Carlisle Castle
Cumbria County Council: Archaeology Section	Now includes extensive 'grey literature' relating to PPG16 driven interventions.
Charles Daniels	Now deceased (1996). Material relating to Mithraism and bridges held in Museum of Antiquities, Newcastle
Dean and Chapter Library, Durham	Contains additional material donated by Dept. of Archaeology, Durham University in 1995. Not fully indexed though some lists exist in draft form.

Mrs J. Du Cane	
Dept. of Archaeology, Durham University	Birley slides and negatives deposited with the university library in 1995. Other material in Palace Green.
University Library, Durham University	Now holds material from Dept. of Archaeology and Dept. of Palaeography and Diplomatic+
EH London	All material now in NMR Swindon
Grace Simpson	
Neil Holbrook	All material now deposited with Tullie House Museum.
Lit and Phil Soc, Newcastle	Now has on-line catalogue of all published material
Mersey Maritime Museum	
NAR, Southampton	Now the National Monument Record, Swindon
Northumberland County Council: Archaeology Section	Now includes extensive 'grey literature' relating to PPG16 driven interventions
Dept. of Archaeology and the Museum of Antiquities, University of Newcastle	Also holds The Archaeological Practice archive and Charles Daniel's material related to Mithraism and bridges.
Northumberland Records Office	Relocating to Woodhorn by late 2006. Work beginning on electronic cataloguing.
National Trust Office, Housesteads	Most material at Housesteads has now been dispersed. Most archives listed are now with Jim Crow.
National Trust, Scots Gap	Correspondence relating to the management of Housesteads from the 1930s and stretches of Wall in the central sector which have come into NT ownership. This includes major repair projects and Wall related work (e.g. Clayton Wall repairs, National Trail), including a substantial photographic archive of works in progress (Pers. comm. Harry Beamish).
Deptartment of Palaeography and Diplomatic, Durham University	Amalgamated with Durham University library in 1990
Geoff Petch	
Alan Reed	
Society of Antiquaries of London	Access to digital catalogue of images, manuscripts and library holdings through the Archives to Archives website and the Archaeological Data Service.
Ray Selkirk	Recently deceased: future of archives uncertain
Tyne and Wear Museums Service	T&W Museums Service act as archaeological curators for Tyne and Wear. The Tyne and Wear HER is held at Jesmond and includes extensive 'grey literature' relating to PPG16 driven interventions on the Wall. Willowford Bridge material held by Paul Bidwell now at Tullie House Museum, Carlisle. Most material from Chester's Bridge now at EH Museum Housesteads, though 1990 material is retained at South Shields.
Tullie House Museum/Carlisle Library	Now holds archives from Carlisle Archaeological Unit and Willowford Bridge archives formerly held by Paul Bidwell and Neil Holbrook
Tyne and Wear Archive Service	Now has digital catalogue accessible via TWAS website
Victoria County Histories	Material still held in London
The Vindolanda Trust	
Vivien Swan	
The Warburg Institute	
David Woolliscroft	

Appendix 2

ALNWICK CASTLE MUSEUM, ALNWICK (NORTHUMBERLAND)

Background
Objects belong to the Duke of Northumberland. Founded in 1769 it contains mainly objects from the Duke's lands in Northumberland, as well as substantial numbers of objects from Lincolnshire and Ireland, and smaller quantities of artefacts from further a field. The main catalogue is still the 1880 Descriptive Catalogue of Antiquities, chiefly British, at Alnwick Castle by J. Collingwood Bruce.

Current Collection Policy
Until recently there have been few further additions, though in recent years objects resulting from fieldwork by Clive Waddington in the area have been added to the collection.

Roman
Roman pottery, including Samian bowl from Corbridge.
Misc objects including Bronze vessel from Newham Bog, fragment of military standard from Halton Chesters and lead pipe from Corbridge.
Collection of miscellaneous small finds (c.70 objects) from High Rochester.
c.50 pieces of stone sculpture and epigraphy.

ENGLISH HERITAGE HADRIAN'S WALL MUSEUMS COLLECTIONS

Housesteads Collection
c.1800 catalogued objects or groups.
Small finds mainly date from the 1930s vicus excavations.
Finds also from commanding officer's house and barrack blocks.
Also included are c.500 stone architectural fragments (in store).
Reserve collection held at Corbridge Site Museum.

Clayton Collection
The Clayton collection was formed by John Clayton between c.1840 and 1890. In addition it comprises a small amount of material acquired at an earlier date, but also includes material acquired after John Clayton's death, mainly as a result of F.G, Simpson's excavations at Haltwhistle Burn, Housesteads.

The material all comes from the central sector of the HW corridor (Halton Chesters to Carvoran) and was acquired either through Clayton's excavations, through his ownership of the land, inheritance or deliberate purchase. The greatest number of items are from Chesters fort itself, but the other main sites represented include Nether Denton, Carvoran, Great Chesters, Vindolanda, Housesteads and Carrawbrugh.

There are c.1900 artefacts on display (almost all Roman).
The 372 items of stone sculpture and inscriptions are of national importance and many items relate directly to the construction of Hadrian's Wall, while others are of importance for the history of the Wall, its units and religious cults.

The wide range of small finds include the Carvoran modius and the objects from Coventina's Well, as well as iron tools and weapons from Chesters.

The remaining reserve collection is store- it includes 4000 catalogued items and c.800-2000 uncatalogued objects. It consists mainly of small finds and pottery. There is not much coarseware, but there are larger quantities of samian and mortaria and probably one of the more interesting collections are the fragments of painted wall-plaster from the commanding officer's house. (Reference: Wallis Budge, E.A. 1903, 1907. *An Account of the Roman Antiquities preserved in the museum at Chester's Northumberland* (Chesters)

Corbridge
The Corbridge Roman Site Museum holds material from the 1906 excavations onwards comprising work done 1906-14 and from 1933 to c.1972 and again 1980. It all comes from the Corbridge Roman site or its immediate environs, the latter including the Shorden Brae mausoleum, the supply base at Beaufront Red House and the A69 bypass excavations.

The museum on display includes material from Red House and also includes other important assemblages such as the Corbridge Hoard. The exhibited material comprises c.5% of the total collections, the rest being stored on site or at the HWM stone store. About 30,000 items are catalogued (including c.6,500 coins)- an estimated 15-20,000 objects remain to be catalogued; the most important collection in this group is the Samian Ware. Most items or groups of items are inventoried and accessible.

MUSEUM OF ANTIQUITIES, UNIVERSITY OF NEWCASTLE, NEWCASTLE UPON TYNE (TYNE AND WEAR)

(Now housed in the Great North Museum)

Background

The museum was opened in 1960 following an agreement with the Society of Antiquaries of Newcastle-upon-Tyne which was first signed in 1956 and has since been twice renewed. The collection now includes a large body of material on loan from the City of Newcastle-upon-Tyne, as well as individual donors and the archaeological collection of the Society of Antiquaries.

The Museum acts as the county museum for Northumberland, as there is no other major archaeological museum in the North of England, which covers all historical periods.

Current Collection Policy

The present collecting area includes the county of Northumberland, the city of Newcastle-upon-Tyne and sites along Hadrian's Wall not provided with a site museum. Whilst actively seeking to acquire objects for collections the Museum has a policy of not buying objects for the Collection except in very special circumstances.

Roman

c.40% of total museum collection.
This is a collection of international significance. Its core is a group of inscriptions from Hadrian's Wall and neighbouring sites. The collections includes 200 altars, 65 tombstones, 200 inscriptions and 133 other sculptural items.

Other important items include, the Aesica hoard of jewellery, the bar cameo from South Shields, Mithraic Sculpture from Housesteads, Carrawburgh and Rudchester and material from the Temple of Antenociticus at Benwell. The domestic artefacts, such as bronze vessels and iron tools, are also of importance.

OLD FULLING MILL MUSEUM, DURHAM (CO. DURHAM)

Background

The Old Fulling Museum was first established in 1833 as part of the University of Durham, and was only the second university museum in the country. Included a typical collection of natural history specimens, foreign curios and antiquities. Antiquities, such as St Cuthbert's coffin, prehistoric flints and coins from Hadrian's Wall, as well as objects from Rome, Carthage and Jerusalem, were supplemented from the Roman fort of Vinovia at Binchester. In 1917 the natural history specimens were dispersed and the rest of the collections were placed in storage. From 1931 the archaeological collections assumed a new importance following the appointment of Eric Birley as the first lecturer in archaeology; he added material from his excavations on Hadrian's Wall. In 1975 the museum returned to the Fulling Mill

Current Collection Policy

The museum will collect archaeological material from Palaeolithic to 19th century, where this enhances existing holdings, but only in consultation with neighbouring museums.

The museum will collect archaeological material from the district of the City of Durham, as agreed with neighbouring museums and the County Archaeological Officer

The acquisition of artefacts must be influenced by the availability of resources for their subsequent care. No material will be acquired without consideration of resource implications.

Collection Size

The Roman ceramic collection, most importantly the Oswald-Plique Samian collection is of international importance, as is the Dean and Chapter's collection of stone inscriptions from and near Hadrian's Wall and other local sites. Other excavated material from Roman sites in the north of England is also an important resource for Roman scholars. There are a total of 2016 accessioned objects from the museum.

TULLIE HOUSE MUSEUM, CARLISLE (CUMBRIA)

Current Collection Policy

Historically, Tullie House has been a repository for archaeological finds from sites throughout the present county of Cumbria. This in part reflected the past lack of alternative local museums. Items relating to recent history have focussed much more clearly on the historic hinterland of the City of Carlisle - which does not necessarily conform to very recently drawn Local Government boundaries.

Future acquisitions in archaeology will normally derive from the Carlisle area, with the following regular exceptions:

- Where the Service already possesses excavated material and documentation from an archaeological site and that site is re-excavated, the finds and documentation will be accepted. This follows current HBMC guidelines that the excavation archive from one site should remain intact.

- Where finds and documentation originate from excavations carried out anywhere in the county under the auspices of the Cumberland & Westmorland Antiquarian and Archaeological Society (CWAAS). (This is in recognition of Tullie House's long-standing association with the CWAAS).

In addition, Tullie House acknowledges its role and responsibility as the largest museum service in the county. In terms of collecting policy, this means that Tullie House reserves the right to collect social history material from other Districts within Cumbria, subject to all three criteria below being satisfied:

- That the artefact(s) in question are judged to be of high importance to the county's heritage.

- That failure to act would result in the item(s) not remaining in or returning to Cumbria and/or being placed at risk of loss or destruction.

- That other relevant interested parties confirm that they not willing or able to proceed with the acquisition.

Artefacts acquired by the Service under the above circumstances would normally be considered strong candidates for loans out to officially Accredited museums of the areas most concerned.

Roman Collection
Material from:

Towns - Carlisle
Forts - Beckfoot, Birdoswald, Bowness-on-Solway, Burgh-by-Sands, Castlesteads, Housesteads and Stanwix
Milecastles - Banks Burn, Banks Head, Dykesfield, Gilsland, Glasson, Harrow's Scar, High House, Kirkland, Poltross Burn, Randylands, and Port Carlisle
Turrets - Appletree, Banks, Beck, Cambeck, Craggle Hill, Garthside, High House, Lea Hill, Pike Hill, Piper Sike, Rindle House and Willowford
Mile Fortlets - Cardurnock, Herd Hill and Mawbray
Towers - Rise Howe

BRITISH MUSEUM- ARCHAEOLOGICAL COLLECTIONS

Background
Founded in the mid-18th century the BM collections include internationally important objects from Britain and abroad. The main collections of material relevant to the north-east are held by the Department of Prehistory and Europe (established in 2003 by a merger of the Department of Prehistory and Early Europe and the Department of Medieval and Modern Europe).

Current Collection Policy
Currently being rewritten.

Collections Size
The museum holds small numbers of finds from the following sites: Benwell, Corbridge, Halton Chesters, 'Hadrian's Wall', Risingham, South Shields and Wallsend.
The museum also currently holds the Vindolanda Tablets.

SENHOUSE MUSEUM COLLECTION

The Museum's main purpose is the safeguarding and displaying of Roman material concerning Maryport and the Cumberland Coast and using those collections for public education. The basic collection areas are:

1) Roman Maryport
2) The Cumberland Coast (Roman material)
3) Archaeological material from Maryport
4) Material concerning the history of The Battery.

The museum would consider other archaeological material from within the Allerdale District, subject to Trustee Approval.

The main collection comprises:

- The Netherhall collection of mainly Roman artefacts from Maryport. The collection includes a few items from elsewhere, such as inscribed stones from Harrington and Beckfoot and some Bronze Age pots. The collection is held on a 125-year loan.
- The Bellhouse archive (but not finds, which are held in Tullie House).
- Finds and archive from MF21 (P. Turnbull).
- The finds and archive from 1966 excavation at Maryport by M. Jarrett
- Finds from Beckfoot Roman cemetery, collected since the mid-1980s, abd coins from unspecified locations between Maryport and Beckfoot.
- Finds (mainly pottery) from Ray Buckingham and Time Team work at Papcastle
- Eclectic collection (Roman and other) of dubious origin said to have been found in an outbuilding at Isel
- Roman coin hoards from Distington and Whitehaven
- Material from Netherhall Furnace (18th century). LUAU excavation.

ARBEIA ROMAN FORT AND SEGEDUNUM ROMAN FORT

Sites

Arbeia Roman Fort (South Shields)

The fort site was opened as the Roman Remains Park in the 1880s, while material from the excavations was put on display in South Shields Museum and Art Gallery in the town centre. In 1953 a small museum was opened on the site, and the archaeological collection was transferred across.

The majority of the collection consists of material and archive from excavations at Arbeia Roman Fort and its surroundings. Most of it comes from the Victorian excavations at the site from 1875 onwards and from excavations carried out since 1983 (still on-going). The collection also includes the Bruce Library of antiquarian books, archive material and ephemera relating to Hadrian's Wall and watercolours by Ronald Embleton.

Segedunum Roman Fort (Wallsend)

The Museum was opened in 2000. Excavation material temporarily stored in Newcastle University and South Shields was transferred into its collection. The collection is made up of material and archives from the excavations at Segedunum Roman Fort and its surroundings from 1975-84 and 1988-2001, including a section of Hadrian's Wall and the Branch Wall.

Current Collection policy

Most acquisitions occur as the result of archaeological excavation, although there are occasional donations by members of the public. The collection covers all archaeological material from the prehistoric to early-medieval period and, in some circumstances, post-medieval. The geographical collections area consists of the five district areas of Tyne and Wear with the following exceptions:

1) City of Newcastle upon Tyne within area of its medieval walls, and the area of its medieval suburbs
2) The Roman fort at Benwell and its surroundings
3) Hadrian's Wall and its associated works in Newcastle District
4) Material from the Anglo-Saxon monastic site at Jarrow

Collection size

Arbeia Roman Fort

Pottery, animal bone, tile, other building material, metalworking debris, sculpture, inscriptions, human remains, environmental samples, and small finds
Small finds: 10,800 artefacts
Bulk finds: very large quantities

Wallsend Roman Fort

Pottery, animal bone, tile, other building material; small quantities of metalworking debris, one inscription, and small finds
Small finds: 5,000 artefacts
Bulk finds: large quantities

THE VINDOLANDA CHARITABLE TRUST: CHESTERHOLM MUSEUM (VINDOLANDA) & THE ROMAN ARMY MUSEUM (CARVORAN)

Background

The Vindolanda Charitable Trust was founded in 1970 to excavate, research and preserve the Roman remains associated with land owned by the Trust - circa 100 acres at Vindolanda and Carvoran. The principal museum for the Trust is situated at Vindolanda with The Roman Army Museum at Carvoran exhibiting parts of the Vindolanda collection and holding copies of archives and documentation associated with the whole collection. Both museums are fully accredited under the MLA Council Museum Accreditation Scheme.

Current Collection Policy

The Vindolanda Trust reserves the right to own, preserve and care for any object found on land belonging to the Trust. The on-going Vindolanda archaeological excavation programme increases the collection on an annual basis. The Trust does not collect artefacts from any other source either by way of gift or purchase. In exceptional circumstances, where an object that has not been found by way of archaeological excavation on Trust land but that has been identified as originating from the same, Trustees then reserve the right to accept such an object by either gift or purchase. The Trust does collect archive material relating to Hadrian's Wall and general Roman research and currently holds the Eric Birley, John Mann & Charles Anderson archives. All of these rights are permissible under the Vindolanda Deed of Trust.

The Collection

The Vindolanda Trust recognises its ownership of an extensive and invaluable site- specific Roman research collection and does not dispose of any part of the collection or offer objects to other museums on permanent loan. The Vindolanda Writing Tablets are deposited with the British Museum after conservation and research and are the only exception to this policy. The collections of organic material (textile, leather and wooden objects) from the Vindolanda anaerobic levels represent the largest single site collection from the Roman World and each of these collections contain several individual pieces of exceptional national and international importance. The collection is fully documented and an advanced documentation programme for selected sections of the collection is now in operation to facilitate planned research. Approximately 35% of the primary collection is on display at any given time. The rest of the collection is in designated and controlled storage and research areas. Collection figures at October 2006 were 10985 'small finds', 160 sculptured & inscribed stones, 1300 coins, 5133 leather objects, 758 textiles, 1370 wooden objects, c 6.5 tons of samian, coarse-ware and other pottery & c. 2.8 tons of bone specimens.

The Vindolanda Trust is committed to the conservation, documentation and care of the collection and all associated archives, including the writing tablet photographic archive. The Trust has a vigorous policy of research, publication, access and education to promote the understanding and value of the collection to the widest possible audience.

ADDITIONAL COLLECTIONS HOLDING MATERIAL FROM HADRIAN'S WALL

Hexham Abbey

Ashmolean Museum

University Museum of Archaeology and Ethnology Cambridge

Durham Cathedral Chapter Library

University of Durham

Hallington Hall

Castlesteads, Walton

Lanercrost Priory (Only those built into fabric remain, others replicas - originals at Birdoswald).

Netherby, Longtown

Kendal Museum and Art Gallery

Yorkshire Museum, York

Appendix 3

Existing Archaeological Research Agendas with Relevance to Hadrian's Wall

Title: 'The Study Group for Roman Pottery: Research Framework Document for the Study of Roman Pottery in Britain, 2004' **Journal for Roman Pottery Studies** 11, 1-21

Authors: Study Group for Roman Pottery (edited and collated by Steve Willis)

Date: 2004

Publishers: SGRP

Content:

1. Introduction
   - 1.1 The need for a Research Framework for Roman pottery study
   - 1.2 The contribution of Roman pottery studies
   - 1.3 The production of Regional Research Frameworks of Roman pottery study and of a National synthesis
   - 1.4 Aim of the Research Framework Documents
2. Summary of the Objectives of Roman Pottery Research
3. Required Research Infrastructure
   - 3.1. The importance of an 'up-to-date' research infrastructure
   - 3.2 A national database catalogue of Roman pottery collections
   - 3.3 National and regional fabric and form series
   - 3.4 Scientific analysis
   - 3.5 Methodology
   - 3.6 Professional standards and expertise
   - 3.7 Strategic publications assisting efficient pottery work

4 Issues and Research Objectives relating to Site Types of the Roman Era: Major Civil Centres ('urban' sites), Military sites, Kiln sites, Rural sites, Smaller Centres and Cemeteries
   - 4.1 Background and potential
   - 4.2 Major civil centres (urban sites) of the Roman period
   - 4.3 Military sites
   - 4.4 Kiln sites
   - 4.5 Rural sites
   - 4.6 Small towns, roadside settlements and smaller centres
   - 4.7 Cemeteries

5 Issues and Research Objectives relating to Themes and Specialist Areas in Roman Pottery Study
   - 5.1 Chronology
   - 5.2 Trade, supply and distribution
   - 5.3 Samian
   - 5.4 Amphorae
   - 5.5 Romanisation; Roman and native interaction and cultural change
   - 5.6 Pottery functions and functional trends
   - 5.7 Site status
   - 5.8 Spatial patterning and integrated finds studies
   - 5.9 Social and cultural identity
   - 5.10 Ritual pots, ritual practice, ritual sites and structured deposition
   - 5.11 Roman pottery production and other Roman industries
   - 5.12 Residuality
   - 5.13 The end of the Romano-British economy

Comments:

4.3.1. Highlights the international. Empire-wide importance of Roman military sites in Britain, particularly Hadrian's Wall.
4.3.2 Notes the importance of pottery in providing chronological information on military sites.
4.3.3. Notes the potential of ceramic assemblages for facilitating spatial analysis on forts. It highlights the potential of the systematic comparison of pottery from barracks, store buildings, administrative buildings and high-status residencies.
4.3.4 Notes the role of pottery studies in relating military sites to wider views on Roman diet, ethnic origins and the politics and culture of food.

4.3.5 Notes the importance of the Northern frontier and makes reference to the Regional Framework for Northern Britain (Evans and Willis 1996).
4.3.6 Notes the importance of pottery studies to inform on aspects of the organisation of the Roman army, including its ethnic composition and movements.
5.8 Discusses the role of pottery studies in analysing spatial patterning within sites and the importance of integrating finds studies. It emphasises the potential of deeply stratified sites for examining spatial and chronological variations and makes explicit mention of northern military sites largely undisturbed by latter activity, including South Shields and Vindolanda. It suggests that research into these sites offers scope for comparison with other limes sites.

Title: Roman Archaeology Beyond the Wall (Chapter 5 of Northumberland National Park's Archaeology Research Agenda)

Authors: Dr. Rob Young, Northumberland National Park Archaeologist

Date: 2005

Publishers: Unpublished

Content:

5.1 Outline History of Previous Archaeological Research in Northumberland and Northumberland National Park
5.2 Assessment of the current state of knowledge relating to the Roman archaeology of the Northumberland National Park beyond Hadrian's Wall
5.3 Unprioritised list of research topics
5.4 References

Comments:
Specficially does not deal with the Hadrian's Wall WHS site because of the EH Management Plan and the forthcoming Hadrian's Wall Research Agenda. Instead focuses on Roman activity to the north of the Wall within the boundaries of the National Park.

Only one fort is within the boundaries of the National Park: High Rochester, though there are seventeen temporary/marching camps and a permanent fortlet at Chew Green. Unlike High Rochester these have seen very little fieldwork.

Research topics highlighted include:

- *Roman forts* focussing particularly on chronology of their construction, development and abandonment. There are also a number of topic related specifically to High Rochester including the relationship between the fort and forts on the Wall, the economic basis of the fort, the impact of a Roman military presence on the surrounding area, the lack of a vicus and further research into the Petty Knowes cemetery.
- *Marching camps* require an improved chronological understanding, greater insight into constructional techniques and comparison with other complexes of camps elsewhere in the Empire. Research questions related to individual camps include a clarification of the relationship between the two earthwork elements at Bagraw, the chronology of the complex of features at Birdhope, as well as investigation into the nature of the possible Roman mausolea at the site. Chew Green required an assessment of the development of the site and a better understanding of the internal roadways and possible ballistaria in Fort IV, and the 'stock enclosures' that in some places overlie the earthworks and run along the course of Dere Street. At Silloans the relationship between the camp and Dere Street, which bisects it, requires further exploration and at Sills Burn North Camp the relationship between the camp and the earthwork visible to its south-east should be clarified.
- *Roads* research should include a consideration of whether the road system was laid out de novo or followed an earlier system of routeways, and the impact of the road system on the physical and 'social' landscape of native settlement in the region.

Title: National Mapping Programme. Hadrian's Wall NMP Project: Bowness on Solway to Carlisle, Cumbria

Authors: Yvonne Boutwood

Date: October 2005

Publishers: Unpublished

Content:

1. Summary
2. Introduction
    2.1 The Physical Landscapes

3. Aerial photograph sources
    3.1 Sources Used
    3.2 Barri Jones Collection
4. Prehistoric and Romano British Settlement
    4.1 Background
    4.2 Aerial reconnaissance
    4.3 Results from NMP
    4.4 Conclusions for the Prehistoric and Romano British Settlement
5. The Solway Frontier
    5.1 Background
    5.2 NMP and Other Data
    5.3 Conclusions for the Solway Frontier
6. Future Research and Recommendations
7. Bibliography

Comments: Mainly a report on the work of the NMP within Block 1 of the Hadrian's Wall NMP, but concludes with a number of recommendations for future research.

- Need for more dating evidence for native sites
- Need to review range of settlement morphology as part of future mapping projects.
- The Solway Frontier defence system should be targeted for future reconnaissance due to the fragmentary nature of the aerial coverage.
- Geophysical survey shuld be used to located possible stretches of linear defence. Particular attention to the area to the west of Biglands House and milefortlet 1 may clarify whether parallel defence ditches do extend further west into the Cardurnock peninsula. Survey of sections flanking Hadrian's Wall and the Vallum, from Bowness on Solway to Port Carlisle may indicate whether these defensive ditches were a phase of the HW defences.

Roman Research Agendas and Overviews

Title: *A Research Framework for Hadrian's Wall: Draft Specification and Brief*

Authors:

Date: 2003 draft

Publishers: n/a

Content:

1. Background
2. Need for a research framework for Hadrian's Wall
3. Scope of framework
    i. Pre-existing landscape
    ii. Roman military network
    iii. Material Culture
    iv. Environmental archaeology
    v. Roman landscape and settlement type
    vi. The *vici*
    vii. The post-Roman transition and post-Roman landscape
    viii. Roman Scotland and the Antonine Wall
    ix. International Context
4. Specification: the production of a Research Framework
5. The process

Comments: Brief written due to the requirement in the WHS Management Plan (2002-7) for an 'academic research framework'. The research framework will cover a much larger area than the area of Hadrian's Wall WHS. Aims to cover entire northern frontier zone, i.e. forts between the Wall and Scotch corner, including Stainmore forts (Greta Bridge, Bowes). Also extends north to include High Rochester and Chew Green (as well as other northern forts outside the NE region). The research framework will also cover wide chronological period, including the pre-Roman landscape and the post-Roman transition.

Title: Review of Roman Small Finds Research

Authors: Lindsay Allason-Jones

Date: 2002

Publishers: in Past, Present and Future: The Archaeology of Northern England, AASDN Research Report 5

Contents:

Historical Review
Military studies
Gender Studies
Technology and Industry
Domestic Life
Future Work

Comments: Based on paper given in 1996. In 'Future Work' Allason-Jones calls for further work on military equipment from the North East, placing it in its national and international context. Secondly, she points out that little is known about funerary habits in the Roman north. Finally, she draws attention to the lack of excavation work carried out on vici. A better understanding of these sites could help elucidate our understanding their role and help broaden our understanding of the end of military occupation on the Wall.

Title: *The Archaeology of Roman Non-Military Sites*

Authors: Mike McCarthy

Date: 2002

Publishers: in Past, Present and Future: The Archaeology of Northern England, AASDN Research Report 5

Content: Based on a paper given at a conference in 1996. Brief review of evidence. Breaks suggestions for further research into macro-approach and micro-approach. The macro-approach involves further study of the wider Roman landscape and environment. Research might focus on the relationships between settlements and the natural environment. Micro- (or site specific) approach includes a more rigorous and analytical approach to data, including site formation processes and cultural assemblages. Creation of 'a series of phased spectra encompassing all finds [which] will help us to compare like with like, phase by phase, site by site.' Archaeo-entomology may prove important - can insects be used as a way of ranking settlements?

Title: *The Current State of Romano-British Pottery Studies*

Authors: Michael Fulford and Karen Huddleston

Date: 1990

Publishers: English Heritage

Content:

1. Achievements of 1970s and 1980s: a review of the literature
2. A review of current working practises and work in progress
3. Assessment of the coverage of towns, major settlements and rural areas in England
4. Conclusions

Recommendations
Appendix
Bibliography

Comments: Written at behest of EH in 1990 (just as EH was reorienting its funding priorities in the light of the introduction of PPG16).

Section 3 includes a brief literature survey of pottery studies on the Northern Frontier and the Pennines- suggests exploring pottery at a fort/vicus level of analysis. Also notes attention will be required to developments in the Roman pottery studies in the nearest legionary fortresses, particularly York.

Main Recommendations
1. Research Designs should be prepared for all ceramic projects. These should be fully integrated with the research design of the wider field project.

2. Potential of ceramic contribution should be considered at earliest stage of planning project (make reference to MAP2)
3. Level of analysis should be appropriate to information required
4. Consistency of analytical technique required. Recommends use of 'weight by war', 'weight by fabric type' and 'Estimated Vessel Equivalents (EVE).
5. Establishment of appropriate national and regional reference collections and syntheses
6. Preparations of manuals and corpora of certain pottery types
7. Additional emphasis on training
8. Regular meetings between EH and specialists

Title: *Britons and Romans: advancing an archaeological agenda*

Authors: Simon James and Martin Millett

Date: 2001

Publishers: CBA Research Report 125

Content:

Introduction *Simon James and Martin Millett*
The Iron Age-Roman Transition *John Creighton*
Romanisation, gender and class: recent approaches to identity in Britain and their possible consequences *JD Hill*
Material Culture and Identity *Lindsay Allason-Jones*
Material approaches to the identification of different Romano-British site types.
A place at the table: the role of vertebrate zooarchaeology within a Roman research agenda *Keith Dobney*
Rural society in Roman Britain *Jeremy Taylor*
Approaches to urban societies *Martin Millett*
Themes for urban research c.100BC to AD 200 *Barry Burnham, John Collis, Colin Dobinson, Colin Haselgrove and Michael Jones*
Soldiers and Civilians: identity and interaction in Roman Britain *Simon James*
The Roman to Medieval Transition *Simon Esmonde Cleary*

Comments: Introduction: arose from the EH sponsored session 'Romano-British Research Agendas' at the Roman Archaeology Conference (Durham 1999). Aims to integrate academic work with opportunities provided by climate provided by PPG16 and related change in funding strategy of EH. Session focused around two themes from EOP1998. 'Transitions and Identities' and 'Characterising settlement and society'.

Comments on individual papers below.

Title: 'Romanisation, gender and class: recent approaches to identity in Britain and their possible consequences'

Authors: JD Hill

Date: 2001

Publishers: in Simon James and Martin Millett (eds.) 2001 Britons and Romans, 12-18

Content:

New Approaches to Identity
Major features of new debates
New identities to consider: where are class or gender in the archaeology of Roman Britain?
Ideology, practice and the everyday
Consequences for field archaeology
Consequences for academic archaeology
Conclusions: Where do you want to go tomorrow?

Comments: Review of new theoretical approaches to Roman archaeology. Suggests field archaeologists to increasingly understand site formation processes and processes leading to the creation of the archaeological record. Calls for more detailed find recording and publication, e.g. distribution plot. Notes lack of specialist training for finds reports.

Title: 'Material culture and identity'

Authors: Lindsay Allason-Jones

Date: 2001

Publishers: in Simon James and Martin Millett (eds.) 2001 Britons and Romans, 19-25

Content: Overview of Roman small finds study. Critique of recommendations in EOP1998. Highlights need to characterise 'typical' finds assemblages, both for wider academic purposes and to help refine excavation strategies. Considers complex and overlapping nature of Roman identities. Emphasises need for more training of finds specialists. Examples mainly drawn from author's work on military sites on HW.

Title: *Town and Country in England: Frameworks for Archaeological Research*

Authors: Dominic Perring, Mark Whyman, Jonathan Finch, Rebecca Roseff, Frances Condron

Date: 2002

Publishers: Council for British Archaeology Research Report 134

Content:

1. Introduction
2. The Research Environment
3. Classes of Evidence and their potential
4. Research Frameworks
5. Conclusions and recommendations

Comments: Based on the Urban Hinterlands Project (1997-8) at the Universities of Leicester and York.
Focuses on dialogue between town and country
-emphasis on urban process rather than urban form
-explores social and economic network

Essentially explores urban-rural relationships though patterns of consumption and discard in the archaeological record

Contains an overview of archaeological and historical approaches to urbanism.
Explores the methodological strengths and limitations of a series of types of evidence, e.g. pottery, faunal assemblages, coinage

Carried out a series of case studies on periods of urban transition or consolidation
- Iron-Age to Roman: focussing on Essex and Colchester
- Coins of Later Roman Britain
- Emporia and early medieval settlement: focussing on Hamwic and Ipswich
- Regionality and the medieval landscape: focussing on Warwickshire and Norfolk
- Town and the Environment: focussing on London

Each case study concludes with a selection of detailed research proposals. The volume concludes with a number of methodological recommendations. These include:
1. Consistent approaches to data collection within the context of regional research agendas. Possibly using the notion of 'recovery levels'.
-suggest standards for pot and faunal remains analysis
-controlled recovery of artefacts from the topsoil/plough horizon
-use of metal detectors
-more research into site formation processes, residuality and taphonomy
2. Creation of more pottery type series and other classificatory systems remains a priority allowing chronologies to be further refined.
3. Better dissemination of existing digital archives
4. Widening the research community

Title: 'Environmental Archaeology: Mesolithic to Roman Period

Authors: J.P. Huntley

Date: 2002

Publishers: Brooks et al. (eds) 2002, 79-93

Content:

The Past
The Present
Environmental Archaeology: Status Today
The Mesolithic Evidence
The Neolithic Period
The Bronze Age
The Iron Age
The Roman Period
The Future
Conclusions
Future (Im)Perfect

Comments: Overview of environmental evidence for prehistoric and Roman periods. Includes considerations of effect of advent of PPG16 on environmental archaeology (e.g. reduced sample sizes, poor reporting).
Calls for more emphasis on charred plant remains and smaller animal bones.
Neolithic settlements need targeting to investigate the nature of domestication of plants and animals. Also needs synthesis of existing pollen work. Metrical analyses of bones and modern DNA work would also assist.
Bronze Age-more work needs to be carried out at an archaeological level on a variety of site types, which may or may not be BA. Particularly large samples needed due to low seed concentrations.

Title: The Romano-British Period Research Agenda for the North West

Authors: Compiled by R. Philpott and M. Brennand with contributions by Peter Carrington, David Shotter and Sue Stallibrass

Date: 2007

Publishers: Part of the North West Archaeological Research Framework.

Content:

Introduction
Improving accessibility of data
Unpublished archives
Chronologies and dating
Identification of new sites
New Research Questions for the Romano-British Period in the North
The Late Pre-Roman Iron Age
Tribal Identity
Environment
Military Activity
Settlement and Landuse
Industrial settlements
'Towns', *vici* and *canabae*
Rural settlement
Ritual, religion and ceremony
Burial
Technology and production
Mineral resources and extraction
Industrial processes
Trade, exchange and interaction
Ports and Maritime Trade
Legacy

Comments: Part of the North-West Regional Research Framework. The agenda covers all aspects of Roman archaeology of the North-West (Cheshire, Cumbria, Greater Manchester, Lancashire and Merseyside). Most of the recommendations have some relevance to Hadrian's Wall, though there are a number of priorities related specifically to military sites. These include:

- Publication and dissemination of unpublished works from military and fort sites
- An investigation of the coastal defences of the western seaboard in the third and fourth centuries.
- An improved understanding of the ethnicity and country of origin of those serving on the province's frontier, particularly capitalising on any opportunity to study surviving bone.

Title: The Roman Research Agenda for the North East

Authors: Compiled by David Petts and Christopher Gerrard

Date: 2006

Publishers: Published as part of the North-East Regional Research Framework. Durham County Council 2006.

Content:

Landscape survey
Forts and vici
Relationship between forts and earlier settlements
Votive deposition
Roman cemeteries
Iron Age to Roman transition
Roads and communication
The Roman military presence
Native and civilian life
Material culture
Trade and industry
Religion
Burial
Landscape and environment
Roman-early medieval transition

Comments: Part of the North-East Regional Research Framework. The agenda covers all aspects of Roman archaeology of the North-East (County Durham, Northumberland, Teeside and Tyne & Wear). All of the recommendations have some relevance to Hadrian's Wall.

Appendix 4

Summary of Aerial Photographs used in HW NMP

This is a summary of the aerial photographs identified during the HW National Mapping Programme based on cover searches carried out by the NMR Air Photos Library, Swindon. The full details of the material are held by the HWRF in Durham as a series of Excel spreadsheets that can be consulted.

Further information about the HW NMP can be found at:
http://www.english-heritage.org.uk/server/show/nav.1162

and

Kersaw, A. 2003. 'Hadrian's Wall National Mapping Programme - a World Heritage Site from the Air' *Archaeol.Prospect.* **10**, 159-61

Abbreviations:
CUCAP = Cambridge University Collection of Air Photographs
MOD = Ministry of Defence
NMR = National Monuments Record

Table 5. Aerial photographs used in HW National Mapping Project
BLOCK 1A (TOTAL 6 QUARTER SHEETS)
NY 15 NE, NY 16 SE, NY 25 NW, NY 25 NE, NY 26 SW, NY 26 SE

Repository	Obliques Total	Obliques BW	Obliques Colour	Verticals
Barri Jones	291	291	0	0
Bob Bewley	75	75	0	0
CUCAP	21	21	0	0
Cumbria Lancs Arch Unit	4	4	0	0
Destroyed (prints held in NMR)	0	0	0	7
MOD	0	0	0	51
NMR	236	176	60	25
Ordnance Survey	0	0	0	11
RH Windsor Collection	1	1	0	0

BLOCK 1B (TOTAL 7 QUARTER SHEETS)
NY 35 NW, NY 35 NE, NY 36 NW, NY 36 SW, NY 36 SE, NY 45 NW, NY 46 SW

Repository	Obliques Total	Obliques BW	Obliques Colour	Verticals
Bob Bewley	48	49	0	0
Barri Jones	217	217	0	0
NMR	345	345	102	22
Cumbria Lancs Arch Unit	5	5	0	0
Cumbria CC	35	35	0	0
CUCAP	9	9	0	0
Destroyed (prints held in NMR)	0	0	0	7
MOD	0	0	0	115
Newcastle University	2	2	0	0
Ordnance Survey	0	0	0	31

BLOCK 2 (TOTAL 9 QUARTER SHEETS)
NY 66 NE, NY 66 SE, NY 67 SE, NY 76 NW, NY 76 NE, NY 76 SW, NY 76 SE, NY 77 SW, NY 77 SE

Repository	Obliques Total	Obliques BW	Obliques Colour	Verticals
Airfotos Ltd	13	0	13	0
CUCAP	31	31	0	0
Anthony Crawshaw	10		10	0
Barri Jones	59	59	0	0
Destroyed (prints held in NMR)	0	0	0	2
MOD	0	0	0	40
Newcastle University	21	21	0	0
NMR	1765	1627	138	116
Ordnance Survey	0	0	0	2

BLOCK 3A (TOTAL 4 QUARTER SHEETS)
NZ 36 NW, NZ 36 NE, NZ 36 SW, NZ 36 SE

Repository	Obliques Total	Obliques BW	Obliques Colour	Verticals
Airfotos Ltd	1	1	0	0
Arbeia Roman Fort	53	?	0	0
Dank Silva	1	1	0	0
Destroyed (prints held in NMR)	39	39	0	29
MOD	402	402	0	192
Newcastle University	55	55	0	0
NMR	511	313	198	81
Ordnance Survey	0	0	0	64
RAF	78	78	0	0

BLOCK 3B (TOTAL 4 QUARTER SHEETS)
NZ 26 NW, NZ 26 NE, NZ 26 SW, NZ 26 SE

Repository	Obliques Total	Obliques BW	Obliques Colour	Verticals
Arbeia Roman Fort	7	7	0	0
Dank Silva	1	1	0	0
Destroyed (prints held in NMR)	40	40	0	14
MOD	441	441	0	181
Newcastle University	15	15	0	0
NMR	491	215	276	88
Ordnance Survey	0	0	0	62

BLOCK 3C (TOTAL 6 QUARTER SHEETS)
NZ 16 NW, NZ 16 NE, NZ 16 SW, NZ 16 SE, NZ 17 SW, NZ 17 SE

Repository	Obliques Total	Obliques BW	Obliques Colour	Verticals
Arbeia Roman Fort	16	0	0	0
CUCAP	6	6	0	0
Destroyed (prints held in NMR)	10	10	0	6
MOD	44	0	0	118
Newcastle University	18	0	0	0
NMR	372	0	68	130
Ordnance Survey	0	0	0	48

BLOCK 4A (TOTAL 6 QUARTER SHEETS)
NY 86 NW, NY 86 NE, NY 87 SW, NY 87 SE, NY 96 NW, NY 97 SW,

BLOCK 4B (TOTAL 6 QUARTER SHEETS)
NY 96 NE, NY 97 SE, NZ 06 NW, NZ 06 NE, NZ 07 SW, NZ 07 SE

Repository	Obliques Total	Obliques BW	Obliques Colour	Verticals
CUCAP	17	17	0	0
Destroyed (prints held in NMR)	1	0	0	0
MOD	0	0	0	36
NMR	491	369	122	25
Ordnance Survey	0	0	0	19

BLOCK 5 (TOTAL 10 QUARTER SHEETS)
NY 45 NE, NY 46 NE, NY 46 SE, NY 55 NW, NY 56 NW, NY 56 NE, NY 56 SW, NY 56 SE, NY 66 NW, NY 66 SW

Repository	Obliques Total	Obliques BW	Obliques Colour	Verticals
CUCAP	24	24	0	0
Cumbria Lancs Arch Unit	4	4	0	0
Anthony Crawshaw	2	2	0	0
Cumbria CC	42	42	0	0
Destroyed (prints held in NMR)	0	0	0	7
MOD	13	13	0	78
Newcastle University	2	2	0	0
NMR	540	322	218	150
Ordnance Survey	0	0	0	16

BLOCK 6A (TOTAL 6 QUARTER SHEETS)
NY 04 NE, NY 05 SE, NY 14 NW, NY 15 NW, NY 15 SW,
NY 15 SE, NY 03 NW, NY 03 NE, NY 04 SE, NY 13 NW, NY 14 SW

Repository	Obliques Total	Obliques BW	Obliques Colour	Verticals
CUCAP	19	0	0	0
Cumbria Lancs Arch Unit	27	0	0	0
Cumbria CC	52	0	0	0
Destroyed (prints held in NMR)	56	0	0	7
MOD	28	0	0	66
Newcastle University	5	0	0	0
NMR	995			58
Ordnance Survey	0	0	0	91
Bob Bewley	24	0	0	0

Appendix 5

Recent Archaeological Interventions on Hadrian's Wall (2000-2006)

Abbreviations:

WB = Watching Brief
Eval - Evaluation
Exc = Excavation
NR = No Results
NPRN = Northumberland Primary Record Number (i.e. event number on Northumberland SMR)

Numbers in brackets are reference numbers of report/event in the relevant SMR

Table 6. Archaeological interventions on Hadrian's Wall 2000-2006

Location	Site Name	Interventions since 2000	Notes	Published References:
Wallsend (Segedunum)		WB 2005: NR (2005/77) NZ 3010 6611 Eval 2002: RB artefacts (2002/89) NZ 3014 6589 WB 2002: Roman layers (2002/90) NZ3014 6589 WB 2002: NR (2002/88)	(2002/89) Three Roman High Water marks recorded. Finds: pot. Coin (2002/90) Roman layers seen. Finds: pot, bone, glass	Britannia 32 (2002), 291-2, figs.7-8
00.00.10	Carrville First School	Eval 2002: NR (2002/8) NZ 296 659		
1.6	Fossway Fire Station	WB 2001: Poss. Ditch (2001/55) NZ 2867 6547		
MC2	Walker	Eval 2005: NR (2005/16) NZ 2809 6526 Eval/WB 2005: Wall ditch (2005/27) NZ 2795 6513	(2005/27) Northern side of foundation and robbing trench; Wall ditch (c.8m wide)	
2.0.5	Newcastle Retail Park	Eval 2004: possible cut features (2004/10) NZ 2754 6488 WB 2004: NR (2004/41) NZ 2766 5506 WB 2004: ditch (2004/39) NZ 275 650 Eval 2003: NR (2003/84) NZ 2766 5506 WB 2003: NR (2003/2) NZ 2166 5506 WB 2002: NR (2004/28) NZ 282 653	(2004/100) Excavation found no evidence of Wall, but probably deeply buried at this point: cut features identified may be Roman features on berm between Wall and ditch	
2.0.5	Tunstall Ave	WB 2004: Wall (2004/117) NZ 2765 6502	2.4m length of Wall. Founds: 0.25m deep layer of sandstone frags in orange clay (width c.2.30-2.9)	
2.1.0	Union Road	Eval 2005: Wall Ditch; cippi pits; prehistoric (2005/42) NZ 2725 6487 Eval 2005: Wall Ditch; cippi pits (2005/42) NZ 265 648		

2.1.3	Corbridge Road	Eval 2005: NR (2005/44) NZ 2722 6478		
2.2.3	65-9 Shields Road	WB 2005: NR (2005/109) NZ 2672 6489		
2.2.5	40-42 Shields Road	Eval 2002: Wall (2002/80) NZ2665 6471	N. face of Wall; core: cobbles/grey sandy material	
2.7	Shields Road	Eval/WB 2005: Wall; ditch (2005/50) NZ 266 647 Eval 2001: NR (2001/80) NZ 266 647	(2005/50) Tr 1: HW in situ; facing walls robbed; overlain by core material; south side of wall ditch also located and possible 'patrol path' to the south of the Wall Core: sandstone and grey/brown silty clay/mortar on tail end of facing stones. Tr 2: Southern side of Wall Ditch and three rows of cippi pits.	
3.15	Byker City Farm	WB 2002: NR (2002/77) NZ2625 6460		
3.20	Ouseburn Village Green	WB 2003: NR (2003/54) NZ 2622 6459		
3.30	Stepney Bank	Eval 2005: Wall features, badly damaged (2005/66) NZ 262 646 Eval 2004: NR (2004/11) NZ 262 646		
3.65	Sallyport Garage	Eval 2004: NR (post-med) (2004/12) NZ 2551 6412		
3.70	Melbourne St/ Gibson St	WB 2004: NR (2004/99) NZ 257 643 Exc 2004: Wall (2004/58) NZ 257 643 Eval 2003: Wall (2003/43) NZ 257 644	(2004/99) Length of wall (2.8m long) located in se corner of site crossing trench at ne-sw angle. At least 2.6m in width. Two courses revealed; foundations not reached. Core: sandstone blocks in brown clay. (2004/58) 13m long stretch of wall; built across stream channel. Two courses high and 2.44m wide. Three rows of cippi pits. Ditch survived (3.1m wide; 1.8m deep).Palaeoen. evidence	
3.80	Melbourne Street	WB 2004: NR (post-med) (2004/50) NZ 2551 6418 Eval 2003: NR (2003/77) NZ 2551 6418		

4.15	14-18 Westgate Road	Eval 2004: Wall (2004/112) NZ249 639	Wal (Broad Wall). Founds: sandstone flags. Walls bonded with brown clay. First course inset 0.12m from founds. Core: sandstone rubble in brown clay	
4.30		Exc 2005: NR (2005/122) NZ 2463 6399		
4.6	Peel Lane/Temple Street	WB 2003: NR (2003/87) NZ 243 639		
4.65	East Blenheim Street	WB 2004: Poss vallum (2004/32) NZ 242 640 Eval 2204: NR (2004/30) NZ242 640	Large site- nine boreholes and three testpits. Land becomes deeper across site, possibly indicating location of the vallum.	
4.65	Carlisle Hotel	Exc 2004: NR (med/post-med) (2004/96) NZ 2426 6407 Eval 2004: Roman features (2004/65) NZ 2426 6407	(2004/65) Stone clay banks - possibly Roman road surface. Gravel-filled gully 8m behind street frontage probably also RB. Finds: pot	
5.40	Westgate Hill School	WB 2002: NR (2004/50) NZ 232 642 WB 2001: NR (2001/43) NZ 218 648		
5.70	Former Nurse's Home, Westgate Road	WB 2005: NR (2005/1) NZ 2280 6444		
5.80	Prospect House, Grainger Park Road	WB 2003: NR (2003/83) NZ 227 644		
5.90	Bowland Lodge/Firestation	Eval 2006: NR (2006/12) NZ 226 645 Eval 2004: NR (2004/83) NZ 2257 6442 WB 2004: NR (2004/97) NZ 225 645		
Benwell *(Condercum)*		WB 2005: structural remains (2005/99) NZ 2158 6471 WB 2005: NR (2005/15) NZ 217 645 Eval 2004: Military Way (2004/44) NZ 215 647 WB 2004: Vallum (2004/59) NZ 218 636 WB 2003: NR (2003/69) NZ 214 649 WB 2002: NR (2002/20) NZ 2162 6483 WB 2002: large cut feature of uncertain date (20002/29) NZ	(2005/99) Internal foundations and flagged floor of granary building and possible remains of E-W transverse wall dividing granary into two portions. Also EW aligned cut, which may be robbing of southern wall of the unnamed building to the west of the hospital Finds: Coin, pot, fe (2004/59) Traces of	

		218 648 Eval 2001: NR (2001/47) NZ 2143 6469 WB 2000: NR (2000/1) NZ 218 647	northern edge of vallum recorded (2004/44) Military Way: No camber or axial/side kerbs; ditches on s. side only.	
6.2.80	St Cuthbert's House	Eval 2003: NR (2003/55) NZ 209 650 WB 2003: NR (2003/70) NZ209 650 WB 2003: NR (2003/40) NZ 209 650 WB 2002: NR (2002/83) NZ 209 650 Eval 2002: NR (2002/38) NZ 209 650		
8.0.30	St Vincent's Home, West Denton	Eval 2004: NR (post-med) (2004/45) NZ 1902 6578		
8.0.30	Roman Way	WB 2001: NR (2005/45) NZ1905 6590		
8.1.20	Union Hall Rd.	WB 2005: NR (2005/52) NZ 1866 6595		
8.1.30	Roman Way, Lemington	WB 2004 : ditch seen in several trenches (2004/60) NZ186661	HW ditch in seen in several trenches. Wall probably south of projected course on map.	
8.1.50	Westlands	WB 2005: NR (2005/76) NZ1838 6611 Eval 2003: HW ditch (2003/37) NZ1842 6611	Possible upper fills of HW ditch. Line of wall probably lies to the south of the projected position	
MC9	Chapel House	Eval 2000: structural remains (Wilmott forthcoming) NZ 1785 6627 WB 2001: Wall Ditch observed (2001/18) NZ1777 6613 - 1783 6631	Finds: Coins, Cu, Stone, Pot,	
9.0.50	Keith's Coaches, Hexham Road, Blucher	Wb/Eval 2003: NR (2003/27) NZ 1760 6640 WB 2003: Vallum ditch and smaller, undated ditch (2003/71) NZ1777 6613 - 1783 6631		
9.1.2	Walbottle Service Station	WB 2004: Wall Ditch located (north side of profile) (2003/29) NZ 170 665 WB 2003: HW ditch (c.8m wide x 2.6m deep), glacis (2003/29) NZ 170 665 WB 2001/14: two sandstone blocks aligned N-S (2001/14) NZ172 664		

T9b	Walbottle	Eval 2005: NR (2005/29) NZ169665 WB 2005: Spread of possible core material (2005/40) NZ170 665	Possible core: sandstone and clay	
9.2.50	Walbottle Campus	Eval 2005: Wall, bank (2005/62) NZ1665 6673	N. face and 2.3m width of wall Found: sandstone slabs, c.0.10m deep and 0.32m wide, bonded with clay Three courses of north face survive in situ at depth of c.0.4m, mortar bonding. First course inset 0.12m from foundation; 2nd/3rd course inset 0.08m from 1st course. Core: yellow clay with sandstone fragments	
MC10	Walbottle Dene	Eval 2000: vallum (Wilmott forthcoming) NZ 1664 6662 Eval 2001: small portion of mound, sealed buried ground surface (2001/76) NZ 165 666		
10.1.50	Throckley	WB 2001: Wall (2001/66) NZ158 668	0.6m x 0.41 m area of Wall recorded: Founds.: sandstone in clay; facing stones with mortar; prehistoric agricultural activity	
10.2.50	Throckley Middle School	Eval 2005: sandstones on wall alignment, but probably not wall (2005/123) NZ 1539 6685 Ex/WB 2004: ditch fill/post-Roman palaeo. (2004/101) NZ155 669 Excav 2004: Wall (2004/43) NZ1544 6685 WB 2003: NR (med/post-med only) (2003/63) NZ 1529 6690 Eval 2003: Wall/cippi pit (2003/60) NZ1543 6686 Eval 2002: NR (LBA pit/med and post-med features) (2002/75) NZ1520 6698 WB 2002: NR (2002/72) NZ1520 6690 Eval 2002: NR (2002/41) NZ1543 6686 WB 2001: Wall (2001/6) NZ155 668	(2004/43) Truncated remains of Hadrian's Wall; Founds.: sandstone slabs and sub-angular blocks bonded with clay (c.2.8m n-s) Core: rubble. Palaeo evidence suggests area cleared by burning before construction (2003/60 Truncated length of HW foundation (max width 1.44m) including south edge. Possible cippi pit 3.5m north of southern face of Wall (0.5m north of postulated north wall) (2001/6) 7m length of HW excavated. 500mm thickness of core material with a single facing of stone. Core: sandstone blocks and snady clay matrix	

10.1.60	Throckley	Eval 2004: lightly packed sandstones, probably not wall (2004/31) NZ1529 6685 WB 2001: Wall (2001/65) NZ1531 6685	Wall. Core: sandstone fragments in clay, width 2.95m. Wall extensively robbed	
T10b	Throckley	WB 2004: NR (2004/8) NZ152 670		
11.0.50	Curtain wall	TT 2005: NR (NEPRN 13451) NZ1428 6684 WB 2005: NR (NEPRN ***) NZ 1452 6687)		
T11b	Great Hill	EX 2002: berm defences, Turret? (NEPRN 340) NZ14296688		
11.2.60	Curtain wall	WB 2003: NR (NEPRN 419) NZ13386697		
MC12	Heddon	TT 2004: NR (NEPRN 13263) NZ13546698		
12.0.5		TT 2004: RM features (NEPRN 13330) NZ 1322 6701 TT 2005: NR (NEPRN 13529) NZ 1322 6701		
T12.1.5	Curtain Wall	WB 2005: NR (NEPRN13258) NZ12756715		
T12b	North Lodge	WB 2002: NR (NEPRN 291) NZ127672		
c.12.2.50	Simpson 1931, 322	TT 2001: wall (NEPRN 308) NZ12406725 TT 2002: NR (NEPRN 367) NZ072682 WB 2003: NR (NEPRN 403) NZ126672 WB 2003: NR (NEPRN 417) NZ126672	CW:111/9.53/2819	
Rudchester (Vindovala)		TT 2000: Roman deposits/vallum (NEPRN 246) NZ1125 6740 WB 2001: NR (NEPRN 198) NZ 1125 6755 WB 2001: re-used masonry (NEPRN 234) NZ1130 6725 WB 2002: undated features (NEPRN 269) NZ11256740 WB 2002: undated features (NEPRN 370) NZ11256740		
MC14	March Burn	EV 2000: wall (NEPRN 248/Wilmott forthcoming) NZ 1068 6768	West and south walls heavily robbed	
MC16	Harlow Hill	WB 2004: Post-med (NEPRN 13305) NY76796639		

	Curtain wall	EV 2005: NR (NEPRN ***) NZ 076 683		
16.2.5	Curtain Wal	WB 2001: NR (NEPRN 282) NZ065682		
c.17.1.50	Curtain wall	WB 2000: building stone frag (NEPRN 186) NZ 0600 6825		
MC18	East Wallhouses	WB 2001: NR (NEPRN 212) NZ 0495 6836 WB 2005: NR (NEPRN 13492) NZ 047682		
18.0.5	CW	EV SV 2000: ditch surveyed (NEPRN 247) NZ04626841		
T18b	Wallhouses West	WB 2005: NR (NEPRN 13578) NZ 0398 6851		
MC20	Halton Shields	TT 2000 Wall (NEPRN 282)		
20.1.00	Curtain wall	WB 2001: NR (NEPRN 164) NZ 011 687		
Halton Chesters *(Onnum)*		WB 2001: building stone (NEPRN 163) NY 9964 6847 TT 2001: HW, str, val (NEPRN 200) NZ018 687		
26.0.40	Curtain wall	WB 2000: NR (NEPRN 190) NY926697 WB 2001: NR (NEPRN 208) NY92896962		
	200m North of T26b	WB 2005: NR (NEPRN 13575) NY9214 7009		
Chesters *(Cilurnum)*		WB 2001: NR (NEPRN191) NY91207025 WB 2001: NR (NEPRN192) NY91247047 GEO 2003: vicus (NEPRN 377) NY91267002		
28.0.5		WB 2003: NR (NEPRN 404) NY90247052		
28.2.5		WB 2003: vallum (NEPRN 416) NY892709		
T29a	Black Carts	WB 2004: NR (NEPRN 13301) NY884712	West wing wall probably 19th century rebuilding Finds: CRM, glass, bone; fe	
T31a	The Strands	SV 2000: mapped vallum (NEPRN 155) NY 8750 7115	Not located	
MC33	Shield on the Wall	WB 2001: NR (NEPRN 145)		

T34a	Grindon West	WB 2003: Wall (NEPRN 13580) NY 8142 7030 WB 2005: Wall (NEPRN ***) NY8142 7030		
T35b	Busy Gap	WB 2001: NR (NEPRN 165) NY 7989 6960		
Housesteads (*Vercovicium*)		GEO 2003: vicus (NEPRN 372) NY790687		
MC38	Hotbank	SV 2002: (NEPRN 13327) NY77266812 WB 2003: NR (NEPRN 13579) NY 7726 6812 WB 2005: NR (NEPRN ***) NY 7726 6812		
T38a	Milking Gap	WB: NR (NPRN 146)		
	Vallum south of MC40	TT 2003: ENV (NEPRN 434) NY 74866687 WB 2002: NR (NEPRN 13323) NY74746683)		
	Military road south of T41b	WB 2004: NR (NEPRN 13272) NY721661		
	Military Road south of MC42	WB 2004: NR (NEPRN 13299) NY71386598		
45.0.90	Curtain wall	WB 2001: NR (NEPRN 148) NY 6646 6604 WB 2001: NR (NEPRN 147) NY 6729 6628		
46.1.60	Curtain wall	WB 2001: NR (NEPRN 149) NY 6540 6598 WB 2001: Med ? (NEPRN 150) NY 6603 6600 WB 2001: NR (NEPRN 151) NY 6603 6593		
T47b	Gap	TT 2005: NR (NEPRN 13458) NY 6399 6623		
47.2.90	Curtain wall	WB 2004: Post-med (NEPRN 13334) NY63546619		
Birdoswald (*Banna*)		Ex 2002 (Wilmott forthcoming) NY 597656 WB 2003: NR (CC 1/04/1250) NY6163 566176		
MC50 TW	High House	WB 2000: NR (CC 1/LUA/00/HIG) NY5960 6560 - NY572 56463		
T50 SW	High House	WB 2000: NR (CC 1/LUA/00/HIG) NY5960 6560 - NY572 56463		

T50a TW		WB 2000: NR (CC 1/LUA/00/HIG) NY5960 6560 - NY572 56463		
T50a SW	High House	WB 2000: NR (CC 1/LUA/00/HIG) NY5960 6560 - NY5725 6463		
T50b TW		WB 2000: NR (CC 1/LUA/00/HIG) NY5960 6560 - NY5725 6463		
T50b SW	Appletree	WB 2000: NR (CC 1/LUA/00/HIG) NY5960 6560 - NY5725 6463		
MC51	Wall Bowers	WB 2000: NR (CC 1/LUA/00/HIG) NY5960 6560 - NY5725 6463		
T51a	Piper Syke	WB 2000: NR (CC 1/LUA/00/HIG) NY5960 6560 - NY5725 6463		
T51b	Lea Hill	WB 2000: NR (CC 1/LUA/00/HIG) NY5960 6560 - NY5725 6463		
MC52	Bankhead	WB 2000: NR (CC 1/LUA/00/HIG) NY5960 6560 - NY5725 6463		
Pike Hill		WB 2000: NR (CC 1/LUA/00/HIG) NY5960 6560 - NY5725 6463		
52.0.99	Curtain wall	WB 2000: NR (CC 1/LUA/00/HIG) NY5960 6560 - NY5725 6463		
T52a	Bank's East	WB 2000: NR (CC 1/LUA/00/HIG) NY5960 6560 - NY5725 6463		
T52.1.70	Curtain wall	Eval 2005: Undated structural remains (CC 1/05/1455) NY57170 64586		
55.0.30	Curtain Wall (High Dovecot Farm)	WB 2003: core/ditch (CC 1/5/1492) NY5334164414 WB 2004: NR (CC1/04/1215)	**Core: rubble**	
MC56	Curtain Wall: Walton	WB 2001: NR (CC 1/LUA/01/WAL), NY5214864476		
57.1.80	Curtain wall: Newtown Farm	Ex/Eval 2002: Core (CC 1/05/1493) NY5015162976 WB 2003: Cut featured ND (CC 1/JAW/03/NE) NY5005362752		

MC58	Newtown	WB 2004: NR (CC 1/04/1248) NY49708 62599 WB 2000: NR (CC 1/LUA/01/NE) Newtown to Old Wall		
MC59	Old Wall	WB 2000: NR (CC 1/LUA/01/NE) Newtown to Old Wall		
c.59.1.50	Curtain Wall (Old Wall Cottage, Irthington)	Eval 2003: NR (CC 1/03/1027) NY48041 61691		
60.9	Curtain Wall (Low Wallhead)	WB 2005: NR (CC 1/05/1515) NY45506, 60860		
62.40	Curtain Wall (Walby Hall)	Eval 2003: Wall ditch (CC1/04/1213) NY43589, 60265	Finds: pot, pb	
64.1.50	Curtain wall	Eval 2003: NR (CC 1/JAW/03/HO) NY41290 58416		
Stanwick *(Uxelodunum/ Petriana)*		WB 2005: NR (CC 1/05/1437) NY40343 57383 WB 2005: NR (CC 1/05/1482) NY4007057146 Eval 2004: parade ground? (CC 1/04/1274) NY40391 57290 Eval 2004: Med/poss R ditch (CC 1/04/1333) NY 40118 57137 WB 2002: Wall/ditch (CC 1/02/476) NY40487 57375 Eval 2000: NR (CC 1/LUA/00/ARC) NY40302 67183 WB 2000: wall/vallum/fort (CC 1/CAL/01/SRD)	Wall at least 1.2m wide; ditch at least 3.5m wide (CC 1/02/476) Stretch of heavily robbed curtain wall with remains of a possibly denuded rampart and an intervallum road inside the wall. Also poss observatio of a stretch of inner and outer defensive ditches of the for and a cobbled surface on the berm between the inner ditch and fort wall (CC 1/CAL/01/SRD)	
66.25	Curtain Wall	WB 2005: NR (CC 1/05/1447) NY39240 56557)		
South of 66.7	Carr's Field, Newtown Rd	Geophys 2004 (CC1/04/1258) NY38193 56227		
67.5	Curtain Wall (Knockupworth Gill)	Pal Ass 2005: Recent soils (CC 1/05/1425) NY37288 56675		
Sw. of 67.6	Carlilse Northern Relief Road	Eval 2002: NR (CC 1/CFA/03/CND) NY36954 56394) Eval 2005: NR (CC 1/05/1426a)		
67.9	Knockupworth Farm	Eval 2005: vallum/wall (CC1/05/1424) NY37075, 57063	Vallum; part of possible patrol track, foundations of wall one course deep, constructed with an inner edge of flat slabs and rubble core. Estimated as much of 2.7m of wall destroyed by erosion from escarpment	

68.8	Curtain wall (Edeholme Farm, Grinsdale)	Eval 2000: Undated ditch (CC 1/LUA/00/GRI) NY36867 57872		
MC69	Sourmilk Bridge	Geophys 1998/2000: milecastle not located (Robinson and Biggins 2000a) NY 351 590 Exc 2000: wall located (Wilmott forthcoming) NY 351 590		
69.7	Curtain Wall (Kirkandrews upon Eden)	WB 2005: NR (CC 1/05/1518) NY35559 58363 Eval 2002: NR (CC1/02/400) NY35252 58435)		
MC70	Braelees	Geophys 2000: milecastle not located (Robinson and Biggins 2000b) NY 351 590		
Vallum s. of T70b	Vallum (Monkhill)	WB 2005: Vallum (CC1/05/1422) NY34341 58626		
MC71	Wormanby	Eval 200:turf wall/milecastle remains (Wilmott forthcoming) NY 3381 5921		
Burgh-by-Sands *(Abballava)*		Eval 2002: Vicus (CC 1/OAN/02/BUR) NY3297359130 WB 2003: Post-med (CC 1/JAW/03/TOC) NY3244359163)	Evidence for extramural settlement; important finds assemblage (CC1/OAN/02/BUR)	
MC72	Fauld Farm	WB 2004: vallum? (CC 1/04/1256) NY32322 59020		
72.2.5	Vallum	Eval 2003: NR (CC 1/03/1049) NY32054 58982)		
Drumburgh *(Coggabata)*		WB 2004: R? occupation layer (CC2/04/1285) NY26601 59776		
T76b	Glasson	WB/Eval 2004: vallum? (CC 2/05/1440) NY 25560 60234		
Vallum wsw of MC77		WB 2003: NR (CC 2/03/1037) NY25260 60462		
MC78	Kirkland	Eval 2000: robbed walls (Wilmott forthcoming) NY 2455 6134		
Bowness on Solway *(Maia)*		Eval 2005: fort remains (CC 2/05/1417) NY22353 62712) WB 2003: NR (CC 2/03/1038) NY22507 62767 Eval 2003: Post-med (CC 2/04/1201) NY22247 62724 WB 2000: Palaeo data (CC 2/CAA/01/RBN) NY22320 62655 WB 2001: Features/sandstone structure, undated (CC 2/02/382) NY22195 62688	Significant structural remains inside fort; including walls, cobbled surfaces, prob Roman, including prob east wall of the fort (CC 2/05/1417)	

		WB 2003: NR (CCC/2003) NY22043 62631 WB 2004: NR (CCC/2004) NY22045 62624		
MF3 CC	Pasture House	Geophys 2004: site identified/poss defensive bank (CC 2/04/1265), NY17887 60351		
T3a CC	Pasture House West	Geophys 2004: not located (CC 2/04/1265), NY17887 60351		
T3b CC	Herd Hill North	Geophys 2004: poss. Disturbance identified (CC 2/04/1265), NY17887 60351		
T15a CC	Bank Mill	WB 2004: NR (CC 2/04/1279) NY 08924 47899		
MF17 CC	Dubmill Point	WB 2005: NR (CC 2/05/1533) NY 07846 46053		
c.800m west of T19b	Mealo Hill Farm	WB 2003: NR (CC 2/04/1219) NY08665 41729		
C2km west of Bank End	Westland's Farm, Crosby	Eval 2004: NR (CC 2/04/1236) NY07332 38436		
Maryport *(Aluana)*		Geophys 2000: vicus (CC 2/TAS/00/MAR) NY 04055 37463 WB 2002: NR (CC 2/NAA/02/ROR) NY04377 36994 Eval 2004: undated pits/stakeholes (CC 2/04/1259) NY04482 36916		
800m NE of Burrow Walls	Lowca Lane, Workington	Eval 2001: NR (2/CAL/01/LOW) NY01132 30965		
Moresby *(Gabrosentum?)*		Geophys 2002: ramparts, poss. structures; tenuous earlier fort (CC 4/02/459) NY98165 21039		

Appendix 6

Portable Antiquities Data and Hadrian's Wall

Rob Collins
PAS/Newcastle University

Introduction

Every year, thousands of artefacts reported by the public are recorded by the Portable Antiquities Scheme. The records of these artefacts are a valuable asset for those engaged in finds research, often indicating historic activity in areas where activity was previously unknown or only presumed. The majority of objects recorded have been recovered by metal detectorists, though a significant percentage are reported by other members of the public due to gardening, walking/running, or walking the dog.

Over the past three years, since the appointment of a fulltime Finds Liaison Officer for both the North East region and another FLO for Cumbria, many hundreds of objects have been recorded from the former Roman frontier. The artefacts provide an opportunity to assess the extent to which Roman finds are recovered outside of scheduled areas, and if such finds conform to any patterns. This paper is a basic assessment and summary of data recorded and held by the Portable Antiquities Scheme (www.finds.org.uk).

There are a number of biases and discrepancies associated with any PAS data, and these must be briefly acknowledged, as they will impact on any interpretation of the data. Primarily, PAS data is a record of voluntary recording of recovered artefacts. The vast majority of recorded objects are reported by metal detectorists, whom employ varied search methods (and regularity), target favoured search areas, and ignore non-metal objects like ceramics. Therefore, data is often skewed toward those parishes that are searched frequently. Many parts of the northern England are less extensively and intensively searched than the Southern counties, and this is reflected in terms of real numbers of recorded finds by county on the PAS database. A secondary issue that must be considered with PAS data is the quality of the identification. Every FLO must accumulate and apply a broad-based knowledge of artefacts from every major archaeological period, and it is simply impossible for every FLO to be a specialist in every major artefact type. To that extent, the quality of each record will vary depending on the individual specialisms of each FLO. Fortunately, this aspect is countered by the excellent training and advice provided by the PAS and the pro-forma of the PAS database, which ensures that specific information is always recorded. A further bias, specific to this research framework is the scheduled status of Roman sites in northern England. Notably, this includes the Hadrian's Wall WHS and very many Roman military installations away from the Wall. This scheduled status means that there will not be many objects recorded that are directly associated with activity on Hadrian's Wall. It should also be noted that no records created after January 20, 2007 were included in this study.

Rather than strictly assessing the few artefacts from the narrow corridor of Hadrian's Wall, a broader approach has been taken to include the majority of the frontier. The actual area that can be considered or defined as the Roman frontier varied throughout the Roman period, but the area examined for this study starts in Cumbria and County Durham, roughly from the Tees north to the Scottish border Within this area, 174 coins and 301 artefacts have been recorded dating to the Roman period, though it should be stated that some of these artefacts, lacking a full archaeological context, may in some instances date to the Medieval period, notably where objects are fragmentary or generic in character. Figure 1 demonstrates a basic distribution of artefacts and coins in the area considered with coins as black circles and artefacts as green squares. At a basic level, this map indicates reported Roman objects rather than every Roman object found in the North. Generally speaking, however, there are relatively few 'blank' swathes of land, with the exception of the Pennines. This blank is due to the lack of searching in the uplands by detectorists. It should also be noted that Scottish data was not incorporated, so the 'blankness' of Scotland should not be taken to indicate anything significant like some sort of chronic material depression.

Summary of Data Available

A variety of artefacts have been recorded via the Portable Antiquities Scheme. A full record of each artefact can be viewed at www.findsdatabase.org.uk using a specific find ID number or through the site search facilities. The majority of objects found along the line of Hadrian's Wall, or in proximity to it, are brooches, coins, and pottery sherds. Most of the artefacts reported are from outside the scheduled area of the WHS, but a small number are from scheduled areas. In such instances, the objects have been recovered from the ground surface due to animal burrowing or land slip, and have been reported by local residents that walk in the area.

At present, there is only one large assemblage of finds from the River Tyne at Corbridge recorded via the PAS (Collins forthcoming); all other objects are single finds that at best were found in the same field with other Roman artefacts. There is another large assemblage from Piercebridge, however, that has also been recorded by the PAS (Walton in prep.). However, it should be noted that higher numbers of finds and the greatest variety of artefact types are found in the vicinity of Roman military installations, both along Hadrian's Wall and in other areas of the frontier. There is also a tendency for Roman objects to be found in proximity to a Roman road or along the coast (Figure 1). This relationship is not a search bias on the part of finders, as there is rarely a concerted effort to target the paths of Roman roads.

Basic Conclusions from PAS Data

A few basic conclusions can be provided from an overview of PAS data in the frontier (Collins, in prep.). Overall, it can be confidently claimed that patterns from PAS data are consistent with those determined through archaeological research.

- There is a contrast between higher numbers of artefacts dated to the early Roman period and higher numbers of coins dated to the 4th century.
- Objects (coins and artefacts) dated to the 4th century seem to have a less geographically extensive distribution in the frontier than objects from the previous centuries.
- The distribution of different types of personal objects, notably brooches, suggests an east-west difference in terms of dress and personal appearance.
- Despite the highly militarized occupation of the frontier, military objects are not frequently found. When they are found, it is almost always in proximity to military installations.
- The date of recorded coins generally concurs with the regional pattern of coin loss, though not the national pattern. Few high value coins (of silver or gold) have been found. Those that have been recorded all date to the early empire.
- Less than half the coins could be attributed to an issue period - a figure that is significantly higher than the percentage from excavated sites. This is probably due to the fact that most PAS data is from land in agricultural use where ploughing regularly destabilizes the depositional environment while most Roman military installations in the North are SAMs.

While these conclusions are rather general, they do offer an important validation of the patterns established through archaeological research in the frontier, in contrast to other regions of Britain. More trends and patterns can be discerned through PAS data, but this requires a more focused approach. Ideally, future research could highlight the degree to which Roman objects permeated the non-military settlements of the frontier, or look for changes in the economic organization of the frontier through an analysis of coinage.

Future research along Hadrian's Wall, particularly finds-based studies or that focusing on economic activity must take account of Portable Antiquities data, as this represents a valuable and constantly growing database for areas that are lacking in archaeological investigation.

Bibliography

Collins, R. *forthcoming*. 'A Riverine Assemblage from the Tyne at Corbridge.'

Collins, R. *in prep*. 'Portable Antiquities in the Roman Frontier', *Proceedings of the 10th Annual Portable Antiquities Scheme Conference*

Walton, P. *in prep*. 'Finds from the River Tees, Piercebridge, County Durham', in H. Cool and D. Mason (eds.), *Excavations at Piercebridge, 1960-1982*

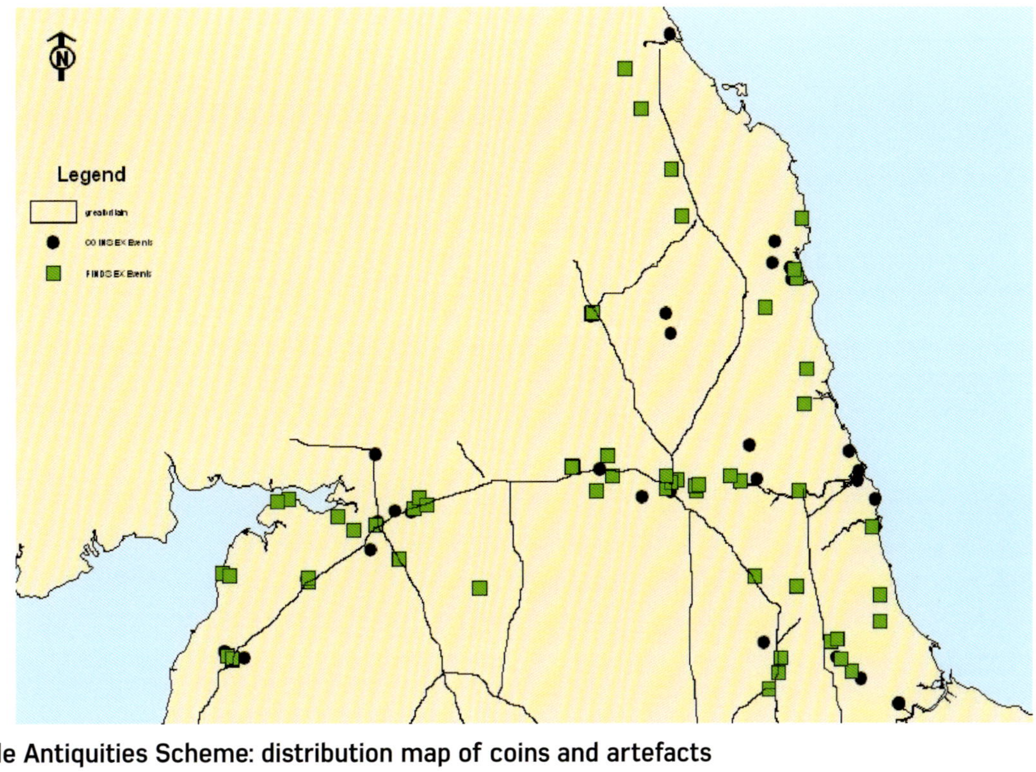

168. Portable Antiquities Scheme: distribution map of coins and artefacts

Tables:

Table 7. PAS data. Roman artefacts listed by material

Primary Material	No. of Finds
Bone	1
Ceramic	125
Copper Alloy	133
Glass	4
Gold	5
Iron	3
Lead	20
Plaster	1
Silver	1
Stone	6
Tin (& Tin Alloy)	2

Table 8. Roman artefacts listed by date.

Date	No. of Finds
Roman (AD 43-410)	239
1st Century AD	4
1st-2nd Century AD	34
2nd Century AD	7
2nd-3rd Century AD	5
3rd Century AD	4
4th Century AD	4
1st-3rd Century AD	2
3rd-4th Century AD	2

Table 9. Roman artefacts listed by category.

Category	No. of Finds
1. Personal Ornaments	67
2. Toilet and Medical Equipment	3
3. Textile Equipment	1
4. Household Utensils and Furniture	117
5. Objects used for Recreational Purposes	4
6. Objects used for Weighing and Measuring	4
7. Objects associated with Written Communications	1
8. Objects associated with Transport	0
9. Buildings and Services	14
10. Tools	7
11. Fasteners and Fittings	42
12. Objects associated with Agriculture	0
13. Military Equipment	29
14. Religious Items	4
15. Objects and Waste associated with Metalworking	5
16. Objects and Waste associated with Bone working	0
17. Objects and Waste associated with the Fired Ceramics	0
18. Miscellaneous	3

Table 10. Roman artefacts listed by type.

Type	No. of Finds
Bead	3
Bracelet	4
Brooch	28
Ear Ring	3
Finger Ring	9
Jewellery	5
Necklace	1
Pendant	4
Pin	9

Table 11. Roman brooches listed by type.

Brooch Type	No. of Finds
Aesica' type	1
Dragonesque	5
Headstud	4
Hod Hill	1
Knee	1
Swastika	1
Trumpet	8
Pins and Fragments	7

Table 12. Coins listed by metal

Material	No. of Coins
Gold	0
Silver	30
Copper Alloy	144

Table 13. Coins listed by date

Date	No. of Coins
Pre 1st Century AD	2
1st Century AD	8
2nd Century AD	29
3rd Century AD	30
4th Century AD	61
1st-3rd Century AD	15
3rd-4th Century AD	27
Illegible Roman	2

Table 14. Coins listed by Reece's issue period.

Issue Period	No. of Coins
1	3
2	0
3	3
4	4
5	6
6	6

7	11
8	3
9	1
10	8
11	1
12	1
13	4
14	2
15	0
16	8
17	9
18	2
19	5
20	1
21	0

Table 15. Fourth century coins listed by imperial house.

House	No. of Coins
House of Constantine	20
House of Valentinian	5
House of Theodosius	1

Bibliography

Abbatt, R, 1849 *A History of the Picts' or Romano-British Wall, and of the Roman Stations and Vallum, London*

Abdy, R, 2003 A Roman coin hoard from Longhorsley, *Archaeol Aeliana* ser **5, 32** 189-91

Adams, J N, 1995 The Latin of the Vindolanda Writing Tablets: an interim report, *J Roman Stud* **85,** 86-134

Allason-Jones, L, 1979 Two unrecognised Roman surgical instruments, *Archaeol Aeliana* ser **5, 7,** 239-241

Allason-Jones, L, 1980 A Zoomorphic Spout from Halton Chesters, *Archaeol Aeliana* ser 5, **8,** 153-154

Allason-Jones, L, 1982 Roman Pottery from Hadrian's Wall Turret 27A, Archaeol Aeliana ser 5, 10, 199-200

Allason-Jones, L, 1983 The small finds, in R Miket, *The Roman Fort at South Shields: Excavation of the Defences,* 1977-81. Newcastle.

Allason-Jones, L, 1988 Small finds from the turrets on Hadrian's Wall, in *Military Equipment and the Identity of Roman Soldiers: Proceedings of the Fourth Roman Military Equipment Conference* (ed J Coulton), BAR Int. Ser. **394,** Oxford, 197-233

Allason-Jones, L, 1989a *Women in Roman Britain,* London

Allason-Jones, L, 1989b Introductory remarks on the nature of Roman trade in the North of Britain, in *Roman Military Equipment: the Sources of Evidence. Proceedings of the Fifth Roman Military Equipment Conference* (ed C van Driel Murray), BAR Int. Ser. 476, Oxford, 13-24

Allason-Jones, L, 1991 Roman and native interaction in Northumberland, in *Roman Frontier Studies 1989: Proceedings of the XVth International Congress of Roman Frontier Studies* (eds V Maxfield and B Dobson), Exeter, 1-5

Allason-Jones, L, 1994 A stone head from Walker, *Archaeol Aeliana* ser 5, **22,** 263-265

Allason-Jones, L, and Jones, J M, 1994 Jet and other materials in Roman artefact studies, *Archaeol Aeliana* ser 5, **22,** 265-72

Allason-Jones, L 1996a *Roman Jet in the Yorkshire Museum* York

Allason-Jones, L 1996b Roman Military and Domestic Artefacts from Great Chesters, *Archaeol Aeliana*, ser 5, **24**, 187- 214.

Allason-Jones, L, 1997 The women of Roman Maryport, in *Roman Maryport and its Setting: Essays in Memory of Michael G. Jarrett* (ed J R A Wilson), Maryport, 105-111

Allason-Jones, L, 1999a Women and the Roman Army in Britain, in *The Roman Army as a Community* (eds A Goldworthy and I Haynes) Portsmouth, Rhode Island, 41-51

Allason-Jones, L, 1999b Health Care in the Roman North, *Britannia* **30,** 133-146

Allason-Jones, L, 2001 The material culture of Hadrian's Wall, in *Limes XVIII - Proceedings of the XVIIIth International Congress of Roman Frontier Studies* held in Amman, Jordan, BAR Int. Ser. **1084,** Oxford, 821 -824

Allason-Jones, L, 2002 The jet industry and allied trades in Roman Yorkshire, in *Aspects of Industry in Roman Yorkshire and the North* (eds P Wilson and J Price) Oxford, 125-132

Allason-Jones, L, 2003 The family in Roman Britain, in *A Companion to Roman Britain* (ed M Todd) 273-87, Oxford

Allason-Jones, L, 2004 Mithras on Hadrian's Wall, in *Roman Mithraism: The Evidence of the Small Finds* (eds M Martens and G de Boc), Brussels, 183-189

Allason-Jones, L, 2005 Germs and the Roman army in Britain, in *Limes XIX: Proceedings of the XIXth International Congress of Roman Frontier Studies.* Pécs, Hungary, September 2003 (ed Z Visy) 309- 313, University of P_cs

Allason-Jones, L, Bennett, J, and Welsby, D, 1984 The finds from milecastle 54, Randylands, *Archaeol Aeliana* ser 5, **12,** 228-235

Allason-Jones, L, and Bishop, M C, 1988 *Excavations at Roman Corbridge: the Hoard,* London

Allason-Jones, L, and Dungworth, D B, 1997 Metalworking on Hadrian's Wall, in *Roman Frontier Studies 1995, Proceedings of the XVIth International Congress of Roman Frontier Studies* (eds W Groenman-van Waateringe, B van Beek, W Willems and S Wynia), Oxford, 317-321

Allason-Jones, L, and Jones, J M, 2001 Identification of 'jet' artefacts by reflected light microscopy, *European Journal of Archaeology* ser 4, **2,** 233-51

Allason-Jones, L, and McKay, B, 1985 *Coventina's Well: A shrine on Hadrian's Wall* Chesters Museum

Allason-Jones, L, and Miket, R F, 1984 *Catalogue of small finds from South Shields Roman Fort,* Newcastle-upon-Tyne

Allen, D, 1983 *Roman Glass from Selected British Sites.* University of Wales PhD thesis.

Allen, D, 1987 Roman glass from Corbridge, in *Corbridge: Excavation of the Roman Fort and Town,* 1947-80 (eds M C Bishop and J N Dore). English Heritage Archaeological Reports, **8,** 287-93.

Allen, D, unpublished a *Glass from excavations by Charles Daniels at Wallsend.* (Written 1987, amended 1997).

Allen, D, unpublished b *Glass from site H 20 at Housesteads.* (Written 1987).

Allen, D, unpublished c *Glass from Milecastle 39 at Castle Nick.* (Wrttten in 1986-6).

Allen, J R L and Fulford, M G, 1999 Fort building and military supply along Britain's eastern Channel and North Sea coasts: the later second and third centuries, *Britannia* **30,** 163-184

Allen, J R M, and Huntley, J P, 2004 South Heddon, Northumberland: palynological investigations of a small hollow, in *An Iron Age or Romano-British enclosure at South Heddon, Northumberland* (eds T Pearson and A Hunt), Vol. AI/5/2004, 40-50

Allison, E P, 2000 The bird bone, in *Roman and Medieval Carlisle: the southern Lanes* (ed M R McCarthy), Carlisle, 89-90

Anon 1905-1906 The third decennial pilgrimage along the line of the Roman Wall, *Proc Soc Antiq Newcastle-on Tyne* ser 3, **2,** 277-296

Anon 1942-1943 Report of the Council, *Proc Soc Antiq Newcastle-on-Tyne* ser 4, **10,** 274-275

Anderson, J D, 1992 *Roman Military Supply in North East England: An analysis of a and an alternative to the Piercebridge formula* BAR Brit. Ser. **224,** Oxford, 35-39

Atkinson, J, 1979 The bronze finger from Carvoran, *Archaeol Aeliana* ser 5, **7**, 241-242
Austen, P S, 1991a *Bewcastle and Old Penrith: A Roman Outpost Fort and a Frontier*
Vicus, Excavations 1977-8, Kendal
Austen, P S, 1991b How big was the second largest fort on Hadrian's Wall at Bowness on Solway?, in *Roman Frontier Studies 1989: Proceedings of the XVth International Congress of Roman Frontier Studies* (eds V Maxfield and B Dobson), Exeter, 6-8
Austen, P S, 1994 Recent excavations on Hadrian's Wall, Burgh-by-Sands, Trans Cumberland Westmorland Antiq *Archaeol Soc* ser 2, **94**, 35-54
Austen, P S, and Breeze, D J, 1979 A new inscription from Chesters on Hadrian's Wall, *Archaeol Aeliana* ser 5, **7**, 115-126
Baatz, D, 1997 The eighth Horsley Memorial Lecture: keeping watch over the limes, *Archaeol Aeliana* ser 5, **25**, 1-20
Baatz, D, 2007 Zur Funktion der Kleinkastelle am Obergermanisch-Raetischen Limes, in *Forschungen zur Funktion des Limes* (ed A Thiel) Bad Homberg, 9-25
Bailey, J B, 1915 Catalogue of Roman inscribed and sculptured stones, coins, earthenware, etc. discovered in and near the Roman fort at Maryport, and preserved at Netherhall, *Trans Cumberland Westmorland Antiq Archaeol Soc* ser 2, **15,** 135-72
Bailey, J B, 1923 Maryport and the Tenth Iter, with further notes on Roman Antiquities, Trans *Cumberland Westmorland Antiq Archaeol Soc* ser 2, **23,** 142-153
Bailey, J B, 1926 Further notes on Roman roads at Maryport and on the Netherhall Collection, *Trans Cumberland Westmorland Antiq Archaeol Soc* ser 2, **26,** 415-222
Bailey, R, and Cramp, R, 1988 *Corpus of Anglo-Saxon Stone Sculpture in England, Vol II: Cumberland, Westmorland and Lancashire-North-of-the-Sands,* Oxford
Barrow, G, 1989 Settlement on the Anglo-Scottish Borders, in *Medieval Frontier Societies* (eds R Bartlett and A MacKay) Oxford, 3-21
Bartle, S H, 1961 Investigations on Hadrian's Wall west of Carlisle, *Trans Cumberland Westmorland Antiq Archaeol Soc* ser 2, **61,** 34-41
Bartley, D D, Chambers, C, and Hart-Jones, B, 1976 The vegetational history of parts of south and east Durham, *New Phytologist* **77**, 437-468
Bates, C J, 1888 A forgotten reference to Roman mile castles, *Trans Cumberland and Westmorland Antiq Archaeol Soc* **9,** 447-451
Bates, C J, 1895 *A History of Northumberland,* Newcastle upon-Tyne
Bayley, J, 1982a *The technological finds from Vindolanda, Northumberland.* Ancient Monuments Laboratory Report **3727**.
Bayley, J, 1982b *Some technological finds from Sewingshields, Hadrian's Wall.* Ancient Monument Laboratory Report **3782**.
Bayley, J, 1984 Technological finds from Sewingshields, in Sewingshields, *Archaeol Aeliana* ser 5, **12,** 33-147 (106-8).
Bayley, J, 1985a *Examination and analysis of small finds from Corbridge,* Northumberland. Ancient Monuments Laboratory Report **4465**.
Bayley, J, 1985b *Examination and analysis of small finds from Housesteads,* Northumberland. Ancient Monuments Laboratory Report 4466.
Bayley, J, 1986 *Analyses of four Roman brooches from Brougham, Cumbria,* Ancient Monuments Laboratory Report 40/1986.
Bayley, J, 1992 *Non-ferrous Metalworking in England: Late Iron Age to Early Medieval.* Unpublished PhD thesis. University of London.
Bayley, J, 2001 Non-ferrous metal technology in Britain in the earlier first millennium AD, in *L'artisanat romain: evolution, continuites et ruptures* (Italie et provences occidentals) (ed M Polfer). Montagnac: Monique Mergoil (*Monographies Instrumentum* **20**), 69-77.
Bayley, J and Butcher, S, 2004 *Roman Brooches in Britain: A Technological and Typological Study Based on the Richborough Collection.* London: Society of Antiquaries of London (Report of the Research Committee **68**).
Bell, R C, 1978 Games played at Corstopitum, *Archaeol Aeliana* ser 5, **6,** 174-176
Bellhouse, R L, 1952 A newly-discovered Roman road from Drumburgh to Kirkbride, *Trans Cumberland Westmorland Antiq Archaeol Soc* ser 2, **52,** 41-45
Bellhouse, R L, 1954 Roman sites on the Cumberland Coast, 1954, *Trans Cumberland Westmorland Antiq Archaeol Soc* ser 2, **54,** 28-55
Bellhouse, R L, 1955 The Roman fort at Burrow Walls, near Workington. *Trans Cumberland Westmorland Antiq Archaeol Soc* ser 2, **55,** 30-55.
Bellhouse, R L, 1957 Roman sites on the Cumberland Coast, 1956, *Trans Cumberland Westmorland Antiq Archaeol Soc* ser 2, **57,** 18-26
Bellhouse, R L, 1960 Excavations in Eskdale: the Muncaster Roman kilns, *Trans Cumberland Westmorland Antiq Archaeol Soc* ser 2, **60,** 1-12
Bellhouse, R L, 1961 Excavations in Eskdale: the Muncaster Roman kilns, *Trans Cumberland Westmorland Antiq Archaeol Soc* ser 2, **61**, 47-56
Bellhouse, R L, 1962 Moricambe in Roman times and Roman sites on the Cumberland Coast, *Trans Cumberland Westmorland Antiq Archaeol Soc* ser 2, **62,** 56-72
Bellhouse, R L, 1963 Roman sites on the Cumberland Coast, 1962, *Trans Cumberland Westmorland Antiq Archaeol Soc* ser 2, **63,** 140-147
Bellhouse, R L, 1966a Roman sites on the Cumberland Coast, 1962-63, *Trans Cumberland Westmorland Antiq Archaeol Soc* ser 2, **66,** 37-41
Bellhouse, R L, 1966b The problem of Burrow Walls, *Trans Cumberland Westmorland Antiq Archaeol Soc* ser 2, **66,** 42-45
Bellhouse, R L, 1969 Roman sites on the Cumberland Coast, 1966-67, *Trans Cumberland Westmorland Antiq Archaeol Soc* ser 2, **69**, 54-101
Bellhouse, R L, 1970 Roman sites on the Cumberland Coast, 1968-69, *Trans Cumberland Westmorland Antiq Archaeol Soc* ser 2, **70**, 9-47
Bellhouse, R L, 1971 The Roman Tileries at Scalesceugh and Brampton, *Trans Cumberland Westmorland Antiq Archaeol Soc* ser 2, **71,** 35-44
Bellhouse, R L, 1973 Roman sites on the Cumberland Coast, 1972, *Trans Cumberland Westmorland Antiq Archaeol Soc* ser 2, **73**, 350-352
Bellhouse, R L, 1979 The case for the Roman Road from

Kirkbride to Carlisle, *CBA group 3 Newsbulletin*. Ser. **2, 9,** 11-12

Bellhouse, R L, 1981a Hadrian's Wall: The limiting ditches in the Cardurnock Peninsula, *Britannia* **12,** 135-42

Bellhouse, R L, 1981b Roman sites on the Cumberland Coast: Milefortlet 20 Low Mire, *Trans Cumberland Westmorland Antiq Archaeol Soc* ser 2, **81,** 7-13

Bellhouse, R L, 1984 Roman Sites on the Cumberland Coast: The New Tower on Rise How, *Trans Cumberland Westmorland Antiq Archaeol Soc* ser 2, **84,** 41-59

Bellhouse, R L, 1986 Roman Sites on the Cumberland Coast: Milefortlet 17, Dubmill Point, *Trans Cumberland Westmorland Antiq Archaeol Soc* ser 2, **86,** 41-47

Bellhouse, R L, 1988 Roman Sites on the Cumberland Coast: Hadrian's Wall. The fort at Bowness-on-Solway, a reappraisal, *Trans Cumberland Westmorland Antiq Archaeol Soc* ser 2, **88,** 33-53

Bellhouse, R L, 1989a *Roman sites on the Cumberland Coast: A new schedule of Coastal sites*. Kendal

Bellhouse, R L, 1989b The Roman forts at Drumburgh, *Trans Cumberland Westmorland Antiq Archaeol Soc* ser 2, **89,** 33-36

Bellhouse, R L, 1991 Rise How: An AMS date for the Iron Age Burial, *Trans Cumberland Westmorland Antiq Archaeol Soc* ser 2, **91,** 266-267

Bellhouse, R L, 1992 Alexander Gordon: Towers or Milefortlets?, *Trans Cumberland Westmorland Antiq Archaeol Soc* ser 2, **92,** 275-276

Bellhouse, R L, and Moffat, I, 1958 Further Roman finds in the Beckfoot cemetery site, *Trans Cumberland Westmorland Antiq Archaeol Soc* ser 2, **58,** 57-62

Bellhouse, R L, and Richardson, G G S, 1975 The Roman site at Kirkbride, Cumberland, *Trans Cumberland Westmorland Antiq Archaeol Soc* ser 2, **75,** 58-90

Bellhouse, R L, and Richardson, G G S 1982 The Trajanic Fort at Kirkbride; the Terminus of the Stanegate Frontier, *Trans Cumberland Westmorland Antiq Archaeol Soc* ser 2, **82,** 35-50

Bennett, J, 1982 The Great Chesters "Pilum Murale", *Archaeol Aeliana* ser 5, **10,** 200-205

Bennett, J, 1983 The Examination of Turret 10A and the Wall and Vallum at Throckley, Tyne and Wear, 1980, *Archaeol Aeliana* ser 5, **11,** 27-60

Bennett, J, 1990 *The Setting, Development and Function of the Hadrianic Frontier in Britain,* unpublished PhD thesis, University of Newcastle upon Tyne

Bennett, J, 1998 The Roman Frontier from Wallsend to Rudchester Burn Reviewed, *Archaeol Aeliana* ser 5, **26,** 17-37

Bennett, J, 2002 A Revised Programme and Chronology for Hadrian's Wall, in *Limes XVIII - proceedings of the XVIIIth International Congress of Roman Frontier Studies held in Amman, Jordan* (eds P Freeman, J Bennett, Z T Fiema and B Hoffmann) BAR Int. Ser. **1084**, Oxford, 825-834

Bennett, J, forthcoming A transection of the linear elements of the Hadrian's Wall system in Wall mile 61 (Crosby-on-Eden, Cumbria), 1980-84, in Hadrian's Wall: *Archaeological Research by English Heritage 1976-2000* (ed T Wilmott), English Heritage Research Report

Bennett, J, Bartlett, D and Holmes, T, 1987 A Watching brief South-east of Moresby Fort, *Trans Cumberland Westmorland Antiq Archaeol Soc* ser 2, **87,** 256-258

Bennett, J, and Turner, R, 1983 The Vallum at Wallhouses, Northumberland: Excavations in 1980 and 1981, *Archaeol Aeliana* ser 5, **11,** 61-78

Berriman, A E, 1956 The Carvoran "modius", *Archaeol Aeliana* ser 4, **34,** 130

Berry, J, and Taylor, D J A, 1997 The Roman fort at Halton Chesters: a geophysical survey *Archaeol Aeliana* ser 5, **25,** 51-60

Berry, J, Taylor, D J A, Biggins, J A, 2000 A report on a Geophysical Survey of the Roman Fort and Vicus at Halton Chesters *Archaeol Aeliana* ser 5, **28,** 37-46

Bewley, R H, 1986 Survey and Excavation in the Solway Plain, Cumbria (1982-4), *Trans Cumberland Westmorland Antiq Archaeol Soc* ser 2, **86,** 19-40

Bewley, R H, 1986 Excavations on Two Crop-Mark Sites in the Solway Plain, Cumbria. Ewanrigg Settlement and Swarthy Hill, Trans Cumberland Westmorland Antiq Archaeol Soc ser 2, **92**, 23-47

Bewley, R, 1994 *Prehistoric and Romano-British Settlement in the Solway Plain* Cumbria Oxford

Bidwell, P T, 1985 *The Roman Fort of Vindolanda, at Chesterholm, Northumberland,* HBMCE, Archaeol Rep **1,** London

Bidwell, P T, 1991 Later Roman Barracks in Britain, in *Roman Frontier Studies 1989: Proceedings of the XVth International Congress of Roman Frontier Studies* (eds V Maxfield and B Dobson), Exeter, 9-15

Bidwell, P T, 1996 Some aspects of the development of later Roman fort plans, *Arbeia Journal* **5,** 1-18

Bidwell, P T, 1997a A water-colour of a culvert through Hadrian's Wall at West Denton, Newcastle upon Tyne, *Archaeol Aeliana* ser 5, **25**, 151-152

Bidwell, P T, 1997b *Roman Forts in Britain,* London

Bidwell, P T, (ed) 1999 *Hadrian's Wall 1989-1999,* Carlisle

Bidwell, P T, 2001 A probable Roman shipwreck on the Herd Sands at South Shields, *Arbeia Journal* **6-7,** 1-23

Bidwell, P T, 2003 The original eastern terminus of Hadrian's Wall, *Archaeol Aeliana* ser 5, **32,** 17 -24

Bidwell, P T, 2005a The system of obstacles on Hadrian's Wall; their extent, date and purpose, *Arbeia Journal* **8,** 53-76

Bidwell, P T, 2005b The dating of Crambeck Parchment Ware, *Journal of Roman Pottery Studies* **12,** 15-21

Bidwell, P T, and Holbrook, N, 1989 *Hadrian's Wall Bridges,* London

Bidwell, P T, Miket, R, and Ford, B, (eds) 1988 *Portae cum turribus: Studies of Roman Stone-built Fort Gates*, BAR Brit. Ser. **206,** Oxford

Bidwell, P T, and Snape, M, 2002 The history and setting of the Roman fort at Newcastle upon Tyne, *Archaeol Aeliana* ser 5, **31,** 251-83

Bidwell, P T, and Speak, S, 1994 *Excavations at South Shields Roman Fort,* Vol 1, Newcastle upon Tyne: Society of Antiquaries of Newcastle upon Tyne Monogr **4**

Bidwell, P T, and Watson, M, 1989 A trial excavation on Hadrian's Wall at Buddle Street, Wallsend, *Archaeol Aeliana* ser 5, **17**, 21-28

Bidwell, P T, and Watson, M, 1996 Excavations on Hadrian's Wall at Denton, Newcastle upon Tyne, 1986-89, *Archaeol Aeliana* ser 5, **24,** 1-56

Biggins, A J, Hall, S, and Taylor, D J A, 2004 A geophysical survey of milecastle 73 and Hadrian's Wall at Burgh-by Sands, Cumbria, *Trans Cumberland Westmorland Antiq Archaeol Soc* ser 3, **4,** 55-70

Biggins, A J, and Taylor, D J A, 1999 A survey of the Roman fort and settlement at Birdoswald, Cumbria, *Britannia* **30,** 91-110

Biggins, A J, and Taylor, D J A, 2000 The Roman fort at Stanwix: a geophysical survey, Cumbria, *Trans Cumberland Westmorland Antiq Archaeol Soc* ser 3, **4,** 55-70

Biggins, A J, and Taylor, D J A, 2004a The Roman fort and vicus at Maryport: geophysical survey, 2000-2004, in *Romans on the Solway, Essays in Honour of Richard Bellhouse* (eds R J A Wilson and I Caruana), 103-133 Kendal

Biggins, J A, and Taylor, D J A, 2004b A geophysical survey at Housesteads Roman fort, April 2003, *Archaeol Aeliana* ser 5, **33,** 51-60

Biggins, A J, and Taylor, D J A, 2004c New discoveries at Chesters Roman Fort, *Archaeology in Northumberland* **14,** 38

Biggins, J A and Taylor, D J A, 2004d Geophysical survey of the *vicus* at Birdoswald Roman fort, Cumbria, *Britannia* **35,** 159 -177

Biggins, A J, and Taylor, D J A, 2007 The Roman Fort at Castlesteads, Cumbria: a Geophysical Survey of the *Vicus, Trans Cumberland Westmorland Antiq Archaeol Soc* ser 3, **7,** 15-30

Bingen, J, 1992 *Mons Claudianus. Ostraca Graeca et Latina I,* Cairo

Bingen, J, 1997 *Mons Claudianus. Ostraca Graeca et Latina II,* Cairo

Binns, A M, 1972 Mains Rigg: Interim Report, June 1971, *CBA Group 3 Archaeological Newsbulletin* **13** (Jan.), 1-6

Birley, A, 1997 Security: the keys and locks, *Vin. Research Report,* N.S., **Vol IV. II,** Greenhead

Birley, A, 2001 *Vindolanda's Military Bath Houses:* report on the pre-Hadrianic military bath house found in 2000, with analysis of the early third century bath house excavated in 1970/71, and possible sites of other bath houses, Greenhead

Birley, A, and Blake, J, 2003 *Vindolanda: the excavations of 2001-2002,* Bardon Mill

Birley, A, and Blake, J, 2000 *Interim Report on the 1999 Excavations,* Greenhead

Birley, A, and Blake, J, 2005 *Vindolanda: the excavations of 2003-2004,* Bardon Mill

Birley, A and Blake, J 2007 *Vindolanda research report: the excavations of 2005-2006,* Hexham

Birley, A R, 1972 Virius Lupus, *Archaeol Aeliana* ser 4, **50,** 179-190

Birley, A R, 1997a *Hadrian, the Restless Emperor,* London

Birley, A R, 1997b Supplying the Batavians at Vindolanda, in *Roman Frontier Studies 1995: Proceedings of the XVIth International Congress of Roman Frontier Studies* (W Groenman-van-Waateringe et al) Oxford, 273-80

Birley, A R, 2002 *Garrison Life at Vindolanda: a Band of Brothers,* Stroud

Birley, B, and Greene, E, 2006 The Roman Jewellery from Vindolanda: beads, intaglios, finger rings, bracelets, ear rings and bracelets, *Vin. Research Report NS* **IV. V,** Greenhead

Birley, B, and Greene E, 2006 *The Vindolanda Jewellery* Greenhead

Birley, E, 1930 Excavations on Hadrian's Wall west of Newcastle upon Tyne in 1929, *Archaeol Aeliana* ser 4, **7,** 143-174

Birley, E, 1931a An introduction to the excavation of Chesterholm-Vindolanda *Archaeol Aeliana* ser 4, **8,** 182-212

Birley, E, 1931b Three notes on Roman Cumberland: Bewcastle, Bowness-on-Solway, Petrianae, *Trans Cumberland Westmorland Antiq Archaeol Soc* ser 2, **31,** 137-147

Birley, E, 1932a A new Roman inscription and a note on the garrisoning of the Wall, *Archaeol Aeliana* ser 4, **9,** 205-215

Birley, E, 1932b Excavations at Chesterholm-Vindolanda, *Archaeol Aeliana* ser 4, **9,** 216-221

Birley, E, 1932c The Stanwix Inscription, *Trans Cumberland Westmorland Antiq Archaeol Soc* ser 2, **32,** 148-9

Birley, E, 1933 Three New Inscriptions, *Archaeol Aeliana* ser 4, **10,** 102-108

Birley, E, 1934a A new inscription from Chesterholm, *Archaeol Aeliana* ser 4, **11,** 127-137

Birley, E, 1934b A note on the date of the Vallum, Archaeol Aeliana ser 4, 11, 146-157

Birley, E, 1935 Excavations *per Lineam Valli* in 1934, *Durham University Journal* **29** (2), 93-98

Birley, E, 1935a Three Roman Inscriptions, *Archaeol Aeliana* ser 4, **12,** 195-203

Birley, E, 1935b A note on the Second Cohort of Tungrians, *Trans Cumberland Westmorland Antiq Archaeol Soc* ser 2, **35,** 56-60

Birley, E, 1936a Another record of Lollius Urbicus from *Corstopitum, Archaeol Aeliana* ser 4, **13,** 274-278

Birley, E, 1936b A Roman Altar from Bankshead, *Trans Cumberland Westmorland Antiq Archaeol Soc* ser 2, **36,** 1-7

Birley, E, 1937 Fifth Report on Excavations at Housesteads, *Archaeol Aeliana* ser 4, **14,** 172 - 184

Birley, E, 1937-193 A modern building at Housesteads, *Proc Soc Antiq Newcastle-on-Tyne* ser 4, **8,** 191-193

Birley, E, 1939a Building-records from Hadrian's Wall, *Archaeol Aeliana* ser 4, **16,** 219-236

Birley, E, 1939b Roman inscriptions from Chesters (Cilurnum), a note on Ala II Asturum and two milestones, *Archaeol Aeliana* ser 4, **16,** 237-259

Birley, E, 1939c The Beaumont Inscription, the Notitia Dignitatum, and the Garrison of Hadrian's Wall, *Trans Cumberland Westmorland Antiq Archaeol Soc* ser 2, **39,** 190-226

Birley, E, 1947 Figured samian from Benwell, 1938, *Archaeol Aeliana* ser 4, **25,** 52-67

Birley, E, 1948 The Roman fort at Moresby, *Trans Cumberland Westmorland Antiq Archaeol Soc* ser 2, **48,** 42-72

Birley, E, 1949 The Roman fort at Moresby: a postscript, *Trans Cumberland Westmorland Antiq Archaeol Soc* ser 2, **49,** 218-219

Birley, E, 1951a Thomas Machell and Hadrian's Wall, *Trans Cumberland Westmorland Antiq Archaeol Soc* ser 2, **51,** 180-182

Birley, E, 1951b Some Roman military inscriptions, Trans Cumberland Westmorland Antiq Archaeol Soc ser 2, **51,** 67-72

Birley, E, 1951c An altar at Tullie House, *Trans Cumberland Westmorland Antiq Archaeol Soc* ser 2, **51,** 182-184

Birley, E, 1952a The Brigantian problem, and the first Roman contact with Scotland, *Transactions of the Dumfriesshire and Galloway Natural History and,*

Archaeological Society ser 3, **29**, 46-65
Birley, E, 1952b A Hadrianic inscription from Castlesteads, *Trans Cumberland Westmorland Antiq Archaeol Soc* ser 2, **52,** 184-185
Birley, E, 1957 A dedication to Belatucadrus, *Trans Cumberland Westmorland Antiq Archaeol Soc* ser 2, **57,** 185-186
Birley, E, 1958a The Roman fort at Ravenglass, *Trans Cumberland Westmorland Antiq Archaeol Soc* ser 2, **58,** 14-30
Birley, E, 1958b The dedication to Belatucadrus from Carlisle, *Trans Cumberland Westmorland Antiq Archaeol Soc* ser 2, **58,** 180-181
Birley, E, 1958c An inscribed fragment from Beckfoot, *Trans Cumberland Westmorland Antiq Archaeol Soc* ser 2, **58,** 182-183
Birley, E 1958d The Roman Wall at Denton Bank, *Archaeol Aeliana* ser 4, **36**, 308-310
Birley, E B, 1958 The genesis of the book, in *Central Gaulish Potters* (eds J A Stanfield and G Simpson) 15-20, Oxford
Birley, E, 1958 The Roman fort at Ravenglass, *Trans Cumberland Westmorland Antiq Archaeol Soc* ser 2, **58,** 14-30
Birley, E, 1959 Excavations at *Corstopitum,* 1906-1958, *Archaeol Aeliana* ser 4, **37,** 1-31
Birley, E, 1960 Hadrian's Wall: Some structural problems, *Archaeol Aeliana* ser 4, **38,** 39-60
Birley, E, 1961a *Research on Hadrian's Wall* Kendal: Titus Wilson & Son Ltd.
Birley, E, 1961b The western sector of Hadrian's Wall, *Trans Cumberland Westmorland Antiq Archaeol Soc* ser 2, **61,** 25-33
Birley, E, 1962 Sir John Clerk's visit to the North of England in 1724, *Transactions of the Architectural and Archaeological Society of Durham and Northumberland,* **11, pts 3-4,** 221-246.
Birley, E, 1963 An inscription from Pike Hill: CIL VII 836, *Trans Cumberland Westmorland Antiq Archaeol Soc* ser 2, **63,** 153-155
Birley, E, 1966 Birdoswald Fort, in *Programme of the Centenary Meeting at Carlisle,* Carlisle
Birley, E, 1974 *Cohors I Tungrorum* and the oracle of Clarian Apollo, *Chiron,* **4,** 511-513
Birley, E, 1986 The deities of Roman Britain in *Aufstieg und Niedergang der Romischen Welt II,* **18, 1** (eds Temporini H and Haase, W), 3-112 (Berlin and New York).
Birley, E, and Bellhouse, R L, 1963 The Roman site at Kirkbride, Cumberland, *Trans Cumberland Westmorland Antiq Archaeol Soc* ser 2, **63,** 126-139
Birley, E, and Bellhouse, R L, 1975 The Roman site at Kirkbride, Cumberland, *Trans Cumberland Westmorland Antiq Archaeol Soc* ser 2, **75,** 58-90
Birley, E, Brewis, P, and Charlton, J, 1933 Report for 1932 of the North of England Excavation Committee, *Archaeol Aeliana* ser 4, **10,** 97-101
Birley, E, Brewis, P, and Charlton, J, 1934 Report for 1933 of the North of England Excavation Committee, *Archaeol Aeliana* ser 4, **11,** 176-184
Birley, E, 1977 A ceramic pilgrim's progress: the growth of Roman pottery studies in northern Britain, in *Roman Pottery Studies in Britain and Beyond* (eds J Dore and K Greene) BAR Suppl. Ser. **30,** 1-3, Oxford
Birley, E, and Birley, M I, 1938 Fourth Report on the excavations at Chesterholm-Vindolanda, *Archaeol Aeliana* ser 4, **15,** 222-237
Birley, E, Birley, R, and Birley, A R, 1993 *The Early Wooden Forts: Reports on the Auxiliaries, the Writing Tablets, Inscriptions, Brands and Graffiti, Vin Research Reports* **NS II,** Hexham
Birley, E, Charlton, J, and Hedley, W P, 1932 Excavations at Housesteads in 1931, *Archaeol Aeliana* ser 4, **9,** 222-237
Birley, E, Charlton J, and Hedley, W P, 1933 Excavations at Housesteads in 1932, *Archaeol Aeliana* ser 4, **10,** 82 - 96
Birley, E, and Charlton, J, 1934 Third Report on Excavations at Housesteads, *Archaeol Aeliana* ser 4, **11,** 185-205
Birley, E, and Gillam, J P, 1948 Mortarium stamps from Corbridge, *Archaeol Aeliana* ser 4, **26,** 172-204
Birley, E, and Keeney, G S, 1935 Fourth Report on Excavations at Housesteads, *Archaeol Aeliana* ser 4, **12,** 204-258
Birley, E, and Richmond, I A, 1938 Excavations at Corbridge, 1936-1938, *Archaeol Aeliana* ser 4, **15,** 243-294
Birley, E, Richmond, I A, and Stanfield, J, 1936 Excavation at Chesterholm-Vindolanda, Third Report, *Archaeol Aeliana* ser 4, **13,** 218-257
Birley, R, 1961 Housesteads civil settlement, 1960, *Archaeol Aeliana* ser 4, **39,** 301-320
Birley, R, 1962a Some excavations at Chesterholm Vindolanda, *Archaeol Aeliana* ser 4, **40,** 97-103
Birley, R, 1962b Housesteads *Vicus, Archaeol Aeliana* ser 4, **40,** 117-134
Birley, R, 1970 Excavations at Chesterholm-Vindolanda 1967-69, *Archaeol Aeliana* ser 4, **48,** 97-157
Birley, R, 1973 Vindolanda-Chesterholm, 1969-1972: some important material from the *Vicus, Archaeol Aeliana* ser 5, **1,** 111-122
Birley, R, 1977a *Vindolanda: A Roman Frontier post on Hadrian's Wall,* London
Birley, R, 1977b *Vindolanda I: 1976 excavations, Interim Report,* Haltwhistle
Birley, R, 1994 *Vindolanda, Vol. 1: The Early Wooden Forts - The Excavations of 1973-76 and 1985-89, with some additional details from the Excavations of 1991-93, Vin Research Reports NS,* Hexham
Birley, R, 1995 *The Making of Modern Vindolanda, with the Life and Work of Anthony Hedley, 1777-1835* Greenhead
Birley, R, 1996 *The Weapons Vin Research Report* **NS IV. I,** Hexham
Birley, R, Blake, J, and Birley, A 1998 *The 1997 Excavations at Vindolanda: the Praetorium site interim report,* Greenhead
Birley, R, 1999 *The writing materials, Vin Research Report* **NS IV. IV,** Hexham
Bishop, M C, 1994 *Corstopitum, An Edwardian Excavation: Photographs from the 1906-14 Excavations of the Roman Site at Corbridge,* London
Bishop, M C, 1995 A "New" Tile-Stamp from Corbridge and Legionary Dispositions on the Tyne-Solway Isthmus, *Archaeol Aeliana* ser 5, **23,** 311-312
Bishop, M C, 1998 An old Corbridge bath-house revisited, *Archaeol Aeliana* ser 5, **26,** 39-47
Bishop, M C, forthcoming The Roman armour, in *The Carlisle Millennium Project: Excavations Within the Roman Fort and Medieval Castle, 1998-2001,* Vol 2 (ed C Howard-Davis)

Bishop, M C, and Dore, J N, 1988 *Corbridge: Excavations of the Roman Fort and Town,* 1947-80 London

Blackburn, K, 1928 Report on an Investigation of the Bottom of the Vallum Ditch at Birdoswald with a view to ascertaining how long the Ditch was open, *Trans Cumberland Westmorland Antiq Archaeol Soc* ser 2, **29,** 308-9

Blackburn, K, 1970 Report on the wood samples from the well in the Headquarters building, 1933, *Archaeol Aeliana* ser 4, **48,** 145

Blagg, T F C, 1985 A relief carving of two female figures from Housesteads, *Archaeol Aeliana* ser 5, **13,** 1-5

Blake, B, 1959 Excavations of Native (Iron Age) sites in Cumberland 1956-1958, *Trans Cumberland Westmorland Antiq Archaeol* soc ser 2, **59,** 1-14

Blake, J, 1999 *The Tools, Vin Research Report* **NS, IV. III,** Greenhead

Blake, J, 2001 *The South-Western Corner of Stone Fort 2,* Greenhead

Blake, J, 2003 *The Excavations of 2001-2002, Vol. II,* Greenhead

Bloemers, T, 1989 Acculturation in the Rhine / Meuse Basin in the Roman Period, in *Barbarians and Romans in North-West Europe* (eds J Barrett, A Fitzpatrick and L Macinnes) BAR. Int. Ser. **471,** 175-97, Oxford

Blood, K, 1987 *Birdoswald (BANNA) Roman Fort and Environs,* unpublished field survey, RCHM (E)

Blood, K, 1999 Wall Mile 43/44, in *Hadrian's Wall 1989 1999* (ed P T Bidwell), 139

Blood, K, and Bowden, M C B, 1990 The Roman Fort at Haltonchesters *Archaeol Aeliana* ser 5, **18,** 55-62

Blood, K, and Pearson, T, 2004 The Roman fort at Ravenglass: a survey by RCHME, in *Romans on the Solway, Essays in honour of Richard Bellhouse* (eds R J A Wilson and I Caruana), 95-101 Kendal

Bosanquet, R C, 1897-1898 Excavations at Housesteads, *Proc Soc Antiq Newcastle-on-Tyne* ser 2, **8,** 247-254

Bosanquet, R C, 1904 Excavations on the line of the Roman Wall in Northumberland: 1. The Roman Camp at Housesteads, *Archaeol Aeliana* ser 2, **25,** 193-300

Bosanquet, R C, 1922a On an altar dedicated to the Alaisiagae, *Archaeol Aeliana* ser 3, **19,** 185-196

Bosanquet, R C, 1922b A newly discovered centurial stone at Housesteads, *Archaeol Aeliana* ser 3, **19,** 198-199

Bosanquet, R C, 1925 Annual meeting 1925, Newcastle upon Tyne 21-29 July, *Archaeol J* **82,** 222-223 Bosanquet, R C, 1929 Dr John Lingard's notes on the Roman Wall, *Archaeol Aeliana* ser 4, **6,** 130-162

Bosanquet, R C, and Birley, E, (ed) 1955 Robert Smith and the "Observations upon the Picts Wall" (1708-9), *Trans Cumberland Westmorland Antiq Archaeol Soc* ser 2, **55,** 154-171

Bosanquet, R C, and Cowen, J D, (ed) 1948 A bone weaving-frame from South Shields, *Archaeol Aeliana* ser 4, **26,** 89-97

Bosanquet, R C, and Richmond, I A, (ed) 1936 A Roman skillet from South Shields, *Archaeol Aeliana* ser 4, **13,** 139-151

Bourne, D, 1967 The Roman Bridge at Corbridge, *Archaeol Aeliana* ser 4, **45,** 17-26

Boutwood, Y, 2005 National Mapping Programme, *Hadrian's Wall NMP Project: Bowness to Carlisle, Cumbria,* English Heritage Document, Aerial Survey Report Series, **AER/3/2005**

Bowden, M C B, and Blood, K, 1991 The Roman fort at Rudchester: an analytical field survey, *Archaeol Aeliana* ser 5, **19,** 25-31

Bowden, M C B, 1999 Wall miles 40/41, in *Hadrian's Wall 1989-1999* (ed P T Bidwell), 137-139

Bowman, A K, 1994 The Roman imperial army: letters and literacy on Rome's northern frontier, in *Literacy and Power in the Ancient World* (eds A Bowman and G Woolf), 109-125, Cambridge

Bowman, A K, 2003 *Life and Letters on the Roman Frontier: Vindolanda and its People,* 3 edn, London

Bowman, A K, 2006 Outposts of empire: Vindolanda, Egypt and the empire of Rome, *Journal of Roman Archaeology* **19,** 75-93

Bowman, A K, and Thomas, J D, 1983 *Vindolanda: the Latin Tablets,* London

Bowman, A K, and Thomas, J D, 1994 *The Vindolanda Writing Tablets: Tabulae Vindolandenses II,* London

Bowman, A K, and Thomas, J D, 2003 The Vindolanda Writing Tablets: Tabulae Vindolandenses III, London

Bowman, A K, Thomas, J D, Crowther, C, and Pearce, J, 2003 Vindolanda Tablets Online, *http://vindolanda.csad.ox.ac.uk.*

Bowman, A K, and Tomlin, R S O, 2005 Wooden stilus tablets from Roman Britain, in *Images and Artefacts of the Ancient World* (eds A Bowman and M Brady) Oxford

Brand, J, 1789 *The History and Antiquities of the Town and County of the Town of Newcastle upon Tyne,* London

Brann, M L, 1985 A Survey of Walls Castle, Ravenglass, Cumbria, *Trans Cumberland Westmorland Antiq Archaeol Soc* ser 2, **85,** 81-85

Breeze, A, 2001 The British-Latin Place-Names *Arbeia, Corstopitum, Dictum,* and *Morbium, Durham Archaeological Journal* **16,** 21-25

Breeze, A, 2004 The Roman place-names Arbeia and Corstopitum: a reply *Archaeol Aeliana* ser 5, **33,** 61-64

Breeze, D J, 1972 Excavations at the Roman fort of Carrawburgh, 1967-1969, Archaeol Aeliana ser 4, **50,** 81-144

Breeze, D J, 1982 *The Northern Frontiers of Roman Britain,* London

Breeze, D J, 1983 *Roman Forts in Britain,* London

Breeze, D J, 1984 Demand and supply on the northern frontier, in *Between and Beyond the Walls* (eds R Miket and C Burgess) Edinburgh, 264-86

Breeze, D J, 1988 The Roman Army in Cumbria, *Trans Cumberland Westmorland Antiq Archaeol Soc* ser 2, **88,** 9-22

Breeze, D J, 1997 The regiments stationed at Maryport and their commanders, in *Roman Maryport and its Setting: Essays in Memory of Michael G. Jarrett* (ed R J A Wilson), Maryport, 67-89

Breeze, D J, 2000 Supplying the Army, in *Kaiser, Heer und Gesellschaft in der römischen Kaiserzeit: Gedenkschrift für Eric Birley* (eds G Alföldy, B Dobson and W Eck), Stuttgart, 59-64

Breeze, D J, 2002a The edge of the world: the imperial frontier and beyond, in *Short Oxford History of the British Isles: the Roman Era* (ed P Salway), Oxford, 173-201

Breeze, D J, 2002b A Pannonian soldier on Hadrian's Wall and the manning of the milecastles, in *Zwischen Rom und dem Barbaricum, Festschrift für T. Kolník zum 70.*

Geburtstag (eds K Kuzmová, K Pieta and J Rajtár), Nitra, 59-63
Breeze, D J, 2003a Warfare in Britain and the building of Hadrian's Wall, *Archaeol Aeliana* ser 5, **32,** 13-16
Breeze, D J, 2003b John Collingwood Bruce and the study of Hadrian's Wall, *Britannia* **34,** 1-18
Breeze, D J, 2004 Roman military sites on the Cumberland coast, in *Romans on the Solway, Essays in Honour of Richard Bellhouse* (eds R J A Wilson and I Caruana), Kendal, 66-94
Breeze, D J, 2005a Why was Hadrian's Wall built across the Tyne-Solway isthmus?, in *Eine ganz normale Inschrift...und ähnliches zum Geburtstag von Ekkehard Weber am 30.* April 2005 (eds F Beutler and W Hameter), Wien, 13 -16
Breeze, D J, 2005b Destruction on Hadrian's Wall, *Arbeia Journal* **8,** 1 -4
Breeze, D J, 2006 *J. Collingwood Bruce's Handbook to the Roman Wall* Newcastle-upon-Tyne
Breeze, D J, and Dobson, B, 1969 Fort types on Hadrian's Wall, *Archaeol Aeliana* ser 4, **47,** 15-32
Breeze, D J, and Dobson, B, 1972 Hadrian's Wall: Some problems, *Britannia* **3,** 182-208
Breeze, D J, and Dobson, B, 2000 *Hadrian's Wall* 4 edn, London
Breeze, D J, and Hill, P R, 2001 Hadrian's Wall began here, *Archaeol Aeliana* ser 5, **29,** 1-2
Breeze, D J, and Rich-Gray, D, 1978-1980 'Fire pits' at Camelon, Stirlingshire, *Proc Soc Antiq Scotl* 110, 513-517
Brennand, M, (ed) 2006 *The Archaeology of North West England. An Archaeological Research Framework for North West England: Volume 1 Resource Assessment,* Manchester
Brennand, M, and Chitty, G, (eds) 2007 The Archaeology of North West England. An Archaeological Research Framework for North West England: Volume 2 Research Agenda and Strategy, Manchester
Brewis, P, 1932 Conjectural construction of turret no. 18a on Hadrian's Wall, *Archaeol Aeliana,* ser 4, **9,** 198-204
Brewis, P, 1936 A cruciform brooch from Benwell, *Archaeol Aeliana,* ser 4, **13,** 117-121
Brewster, N H, 1972 Corbridge: its significance for the study of Rhenish Ware, *Archaeol Aeliana* ser 4, **50,** 205-216
Brock, R, and Fulford, M, 2005 The Leeds index of samian potter's stamps pilot project, *http://www.leeds.ac.uk/lhri/documents/news_stories/the_leeds_index_of_samian_potters_stamps.pdf*
Bruce, J C, 1851a *The Roman Wall,* 1 edn, London and Newcastle-upon-Tyne
Bruce, J C, 1851b *Views on the Line of the Roman Wall in the North of England,* Newcastle-upon-Tyne
Bruce, J C, 1853 *The Roman Wall,* 2 edn, London and Newcastle upon Tyne
Bruce, J C, 1857 Visit to Cilurnum, Borcovicus etc., *Proc Soc Antiqs Newcastle-upon-Tyne,* 1, nr. **27,** 255-260
Bruce, J C, 1863 *The Wallet Book of the Roman Wall,* London and Newcastle upon Tyne
Bruce, J C, 1865 Mural Notes, *Archaeol Aeliana* ser 1, **6,** 220-224
Bruce, J C, 1867 The Roman Wall, 3 edn, London and Newcastle-upon-Tyne
Bruce, J C, 1874 On the Altars recently found in the Roman Camp at Maryport, *Trans Cumberland Westmorland Antiq Archaeol Soc* ser 1, **I,** 175-188
Bruce, J C, 1875 *Lapidarium Septentrionale: or a Description of the Monuments of Roman Rule in the north of England,* Newcastle-upon-Tyne
Bruce, J C, 1880 An account of the Excavation of the South Gateway of the station of *Cilurnum, Archaeol Aeliana* ser 2, **8,** 211-221
Bruce, J C, 1884 *The Handbook to the Roman Wall,* 2 edn, London and Newcastle upon Tyne
Bruce, J C, 1885 *The Handbook to the Roman Wall,* 3 edn, London and Newcastle-upon-Tyne
Bruce, J C, 1889 A Christian inscription from Chesterholm, *Archaeol Aeliana* ser 2, **13,** 367-369
Bruce, J C, 1889a Some Excavations at Chesters, *Archaeol Aeliana* ser 2, **13,** 374-377
Budge, E A W, 1902 *The Roman Antiquities in the Museum at Chesters,* London
Bulmer, W, 1943 A fragmentary inscription of Marcus Aurelius and Lucius Verus from Corbridge, *Archaeol Aeliana* ser 4, **21,** 239-247
Bulmer, W, 1955 Roman glass vessels in the Corstopitum museum, Corbridge, *Archaeol Aeliana* ser 4, **33,** 116-133
Burgers, A, 2001 *The Water Supplies and Related Structures of Roman Britain,* BAR Brit. Ser. **324,** Oxford
Burgess, C, 1984 The Prehistoric Settlement of Northumberland: A Speculative Survey, in *Between and Beyond the Walls: Essays on the Prehistory and History of North Britain in Honour of George Jobey* (eds R Miket and C Burgess), 126-175, Edinburgh
Burn, A R, 1969 *The Romans in Britain. An Anthology of Inscriptions,* 2 edn, Oxford
Burnham, B, Hunter, F, Fitzpatrick, A, Worrell, S, Hassall, M and Tomlin, R, 2004 Roman Britain in 2003, *Britannia* **35:** 253-349
Burnham, B C, Keppie, L J F, Esmonde Cleary, A S, Hassall, M W C, and Tomlin, R S O, 1995 Roman Britain in 1994, *Britannia* **26,** 325-390
Burnham, B C, Keppie, L J F, Esmonde Cleary, A S, Hassall, M W C, and Tomlin, R S O, 1998 Roman Britain in 1997, *Britannia* **29,** 365-445
Burnham, B C, Keppie, L J F, Tomlin, R S O, 1997 Roman Britain in 1996, *Britannia* **28,** 395-472
Burnham, B, Keppie, L, Fitzpatrick, A, Hassall, M, Tomlin, R, 2001 Roman Britain in 2000, *Britannia* **32,** 311-400
Busby, P A, 1988 *A Study of Plant Macro-Fossils from a Roman Well: Laws Lane, Carlisle*
Bushe-Fox, J P, 1913 The use of samian pottery in dating the early occupation of the north of Britain, *Archaeologia* **64,** 295-314
Button, J, and Caruana, I, 1984 Samian Pottery from Milecastle 64, *Trans Cumberland Westmorland Antiq Archaeol Soc* ser 2, **84,** 260
Buxton, K, and Howard-Davis, C L E, 2000 *Bremetenacum: Excavations at Ribchester, 1980, 1989-90.* Lancaster
Calkin, J B, 1955 Kimmeridge coal money and the Romano-British shale armlet industry, *Proceedings of the Dorset Natural History and Archaeological Society* **75,** 45-71
Callender, M H, 1949 Amphora stamps from Corbridge *Archaeol Aeliana* ser 4, **27,** 60-121
Callender, M H, 1965 *Roman Amphorae: with an Index of Stamps,* London
Camden, W, 1722 *Britannia.* (ed. E. Gibson), London

Caplan, C, 1976 To Neptune and to Oceanus, *Archaeol Aeliana* ser 5, **4,** 171-176

Carréras Monfort, C, and Funari, P P A, 1998 *Britannia y el Mediterráneo: estudios sobre el abastecimiento de aceite bético y africano en Britannia,* Barcelona

Carrington, P, 2008 Feeding the wolf in Cheshire: models and (a few) facts, in *Feeding the Roman Army* (eds R Thomas and S Stallibrass) Oxford

Caruana, I D, 1986a The Provenance of RIB 2028, *Trans Cumberland Westmorland Antiq Archaeol Soc* ser 2, **86,** 259-260

Caruana, I D, 1986b An Altar to Victory from the Birdoswald sector of Hadrian's Wall, *Trans Cumberland Westmorland Antiq Archaeol Soc* ser 2, **86,** 260-264

Caruana, I D, 1989 Fieldwalking in the Solway Plain, *Trans Cumberland Westmorland Antiq Archaeol Soc* ser 2, **89,** 51-68

Caruana, I D, 1989 Carlisle, *Tullie House Extension, 1989: Interim Report,* Carlisle Archaeol Unit, unpubl rep

Caruana, I D, 1992 Carlisle: excavation of a section of the annexe ditch of the first Flavian fort, 1990, *Britannia* **23,** 45-109

Caruana, I D, 1994 On the Trail of the Lonesome Pine Cone, *Archaeol Aeliana* ser 5, **22,** 274-276

Caruana, I D, 2000 Observations in the *vicus* of Stanwix Roman fort on the site of the Miles MacInnes Hall, 1986, *Trans Cumberland Westmorland Antiq Archaeol Soc* ser 2, **100,** 2000, 55-78

Caruana, I D, 2004a The cemetery at Beckfoot Roman fort, in *Romans on the Solway, Essays in Honour of Richard Bellhouse* (eds R J A Wilson and I Caruana), Kendal, 134-173

Caruana, I D, 2004b Timber towers on the Solway frontier?, in *Romans on the Solway, Essays in Honour of Richard Bellhouse* (eds R J A Wilson and I Caruana) Kendal, 184-85

Caruana, I D, in preparation *The Roman Forts at Carlisle: Excavations at Annetwell Street 1973-84*

Caruana, I D, and Coulston, J C, 1987 A Roman Bridge Stone from the River Eden, *Trans Cumberland Westmorland Antiq Archaeol Soc* ser 2, **87,** 43-51

Caruana, I D, and Fane-Gladwyn, Col P F, 1980 Unpublished Excavations on the Line of the Roman Wall in Hadrian's Camp, *Trans Cumberland Westmorland Antiq Archaeol Soc* ser 2, **80,** 17-24

Caruana, I D, and James, A, 1987 Observations in the Roman *Vicus* at Bowness-on-Solway, *Trans Cumberland Westmorland Antiq Archaeol Soc* ser 2, **87,** 256

Caruana, I D, Shotter, D C A, and Pirie, E J E, 1994 Roman and medieval coins found during sewer renewal in Carlisle, 1983-87 *Trans Cumberland Westmorland Antiq Archaeol Soc* ser 2, **94,** 65-76

Casey, P J, 1993 The end of garrisons on Hadrian's Wall: an historico-environmental model, in *The Later Roman Empire Today* (eds D Clark, M Roxan, and J Wilkes), London, 69-80

Casey, P J, and Hoffmann, B, 1995 Excavations on the Corbridge Bypass, 1974, *Archaeol Aeliana* ser 5, 23, 17-45

Charlesworth, D, 1959a Roman glass in Northern Britain, *Archaeol Aeliana* ser 4, **37,** 33-58

Charlesworth, D, 1959b Roman Glass in Tullie House Museum, *Trans Cumberland Westmorland Antiq Archaeol Soc* ser 2, **59,** 32-39

Charlesworth, D, 1959c The glass, in The Roman Bath House at Red House, Beaufront, near Corbridge (C M Daniels), *Archaeol Aeliana* ser 4, **37,** 164-6.

Charlesworth, D, 1960 A Roman well at Benwell, *Archaeol Aeliana* ser 4, **38,** 233-235

Charlesworth, D, 1961 Glass, in An excavation at Chesters, 1960 (R P Harper), *Archaeol Aeliana* ser 4, **39,** 326.

Charlesworth, D, 1962 Glass, in The shrine of the nymphs and the *genius loci* at Carrawburgh (D J Smith), *Archaeol Aeliana* ser 4, **40,** 80.

Charlesworth, D, 1963 The Roman Wall at Cawfields, Archaeol Aeliana ser 4, **41,** 217-218

Charlesworth, D, 1967a Excavations in the Carrawburgh car-park site 1964, *Archaeol Aeliana* ser 4, **45,** 1-16

Charlesworth, D, 1967b Preliminary work on the Portgate, *Archaeol Aeliana* ser 4, **45,** 208

Charlesworth, D, 1967c Poltross Burn, Milecastle 48, *Trans Cumberland Westmorland Antiq Archaeol Soc* ser 2, **67,** 233-235

Charlesworth, D, 1968 Recent work on Hadrian's Wall, Cawfields, *Archaeol Aeliana* ser 4, **46,** 69-74

Charlesworth, D, 1969a A gold signet ring from Housesteads, *Archaeol Aeliana* ser 4, **47,** 39-42

Charlesworth, D, 1969b The Roman Wall at Cambeckhill Farm (NY 507637), *Trans Cumberland Westmorland Antiq Archaeol Soc* ser 2, **69,** 346

Charlesworth, D, 1971a Housesteads west ditch and its relationship to Hadrian's Wall, *Archaeol Aeliana* ser 4, **49,** 95-99

Charlesworth, D, 1971b A group of vessels from the commandant's house, Housesteads, *Journal of Glass Studies,* **13,** 34-37 Charlesworth, D, 1973a A re examination of two turrets on Hadrian's Wall, *Archaeol Aeliana* ser 5, **1,** 97-109

Charlesworth, D, 1973b The Aesica Hoard, *Archaeol Aeliana* ser 5, **1,** 225-234

Charlesworth, D, 1973c Hadrian's Wall, turret 51A (Piper Sike), *Trans Cumberland Westmorland Antiq Archaeol Soc* ser 2, **73,** 67-78

Charlesworth, D, 1975 The commandant's house, Housesteads, *Archaeol Aeliana* ser 5, **3,** 17-42

Charlesworth, D, 1976 The hospital, Housesteads, *Archaeol Aeliana* ser 5, **4,** 17-30

Charlesworth, D, 1977 The turrets on Hadrian's Wall, in *Ancient Monuments and their Interpretation* (eds M R Apted, R Gilliard-Beer and A D Saunders), 13-26, London

Charlesworth, D, 1978 Roman Carlisle, *Archaeol J* **149,** 69-81

Charlesworth, D, 1979a Glass, in (W Hanson et al) The Agricolan supply-base at Red House, Corbridge. *Archaeol Aeliana* ser 5, **7,** 58-61.

Charlesworth, D, 1979b Glass, in (J N Dore and J P Gillam) *The Roman Fort at South Shields.* The Society of Antiquaries of Newcastle upon Tyne, Monograph ser **1,** 166-7.

Charlesworth, D, 1979c Plough-marks beneath 21 Annetwell St. Carlisle, *Trans Cumberland Westmorland Antiq Archaeol Soc* ser 2, **79,** 146

Charlesworth, D, 1979d Glass, in (T W Potter) *The Romans in North West England: Excavations at the Roman Forts of Ravenglass, Watercrook and Bowness on Solway,* Kendal, 99-100.

Charlton, J, 2004 Saving the Wall: quarries and

conservation *Archaeol Aeliana* ser **5,** 33, 5 -8
Cherry, J, and Caruana, I, 1989 A Romano-British glass bangle from Ravenglass *Vicus, Trans Cumberland Westmorland Antiq Archaeol Soc* ser 2, **89,** 277-278
Clare, T, 2000 The distribution of some archaeological sites in relation to features of Holocene coastal change, *Trans Cumberland Westmorland Antiq Archaeol Soc* ser 2, **100,** 1-23
Clare, T, 2004 Coastal change and the western end of Hadrian's Wall, in *Romans on the Solway, Essays in Honour of Richard Bellhouse* (eds R J A Wilson and I Caruana), Kendal, 39-51
Clayton, J, 1848 Account of Excavations at the Mile Castle of Cawfields, on the Roman Wall, *Archaeol Aeliana* ser 1, **4,** 54-59
Clayton, J, 1855-1857a The Roman Wall, *Proc Soc Antiq Newcastle-on-Tyne* ser 1, **1,** 56-57
Clayton, J, 1855-1857b Borcovicus (Housesteads) *Proc Soc Antiq Newcastle-on-Tyne* ser 1, **1,** 201-203
Clayton, J, 1876 Notes of an excavation at Cilurnum, *Archaeol Aeliana* ser 2, **7,** 171-176
Clayton, J, 1880 Excavations at Carrawburgh, *Archaeol Aeliana* ser 2, **8,** 1-19
Clayton, J, Watkin, W T, Hubner, E, and Stephens, G, 1885 On the discovery of Roman inscribed altars etc., at Housesteads, November 1883, *Archaeol Aeliana* ser 2, **10,** 148-150, 169-171.
Coles, B, 2006 *Beavers in Britain's Past* Oxbow Books and WARP (Wetland Archaeology Research Project), Oxford Collingwood, R G, 1921a Hadrian's Wall; a history of the problem, *J Roman Stud* **11,** 37-66
Collingwood, R G, 1921b The purpose of the Roman Wall, *Vasculum* 8, 4-9
Collingwood, R G, 1922a The Roman Fort at Bewcastle, *Trans Cumberland Westmorland Antiq Archaeol* Soc ser 2, **22,** 169-185
Collingwood, R G, 1922b The Roman Fort at Bewcastle, *Trans Cumberland Westmorland Antiq Archaeol Soc* ser 2, **22,** 198-233
Collingwood, R G, 1923a Explorations of the Roman fort at Burgh-by-Sands, *Trans Cumberland Westmorland Antiq Archaeol Soc* ser 2, **23,** 2-12
Collingwood, R G, 1923b A Tombstone from Birdoswald, *Trans Cumberland Westmorland Antiq Archaeol Soc* ser 2, **23**, 13-16
Collingwood, R G, 1924 The End of the Maiden Way, *Trans Cumberland Westmorland Antiq Archaeol Soc* ser 2, **24,** 110-116
Collingwood, R G, 1928 Roman Ravenglass, *Trans Cumberland Westmorland Antiq Archaeol Soc* ser 2, **28,** 353-366
Collingwood, R G, 1929a Roman signal-stations on the Cumberland Coast, *Trans Cumberland Westmorland Antiq Archaeol Soc* ser 2, **29,** 138-65
Collingwood, R G, 1929b Roman Eskdale, Whitehaven
Collingwood, R G, 1929-1930 Hadrian's Wall. A system of numerical references, *Proc Soc Antiq Newcastle-on-Tyne* ser 4, **4,** 179-187
Collingwood, R G, 1930a A System of numerical references to the parts of Hadrian's Wall and the structures along its line, *Trans Cumberland Westmorland Antiq Archaeol Soc* ser 2, **30,** 108-115
Collingwood, R G, 1930b *The Book of the Pilgrimage of Hadrian's Wall, July 1st to 4th 1930* Newcastle upon Tyne.
Collingwood, R G, 1931a Roman objects from Stanwix, *Trans Cumberland Westmorland Antiq Archaeol Soc* ser 2, **31,** 69-80
Collingwood, R G, 1931b Ten Years' Work on Hadrian's Wall, *Trans Cumberland Westmorland Antiq Archaeol Soc* ser 2, **31,** 87-110
Collingwood, R G, 1935a The Bewcastle Cross, *Trans Cumberland Westmorland Antiq Archaeol Soc* ser 2, **35,** 1-29
Collingwood, R G, 1935b The Inscription from the Turf Wall at High House, in Report of the Cumberland Excavation Committee for 1934, *Trans Cumberland Westmorland Antiq Archaeol Soc* ser 2, **35,** 229-232
Collingwood, R G, 1936a The Roman Fort at Beckfoot, *Trans Cumberland Westmorland Antiq Archaeol Soc* ser 2, **36,** 76-84
Collingwood, R G, 1936b The Roman Fort and settlement at Beckfoot, *Trans Cumberland Westmorland Antiq Archaeol Soc* ser 2, **36,** 85-99
Collingwood, R G, 1938 John Horsley and Hadrian's Wall, *Archaeol Aeliana* ser 4, **15,** 1-42
Collingwood, R G, and Myers, J N L, 1937 *Roman Britain and the English Settlements,* Oxford
Collingwood, W G, 1915 Notes on Early Crosses at Carlisle, Bewcastle and Beckermet, *Trans Cumberland Westmorland Antiq Archaeol Soc* ser 2, **15,** 125-131
Collins, R, 2004 Before 'the End': Hadrian's Wall in the fourth century and after, in *Debating Late Antiquity in Britain AD300-700* (eds R Collins and J Gerrard) BAR Brit. Ser. **365,** 123 -32
Collins, R, 2007 *Decline, Collapse or Transformation? Hadrian's Wall in the fourth - fifth Centuries,* Unpublished PhD. Thesis, Department of Archaeology, University of York
Collins, R, forthcoming Hadrian's Wall and the Collapse of Roman Frontiers, in *Roman Frontier Studies XXI* (eds Morillo et al) Leon Spain
Connolly, P, and van Driel-Murray, C, 1991 The Roman Cavalry Saddle, *Britannia* **22,** 33-50
Cool, H E M, unpublished a *Glass from the Roman forts in Carlisle: excavations in Annetwell Street in 1990.*
Cool, H E M, unpublished b *Small finds and vessel glass from Birdoswald sites 585, 590 and BRD99.*
Cool, H E M, 1992 Glass, in (I Caruana) Carlisle: excavation of a section of the annexe ditch of the first Flavian fort. *Britannia* **23,** 63-8.
Cool, H E M, 2000 The parts left over: material culture into the fifth century, in *The Late Roman Transition in the North,* (eds T Wilmott and P Wilson) BAR Brit. Ser. **299,** Oxford, 47 65
Cool, H E M, 2004 *The Roman Cemetery at Brougham, Cumbria: Excavations 1966 and 1967,* Britannia Monograph **21** (London)
Cool, H E M and Price, J 1991 Roman vessel and window glass, in *Roman Waterlogged Remains at Castle Street, Carlisle: fascicule 2: Metalwork, Glass and Stone Objects from Castle street, Excavations 1981-2* (M R McCarthy). Cumberland and Westmoreland Antiquarian and Archaeological Society Research series **5,** 165-76.
Cool, H E M and Price, J unpublished *The Glass from Roman Forts in Carlisle; Excavations in Annetwell Street in 1973-4* (written 1980-84).

Coulston, J C N, 1981 A Sculptured Dacian falx from Birdoswald, *Archaeol Aeliana,* ser 5, **9,** 348-350
Coulston, J C N, 1983 A Fragmentary Altar to Jupiter from Wallsend, *Archaeol Aeliana* ser 5, **11,** 309-313
Coulston, J C N, 1997 The stone sculptures, in *Romans on the Solway, Essays in Honour of Richard Bellhouse* (eds R J A Wilson and I Caruana), 112-131 Kendal
Coulston, J C N, and Phillips, E J, 1988 *Corpus Signorum Imperii Romani: Great Britain* I, 6; *Hadrian's Wall West of the North Tyne, and Carlisle,* Oxford
Cox, C, Chandler, M, Cox, M, Jones, J and Tinsleey, H, 2000 Early medieval hemp-retting at Glason Moss, Cumbria in the context of the use of *Cannabis sativea* during the historic period, *Trans Cumberland Westmorland Antiq Archaeol Soc,* ser 2, **100,** 131-150
Cowen, J D, 1965 The Crawhall Collection, *Archaeol Aeliana,* ser 4, **43,** 1-20
Cowen, J D, 1966 Sir Ian Richmond. A memoir, *Archaeol Aeliana* ser 4, **44,** 1-5
Cowen, J D, and Richmond, I A, 1935 The Rudge Cup, *Archaeol Aeliana* ser 4, **12,** 310-342
Cracknell, P, 2004 A piece of Roman metalwork from Bowness-on-Solway, *Trans Cumberland Westmoreland Antiq Archaeol Soc* Ser 3, **4,** 251-252
Cramp, R 1964 An Anglo-Saxon pin from Birdoswald, *Trans Cumberland Westmorland Antiq Archaeol* Soc ser 2, **64,** 90-93
Cramp, S, 1980 Handbook of the Birds of Europe, the Middle East and North Africa. Volume 2: Hawks to Bustards, Oxford
Creighton, J, and Wilson, R J A, (eds) 1999 Roman Germany: studies in Cultural Interaction, *JRA* Supplementary Series **32,** Portsmouth
Croom, A T, 2001 A Ring Mail shirt from South Shield's Roman Fort, *Arbeia Journal* **6-7,** 55-60
Croom, A T, 2001 Torc beads from South Shields Roman Fort, *Arbeia Journal* **6-7,** 60 -63
Croom, A T, 2001 Some finds from the 1997 -8 excavations at South Shields Roman fort, *Arbeia Journal* **6-7,** 68 -73
Croom, A T, 2005 *Roman Furniture,* Stroud
Croom, A T, and Caffell, A, 2005 Human remains from South Shields fort and its cemetery, *Arbeia Journal* **8,** 101-118
Crow, J G, 1986 The function of Hadrian's Wall and comparative evidence of Late Roman Long Walls, *Studien zur Militärgrenzen Roms III, 13 Internationaler Limes Kongress Aalen 1983,* Stuttgart, 724-729
Crow, J G, 1988 Notes on the north gateway of milecastle 39, Castle Nick, in *Portae cum Turribus* (eds P Bidwell, R Miket and B Ford), BAR Brit. Ser. **206,** 143-154, Oxford
Crow, J G, 1991a Construction and reconstruction in the central sector of Hadrian's Wall, in *Roman Frontier Studies 1989: Proceedings of the XVth International Congress of Roman Frontier Studies* (eds V Maxfield and M Dobson), Exeter, 44-47
Crow, J G, 1991b A Review of Current Research on the turrets and curtain of Hadrian's Wall, *Britannia* **22,** 51-63
Crow, J G, 2004a *English Heritage Book of Housesteads,* London
Crow, J G, 2004b The northern frontier of Britain from Trajan to Antoninus Pius: Roman builders and native Britons, in *A Companion to Roman Britain* (ed M Todd), 114-135, Oxford
Crow, J G, and Jackson, M, 1997 The Excavation of Hadrians Wall at Sewingshields and the Discovery of a Long Cist Burial, *Archaeol Aeliana,* ser 5, **25,** 61-69
Crutchley, S, 2006 Light detection and ranging (lidar) in the Witham Valley, Lincolnshire: an assessment of new remote sensing techniques, *Archaeological Prospection* **13,** 251-257
Cunliffe, B, 1983 The Iron Age of Northern Britain: A view from the south, in *Settlement in North Britain 1000 BC - AD 1000* (eds J Chapman and H Mytum) BAR Brit. Ser. **118,** Oxford, 83-102
Curle, J, 1911 *A Roman Frontier Post and its People: the Fort of Newstead in the Parish of Melrose,* Glasgow
Dacre, J A, 1985 An excavation on the Roman fort at Stanwix, Carlisle, *Trans Cumberland Westmorland Antiq Archaeol* Soc ser 2, **85,** 53-69
Dannell, G B, and Irving, P, 2005 Chronological list of the published works of K. F. Hartley, *Journal of Roman Pottery Studies* **12,** 2-10
Daniels, C M, 1959 The Roman bath house at Red house, Beaufront, near Corbridge, *Archaeol Aeliana* ser 4, **37,** 85-176
Daniels, C M, 1960 Excavations at Bowness on Solway, 1955, *Trans Cumberland Westmorland Antiq Archaeol Soc* ser 2, **60,** 13-19
Daniels, C M, 1962 *Mithras Saecularis,* the Housesteads mithraeum and a fragment from Carrawburgh, *Archaeol Aeliana* ser 4, **40,** 105-116
Daniels, C M, 1968 A hoard of iron and other materials from Corbridge, *Archaeol Aeliana* ser 4, **46,** 115-126
Daniels, C M, 1970 Problems of the Northern Frontier, *Scottish Archaeological Forum* **12,** 91-101
Daniels, C M, 1978 *J Collingwood Bruce's Handbook to the Roman Wall,* 13 edn, Newcastle upon Tyne
Daniels, C M, 1980 Excavation at Wallsend and the fourth century barracks on Hadrian's Wall, in *Roman Frontier Studies 1979* (eds W S Hanson and L J F Keppie), Oxford, 173-93
Daniels, C M, (ed) 1989 *The Eleventh Pilgrimage of Hadrian's Wall,* Newcastle-upon-Tyne
Daniels, C M, 1990 How many miles on the Cumberland Coast?, *Britannia* **21,** 401-406
Daniels, C M, and Harbottle, B, 1980 A new inscription of Julia Domina from Newcastle, *Archaeol Aeliana* ser 5, **8,** 65-73
Daniels, C M, and Jones, G D B, 1969 The Roman camps on Llandrindod Common, *Archaeol Cambrensis* **118,** 124-34
Dark, K, 1992 A Sub-Roman Re-defence of Hadrian's Wall?, *Britannia* **23,** 111-120
Dark, K, and Dark, P, 1996 New Archaeological and Palynological Evidence for a Sub-Roman Reoccupation of Hadrian's Wall, *Archaeol Aeliana,* ser 5 **24,** 57-72
Dark, P, 2000 *The Environment of Britain in the First Millennium* A.D., London
Dark, P, 2005 Mid- to late-Holocene vegetational and land-use change in the Hadrian's Wall region: a radiocarbon-dated pollen sequence from Crag Lough, Northumberland, England, *Journal of Archaeological Science* **32,** 601-618
Dark, P, 2006 Climate deterioration and land-use change in the first millenium BC: perspectives from the British palynological record, *Journal of Archaeological Science*

33, 1381-1395
Darrah, R, forthcoming The Structural Timber, in Howard Davis, (ed) forthcoming
Davies, G, and Turner, J, 1979 Pollen diagrams from Northumberland, *New Phytologist,* **82,** 783-804
Davies, H F, 1936 The shale industries at Kimmeridge, *Archaeol J* **93,** 200-13
Davies, J L, 2002 Soldiers, peasants, industry and towns, in P Erdkamp (ed), 169-203.
Davies, J L, and Jones, R H, 2002 Recent research on Roman camps in Wales, in *Proceedings of the XVIIIth International Congress of Roman Frontier Studies* (eds P Freeman, J Bennett, Z T Fiema and B Hoffman), BAR Int. Ser. **1084** (II), Oxford, 835-41
Davies Pryce, T, and Birley, E, 1935 The first Roman occupation of Scotland, *J Roman Stud* **25** (i), 59-80
Davies, R W, 1968 A note on some Roman soldiers in quarries, *Trans Cumberland Westmorland Antiq Archaeol Soc* ser 2, **68,** 22-26
Davies, R W, 1971 The Roman military diet, *Britannia* **2, 122-143**
Davies, R W, 1977 *Cohors I Hispanorum* and the Garrisons of Maryport, *Trans Cumberland Westmorland Antiq Archaeol Soc* ser 2, **77,** 7-16
Delaine, J, 1997 *The Baths of Caracalla: A Study in the Design, Construction, and Economics of Large-Scale Building Projects in Imperial Rome, JRA* Suppl Ser **25,** Rhode Island
Derks, T, & Roymans, N, 2002 Seal boxes and the spread of Latin literacy in the Rhine delta, in *Becoming Roman, Writing Latin? Literacy and Epigraphy in the Roman West* (ed A Cooley), Portsmouth and Rhode Island, 87-134
Detsicas, A P, 1962 Figured samian from Birdoswald, *Trans Cumberland Westmorland Antiq Archaeol Soc* ser 2, **62,** 31-55
Dickinson, B M, 1990 The samian ware, in *A Roman, Anglian and Medieval Site at Blackfriars Street, Carlisle: Excavations 1977-9* (ed M R McCarthy), 213-36, Kendal
Dickinson, B M, 1991 The samian ware, in *The Roman Pottery from Castle Street, Carlisle: Excavations 1981-82* (ed J Taylor), 344-365, Kendal
Dickinson, B M, 1992 Samian ware, in I D Caruana, Carlisle: excavation of a section of the annexe ditch of the first Flavian fort 1990, *Britannia* **23,** 51-58
Dickinson, B M, 1994 Samian, in P Ellis, J Evans, H Hanaford, G Hughes and A Jones, Excavations in the Wroxeter hinterland 1988-1990: the archaeology of the Shrewsbury bypass, *Transactions of the Shropshire Archaeological and Historical Society* **69,** 85-87
Dickinson, B M, 1997 Decorated samian and potter's stamps, in T Wilmott, *Birdoswald,* English Heritage Archaeological Report **14,** London, 256-267
Dickinson, B M, 2000 Samian ware, in I Caruana, Observations in the vicus of Stanwix Roman fort on the site of the Miles MacInnes Hall 1986, *Trans Cumberland Westmorland Antiq Archaeol Soc* ser 2, **100,** 62-66
Dickinson, B M, and Hartley, B R, 1979 Samian, in W S Hanson, C M Daniels, J N Dore, and J P Gillam, The Agricolan supply base at Red House, Corbridge, *Archaeol Aeliana* ser 5, **7,** 1-98.
Dickinson, B M, and Hartley, B R, 1988 Samian potters' stamps from Corbridge, and, Selected Dr.29s, in M C Bishop and J N Dore, *Corbridge: Excavations of the Roman Fort and Town, 1947-80,* English Heritage Archaeological Report **8,** London, 221-8 and 243-6
Dickinson, B M, and Hartley, B R, 2000 The samian, in P Rush, B M Dickinson, B R Hartley, and K F Hartley, *Roman Castleford, Excavations 1974-85, Vol. III: The Pottery,* Leeds, 5-88
Dixon, D, 1903 *Upper Coquetdale, Northumberland: Its History, Traditions, Folk-lore and Scenery* Newcastle-upon Tyne
Dixon, K, 1989 A Roman Bronze Openwork Buckle from Corbridge, *Archaeol Aeliana* ser 5, **17,** 211-213
Dobney, K, Jacques, D, & Irving, B, 1995 Of butchers and breeds. *Report on Vertebrate Remains from Various Sites in the City of Lincoln,* Lincoln Archaeological Studies **5,** Lincoln
Dobson, B, 1986 The function of Hadrian's Wall, *Archaeol Aeliana* ser 5, **14,** 1-30
Dobson, B, 1990 P.T.Bidwell and N.Holbrook Hadrian's Wall Bridges, *Archaeol Aeliana* ser 5, **18,** 236-237
Dockerill, J, 1969 *Pottery from the Milecastles and Turrets on Hadrian's Wall,* Unpublished MA thesis, University of Durham
Dodds, W, 1965 Fragment of Roman sculpture in Hexham Abbey, *Archaeol Aeliana* ser 4, **43,** 319-321
Dodds, W, 1973 Metal object from Milefortlet 16 Mawbray, *Trans Cumberland Westmorland Antiq Archaeol Soc* ser 2, **73,** 360-361
Donaldson, A M, & Turner, J, 1977 A pollen diagram from Hallowell Moss, near Durham City, UK, *Journal of Biogeography* **4,** 25-33
Donaldson, G H, 1985 Roman Military Signalling on the North British Frontiers, *Archaeol Aeliana* ser 5, **13,** 19-26
Donaldson, G H, 1988 Thoughts on a military appreciation of the design of Hadrian's Wall, *Archaeol Aeliana* ser 5, **16,** 125-137
Donaldson, G H, 1989 Tormenta, Auxilia and Ballistaria in the Environs of Hadrian's Wall, *Archaeol Aeliana* ser 5, **17,** 217-219
Donaldson, G H, 1990 A Reinterpretation of RIB 1912 from Birdoswald, *Britannia* **21,** 207-14
Dore, J N, 1976 Excavations at South Shields, *Archaeol Aeliana* ser 5, **4,** 185-186
Dore, J N, and Gillam, J P, 1979 *The Roman Fort at South Shields: Excavations 1875-1975,* Newcastle upon Tyne
Dore, J N, and Greene, K, 1976 North African pottery from South Shields, *Archaeol Aeliana* ser 5, **4,** 187-189
Dornier, A, 1968 Knag Burn, Housesteads, Northumberland, *Archaeological Newsbulletin for Northumberland, Cumberland and Westmorland* **1** (Jan. 1968), 2-4
Dornier, A, 1969 Knag Burn, Housesteads, Northumberland, *Archaeological Newsbulletin for Northumberland, Cumberland and Westmorland* **4** (Jan. 1969), 5
Drury, D, 1996 Crossing Hadrian's Wall: the 1991 excavation, in Lambert, J, (ed) *Transect through Time; the Archaeological Landscape of the Shell North Western Ethylene Pipeline,* Lancaster Imprints **1,** 84-86, Lancaster
Dryden, J S, & Withell, A R, 1978 The Pottery from Turret 52a, Banks East, *Trans Cumberland Westmorland Antiq Archaeol Soc* ser 2, **78,** 37-46
Duff, H, 1939 Roman Remains at Bowness-on-Solway, *Trans Cumberland Westmorland Antiq Archaeol Soc* ser 2, **39,** 327-329
Dumayne, L, & Barber, K E, 1994 The impact of the

Romans on the environment of northern England: pollen data from three sites close to Hadrian's Wall, *The Holocene* **4,** 165-173
Dumayne-Peaty, L, 1998 Forest Clearance in northern Britain during the Romano-British times: re-addressing the palynological evidence, *Brittania* **29**, 315-322
Dumayne-Peaty, L, & Barber, K E, 1997 Archaeological and environmental evidence for Roman impact on vegetation near Carlisle, Cumbria: a comment on McCarthy, *The Holocene* **7,** 243-245
Dungworth, D B, 1995 *Iron Age and Roman Copper Alloys from Northern Britain.* Unpublished PhD thesis, Durham University.
Dungworth, D B, 2001 *Metal-working Evidence from Housesteads Roman Fort, Northumberland.* Centre for Archaeology Report **109**/2001.
Dykes, F L B, 1870 A survey of the Roman Road from Maryport to Papcastle, *Trans Cumberland Westmorland Antiq Archaeol Soc* ser 1, **1**, 169-75
Eden, W A, 1937 The Housesteads Terraces, *Liverpool Annals of Archaeology* **24,** 156-164
Edwards, B J N, 2003 Red Rock Fault: lime and Hadrian's Wall, *Trans Cumberland Westmorland Antiq Archaeol Soc* ser 3, **3,** 226-228
Edwards, B J N, 2006 The "caput Carvetiorum" and the putative god of the tribe, *Trans Cumberland Westmorland Antiq Archaeol Soc* ser 3, **6,** 221-226
Edwards, B J N, & Shannon, W D, 2001 Raphaell Holinshed's description of Hadrian's Wall, *Trans Cumberland Westmorland Antiq Archaeol Soc* ser 3, **1,** 196-201
Edwards, B J N, & Shotter, D C A, 2005 Two Roman Milestones from the Penrith Are, *Trans Cumberland Westmorland Antiq Archaeol Soc* ser 3, **5,** 65-77
Edwards, B J N, & Shotter, D C A, 2006 The Langwathby Roman Milestone - a postscript, *Trans Cumberland Westmorland Antiq Archaeol Soc* ser 3, **6,** 235-237
Edwards, D A, & Green, C J S, 1977 *The Saxon Shore* fort and settlement at Brancaster, Norfolk, in The Saxon Shore (ed D E Johnston) CBA Research Report **18,** London, 21-29
Elton, H, 1996 *Frontiers of the Roman Empire,* London
Erdkamp, P, (ed) 2002 *The Roman Army and the Economy,* Amsterdam
Evans, J, 2000 The end of Roman pottery in the north, in *The Late Roman Transition in the North. Papers from the Roman Archaeology Conference Durham 1999* (eds T Wilmott and P Wilson) Oxford: Archaeopress BAR Brit Ser **299,** Oxford, 39-46
Evans, J, in preparation Supply zones of the Roman army: pottery from King Street and beyond.
Evans, J, & Willis, S H, 1997 Research Framework for the Study of Roman Pottery in the North of Britain, in *Research Frameworks for the Study of Roman Pottery* (ed S H Willis) Milton Keynes
Fair, M C, 1948 Roman finds on the Cumberland coast, *Trans Cumberland Westmorland Antiq Archaeol Soc* ser 2 **48,** 218-21
Ferguson, R, 1864 Discoveries on the south side of the city (Carlisle), *Journ British Archaeol Assoc* **20,** 84-5.
Ferguson, R S, 1878 Report on the Remains of a Roman Mile Castle, *Trans Cumberland Westmorland Antiq Archaeol Soc* ser 1, **1,** 214-215
Ferguson, R S, 1881 An attempt at a survey of Roman Cumberland and Westmorland V, *Trans Cumberland Westmorland Antiq Archaeol Soc* ser 1, **5,** 124-131
Ferguson, R S, 1886 Excavations on the line of the Roman Wall, *Trans Cumberland Westmorland Antiq Archaeol Soc* ser 1, **9,** 162-177
Ferguson, R S, 1888 The Roman camp at Muncaster *Trans Cumberland Westmorland Antiq Archaeol Soc* ser 1, **9,** 296-7
Fitts, R, Haselgrove, C, Lowther, P & Turnbull, P, 1994 An Iron Age farmstead at Rock Castle, Gilling West, North Yorkshire, *Durham Archaeological Journal* **10,** 13-42
Flynn, P, 1994 A watching brief at 46-52 Lowther Street, Carlisle, *Trans Cumberland Westmorland Antiq Archaeol Soc* ser 2, **94,** 289-291
Forster, M, 1997 *Rich Desserts and Captain's Thins: A Family and their Times 1831-1931,* London
Forster, R H, 1881 *History of Corbridge and its Antiquities,* Newcastle-upon-Tyne
Forster, R H, 1908 *Corstopitum.* Report of the excavations in 1907, *Archaeol Aeliana* ser 3, **4,** 205-303
Forster, R H, & Knowles, W H, 1910 *Corstopitum.* Report of the excavations in 1909, *Archaeol Aeliana* ser 3, **6,** 205-72
Forster, R H, & Knowles, W H, 1911 *Corstopitum.* Report of the excavations in 1910, *Archaeol Aeliana* ser 3, **7,** 143-267
Forster, R H, & Knowles, W H, 1912 *Corstopitum.* Report of the excavations in 1911, *Archaeol Aeliana* ser 3, **8,** 137-263
Forster, R H, & Knowles, W H, 1913 *Corstopitum.* Report of the excavations in 1912, *Archaeol Aeliana* ser 3, **10,** 230-80
Forster, R H, & Knowles, W H, 1914 *Corstopitum.* Report of the excavations in 1913, *Archaeol Aeliana* ser 3, **11,** 279-310
Forster, R H, & Knowles, W H, 1915 *Corstopitum.* Report of the excavations in 1914, *Archaeol Aeliana* ser 3, **12,** 227-86
Fowler, M J F, 2004 Archaeology through the keyhole: the serendipity effect of aerial reconnaissance revisited, *Interdisciplinary Science Reviews* **29,** 118-134
Fowler, P, 1983 *The Farming of Prehistoric Britain* Cambridge
Frain, T, McKelvey, J, & Bidwell, P T, The excavation of prehistoric features and Hadrian's Wall at Nos 224 -228, Shields Road, Newcastle upon Tyne, *Arbeia Journal* **8**, 5-28
Frain, T, McKelvey, J, & Bidwell, P T, 2005 Excavations and watching briefs along the berm of Hadrian's Wall at Throckley, Newcastle upon Tyne, in 2001-2002, *Arbeia Journal* **8,** 29-52
Frere, S S, 1987 *Britannia: A History of Roman Britain* London
Frere, S S, Hassall, M C W, & Tomlin, R S O, 1977 Roman Britain in 1976, *Britannia* **8,** 356-449
Frere, S S, Hassall, M C W, & Tomlin, R S O, 1984 Roman Britain in 1983, *Britannia* **15,** 266-356
Frere, S S, Hassall, M C W, & Tomlin, R S O, 1985 Roman Britain in 1984, *Britannia* **16,** 252-332
Frere, S S, Hassall, M C W, & Tomlin, R S O, 1986 Roman Britain in 1985, *Britannia* **17,** 363-454
Frere, S S, Frere, S S, Hassall, M C W, & Tomlin, R S O, 1977 Roman Britain in 1976, *Britannia* **8,** 356-449
Frere, S S, Hassall, M C W, & Tomlin, R S O, 1984 Roman Britain in 1983, *Britannia* **15,** 266-356

Frere, S S, Hassall, M C W, & Tomlin, R S O, 1985 Roman Britain in 1984, *Britannia* **16,** 252-332

Frere, S S, Hassall, M C W, & Tomlin, R S O, 1988 Roman Britain in 1987, *Britannia* **19,** 415-508

Frere, S S, Hassall, M C W, & Tomlin, R S O, 1989 Roman Britain in 1988, *Britannia* **20,** 257-345

Frere, S S, Hassall, M C W, & Tomlin, R S O, 1990 Roman Britain in 1989, *Britannia* **21,** 303-364

Frere, S S, 2000 M. Maenius Agrippa, the Expedition Britannica and Maryport, *Britannia* **31,** 23-26

Frere, S S, & St Joseph, J K, 1983 *Roman Britain from the Air* Cambridge

Frere, S S, & Tomlin, R S O, 1992, *The Roman Inscriptions of Britain volume II Instrumentum Domesticum, Fascicule 4,*

Frodsham, P, 2000 Worlds without ends: towards a new prehistory for Central Britain, in *Northern Pasts: Interpretations of the Later Prehistory of Northern England and Southern Scotland* (ed J Harding) BAR Brit. Ser. 302, 15-31, Oxford

Frodsham, P, (ed) 2004 *Archaeology in Northumberland National Park* CBA Research Report **136,** York

Fulford, M, 2004 Economic structures, in *A Companion to Roman Britain* (ed M Todd), Oxford, 309-326

Funari, P P A, 1996 *Dressel 20 Inscriptions from Britain and the Consumption of Spanish Olive Oil: With a vCatalogue of Stamps,* BAR Brit.Ser. **250**, Oxford

Gardner, A, 2002 Social identity and the duality of structure in late Roman-period Britain, *Journal of Social Archaeology* **2,** No. 3, 323-351

Gardner, A, 2007 Artefacts, contexts and the archaeology of social practices, in *Roman Finds: Context and Theory* (eds R. Hingley and S H Willis), 128-39, Oxford

Gardner, J, 1986 *Women in Roman Law and Society* London

Gater, J A, 1981 *Hadrians Wall, Geophysics 24/1981,* Ancient Monuments Laboratory Report, **3508**

Gates, T, 1983 Unenclosed Settlements in Northumberland, in *Settlement in North Britain 1000 BC - AD 1000* (eds J Chapman and H Mytum) BAR Brit. Ser. **118,** 103-147

Gates, T, 1999 *The Hadrian's Wall Landscape from Chesters to Greenhead: an Air Photographic Survey,* Northumberland National Park.

Gates, T, 2004a *The Hadrian's Wall Landscape from Chesters to Greenhead: an Air Photographic Survey,* Northumberland National Park.

Gates, T, 2004b Flying on the Frontier: Recent archaeological air photography in the Hadrian's Wall corridor, in *Archaeology in Northumberland National Park* (ed P Frodsham) CBA Research Report **136,** 236-245

Gates, T, & Hewitt, R, 2007 Some newly identified Roman temporary camps in Northumberland and their relation to the Devil's Causeway, *Archaeol Aeliana* ser 5, **36,** 11-30

Gerrard, J, & Mills, S 2002 Some stray finds from the Ravenglass area, Cumbria and their implications, *Trans Cumberland Westmorland Antiq Archaeol Soc* ser 3, **2,** 59-66

Gibson, B E, 1722 *Camden's Britannia: or a Chorographical Description of the Flourishing Kingdoms of England, Scotland and Ireland and the Islands Adjacent; from the Earliest Antiquity* London

Gibson, J P, 1903 On Excavations at Great Chesters (Aesica) in 1894, 1895, and 1897, *Archaeol Aeliana,* ser 2, **24,** 19-64.

Gibson, J P, & Simpson, F G, 1909a Recently Discovered Roman Inscriptions, *Archaeol Aeliana,* ser 3, **5,** 158 - 167

Gibson, J P, & Simpson, F G, 1909b The Roman fort on the Stanegate at Haltwhistle Burn, in *Archaeol Aeliana* ser 3, **5,** 213-85

Gibson, J P, and Simpson, F G, 1911 The milecastle on the Wall of Hadrian at the Poltross Burn, *Trans Cumberland Westmorland Antiq Archaeol Soc* ser 2, **11,** 390-461

Gillam, J P, 1949a "Also, along the Line of the Wall", *Trans Cumberland Westmorland Antiq Archaeol Soc* ser 2, **49,** 38-58

Gillam, J P, 1949b Trial trenching at Bewcastle, *Trans Cumberland Westmorland Antiq Archaeol Soc* ser 2, **49,** 216-218

Gillam, J P, 1950 Recent excavations at Birdoswald, *Trans Cumberland Westmorland Antiq Archaeol Soc* ser 2, **50,** 63-8

Gillam, J P, 1952a *Birdoswald 1952,* Unpublished manuscript notes lodged with excavation archive at Tullie House Museum

Gilliam, J P, 1952b Antonine pits and a pre-Hadrianic ditch at Corbridge, in Further exploration of the Antonine fort at Corbridge (I A Richmond and J P Gillam), *Archaeol Aeliana* ser 4, **30,** 251-66

Gillam, J P, 1953 Excavations at Low Brunton milecastle, No. 27, in 1952, *Archaeol Aeliana* ser 4, **31,** 165-173

Gillam, J P, 1954 The Roman bath-house at Bewcastle, *Trans Cumberland Westmorland Antiq Archaeol Soc* ser 2, **54,** 265-267

Gillam, J P, 1955 Centurial stones from Hadrian's Wall near Gilsland, *Trans Cumberland Westmorland Antiq Archaeol Soc* ser 2, **55,** 320-322

Gillam, J P, 1957 Types of Roman coarse pottery vessels in Northern Britain, *Archaeol Aeliana* ser 4, **35,** 180-251

Gillam, J P, 1970 The Northern British frontier from Antoninus Pius to Caracalla, *Archaeol Aeliana* ser 4, **48,** 1-44

Gillam, J P, 1974 The frontier after Hadrian - a history of the problem, *Archaeol Aeliana* ser 5, **2,** 1-15

Gillam, J P, 1976 Possible changes in plan in the course of the construction of the Antonine Wall, *Scottish Archaeological Forum* **7,** 51-6

Gillam, J P, 1976 Coarse fumed ware in North Britain and beyond, *Glasgow Archaeological Journal* **4,** 57-80

Gillam, J P, 1977 The Roman forts at Corbridge, *Archaeol Aeliana* ser 5, **5,** 47-74

Gillam, J P, and Daniels, C M, 1961 The Roman mausoleum on Shorden Brae, Beaufront, Corbridge, Northumberland, *Archaeol Aeliana* ser 4, **39,** 37-62

Gillam, J P, Jobey, I M and Welsby, D A, 1993 *The Roman Bath-house at Bewcastle, Cumbria.* Cumberland and Westmoreland Antiquarian and Archaeological Society Research Series **7.**

Gillam, J P, MacIvor, I, Birley, E, 1954 The temple of Mithras at Rudchester, *Archaeol Aeliana* ser 4, **32,** 176-219

Gillam, J P, Harrison, R M, and Newman, T G, 1973 Interim report on excavations at the Roman fort of Rudchester, 1972, *Archaeol Aeliana,* ser 5, **1,** 81-85

Gillam, J P, and Richmond, I A, 1959 Second century defences at Corbridge, *Archaeol Aeliana* ser 4, **37,** 59-84

Gillam, J P, and Tait, J, 1971 The investigation of the Commander's House area, on Site XI, Corbridge, 1958

1970: the structures, *Archaeol Aeliana* ser 4, **49,** 1-28
Gilson, A, 1978 The Doctor at Housesteads, *Archaeol Aeliana* ser 5, **6,** 162-165
Goodburn, R, Hassall, M, and Tomlin, R, 1979 Roman Britain in 1978, *Britannia* **10,** 268-356
Greene, K T, 1978 Apperley Dene 'Roman fortlet': a re examination 1974-5, *Archaeol Aeliana* ser 5, **6,** 29-59
Griffiths, W B, 1993 Excavation to the north-east of Wallsend Roman fort - 1993, *Arbeia Journal* **2,** 25-36
Groenmann-van Waateringe, W, 1980 Urbanisation and the north-west frontier of the Roman empire, in *Roman Frontier Studies 1979* (eds W Hanson and L Keppie) BAR Int. Ser. **71,** 1037-1044
Goldsworthy, A, and Haynes, I, (eds) 1999 *The Roman Army as a Community,* Portsmouth and Rhode Island
Goodburn, R, Wright, R P, Hassall, M C W, and Tomlin, R S O, 1976 Roman Britain in 1975, *Britannia* **7,** 290-392
Goodburn, R, Hassall, M W C, and Tomlin, R S O, 1978 Roman Britain in 1977, *Britannia* **9,** 403-485
Goodburn, R, Hassall, M W C, and Tomlin, R S O, 1979 Roman Britain in 1978, *Britannia* **10,** 267-356
Gordon, A 1726 *Itinerarium Septentrionale: or a Journey thro'most of the Counties of Scotland and those in the North of England.* London
Gough, R 1769 *Camden's Britannia: or a Chorographical Description of the Flourishing Kingdoms of England, Scotland and Ireland and the Islands Adjacent; from the Earliest Antiquity.* London.
Groves, C M, 2000 The dendrochronology, in *Roman and Medieval Carlisle: the Southern Lanes* (ed M R McCarthy), 69-70, Carlisle
Groves, C, in preparation The dendrochronology, in Caruana in prep
Guido, M, 1985 *The Glass Beads of the Prehistoric and Roman Periods in Britain and Ireland.* Society of Antiquaries of London Research Report, **35**. London.
Haffner, A, and von Schnurbein, S, 1996 Kelten, Germanen, Römer im Mittelgebirgsraum zwischen Luxemburg und Thüringen, *Archäologisches Nachrichtenblatt* **1,** 70-7
Haigh, D, and Savage, M, 1984 Sewingshields, *Archaeol Aeliana* ser 5, **12,** 33-148
Hall, A, and Kenward, H, 2003 Can we identify biological indicator groups for craft, industry and other activities?, in *The Environmental Archaeology of Industry* (eds P Murphy and P E J Wiltshire), 114-130, Oxford
Hall, A, Kenward, H, Large, F, and Usai, R, 1994 *Assessment of Biological Remains and Sediments from Roman deposits at Cumbria College of Art, Stanwix, Carlisle* (site code ARC94), Reports from the Environmental Archaeology Unit, York **94/56**
Halliday, W 1971 *Roman Glass with Special Reference to Material in Northern Britain.* Unpublished MA thesis, Univ of Durham.
Hanson, W S, 1987 *Agricola and the Conquest of the North,* London.
Hanson, W S, 1996 Forest Clearance and the Roman Army, *Britannia* **27,** 354-358
Hanson, W S, 1997 The Roman Presence: brief interludes, in Scotland; *Environment and Archaeology, 8000 BC - AD 1000* (eds K Edwards and I Ralston), 195-216, Chichester
Hanson, W S, and Breeze, D J, 1991 The Future of Roman Scotland, in *Scottish Archaeology:* new perceptions (eds W S Hanson and L Slater)Aberdeen, Aberdeen University Press
Hanson, W S, Daniels, C M, Dore, J N, and Gillam, J P, 1979 The Agricolan supply base at Red House, Corbridge, *Archaeol Aeliana* ser 5, **7,** 1-98
Hanson, W S, and Macinnes, L, 1980 Agricola's campaigns in Scotland, Forests, forts and fields: a discussion, *Scottish Archaeolgoical Forum* **12,** 98-113
Hanson, W S, and Maxwell, G, 1983 *Rome's North West Frontier: the Antonine Wall* Edinburgh
Harbottle, B, Fraser, R, and Burton, F C, 1988 The Westgate Road milecastle, Newcastle upon Tyne, *Britannia* **19,** 153-274
Harding, D, 2004 *The Iron Age in Northern Britain: Celts, Romans, Natives and Invaders,* Abingdon
Harrison, D, 1956 *Along Hadrian's Wall,* London
Harper, R P, 1961 An excavation at Chesters, 1960, *Archaeol Aeliana* ser 4, **39,** 321-326.
Hartley, B R, 1959 Samian ware, in C M Daniels, The Roman bath house at Red House, Beaufront, near Corbridge, *Archaeol Aeliana,* ser 4, **37,** 158-60
Hartley, B R, 1965 Samian identifications, in C Woodfield, Six turrets on Hadrian's Wall, *Archaeologia Aeliana,* ser 4, **43,** 87-200
Hartley, B R, 1966 Some problems of the Roman Military Occupation of the North of England, *Northern History* **1,** 7-20
Hartley, B R, 1969 Samian ware or terra sigillata, in *The Archaeology of Roman Britain* (eds R G Collingwood and I A Richmond) London, 235-251
Hartley, B R, 1972 The Roman occupations of Scotland: the evidence of samian ware, *Britannia* **3,** 1-55.
Hartley, B R, 1994 The samian stamps in the Period 1 ditch, in R Birley, *Vindolanda, Vol. 1: The Early Wooden Forts - The Excavations of 1973-76 and 1985-89, with Some Additional Details from the Excavations of 1991-93,* Vindolanda Research Reports, New Series, Hexham, 23-24.
Hartley, B R and Dickinson, B M 1994 The samian ware, in P T Bidwell and S Speak, *Excavations at South Shields Roman Fort.* Vol. I, Newcastle, 206-208
Haselgrove, C, 1984 The later pre-Roman Iron Age between the Humber and the Tyne, in *Settlement and Society in the Roman North* (eds P Wilson, R Jones and D Evans), 9-25, Bradford/Leeds
Haselgrove, C, 2002 The Later Bronze Age and the Iron Age in the Lowlands, in *Past, Present and Future: The Archaeology of Northern England* (eds C Brooks, R Daniels and A Harding), Durham, 49-77
Hassall, M W C, 1978 Britain and the Rhine Provinces: epigraphic evidence for Roman trade, in *Roman Shipping and Trade: Britain and the Rhine Provinces* (eds J du Plat Taylor and H Cleere), London, 41-48
Hassall, M W C, Wilson, D R and Wright, R P, 1972 Roman Britain in 1971, *Britannia* **3,** 299-367
Haverfield, F, 1888 Excavations on the line of the Roman Wall; Report of the Committee appointed April 20th 1886, laid before the Society at Kendal, September 8th 1886, *Trans Cumberland Westmorland Antiq Archaeol Soc* ser 1, **9,** 162-77
Haverfield, F, 1895 Report of the Cumberland Excavation Committee for 1894, *Trans Cumberland Westmorland Antiq Archaeol Soc* ser 1, **12,** 453-469

Haverfield, F, 1897 Report of the Cumberland Excavation Committee, 1895, *Trans Cumberland Westmorland Antiq Archaeol Soc* ser 1, **14,** 185-197
Haverfield, F, 1898a Report of the Cumberland Excavation Committee, 1897, *Trans Cumberland Westmorland Antiq Archaeol Soc* ser 1, **15,** 172-190
Haverfield, F, 1898b Inscriptions Preserved at Birdoswald, *Trans Cumberland Westmorland Antiq Archaeol Soc* ser 1, **15,** 197-200
Haverfield, F, 1899 Report of the Cumberland Excavation Committee for 1898, *Trans Cumberland Westmorland Antiq Archaeol Soc* ser 1, **15,** 345-64
Haverfield, F, 1900 Report of the Cumberland Excavation Committee for 1899, *Trans Cumberland Westmorland Antiq Archaeol Soc* ser 1, **16,** 35-54
Haverfield, F, 1901 Report of the Cumberland Excavation Committee for 1900, *Trans Cumberland Westmorland Antiq Archaeol* Soc ser 2, **1,** 75-92
Haverfield, F, 1902 Report of the Cumberland Excavation Committee for 1901, *Trans Cumberland Westmorland Antiq Archaeol Soc* ser 2, **2,** 384-392
Haverfield, F, 1903 Report of the Cumberland Excavation Committee for 1902, *Trans Cumberland Westmorland Antiq Archaeol Soc* ser 2, **3,** 328-349
Haverfield, F, 1904 Report of the Cumberland Excavation Committee, 1903, *Trans Cumberland Westmorland Antiq Archaeol Soc* ser 2, **4,** 239-249
Haverfield, F, 1911 Coton Iulius F.VI. Notes on Reginald Bainbrigg of Appleby, on William Camden and on some Roman Inscriptions, *Trans Cumberland Westmorland Antiq Archaeol Soc* ser 2, **11,** 343-78
Haverfield, F, 1915-1916 Roman Notes, *Trans Cumberland Westmorland Antiq Archaeol Soc* ser 2, **16,** 282-286
Haverfield, F, 1918 The Roman name of Birdoswald fort, *Trans Cumberland Westmorland Antiq Archaeol Soc* ser 2, **18,** 223-9
Haverfield, F, 1919 The Tullie House Fibulae, *Trans Cumberland Westmorland Antiq Archaeol Soc* ser 2, **19,** 1-16
Haverfield, F, and Atkinson, D, 1916-1917 The First Days of Carlisle, *Trans Cumberland Westmorland Antiq Archaeol Soc* ser 2, **17,** 235-250
Haynes, I, 2002 Britain's first information revolution. The Roman army and the transformation of economic life, in *The Roman Army and the Economy* (ed P Erdkamp) Amsterdam, 111-126 Head, Revd, 1773 An account of some antiquities discovered, on digging into a large Roman barrow, at Ellenborough, in Cumberland 1763, *Archaeol* **2,** 54-57
Healey, C, 2007 *Beckfoot Roman Cemetery and Milefortlet, Cumbria* (Unpublished report for English Heritage)
Hedley, A, 1822 An account of a sepulchral inscription discovered at Little Chesters in the County of Northumberland, *Archaeol Aeliana* ser 1, **1,** 208-212
Hedley, J P, 1937 The last days of *Corstopitum* and the Roman Wall - the coin evidence, *Archaeol Aeliana* ser 4, **14,** 95-102
Hedley, W P, 1931a The Walbottle (Throckley) hoard of Roman coins, *Archaeol Aeliana* ser 4, **8,** 12-48
Hedley, W P, 1931b Ancient cultivations at Housesteads, Antiquity 5, 351-354 Heichelheim, F M, 1935 *Genii Cucullati, Archaeol Aeliana* ser 4, **12,** 187-194
Henderson, J 1991 The glass artefacts, in *Roman Waterlogged Remains at Castle Street, Carlisle. Fascicule 2: Metalwork, Glass and Stone Objects from Castle Street Excavations 1981-2* (M R McCarthy). Cumberland and Westmoreland Antiiq and Archaeol Soc Research series **5,** 177-80.
Hendon, D, Charman, D J, and Kent, M, 2001 Palaeohydrological records derived from testate amoebae analysis from peatlands in northern England: within-site variability, between-site comparability and palaeoclimatic implications, *The Holocene* **11,** 127-148
Henig, M, 1971 The huntsman intaglio from South Shields, *Archaeol Aeliana* ser 4, **49,** 215-230
Henig, M, 1972a The Aesica amulet and its significance, *Archaeol Aeliana* ser 4, **50,** 282-286
Henig, M, 1972b Intaglios from Castlesteads and the Roman fort at Kirkbride, Trans Cumberland Westmorland Antiq Archaeol Soc ser 2, **72,** 57-65
Henig, M, 1973 Baal at Corbridge, *Archaeol Aeliana* ser 5, **1,** 241
Henig, M, 1980 An intaglio from Roman Corbridge, *Archaeol Aeliana* ser 5, **8,** 161-163
Henig, M, 1984 *Religion in Roman Britain,* London
Henig, M, 2004a *Roman Sculpture from the North West Midlands. Fascicule 9 of Corpus Signorum Imperii Romani Great Britain* Vol.1
Henig, M, 2004 *Murum civitatis, et fontem in ea a Romanis mire olim constructum*: The Arts of Rome in Carlisle and the Civitas of the Carvetii and their Influence, in *Carlisle and Cumbria: Roman and Medieval Architecture, Art and Archaeology* (eds M McCarthy and D Wilson) British Archaeological Associations Conference Transactions **27,** Leeds, 10 -28
Henig, M, and Allason-Jones, L, 1986 The Sewingshields Finger-Ring, *Archaeol Aeliana* ser 5, **14,** 181-182
Henig, M, and Millet, M, 1986 An intaglio from Carlisle, *Trans Cumberland Westmorland Antiq Archaeol Soc* ser 2, **86,** 258-259
Hepple, L W, 1999 Sir Robert Cotton,Camden's Britannia and the Early History of Roman Wall Studies, *Archaeol Aeliana* ser 5, **27,** 1-19
Heslop, D, 1987 *The Excavation of an Iron Age Settlement at Thorpe Thewles, Cleveland 1980-2,* London
Hetherington, D A, Lord, T C, & Jacobi, R M, 2005 New evidence for the occurrence of Eurasian lynx (Lynx lynx) in medieval Britain, *Journal Of Quaternary Science* **21,** 3-8
Heywood, B, 1965 The Vallum- its problems restated, in *Britain and Rome: Essays Presented to Eric Birley on His Sixtieth Birthday* (eds M G Jarrett and B Dobson) 85 94, Kendal
Higham, N, & Jones, G, 1975 Frontier, forts and farmers, *Archaeol J* **132,** 16-53.
Higham, N J, & Jones, G B D, 1985 *The Carvetii* Sutton
Higham, N J, 1989 Roman and Native in England North of the Tees: acculturation and its limitations, in *Barbarians and Romans in North-West Europe* (eds J Barrett, A Fitzpatrick & L Macinnes) BAR Int. Ser. 471, Oxford, 153-74
Hill, P, 1982 Broxmouth Hill-fort excavations, 1977-78: An interim report, *in Later Prehistoric Settlement in SE Scotland* (ed D Harding), Edinburgh, 141-188
Hill, P R, 1981 Stonework and the Archaeologist including a Stonemason's View of Hadrian's Wall, *Archaeol Aeliana* ser 5, **9,** 1-22
Hill, P R, 1991 Hadrian's Wall: some aspects of its execution,

Archaeol Aeliana ser 5, **19,** 33-39
Hill, P R, 1997 The Stone Wall turrets of Hadrian's Wall, *Archaeol Aeliana* ser 5, **25,** 27-50
Hill, P R, 2001 Hadrian's Wall from MC0 to MC9, *Archaeol Aeliana* ser 5, **20,** 3-18
Hill, P R, 2002 The development of the Stanegate: alternative thoughts, in *Polybius to Vegetius, Essays on the Roman Army and Hadrian's Wall Presented to Brian Dobson to Mark his 70th Birthday* (ed P R Hill), 87 102, England
Hill, P R, 2004 *The Construction of Hadrian's Wall,* BAR Brit. Ser. **375**, Oxford
Hill, P R, 2006 *The Construction of Hadrian's Wall Stroud*
Hill, P R, 1992 Survey of Standing and Excavated stone: Birdoswald Roman fort 1990 and 1992, unpublished report to English Heritage]
Hill, P R, forthcoming The Gateways: Technical survey of the masonry, in *The Grandest Station: Excavation and Survey at Housesteads Roman Fort* by C.M.Daniels, J. P. Gillam, J.G. Crow, D. J. Smith and the RCHME 1954-88 (ed A Rushworth) English Heritage Archaeological Report, London
Hill, P R, & Dobson, B, 1992 The design of Hadrian's Wall and its implications, *Archaeol Aeliana* ser 5, **20,** 27-52
Hill, S, & Welfare, H, 1975 The pottery from Turret 19B, West Clarewood, *Archaeol Aeliana* ser 5, **3,** 222-226
Hingley, R, 2000 *Roman officers and English Gentlemen: the Imperial Origins of Roman Archaeology,* London
Hingley, R, 2002 Later Prehistory: Introduction, in *Past, Present and Future: The Archaeology of Northern England* (eds C. Brooks, R. Daniels and A Harding), 45-47, Durham
Hingley, R, 2004 Rural settlement in Northern Britain, in *A Companion to Roman Britain* (ed M Todd) 327-348, Oxford
Hingley, R, 2005 *Globalizing Roman Culture: Unity, Diversity and Empire,* London
Hingley, R, (forthcoming) Cultural Diversity and Unity: empire and Rome, in *Local and Global Identities: Rethinking Identity and Material Culture in the Ancient Mediterranean* (eds S Hales and T Hodos), Cambridge
Hird, L, 1977 *A Report on the Pottery Found in Pre Hadrianic Levels at Vindolanda during the Excavations of 1972-1975,* Hexham
Hird, M L, & Brooks, C M, forthcoming *Roman and Medieval Carlisle: the Southern Lanes: Excavations 1981-2: Fasc. 3 The Roman and Medieval Pottery.*
Hodgson, E, 1897 Notes on the Excavations on the line of the Roman Wall in Cumberland in 1894 and 1895, *Trans Cumberland Westmorland Antiq Archaeol Soc* ser 1, **14,** 390-407
Hodgson, E, 1899 Notes on the Excavations on the Line of the Roman Wall in Cumberland, in 1898, *Trans Cumberland Westmorland Antiq Archaeol Soc* ser 1, **15,** 365-76
Hodgson, E, 1920 Appletree, in The 5th Pilgrimage of Hadrian's Wall, *Proc Soc Antiqs Newcastle-on-Tyne* ser 3, **9,** 283
Hodgson, G W I, 1968 A comparative account of the animal remains from *Corstopitum* and the Iron Age site of Catcote near Hartlepool, Co. Durham, *Archaeol Aeliana* ser 4, **46,** 127-162
Hodgson, G W I, 1971 Report on the animal remains recovered from the site of the Roman fort at South Shields, County Durham, *Archaeol Aeliana* ser 4, **49,** 135-138
Hodgson, J, n.d., post 1810 *A Topographical and Historical Description of the County of Northumberland.* (in 'The Beauties of England and Wales' series).
Hodgson, J, 1822 Observations on the Roman Station of Housesteads, *Archaeol Aeliana* ser 1, **1,** 263-320
Hodgson, J, 1828 *History of Northumberland, part 3, vol 2,* Newcastle-upon-Tyne
Hodgson, J, 1840 *History of Northumberland Part 2, vol 2,* Newcastle-upon-Tyne
Hodgson, J, 1832 *MSS notebook,* NRO M15, A39, 355
Hodgson, J, and Brennand, M, 2006 Prehistoric Period Resource Assessment, in *The Archaeology of North West England, An Archaeological Research Framework for North West England: Volume 1 Resource Assessment* (ed M Brennand), Manchester
Hodgson, N, 1995 ere there two Antonine occupations of Scotland?, *Britannia* **26,** 29-49
Hodgson, N, 1996 A late Roman courtyard house at South Shields and its parallels, in *Architecture in Roman Britain* (eds P Johnson and I Haynes), York, 135-51
Hodgson, N. 1997 Relationships between Roman river frontiers and artificial frontiers, in *Roman Frontier Studies 1995, Proceedings of the XVIth International Congress of Roman Frontier Studies* (eds W Groenman van Waateringe, B van Beek, W Willems and S Wynia), Oxford, 61-66
Hodgson, N, 2000 The Stanegate: A Frontier Rehabilitated, *Britannia* **31,** 11-22
Hodgson, N, 2001 The origins and development of the Roman military supply-base at South Shields: an interim report on the results of excavations in the eastern quadrant and central area, 1990-2000, *Arbeia Journal* **6-7,** 25-36
Hodgson, N, 2002 The Roman place-names Arbeia and Corstopitum: a rejection of recently suggested meanings, *Archaeol Aeliana* ser 5, **30,** 173-4
Hodgson, N, 2003 *The Roman Fort at Wallsend: Excavations in 1997-8* (Tyne and Wear Museums Archaeological Monograph **2**), Newcastle upon Tyne
Hodgson, N, 2005 Destruction by the enemy? Military equipment and the interpretation of a late-third century fire at South Shields, in *Archäologie der Schlachtfelder - Militaria aus Zerstörungshorizonten: Akten der 14. Internationalen Roman Military Equipment Conference,* Carnuntum Jahrbuch, 207-216
Hodgson, N, & Bidwell, P T, 2004 Auxiliary barracks in a new light: recent discoveries on Hadrian's Wall, *Britannia* **35,** 121-57
Hodgson, N, & Griffiths, B, 1999 Wallsend: Where did they keep the Horses in Roman Forts? *Current Archaeology* **164,** 234-289
Hodgson, N, & McKelvey, J, 2006 An excavation on Hadrian's Wall at Hare Hill, wall mile 53, Cumbria, *Trans Cumberland Westmorland Antiq Archaeol Soc* ser 3, **6,** 45-60
Hodgson, N, Stobbs, G, & van der Veen, M, 2001 An Iron Age Settlement and Remains of Earlier Prehistoric Date beneath South Shields Roman Fort, Tyne and Wear, *Archaeol J* **158,** 62-160
Hodgson, T, 1909-1910 The 'praetorium' at Chesters, *Proc*

Soc Antiq Newcastle ser 3, **4,** 134-143
Hoffmann, B, 1995 The quarters of Legionary centurions of the Principate, *Britannia* **26,** 107-52
Hoffman, B, 2003 Roman glass from Newstead and Vindolanda. *Annales du 15e Congres de l'Association Internationale pour Histoire du Verre.* New York-Corning, 41-44.
Hogg, R, 1949 A Roman cemetery site at Beckfoot, Cumberland *Trans Cumberland Westmorland Antiq Archaeol Soc* ser 2, **49,** 32-37
Hogg, R, 1952 The historic crossings of the river Eden at Stanwix, and their associated road systems, *Trans Cumberland Westmorland Antiq Archaeol Soc* ser 2, **52,** 131-59
Hogg, R, 1953 Notes on Drumburgh, *Trans Cumberland Westmorland Antiq Archaeol Soc* ser 2, **53,** 215-216
Hogg, R, 1955 Excavations in Carlisle, 1953, *Trans Cumberland Westmorland Antiq Archaeol Soc* ser 2, **55,** 59-107
Hogg, R, 1962a Millstone, Birdoswald, *Trans Cumberland Westmorland Antiq Archaeol Soc* ser 2, **62,** 321-323
Hogg, R, 1962b Beckfoot fort, cemetery site, *Trans Cumberland Westmorland Antiq Archaeol Soc* ser 2, **62,** 321-323
Hogg, R, 1964 Excavations at Tullie House, Carlisle, 1954 56, Trans Cumberland Westmorland Antiq Archaeol Soc ser 2, **64**, 14-62
Hogg, R, 1965 Excavation of the Roman auxiliary tilery, Brampton, *Trans Cumberland Westmorland Antiq Archaeol Soc* ser 2, **65,** 133-68
Hogg, R, 1972 Romano-British P-shaped brooch, Beckfoot, *Trans Cumberland Westmorland Antiq Archaeol Soc* ser 2, **72,** 331
Hogg, R, 1974 Roman glass phalera from Stanwix, *Trans Cumberland Westmorland Antiq Archaeol Soc* ser 2, **74,** 217-8
Holbrook, N, 1991 A watching brief at the Roman fort of Benwell-Condercum 1990, *Archaeol Aeliana* ser 5, **19,** 41-5
Holbrook, N, and Speak, S C, 1994 Washing Wells Roman Fort: a transcription of the aerial photographs and an assessment of the evidence, *Arbeia Journal* **3,** 33-45
Holder, P A, 2004 Roman place-names on the Cumbrian coast, in *Romans on the Solway, Essays in Honour of Richard Bellhouse* (eds R J A Wilson and I Caruana), 52 65, Kendal
Holder, P A, 1997 A Roman military diploma from Ravenglass, Cumbria, *Bull John Rylands Univ Library* Manchester **79,** 3-41
Holmes, S, 1893 Notes on the cuttings through the vallum on the hill a little to the east of Heddon, *Proc Soc Antiq Newcastle-on-Tyne* ser 1, **6,** 58-60
Honeyman, H L, 1936 A grave at Condercum, *Proc Soc Antiq Newcastle* ser 4, **7,** 50-4.
Hooley, J, and Breeze, D J, 1968 The building of Hadrian's Wall: a reconsideration, *Archaeol Aeliana* ser 4, 46, 97-114
Hooper, W D, 1935 *Cato and Varro on Agriculture* Cambridge, Massachusets
Hope, L E, 1905 Recent finds, Medieval, and Romano British, in and near Carlisle, *Trans Cumberland Westmorland Antiq Archaeol Soc* ser 2, **5,** 266-269
Hopewell, D, 2005 Roman fort environs in North West Wales, *Britannia* **36,** 225-69.
Hornshaw, T R, 2000 The Wall of Severus? *Archaeol Aeliana* ser 5, **28,** 27-36
Horsley, J, 1732 *Britannia Romana,* London
Howard, P, 1979 *Camboglanna, Birdoswald Fort on Hadrian's Wall; A Short History and Guide,* Newcastle upon-Tyne
Howard-Davis, C (ed), Unpublished glass from the Roman forts in Carlisle: the Millennium site.
Howard-Davis, C, (ed) forthcoming *The Carlisle Millennium Project: Excavations within the Roman Fort and Medieval castle, 1998-2001, Vol 2*
Hughes, M J, 1980 The analysis of Roman tin and pewter ingots, in *Aspects of Early Metallurgy* (ed W A Oddy). London: British Museum (Occasional Paper No. **17**), 41-50.
Hughes, P D M, Mauquoy, D, Barber, K E, and Langdon, P G, 2000 Mire-development pathways and palaeoclimatic records from a full Holocene peat archive at Walton Moss, Cumbria, England, *Holocene* **10,** 465-479
Hull, M R, 1926 The Excavations at Aesica, 1925 Interim Report, *Archaeol Aeliana,* ser 4, **2,** 197 - 202
Hunneysett, R, 1980 The milecastles on Hadrian's Wall: an alternative interpretation, *Archaeol Aeliana* ser 5, **8,** 95-107
Hunter Blair, P, 1934 Housesteads milecastle, *Archaeol Aeliana* ser 4, **11,** 103-121
Hunter, C, 1702 (Letter in) *Philosophical Transactions of the Royal Society* **23,** no.278, p.1131
Hunter, F, 2007 Artefacts, regions, and identities in the northern British Iron Age, in *The Later Iron Age in Britain and Beyond* (eds C Haselgrove and T Moore) 286 96, Oxford
Huntley, J P, 1987 *Woodland Management Studies from Carlisle: Castle Street 1981,* Ancient Monuments Laboratory Report, **119/87**
Huntley, J P, 1988 Palaeoenvironmental investigations, in The Westgate Road milecastle, Newcastle upon Tyne (B Harbottle, R Fraser and F C Burton), *Britannia* 19, 160-163
Huntley, J P, 1989a *Plant Remains from Annetwell Street, Carlisle, Cumbria: the Bulk Samples.* Ancient Monuments Laboratory Report, 1/89, 103.
Huntley, J P, 1989b *Waterlogged Plant Remains from Annetwell Street, Carlisle, Cumbria, part 2: Data analysis.* Ancient Monuments Laboratory Report, **37/89**
Huntley, J P, 1989c Woodland Management Studies from Carlisle: Annetwell Street, 1983-4, Ancient Monuments Laboratory Report, 51/89
Huntley, J P, 1990 *Macrobotanical Remains from the Roman Fort of Banna* (Birdoswald, Cumbria), Ancient Monuments Laboratory Report **104/91**
Huntley, J P, 1991 *Botanical Remains in Samples from the Tullie House Extension* (ANN D and ANN E) and Tullie House Basement (ABB B) sites (Carlisle). Durham Environmental Archaeology Report, 1/91
Huntley, J P, 1992a Botanical samples. pp49-51. In Carlisle: excavation of a section of the Annexe Ditch of the first *Britannia* Flavian fort, 1990 (ed I D Caruana), **23,** pp. 45-109
Huntley, J P, 1992b *Plant Remains from Excavations at The Lanes, Carlisle, Cumbria: part I* - CAL, OGL, OBL and LEL Ancient Monuments Laboratory Report, 51/92, 201.
Huntley, J P, 1997 Macrobotanical evidence from the horrea. pp 141-144. In *Birdoswald. Excavation of a Roman Fort on Hadrian's Wall and its Successor Settlements:*

1987-92 (ed T Wilmott), Archaeological Report No. **14,** pp. 461. English Heritage, London.
Huntley, J P, 1998a The environmental samples, in' *Vindolanda. 1997 excavations. Praetorium site. Interim Report* (eds R Birley, J Blake and A Birley) Greenhead, 68-80
Huntley, J P, 1998b *Excavations at Wallsend, Tyne and Wear: WV97. Evaluation of the Environmental Samples from the Roman fort of Segedunum.* Durham Environmental Archaeology Report, **37/98.**
Huntley, J P, 1998c *Black Carts, Northumberland: CAS-623. Assessment of Bulk Environmental Samples and Pollen Monoliths from Sections Across Hadrian's Wall, Durham* Environmental Archaeology Report, 18/98
Huntley, J P, 1999 Environmental evidence from Hadrian's Wall, in *Hadrian's Wall 1989-1999* (ed P. Bidwell), 48-64, Carlisle
Huntley, J P, 2000a The plant and wood remains. In *Roman and Medieval Carlisle: the Southern Lanes* (ed M.R. McCarthy), pp. 71-79. Carlisle Archaeology Ltd, Carlisle.
Huntley, J P, 2000b Late Roman transition in the north: the palynological evidence, in *The Late Roman Transition in the North. Papers from the Roman Archaeology* Conference, Durham 1999 (eds T. Wilmott & P.R. Wilson), BAR Brit. Ser. **299,** 67-72, Oxford
Huntley, J P, 2003 Vindolanda: analysis of environmental samples. 1998-2002 excavations, in *The Excavations of 2001-2002* (ed A. Birley), 256-279, Hexham
Huntley, J P, & Daniell, J R G, 2000 *Blackgate, Newcastle upon Tyne: BG85, BG90 and BG92. Analysis of Plant Remains from Roman Deposits.* Durham Environmental Archaeology Report, **01/2000.**
Huntley, J P, & Stallibrass, S M, 1995 *Plant and Vertebrate Remains from Archaeological Sites in Northern England: Data reviews and Future Directions,* Research Report **4,** Durham
Hutchinson, W, 1776 *An Excursion to the Lakes in Westmorland and Cumberland; with a Tour through Part of the Northern Counties in the Years 1773 and 1774* Newcastle
Hutchinson, W, 1794 *The History of the County of Cumberland, and some Places Adjacent* (2 vols). Carlisle.
Hutton, W, 1802 *The History of the Roman Wall, which Crosses the Island of Britain, from the German Ocean to the Irish Sea. Describing its Ancient State and its Appearance in the Year 1801.* London
Hutton, W, 1813 *The History of the Roman Wall* London
Iley, W 1974 The stones of St. Andrew's, Corbridge, *Archaeol Aeliana* ser 5, **2,** 201-211
Izard, K, 1993 *The Animal Bones from Birdoswald, CAS Site 420, Cumbria, 1987-90,* Ancient Monuments Laboratory Report **13/93**
Jackman, J, 1990 Conservation of Roman leather from Vindolanda, *World Leather,* 62-64
Jackson, K H, 1982 Brigomaglos and St. Briog, *Archaeol Aeliana* ser 5, **10,** 61-65
Jackson, W, 1883 An account of some excavations made at Walls Castle in 1881, *Trans Cumberland Westmorland Antiq Archaeol Soc* ser 1, **6,** 216-24
Jalas, J, & Suominen, J, 1972 *Atlas Flora Europaeae,* Cambridge
James, S T, 1984 Britain and the Late Roman Army, in T. F. C. Blagg and A. C. King (eds.) *Military and Civilian in Roman Britain.* BAR Int Ser **136,** Oxford: 161-186.
James, S. 2001. 'Soldiers and civilians: identity and interaction in Roman Britain', in S. James and M. Millett, (eds) *Britons and Romans: Advancing an Archaeological Agenda,* York: CBA, 77-89.
Jarret, M G, 1954a A Christian monogram from Roman Maryport, *Trans Cumberland Westmorland Antiq Archaeol Soc* ser 2, **54,** 268-270
Jarret, M G, 1954b A Roman mortar from Maryport, *Trans Cumberland Westmorland Antiq Archaeol Soc* ser 2, **54,** 270-271
Jarret, M G, 1958 The pre-Hadrianic occupation of Roman Maryport, *Trans Cumberland Westmorland Antiq Archaeol Soc* ser 2, **58,** 63-67
Jarrett, M G, 1959 The defences of the Roman fort at Halton Chesters, *Archaeol Aeliana* ser 4, 37, 177-190
Jarrett, M G, 1959 Excavations at Halton Chesters, *Archaeol Aeliana* ser 4, **37,** 177-90
Jarrett, M G, 1960 Roman coins and potters' stamps from Halton Chesters, *Archaeol Aeliana* ser 4, **38,** 153-160
Jarrett, M G, 1965 Roman officers at Maryport, Trans Cumberland Westmorland Antiq Archaeol Soc ser 2, **65,** 115-132
Jarrett, M G, 1976 *Maryport, Cumbria: a Roman Fort and its Garrison* (Trans Cumberland Westmorland Antiq Archaeol Soc Extra Series **22,** Kendal)
Jarret, M G, & Stephens, G R, 1987 The Roman garrisons of Maryport, *Trans Cumberland Westmorland Antiq Archaeol Soc* ser 2, **87,** 61-66
Jefferson, S, 1842 *The History and Antiquities of Cumberland II* Carlisle
Jilek, S, & Breeze, D J, 2007 The detritus of life: the contribution of small finds to understanding smaller military installations, in *Roman Finds: Context and Theory* (eds R Hingley & S H Willis), 199-213, Oxford
Jobey, G, 1958a The Wall ditch, Bays Leap, Heddon on the Wall, *Archaeol Aeliana* ser 4, **36,** 55-60
Jobey, G, 1958a An altar to Minerva from Benwell, *Archaeol Aeliana* ser 4, **36,** 307-308
Jobey, G, 1960 Some rectilinear settlements of the Roman period in Northumberland, *Archaeol Aeliana* ser 4, **38,** 1-38
Jobey, G, 1962 An Iron Age homestead at West Brandon, Durham, *Archaeol Aeliana* ser 4, **40,** 1-34
Jobey, G, 1965a Hillforts and settlements in Northumberland, *Archaeol Aeliana* ser 4, **43,** 21-64
Jobey, G, 1965a Stott's House "Tumulus" and the military way, Walker, *Archaeol Aeliana* ser 4, **43,** 77-86
Jobey, G, 1969 Barcombe Hill Signal Station, Thorngrafton, *Archaeol Aeliana* ser 4, **47,** 183-185
Jobey, G, 1974 Notes on some population problems in the area between the two Roman walls, *Archaeol Aeliana* ser 5, **2,** 17-26
Jobey, G, 1979 Palisaded enclosures, a Roman temporary camp and Roman gravel quarries on Bishop Rigg, Corbridge, *Archaeol Aeliana* ser 5, **7,** 99-113
Jobey, G, & Maxwell, D, 1957 A square-headed brooch from Benwell, *Archaeol Aeliana,* ser 4, **35,** 282-4
Jobey, I, 1979 Housesteads ware - a Frisian tradition on Hadrian's Wall, *Archaeol Aeliana,* ser 5, **7,** 127-143
Jobey, I and Jobey, G, 1987 Prehistoric, Romano-British and later remains on Murton High Crags, Northumberland. *Archaeol Aeliana* ser 5, **15,** 151-98.

Johnson, M & Cameron, K, in prep. The excavations of two Roman pottery kilns at7Fisher Street, Carlisle

Johnstone, C, 2005 Those elusive mules: investigating osteometric methods for their investigation, in *Equids in Time and Space* (ed M Mashkour), 183-191, Oxford

Johnstone, C, 2008 Commodities or logistics? The role of equids in Roman supply networks, in *Feeding the Roman Army* (eds R Thomas and S Stallibrass) Oxford

Jones, C P, 2005 Ten Dedications "To the gods and goddesses" and the Antonine Plague, *J Roman Archaeol* **18**, 293-301

Jones, G D B, 1976 The western extension of Hadrian's Wall, *Britannia* **7**, 236-43

Jones, G D B, 1982 The Solway Frontier: Interim report 1976-81, *Britannia* **13**, 283-97

Jones, G D B, 2004 Excavations on a coastal tower: Campfield Tower 2b, Bowness-on-Solway, in *Romans on the Solway, Essays in Honour of Richard Bellhouse* (eds R J A Wilson & I Caruana),174-183, Kendal

Jones, G D B, & Maude, K, 1987 The Solway frontier 1984: Roman Frontier Studies, *Manchester Archaeological Bulletin* **1**, 3-9

Jones, G D B, and Woolliscroft, D J, 2001 *Hadrian's Wall from the Air.* Brimscombe Port

Keays, L, forthcoming The metalworking debris, in *The Carlisle Millennium Project: Excavations within the Roman Fort and Medieval Castle, 1998-2001, Vol 2* (ed C Howard-Davis)

Keeley, H C M, 1989 *A Report on Some Soil Samples from Carlisle, Cumbria.* Ancient Monuments Laboratory Report, 48/1989

Keeney, G S, 1934 *Corstopitum* as a civil centre, *Archaeol Aeliana* ser 4, **11**, 158-175

Keevill, G D, Shotter, D C A, & McCarthy, M R, 1989 A solidus of Valentinian II from Scotch Street, Carlisle, *Britannia* **20**, 254-255

Kendal, R, 1996 Transport logistics associated with the building of Hadrian's Wall, *Britannia* **27,** 129-52

Kennedy, D L, 1986 The place-name Arbeia, *Britannia* **17,** 332-3

Kent, J P C, 1951 Coin evidence, and the evacuation of Hadrian's Wall, *Trans Cumberland Westmorland Antiq Archaeol Soc* ser 2, **51,** 4-15

Kenward, H K, 2000 *Assessment of Insect Remains from a Sample from the Flodden Hill Rectilinear Enclosure.* Reports from the Environmental Archaeology Unit, York, **2000/79**

Kenward, H K, in press *Northern Regional Review of Environmental Archaeology. Invertebrates in Archaeology* in the North of England, Centre for Archaeology Reports.

Kenward, H K, Allison, E P, Dainton, M, Kemenés, I K, & Carrott, J B, 2000 The insect and parasite remains, in *Roman and Medieval Carlisle: the Southern Lanes* (ed M R McCarthy) Carlisle, 81-83

Kenward, H K, Allison, E P, Morgan, L M, Jones, A K G, & Hutchinson, A, 1991 The insect and parasite remains, in *The Structural Sequence and Environmental Remains from Castle Street, Carlisle: excavations 1981-2.* (ed M R McCarthy) Carlisle, 65-72

Kenward, H, & Hall, A, 1997 Enhancing bioarchaeological interpretation using indicator groups: stable manure as a paradigm, *Journal of Archaeological Science* **24,** 663-673

Keppie, L, 1989 Beyond the Northern Frontier: Romans and Natives in Scotland, in *Research on Roman Britain 1960-89* (ed M Todd) *Britannia* Monograph Series No. **11**, London, 61-74

Kershaw, A, 2003 Hadrian's Wall National Mapping Programme - a World Heritage Site from the air, *Archaeological Prospection* **10,** 2, 159-161

Kewley, J, 1973 Three altars from Chesterholm, *Archaeol Aeliana* ser 5, **1,** 123-127

Kilbride-Jones, H E, 1938 The excavation of a native settlement at Milking Gap, High Shield, Northumberland, Archaeol Aeliana, ser 4, **15**, 303-350

Knowles, W H, & Forster, R H, 1909 Corstopitum. Report of the excavations in 1908, *Archaeol Aeliana* ser 3, **5**, 305-424

Lawson, W, 1966 The origin of the Military Road from Newcastle to Carlisle, *Archaeol Aeliana* ser 4, **44,** 185-207

Lawson, W, 1973 The Construction of the Military Road in Northumberland 1751-1757, *Archaeol Aeliana* ser 5, **1,** 177-93

Lax, A, & Blood, K, 1997 The earthworks of the Maryport fort: and analytical field survey by the Royal Commission on the Historical Monuments of England, in *Roman Maryport and its Setting: Essays in Memory of Michael G. Jarrett* (ed R J A Wilson), 52-66, Great Britain

Leach, J, 1962 Note on the figure of a *Genius Cucullatus* from Corbridge, *Archaeol Aeliana* ser 4, **40,** 280

Leach, J, & Wilkes, J J, 1962 Excavations in the Roman fort at Housesteads, 1961, *Archaeol Aeliana* ser 4, **40,** 83-96

Lewis, M, 1993 *A Palynological Investigation of Deposits from Midgeholme Moss, a Valley Mire Adjacent to Birdoswald Roman Fort,* Hadrian's Wall, Cumbria, unpubl. BA dissertation, Kings College London

Lewis, M J T, 1995 A *Festuca* from Chesters? *Archaeol Aeliana* ser 5, **23,** 47-50

Lewis, M J T, 2001 *Surveying Instruments of Greece and Rome.* Cambridge

Leland, J, (ed T Hearne) 1710-12 *The Itinerary of John Leland.* Oxford

Lingard, J, 1807 *Mural Tourification,* August 24th 1807 (Second Notebook) = *Archaeol Aeliana* ser 4, **6** (1929)

Macdonald, G, 1931a Julius Verus and Hadrian's Wall *Archaeol Aeliana* ser 4, **8**, 6-11

Macdonald, G, 1931b The bath-house at the fort of Chesters, *Archaeol Aeliana* ser 4, **8,** 219-304

Macdonald, G, 1933 John Horsley, scholar and gentleman, *Archaeol Aeliana* ser 4, **10**, 1-57

MacGregor, M, 1976 *Early Celtic Art in Northern Britain,* Leicester

Mackay, D A, 1990 The Great Chesters Aqueduct: A New Survey, *Britannia* **21,** 285 - 289.

MacLauchlan, H, 1857 *The Roman Wall and Illustrations of the Principal Vestiges of Roman Occupation in the North of England.* London.

MacLauchlan, H, 1858 *Memoir Written during a Survey of the Roman Wall, Through the Counties of Northumberland and Cumberland in the Years 1852-1854,* London

MacPherson, S, and Bidwell, P T, 2001 Excavations at Westgate Road, Newcastle upon Tyne and the position of Hadrian's Wall and the Vallum, *Arbeia Journal* **6-7**, 49 -54

Mann, J C, 1969 The northern frontier in *Britain from Hadrian to Honorius. Literary and Epigraphic Sources,* Newcastle-upon-Tyne

Mann, J C, 1984 A note on Inscriptions from Carvoran, *Archaeol Aeliana* ser 5, **12**, 243-245
Mann, J C, 1989a The Housesteads latrine, Archaeol Aeliana ser 5, **17**, 1-4
Mann, J C, 1989b Birdoswald to Ravenglass, *Britannia* **20,** 75-9
Mann, J C, 1990a Hadrian's Wall west of the Irthing: the role of VI Victrix, *Britannia* **21,** 289-92
Mann, J C, 1990b The function of Hadrian's Wall, *Archaeol Aeliana* ser 5, **18,** 51-54
Mann, J C, 2002 The Settlement of Veterans Discharged from Auxiliary Units Stationed in Britain, *Britannia,* **33**, 183-188
Manning, W H, 1966 A hoard of Romano-British ironwork from Brampton, Cumberland, *Trans Cumberland Westmorland Antiq Archaeol Soc* ser 2, **66,** 1-36
Manning, W H, 1972 Ironwork hoards in Iron Age and Roman Britain, *Britannia* **3,** 224-49
Margary, I D, 1967 *Roman Roads in Britain,* London
Marlière, E, 2003 Tonneaux et amphores à Vindolanda: contribution à la connaissance de l'approvisionnement des troupes stationnées sur la frontiére Nord de l'Empire, in *The Excavations of 2001 and 2002: Civilian Settlement, Severan and Second Century Forts, and the Pre Hadrianic Occupation, With a Report on the Trial Excavations at Carvoran* (A Birley), Vindolanda Research Report, Vol. 1, 128-79
Marichal, R, 1992 *Les ostraca de Bu Njem, Tripoli*
Marlière, E, & Costa, J T, 2005 Tonneaux et amphores à Vindolanda: contribution à la connaissance de l'approvisionnement des troupes stationnées sur le mur d'Hadrien, in *Vindolanda Excavations 2003-2004* (A Birley and J Blake), Bardon Mill, 214-36
Masser, P, & Evans, J 2005 Excavations within the *vicus* settlement at Burgh by Sands, 2002 *Trans Cumberland Westmoreland Antiq Archaeol Soc* ser 3, **5,** 31-64
Mattingly, D, 2004 Being Roman: expressing identity in a provincial setting, *J Roman Archaeol* **17**, 5-25
Mattingly, D, 2006 *An Imperial Possession: Britain in the Roman Empire,* London
Maxfield, V A, 1974 The Benwell Torc - Roman or native?, *Archaeol Aeliana* ser 5, **2,** 41-47
Maxfield, V A, 1982 Mural Controversies, in Problems and Case Studies in *Archaeological Dating* (ed B Orme), 57-81, Exeter
Maxfield, V A, 1990 Hadrian's Wall in its imperial setting, *Archaeol Aeliana* ser 5, **18**, 1-27
Maxwell, G S, 1998 *A Gathering of the Eagles, Scenes from Roman Scotland,* Edinburgh.
Maxwell, G S, & Wilson, D R, 1987 Air Reconnaissance in Roman Britain 1977-84, *Britannia* **18,** 1-48
May, T, 1916-1917 Catalogue of the Roman Pottery in the Museum, Tullie House, Carlisle, *Trans Cumberland Westmorland Antiq Archaeol Soc* ser 2, **17,** 114-197
McCarthy, M R, 1990 *A Roman, Anglian and Medieval Site at Blackfriars Street, Carlisle: Excavations 1977-79,* Cumberland Westmorland Archaeol Antiq Soc Res Ser **4,** Kendal
McCarthy, M R, 1991 *Roman Waterlogged Remains and Later Features at Castle Street, Carlisle, excavations: 1981,* Cumberland Westmorland Antiq Archaeol Soc Res Ser, **5,** Kendal
McCarthy, M R, 1997 Archaeological and environmental evidence for Roman impact on vegetation near Carlisle, Cumbria: a reply to Dumayne-Peaty and Barber, *The Holocene* **7**, 245-246
McCarthy, M R, 1999a Stanwix - Petriana, in *Hadrian's Wall 1989-1999* (ed P T Bidwell), 162-168, Kendal
McCarthy, M R, 1999b Netherby, in *Hadrian's Wall 1989 1999* (ed P T Bidwell), 202, Kendal
McCarthy, M R, 2000 *Roman and Medieval Carlisle: the Southern Lanes: Excavations 1981-82,* Carlisle
McCarthy, M R, 2002 *Roman Carlisle and the Lands of the Solway,* Stroud
McCarthy, M R, 2003 Luguvalium (Carlisle): a civitas capital on the northern frontier in *The Archaeology of Roman Towns: Studies in Honour of John S. Wacher* (ed P Wilson) Oxbow Monographs
McCarthy, M R, 2004 The Roman Town of Luguvalium and the Post-Roman Settlement, in *Carlisle and Cumbria: Roman and Medieval Architecture, Art and Archaeology* (eds M McCarthy & D Wilson) British Archaeological Associations Conference Transactions 27, Leeds, 1-10
McCarthy, M R, 2005 Social dynamics on the northern frontier of Roman Britain, *Oxford Journal of Archaeology* **24/1,** 47-71
McCarthy, M R, Bishop, M, & Richardson, T, 2001 Roman armour and metalworking at Carlisle, Cumbria, England, *Antiquity* **75,** 507 -508
McCarthy, M R, & Padley, T G, 2000 *Roman and medieval Carlisle, The Lanes, Vol 1. Excavations at Old Grapes, Crown and Anchor, and Lewthwaite Lane. Fasc 2. The Roman and Medieval Finds,* Carlisle
McCarthy, M R, Padley, T G, & Henig, M, 1982 Excavations and finds from The Lanes, Carlisle, *Britannia* **13**, 79-89
McCarthy, M R, & Wilson, D, (eds) 2004 *Carlisle and Cumbria: Roman and Medieval Architecture, Art and Archaeology*, British Archaeological Associations Conference Transactions **27,** Leeds
McCord, N, & Jobey, G, 1971 Notes on air reconnaissance in Northumberland and Durham - II, *Archaeol Aeliana* ser 4, **49,** 119-130
McGowan, P, Crow, J, & Rushworth, A, 2002 *Housesteads Roman Fort Conservation Plan* English Heritage/National Trust, 2 vols.
McIntyre, J, & Richmond, I A, 1934 Tents of the Roman Army and leather from Birdoswald, *Trans Cumberland Westmorland Antiq Archaeol Soc* ser 2, **34,** 62-90
McIntyre, W T, 1939 The Fords of the Solway, *Trans Cumberland Westmorland Antiq Archaeol Soc* ser 2, **39,** 152-170
McKelvey, J, 2003 Recent discoveries of defensive features at the eastern end of Hadrian's Wall, Newcastle, *Archaeology North* **21,** 12 -13
McKelvey, J, & Bidwell, P T, 2005 The excavation of prehistoric features and Hadrian's Wall at Nos 224-228, Shields Road, Byker, Newcastle upon Tyne, *Arbeia Journal,* **8,** 5-28
McKinley, J, 2004 The human remains and aspects of pyre technology and cremation rituals, in *The Roman Cemetery at Brougham, Cumbria: Excavations 1966 and 1967,* (H E M Cool) *Britannia* Monograph **21,** London, 283-308
Miket, R, 1978 Two early Anglo-Saxon brooches from Chesters and Chesterholm *Archaeol Aeliana* ser 5, **6,** 177-180

Miket, R, 1983 *The Roman Fort at South Shields: Excavation of the Defences, 1977-81,* Newcastle upon Tyne
Miket, R, and Maxfield, V A, 1972 The excavation of Turret 33B (Coesike) *Archaeol Aeliana* ser 4, **50,** 145-178
Miller, I, forthcoming *Excavation of a Roman Suburb: 53-55 Botchergate, Carlisle*
Mills, J M, 1997 *Catalogue and Summary of the Plain Samian from the 1987-92 Excavations at Birdoswald,* Archive Report for English Heritage, Tullie House Museum, Carlisle
Morris, J, 1950 The Vallum again, *Trans Cumberland Westmorland Antiq Archaeol Soc* ser 2, **50,** 43-53
Mould, Q, 1997 Leather, in *Birdoswald. Excavation of a Roman Fort on Hadrian's Wall and its Successor Settlements: 1987-92* (T Wilmott,), English Heritage Archaeological Reports **14,** London, 326-41
McDonnell, J G, 1991, *The Ironworking Evidence from Birdoswald Roman Fort, Cumbria,* Ancient Monuments Laboratory Report 100/91
Nelis-Clément, J, 2000 *Les beneficiarii: Militaires et Administrateurs au Service de l'empire* (1er s. AC - VIe s. PC), Bordeaux
Nevell, M, & Fielding, A, 2005 *Brine in Britannia: Recent Archaeological Work on the Roman Salt Industry in Cheshire,* Archaeology North West 7. Manchester: Council for British Archaeology North West, University of Manchester and The Lion Saltworks Trust
Newbold, P, 1913 The pottery and the periods of occupation, in Excavations on the line of the Roman Wall in Cumberland during the years 1909-12 (F G Simpson), *Trans Cumberland Westmorland Antiq Archaeol Soc* ser 2, **13,** 339-59
Newman, R, 2006 The Early Medieval Period Resource Assessment, in *The Archaeology of North West England. An Archaeological Research Framework for North West England: Volume 1 Resource Assessment* (ed M Brennand), Manchester
Nikolaus-Havé, F, 1986 Der Herkules von Birdoswald Unikum oder Fälschung, *Archäeologische Anzeiger* **3,** 571-81
Norman, H, 1860 An Account of Recent Excavations at Amboglanna (Birdoswald), *Archaeol Aeliana* ser 2, **4** (15), 249
Ordnance Survey 1972 Map of Hadrian's Wall Southampton.
Ornsby, G, (ed) 1878 Selections from the Household Books of the Lord William Howard of Naworth Castle, *Surtees Society* **68,** Durham
O'Sullivan, D, 1993 Sub-Roman and Anglo-Saxon Finds from Cumbria, *Trans Cumberland Westmorland Antiq Archaeol Soc* ser 2, **93,** 25-42
Oswald, A, Ainsworth, S, & Pearson, P, 2006 *Hillforts: Prehistoric Strongholds of Northumberland National Park,* Swindon
Padley, T G, 1991 The metalwork, glass and stone objects from Castle Street, Carlisle: excavations 1981-2
Padley, T G, and Winterbottom, S, 1991 *The Roman waterlogged remains and later features at Castle Street, Carlisle: Excavations 1981-2; Fascicule 3 The Wooden, leather and bone objects,* Cumberland and Westmorland Antiquarian and Archaeological Society Research Series **5,** 1991, Kendal
Parker, A J, 1988 The birds of Roman Britain, *Oxford Journal of Archaeology* **7,** 197-226
Passmore, D G, Waddington, C, & van der Schriek, T, 2006 Enhancing evaluation and management of river valley archaeology; geoarchaeology in the Till-Tweed catchment, northern England, *Archaeological Prospection* **13,** 269-281
Patten, T, 1974 The Roman cemetery on London Road, Carlisle, *Trans Cumberland Westmorland Antiq Archaeol Soc* ser 2, **74,** 8-13
Peachin, M, 1999 Five Vindolanda tablets, soldiers and the law, *Tyche* **14,** 223-235.
Pearce, J, 2002 Food as substance and symbol in the Roman army: a case study from Roman Vindolanda, in Limes XVIII - *Proceedings of the XVIIIth International Congress of Roman Frontier Studies held in Amman, Jordan* (eds P Freeman, J Bennett, Z T Fiema and B Hoffmann), BAR Int. Ser. **1084,** Oxford, 931-944
Pearce, J, 2004 Archaeology, writing tablets and literacy in Roman Britain, *Gallia* **61,** 43-51
Pearson, T, & Hunt, A, 2004 *An Iron Age or Romano-British enclosure at South Heddon, Northumberland.* Archaeological Investigations Report Series, AI/5/2004
Pengelly, H, 1975 The samian ware, in The Commandant's House, Housesteads (D Charlesworth), *Archaeol Aeliana* ser 5, **3,** 30-37
Pengelly, H, 1985 The samian ware, in P T Bidwell, *The Roman Fort of Vindolanda, at Chesterholm,* Northumberland, HBMCE, Archaeological Report **1,** London, 166-171
Petch, J A, 1928 Excavations at Benwell (Condercum), *Archaeol Aeliana* ser 4, **5,** 46-74
Petts, D, 2006 *Shared Visions: The North-East Regional Research Framework for the Historic Environment,* Durham
Pevsner, N, (eds J Grundy, G McCombie, P F Ryder, H Welfare) 1992 *The Buildings of England: Northumberland,* 2 edn, London.
Phillips, E J, 1977 *Corpus Signorum Imperii Romani: Great* Britain I, 1; Corbridge Hadrian's Wall East of the North Tyne Oxford
Piggott, C, 1948 Excavations at Hownam Rings, Roxburghshire, 1948, *Proc Soc Antiq Scotl* **82,** 193-225
Piggot, C, 1958 Native Economies and the Roman Occupation of North Britain, in *Roman and Native in North Britain* (ed I A Richmond), 1-27, London
Piggott, S, 1985 *William Stukeley, An Eighteenth Century Antiquary,* 2 edn, London
Potter, H G, 1855a Amboglanna: Communicated to the Society of Antiquaries of Newcastle-upon-Tyne, Nov. 6, 1850, *Archaeol Aeliana* ser 1, **4,** 63-9
Potter, H G, 1855b Amboglanna: Communicated to the Society of Antiquaries of Newcastle-upon-Tyne, Nov. 5, 1851, *Archaeol Aeliana* ser 1, **4,** 69-75
Potter, H G, 1855c Amboglanna: Communicated to the Society of Antiquaries of Newcastle-upon-Tyne, Dec. 1852, *Archaeol Aeliana,* ser 1, **4,** 141-49
Potter, T W, 1975 Excavations at Bowness-on-Solway, *Trans Cumberland Westmorland Antiq Archaeol Soc* ser 2, **75,** 29-57
Potter, T W, 1977 The Biglands milefortlet and the Cumberland Coast defences, *Britannia* **8,** 149-183
Potter, T W, 1979a *Romans in North West England: Excavations at the Roman Forts of Ravenglass, Watercrook and Bowness on Solway,* Kendal
Potter, T W, 1979b The Roman frontier in Cumbria, in *Roman Frontier Studies 1979* (eds W Hanson & L Keppie),

BAR Int. ser. **71**(i), 195-200 Oxford
Potter, T W, & Turner, R C, 1979 The Roman fort at Ravenglass, in *Romans in North-West England: Excavations at the Roman forts of Ravenglass, Watercrook and Bowness on Solway* (T W Potter), 1-64, Kendal
Poulter, J S, 1998 The date of the Stanegate and a hypothesis about the manner and timing of the construction of Roman roads in Britain, *Archaeol Aeliana*, ser 5, **26,** 49-56
Poulter, J S, 2005 The direction of planning of the eastern sector of Hadrian's Wall and the Vallum, from the River North Tyne to Benwell, west of Newcastle upon Tyne, *Arbeia Journal* **8,** 87-99
Poulter, J S, forthcoming (a) The directions of planning of Hadrian's Wall and the Vallum between the River North Tyne and Bowness-on-Solway, *Arbeia Journal*
Poulter, J S, forthcoming (b) The planning of Roman Dere Street from the Vale of York to Newstead by the Tweed, *Arbeia Journal*
Pratt, K E, 1996 *Development of Methods for Investigating Settlement and Land-Use Using Pollen Data: a Case Study from North-East England circa 8000 cal BC - cal AD 500,* unpubl. PhD thesis, University of Durham
Price, J, 1976 Glass, in M G Jarrett, *Maryport, Cumbria: A Roman Fort and its Garrison.* Cumberland and Westmorland Antiquarian and Archaeological Society extra series **22,** 49-54.
Price, J, 1985 The glass, in P T Bidwell, *The Roman Fort of Vindolanda.* English Heritage Archaeological Report **1,** 206-14.
Price, J, 1990 Roman vessel and window glass, in M R McCarthy, *A Roman, Anglian and Medieval Site at Blackfriars Street, Carlisle.* Cumberland and Westmorland Antiquarian and Archaeological Society Research Series, **4,** 163-79.
Price, J and Cottam, S, 1997 Glass armlets and beads, finger ring, vessels and window fragments, in T Wilmott, *Birdoswald: Excavation of a Roman Fort and its Successor Settlements, 1987-92.* English Heritage Archaeological Report **14,** 272-6, 283, 341-55.
Price, J and Cottam, S, 2000 The finds: Glass, in M R McCarthy, *Roman and Medieval Carlisle: the Southern Lanes.* Dept Archaeological Sciences, University of Bradford Research Report **1**, 96-7, 103-5 (full report not published).
Price, J and Worrell, S, unpublished *The Glass from the Northern Lanes, Carlisle.* (Catalogue prepared in 1999).
Pringle, S, & Swan, V G, forthcoming The ceramic building materials, in *The Carlisle Millennium Project: Excavations within the Roman Fort and Medieval Castle, 1998-2001,* Vol 2 (ed C Howard-Davis)
Quartermaine, J, Brennand, M, and Newman, R, 2006 *ALSF Aggregate Extraction in the Lower Ribble Valley. Final Report.,* Liverpool University
Rasmussen, P, 1989 Leaf-foddering of Livestock in the Neolithic: Archaeobotanical Evidence from Weier, Switzerland, *Journal of Danish Archaeology* **8,** 51-71
Reed, A, 1995 The Stanegate at Foustones, in *Archaeology in Northumberland 1994-1995* (ed C Hardie) NCC. Morpeth, 41
Redfern, H, 1921 Notes on a Roman Well discovered in the Courtyard of the Blue Bell Inn, Scotch Street, Carlisle, *Trans Cumberland Westmorland Antiq Archaeol Soc* ser 2, **21,** 253-256
Riccobono, S, Baviera, J, Ferrini, C, Furlani, J and Arangio Riuz (eds) 1968-1969 *Fontes Iuris Romani Antejustiniani,* Florence
Richardson, A, 2000 The numerical basis of Roman camps, *Oxford Journal of Archaeology* **19(4)**, 425-37
Richardson, A, 2001 The order of battle in the Roman army: evidence from marching camps, *Oxford Journal of Archaeology* **20(2),** 171-85
Richardson, A, 2002 Camps and forts of units and formations of the Roman army, *Oxford Journal of Archaeology* **21(1)**, 93-107
Richardson, A, 2004 Granaries and garrisons in Roman forts, *Oxford Journal of Archaeology* **23(4),** 429-442
Richardson, G G S, 1972a A new cross-section of the Vallum ditch near Irthington, *Trans Cumberland Westmorland Antiq Archaeol Soc* ser 2, **72,** 325-327
Richardson, G G S, 1972b Hadrian's Wall: a section at Hadrian's Camp, Carlisle (NY414585), *Trans Cumberland Westmorland Antiq Archaeol Soc* ser 2, **72,** 330-331
Richardson, G G S, 1973 The Roman tilery, Scalesceugh, 1970-1971, *Trans Cumberland Westmorland Antiq Archaeol Soc* ser 2, **73**, 79-89
Richardson, G G S, 1975 The Stanegate, Boothby, Cumbria, *CBA group 3 Newsbulletin* **10**, 6-7
Richardson, G G S, 1977 A Romano-British Farmstead at Fingland, *Trans Cumberland Westmorland Antiq Archaeol Soc* ser 2, **77,** 53-9
Richardson, G G S, 1978 A Section of the Stanegate at Boothby, Cumbria, *Trans Cumberland Westmorland Antiq Archaeol Soc* ser 2, **78,** 206-208
Richardson, G G S, 1978 The North Sea Gas-pipeline through North Cumbria, *Trans Cumberland Westmorland Antiq Archaeol Soc* ser 2, **78,** 325-327
Richmond, I A, 1929 Excavations on Hadrian's Wall in the Gilsland-Birdoswald-Pike Hill Sector, 1928, *Trans Cumberland Westmorland Antiq Archaeol Soc* ser 2, **29,** 303-315
Richmond, I A, 1930a The University Excavations on Hadrian's Wall, 1929, *Durham Univ J,* **March 1930,** 1-7
Richmond, I A, 1930b The University Excavations on Hadrian's Wall, 1930, *Durham Univ J,* **December 1930,** 1-7
Richmond, I A, 1931 Excavations on Hadrian's Wall in the Birdoswald - Pike Hill Sector, 1930, *Trans Cumberland Westmorland Antiq Archaeol Soc* ser 2, **31,** 122-134
Richmond, I A, 1933 The Tower at Gillalees Beacon, called Robin Hood's Butt, *Trans Cumberland Westmorland Antiq Archaeol Soc* ser 2, **33,** 241-245
Richmond, I A, 1934 The Roman fort at South Shields, *Archaeol Aeliana,* ser 4, **11,** 83-102
Richmond, I A, 1939 Hadrian's Wall, 1938, *Archaeol Aeliana,* ser 4, **16,** 264-277
Richmond, I A, 1940 Roman Britain in 1939, J Roman Stud **30,** 162 - 165
Richmond, I A, 1943 Roman legionaries at Corbridge, their supply-base, temples and religious cults, *Archaeol Aeliana* ser 4, **21,** 127-224
Richmond, I A, 1950 A Roman wrist-purse from Birdoswald, *Trans Cumberland Westmorland Antiq Archaeol Soc* ser **2,** 50, 69
Richmond, I A, 1953a *The Roman fort at South Shields: a Guide,* South Shields

Richmond, I A, 1953b Excavation at Milecastle 49 (Harrows Scar), *Trans Cumberland Westmorland Antiq Archaeol Soc* ser 2, **53,** 212-213
Richmond, I A, 1954 The Birdoswald hoard and its composition, *Trans Cumberland Westmorland Antiq Archaeol Soc* ser 2, **54,** 56-60
Richmond, I A, 1956a Frank Gerald Simpson, *Archaeol Aeliana,* ser 4, **34,** 219-221
Richmond, I A, 1956b Excavations at Milecastle 49 (Harrow's Scar), 1953, *Trans Cumberland Westmorland Antiq Archaeol Soc* ser 2, **56,** 18-27
Richmond, I A, 1956c Cote How Tower (16a), on the Cumberland coast, *Trans Cumberland Westmorland Antiq Archaeol Soc* ser 2, **56,** 62-66
Richmond, I A, & Birley, E B, 1930 Excavations on Hadrian's Wall in the Birdoswald-Pike Hill Sector, 1929, *Trans Cumberland Westmorland Antiq Archaeol Soc* ser 2, **30** 169-205
Richmond, I A, & Birley, E, 1937 Centurial stones from the Vallum west of Denton Burn, *Archaeol Aeliana* ser 4, **14,** 227-242
Richmond, I A, & Birley, E, 1940 Excavations at Corbridge, 1938-9, *Archaeol Aeliana* ser 4, **17,** 85-115
Richmond, I A, & Childe, F A, 1942 Gateways of Forts on Hadrian's Wall, Archaeol Aeliana ser 4, **20,** 134-154
Richmond, I A, & Gillam, J P, 1950 Excavations on the Roman site at Corbridge 1946-1949, *Archaeol Aeliana* ser 4, **28,** 152-201
Richmond, I A, & Gillam, J P, 1951 The temple of Mithras at Carrawburgh, *Archaeol Aeliana* **29,** 1-92
Richmond, I A, & Gillam, J P, 1952a Further exploration of the Antonine fort at Corbridge 1946-1949, *Archaeol Aeliana* ser 4, **30,** 239-266
Richmond, I A, & Gillam, J P, 1952b Milecastle 79 (Solway), in Report of the Cumberland Excavation Committee for 1947-1949, *Trans Cumberland Westmorland Antiq Archaeol Soc* ser 2, **52,** 17-40
Richmond, I A, & Gillam, J P, 1953 Buildings of the first and second centuries north of the granaries at Corbridge, *Archaeol Aeliana,* ser 4, **31,** 205-253
Richmond, I A, & Gillam, J P, 1955 Some excavations at Corbridge 1952-54, *Archaeol Aeliana,* ser 4, **33,** 218-252
Richmond, I A, & Hodgson, K S, 1934 Excavations at Castlesteads, *Trans Cumberland Westmorland Antiq Archaeol Soc* ser 2, 34, 159-165
Richmond, I A & Hodgson, K S, 1936 The Roman Temporary Camp at Watchcross, in Report of the Cumberland Excavation Committee for 1935, *Trans Cumberland Westmorland Antiq Archaeol Soc* ser 2, **36,** 170-172
Richmond, I A, Hodgson, K S, & St. Joseph, K, 1938 The Roman fort at Bewcastle, in Report of the Cumberland Excavation Committee, *Trans Cumberland Westmorland Antiq Archaeol Soc* ser 2, **38,** 195-237
Richmond, I A, & Simpson F G, 1935 The use of clay instead of turf in the Great Wall at Randylands and Garthside, in Report of the Cumberland Excavation Committee for 1934, *Trans Cumberland Westmorland Antiq Archaeol Soc* ser 2, **35,** 244-247
Richmond, I A, & Wright, R P, 1943 Stones from a Hadrianic war memorial on Tyneside, *Archaeol Aeliana,* ser 4, **21,** 93-120
Rivet, A L F, and Smith, C, 1981 *The Place-Names of Roman Britain* 2 edn, London
Roach Smith, C, 1852 *Collectanea Antiqua,* London
Robertson, A S, 1968 Two groups of Roman asses from North Britain, *Numismatic Chronicle* ser 7, **8,** 61-6
Robertson, A S, 1975 *Birrens (Blatobulgium).* Edinburgh.
Robinson, J, 1881, Notes on the excavations near the Roman camp, Maryport, during the year 1880, *Trans Cumberland Westmorland Antiq Archaeol Soc* ser 2, **5,** 237-55
Rooke, H, 1792 An account of some antiquities in Cumberland hitherto unnoticed, *Archaeol* **10,** 137-42
Ross, A, 1961 The horned god of the Brigantes, *Archaeol Aeliana* ser 4, **39,** 63-86
Roth, J P, 1998 *The Logistics of the Roman Army at War* (264 BC - AD 235), Leiden
Roxan, M M, 1989 Women on the frontiers, in *Roman Frontier Studies 1989. Proceedings of the XVth International Congress on Roman Frontier Studies* (eds V A Maxfield and M J Dobson), 462-7, Exeter
Roymans, N, Derks, T, et al 2007 *Bataafse gemeenschap in de wereld van het Romeinse rijk: Opgravingen te Tiel Passewaaij,* Utrecht
Rushworth, A, (ed) forthcoming *The Grandest Station: Excavation and Survey at Housesteads Roman Fort* by *C.M.Daniels, J. P. Gillam, J.G. Crow, D. J. Smith and the RCHME 1954-88,* English Heritage Archaeological Report, London
Rushworth, A, & Barker, L, 1997 *Hadrian's Wall at Winshield Crags, Cawfield Crags and Walltown Crags,* Unpublished report for English Heritage Historic Properties North.
Sainsbury, I, & Welfare, H, 1990 The Roman fort at Bewcastle; an analytical field survey *Trans Cumberland Westmorland Antiq Archaeol Soc* ser 2, **90,** 139-46
Schwinden, L, 1985 Römerzeitliche Bleietiketten aus Trier. Zum Handel mit Pfeffer, Arznei und Kork, *Trierer Zeitschrift* **48,** 121-37
Salway, P, 1958 Civilians in the Roman frontier region, *Archaeol Aeliana,* ser 4, **36,** 227-244
Salway, P, 1965 *The Frontier People of Roman Britain,* Cambridge
Sealey, P R, 1985 *Amphoras from the 1970 Excavations at Colchester Sheepen,* BAR Brit. Ser. **142,** Oxford
Sekulla, M, 1981 A Phantom Hoard from Hadrian's Wall?, *Archaeol Aeliana* ser 5, **9,** 253-255
Selkirk, R, 1983 *The Piercebridge Formula: a Dramatic New View of Roman History,* Cambridge
Selkirk, R, 1995 *On the Trail of the Legions,* Ipswich
Serjeantson, D, 1989 Animal remains and the tanning trade, in *Diet and Crafts in Towns: the Evidence of Animal Remains from the Roman to the Post-Medieval Period* (eds D Serjeantson and T Waldron) BAR Brit. Ser. **199,** 129-146
Shaw, R C, 1924 Romano-British Carlisle: its structural remains, *Trans Cumberland Westmorland Antiq Archaeol Soc* ser 2, **24,** 95-109
Shaw, R C, 1926 Excavations at Willowford, *Trans Cumberland Westmorland Antiq Archaeol Soc* ser 2, **26,** 429-506
Sherlock, D, 1999 Silver spoon from Benwell Roman fort, *Archaeol Aeliana* ser 5, **27,** 176-178
Shiel, N, 1972 An unpublished intaglio from Corstopitum, *Archaeol Aeliana* ser 4, **50,** 294-297
Shiel, N, 1975 Casual finds from South Shields, *Archaeol Aeliana* ser 5, **3,** 221-222

Shiel, N, 1977 Carausian and Allectan coin evidence from the Northern Frontier, *Archaeol Aeliana* ser 5, **5,** 75-79
Shipman, T T, 1874 The Recently Discovered Remains at Nether Denton Parsonage, *Trans Cumberland Westmorland Antiq Archaeol Soc* ser 1, **1,** 88-93
Shirley, E, 2000 *The Construction of the Legionary Fortress at Inchtuthil,* BAR Brit. Ser. **298,** Oxford
Shorer, P, 1977 An unusual dragonesque brooch from South Shields, *Archaeol Aeliana* ser 5, **5,** 197-198
Shotter, D C A, 1977 A Roman As from Carlisle, *Trans Cumberland Westmorland Antiq Archaeol Soc* ser 2, **77,** 178
Shotter, D C A, 1978 Roman Coins from Carlisle, *Trans Cumberland Westmorland Antiq Archaeol Soc* ser 2, **78,** 201-204
Shotter, D C A, 1979 Roman Coin Hoards from Cumbria, *Trans Cumberland Westmorland Antiq Archaeol Soc* ser 2, **79,** 5-17
Shotter, D C A, 1980 The Roman occupation of North-west England: The coin evidence, *Trans Cumberland Westmorland Antiq Archaeol Soc* ser 2, **80,** 1-15
Shotter, D C A, 1989 Roman Coin-finds in Cumbria, *Trans Cumberland Westmorland Antiq Archaeol Soc* ser 2, **89,** 41-50
Shotter, D C A, 1994a Rome and the Brigantes: Early Hostilities, *Trans Cumberland Westmorland Antiq Archaeol Soc* ser 2, **94,** 21-34
Shotter, D C A, 1994a Recent finds of Roman coins in Cumbria, *Trans Cumberland Westmorland Antiq Archaeol Soc* ser 2, **94,** 291-294
Shotter, D C A, 1996 *The Roman Frontier in Britain,* Preston
Shotter, D C A, 2000 The Roman Conquest of the North West, *Trans Cumberland Westmorland Antiq Archaeol Soc* ser 2, **100,** 33-53
Shotter, D C A, 2001 Petillius Cerialis in Carlisle: a numismatic contribution, *Trans Cumberland Westmorland Antiq Archaeol Soc* ser 3, **1,** 21-29
Shotter, D C A, 2002 Recent Roman coin finds from Cumbria, *Trans Cumberland Westmoreland Antiq Archaeol Soc* Ser 3, **2,** 305 -306
Shotter, D C A, 2004 The Cumberland coast and the evidence of Roman coin loss, in *Romans on the Solway, Essays in Honour of Richard Bellhouse* (eds R J A Wilson and I Caruana) Kendal, 195-204
Shotter, D C A, 2004 *Romans and Britons in North-West England,* Lancaster
Shotter, D C A, 2006 Recent finds of Roman coins in Cumbria, *Trans Cumberland Westmorland Antiq Archaeol Soc* ser 3, **6,** 229-233
Shotter, D C A, 2006 A hoard of Roman coins from Beckfoot, Cumbria, *Trans Cumberland Westmorland Antiq Archaeol Soc* ser 3, **6,** 233-235
Shotter, D C A, forthcoming The Roman coins, in *The Carlisle Millennium Project: Excavations within the Roman Fort and Medieval Castle, 1998-2001, Vol 2* (ed C Howard Davis)
Simpson, F G, 1913 Excavation on the line of the Roman Wall in Cumberland during the years 1909-12, *Trans Cumberland Westmorland Antiq Archaeol Soc* ser 2, **13,** 297-397
Simpson, F G, 1921-1922 An Excavation at Chesters in October 1921, *Proc Soc Antiq Newcastle-on-Tyne* ser 3, **10,** 216-218
Simpson, F G, 1928 Excavations on Hadrian's Wall in the Gilsland-Birdoswald-Pike Hill sector, 1927, *Trans Cumberland Westmorland Antiq Archaeol Soc* ser 2, **28,** 377-388
Simpson, F G, 1929-1930 The Roman Fort at Newbrough, *Proc Soc Antiq Newcastle-on-Tyne ser* 4, **4,** 163-165
Simpson, F G, 1931 Excavations on Hadrian's Wall between Heddon-on-the-Wall and North Tyne in 1930, *Archaeol Aeliana* ser 4, **8,** 305-327
Simpson, F G, 1932a Stanwix, in Report of the Cumberland Excavation Committee for 1931 *Trans Cumberland Westmorland Antiq Archaeol Soc* ser 2, **32,** 147-148
Simpson, F G, 1932b The Wall at the Sewage Disposal Works, Carlisle, in Report of the Cumberland Excavation Committee for 1931 *Trans Cumberland Westmorland Antiq Archaeol Soc* ser 2, **32,** 149-151
Simpson, F G, 1933 Carlisle and Stanwix, in Report of the Cumberland Excavation Committee for 1932, *Trans Cumberland Westmorland Antiq Archaeol Soc* ser 2, **33,** 275-276
Simpson, F G, 1934a Boothby, Castle Hill, in Report of the Cumberland Excavation Committee for 1933 *Trans Cumberland Westmorland Antiq Archaeol Soc* ser 2, **34,** 154-5
Simpson, F G, 1934b The Vallum at Stanwix, in Report of the Cumberland Excavation Committee for 1933, *Trans Cumberland Westmorland Antiq Archaeol Soc* ser 2, **34,** 155-157
Simpson, F G, 1941 Stanwix Roman fort, *Trans Cumberland Westmorland Antiq Archaeol Soc* ser 2, **41,** 210-13
Simpson, F G, 1972 Samian pottery and a Roman road at Corbridge, *Archaeol Aeliana* ser 4, **l,** 217-233
Simpson, F G, & Hodgson, K S, 1947 The Coastal Mile Fortlet at Cardurnock, *Trans Cumberland Westmorland Antiq Archaeol Soc* ser 2, **47,** 78-125
Simpson, F G, Hodgson, K S, & Richmond, I A, 1934 New turret-sites on the line of the Turf Wall, and the type of Stone Wall later associated with them, in Report of the Cumberland Excavation Committee for 1933, *Trans Cumberland Westmorland Antiq Archaeol Soc* ser 2, **34,** 130-37
Simpson, F G, Hodgson, K S, & Richmond, I A, 1952 Turrets and Milecastles between Burgh-by-Sands and Bowness-on-Solway, in Report of the Cumberland Excavation Committee for 1947-1949, *Trans Cumberland Westmorland Antiq Archaeol Soc* ser 2, **52,** 14-16
Simpson, F G & Hogg, R, 1935 Stanwix, in Report of the Cumberland Excavation Committee for 1934, *Trans Cumberland Westmorland Antiq Archaeol Soc* ser 2, **35,** 256-258
Simpson, F G, & McIntyre, J, 1932 Pike Hill, in Report of the Cumberland Excavation Committee for 1931, *Trans Cumberland Westmorland Antiq Archaeol Soc* ser 2, **32,** 145-147
Simpson, F G, & McIntyre, J, 1933a Banks Burn to Randylands, in Report of the Cumberland Excavation Committee for 1932, *Trans Cumberland Westmorland Antiq Archaeol Soc* ser 2, **33,** 262-270
Simpson, F G, & McIntyre, J, 1933b Pike Hill, in Report of the Cumberland Excavation Committee for 1932, *Trans Cumberland Westmorland Antiq Archaeol Soc* ser 2, **33,** 271-275
Simpson, F G, & Richmond, I A, 1932 Birdoswald, in Report

of the Cumberland Excavation Committee for 1931, *Trans Cumberland Westmorland Antiq Archaeol Soc* ser 2, **32,** 140-45

Simpson, F G, & Richmond, I A, 1933 Birdoswald, in Report of the Cumberland Excavation Committee for 1932, *Trans Cumberland Westmorland Antiq Archaeol Soc* ser 2, **33,** 246-262

Simpson, F G & Richmond, I A, 1934a Birdoswald, in Report of the Cumberland Excavation Committee for 1933, *Trans Cumberland Westmorland Antiq Archaeol Soc* ser 2, **34,** 120-30

Simpson, F G, & Richmond I A, 1934b Banks East Turret, 52a, in Report of the Cumberland Excavation Committee for 1933, *Trans Cumberland Westmorland Antiq Archaeol Soc* ser 2, **34,** 148-152

Simpson, F G, & Richmond, I A, 1935a Randylands Milecastle 54, in Report of the Cumberland Excavation Committee for 1934, *Trans Cumberland Westmorland Antiq Archaeol Soc* ser 2, **35,** 236-244

Simpson, F G, & Richmond, I A, 1935b The use of clay instead of turf in the Great Wall at Randylands and Garthside, in Report of the Cumberland Excavation Committee for 1934, *Trans Cumberland Westmorland Antiq Archaeol Soc* ser 2, **35,** 244-247

Simpson, F G, & Richmond, I A, 1935c Bankshead Milecastle 52, in Report of the Cumberland Excavation Committee for 1934, *Trans Cumberland Westmorland Antiq Archaeol Soc* ser 2, **35,** 247-256

Simpson, F G, & Richmond, I A, 1936 The Roman fort on the Stanegate, and other remains, at Old Church, Brampton, in Report of the Cumberland Excavation Committee for 1935 *Trans Cumberland Westmorland Antiq Archaeol Soc* ser 2, **36,** 172-182

Simpson, F G, & Richmond, I A, 1937a The Fort on Hadrian's Wall at Halton, *Archaeol Aeliana* ser 4, **14,** 151-171

Simpson, F G, & Richmond, I A, 1937b The Vallum at milecastles 51, Wall Bowers, and 50 TW, High House, *Trans Cumberland Westmorland Antiq Archaeol Soc* ser 2, **37,** 157-177

Simpson, F G, & Richmond, I A, 1937 Recent excavations at Hunnum, *Archaeol Aeliana* ser 4, **14,** 151-70

Simpson, F G, & Richmond, I A, 1941a The Roman fort at Benwell on Hadrian's Wall, *Archaeol Aeliana* ser 4, **19,** 1-43

Simpson, F G, & Richmond, I A, 1941b *Petriana* and the tactical arrangement of Hadrian's Wall in Cumberland, *Durham University Journal* **33,** 2, 102-10

Simpson, F G, & Richmond I A, 1952 The Roman fort at Drumburgh, in Report of the Cumberland Excavation Committee for 1947-1949, *Trans Cumberland Westmorland Antiq Archaeol Soc* ser 2, **52,** 9-14

Simpson, F G, Richmond, I A, Birley, E, Keeney, G S, & Steer, K A, 1936 Milecastles on Hadrian's wall explored in 1935 36, *Archaeol Aeliana* ser 4, **13,** 258-273

Simpson, F G, Richmond, I A, Hodgson, K S, & St. Joseph, J K, 1936 The Stanegate, in Report of the Cumberland Excavation Committee for 1934, *Trans Cumberland Westmorland Antiq Archaeol Soc* ser 2, **36,** 182-191

Simpson, F G, Richmond, I A, & McIntyre, J, 1934a Garthside Turrets, 54a, in Report of the Cumberland Excavation Committee for 1933, *Trans Cumberland Westmorland Antiq Archaeol Soc* ser 2, **34,** 138-44

Simpson, F G, Richmond, I A, & McIntyre, J, 1934b Milecastles on the line of the Turf Wall, in Report of the Cumberland Excavation Committee for 1933, *Trans Cumberland Westmorland Antiq Archaeol Soc* ser 2, **34,** 144-148

Simpson, F G, Richmond, I A, & McIntyre, J, 1935 The Stone Wall, Turf Wall and Vallum west of Burgh-by-Sands, in Report of the Cumberland Excavation Committee for 1934, *Trans Cumberland Westmorland Antiq Archaeol Soc* ser 2, **35,** 213-220

Simpson, F G, Richmond I A, & St Joseph, K, 1935a The Turf-Wall milecastle at High House, in Report of the Cumberland Excavation Committee for 1934, *Trans Cumberland Westmorland Antiq Archaeol Soc* ser 2, **35,** 220-229

Simpson, F G, Richmond I A, & St Joseph, K, 1935b The Turf-Wall turrets between Wallbowers and Harrow's Scar, in Report of the Cumberland Excavation Committee for 1934, *Trans Cumberland Westmorland Antiq Archaeol Soc* ser 2, **35,** 232-236

Simpson, F G, Richmond I A, & St Joseph, K, 1936 The Vallum at High House Turf-Wall Milecastle, 50 TW, in Report of the Cumberland Excavation Committee for 1935, *Trans Cumberland Westmorland Antiq Archaeol Soc* ser 2, **36,** 158-170

Simpson, F G & Shaw, R C, 1922 The purpose and date of the Vallum and its crossings, *Archaeol Aeliana* ser 2, **22,** 353-433

Simpson, F G, & St Joseph , J K S, 1934 Nether Denton, in Report of the Cumberland Excavation Committee for 1933, *Trans Cumberland Westmorland Antiq Archaeol Soc* ser 2, **34,** 152-4

Simpson, G, 1971 The close of period IA on Hadrian's Wall, and some Gaulish potters, *Archaeol Aeliana* ser 4, **49,** 109-118

Simpson, G, 1972 Samian pottery and a Roman road at Corbridge, *Archaeol Aeliana* ser 4, **50,** 217-234

Simpson, G, 1974 Haltwhistle Burn, *Corstopitum* and the Antonine Wall: A Reconsideration, *Britannia* **5,** 317-39

Simpson, G, 1975 The moving milecastle: or how Turret 0B came to be called milecastle 1, *Archaeol Aeliana* ser 5, **3,** 105-115

Simpson, G, 1976 *Watermills and Military Works on Hadrian's Wall: Excavations in Northumberland* (ed G. Simpson), 1907-1913 Kendal

Skinner, J, (ed H & P Coombs) 1978 *Hadrian's Wall in 1801: Observations on the Roman Wall,* Bath

Smith, G S, 1978 Excavations near Hadrian's Wall at Tarraby Lane, 1976, *Britannia* **9,** 19 56

Smith, D, 1962 The shrine of the nymphs and the Genius Loci at Carrawburgh, *Archaeol Aeliana* ser 4, **40,** 59-81

Smith, D J, 1959a A Palmyrene sculptor at South Shields?, *Archaeol Aeliana* ser 4, **37,** 203-210

Smith, D J, 1959b Models of Hadrian's Wall and its component works, *Archaeol Aeliana* ser 4, **37,** 339-340

Smith, D J, 1960 A Roman silver pin from Halton Chesters, *Archaeol Aeliana* ser 4, **38,** 231

Smith, D J, 1962a The shrine of the nymphs and the genius loci at Carrawburgh, *Archaeol Aeliana* ser 4, **40,** 59-82

Smith, D J, 1962b The restoration of the "Birth of Mithras" from Housesteads, *Archaeol Aeliana* ser 4, **40,** 277-280

Smith, D J, 1963 The restoration of the Housesteads Tauroctony, *Archaeol Aeliana* ser 4, **41,** 226-227

Smith, D J, 1968 The Archer's tombstone from Housesteads, *Archaeol Aeliana* ser 4, **46,** 284-291

Smith, D J, 1969 Two pricks of Roman spurs from South Shields, *Archaeol Aeliana* ser 4, **47,** 172

Smith, D J forthcoming Excavations in the *Principia,* in *The Grandest Station: Excavation and Survey at Housesteads Roman Fort by C.M. Daniels, J.P. Gillam, J.G. Crow, D.J. Smith and the RCHME 1954-88* (ed A Rushworth), English Heritage Archaeological Report, London.

Smith, I, 1996 The origins and development of Christianity in northern Britian and southern Pictland, in *Church Archaeology, Research Directions for the Future* (eds J Blair and C Pyrah) CBA Research Report **104,** York.

Smith, R A, 1922 On some recent exhibits. Antiquaries *Journal,* **2,** 93-104.

Smythe, J A, 1937/8 Notes on ancient and Roman tin and its alloys with lead. *Transactions of the Newcomen Society,* **18,** 255-66.

Snape, M E, 1991 Roman and Native: vici on the north British frontier, in *Roman Frontier Studies 1989: Proceedings of the XVth International Congress of Roman Frontier Studies* (eds V Maxfield and B Dobson), Exeter, 468-471

Snape, M E, 1992 Sub-Roman brooches from Roman sites on the northern frontier, *Archaeol Aeliana* ser 5, **20,** 158-160

Snape, M E, 1993 *Roman Brooches from North Britain: A Classification and a Catalogue of Brooches from Sites on the Stanegate,* BAR Brit. Ser. **235,** Oxford

Snape, M E 1994 An excavation in the Roman cemetery at South Shields, *Archaeol Aeliana* ser 5, **22,** 43-66

Snape, M E & Bidwell, P T, 1994 The *vicus* of the Roman fort at Wallsend, Tyne and Wear, *Arbeia Journal* **3,** 13-32

Snape, M E, 2001 Roman Brooches of a Dacian Type found at South Shields fort' *Arbeia Journal* **6-7,** 63 -64

Snape, M E, & Bidwell, P T, 2002 Excavations at Castle Garth, Newcastle upon Tyne, 1976-92 and 1995-6: the excavation of the Roman fort, *Archaeol Aeliana* ser 5, **31,** 1-249

Sockett, E W, 1973 The Stanegate at Homer's Lane, *Archaeol Aeliana* ser 5, **1,** 241-243

Sockett, E W, 1986 A Note on Major Donaldson's Article on Roman Military Signalling, *Archaeol Aeliana* ser 5, **14,** 187

Sockett, E W, 1993 *The Stanegate Crossing of North Tyne,* Tyne and Tweed **47,** 7

Sommer, C S, 1984 *The Military Vici in Roman Britain. Aspects of their Location, Layout, Administration, Function and End.* BAR Brit. Ser. **129,** Oxford

Sommer, C S, 2006 Military *vici* in Roman Britain revisited, in *Romanitas: Essays on Roman Archaeology in Honour of Sheppard Frere on the Occasion of his Ninetieth Birthday* (ed R J A Wilson). Oxford, 95-146.

Southern, P, The *numeri* of the Roman army, *Britannia* **20,** 81-140

Southern, P, 2004 The Army in late Roman Britain, in *A Companion to Roman Britain* (ed M Todd), Oxford, 393-408

Spain, G R B, 1922 The Black Dyke, Archaeol Aeliana ser 3, **19,** 121-168

Spain, G R B, 1930 The Treasure vault of the Roman Fort at Benwell (Condercum), *Archaeol Aeliana* ser 4, **7,** 126-130

Spain, G R B, 1933 An altar dedicated to Jupiter found in Newcastle-upon-Tyne, *Archaeol Aeliana* ser 4, **10,** 109-110

Spain, G R B, 1934 The Roman Wall in Westgate, Newcastle upon Tyne, *Archaeol Aeliana* ser 4, **11,** 227-233

Speak, S, & Walker, I, 2001 A New building record from Hadrian's Wall, *Arbeia Journal* **6-7,** 65 -67

Spiedel, M P, 1989 The soldiers' servants, *Ant. Soc.* **20,** 239-247

Stallibrass, S, 1991 *Animal Bones from Excavations at Annetwell Street, Carlisle, 1982-4. Period 3: the Earlier Timber Fort,* Ancient Monuments Laboratory Report 132/91

Stallibrass, S, 1998a *Mitchell's Brewery, Church Street, Lancaster: LB88 & LB92: The Animal Bones from Urban Deposits Spanning the Roman to Post-Medieval Periods,* Durham Environmental Archaeology Report, **19/98**

Stallibrass, S, 1998b Vindolanda, Northumberland: VIN97. An assessment of the animal bones from the area of the 3rd/4th century praetorium of the second stone fort. Durham Environmental Archaeology Report, 33/98

Stallibrass, S, 2000a Cattle, culture, soldiers and status, in TRAC 1999. *Proceedings of the ninth annual Theoretical Roman Archaeology Conference* (eds G Fincham, G Harrison, R Rodgers Holland and L Revell), 64-73, Oxford

Stallibrass, S, 2000b How little we know, and how much there is to learn: what can animal and human bones tell us about the late Roman transition in northern England? in *The Late Roman Transition in the North. Papers from the Roman Archaeology Conerence Durham 1999* (eds T Wilmott and P Wilson) BAR Brit. Ser. **299,** Oxford, 73-79

Stallibrass, S, 2002 An overview of the animal bones: what would we like to know, what do we know so far, and where do we go from here?, in *Catteractonium: Roman Catterick and its Hinterland. Excavations and Research 1958-1997. Part II.* (ed P R Wilson), York, 392-415

Stanfield, J A, 1935 A Samian Bowl from Bewcastle, with a note on the potters Casurius and Apolauster, *Trans Cumberland Westmorland Antiq Archaeol Soc* ser 2, **35,** 182-205

Stanfield, J A, & Simpson, G, 1958 Central Gaulish Potters, London

Stanfield, J A, & Simpson, G, 1990 *Les Potiers de la Gaule Centrale,* Revue Archéologiques Sites, Hors-série **37,** Gonfaron.

Stephens, G R, 1984 The Metrical Inscription from Carvoran, *Archaeol Aeliana* ser 5, **12,** 149-156

Stephens, G R, & Jarret, M G, 1985 Two Altars of cohors IV Gallorum from Castlesteads, *Trans Cumberland Westmorland Antiq Archaeol Soc* ser 2, **85,** 77-80

Stephens, G R, 1987 G. Julius Marcus, *Trans Cumberland Westmorland Antiq Archaeol Soc* ser 2, **87,** 53-60

Stephens, G R, 1988 An Altar to Vulcan from Maryport, *Trans Cumberland Westmorland Antiq Archaeol Soc* ser 2, **88,** 29-31

Stevens, C E, 1948 The building of Hadrian's Wall, *Archaeol Aeliana* ser 4, **26,** 1-46

Stevens, C E, 1950 A Roman author in north-west Britain, *Trans Cumberland Westmorland Antiq Archaeol Soc* ser 2, **50,** 70-79

Stevens, C E, 1966 *The Building of Hadrian's Wall,* Kendal

St Joseph, J K S, 1951 Air Reconnaissance of North Britain, *J Roman Stud* **41,** 52-65

Stukeley, W, 1759 *The Medallic History of Carausius,* London

Stukeley, W, 1776 Iter Boreale of 1725, in *Itinerarium Curiosum,* 2 edn, London

Stukeley, W, 1776 *Itinerarium Curiosum,* 2 edn, London
Swan, V 1992 Legio VI and its men: African legionaries in Britain, *Journ. Roman Pottery Studies* **5,** 1-33.
Swan, V G, 1999 The twentieth legion and the history of the Antonine Wall reconsidered, *Proc Soc Antiq Scotl* **129,** 399-480
Swan, V G, forthcoming *The Roman Coarse Pottery, in The Carlisle Millennium Project: Excavations within the Roman Fort and Medieval Castle, 1998-2001, Vol 2* (ed C Howard-Davis)
Swinbank, B, 1951 A trial excavation at Moresby, *Trans Cumberland Westmorland Antiq Archaeol Soc* ser 2, **51,** 176-177
Swinbank, B,1952 Excavations in High House paddock, Cumberland, *Trans Cumberland Westmorland Antiq Archaeol Soc* ser 2, **52,** 46-54
Swinbank, B, 1953 The problem of the vallum at Carvoran, *Archaeol Aeliana* ser 4, **31**, 82-94
Swinbank, B, 1955 Pottery from levels of the second and third century, covering the Vallum at Benwell, *Archaeol Aeliana* ser 4, **33**, 142-162
Swinbank, B, & Gillam, J P, 1950 Pottery from the Vallum Filling at Birdoswald, *Trans Cumberland Westmorland Antiq Archaeol Soc* ser 2, **50,** 54-62
Swinbank, B, & Spaul, J E H, 1951 The spacing of the forts on Hadrian's Wall, *Archaeol Aeliana* ser 4, **29,** 221-238
Sykes, N, & O'Connor, T P, in preparation *Introductions and extinctions.*
Symonds, M, 2005 The Construction Order of the Milecastles on Hadrian's Wall, *Archaeol Aeliana* ser 5, **34,** 67-81
Symonds, M, 2007 *The Design and Purpose of Roman Fortlets in the North-Western Frontier Provinces of the Empire,* Unpublished D.Phil thesis, The University of Oxford
Symonds, M, forthcoming Fortlets and their adaptation for artificial frontiers, in *Roman Frontier Studies XXI* (eds Morillo et al) Leon Spain
Tait, J, 1962 The Vallum at West Denton and Heddon-on the-Wall, *Archaeol Aeliana,* ser 4, **40,** 135-143
Tait, J, 1963 An excavation at Housesteads, 1962, *Archaeol Aeliana,* ser 4, **41,** 37-44
Taylor, C, 1982 *Roads and Tracks of Britain,* London
Taylor, D J A, 2000 *Forts on Hadrian's Wall, a Comparative Analysis of the Form and Construction of Some Buildings* BAR Brit. Ser. **305**, Oxford
Taylor, D J A, Robinson, J, & Biggins, J A, 2000 A report on a geophysical survey of the Roman fort and vicus at Halton Chesters, *Archaeol Aeliana* ser 5, **28,** 37-46
Taylor, J, 1991 *The Roman Pottery from Castle Street, Carlisle: Excavations 1981-2,* Kendal
Terras, M, 2006 *Image to Interpretation: An Intelligent System to Aid Historians in Reading the Vindolanda Texts,* Oxford
Tipping, R, 1997 Pollen analysis and the impact of Rome on native agriculture around Hadrian's Wall, in *Reconstructing Iron Age Societies* (eds A Gwilt and C Haselgrove), Oxbow Monograph **71,** 239-247, Oxford
Todd, M, (ed.) 2004 *A companion to Roman Britain,* Oxford
Tomlin, R S O, 1992a The Roman "carrot" amphora and its Egyptian provenance, *Journal of Egyptian Archaeology* **78,** 307-312
Tomlin, R S O, 1992b The Twentieth Legion at Wroxeter and Carlisle in the first century: the epigraphic evidence, *Britannia* **23,** 141-58
Tomlin, R S O 1996a A five-acre wood in Roman Kent, in *Interpreting Roman London: Papers in Memory of Hugh Chapman* (eds J Bird, M Hassall and H Sheldon), 209-215 Oxford
Tomlin, R S O, 1996b The Vindolanda tablets (review article), *Britannia* **27,** 459-63
Tomlin, R S O, 1998 Roman manuscripts from Carlisle: the ink-written tablets, *Britannia* **29,** 31-84
Tomlin, R S O 1999 The missing lances, or making the machine work, in *The Roman Army as a Community* (eds A Goldsworthy and I Haynes) Portsmouth and Rhode Island, 127-138
Tomlin, R S O, 2003a 'The Girl in Question': a new text from Roman London, *Britannia* **34,** 41-51
Tomlin, R S O, 2003b Documenting the Roman army at Carlisle, in *Documenting the Roman Army: Essays in honour of Margaret Roxan* (ed J J Wilkes), Bulletin of the Institute of Classical Studies Supplement **81,** London, 175-186
Tomlin, R S O, & Annis, R G, 1989 A Roman Altar from Carlisle Castle, *Trans Cumberland Westmorland Antiq Archaeol Soc* ser 2, **89,** 78-91
Topping, P, 1989a The context of Cord Rig cultivation in later prehistoric Northumberland, in *From Cornwall to Caithness: Some Aspects of British Field Archaeology: Papers presented to Norman V. Quinnell* (eds M Bowden, D Mackay and P Topping) BAR Brit. Ser. **209,** 145-158
Topping, P, 1989b Early Cultivation in Northumberland and the Borders, *Proc Prehist Soc* **55,** 161-179
Toynbee, J M C, & Richmond, I A, 1953 A Roman glass phalera from Carlisle, *Trans Cumberland Westmorland Antiq Archaeol Soc* ser 2, **53,** 40-48
Turnbull, P, 1991 The position of Milefortlet 10 (Silloth), *Trans Cumberland Westmorland Antiq Archaeol Soc* ser 2, **91,** 267-268
Turnbull, P, 1996 The supposed Roman harbour at Maryport, *Trans Cumberland Westmorland Antiq Archaeol Soc* ser 2, **96,** 233-5
Turnbull, P, 1998 Excavations at milefortlet 21, *Trans Cumberland Westmorland Antiq Archaeol Soc* ser 2, **98,** 61-106
Turner, J, & Kershaw, A P, 1973 A late - and post-glacial pollen diagram from Cranberry Bog, near Beamish, County Durham, *New Phytologist* **72**, 915-928
Turner, R C, 1980 A Roman Gaming Board from near Bowness-on-Solway, *Trans Cumberland Westmorland Antiq Archaeol Soc* ser 2, **80,** 159-160
Turner, R C, 1988 A Cumbrian Bog Body from Scaleby, *Trans Cumberland Westmorland Antiq Archaeol Soc* ser 2, **88,** 1-7
Tyers, I, & Groves, C, forthcoming The dendrochronology, in *The Carlisle Millennium Project: Excavations within the Roman Fort and Medieval Castle, 1998-2001,* Vol 2 (ed C Howard-Davis)
Tyers, P, 1996 *Roman Pottery in Britain,* London
Usai, M R, 1999 *Assessment of Soils and Sediments from Excavations along Hadrian's Wall, near Black Carts, Northumberland* (Site Code CAS 623). Reports from the Environmental Archaeology Unit, York, **99/25.**
Usai, M R, 2001 Textural pedofeatures and pre-Hadrian's Wall ploughed paleosols at Stanwix, Carlisle, Cumbria,

U.K., *Journal of Archaeological Science* **28** (5), 541 -553

Usai, M R, 2002 *Northern Regional Review of Environmental Archaeology: Geoarchaeology in Northern England II: Site Review, Discussion and Research Priorities,* Centre for Archaeology Reports, **24/2002**

Van der Veen, M, 1988 Carbonised grain from a Roman granary at South Shields, north east England, in *Der Praehistoriche Mensch und seine Umwelt* (ed K Küster), Forschungen und Berichte zur Vor- und Frügeschichte in Baden-Württemberg **21,** 353-65

Van der Veen, M, 1992 *Crop Husbandry Regimes: an Archaeobotanical Study of Farming in Northern England 1000 BC - AD 500,* Sheffield

Van der Veen, M, 1998 A life of luxury in the desert? The food and fodder supply of Mons Claudianus, *J Roman Archaeol* **11,** 101-16

Van Driel-Murray, C, 1985 The production and supply of military leatherwork in the first and second centuries AD, a review of the archaeological evidence, in *The Production and Distribution of Roman Military Equipment* (ed M C Bishop) Oxford, BAR Int. Ser. **275,** 42-81

Van Driel-Murray, C, 1989 The Vindolanda chamfrons and miscellaneous items of leather horse gear, in *Roman Military Equipment: the Sources of Evidence* (ed C van Driel-Murray) BAR Int. Ser. **476,** 281-318

Van Driel-Murray, C, 1990 New light on old tents: the evidence from Vindolanda, *Journal of Roman Military Studies* **1,** 109-38

Van Driel-Murray, C, 1993 *The Early Wooden Forts: Preliminary Reports on the Leather, Textiles, Environmental Evidence and Dendrochronology,* Vin Research Reports NS **3,** Bardon Mill

Van Driel-Murray, C, 1995 Gender in question, in *Theoretical Roman Archaeology: Second Conference Proceedings* (ed P Rush) Aldershot, 3-21

Van Driel-Murray, C, 1998 A question of gender in a military context, *Helinium* **34,** 342-362

Van Driel-Murray, C, 2001 Vindolanda and the dating of Roman footwear, *Britannia* **32,** 185-197

Van Driel-Murray, C, 2002 Ethnic Soldiers: The Experience of the Lower Rhine Tribes, in *Kontinuität und Diskontinuität: Germania inferior am Beginn und am Ende der römischen Herrschaft.* Beiträge des deutsch niederländischen Kolloquiums in der Katholieke Universiteit Nijmegen (27. bis 30.06.2001) (eds T Grünewald and S Seibel), Berlin, 200-17

Wallis, J, 1769 *The Natural History and Antiquities of Northumberland,* London

Wallis-Budge, E A, 1907 *An Account of the Roman Antiquities Preserved in the Museum at Chesters, Northumberland.* London.

Warburton, J, 1716 *A Map of the County of Northumberland,* London

Warburton, J, 1753 *Vallum Romanum or, the History and Antiquities of the Roman Wall, Commonly Called the Picts Wall, in Cumberland and Northumberland, Built by Hadrian and Severus,* London

Ward, M, forthcoming The samian pottery, in *The Carlisle Millennium Project: Excavations within the Roman Fort and Medieval castle, 1998-2001, Vol 2* (ed C Howard-Davis)

Watson, G R, 1954 The Birdoswald Hoard; the Pay and the Purse, *Trans Cumberland Westmorland Antiq Archaeol Soc,* ser 2, **54,** 61-65

Webster, J 1973 A bronze incense container in the form of Bacchus from Carlisle, *Trans Cumberland Westmorland Antiq Archaeol Soc* ser 2, **73,** 90-93

Webster, J 1986 Roman Bronzes from Maryport in the Netherhall Collection, *Trans Cumberland Westmorland Antiq Archaeol Soc* ser 2, **86,** 49-70

Webster, P V, 1972 Severn Valley Ware on Hadrian's Wall *Archaeol Aeliana* ser 4, **50,** 191-204

Welfare, A T, 1985 The Greenlee Lough (Northumberland) Palimpsest: an Interim Report on the 1985 season. *Northern Archaeology,* **7** part 2, 35-37

Welfare, H G, 1974 A cemetery at High Nook, Nether Denton, *Trans Cumberland Westmorland Antiq Archaeol Soc* ser 2, **74,** 14-7

Welfare, H G, 2000 Causeways, at milecastles across the ditch of Hadrian's Wall, *Archaeol Aeliana* ser 5, 28, 13-25

Welfare, H G, 2002 The Uplands of the Northern Counties in the First Millennium BC, in *Past, Present and Future: The Archaeology of Northern England* (eds C. Brooks, R. Daniels & A Harding), 71-77, Durham

Welfare, H G, 2004 Variation in the form of the Ditch, and of its equivalents, on Hadrian's Wall, *Archaeol Aeliana* ser 5, **33,** 9-23

Welfare, H G, forthcoming Survey of Housesteads environs, in *The Grandest Station: Excavation and Survey at Housesteads Roman Fort by C.M.Daniels, J. P. Gillam, J.G. Crow, D. J. Smith and the RCHME 1954-88* (ed A. Rushworth), English Heritage Archaeological Report, London.

Welfare, H G, & Swan, V, 1995 *Roman Camps in England: The Field Archaeology,* London

Wells, C, 2003 Environmental changes in Roman north west England: a synoptic overview of events north of the Ribble. *Trans Cumberland Westmorland Antiq Archaeol* Soc, **3,** 67-84

Welsby, D A, 1980 Roman building inscriptions, recording buildings collapsed through age or destroyed by the enemy?, *Archaeol Aeliana* ser 5, **8,** 89-94

Welsby, D A, 1982 *The Roman Military Defence of the British Provinces in its Later Phases,* BAR Brit. Ser. **101,** Oxford

Welsby, D A, 1985 The Pottery from the Two Towers at Garthside on Hadrian's Wall, *Trans Cumberland Westmorland Antiq Archaeol Soc* ser 2, **85,** 71-76

Welsby, D A, 1989 *Report on the Carved Stonework at Housesteads,* English Heritage.

Wenham, L P, 1939 Notes on the garrisoning of Maryport, *Trans Cumberland Westmorland Antiq Archaeol Soc* ser 2, **39,** 19-30

Whellan, W, 1860 *History and Topography of Cumberland and Westmorland,* Pontefract

Whittaker, C R, 1994 *Frontiers of the Roman Empire: a Social and Economic Study,* Baltimore/London

Whittaker, C R, 2000 Frontiers, in *The High Empire, A.D. 70-192,* The Cambridge Ancient History **XI** (eds A K Bowman, P Garnsey and D Rathbone) 2 edn, Cambridge

Whittaker, C R, 2002 Supplying the Roman army. Evidence from Vindolanda, in P. Erdkamp (ed), 204-234.

Whitworth, A M, 1990 The Housesteads bastle, *Archaeol Aeliana* ser 5, **18,** 127-129

Whitworth, A M, 1992 The cutting of the Turf Wall at Appletree, *Trans Cumberland Westmorland Antiq*

Archaeol Soc ser 2, **92,** 49-65
Whitworth, A M, 1994 Recording the Roman Wall, *Archaeol Aeliana* ser 5, **22,** 67-77
Whitworth, A M, 1997a Five Stones from Great Chesters Fort, *Archaeol Aeliana* ser 5, **25,** 153 - 159
Whitworth, A M, 1997b Recording of Hadrian's Wall at Willowford Farm, *Trans Cumberland Westmorland Antiq Archaeol Soc* ser 2, **97,** 57-61
Whitworth, A, forthcoming A nineteenth-century condition survey of Hadrian's Wall: the James Irwin Coates archive, 1877-1896, in Wilmott, T (ed), forthcoming, *Hadrian's Wall: Archaeological Research by English Heritage 1976-2000,* English Heritage Research Report
Wild, J P, 1971 The South Shields heddle, *Archaeol Aeliana* ser 4, **49,** 230-231
Wild, J P, 2002 The textile industries of Roman Britain, *Britannia* **33,** 1-42
Wilkes, J J, 1960 Excavations at Housesteads in 1959, *Archaeol Aeliana* ser 4, **38,** 61-71
Wilkes, J J, 1961 Excavations in Housesteads fort, 1960, *Archaeol Aeliana* ser 4, **39,** 279-300
Wilkes, J J, 1966 Early fourth-century rebuilding in Hadrian's Wall forts, in *Britain and Rome: Essays Presented to Eric Birley on His Sixtieth Birthday* (eds M G Jarret and B Dobson) Kendal, 114-138
Williams, D, 1983 The Vallum's Original Intention: a Multi Purpose Work of Frontier Support, *Trans Cumberland Westmorland Antiq Archaeol Soc* ser 2, **83,** 33-39
Willis, S H, 1994 Roman imports into late Iron Age British societies: towards a critique of existing models, in *TRAC94: Proceedings of the 4th Theoretical Roman Archaeology Conference,* Durham 1994 (eds S Cottam, D Dungworth, S Scott and J Taylor) Oxford, 141-150
Willis, S H, 1997a. Samian: beyond dating, in *TRAC96: Proceedings of the 6th Theoretical Roman Archaeology Conference,* Sheffield 1996 (K I Meadows, C R Lemke and J Heron) Oxford, 38-54
Willis, S H, 1997b *The English Heritage Samian Project. Report on the Results of Phase 1,* Durham
Willis, S H, 1998 Samian pottery in Britain: exploring its distribution and archaeological potential, *Archaeol J* **155,** 82-133
Willis, S H. 1999 Without and within: aspects of culture and community in the Iron Age of north-eastern England, in *Northern Exposure: Interpretative Devolution and the Iron Ages in Britain* (ed B Bevan) Leicester Archaeological Monograph **4,** Leicester, 81-110
Willis, S H, 2004 The Study Group for Roman Pottery: Research Framework Document for the Study of Roman Pottery in Britain, 2004, *Journal of Roman Pottery Studies* **11,** 1-20
Willis, S H, 2005a Samian pottery, a resource for the study of Roman Britain and beyond: The results of the English Heritage funded Samian Project. An E-monograph, in *Internet Archaeology*, 17. http://intarch.ac.uk/journal/issue17/willis_toc.html
Willis, S H, 2005b The context of writing and written records in ink: the archaeology of samian inkwells in Roman Britain, *Archaeol J* **162,** 96-145
Willis, S H, in press (a) The samian ware, in T Wilmott, *Excavations at Birdoswald Study Centre site, 1997and 1998*
Willis, S H, in press (b) The samian ware, in *T Wilmott, Excavations on the Spur at Birdoswald, 1998*
Willis, S H, in press (c) The samian associated with Turrets 49b, 50a, and 50b and Milecastle 50: A review, in T Wilmott, *Excavations at Birdoswald Study Centre Site, 1997 and 1998*
Willis, S H, in press (d) The samian from the excavations at Birdoswald by Time Team, 1999: Dated catalogue and report, in T Wilmott, *Excavations in the western vicus and cemetery, Birdoswald 1999*
Willis, S H, forthcoming (a) The Samian associated with Turrets 49b, 50a and 50b and Milecastle 50: a Review, in *Hadrian's Wall: English Heritage Research 1980 - 2000* (ed T Wilmott) English Heritage Archaeological Report
Willis, S H, forthcoming (b) The pottery assemblage from the excavations and fieldwork, Newcastle Great Park Excavations, Tyne and Wear Museums.
Wilmott, T, 1987 Birdoswald Excavations 1987, *English Heritage Conservation Bull* **3,** 12
Wilmott, T, 1989a Birdoswald: Dark Age Halls in a Roman Fort? *Current Archaeology* **116,** 288-91
Wilmott, T, 1991 Archaeology and the Public at Birdoswald, *The Field Archaeologist* **15,** 264-66
Wilmott, T, 1991 A Military basilica at Birdoswald, *Roman Research News* **3,** 8
Wilmott, T, 1993 The Roman Cremation Cemetery in New Field, Birdoswald, *Trans Cumberland Westmorland Antiq Archaeol Soc* ser 2, **93,** 79-85
Wilmott, T, 1997a *Birdoswald: Excavations of a Roman fort on Hadrian's Wall and its Successor Settlements: 1987-92,* English Heritage Archaeological Report **14**, London
Wilmott, T, 1997b A new type of building in an Expeditio fort; the Birdoswald basilica, in *Roman Frontier Studies 1995. Proceedings of the XVIth International Congress of Roman Frontier Studies* (eds W Groenman van Waateringe, B L van Beek, W J H Willems, S L Wynia) Oxbow Monograph **91,** Oxford, 581-6
Wilmott, T, 1999b Birdoswald, in *Hadrian's Wall 1989-1999* (ed P T Bidwell), 145-57, Kendal
Wilmott, T, 2000 The Late Roman Transition at Birdoswald and on Hadrian's Wall, in *The Late Roman Transition in the North. Papers from the Roman Archaeology Conerence Durham 1999* (eds T Wilmott and P Wilson) BAR Brit. Ser. **299,** Oxford, 13-24
Wilmott, T, 2001a *Birdoswald Roman Fort: 1,800 years on Hadrian's Wall,* London
Wilmott, T, 2001b *Cohors I Aelia Dacorum;* A Dacian unit on Hadrian's Wall, *Acta Musei Napocensis,* **38/1,** 103-122
Wilmott, T, 2002 Research and development in the Birdoswald sector of Hadrian's Wall, 1949-1989', in *Limes XVIII: Proceedings of the XVIIIth International Congress of Roman Frontier Studies Held in Amman, Jordan* (September 2000) (eds P Freeman, J Bennett, Z Fiema & B Hoffman) BAR Int. Ser. **1084** (II), Oxford, 851-858,
Wilmott, T, 2004 A possible prehistoric cist from Birdoswald, Cumbria, *Trans Cumberland Westmorland Antiq Archaeol Soc,* ser 3, **4,** 27-38
Wilmott, T, 2004 Aspects of recent archaeology on Hadrian's Wall, in *Archaeology in Northumberland National Park* (P Frodsham) CBA Research Report **136,** York, 224-235
Wilmott, T, 2006 The Profile of the Ditch of Hadrian's Wall, *Archaeol Aeliana* ser 5, **35,** 33-38
Wilmott, T, 2006 Warfare and the construction of Hadrian's Wall: a problem, *Archaeol Aeliana* ser 5, **35,** 27-31

Wilmott, T, forthcoming (a) Four investigations of the linear elements of Hadrian's Frontier works, 1980-2000, in *Hadrian's Wall: Archaeological Research by English Heritage 1976-2000* (ed T Wilmott), English Heritage Research Report
Wilmott, T, forthcoming (b) The linear elements of the Hadrian's Wall complex; excavation and evaluation, 1976 2000, in *Hadrian's Wall: English Heritage Research 1980-2000* (ed T Wilmott), English Heritage Archaeological Report
Wilmott, T, & Wilson, P, (eds), 2000 *The Late Roman Transition in the North,* BAR Brit. Ser. **299,** Oxford, 13-24
Wilmott, T, Cool, H, & Evans, J, forthcoming Excavations at the Hadrian's Wall fort of Birdoswald (Banna), Cumbria: 1996-2000, in *Hadrian's Wall: English Heritage Research 1976-2000* (ed T Wilmott), English Heritage Archaeological Report
Wilson, A, 2002 Machines, power and the ancient economy, *J Roman Stud,* **92,** 1-32
Wilson, A, 2003 Roman and Native in Dumfriesshire, *Transactions of the Dumfries and Galloway Natural History and Archaeology Society* **77,** 103 -60
Wilson, D, Wright, P & Hassall, M, 1974 Roman Britain in 1973, *Britannia* **5:** 396-480
Wilson, D G, 1979 Horse Dung from Roman Lancaster: A Botanical Report, *Archaeo Physika,* **8,** 331-350
Wilson, D G, 1988 Horse dung from Roman Lancaster: a botanical report, in *Roman Lancaster. Rescue Archaeology in an historic city 1970-75* (eds G D B Jones and D C A Shotter), Manchester, 170-176
Wilson, P R, 2002 *Cataractonium. Roman Catterick and its Hinterland* (Vol. I), York
Wilson, R J A, (ed.) 1997a *Roman Maryport and its Setting: Essays in Memory of Michael G. Jarrett.*
Wilson, R J A, 1997b Maryport from the first to the fourth centuries: some current problems, in *Roman Maryport and its Setting: Essays in Memory of Michael G. Jarrett* (ed J R A Wilson), Maryport, 17-39
Wilson, R J A, 2003a Journeymen's jottings: two Roman inscriptions from Hadrian's Wall, *Archaeol Aeliana* **32,** 25 -35
Wilson, R J A, 2003b Roman vaulting tubes (*tubi fittili*) from Chesters: an addendum *Archaeol Aeliana* **32,** 192-3
Wilson, R J A, 2004 Introduction: the Roman frontier on the Solway, in *Romans on the Solway, Essays in Honour of Richard Bellhouse* (eds R J A Wilson and I Caruana), Kendal, 19 -38
Wilson, R J A & Caruana, I D, (eds) 2004 *Romans on the Solway. Essays in Honour of Richard Bellhouse,* Kendal
Wilthew, P, 1985 *Examination of a Crucible from Carlisle.* Ancient Monuments Laboratory Report, **4452.**
Wiltshire, P, 1997 The pre-Roman environment, in *Birdoswald: Excavations of a Roman Fort on Hadrian's Wall and its Successor Settlements* (T Wilmott) London
Winterbottom, S, 1989 Saddle covers, chamfrons and possible horse armour from Carlisle, in Roman Military Equipment: the Sources of Evidence (ed C van Driel Murray), BAR Int. Ser. **476,** Oxford, 319-36
Woodfield, C, 1965 Six turrets on Hadrian's Wall, Archaeol Aeliana ser 4, **43,** 87-200
Woodfield, P, 1966 Barcombe Hill, Thorngrafton, *Archaeol Aeliana* ser 4, **44,** 71-77
Woodside, R, & Crow, J 1999 *Hadrian's Wall: an Historic landscape,* Cirencester
Woodward, T, 1983 Shell table, in *The Roman Fort at South Shields: Excavation of the Defences 1977-1981* (ed R. Miket), Newcastle-upon-Tyne, 150-153
Woolley, C L, 1907 *Corstopitum:* provisional report of the excavations in 1906, *Archaeol Aeliana* ser 3, **3,** 161-86
Woolliscroft, D J, 1988 The Outpost System of Hadrian's Wall, *Trans Cumberland Westmorland Antiq Archaeol Soc* ser 2, **88,** 23-28
Woolliscroft, D J, 1989 Signalling and the design of Hadrian's Wall, *Archaeol Aeliana* ser 5, **17,** 5-19
Woolliscroft, D J, 1994 Signalling and the design of the Cumberland Coast system, *Trans Cumberland Westmorland Antiq Archaeol Soc* ser 2, **94,** 55-64
Woolliscroft, D J, 1999 More thoughts on the Vallum, *Trans Cumberland Westmorland Antiq Archaeol Soc* ser 2, **99,** 53-65
Woolliscroft, D J, 2001 *Roman Military Signalling,* Stroud
Woolliscroft, D J, 2004 Excavations on the Cumberland coast at Silloth and at Finland Rigg, 1994, *in Romans on the Solway, Essays in Honour of Richard Bellhouse* (eds R J A Wilson and I Caruana),186-194, Kendal
Woolliscroft, DJ. & Jones, G.D.B. 2004. Excavations on the Cumberland coast at Silloth and at Fingland Rigg, 1994 in RJ. Wilson and I. Caruana (eds) 2004, 186-94
Woolliscroft, D J, Nevell, M D, & Swain, S A M, 1989 The Roman Site on Grey Hill, Bewcastle, Cumbria, *Trans Cumberland Westmorland Antiq Archaeol Soc* ser 2, **89,** 69-75
Woolliscroft, D J, Swain, S A M, & Lockett, N J, 1992 Barcombe B, a Second Roman 'Signal' Tower on Barcombe Hill, *Archaeol Aeliana* ser 5, **20,** 57-62
Wright, R P, 1936 The Stanegate at North Tyne, *Archaeol Aeliana* ser 4 **13,** 199-206
Wright, R P, 1937 The Stanegate at Chesterholm, *Archaeol Aeliana* ser 4, **14,** 185-193
Wright, R P, 1939 The Stanegate at Walwick Grange, *Archaeol Aeliana* ser 4, **16,** 140-147
Wright, R P, 1940a The Wrekendyke and the Roman Road Junction on Gateshead Fell, *Archaeol Aeliana* ser 4, **17,** 54-64
Wright, R P, 1940b A note on two milestones of Severus Alexander, *Archaeol Aeliana* ser 4, **17,** 116-120
Wright, R P, 1941 The Stanegate at Corbridge, *Archaeol Aeliana* ser 4, **19,** 194-209
Wright, R P, 1942 Roman Inscriptions from Cumberland, *Trans Cumberland Westmorland Antiq Archaeol Soc* ser 2, **42,** 154-158
Wright, R P, 1953 A centurial stone from Carlisle, *Trans Cumberland Westmorland Antiq Archaeol Soc* ser 2, **53,** 215
Wright, R P, 1954 Some Roman inscriptions from Cumberland and Westmorland, *Trans Cumberland Westmorland Antiq Archaeol Soc* ser 2, **54,** 215
Wright, R P, 1957 Roman Britain in 1956, *J Roman Stud* **47,** 198-234
Wright, R P, 1958 The Stanegate at Newbrough, *Archaeol Aeliana* ser 4, **36,** 316
Wright, R P, 1961 Roman Britain in 1960, *J Roman Stud* **51,** 157-198
Wright, R P, 1975 The discovery of Roman altars at Busbridge Hall, near Godalming, Surrey, *Trans Cumberland Westmorland Antiq Archaeol Soc* ser 2, **75,**

91-95
Wright, R P, 1985 The locating of Roman Structures along the Line of Hadrian's Wall between Wallsend (Segedunum) and Milecastle 2, *Archaeol Aeliana* ser 5, **13,** 213-214
Wright, R P, and Phillips, E J, 1975 *The Roman Inscribed and Sculptured Stones in Carlisle Museum,* Carlisle
Wright, R P, and Hill, S, 1975 A sculptured and inscribed tombstone from Halton Chesters, Northumberland, *Archaeol Aeliana* ser 5, **3,** 212-214
Young, R 2005 *Archaeological Research Strategy for Northumberland National Park Authority: Resource Assessment and Research Agenda,* Northumberland
Younger, D A, 1994 The small mammals from the forecourt granary and the south west fort ditch., in *Excavations at South Shields Roman Fort* (eds P T Bidwell and S Speak), Vol. 1, Society of Antiquaries of Newcastle upon Tyne Monograph Series No. **4,** Newcastle-upon-Tyne, 266-268
Zant, J M, 1997 Evaluation and excavation at Stanwix Primary School, Carlisle, *Archaeology North* **14,** 30-34
Zant, J M 1998 An excavation at Low Crosby, Carlisle, *Trans Cumberland Westmorland Antiq Archaeol Soc* ser 2, **98,** 299-303
Zant, J M, 2000 Recent excavations on Castle Green and Castle Way, Carlisle, *Archaeology North* **17,** 7-8
Zant, J M, in press *The Carlisle Millennium Project: Excavations within the Roman Fort and Medieval Castle, 1998-2001, Vol 1*

Index

(1. and 2. refer to Volumes I & II. Figures in bold refer to illustrations).